Allied Intelligence and the Cover-Up at Pointe du Hoc

The Greek historian, Polybius, who was born circa 203 BC, defined history thus:

If you take the truth from History, what is left is but an idle unprofitable tale. Therefore, one must not shrink either from blaming one's friends or praising one's enemies: or be afraid of finding fault with and commending the same persons at different times. For it is impossible that men engaged in public affairs should always be right, and unlikely that they should always be wrong. Holding ourselves, therefore entirely aloof from the actors, we must as historians make statements and pronounce judgements in accordance with the actions themselves.

Allied Intelligence and the Cover-Up at Pointe du Hoc

2nd & 5th US Army Rangers 1943 – 30 April 1944

Volume 1

Gary Sterne

Pen & Sword
MILITARY

First published in Great Britain in 2018
by Pen & Sword Military
An imprint of Pen & Sword Books Limited
47 Church Street
Barnsley
South Yorkshire
S70 2AS

ISBN 978 1 52675 222 2

A CIP catalogue record for this book is
available from the British Library

Typeset in Ehrhardt
by Mac Style

Printed and bound in the UK
by CPI Group (UK) Ltd, Croydon, CR0 4YY

Pen & Sword Books Limited incorporates the imprints of Atlas,
Archaeology, Aviation, Discovery, Family History, Fiction, History, Maritime,
Military, Military Classics, Politics, Select, Transport,
True Crime, Air World, Frontline Publishing, Leo Cooper,
Remember When, Seaforth Publishing, The Praetorian Press,
Wharncliffe Local History, Wharncliffe Transport,
Wharncliffe True Crime and White Owl.

For a complete list of Pen & Sword titles please contact
PEN & SWORD BOOKS LIMITED
47 Church Street, Barnsley, South Yorkshire, S70 2AS, England
E-mail: enquiries@pen-and-sword. co. uk
Website: www. pen-and-sword. co. uk

Contents

Introduction

For almost seventy-five years the historical importance and the facts surrounding the D-Day attack on the famous gun battery at Pointe du Hoc in Normandy have been known to everyone. Millions of words and tens of thousands of books have covered this subject – and yet, during my research through recently released documents I have been able to uncover serious differences between the events as we have been told them, and a reality which is a lot more disturbing.

It is a bold claim – after all, why would battle accounts and reports of what happened there not be 100 per cent accurate and proven correct after all this time? Surely we must know everything there is to know about that battle and its participants by now, you could argue!

I would have agreed wholeheartedly with that, until I started my research into the role played by the Maisy Batteries in the coastal defence of that area of Normandy in 1944. It was during this very focused research that I came across paperwork which has opened my eyes to an alternative series of events surrounding the battle for Pointe du Hoc – and a very different outcome to the events as they have been portrayed historically since the war.

In this, the first of two volumes, we look at the critical months leading up to D-Day, as well as the orders and intelligence being received by the Rangers at that time. Vol. 2 takes the reader through hectic weeks of training until its climax on 6 June – the assault on Normandy. The aftermath of the Rangers' battles can then be seen through the eyes of the original After Actions Reports for all the units involved. Then there follows a critical examination of those missions and the inevitable question: … is our present understanding of the Pointe du Hoc battle a flawed one? A later book will study the Rangers' WW2 training methods, equipment, uniforms, and tactics.

The laws surrounding the retention of documents by the US and British governments effectively removed from circulation any paperwork marked 'Top Secret' and this prevented many of those documents from being viewed for at least sixty years. These restrictions have now been lifted and slowly more and more elusive paperwork has been processed and released. Some of these papers have taken four or five years beyond the sixty-year rule to surface.

As you can imagine, the volume of TOP SECRET marked paperwork from that era means the US Archives have been inundated with work to catalogue and publish everything – and especially the vast amounts which were generated relating to the most secret mission of all – D-Day.

My historical interest in this subject goes back some twelve years to when the gun batteries at Maisy in Normandy started to be uncovered and made headline news all around the world. The reason for the media interest at the time was quite simple, no-one knew that the huge German gun position was still there lying buried under the French countryside and even Ranger veterans thought that it had been completely destroyed after the battle. Nobody mentioned Maisy and nobody cared about Maisy, because all the interest in the area was focused on Omaha Beach and Pointe du Hoc. This was further fuelled by the films *Saving Private Ryan* and *The Longest Day* which heavily featured the battles at these two locations and created a focus for a new generation of history buffs.

I received a vast amount of publicity during my initial digging at Maisy. Not even the local residents, the local police, the mayor's office, etc. had a clue about the site. There were only a very small number of people who were children during the war who remembered it from their childhood. Beyond that, there was nothing recorded in the area, so it is understandable why so many books have not included any mention of the site. When the news of Maisy hit the world news media, the first thing that TV crews and journalists did was to call the town mayor's office to see what had been found. They needed to check it was something interesting before they flew thousands of miles to photograph the site and interview me. It would not really have been newsworthy, if everyone had known about the place already.

The reporters came in their dozens and they wrote their stories. Some sensationalised the find in ridiculous ways, and while others took their time to do a serious piece; but there were a lot of sceptics. I remember well that a number of authors and historians jumped up and said 'yes we know all about Maisy' but in reality during my own private research prior to buying the land, I could find no mention of Maisy's existence.

Where were all the books talking about Maisy before mine – The *Cover up at Omaha Beach: The Maisy Battery and the US Rangers* – was published in 2014? The answer was easy to prove. Maisy did not exist in any of the million-selling D-Day books and to a large degree it still does not. It has literally been written out of history inadvertently by authors around the world – one assumes because they did NOT have access to the documention that has now been released.

Over the last few years I have heard dozens of historians and experts provide me with reasons why Maisy was buried, covered over or simply lost, or why it had no role to play on D-Day, or why it was not a D-Day mission for anyone etc. And yet many have only the work of others upon which to base their arguments. Maisy sits right in the centre of the US invasion area and could fire on the Omaha and Utah landing sectors – not Omaha Beach – Omaha Sector, there is a big difference – so logically it would have had some role to play on D-Day.

As well as visiting and communicating with the surviving Ranger veterans, I was digging up battle-scarred bunkers, live shells and equipment with a regularity which implied that Maisy was NOT an insignificant establishment for the Germans. On one occasion I found the complete skeleton of a German officer lying in a buried trench.

Over time the biggest motivation for me to continue researching the role Maisy played came from a strange source. It was as a result of the reaction I received from a US Museum to the whole Maisy story. They told me that no factual evidence existed proving that Maisy had played a significant role on D-Day and that basically my 'claims' were unsubstantiated by 'their veterans'. They were politely saying that my claims were *untrue*. More on this later …

So I had a challenge. I decided to build the Rangers' history day by day and reproduce the documents in their original form for others to read. The research behind this work has taken around three years to compile and although the conclusions drawn at the end are mine, the rest of the evidence is shown in such a way that it cannot now in any way be labelled as unsubstantiated.

For the first time historians have ALL the evidence – a lot of which I guarantee NO book you own has produced in this form before. I hope that now the debate can move on and be about how this evidence fits in with D-Day as we know it – and I ask that you do not disregard the historical implications that this throws up. These are fresh historical facts and in my view they do tell a different story to the accepted one.

Quite simply – **here for the first time are the period documents which prove that Maisy was a major part of the Atlantic Wall and that it was huge problem for the US Army on D-Day… and that it WAS a Rangers' D-Day objective.**

This book offers a new look at the workings of the US Army Rangers as they prepare for D-Day and it has been drawn together using their own Battalion archive documents. It is of the greatest historical importance that readers can now explore the many previously unavailable papers detailing their orders and objectives for D-Day. You now know what they knew then, and for the first time can see everything they did and judge if the decisions that the Rangers' leaders made align with their orders and objectives. You can judge if the events of the day as we **had** understood them, are in fact now accurate.

Forget what you have read before about the missions and personalities of the Rangers – this book is going to make you rethink all of that.

The information has been gathered and presented in chronological order using period papers. Intelligence information relating to Omaha Beach, the Radar Station at Englesqueville, Pointe du Hoc and Maisy is all here, as are the After Action Reports for all of the units involved – just as they were written in the days that followed.

In short, there is no more room for speculation as to the orders and objectives of the Rangers – there can be no more questions about how much intelligence the Allies had on Pointe du Hoc, Maisy and the German units in the vicinity.

But the story of the US Army Rangers needs to start early in their conception and they were the end result of the US Army needing more specialist troops. I have looked at the time period covering their formation, training and then the deployment of the 2nd and 5th Ranger Infantry Battalions in Europe. There were obvious direct links between their US and UK based training and then the events which took place during their assault on Normandy in 1944, and of great interest was the physical intelligence supplied to the Rangers prior to their landings. In my opinion, much of this detailed information is missing in other works and often it appears the information stated is either created from supposition or as a repetition of another writer's work – not to mention public talks given on the subject which are lacking facts, often in favour of glorification or even, as will be shown in the conclusion to Vol 2, made up and pure fantasy.

I wanted to look at events as they unfolded in England and then Normandy as the two are directly related. The training of the men, even during the early months of 1944, had to educate and equip them for their D-Day roles, so it is interesting to watch how that was tuned in the months leading up to June.

You may not agree with my conclusions and you may have your own theories and opinions – but for the first time I have made my reasoning clear and you can see where I have my information from. I also know that my thoughts are at odds with many other historians and virtually every other book written about Pointe du Hoc. A good percentage of the paperwork here is new and for the greater part that makes it historically relevant in its own right. When you read it in its original form, you know that it was written more than seventy years ago by the men who were actually involved.

A note of caution however, you must understand that there is a big difference between physical orders issued before D-Day by commanding generals, which are 100 per cent accurate historically, and the orders that individual Rangers received verbally from their commanding officer on D-Day. This is a distinction that needs to be understood very clearly from the start when you compare this book with others on the subject. The orders from the commanding generals are facts that we have on paper. The other orders at battalion level that we have been told about post war are more often than not a Ranger's personal interpretation or personal account of events that happened to him. As such, these latter remembrances must be subject to a higher degree of scrutiny, and too many books in the past have relied on these personal accounts alone to form their narrative and then they have based their conclusions upon them.

On paper this is a subject which has already been covered by thousands of authors, so I should have very little new to add to the story. But when reading many of these books, it soon became clear to me that there *was* a much bigger story to tell. It is a story that had a direct bearing on the outcome of the beach landings in the Omaha Sector and it was obvious that the Rangers had a wider and more important scope of operations than has ever been acknowledged – and by the same measure, it is also one which they have NEVER been given credit for. Most books and documentaries only really cover the Rangers' training in brief and often by simplifying things – for example some will just say '*they climbed cliffs in Cornwall and on the Isle of Wight*' and the majority of authors focus more on the action and events of D-Day. By doing so, I think that they have missed many clues as to the Rangers' real objectives which are clear in their paperwork and training methods leading up to D-Day – once the period paperwork was released.

I wanted to do almost the opposite of other books, and look at every day before D-Day with as much detail as I could, for that is where much of the real intelligence story lies. To show this, I have also included mundane and perhaps trivial information to present as full a picture as it is possible to do. The mundane can also be interesting. A good personal friend of mine, Ranger veteran James W. Gabaree, told me of a couple of key events in his time prior to D-Day that nearly stopped him taking part in the landings. My seeing mention of those things in the Morning Reports was a confirmation of what had happened to him and when. His own memoirs had one of these events happening in one month – when in reality they happened in a different month and the Morning Reports proved that to us both. So even though he was there – his recollection of things was actually one month out.

I have used the Rangers Company Morning Reports as my skeleton and my backbone – but it is worth remembering also, that these reports were written by men who did not always spell other men's names correctly, perhaps because they did not know them or they were filling in for the day – in some cases they do not even record the man's correct rank. Over the duration of the reports, I found names spelt in a myriad of ways. The spelling of Pointe du Hoc is another example. On most period US papers it is spelt "Point du Hoe" and yet the correct French spelling is "Pointe du Hoc".

The Morning Report pages run into their thousands for these men – so when appropriate, I have condensed them to save repetition, particularly when different companies of the same unit were in the same place, on the same day. It does get more complex when different companies are doing different things on the same day – then I have listed that as well. What I have not done is include every aspect of the day-to-day running of each company as one would sometimes find included within these reports.

A typical Morning Report might list a man being promoted from perhaps Private (Pvt.) to Private First Class (Pfc.) one rank up. Or it might state that a number of men were sent on leave – and a given number of men returned from leave another day. There are officers going on a course, men injured, sick or being disciplined, all regularly marked on these pages. The problem with providing it all, is that it would get in the way of the main story. Thus the only way to write this book was to remove some of the daily grind. Each date therefore describes the action and activities of the men as briefly as possible and includes any intelligence or papers made available on that day from all sources that apply directly to the Rangers, their missions and/or would be within their sphere of operations.

Some of the many general orders given to these men and to their superiors every day are also included. Under each date you will see what they were doing as companies and then as a battalion, whilst for the first time seeing what their commanders were receiving by way of intelligence and how that was used to formulate the men's training. Also included are a number of regular pieces of information that the US Army was producing as General Orders including subjects ranging from how men were to conduct themselves when in contact with the British, to handing in anti-gas clothing.

I have used excerpts from a period document written by Pfc. Maurice Prince of the 2nd Battalion Rangers, which is held in the US National Archives. His wartime written diary helps tell the story on behalf of the 2nd Battalion. Prince was tasked with writing a chronological history of the 2nd Ranger Battalion and it is in effect (short of individual Ranger interviews) the most accurate general report of what his battalion was doing. At times he does focus specifically on the activities of A Company 2nd Battalion, which he was part of.

The same type of battalion history was done to a lesser degree by T-4 Henry S. Glassman of HQ Company 5th Battalion, who wrote a similar, but less detailed narrative of their activities. When appropriate I have also used that.

I have included period US Army documents whenever possible. Reports such as the Operation Neptune Planning papers are reproduced in full because of their historical significance. As D-Day looms, I have used the US Army After Action Reports for each unit and marked them as 'AAR' – to identify them to the reader. These are words taken exactly as written from the reports and as they were filed by the men concerned. There are two slightly different sets which exist for the 2nd Battalion covering 1–10 June as they had split up. The same goes for the 5th Battalion Situation Reports, which go a degree further from 6–10 June. HQ Company were tasked with recording what they called 'Incidents, Messages and Orders' as they happened. I have shown these with the precursor 'IMO' in the text.

I have also drawn upon a wealth of information contained within a report called the 'Small Unit Actions Report – Pointe du Hoc'. It is a document held at the US Army Centre for Military History – Historical Section. When I have quoted this report, it is abbreviated 'SUA' and this report is unique because it was written within a month of the Action at Pointe du Hoc, and the report's authors interviewed surviving Rangers who took part. It is the best official first-hand narrative of the events of that action ever written.

Additionally, inserted on the dates at which they were released, are some of the many documents written by the Army Training Centre and issued to the assault troops to enhance their training.

All of these papers are most representative of the time and now publicly available from the US National Archives – thus they are not open to any suggestion of speculation on the part of the author. The Small Unit Actions report Pointe du Hoc, tells the story of that battle in a way which not many other works can. But alongside it, I have added to its content by using the Morning Reports covering unit movements and casualties – some of which contain information not included in the SUA report.

I have included the memoirs of a Naval Shore Fire Control Officer – Coit Coker, who was attached to the 5th Rangers during their advance inland on 6 June. His diary of events surrounding the movements of the 5th Battalion are in my opinion one of the most accurate available. He is defined as 'Coker' when quoted. Other Rangers are quoted by name and their comments have been taken from interviews with the author and add context and expanded content. During my personal interviews and filming with the veterans, I asked them to tell me of incidents where often they were the only witnesses. When available, I have added any relevant 'official US Army After Action Report' comments to expand on some of these actions.

I opened up some of the US Army Training Manuals to expose the myriad of things that each Ranger was expected to learn and understand prior to going into battle. The sheer volume of information that was given to these men is overwhelming and this book does not come close to covering everything that was required to be absorbed by the individual Ranger. The inclusion of just some of this information gives you an idea of the wide scope and variety of their training. Indeed, there was so much additional training information that I decided that it warranted a separate book and that will be available in the future.

We now no longer need to accept events as being accurate simply because an author wrote about them twenty years ago. Equally, as will be proved, Rangers were only told what their commanders wanted them to know – and often the true battle objectives differed considerably from that. But a word of caution, After Action Reports and even Morning Reports which have been around for years can and were used to present to their superiors what their writers at the time wanted them to read. Sometimes omission is deliberate and inclusion is done to aid someone's prospective or career/military agenda. It all has to be taken in the round and without all the pieces of the jigsaw, a decent study of this subject would have been impossible.

Using all the documents available, this book aims to allow you to delve into the lives of the US Army Rangers in England and Normandy in a way that no other has done before. Yes, it's complex and it does not always read like a novel… but that is somewhat the point. Not every soldier would have had all the information available to him at any one time and it builds for individuals and then units as a whole. Information on a certain subject may have been given out on a need-to-know basis. A good example of this would be the operational working of the ladders fitted to the DUKWs (to be covered in a future work). Only a small number of Rangers were involved in that aspect of the equipment training – yet I found that it was necessary to discuss this piece of equipment in full – in one go. Inevitably you will find that on some days there is a lot of information being processed by a wide number of different groups of Rangers – and on other days the men were simply training together or working on a particular 'problem' as the veterans liked to call them.

The one thing of which we can be sure – the officer in charge of the two Ranger battalions (2nd and 5th) Lieutenant Colonel James Earl Rudder was briefed on **all** the intelligence available to the Allies before the assault. Not only were some of the documents shown in this book actually signed off by him as CO (Commanding Officer) – but multiple copies were provided to the Rangers for him to delegate to those beneath him. Now we know what he knew – and on the days when he knew it. Thus, going forward, there can be no misinterpretation of what he knew before landing. More to the point, I hope that this book will put an end to the many variations of the Rangers' history that are out there.

Inevitably, Lt. Col. Rudder could not control everything. He alone could not organise the many and various aspects of training for all of the men, so that was delegated to junior officers. The men had to train for cliff climbing, demolition, marksmanship, map reading, orientation, weaponry and much more – and they needed a thorough understanding of enemy weapons as well as their own. They had to be at the top of their physical game at all times, and above all, they needed the individual skills to complete their own specific company missions – even though, until some weeks before D-Day, they would not actually be told what those missions were.

But Lt. Colonel Rudder was in control of how much of the intelligence his men had access to – and this is a major factor which will be discussed later in the book. Just how much of this information did Lt. Colonel Rudder disseminate to his men has long been a tricky subject for me to understand. One reason is that many books on the subject of D-Day and the Rangers make him out to have been the leading force behind the 'success' of the Pointe du Hoc mission and yet I can see flaws in that.

Each document should provide you with a good overview of the intelligence gathering process and how the planning worked for the whole division in the build up to D-Day. This fact alone puts us in the unique position to now see what the eyes of a commanding officer could see prior to D-Day. With the benefit of hindsight, we can judge – if we think the decisions he made were the right ones or not.

Chapter 1

The Formation of the Rangers

The 2nd and 5th Ranger companies consisted of approximately sixty-five men per company and three officers – although these were increased by around fifteen per cent before D-Day to allow for expected casualties. The 2nd and 5th Ranger Battalions each contained a number of companies, namely A, B, C, D, E, F as well as a Medical Company, a Headquarters Company for each battalion and, towards D-Day, a few additional split-off elements such as the 2nd Battalion Cannon Company. When required, some elements became 'Detachment A' who were given the task of organising replacements or preparing accommodation in advance of the main body arriving etc.

Essentially there were two battalions training in the US, then they came to England and from there they were fighting in Normandy. They were called the 2nd and 5th US Army Ranger Infantry Battalions and accounted for around 1,100 men in total.

Every day, every single man had to be accounted for in a Morning Report. It was recorded where he was and who he was with. At all times the leadership would know what every group was doing and when it came to combat, they could keep abreast of the figures by looking at the Morning Reports and from those reports, they could gain an accurate view of the number of casualties. Also, at the very least, they had a simplified understanding of what each company had been involved in during the previous day. The men could all be doing different things and yet the company commanders, battalion HQ Company and ultimately the battalion commander knew on any given day the status of each group and its activities – and of most importance, how many men he had ready to fight at a moment's notice.

What each unit was to be doing at any given time during training was directed by the battalion leadership and once in combat, it was guided by those same men and given overall direction by divisional orders with objectives and timings set out well in advance.

The chain of command was pivotal in the way that the Rangers functioned. They were to be at the dictate of others above them – yet, they were to play a strategic role in the direction and advance of the war. An important aspect of the Rangers' DNA was their ability to take a mission and decide for themselves how it would be conducted. They were to be assault troops who (for the first time in military history) were trained to adapt and develop as the battle unfolded using their own initiative. We are told by historians that ALL of the Rangers were informed of their own mission and that of those around them. They were to act independently or in small groups when necessary and above all, they were to complete the mission given to them – whatever the individual hardship and losses the larger unit suffered.

To suggest they were expendable is not accurate and nor were they on a 'suicide mission'. One of the reasons that they, as a unit, were created was to make surgical incisions into enemy territory to achieve advantage by surprise and speed – and often to make gains and consolidations for the divisions around them. As happened later on in the war, their participation in particular battles was often the turning point and the edge needed for an operation to succeed.

On D-Day the Rangers were given a number of such vital missions and pre-assault intelligence played a huge role in their story. During the planning stages for Operation Overlord (the code name for the Normandy landings), once individual unit missions were delegated from General Eisenhower's office down through to division and then to individual combat leaders for their battalion, it was then those leaders that were the ones who received the intelligence directly thereafter for their assault area. If the intelligence changed – the battalion commanders were some of the first to know.

It makes perfect sense that only Lt. Col. Rudder (the 2nd and 5th Rangers' commanding officer) would receive intelligence information about the Pointe du Hoc Battery, Maisy Batteries and the Radar Station at Pointe et Raz de la Percée each day. Equally he would not receive intelligence concerning Pegasus Bridge, the proposed attack on Merville Battery or the Sainte-Mère-Église town assault. Each commander was delegated his mission for his unit and, although an overview was given to surrounding troops, it was the Rangers' mission to carry out their own individual orders as part of the larger whole. Failure of any one part of the D-Day landings could be catastrophic for other elements and perhaps lead to the failure of the whole invasion.

Therefore once Colonel Rudder had been briefed on his missions, any and all intelligence related to those targets was being provided directly to him by military intelligence after that initial introduction – and the introduction was a good one. It is repeatedly stated in other works that Allied Supreme Commander Dwight Eisenhower told Lt. Col. Rudder that he had *'the most important mission on D-Day…'* – and he may well have said that – and this is generally the perceived level of importance that had been placed on Pointe du Hoc as a target in the early months of 1944.

When we find an illustration of the Pointe du Hoc area, for example the one from April 1944, it was hand drawn specifically for the Rangers to use. The exact detail of the mission and the assault itself would not have been the concern of the intelligence operatives drawing the maps from aerial reconnaissance photos. It was for the Rangers to decide for themselves on the battle plan and how that fitted in with their overall orders.

Information was continually being updated, often daily. I have shown that information in whatever format it was produced, so we know what was being seen by Lt. Col. Rudder. This is not supposition on my part, as these are the actual documents the Rangers received; one assumes after that, it was then processed down to the individual Rangers beneath them. As target sites changed and overhead aerial reconnaissance flights took place, changes to the topography or layout of a position would be noted and often within hours new maps were issued. Thus the process went on until D-Day. It was imperative that all assault groups had the most up-to-date maps available to allow them to complete their missions and this was actually done at the expense of the later following units, some of whom did not need to have such a specific understanding of the Normandy coastline.

The formation of the Rangers and their 'special forces' status depended upon their having a role to play in the operations to come in Europe. The role of the 29th Provisional Ranger Battalion as it was originally known, was short lived and it was wondered at the time, if it was necessary to actually create another specialist combat unit.

Following interviews carried out in 1943 with Major Gilbert Embury (of Combined Operations), Major Cleaves Jones, Lieutenant Colonel Jock Lawrence P.R.C. S.O.S. and Major Manning Jacob, the American Military Attaché, American Embassy, the following document was drawn up based on information provided by them and by the men under their command:

> *Early in the spring of 1942, General George C. Marshall and the Lord Louis Mountbatten (at that time Chief of Combined Operations) met in London. Among the items discussed at this conference was the creation of an American Staff to work with and study the methods, organisation etc. of the British at Combined Operations HQ. One organisation in particular they were to study thoroughly, the British Commandos, so that if and when the then germinating idea for the establishment of a comparable organisation in the US Army became more than just an idea, these Staff Officers would be in a position to supervise the organisation, constitution and training of such an organisation.*
>
> *The machinery to place a group of American Officers with Combined Operations Headquarters began with an order from General Marshall to Col. Lucian K. Truscott, Jr. The order was dated April 30th 1942 and in effect it read as follows:*
>
> *Missions of this group which was to be headed by Colonel Truscott:*
> *To study the planning, organisation, preparation and conduct of Combined Operations, especially those of Commando type and to keep the CO. W.D. informed as to development in the training techniques and equipment pertaining to these and related operations.*
>
> *To initiate plans for the participation by American troops in these operations to the fullest possible and practicable extent with a view to affording actual battle experience to maximum personal and to plan and co-ordinate the training of the detachment designated for such participation. (Note this was carried out to a very little extent with the participation of a small detachment of the 1st Ranger Battalion with the Dieppe Raid… see below).*
>
> *To provide information and recommendations relative to the techniques, training and equipment involved in those and related operations. To assist the Headquarters of Army Ground Forces in planning, organising and conducting training in such operations in the United States.*
>
> *The following officers were assigned by W.D. order to Combined Ops on 18 May 1942: Brigadier General Lucian K. Truscott Jr, Lieutenant Colonel Lawrence B. Hilsinger, Major Theodor J. Conway and Lieutenant Colonel Haskell H. Cleaves.*

A letter dated 1 June 1942 HQ USAFBI contained a series of directives upon which this group was to base the coming Ranger unit. A letter dated 13 June 1942 HQ ETOUSA authorized the organization of the 1st Provisional Ranger Battalion.

According to Major Jacob, much of the idea for a Ranger unit can be credited to Lieutenant Colonel Darby, (at that time, Captain, aide to General Hartle) and when the authorization for it was made, he was placed in command. By order, Major T. Conway was assigned the task of drawing up the T/O etc. for the Rangers. In carrying out his task he went to Northern Ireland and with the assistance and co-operation of the officers and men of the American forces there, the selection and organization of the 1st Provisional Rangers Battalion began. (Originally based on No.1 Commando).

It was composed entirely of volunteers from all American units in the British Isles. Service requirements were rigid and exacting, the highest physical and mental standards were demanded of the volunteers, and another important point used for the selection was the past military record of the applicant and their ability to speak one or more foreign language.

Each candidate was given a questionnaire and after he had filled it out and it had been studied by the board, he was interviewed. This board consisted of (then) Major Darby, his Executive Officer Captain Herman W. Dammer and Captain Steve Meade. Organization and equipment completed during June, the unit was then ready for training. It was ordered to report to the Commando Depot, Achnacarry, Spean Bridge, Inverness-shire, Scotland for training where, under trained personnel from the Commando units, it was put through a rigid and exacting training programme for four weeks. This programme, in brief, consisted of all forms of toughening up exercises, calisthenics, marches, speed marches, obstacle and assault courses, unarmed combat, much field-craft, weapon training, boat training, swimming, climbing, use of assault craft, and several exercises involving landing and assaults under very real, but simulated battle conditions. Considerable emphasis was put on the idea of night fighting, patroling, street fighting, etc.

The first practical application of this intensive training was made during the Dieppe Raid, 19 August 1943, when a small detachment consisting of six officers and forty-four enlisted men were assigned to the units which were to make the raid on Dieppe. Of the participants, the Rangers suffered some casualties. Two officers and some enlisted men were missing, six enlisted men were wounded. The lessons brought forth from this raid were immediately incorporated into the renewed training programme, which was continuous.

Emphasis went on to more concentrated work on assault with landing craft etc., until the Ranger Battalion left the UK to participate in the landing and subsequent operations in North Africa. After the initial work in North Africa, the battalion was withdrawn from combat and used in various capacities as MPs etc.

Briefly the battalion was organized as follows: (approximate numbers)

HQ and HQ Companies: 9 officers and 94 enlisted men (103 total).
Six line companies: 3 officers and 65 enlisted men each.
Aggregate strength of 511 officers and enlisted men.

After the 1st was assigned to the Fifth Army Assault Training Centre as a demonstration unit, Lieutenant Colonel Darby broke the unit into groups and made three new battalions using the original first as a cadre to produce the new units.

1st Rangers – Lieutenant Colonel Darby, Commanding Officer, Ex.O. Captain Martin.
3rd Rangers – Major Herman W. Dammer, Commanding Office, Ex.O. Captain Miller.
4th Rangers – Major Roy Murray, Ex.O. Captain Schneider.

There is a 2nd Ranger Battalion at present in training at Camp Forrest Tennessee. In the UK there is at present only one other Ranger Type organization. That is the 29th Provisional Ranger Battalion commanded by Major Randolph Millholland. It is a Bastard outfit having no official existence… no approved Training Organisation. Yet it is training and while differently composed (HQ detachment and 4 line Companies) – as contrasted with the 1st Ranger Battalion (see above) one cannot simply say that the unit does not exist, because it has no official birth.

Tactical employment of the Rangers: Primarily, like the commandos, the Rangers are to be used as an advance striking force in ship to shore landing assaults against a hostile coast. All of the training has been directed towards *the achievement of that goal, amphibious work, street fighting and night operations. In the land fighting in Tunisia the Rangers have been used as large fighting patrols, to make land raids or used in combination with the British Commandos as a tactical group with which large scale land raids may be made.*

To date, despite strong recommendations from many sources, the Army Ground Forces have been unable or unwilling to come to a decision on whether or not to have more Ranger type units… whether if they did have such a unit, it should be made of men drawn from the Infantry Divisions, given the specialised training and then returned to be attached to the Division as a Division task force, so to speak… or whether they should behave as a Ranger Division similar to the Special Services Brigade of the British.

The Commandos. This is commanded by Brigadier Laycock, and, is directly under Combined Operations HQ, constituting what one might call the troops of Combined Ops HQ. At present there are some 2 paratroop Commando (term Commando being used here to indicate a unit comparable in size and scope to our Ranger Battalion which is patterned largely on the Commando), 4 Marine Commandos and 10 Commando.

It is difficult to understand why there has been such a tremendous amount of hedging on the Rangers. They are proving to be of inestimable value. Major Manning Jacob told me 'that one of the other so-called stumbling blocks which beset the Army Ground Forces was whether or not to adopt Ranger type training for all Infantry.' I asked him what time he would estimate that it would take to carry through such a training program, assuming that all of the equipment and instructors personnel were available at the beginning… He replied '4 months'.

Major Gilbert W. Embury has done another large bit of research on this subject of the Rangers. He has suggested the creation of a Ranger Planning Officer to plan and provide for a Ranger Division. There is a definite and concrete need for such an organisation in our total war organisation.

Both the 29th and the 1st Ranger Battalion have carried out a number of tests of equipment and rations, results of which have been of great value, in providing practical knowledge of how the equipment or rations work or fail to work practicably under test conditions.

Certainly the lessons which have been brought back to the experiences of the 1st Ranger Battalion in its combat in the Tunisian and subsequent Sicilian campaign cannot be ignored. They have inestimable value for future training of our soldiers.

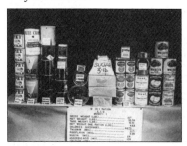

Members of the 29th Rangers taking part in rations trials.

The 29th Ranger Battalion (Provisional). 21 December 1942 – 16 October 1943

The following information comes from a discussion with Major Millholland, C.O. of the Ranger Battalion during its short unofficial life:

This Battalion began when Major Millholland, who returned from the British G.H.Q. Battle School on the 8th of December 1942 was asked by General Gerow, the then Division Commander, if he would like to volunteer to organise and train a Ranger unit out of the 29th. This was enthusiastically accepted by Major Millholland and he set straightaway to the task.

First it was necessary to choose officers for the 2 companies of which the battalion was to consist. This was done in much the same manner as was done with the selection of the officers for the 1st Ranger Battalion. Volunteers were called for, and from the group which responded, Millholland made his selection…. taking sufficient officers for the 2 companies and a headquarters detachment.

Next came the selection of enlisted personnel. Volunteers were requested, and of the number who volunteered, some 40% were finally accepted after thorough examination and personal interview by Millholland and his chosen group of officers. These enlisted men, some 170 in all were placed on D.S. with the Rangers on the 21st of December 1942.

From this group, Millholland formed and trained a battalion on the lines of training that he had received while at the Battle School. Then, on the 2nd of February 1943, the unit moved to the Commando Depot at Achnacarry, Scotland to undergo five weeks of rigorous training under the direction of, and with the Commandos.

US Army Signal Corps photograph which is captioned: US Rangers boarding a cutter for boating practice, somewhere in Britain. Their workouts are done in conjunction with Commando Training. Spean Bridge, Scotland – 10 February 1943.

Lt. Colonel C.E. Vaughan, Commandant of a Commando Depot confers with his Second in Command, Major Peter Cockraft on the day's schedule for a Ranger Unit. Spean Bridge, Scotland – 12 February 1943. US Army Signal Corps.

Major Peter Cockraft, Second in Command at Commando Depot, somewhere in Britain. Commando Depot, Spean Bridge, Scotland – 7 February 1943. US Army Signal Corps.

Sgt. Major Thomas Sawkins of a Commando Depot gives special instructions on the use of a Tommy Gun to the US Rangers in the foreground. (L-R). Cpl. Chas. Shaw of Philadelphia, Pa., and Pvt. James Yingling of Johnstown, Pa., and Pvt. Anton Karpowish of Perth Amboy, N.J. – Scotland 1943. US Army Signal Corps.

Lt. Derek Burr of a Commando Depot stands behind four men of a Ranger unit whom he is instructing in the use of a M1 Rifle. (L-R) Pfc. Vernon Dougherty of Altoona, Pa., Pfc. Chas. Perachka of Mercer, Pa., Cpl. Alonzo Colds of Todd, N.C., and Cpl. Laurence Hickman, Md. – Scotland 1943. US Army Signal Corps.

Members of a US Army Ranger Battalion taking a 10 mile speed march somewhere in Britain – Members of US 29th Rangers Spean Bridge, Scotland. US Army Signal Corps.

Two British officers take tea with a 29th Ranger.

Lt. John Lee Warner, British Rifle Instructor at a Commando Depot, giving instructions to US Rangers, who are training there – Spean Bridge, Scotland. US Army Signal Corps.

29th Rangers training and running with logs.

During this training period Millholland's men shattered several of the previous records for speed marches which had been set up by the Commandos and the first Ranger Battalion. At the conclusion of this rigorous course, the unit was returned to Tidworth, where the men and officers were given a well-earned 4 day leave in London. How poor London must have caught it with this rough and trim bunch of fighting manpower descending after having been in little contact with the so-called society life for five weeks.

At the conclusion of this heavenly, but expensive rest, the unit went back to work again. This time they reported to East Leigh where they were 'billeted out'... with British civvies homes as their quarters. Here they were attached to Lord Lovett's 4th Commando for additional training.

During this time, they took part in the huge exercise Seaweed... which among other things involved several different landing operations (practice not actual battle operations). From this service with the 4th Commando the unit returned to Tidworth (Perham Downs) on the 10th of April 1943 much better trained, seasoned with valuable experience. One officer and four enlisted men had been attached to another British Commando unit, and while with them had participated in three separate landing operations in Norway... these men returned to the unit on the 26th of April 1943.

Meanwhile the rest of the Battalion, back at Perham Downs Camp in the Tidworth area, had not been idle. Two more companies were formed, by the same process of calling for volunteers and again only about 40% of those who came forward were accepted. These two new companies were sent speedily to Achnacarry where during a shorter course broke some of the records which had been set by the first group of the 29th Rangers.

Returning to the unit on the 27th of May, the entire outfit participated in the Exercise 'Columbus'... 175th C.T., plus attached units against a British Armoured Division. The Rangers almost stole the show when they made a wide sweep around the flank and deep into 'enemy' territory to smash the command post, and gather in the plans of campaign. Returning to the Combat Team, the Rangers acted as a covering force for the withdrawal of the C.T., smashing bridges built at night by the British and blocking their access to another bridge. In all of their work, the Rangers acquitted themselves most admirably. 'The commandos have rated this unit the best of all troops, British, Canadian or American to go through the commando course.'

Once again the Rangers moved. This time to Bude in North Devon, on the 3rd of June 1943 where they received all types of specialised training.... such as cliff scaling, demolitions, use of semaphores in signaling (all the men were made accomplished signalers), morse code. Here also they made an 11-day ration test.

One company was placed on C rations alone for the period ... another on K ration. A third on K ration plus D ration for one day, then on C & D for the next... alternating with this ration right along. They covered over 150 miles, with several small unit problems worked into the day march. Each man carried his full equipment with rations for one day.

On returning from this 11 day trip, the battalion watched a Training Film entitled 'Preparation for Assault Operations'. The results were highly gratifying to the War Department and Major Millholland said that he understood that this film was being used as one of the basic training aids for instruction in assault techniques back in the states.

On the 2nd of September 1943 they went to Dorlin House in Scotland where they received some advanced assault training. They also received the highest commendation from their instructors as the best all round group of men, and SOLDIERS ever to pass through the training. Two men were sent to A Commando for an operation onto some islands off the coast of France. Both received the highest praise. One of the men, in covering the withdrawal of the unit to the boats, accounted certainly for three Germans, and probably for three more.

One full company went to Dover on September 20th 1943 to be used in a large-scale raid against the continent. They had a specific mission all to themselves. This raid was to have been the runner up for a large scale raid that was cancelled. Unfortunately for battle experience, the company did not go as the smaller raid was cancelled.

But the life of the unit was coming to an unnatural end. It was to be returned to its basic bits... because the 'War Department felt that they could bring over better trained Ranger type units from the states.' What a lot of waste has gone into this. These men, while benefitting tremendously from their training as Rangers, are now no longer a striking force. Their experience will probably not be put to great use in the division if past conduct of the division is any criterion. The men themselves are terribly broken up over the fate of their unit. AWOL's have already started ... a thing which was rare indeed in Ranger or Commando units. However, one ray of hope, is Gerhardt's evident desire to make full use of these men.

322 RANGERS

2 December 1942
AG 320.2MGC
Activation of Ranger Bn.

TO : TAG, W.D., Washington, D.C.

FROM: Theater Commander.

1. 1st Ranger Bn. was organized in this theatre early in June 1942, tr at Br. Comm. T.C.; used in Dieppe raid and assault near Oran. Now in Mediterranean; will not return to England.

2. Request 2nd Ranger Bn. be organized now.

3. Shortage of combat personnel here; small tr being organized in 29th Division; to be returned after training.

4. All personnel should be volunteers; Age field - not over 40; others not over 30 to be tr. with the Br.

5. Request 2nd Ranger Bn. (less one Co.) be activated in U.S. at early date and shipped to U.K.

6. C.G., E.T.O., be authorized to activate one Co. Ranger Bn. from personnel in E.T.O.

7. 10% overstrength

1st. Ind from W.D. --
T/O not favorably considered.

No object to utilize of a bn. or regt. of Infantry of an Infantry Division within U.K. which permits organization within unit similiar to Ranger Bn. Since it is possible to again reintegrate personnel into parent unit.
One company may be organized under same provisions.

Ltr to C.G., 29th Infantry Division, 14 February 1943 320.2MGC

Activation of 2nd Ranger Bn.

1. Request for permanent Ranger Bn. desired by W.D.

2. Ranger Bn, 29th Infantry Division will continue to function on a provisional basis

AG 320.2MGC - 12 March 1943 - Ranger Battalion, To TAG, Wash DC

Reopen question of act of Ranger Battalion for 29th Inf. Division -- Lord Louis Marlbatten states Gen Marshall at Casa blanca wants more rangers, Request Ranger Bn be designated 29th Ranger Bn.

1st Ind., 23 April 1943 - To C.G. ETO from W.D.

Provisional act of 29th Ranger Bn is approved.

2nd Ranger Bn is organized and earmarked for E.T.O.

Another letter at the time was entitled: Activation of 2nd Ranger Battalion (3-11-43)

HEADQUARTERS SECOND ARMY, Memphis, Tennessee
To: Commanding Officer, 11th Detachment Special Troops. Second Army Camp Forrest, Tennessee.
1. *For compliance with applicable provisions of basic communication as amended.*
2. *Unit will be housed in tents in bivouac area.*
3. *You are directed to:-*
   a) *Issue the necessary Letter Orders activating the 2nd Ranger Battalion on April 1st 1943.*
   b) *Observe the transfer of personnel and equipment to this Battalion.*
   c) *Assist the Commanding Officer, 2nd Ranger Battalion in obtaining necessary supplies through Director of Supplies, Camp Forrest, Tennessee.*
   d) *Report observations and completion of activation to Headquarters Second Army.*
4. *Two copies activation directive as amended, Army Ground Forces enclosed.*
By Command of Lieutenant General Lear

So began the formation of the 2nd Ranger Infantry Battalion.

```
------------------------------------------------

23 June 1943 - To Tag, W.D.

      Request tha another Ranger Bn be activated for ETO ar-
rive December 1943

25 March 1943, Ltr to Lord Louis Mountbatten from Gen Barker

      Request additional increment of 12 officers and 165 EM
Can this personnel be trained at a Commando T.C.  This is
2 Co and overhead personnel

29 November 1942 - C.G., 29th Inf. Division

      Authority to form a provisional Ranger Battalion.

9 August 1943 - To C.G. ETOUSA (on 28 August Gen Noce said
no answer required, 1 oral discussion for the present)

Activation of a Ranger Batallion for Gen Gerow.

      Request that W.D. be req. to reconsider dec. ad to
authorize act of Ranger Bn in 29th Infantry Div.

16 August 1943 - Memo to Gen Abbott from Gen. Edwards.

      1. 2d Ranger Bn arrives in United Kinggom in October
      2. 5th Ranger Bn arrives in United Kingdom in December.
      3. Activation of 29th Ranger Bn disapproved.
      4. Theatre must justify Ranger Bn in theatre to 3 -
         justified in overload.
      5. Overall troop basis of Army provides only for 5 Ranger
         Bns; 3 in W.A.; 2 in U.K.  One more requires change in
         Overall.

See 322 Infantry for Disbandment of 29th Ranger Battalion

Memo to Gen Chambers from Gen Noce - 28 September 1943

      Reasons why 29th being deactivated 99th Sep Bn (Norwegian)
in U.K. will receive Ranger Training and 2 more Ranger Ranger
Bns to arrive in theatre at an early date -- 1st Ind - Hq.
Cossac 28 September 1943.  Cassac agrees disbanding of the
Ranger Bn, 29th Division will not jeopardize commando opera-
tion contemplated by him.

AG 322 - MGC - Subject; Disbandment of Provisional Unit
            To    : C.G. V Corps
            From  : Gen Devers.

      1. 29th Ranger Bn to be disbanded.  Personnel to return
to 29th Infantry Battalion.

      2. 1st Ind -- Hq V Corps -- 4 October 1943 to 29th Inf Div
         2nd Ind -- 18 October 1943 -- 29th Ranger Bn disbanded
         effective 18 October 1943.

------------------------------------------------
```

```
------------------------------------------------

Memo 8 June 1943 to C/s from Gen. Noce.

      Assignment of 1st Special Service Force.

      On arrival Service Force to be assigned V corps; C.G.
V Corps, training C.G. to be stationed at Perham, Downs.

Filed in 370.2 S/G

      A need for Ranger Bns in ETOUSA - 10 August 1943.

      Gen Cota to C.G. Etousa.

312.1 Off. only -- serial 30 Vol 1

      Use of U.S. rangers in raids and reconna.

------------------------------------------------
```

25 February 1943 dated memo discussing the requirements and attributes of the Assault Training Centre land.

CONFIDENTIAL

HEADQUARTERS
EUROPEAN THEATER OF OPERATIONS
UNITED STATES ARMY

25 February 1943

MEMORANDUM (No.9) FOR: General Barker.

SUBJECT   : Estimate of the terrain, proposed Training Center.

1. **Size and shape.** The proposed site for the combined amphibian-assault Training Center has the following general dimensions:
Width parallel to front: 10,000 yards.
Depth perpendicular to front: 6,000 yards.

Deduction: firing by anything other than small-caliber weapons and infantry mortars is out of the question. Even such firing is out of the question anywhere except along or very close to the front (beaches).

2. **General terrain characteristics.**

a. **Beaches.** There are two beaches along the front of the area. The chief one, Morte Bay Beach, is about 4,000 yards long. The other one, Croyde Bay Beach, is about 800 yards long, and is separated from Morte Bay Beach by the 1500-yard-wide Baggy Point. The beaches are sandy and flat (about 1 to 100 slope). There is not any appreciable quantity of "shingle" on them. Between the beaches and the mainland bluffs there is a narrow (100 yard wide) belt of rough sand dunes.

b. **Tides and surf.** The range of tide at the site varies from 20 feet to 25 feet. There is normally a strong surf running. Deduction: with the exception of the lack of "shingle", the beaches and oceanographic conditions at the proposed site simulate closely the conditions to be encountered at many points along the western coast of Europe.

c. **Terrain at beaches.** The main beach (Morte Bay Beach) is dominated throughout its entire length by the steep bluff barrier extending from Potter's Hill south to near Putsborough. In general, the barrier is all but unscalable, (for infantry, combat equipped), except at points where it is broken by creeks and sloughs. These points form the entrances to the Terrain "corridors" described in d. below. The secondary beach (Croyde Bay Beach) is flanked by unscalable bluffs, but it opens on the corridor formed by Croyde Creek. Deduction. Assault forces will be able to advance from the beaches inland only along the corridors which break through the almost-unscalable bluffs flanking and fronting on the beaches.

d. **Terrain corridors.** As already indicated, the heights overlooking the beaches are broken by natural terrain corridors. There are two primary and four secondary corridors as follows:

(1) Valley of Woolacombe Creek. This is a primary corridor, extending due east and leading to the controlling heights, Hill 688. A two-way all-weather road runs along the northern slopes of the corridor. The village of Woolacombe lies astride the mouth of the corridor.

(2) Valley of Croyde Creek. This is a primary corridor, extending due east and leading to the controlling heights, Oxford Cross - Hill 510. A one-way all-weather road runs up the corridor. The villages of Croyde and

CONFIDENTIAL

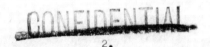

2.

Georgeham lie astride and block the corridor practically completely.

(3) Resevoir Slough. This is a secondary corridor, debouching on the beach just south of the mouth of Woolacombe Creek, and extending southeastward there-from. The corridor leads to the controlling heights, Potter's Hill and Hill 630. It complements the Woolacombe Creek Corridor. A one-way all-weather road runs up the corridor.

(4) Old Hotel Slough. This is a secondary corridor, debouching on the beach opposite Old Hotel, and extending northwestward therefrom. The corridor leads to the controlling heights, Hill 630. It complements the Resevoir Slough Corridor.

(5) Pickwell Slope. This is a secondary corridor, debouching on the beach opposite Pickwell and extending due east therefrom. The corridor leads to the controlling heights, Oxford Cross-hill 510. It complements the Croyde Creek Corridor.

(6) Twitchen Creek. This a secondary corridor, debouching in a rocky cove just north of Woolacombe, and extending east-northeastward therefrom. The corridor leads to the controlling heights overlooking the Woolacombe Creek corridor from the north. It complements the Woolacombe Creek Corridor.

(7) Spreacombe Creek. This is a secondary reverse corridor, leading from the controlling heights, Hill 688, southeastward to the terrain compartment formed by the valley of Braunton River.

Deduction: Any advance inland following a landing on the beaches must be along these corridors.

e. Terrain"Compartment". The valley of Braunton Creek, running along the rear boundary of the area, forms a broad terrain compartment which cuts perpendicularly across the entire front, at an average distance of 6,000 yards from the beaches. A two-way all-weather highway and a double-tracked railway run up this compartment.

f. Controlling heights.

(1) Beaches. Morte Bay Beach is controlled directly by the line of sand dune and the line of bluffs running from Potter's Hill south to Pickwell Hill. The Beach is controlled in enfilade by the heights on Morte Hoe Point and Baggy Point. Croyde Bay Beach similarly is controlled by nearby high ground, both directly and in enfilade.
Deduction. The first assault objective of the landing force must be the heights controlling the beaches.

(2) Hinterland. The hinterland of the area is a rolling plateau. The controlling terrain feature is the long curved ridge, Hill688-Hill 656 - Hill 630 - Oxford Cross. Deduction: The second assault objective of the landing forces must include the ridge just defined.

3. The five "terrain factors". The analysis in this paragraph pertains to the five "terrain factors" listed in Engineer Field Manual 5-15 (observation, fields of fire, cover, and concealment, obstacles, communications).

a. Observation. Excellent observation characterizes the entire

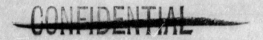

CONFIDENTIAL

3.

area. There is scarcely a square yard of the terrain that is not covered completely, and from several angles, by good observation. The beaches themselves are covered directly and in enfilade. Paucity of cover (see c. below) ensures almost perfect observation from any commanding elevation.

b. Fields of fire. Excellent fields of fire, long and unobstructed, characterize the entire area. There are few dead areas. Enfilade fire is practicable at most points.

c. Cover and concealment. Lack of extensive cover characterizes the entire area. The only cover consists of infrequent patches of thin woods, somewhat more extensive patches of thickets (bushes five feet high), solid walls and hedges (four feet high) which cross and criss-cross the fields, and villages and farm buildings. Some important terrain features - Potter's Hill, for example -are completely devoid of cover. From the standpoint of creating cover the area is unpromising. Through much of the area, hard rock underlies the ground surface at shallow depths. Deduction: The operation of digging in will be difficult, and in places impossible.

d. Obstacles. Except for the practically unscalable slopes facing the beaches, there are no important natural obstacles in the area. The walls and hedges which cross and criss-cross the fields are earth and rock structures, about two feet thick by four feet high. They constitute effective obstacles against wheeled vehicles, but not against tanks. The villages constitute obstacles in some cases blocking important natural avenues of advance.

e. Communications. The northern and southern parts of the area are served respectively, each, by one two-way and one one-way all-weather road. These roads either debouch onto the beaches, or pass within a few yards of them. The roads generally run due east. In a north-south direction, the area is served by one one-way all-weather road paralleling the beaches at a distance of approximately 2000 yards, and by one two-way all-weather trunk-line highway, paralleling the beaches at a distance of approximately 6000 yards. A two-track railway runs adjacent to the latter road. The railway marks the rear boundary of the area. Deduction. The road system serving the area will permit of handling a daily tonnage inland of about 5,400 tons.

4. Conclusions. The area in question offers advantages and disadvantages as follows:

Advantages.	Disadvantages.
Favorable beaches and oceanographic conditions, similar to what our forces will encounter along the western coast of Europe.	Small size of area permitting little, or no, tactical firing.
Favorable terrain for maneuver, including definite objectives, and good avenues of approach.	Lack of cover, dissimilar to terrain our forces will encounter near the beaches of western Europe.
Good communications from beaches rearward.	Unfavorable soil, complicating the operation of digging in.

All in all, I feel that, witht the area bounded as proposed in my Memorandum No.6, we can, so far as terrain is concerned substantially accomplish the mission of the Training Center.

Paul W. Thompson,
Lt. Col., C.E.

CONFIDENTIAL

Land acquition for ATC

"Exploratory investigation re: acquisition of land for
Assault Training Center, ETOUSA."

PWT/11p

1. A.G. Assault   7 April" Request letter substantially as follows
    Training   1943   be directed to C.G., SQO.S., ETOUSA."
    Center

1. Reference is made to conversations
you had recently with the Commandant ATC concerning boundaries of reservation.

2. Map included, plotting prosposed
boundaries. "The vital areas from the stadpoint of training are the three
beaches, SaantonSands, Croyde Beach and Woolacombe Sands, together with
the corridors and terrain features complementing and controlling them.
The areas along the rivers Taw and Torridge, forming the harbor for the
naval craft of the Center, are also vital. These areas consitute the
'minim requirement' for the reservation."

3. Realized may"include structures and
areas of especial importance to British civilians or governmental interests."
Believed problems arising in connections with such interests "can be resolved
successfully without unde adverse effect" on ATC's mission. Following
arrangem nts will be acceptable:

a. "The three villages - Woolacombe,
Georgeham, and Croyde - included within the proposed boundaries are to be
evacuated if possible. In any event, rights to maneuver through the villages
streets and yards are to be obtained. If the villages can be evacuated,
every effort will be made to ensure buildings against permanent damage. If i
it proves impracticable to evacuate the villages, every effort will be made
to conduct training with minimum disturbance to the village populations.
In that event, no firing will be permitted within range of the villages, and
no explosives will be used in or near them.

b." Small areas of especial importance
to the British can be fenced and placed 'off-limits' in cases where such
action will not compromise unduly the mission" of the ATC, including
individual structures. Merits of each case, will be decided upon, after
consultation with Commandant of Center.

4. Areas to be used for realistic field
maneuvers of invasion conditions. "Therefore (but with exeptions as
noted in the preceding paragraphs), we must have the right to use the
properties inany indicated way: that is, to erect fortifications, to gt
dig-in, to demolish fences and hedges, to close roads to civil traffic, to
use explosives and fire power(when such will not endanger civilian lives
and property outside the boundaries), to maneuver at will, and to construct
buildings and facilities of various types."

5. "Alll available billieting facilities
in the villages of Woolacombe and Ilfracombe, and perhaps in other
nearby villages, are to be acquired."

6. Desired exploratory investigation
be made to determine practicability of acquiring the land under letter's
conditions. Investigation to precede acquisition itself. Commandant will
assist in all ways possible.

7. As plans for Center dependant on
land qcquisition, desires such investigation be undertaken at once and
completed by 13 April.

P.W.T.

AG RECORDS.

HEADQUARTERS
EUROPEAN THEATER OF OPERATIONS
UNITED STATES ARMY   RPF/rls

AG 322.3 MGC   6 May 1943

SUBJECT: Duties of the Assault Training Center, ETOUSA

TO: Commandant, Assault Training Center, ETOUSA.

    1. The Assault Training Center, ETOUSA, has been established with the following missions:

      a. To develop and keep up-to-date the doctrines and methods covering the assault of enemy-held coasts, particularly of Western Europe.
      b. To prepare and operate the Assault Training Center for the reception and training of such organizations as my be selected for this type of training.
      c. To train the demonstration troops in the approved methods.
      d. To stage demonstrations of approved methods for the benefit of organizations being trained.
      e. To instruct and supervise the assault training of such organizations as may be designated to receive this training.

    2. The Assault Training Center will operate directly under the control of this headquarters and, until further notice, will coordinate its activities through the G-3 Section.

    3. Plans for the accomplishment of the mission outlined will be prepared and submitted to this headquarters for approval. These should be submitted without delay.

    4. Authorization is granted to establish informal liaison with British and United States agencies engaged in similar development and training. Liaison with British Combined Operations Headquarters will be through the Combined Operations Liaison Officer, this headquarters. Formal commitments and agreements will be sumitted through normal command channels for approval.

    By Command of Major General KEY:

                RICHARD P. FISK,
                Lt. Colonel, A.G.D.,
              Assistant Adjutant General.

14 February dated 'Mission statement' which breaks down the function of the newly formed Army Training Centre.

CONFIDENTIAL

HEADQUARTERS
EUROPEAN THEATRE OF OPERATIONS
UNITED STATES ARMY

14 February 1943

MEMORANDUM (NO. 1) FOR: General Barker

SUBJECT   :   Mission of Combined Operations Assault Training Center.

    1. General statement of mission. My mission is to set up a training center "to develop the special tactics and technique involved in the assault of a heavily-defended shore", and "to train units which will be employed in such operations". The mission thus is double-barrelled: to develop, and to train.

    2. Specific break-down of mission. As I now understand it, the general mission quoted above embraces specific operations as follows:
        a. Embarkation of assault teams in landing craft on the near shore.

        b. Shore services incident to embarkation on the near shore.

        c. transport of assault troops across water to the far shore, including the incident navigational operations.

        d. Landing (debarkation) from landing craft on the far shore.

        e. Shore services incident to landing on the far shore.

        f. Assault by the landed assault teams against enemy positions on the far shore, including:

                overcoming of on- and off-shore obstacles,
                reductions of fortifications,
                repulsing of counter-attacks,
                establishing of the beach-head.

        g. Supply of assault teams, including rations, ammunition and fuel, throughout the entire operation.

        h. Reinforcing and supporting of assault teams throughout the entire operation.

    3. Discussion. My mission, as thus broken down, is indeed a large order. It embraces the most difficult type of military operation: crossing of a great obstacle in the face of the strongest enemy resistance. It embraces combined operations of ground, naval, air, and supply forces. It lies in a field not covered completely be previous experience.

    4. The difficulties and ramifications of my mission, however, are fully matched by the vital importance of the operations involved. My only object in dwelling on the difficulties and ramifications is to establish this point that the job at hand is a big and tough one, and that I must have authority and means consistent therewith.

2.

Course are to act as instructors. Thus, every new division arriving in England will have been indoctrinated with the Engineer School conception of assault tactics and technique - which, as I have pointed out, is based largely on theoretical analysis of what we think has happened in recent campaigns.

e. North African Battle School. I am informed that a "Battle School" has been, or is about to be, established in the North African theater. I also understand that the Engineer Amphibian Brigade in that theater will set up a school (possibly in conjunction with the Battle School). No details are available, but it is evident that something along the lines of our proposed center is also brewing in North Africa.

f. American Navy and Marine Corps. Without having availabel any details, I know that our Navy and Marine Corps have done, and are doing, aa great deal of intensive work on all aspects of amphibian-assault operations. it goes without saying that in this work, the Navy and Marine Corps are incorporating the results of much valuable recent experience.

g. British agencies. Several British agencies are engaged constantly in development and training relative to amphian-assault operations. There is no doubt but that in many aspects of the problem the British are out ahead of the field. Among other items, the British have available an unparalleled volume of data based on actual experience.

2. Needfor liaison. With the various agencies described above (plus some others probably) there is already considerable overlapping and inconsistency in what American soldiers are being taught about amphibian-assault operations. The overlapping may not be so important; but, the teaching of inconsistent doctrines at different establishments is important. It is essential that our Center incorporate the results of the vast efforts of these long-existing establishments. It is essential that we complement rather than duplicate or oppose research work already done or under way. It is essential, in short, that we maintain with these agencies the closest liaison.

Paul W. Thompson,
Lt. Col., C.E.

Dated 20 May, the Army started to produce illustrations to show soldiers and engineers the types of German emplacements now being constructed along the Atlantic Wall.

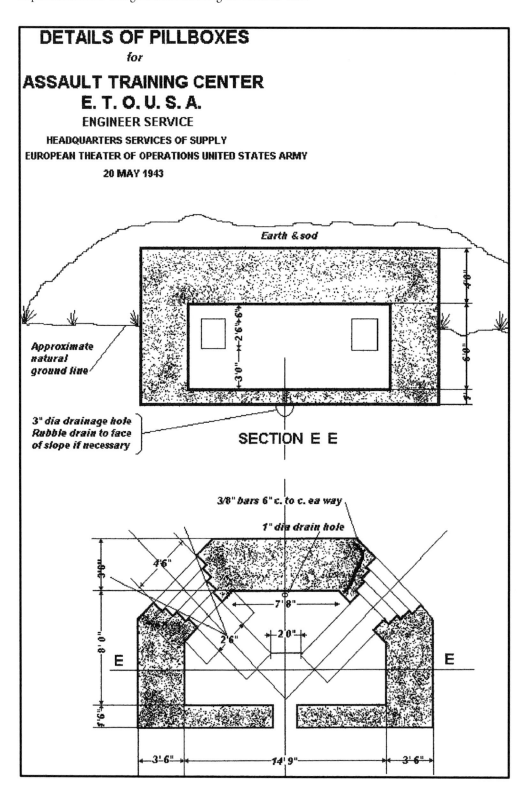

Between 8 and 13 July the Rangers were involved in field exercises at the Assault Training Centre in Woolacombe, North Devon.

It has long been thought that Lieutenant Colonel Rudder was the instigator of the planning and execution of the Pointe du Hoc raid. This was not the case, as the Omaha Beach / Pointe du Hoc landings of 1944 mimic almost exactly the British-based training missions for the prior Ranger units in 1943, the only difference being the individual units of the Rangers involved.

In 1943, the 2nd and 5th Ranger Battalions were still forming up in the States. These early exercises were being undertaken by the vanguard of the Ranger units who were training in England at that time. Ironically, these were Ranger units who would not take part in D-Day on the Normandy coast. They had missions to other parts of the world and therefore fall outside the remit of this book. However, their briefing on this style of assault is very relevant to events as they unfolded in Normandy – so they have been included here.

The format for the training of the Rangers at the ATC (Army Training Centre) was as follows:

TRAINING PROGRAMME – CBTC – times were divided up into 40-minute modules.
No 21 – Intake.

Opening Address	2	Medical Lecture	6
Physical Training	17	Training Films	4
Unarmed Combat	8	Forced Marches	19
Rope Work	10	Cross Country Marches	33
Drill	15	Range Work	37
Weapon Training	50	Demolitions	15
Fieldcraft	40	Commando Day	11
Boating	28	Make and Mend	55
Climbing	10	Preparing for Course, etc.	33
Map Reading	30	Interior Economy	9
Assault Courses	5	Competitions	11
Woodcraft	3	Spare	11

Total Number of 40 minute periods = 462

At the same time as the 2nd and 5th Rangers were forming and training in the US, all manner of information gathering was taking place along the Normandy coast. Much of it was gained from aerial reconnaissance photographs and in some instances Top Secret missions were sent to the beaches to take soil and sand samples and also to examine beach obstacles, etc.

For example, the following are comments made after various 1943 RAF aerial reconnaissance overflights of the Maisy Batteries.

Maisy: 17 April 1943 (B512): *Constructional activity is taking place at this battery. Four excavations are being dug, and a casemate/shelter approximately 35' x 45' is in early stages of construction in an excavation to the left of No. 3 gun. The four emplacements are occupied and are approximately 30' in diameter. (5006/7 of sortie RA/187, 13 April 1943, 1/8,500, quality fair).*

Overleaf: details of a typical Assault Training Centre officers' training course.

TRAINING PROGRAMME - C.B.T.C.

NO. 20 OFFICERS' COURSE

KEY.	PERIODS.	SUBJECT.
OA	1 - ½	Opening Address.
LECTURES.		
L1	1	Commando Organisation.
L2	1	Psychology of fire, location of fire, Trg Tps
L3	3	Discussion tactics and organisation.
L4	1	Tp Attacks.
L5	1	Tp in Defence.
	3	Sandtable TEWT. Cdo attack with Supp Arms.
	4	TEWT
L6	4 - 18	Lecturettes.
TRAINING FILMS.		
F1	1	Eastern Battleground.
TF1	1	Cliff Assault.
TF2	1	Use of Fire and Fieldcraft.
TF4	1	You too can get Malaria.
F12	1	Fighting patrol.
TF5	1 - 6	DDZ.
TACTICAL AND ENDURANCE EXERCISES.		
CC1	10	Endurance and Map Reading cross country March.
CC2	37 - 47	Exercise followed by B6
FORCED MARCHES.		
5M	2	5 Mile March (1 hour)
7M(S)	3	7 Mile March followed by shooting (1 hr 10 mins)
9M(D)	3	9 Mile March followed by digging (1 hr 30 min)
12M(DR)	5 - 13	12 Mile March followed by Drill (2 hr 10 min)
FIELDCRAFT.		
F10	4	Keeping direction and memorising a route.
F13	1	Lecture Patrols.
F14	4	Practical - Patrols and Ambushes.
F16	3 - 12	Attack on a Bunker posn (field firing)
MEDICAL.		
ML1	1	Lecture - MO
M.	1 - 2	Lecture MO.
MISCELLANEOUS.		
MM	30	Make and Mend.
-	8	Sport, (Min.Range, Football, Badminton, Netball, Killing)
PE	10	Physical Efficiency Tests.
P	11	Physical Trg.
R	8	Ropework and Tarzan Course.
D	7	Drill.
C	6	Climbing.
DM (2,3,4,6,8,9)	8	Demolitions.
WD	2	Woodcraft.
S	3	Spare.
A1	2	Assault Course.
A2	2	Camp Assault Course.
A3	1	Death Ride.
B (2,3)	4	Boating.
B.6	3	Disembarking, negotiating obstacles and fd firing.
S8	2	Jungle snap shooting Range.
S9	3	Tree Top Range.
J (2,3,4)	3	Unarmed Combat.
B7	8 - 121	LCA Day Exercise, Dories, Cliff Assault.

Another such secretive study was dated 1 May 1943. The Inter-Service Topographical Department report as it was known, was a complete study of the cliffs at Pointe et Raz de la Percée and along the coast to Pointe du Hoc:

SPECIAL REPORT

on

THE COAST BETWEEN

POINTE ET RAZ DE LA PERCÉE and POINTE DU HOC

(638930 to 586940, Sheet 6 E/6)

Coast and beach   (Admiralty Chart 2073)

The coast between these two points consists of precipitous chalk cliffs from 80 to 100 feet high. There are thin layers of flints in the cliff face, but these do not provide hand-hold as they are likely to break away if any weight is placed on them. Similarly the nature of the chalk does not favour the use of climbing irons or steel spikes and these cliffs are unscalable over the length under report, except at the semaphore station, 1600 yards west of Pointe de la Percée, where the cliff has fallen and is accessible to specially trained and lightly equipped men. The beach is composed of drying rocky ledges with scattered boulders fallen from the cliffs.

Dimensions and gradient

The beach is 5,500 yards long and about 50 yards wide. The gradient from the chart datum line of low water is 1 in 7. The 18 feet depth contour line lies 200 yards off-shore near Pointe de la Percée and this distance increases regularly to 700 yards near Pointe du Hoc.

Landing

The beach is only suitable for small boats in calm weather. With these limitations a landing can be effected at any state of the tide. At low water the going over the beach will be rough and laborious. At high water springs the sea washes the foot of the cliffs.

Weather

Winds from north-west, through north to east-north-east will cause a surf on the beach and make landing and re-embarkation very difficult and dangerous.

Approach

Approach is clear. The semaphore station was conspicuous in peace-time.

Anchorage

There is anchorage in depths of 30 feet from 500 to 1000 yards off-shore.

Tides

Spring rise above chart datum :   23 feet.
Neap rise above chart datum :   19 feet.
Mean level above chart datum :   13 feet.

Tidal streams

Tidal streams set east and west and attain a rate of 2.8 knots at Springs.

General description

The area under consideration in this report is taken as the coastal strip lying between the two points mentioned above and extending from the cliff-top inland to a minor motor road (G.C. 32) running parallel to the coast and keeping fairly constantly at a distance of half a mile from the cliff edge.

There is no variation whatever in the type of country between these two points and the following description applies all the way along

The ground slopes up gently from the cliff edge with an average gradient of 1 in 40.   The soil is chalky and movement across ploughed fields would be heavy after rain, but easy in dry weather.   A strip of land, about 550 yards wide, extending inland from the cliff edge, consists of open fields, rectangular in shape and enclosed by thin low hedges.   These fields naturally vary in size, but a fair average dimension is 200 x 200 yards which gives four fields between the edge of the cliff and the road (G.C.32). This number naturally varies in places, the fields tending to become smaller near the houses along the road

This 550-yard strip consists almost entirely of ploughed land. South of this strip, for the remaining 250 yards or so to the road there is a broken belt of orchards.   These do not extend continuously along the seaward side of the road, but are clustered round farmhouses and hamlets. Almost all these orchards are indicated on the G.S.G.S. map, with the exception of an orchard on the north side of the road which would mask the "ville" of Château d'Englesqueville (610830).   Between the orchards grassland predominates.   This is more particularly noticeable at the west end of the area, where the orchards are closer together.   At the east end where the orchards are more widely spaced, ploughed land may extend right up to the roadside.

Hedges and walls

Along the top of the cliff there appears to be a low earthen mound.   It is not continuous, being broken in several places, the longest broken stretch being some 370 yards west of the semaphore at 624935.   At one or two points the mound is either replaced or backed by a tree-hedge. A path appears to run along the edge of the cliff-top.

The hedges appear in general to be some eight to ten feet high and to consist of thick bushes, probably blackthorn or some similar shrub, with tall spindly trees, mostly poplars, planted along the hedgerow at intervals of about five feet.

4.

The hedges may probably be too thick for infantry to break through without considerable effort, but there are gaps generally at the corners of the fields. Working inland from the cliff top, these gaps are usually situated at or near the junction of the hedges running inland with the hedges running parallel to the coast.

At no point between Pointe et Raz de la Percée and Pointe du Hoc is it possible to move straight inland from the cliff edge to the road (G.C.32) without encountering hedges unless the footpaths (see below) are used.

In spring and early summer these hedges would hold many nesting birds. The blackbird, for instance, when disturbed emits a strident alarm, and if defending troops were country-bred they would probably realize that movement was taking place. Birds are less likely to be disturbed along the tracks where they are more accustomed to human traffic. It is also considered that partridge and pheasant would be likely to occur in this area.

Orchards

As previously pointed out, orchards only occur near houses. The trees are planted in straight rows, but from the size of the trees and the gaps these orchards appear to be rather old. The trees are planted at an average distance of 10 yards apart.

Only once, at La Cavée (624928) does an orchard extend as much as 400 yards to seaward of the road; elsewhere the orchards are only about 250 yards wide from the road, northward towards the cliff edge. Infantry moving inland would, therefore, know that they were getting close to the road when they started to cross the orchards. They would also know that they were near houses.

Habitations

All the buildings shown on the G.S.G.S. map are seen on aerial photographs still to be in existence. New construction, not shown on the map and probably of a military nature has only taken place at two points: at the semaphore (624935) where there are a number of buildings at the edge of the cliff and at Pointe du Hoc where a considerable amount of excavation has occurred and there are buildings to left and right of the path leading inland from this point.

5.

Most of the houses consist of small detached buildings of the small holding or labourer's cottage type. These are usually built in small clusters and form the hamlets shown on the map as Au Guay, Le Févre, La Cavée etc.

There are larger farms, consisting of low single-storey barns and a two-storey house built round three sides of a square. This type of building is found at 618927, on the south side of G.C.32, at 612927 (Château d'Englesqueville, a large farm or manor house) and at 590930 (Château: similar to Englesqueville).

There is a distinct tendency for the houses in this area to be strung out along the road (G.C.32) or for about 200 yards along the by-roads leading north, i.e. aseaward. The only isolated houses within 500 yards of the cliff top are those shown on the G.S.G.S. map (Le Guay: 618934, and south of Pointe du Hoe: 585936).

Paths and tracks

All the paths and tracks shown on the G.S.G.S. map appear in recent air photographs, with the addition of a new, straight, track leading inland from the semaphore to G.C.32 which it joins at the south-west corner of the orchard (623928).

There are the following tracks leading inland from the edge of the cliff :-

(a) From the semaphore to 623928. Not shown on the
    G.S.G.S. map. From a point about 175 yards north
    of its junction with G.C.32 this track appears to be
    surfaced as far as the junction. This track is
    hedged on the east side from approximately 623930 to
    the junction with G.C.32.

6.

(b) From 618936 to 618928.   This track is hedged on both sides from about 618935 to its junction with G.C.32.   It passes the farmhouse at Le Guay and then runs beside a small orchard with very widely spaced trees, on the east side of the track, and joins G.C.32 beside a small cluster of houses (St.Hilaire).

(c) From 612937 to 612928.   A wide and absolutely straight cart track, hedged on both sides all the way from the edge of the cliff to the junction with G.C.32.   For the first 100 yards inland from the edge of the cliff the track is narrow, but at 612936 there is a circular clearing, probably a turning place for carts, and from this point onward the track is very wide.   This track does not pass near any houses until it reaches G.C. 32 opposite the Château d'Englesqueville.

(d) From 601938 to 598928.   A rather winding track which joins G.C.32 at the hamlet of Le Févre.   The houses of this hamlet face on to the east side of this track, being strung along it for the last 230 yards to the junction with the road.   This track is hedged on its east side all the way along and on its west side from a point about 190 yards from the cliff top to the junction with G.C.32.

(e) From 591937 to 591929.   An ill-defined cart track running along the edge of ploughed fields, paralleled by hedges on its west side.   This track joins G.C.32 at the manor house, shown as Château on the G.S.G.S. map.   It does not pass any houses until it reaches G.C.32 adjacent to the Château.

7.

(f) From 588937 to 588930.   A fairly straight cart-track.
Unhedged for the first 130 yards in from the cliff top
and then hedged on both sides to the junction with
G.C.32.   For the last 145 yards to the junction with
G.C. 32 this track runs between two hedged orchards.
The nearest building to this road is 150 yards distant,
on the west side, near the junction with G.C. 32.

(g) From Pointe du Hoe (586940) to 585931.   A fairly
straight track which appears to be surfaced.   This
is likely, in view of the construction activity at the
point.   There are buildings on both sides of the track
for about 300 yards inland from the cliff top and at
the two points on the west side of it, as shown on the
G.S.G.S. map.   This track is only hedged at one point:
on both sides for about 60 yards south of the southern-
most building of those stretching inland from Pointe
du Hoe.

Obstacles

There are no water obstacles between the cliff edge and the road
(G.C.32).

The most important obstacles to movement straight across country are
the hedges mentioned above.   Infantry should also take note of the buildings
round the semaphore and at Pointe du Hoe.

At the cliff edge at 617937 there is a rectangular excavation where
a sloping field has been ploughed level.   The dimensions of this are about
80 yards from north to south and 30 yards from west to east.   The southern
side of the rectangle is in the form of a vertical ridge probably about six
feet high.   This ridge is caused by the difference in level between the back
of the field and the seaward edge of it and the fact that the ground has been
ploughed level.   This ridge should be avoided at night.

Intelligence gathering also started with low flying reconnaissance fights in June and more detailed studies began to appear of the area that would become known as the 'Omaha Sector'.

The Army also issued an Intelligence Bulletin No.1 on the subject of understanding beach obstacles and coastal defences. This included mock beach maps to orientate soldiers on what type of obstacles the heavily defended beaches could contain.

This map was produced and entitled 'Hypothetical layout of beach defences'. It is followed by a description of the problems being encountered interpreting aerial photographs.

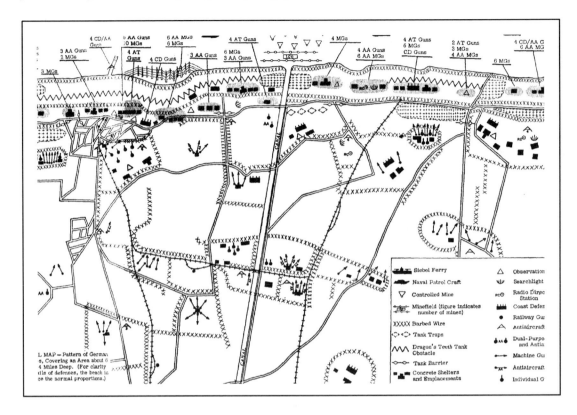

GERMAN COASTAL DEFENSES

Dummy installations.—The use of dummy works and weapons is extensive and serves the double purpose of distracting aerial observation from actual defenses and of inducing the enemy to make wasteful attacks on barren areas while the real defenses remain in operation. A common practice is to install dummy antiaircraft-gun positions and dummy guns, and even to simulate gun flashes in such positions, usually along lines of probable air approach. Sometimes real, mobile guns fire from the dummy positions in an effort to confound aerial reconnaissance. The practice is also extended to other types of artillery. Railway-gun turntables suspected of being faked have been noted in aerial reconnaissance. Dummy observation posts have also been reported. In some places that are heavily mined and wired but do not have a great many weapons, sham turrets and wooden guns are planted in barbed-wire lines.

Many dummy airfields exist along the coast of western Europe. Mock or disused planes and dummy buildings are installed on these fields, and at night they are likely to flash landing lights. From time to time the dummy aircraft are moved around to help fill out the impression of a field in actual operation.

Dummy installations are likely to be deliberately ostentatious or poorly camouflaged, in order to draw fire and distract attention from real and cleverly concealed fortifications.

The Omaha Beach, Vierville exit was filmed from high altitude, so as not to raise any undue suspicions.

Flying low and fast over beaches also provided oblique photographs which were useful in determining the size of any obstacles.

This photograph of Omaha beach is dated 30 June 1943.

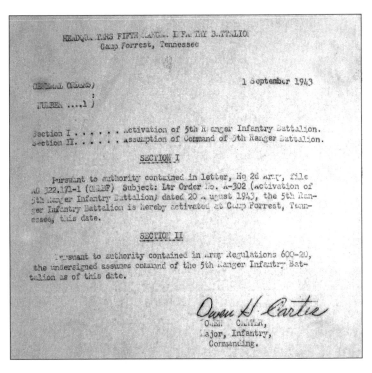

By 21 June the ATC started to produce briefings for mock attacks on enemy positions. They were produced in a fashion to mimic as closely as possible the German-held coastline in France. These mock battles included the use of Ranger elements within them and it goes some way to indicate that the Army had a definitive idea of what they wanted the Rangers to do as early as 1943.

Coastal batteries were located at different parts of the mock invasion area and one was on top of a cliff bearing more than a passing resemblance to Pointe du Hoc. One battery was an INITIAL OBJECTIVE and the other an INTERMEDIATE OBJECTIVE.

Also of note, beyond the two gun battery targets is the advancement inland indicated for all units on D-Day and the dropping of paratroopers to the rear. As we will see later, the real D-Day maps bear a striking similarity to the actual objectives and advancement lines indicated here. The Ranger objectives here are highlighted in grey.

ASSAULT TRAINING CENTER
CONFERENCE
HQ ETOUSA

21 June 1943
KM

Exercise No. 1

General Situation

1. The BARNSTAPLE BAY area is assumed to be part of the coast of FRANCE. The coast is assumed to be as shown on the map between MORTE POINT and HARTLAND POINT (both inclusive). It is assumed to run due north from ROCKHAM BAY (on the north side of MORTE POINT), and due south from HARTLAND POINT. All is land east of this assumed coastline.

2. The enemy holds the entire coast, in both directions from the BARNSTAPLE BAY area, in considerable strength, divisions holding sectors measuring about 25 to 35 miles in width. All sectors are topographically similar to the BARNSTAPLE BAY sector, and are fortified. on about the same scale.

3. A panzer division is located in the EXETER area. This division can close in the BARNSTAPLE BAY area within 24 hours after the beginning of an assault. Another panzer division can be expected to close in the area within 48 hours of an assault.

4. The I Corps (reinforced) has been designated to invade FRANCE near BARNSTAPLE BAY. The I Corps is at present located in the vicinity of embarkation points approximately 80 miles by water from the coast of FRANCE.

First Special Situation

1. On   the CG 1st Infantry Division was called to the Headquarters I Corps, where he received the following information:

   a. The I Corps with 1st and 2d Infantry Divisions abreast as Assault Divisions (1st Inf Div on the left) will invade FRANCE near BARNSTAPLE. (See operations map).

   b. D-Day will be announced later.

   c. H-Hour - 3 hours prior to nautical twilight.

   d. NAVAL SUPPORT The Navy is prepared to support the landing by the following means:

      (1) Furnish naval gunfire support.

      (2) Furnish support craft of the following types:

         (a) LCS(S)

         (b) LCS(M)

         (c) LCS(L)

         (d) LCT(R)

         (e) LCF(L)

         (f) LCG

-1-

(3) Trained Naval shore fire control parties each consisting of 1 Army Officer, 2 Naval Officers, and 4 Privates with necessary communication equipment will be furnished on the basis of one team for each battalion landing team.

(4) One Army gunfire support liaison officer will be aboard each firing ship.

e. AIR SUPPORT All indications point to definite air superiority for the landing forces. However, it is known that the enemy has available a large enemy fighter force and at least 150 bombers prepared to oppose both the passage of the convoy and the landing proper. Despite our air superiority isolated air attacks can be expected.

The Air Force is prepared to support the landing by the following means:

(1) Preparatory bombardment from D-7.

(2) Provide fighter cover and escort except during hours of darkness in amounts required from time convoy leaves embarkation point.

(3) Night area bombing missions.

(4) Day low level bombing missions.

(5) Day high level bombing missions.

(6) Fighter bomber missions.

(7) Dive bomber missions.

(8) Photo reconnaissance missions.

(9) Smoke laying missions.

(10) Cannon fighter straffing.

(11) Transport of such airborne units as may be required.

(12) Provide antisubmarine patrol.

The 1st Infantry Division will be furnished four (4) trained Air Support Parties.

Air Support Control will be operated at Headquarters I Corps.

f. 1st Infantry Division reinforced will land in its zone of action on D-DAY at H-HOUR and seize and hold the line of the RIVER YEO (BARNSTAPLE exclusive) as a beach head line. See operations map. Maintain contact with 2d Div on right (south) and II Corps on left (North). CG 1st Inf Div responsible for establishment and operation of beach maintenance area until relieved by orders of CG, I Corps.

g. Composition 1st Infantry Division, reinforced.

See Annex #1, attached.

h. Scales of MT personnel and equipment

(1) Motor Transport: Motor transport will be limited to assault scale and to following types of vehicles:

1/4 ton Jeeps (Land and amphibious)
3/4 ton Command and Reconnaissance
3/4 ton Weapons Carriers

-2-

2.1/2 ton Trucks (Land and Amphibious).
1/4 ton Trailers.
1 ton Trailers.
Such special vehicles as required by Beach Maintenance
  Group.

(2) Personnel: Personnel will be figures on the elimina-
tion from T/O strength of the following:

Bands
Basics
Chauffeurs for motor vehicles remaining at home stations
Motorcyclists
Reduction of rifle squads to 10 men.

Final T/O strength after above eliminations will be reduced by 3% for
figuring boat space required.

In no case will tactical units such as platoons and companies be eliminated.

(3) Equipment -(a) Organizational equipment will be
reduced to the minimum required for combat.

(b) Personal equipment will be reduced to absolute
minimum for combat over a period of three (3) days.

(c) In determining required equipment, the following
factors will be considered:

Assault troops are physically fit and tough and
  can live on emergency rations without loss of
  combat effectiveness for a period of three (3)
  days.

Assault troops must be prepared to fight immediately
  they leave landing craft.

Means must be provided for passage of underwater
  and beach obstacles, and minefields.

Means must be provided for attack of concrete gun
  emplacements, and destruction of antitank
  obstacles.

The enemy may use gas.

FIRST EQUIPMENT

1. Tactical plan prepared by CG 1st Infantry Division (show scheme
of maneuver on operations map).

2. Number and type of motor transport to be embarked for landing
on D-day.

3. Administrative plan of CG 1st Infantry Division to include means
of providing for the period D to D ≠ 3 of:

a. Rations.

b. Water

c. Ammunition

d. Care and evacuation of wounded.

4. Requests made by CG 1st Infantry Division relative to:

   a. Naval gunfire support desired.

   b. Support craft desired.

   c. Air support desired.

   d. Type and number of ships and craft required to transport division and attached troops.

   e. Special equipment (not included in Table of Basic Allowances) required for the division and attached troops.

5. Show by sketch plan for beach maintenance area to include:

   a. Beach exits.

   b. Location of Dumps.

   c. Medical establishment

   d. Transportation Park.

   e. Communication plan.

   f. Assembly areas for "follow up" troops.

SECOND REQUIREMENT

   1. Based on solution of FIRST REQUIREMENT, give the tactical plan prepared by the CO, CT 1 (show scheme of maneuver on operations map).

THIRD REQUIREMENT

   1. Based on solution of SECOND REQUIREMENT give the tactical plan prepared by the CO 2d Bn 1st Infantry Regiment (show scheme of maneuver on operations map).

   2. Show by diagram the boat formation used by this battalion during approach to shore. Include loading of each boat.

FOURTH REQUIREMENT

   1. Based on solution of THIRD REQUIREMENT state pars 2 and 3 of Field Order issued by CO E Company 2d Bn, 1st Infantry.

FIFTH REQUIREMENT

   1. Based on solution of FOURTH REQUIREMENT state pars 2 and 3 of Orders issued by CO 2d Platoon E Company 2d Bn 1st Infantry.

SIXTH REQUIREMENT

   1. Based on solution of FIFTH REQUIREMENT state pars 2 and 3 of Orders issued by the Squad leader of 1st Squad 2d Platoon E Company 2d Bn 1st Infantry.

-4-

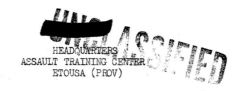

HEADQUARTERS
ASSAULT TRAINING CENTER
ETOUSA (PROV)

Solution to Par 1, First Requirement

2.   This Division reinforced (see Annex #1) will land at beaches between the river TAW estuary and BULL POINT, quickly capture and (improve) beach exits near WOOLACOMBE and CROYDE BAY, seize and hold the line of the RIVER YEO (BARNSTAPLE exclusive) and establish and maintain a beachhead for further operations.

      Landing Beaches: See Operations Map
      Formation   :   See Operations Map
      Boundaries   :   See Operations Map
      Time of landing: D-day (to be announced later); H-hour, 3 hours before nautical twilight.

3.   a.   CT 2 (see Annex #1 attached) will land at Beaches "A" and "B" immediately capture the beach exit at CROYDE BAY and in accordance with scheme of maneuver indicated on Operations Map, seize the objectives within the zone of action of the CT.   It will protect the right flank of the Division and maintain contact with the Division on the right. CHIVENOR AIRFIELD will be captured with utmost speed, and Division Hq notified immediately on capture of same.   Advance beyond first objective will be made only on orders from Division.

    b.   CT 1, with 3d Ranger Bn attached (see Annex #1) will land at Beaches "C" and "D";   immediately capture the beach exit near WOOLACOMBE and, in accordance with the scheme of maneuver indicated on Operations Map, seize the objectives within the zone of action of the CT.   It will protect the left flank of the Division and maintain contact with the unit on the left.   Advance beyond first objective will be made only on orders from Division.

    c.   The CT 3 (see Annex #1) in floating reserve will be prepared to land on orders in the zone of action of either assault regiment.   For this purpose it will establish and maintain liaison with each assault regiment.

    d.   The 1st Ranger Bn will land along the coast near BAGGY POINT at H-1 hour and reduce coast artillery guns located near CROYDE HOE. (For Bomber support see Air Force Annex).   The Bn will then assist the 2nd CT in capturing the beach exit at CROYDE BAY by flanking action to the north.   Attached to CT 2 after capture of beach exit at CROYDE BAY.

    e.   The 2nd Ranger Bn. will land at Beach "E" at H-1 hour, capture the hostile coast artillery guns located near MORTE POINT and then assist CT 1 in capturing the high ground north of WOOLACOMBE by flanking action to the south.   (For Bomber support see Air Force Annex).   The 2nd Ranger Bn will establish contact with the 3d Ranger Bn which will land at Beach "C" at H hour, and thereafter is attached to following CT 1.

    f.   Division Artillery (less CT attachments) will land at Beach "D" immediately following CT 1 and support the attack with special attention to the support of CT 1.   The CG Division Artillery will make plans for bringing all supporting artillery under his control with least practicable delay after landing.

    g.   Anti-aircraft Artillery (less CT attachments) will land at Beach "B" immediately following CT 2.   It will proceed without delay to

Solution to Second Requirement

2. CT 1 with the 3d Ranger Bn attached will land on Beaches in
the Woolacombe area, immediately capture the high ground to the north
and south of Woolacombe and then advance eastward to the Southern
Railway and the highway running north thru INN ($\frac{1}{2}$ mi west of West
Down) to ILFRACOMBE, where units will prepare for advance to the west
bank of Colom Stream (see map).

Formation: 1st, 2d Bns and 2nd Rangers abreast from right to left
Landing Beaches: C.D.E. Boundary between BNCT (see map)

3. a. The 1st Bn CT will land at Beach "C" penetrate the
hostile beach defenses near the boundary between Bns and the northern
half of the enemy combat post defending the southern end of Woolacombe
Beach and capture the high ground north of Rickwell Down. It will
then seize the hill south of Willingcott and advance thereafter to
the line of the Southern Railway - Dean. The 1st Bn will maintain
contact with the 2nd Inf on the right.

b. The 2nd Bn Combat Team will land at Beach "D" and immediately
capture Woolacombe and the high ground north and south thereof. It
will then advance to the east and seize the general line of the DEAN -
ILFRACOMBE road within the battalion zone of action and prepare without
delay for further advance. The 2nd Bn will protect the left flank of
the regiment.

c. The 3d Ranger Bn will land at Beach "E", establish contact
with the 2nd Ranger Bn operating near Mortehoe. It will then advance
southwest generally along the Mortehoe - Mortehoe Sta Road and assist
the 2nd Bn in capturing the high ground near Mortehoe Sta, and assist
the advance of the 2nd Bn CT to the line of the Dean - Ilfracombe
Road and await further orders.

d. The 3d Bn Ct with the anti-tank company and the Cannon Platoon
attached (Reg Reserve) will be prepared to land at Beach "C" or "D".
One liaison group of 1 officer, 2 messengers and 1 radio operator
equipped with radios will land with each assault Bn CT, establish
close contact with them and facilitate employment of the Reserve CT
in the zone of action of either assault Bn.

x. Bayonets will be fixed during hours of darkness. Weapons
will be fired on orders of Platoon leaders only.

ASSAULT TRAINING CENTER
CONFERENCE
HQ ETOUSA

Annex II - AIR

DETAIL AIR PLAN DURING INITIAL ASSAULT

D-1
23.10   1.   High level Strat. Bomb to be stopped on assault
             area at H-3.

D
02.00   2.   1 sqd A-20 to attack targets 6, 7, & 8, with
02.05   gunfire and para-frag bombs low level alt.

02.00   3.   Fighter cover patrol beach area.
             3 sqd 1-P-47, 2 P-51 to be increased or decreased
             as enemy situation allows.

02.05   4.   1 Flight B-26 attack target 4, preceded by gun attack
             from 2-P-51.

01.55   5.   Smoke in plan A to be placed so to cover from MORTE
             POINT south to RIVER TAW, smoke screen.

02.10   6.   Smoke bombs on MORTE POINT, BAGGY POINT, and SAUNTON
3.25   DOWNS, to be maintained.

02.10   7.   1 Sqd B-25 target 5 and area.

02.30   8.   1 Sqd B-26 target 3.

02.25   9.   4 sqd P-51 used in close cover support of mainland
             advance.

02.45 10.   Tactical Reconnaissance of roads Bridgehead area.
onward

02.30 11.   4 Med, 2 light, at 60 min. notice.
onward

02.35 12.   2 Dive bomb sqd assist Rangers on target 1 and 2
             if necessary.

01.30 13.   Dropping of one bn Paratroopers to attack target
             area f on dropping zone 972660, 2½ miles from
             target.

02.00 14.   Dropping of one Airborne Div along line of road
             from 972660 to road junction 980610.

UNCLASSIFIED

-16-

The Rangers were to attack two distinctly different German gun batteries during the mock assault.

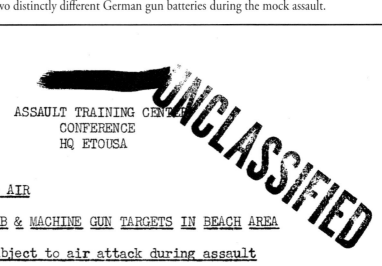

ASSAULT TRAINING CENTER
CONFERENCE
HQ ETOUSA

UNCLASSIFIED

Annex II - AIR

BOMB & MACHINE GUN TARGETS IN BEACH AREA

Subject to air attack during assault

1.   4 fixed coastal guns
      1 light AA
      892   675

2.   4 fixed coastal guns
      1 light AA
      865   626

3.   Headquarters
      705   630

4.   7 Heavy AA
      700   644

5.   2 Hv Railroad guns
      928   639

6.   3 Light machine guns
      1 AT
      884   629

7.   2 AT
      1 LMG
      893   599

Chapter 2

September–November 1943 – Training

The Rangers were to attack the cliff top gun battery position before advancing inland to a divisional first objective, then a second and then a final objective.

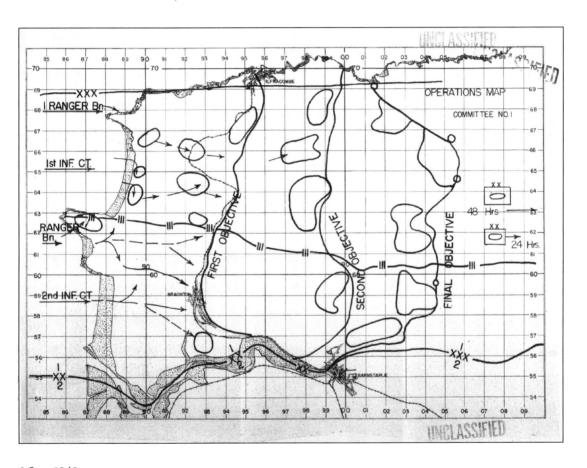

2 Sept 1943

The Army issued this instructional letter:

Ireland. No person subject to American military control under this headquarters will visit Eire except on specific authority issued by Headquarters ETOUSA and then only in the performance of official duties.

Bus Queues: Improper queueing (lining up and awaiting your turn) or failure to queue (line up) for public vehicle transportation is unlawful.

Objects of enemy origin: All such objects dropped from the air or otherwise, whether war material or private property of members of enemy forces, will be delivered or reported immediately to the proper military authorities or to the police.

Telescope and binoculars may not be carried in regulated areas without a permit.

Waste. It is unlawful to waste food, water, or fuel including petrol or to destroy the salvageable value of waste paper, rags, rope, string or rubber.

As the 2nd and 5th Rangers were forming, here are two typical stories of men who joined and then stayed with the Rangers – the first is Lee Brown, here told by his son.

Lee Brown HQ Company 5th Battalion: *He was living in New Haven, Connecticut, with his mother and sister, before he was an army draftee on January 29th 1943 – his 18th birthday. He went into the army on March 23, 1943 at Ft Devens in Massachusetts. He was then transferred to Ft Leonard Wood in Missouri as a member of the 75th Infantry Division for boot camp and arrived there in late March and received his first 'buzz' haircut. Dad almost became a member of the Airborne forces when an announcement came looking for volunteers. Dad was miserable at Ft Leonard Wood and wanted out – no matter where it was! He describes Ft Leonard Wood as a 'hell-hole' and says that it was an unbearably hot summer and the dirt was hard as rocks. Dad made the mistake of letting his mother know of his intent to 'join the paratroopers' (I assume by telegraph) and she became extremely upset and begged him not to do so.*

A little background – Dad's older brother, H.H. 'Larry' Brown Jr., was a 1st Sgt at the time in the Army Signal Corps stationed at Camp Crowder, Missouri, having joined the army in 1938 at 18 years of age (5 years older than Dad). Dad's mother was already extremely worried that Larry would be in very dangerous situations in his role and feared that Dad would be in too dangerous of a situation as a 'paratrooper'. Dad had to back off his plan to try and join the Airborne, but learned a valuable lesson for the future – 'don't ask permission in advance, just ask for forgiveness afterwards'. This new strategy came in very handy when a 'mountain of a Ranger Captain' (as Dad describes him), 'who stood almost 6 feet 6 inches tall with a little waist, but shoulders as broad as mountains' came looking for volunteers for the Rangers sometime in August or September 1943. The Ranger Captain guaranteed them that anyone who made the cut as a Ranger would be overseas by January 1944 and that ultimately proved true – just barely. Dad and his boot camp buddy wanted to get out of that godforsaken hell hole known as Ft Leonard Wood and volunteered to 'try out' for the Rangers. Many tried out (50 or more), but Dad and his buddy were two of the few who made it.

This is when Dad decided to 'ask forgiveness later', so he wrote his mother and let her know that he had been transferred to the Rangers. She was thrilled because she thought he meant the US Forest Rangers that oversee the US national forests! Well she soon found out otherwise when my Uncle Larry called home to talk with their mother and she excitedly told Larry than Dad had joined the Rangers! Larry's response was 'how did that little SOB get into the Rangers – that's the toughest outfit in the Army!' It took smelling salts to revive her!

The second is from John Raaen, HQ Co. 5th Battalion:

Before I graduated from West Point, Darby had organized the 1st Ranger Battalion and had landed in Africa. He and his Rangers were quite the rage in the media. I said to myself, I've got to get into the Rangers. But it was not to be. I graduated into the Corps of Engineers and was assigned to the 55th Armored Engineer Battalion of the 10th Armored Division. On Tennessee maneuvers, I learned that the Armored Force was not for me. In combat situations, I reacted like an Infantryman, set up a base of fire, envelop. Not like an armored man, step on the gas and smash through with guns blazing. I had to get out of armor, and back to the ground pounders.

I saw my classmates driving their Infantry platoons along the dirt roads of Tennessee while I sped by in my 'peep', covered with mud from the dust. I envied those lucky friends.

One day there was an announcement that anyone who wanted to volunteer for a new Ranger Battalion should report to some nearby location. I did. Major Carter told me he was looking for a demolition, mines and field fortification expert. I fitted that bill. I was surprised when I got my orders to join the 5th at Camp Forrest. I got my wish. I was a platoon leader in a Ranger Battalion.

On 6 Sept 1943 the ATC produced a detailed overview for troops who would be *'landing on hostile shores'*. It is worth remembering that all of this type of training was very much in its infancy at this time, so even the basic elements of it had to be explained.

UNITED STATES ASSAULT TRAINING CENTER ETOUSA

TRAINING MEMORANDUM: 6 September 1943

LANDING ON HOSTILE SHORES

NAVAL ORIENTATION

CHAPTER 1

ATTACK ON OVERSEA OBJECTIVE

1. SCOPE OF THIS MEMORANDUM. This training memorandum is a description of amphibious operations in general, and a description of Navy functions in the transportation and landing of Army troops. Detailed instructions concerning the functions of Army units in movements in Navy boats and ships will be issued separately. The corresponding Navy Publications are FTP 167 and FTP 211.

2. PRINCIPLES INVOLVED. a. An operation involving a landing is conducted in accordance with the same military principles as military operations conducted entirely on land. These principles are set forth in FM 100-5 (Operations), those particularly applicable being contained in Chapter 9 (The Offensive).

b. Three characteristics of such an operation are unusually favorable to the attacker. The attackers may usually make thorough preparation for attack on a particular portion of the enemy's coast line, and attack only after such preparation is complete. Within the sea area the attacking forces have great mobility as to movement of large, compact bodies of troops and their supporting elements. The enemy surface reconnaissance seaward from his shore line is usually extremely difficult. These characteristics permit great and unexpected concentration of force in a given landing area, facilitating strategic surprise. The initial landing often finds the defender psychologically unprepared.

c. Numerous characteristics of the operation are highly unfavorable to the attacker. Assault troops approaching shore and landing are highly vulnerable. During certain periods the Army units supporting arms and services function in a limited manner or not at all. Necessary detailed intelligence is difficult to obtain. Coordination and cooperation of many elements are required. The places at which large forces can cross the shore line are limited. Landing operations are highly vulnerable to air and submarine attack. The number of boats and suitable ships desired may not be available.

3.   FORCES INVOLVED. In this type of operation many elements are required to supplement the troops needed for the landing operation. The troops and their supplies are carried in Navy Vessels or air transport. Navy combatant ships, and Army or Navy aircraft are required to protect and support the troops.

4.   JOINT TASK FORCES. The forces involved are usually combined into a joint task force. The responsibility and authority of the commanders of Army elements and Navy elements are usually embodied in the directive for the operation, based on joint agreements embodied in War Department publication entitled "Joint Action of the Army and the Navy". The joint task force is given a code designation. The Army elements and the Navy elements may be called an Army task force and a Navy task force respectively. Alternatively, the Navy element may be called a naval attack force, and the Army element a landing force.

5.   THE NAVAL TASK FORCE. This force is usually divided into task groups based primarily on the various missions to be performed Thus, the light combat vessels which may be sent ahead or to a flank for reconnaissance may be designated a reconnaissance group, and a covering force of battleships and a lighter craft which protects the main body of transports from a distance called a covering group. On occasion types of ships are grouped, as submarines or aircraft carriers with their supporting elements and their aircraft. The naval elements which transport, and protect closely and support an infantry division are often organized into a task group. So may be those of a small force operating at a distance from the main body of the task force. The transports of a Navy task force may constitute a task group.

6.   THE NAVAL TASK GROUP. - a. The transports of the task group are organized into transport divisions. Such divisions often are constituted of the ships which carry a reinforced regimental combat team. Such a division will usually be composed of about four assault transports and one or two freight ships, depending upon the constitutents of the reinforced regimental combat team, and the ships available. A transport division may be made up of ships carrying service elements, Army Air Force elements, etc.

b.   Large, seagoing landing craft and landing ships of a task group are usually organized into divisions and flotillas, so constituted as to carry balanced Army forces or to provide sea transport for material too heavy to be unloaded from transports in the open sea.

c.   Remaining elements of the naval task group which carries and lands army troops include gunfire support ships, screening vessels, mine sweepers, control vessels, and destroyer transports.

7.   THE ARMY TASK FORCE. - a. The Army elements of the joint task force is so constituted as to strength and composition that it will be able to seize and hold the objective. The main body will be composed primarily of infantry divisions, together with armored, antiaircraft, and service elements. Army Air Force units to be flown on to captured airfields prior to the completion of the operation are often included, as are airborne troops and the air transport.

b. Army task forces are often divided into sub-task forces, usually of the strength of a reinforced infantry division. A smaller force to land at some distance from the main attack may be called a sub-task force. The sub-task force is usually embarked in the ships of a Navy task group.

c. The Army units are organized for combat in accordance with the principles of land warfare. Among primary factors is the necessity for unusual attachment of reinforcements to infantry assault units due to lack of centralized control during the early phases of the landing attack.

d. The Army elements have a certain amount of special training and equipment. This applies particularly to engineer units, called shore engineers, designed to facilitate movement of supplies and reserve troops across beaches, to infantry intended to land by rubber boat in difficult places, called raiders, and to commanders and staffs (especially transport loading officers), and certain communications personnel. If strong opposition is to be expected at the shore line, the army elements may have considerable additions and changes in organization and equipment to suit the problem

3. GENERAL PLAN OF OPERATION. - a. Army troops are landed in accordance with the joint plan of operations. Assault elements are usually landed from transports by landing craft carried by ships. Other elements, including reserves, may be landed by this means, or by seagoing landing ships. Troops may travel the entire overwater distance in landing boats (shore-to-shore operations).

b. Initial landings are made by reinforced battalions. Each assault battalion is assigned a portion or portions of shoreline on which it lands and around which it establishes a battalion beachhead. Reserve battalions and regimental headquarters land behind successful assault battalions. Battalions advance, and close toward each other if necessary, for the establishment of the regimental beachhead. Similarly division beachheads are formed by regimental action and the landing of division command elements. The establishment of the task force beachhead follows.

c. A beachhead is an area seized immediately upon landing to permit uninterrupted movement ashore of troops and supplies and for organization of further advance.

d. After the establishment of the task force beachhead the task force may seize ports and airfields and place them in condition for operation, or may first proceed to its objective. Until supply across beaches and oversea air support ceases, the operation continues to have important amphibious aspects.

9. COOPERATION WITH NAVY. - a. A high degree of cooperation must be exchanged between Army commanders and their associated Navy commanders. The cooperation must be particularly close, as to planning and execution, between the Army task force commander and his staff, and the Navy task force commander and his staff. This applies to quite an extent between the Army sub-task force commander and the Navy task group commander. In execution, all units must cooperate fully, including the battalion, company, and platoon commander working with the boat group, boat wave, and boat division commander.

> b. An army commander who is thoroughly familiar with landing opera-
> tions, and whose unit has the appearance and esprit of a good unit, will
> have little difficulty in obtaining cooperation of naval elements within
> the limits of their ability.
>
> 10. SEQUENCE OF STUDY. - The planning and proper execution of each
> phase of an amphibious operation depends to an unusual degree on the
> succeeding phases. Hence study of landing operations must take place in
> reverse chronological order beginning with the operations contemplated
> ashore, next taking up the landing, then the debarkation from ships, and
> finally the embarkation in the ships.

22 September 1943

Army circular No.77 was issued to deal with the huge influx of US Army personnel into London:

Registration of officers on temporary duty in London.
Every officer visiting London on temporary duty with HQ, ETOUSA will, upon arrival and departure register in
person at the officer of the Adjutant General Flat 227, 20 Grosvenor Square, London.

These extra US Service personnel created the necessity for identity cards and on 26 September a set of guidelines was
issued for all personnel to follow:

1) *A typewriter will be used in entering personal description etc.*
2) *Care will be exercised in taking of fingerprints to insure clear, legible impression.*
3) *An official seal will be impressed on the lower part of the photograph after it has been securely attached by glue*
   in the space provided on the card. Issuing headquarters not possessing an official impression seal will, prior to
   their issue, forward all cards to HQ SOS, ETOUSA, for affixation of an official seal and return seals of tactical
   organisations and headquarters will not be used.
4) *The holder's card will not be issued merely because of a change in the holder's grade or branch (arm of service).*
5) *In each such case, the holder will make the necessary correction in pen and ink, recording and authenticating the*
   correction in the right hand corner of the space provided for fingerprints.

ENLISTED MEN
Each enlisted man who does not already have in his possession a War Department identification card will be
issued a yellow identification card.

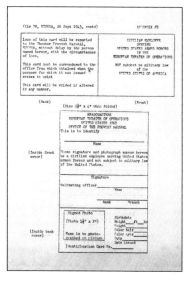
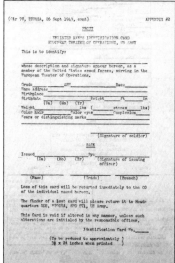
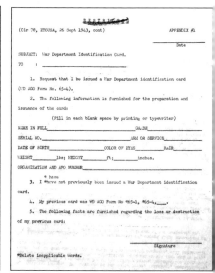

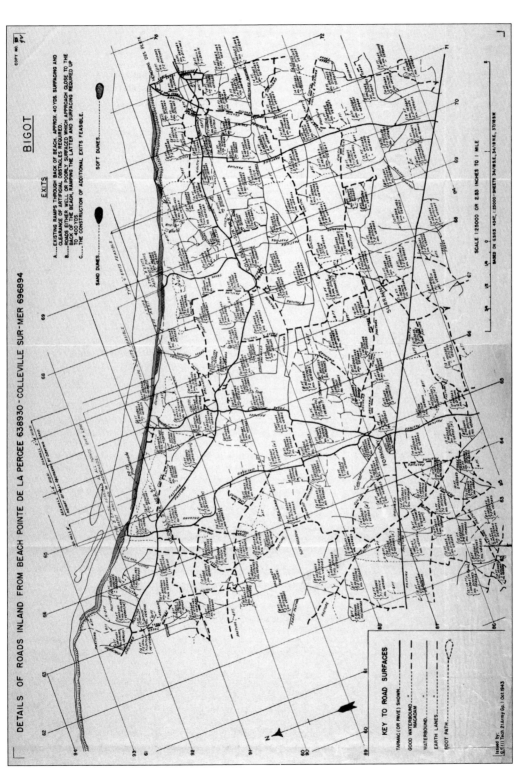

A highly detailed plan of the terrain behind Omaha Beach was drawn. It contained the heights of bushes and hedgerows etc. and it goes some way to confirm that Omaha Beach was very much considered the perfect landing beach at this time.

Over time the types and style of missions for the Rangers and other assault troops developed and the specifics of what the army called 'raider' training was developed. Here is an evaluation dated 22 October 1943.

22 Oct.

Colonel Ely:

The practice of landing small groups by rubber boats in odd places has been sufficently successful, to lead, to the attempt to make a much more important factor of it. It is referred to as "Infiltration Landings". See Capt. Melody for further detail. In several of the early trials he made successful landings on the rocks, particularly impressive being those on Baggy Point.

Capt. Melody:

About the first of September a "raider" section of one officer and 29 men was set up for specialized training in raider tactics and technique. Subjects stressed were:
  a. Handling rubber boats, particularly in surf.
  b. Cliff scaling
  c. Forced Marches
  d. Hand-to-hand combat
  e. Night operations.

The mission was to land on rocky shores, inacessible to ordinary craft and establish a small bridgehead.
The experiment was so successful that an infantry company is now being trained in these tactics. The ultimate aim is to make this the nucleus of a larger group which will land on an unfavorable - hence weakly defended coast, and establish a strong bridgehead which will neutralize enemy coast artillery fire on the assault troops on the beaches.
Note that the concept has departed from that of raiding in its usual sense. These forces, to be known as infiltration troops, are not to hit and run- but to hold on to what they size till the main force can take over. In this point they resemble airborne units and are in fact intended to be used in conjunction with them. They carry enough supplies for 48 to 72 hours - counting on resupply over the beaches or by air as the situation permits.

SECRET

Minutes of Conference held in Office of the Commanding Officer
(Morning of 25 October 1943).

Technique of Assault Section.

1. Colonel Thompson opened the discussion by introducing a chart showing
the minute-by-minute breakdown of the operations of an assault section in
attacking a pill box-obstacle installation. It was pointed out that the rifle
group, which is first off the landing craft, reconnoiters the obstacle, selects
the location of the proposed breach and lays a tape from that point back to the
wire-cutting group. Only then the latter goes forward to make the breach. By
this process it is perhaps (6) minutes before the breaching operations actually
begins. It was further pointed out that the breaching operations actually begins
It was further pointed out that the breaching operation itself requires perhaps
(8) minutes, of which as much as half are consumed in grappling for trip wires.
Colonel Thompson pointed out that this procedure results in the mass of the
section lying on the beach for the extended period of time. Although in shell
holes, these soldiers never the less are highly vulnerable, expecially to observed mortar and artillery fire.

2. Colonel Thompson also pointed out that by our doctrine something like
eight assault sections normally are landed over a length of beach which normally
includes not more than two pill boxes. Colonel Chase pointed out that these
sections are within 50 yards of each other and that therefore there is not much
room in any case for deliberate reconnaissance along the obstacle.

3. In view of the above considerations, it was decided:

    a. To adopt as doctrine a procedure whereby the rifle and wire-cutting
group will push ahead rapidly from the point where it leaves the landing craft
and will proceed to breach the obstacle in the shortest possible time without
detailed reconnaissance.

    b. To eliminate or reduce drastically the time consumed in grappling
operations while on the beach. To remove trip wires principally by cutting them
manually.

    c. To eliminate or partially eliminate from assault operations over the
beach the practice of cutting through bands of barbed wire. To breach the
barbed wire principally by means of bangalore torpedoes.

4. There followed a discussion of the relative merit of the BAR versus the
LMG in the assault section. It was decided to replace the LMG by the BAR in the
assault section.

At this time the decision to replace the light machine gun (.30 Browning) in favour of the more portable Browning
Automatic Rifle was implemented. The conference report continues:

5.   The question of placing the LMG's made surplus by the step taken above was discussed at length. No final conclusions were reached, but it was the consensus that LMG's should be included in the support waves, in such manner that they would be at the disposal of the company commanders. The desirability of attaining an organization as close as practicable to existing infantry organizations was emphasized.

6.   The modifications in technique and organization as discussed above are to be effected for the next (115th) RCT.

Landing Assault Exercises:

7.   Colonel Thompson introduced the question of possible improvement in our present landing-assault exercises. He referred specifically to the matter of umpiring and stated that the plan for providing a junior officer umpire with each assault section is something for the future, to be accomplished as soon as practicable; meanwhile, one senior officer, preferably a colonel, is to accompany each assault company through the exercises beginning with the one for today. It was emphasized that an adequate system of umpiring must be established for the next RCTs.

8.   Following a detailed discussion and in view of the umpiring system which will be installed as described above, it was decided to effect the following changes in the landing-assault exercises for the next RCT:

      a.   To eliminate the simulated enemy troops.

      b.   To employ live fire by the landing forces, this fire to include all short-range high-trajectory weapons such as: Infantry Mortars, 105mm HE artillery, aerial bombs, offensive hand grenades, etc.

      c.   To employ actual smoke on a scale comparable to that which would be required for an actual operation; to place the smoke partly by means of 81mm mortars and 105mm artillery firing ahead of the assault waves from positions on Baggy Point.

9.   Colonel Thompson stated that negotiations looking to acquiring rights to fire inland from Woolacombe Beach through the depth of our area are proceeding satisfactorily.

10.   Except for the providing of senior officer umpires, which is to take effect immediately the modifications described above are to be effected for the next (115th) RCT.

Platoon and company assault training aids.

11.   Colonel Thompson called attention to the gap existing in our present training programs: the lack of adequate training in platoon and company formations. It was brought out that under our present system the training proceeds from the individual section to the battalion. The plan for converting the Baggy Point plateau into an area for training on platoon and company scale was discussed, and it was directed that the necessary aids be laid out and the construction effected without delay, on highest priority.

As more and more US personnel were arriving in Britain, the US Army issued an endless stream of orders dealing with various situations as they appeared. The following is just one of many sets; in all they cover a multitude of subjects. Often HQ Company for each battalion would be sent these and they would apply and distribute them as necessary. Some would be appropriate to the Rangers and others would not.

Command Responsibility: All commanders are charged with the responsibility for operation of motor vehicles of their command for authorised purposes only.

Control and maintenance of motor vehicles: Tactical vehicles will remain with their organisations and will be utilised as tactical transportation. Vehicles other than those operated under tactical conditions will be operated through a motor pool. Records showing operation will be prepared and maintained for inspection at any time.

Officers: All officers are required to have in their possession at all times an official War Department identification card. An officer requiring a card will submit a request, approved by this commanding officer, in form to the nearest issuing headquarters of his command, which will take the necessary action to issue and record the card and to obtain a receipt therefor.

Each issuing headquarters will, at the end of each month, submit to HQ SOS, ETOUSA, APO 871 in duplicate, a report in the following form on the cards issued during such month.

Serial number of card.	Branch of Army or Service
Name of officer to whom issued.	Initial or replacement issue.
Army Serial Number.	Serial No. of old card, if replacement.
Grade.	

Invitations from local civilians: Care must be exercised to reply promptly to correspondence from local civilians, especially when invitations to visit their homes are involved, as the British public are very generous in their offers to share the limited supplies which they have, but are most punctilious in replies to invitations between themselves. They expect, and rightfully so, the same courteous treatment from our officers and men. In the event that an invitation has been accepted and it becomes impossible to attend, every effort must be made to advise the host so that supplies may not be wasted and an impression of ingratitude be created.

Subsistence: Officers may be reimbursed for expenses involved in retaining quarters at their permanent station for not exceeding 15 days of hospitalisation. No subsistence allowance will be paid to officers while sick in government hospitals.

Travel: Officers on temporary duty away from permanent station will make application for government quarters. If government quarters are not available, they will be reimbursed for the actual cost of quarters. The maximum rate of reimbursement will not exceed $4.00 per day and is in addition to government allowances at permanent station. If temporary duty exceeds 30 days the officer will be required to terminate quarters at permanent station prior to departure on temporary duty.

No military personnel will be permitted to live in Red Cross hostels or government subsidised institutions while in receipt of a monetary allowance for quarters at their permanent station. This ruling does not apply to individuals away from their permanent station on leave, pass, or furlough.

Driving in the UK: Most motor vehicles in the British Isles have right-hand drive. For this reason, drivers of British cars and trucks are accustomed to receive traffic signals from the right hand side of other vehicles. In the interests of safety, drivers and assistant drivers of American cargo vehicles are directed to give proper traffic signals at all times. The operators of passenger vehicles, in addition to giving the prescribed signals, will assure themselves that vehicles in their rear are in no danger of collision before making a turn.

Each officer responsible for maintenance will use the utmost discretion in discarding motor parts. No parts will be discarded until it is impossible to make repairs. The automotive officer of each unit will make careful check to determine compliance with this provision.

Officers responsible for the operation of motor vehicles will see that their use is reduced to military necessities. Every effort will be made to conserve gasoline, oil, tires and parts.

The first requirement of a military motor vehicle is its reliability. Vehicles will be constantly checked by the responsible officer for any deficiencies or necessary adjustment. Vehicles out of service and on the dead line will be reduced to the minimum. Every effort will be made to maintain all motor vehicles in operating condition.

<u>*Road discipline for military personnel on foot*</u>*: Troops on foot on roads in the UK will be marched in not more than a column of threes. Columns will march on the left side of the road in the same direction as moving vehicular traffic. The senior officer or non-commissioned officer present with the column is responsible for adequate safety precautions and for observance of the following instructions.*

Advance and Rear Guards. Two men will be designated from the column to act as advance and rear guards. They will march not less than 50 paces to the front or rear of the main body, as the case may be. During daylight, they will warn approaching traffic of the presence of the column by means of appropriate hands signals or signs. During hours of darkness, they will carry lighted lanterns or lamps with defused light to warn and slow down approaching traffic; the advance guard carrying a white lantern and the rear guard a red lantern.

U.S. Army Here Blueprint The 'Invasion'

MAN FROM INSIDE WEHRMACHT LEADS

By VICTOR LEWIS, 'Daily Sketch' Special Correspondent, At a U.S. Assault Training Centre, Monday

THE fight for every foot of the first 1,000 yards of the Fortress of Europe by American assault troops has been worked out in detail. Every man who will take part in this vital amphibious operation has been, or is being, trained to a split second in what he will do.

In this "somewhere-in-England" assault centre he is learning hour after hour, under hazardous, realistic conditions, to overcome the obstacles he will meet. This, so far as the American army is concerned, is where the invasion is being hatched.

Beaches Reproduced

Under a man who for years up to the early days of the war studied German army tactics—from inside the German Army—American assault forces are learning each move in what may be one of the greatest battles in history when the first assault forces must break down the heavily fortified beaches of Europe.

Every detail of the beaches has been reproduced with pillbox positions with their interlocking bands of fire, barbed-wire used exactly as the Germans use it, every known German type of tank obstacle, anti-tank and anti-personnel mines, mortars and artillery.

Officers from the landing at Salerno are passing on valuable information. Men are briefed from huge relief models. The technique of close air support is part of the "course."

Each man is becoming highly skilled in the weapon he will handle. The weapons are not secret—it is the method of their use that will be secret. The invasion has been worked out like a bridge hand.

This is a tough school, and there are casualties. But the battle innoculation is complete and invaluable.

Flame Throwers At Work

The precision training is so accurate that I was able to stand on high ground at the climax of the attack after the assault troops had established the bridgehead.

Live artillery fire concentrated on a point not 200 yards ahead. Rifle and light machine gun fire passed a few feet over me.

Ground strafing from air support threw up the ground 50 yards away. Flame-throwers and wire-wrecking parties worked under my nose and tanks passed through to the assault near enough for me to feel the ground tremble.

The man behind it all—36-year-old Nebraska-born Colonel Paul W. Thompson, once an engineer with a brilliant career before him, told me that he spent several years in Germany studying Army organisation and was attached to several units of the German Army.

In February this year he was assigned to form this assault training centre in Britain.

A new tank capable of fording rivers advances over difficult country during the great assault exercise. The purpose of the two objects resembling ventilators on the tank is a military secret.

Traffic Control: Signals. Marching columns will observe highway traffic control signals in the same manner as vehicles. When a traffic light turns to red, that portion of the column which has not passed the light will halt, the interval thus caused normally being made up through a decrease in pace by the leading portion of the column. Only in exceptional circumstances or urgent combat contingencies will the strict observation of traffic lights be waived.

Not in Formation: Military personnel walking in the UK not in formation will, where possible, utilise side-walks and footpaths and not the travelled portion of the highway. Where no sidewalk of footpath is provided, such personnel will walk well to the right edge of the road, facing the oncoming traffic.

By command of General Eisenhower. 19th October 1943.

In November 1943 the US Army started to allow certain aspects of the US training to become public knowledge. It was important politically to let the public know that training for the assault on Nazi occupied Europe was underway and it was very much seen as a propaganda boost aimed at the battered British public. A series of articles were released to the press in England for this purpose and heavily featured new equipment and tactics being put into operation.

'School' for Invaders

Secret Tactics

By Daily Mail Reporter

U.S. ARMY ASSAULT TRAINING CENTRE, " SOMEWHERE IN ENGLAND," Monday.

AMERICAN shock troops who will land on the coast of German-held Europe to carve bridgeheads for the U.S. armies that follow them are being trained here in secret tactics by an American colonel who, until late in 1939, was serving with units of the German Army.

Colonel Paul Thompson, commandant of this battle school, is 36 years of age, short, cheery—and tough. He had a close-up, inside view of the Wehrmacht for many months while he was attached for special duties to the American Attaché in Berlin.

His " scholars " are taught tactics modelled on lessons learned in all the Allied landings from Dieppe to Salerno.

Casualties

Around the bays and among the sand dunes here—in peace-time the haunt of bathers and picnickers—conditions reproduce those which the men who train will find when they do their real fighting.

Casualties from shell splinters and ricocheting bullets are not uncommon during an attack by a battalion of infantry on a German " hedgehog " collection of strongly defended pill-boxes.

As I stood on the sand dunes watching an infantry assault battalion coming ashore in successive waves Colonel Thompson told me :

" All the U.S. assault units who will form the spearhead of the American invasion will pass through this type of course."

The enthusiasm and hopes of the men taking this course is summed up in the words, printed at the end of the programme for my visit : " When we see you across the Channel, we will tell you how it all worked out."

DAILY · MAIL ·

· 2 · NOV · 43 ·

"REAL-LIFE" INVASION PRACTICE BY U.S. ARMY HERE

ON a site specially selected because of its resemblance to the German-occupied coast and with replicas of the enemy's anti-invasion defences the U.S. Army in Britain, using live ammunition—and suffering inevitable casualties—is rehearsing its 1944 task of smashing Hitler's west wall.

By day and by night the troops toil to perfect their secret plans and methods of reducing and overcoming the enemy's defences.

' Our problem is the first

DAILY · MIRROR·

2. NOV· 1943

few hundred yards of Europe," said the commanding officer of this training assault centre, Colonel Paul W. Thompson, yesterday.

Not yet forty, the colonel is an expert on the German Army. For several years he was attached to German military units, and was U.S. military attache in Berlin till after the European war started.

In this grim battle school, which covers thousands of acres, there is no question of blank ammunition or simulated effects.

Using every weapon in its armoury, working always with the Navy and the Air Force, the U.S Army concentrates on what will follow the initial landing.

' There is no real precedent

for this business. There has never in history been a landing assault such as is facing us," says Colonel Thompson.

He has devised his own technique for the job with advice from those who know all about Dieppe and Salerno.

The landings start when the Duks crash through the surf, and, transformed from ships to cars, come waddling ashore.

They deposit their cargoes—bull-dozers, " Seaps," which are amphibious " Jeeps," tanks, guns, and all the paraphernalia of an invasion force.

Primarily, however, the first 1,000 yards to Europe is a job for the infantry.

It is on their training that the assault centre concentrates.

Spectacular Assault

Observers saw these small self - contained " task forces " concentrate first on the destruction of beach defences and afterwards join forces in a spectacular assault on a hedgehog position.

A preliminary softening filled the air with shells, bombs and grenades.

Infantry followed closely under the hail of lead.

Flame throwers came up to project great jets of fire at picked targets, bazookas, with their secret explosives, smashed through thick walls of concrete.

Replicas have been built so that, with drill and discipline, troops and all their equipment can be passed from ship to landing craft in less than three minutes.

The scaling of massive concrete walls had been brought to a swift, fine art.

Flame-thrower squads were perfecting their aim in an inferno of smoke and heat.

Before the winter is over many thousands of American soldiers will have passed through this training centre.

3 November 1943

US WAR DEPARTMENT DIRECTIVE

> *War Department prohibition of marriage without approval: 'No military personnel on duty in any foreign country or possession may marry without the approval of the commanding officer of the United States army forces station in such foreign country or possession.'*
>
> *General officers are authorised to approve or disapprove applications for permission to marry by commissioned, warrant and flight officers under their command.*
>
> *Regimental and corresponding commanders are authorised to approve or disprove application for permission to marry by enlisted personnel under their command.*
>
> *Such an application may be approved when, in the judgement of the commander specified above, the marriage contemplated would not bring discredit to the military service.*
>
> *Applications will state full name and address of the person who applicant proposes to marry and will be accompanied by a letter from such person stating her or his acquiescence.*
>
> *Application and accompanying papers will be signed in triplicate. All three copies will be presented by the applicant to his immediate commanding officer.*

5 November 1943 there was an aerial reconnaissance report produced covering La Martinière Battery, Maisy II:

> *The sunken casemate/shelter, reported as being in the early stages of construction in B512, appears complete and the excavation which was to the right of No.2 gun now presents a similar appearance to the completed casemate/shelter. Two of the three long huts behind the battery have been removed. The guns have been camouflaged and signs of the previously reported activity toned down. (1011/12 of sortie RA/867, 24 October 1943, 1/12,600, quality good)*

5 November 1943 a report covering Les Perruques Battery, Maisy I:

> *A dummy battery [at GR 532923] for battery Maisy I, 600 yards in front of this battery and similar to it in layout. Emplacements are 25' in diameter and contain objects. (1011 of sortie RA/867, 24 October 1943, 1/12,600, quality good)*

On 5 November 1943 the whole 5th Ranger Battalion moved to Fort Pierce in Florida for amphibious training. One training exercise involved capturing areas of the North and South islands at Fort Pierce and various objectives including capturing a Coast Guard security tower and boat. It was an exercise that had never been completed before – so the Rangers were going to have to use all their skill, inventiveness and expertise to accomplish it.

The men had two rubber boats with which to cross a fast moving area of water and this was where other units had fallen foul of being spotted making the crossing – even at night. The Rangers decided to send a man swimming across the channel on his own to capture the observation tower – which he did by climbing a 50ft ladder and taking the three lookouts by surprise. They were looking for boats crossing the water and had never expected the man who arrived behind them.

So that was one major part of the exercise mastered as none of these men could now participate and importantly, could not call or make telephone calls. Whilst the tower was being neutralised, a group of eleven men headed for the North Island in their boats. It was dark and the men submerged themselves in seawater to hide their scent from the sentry dogs which patrolled the road with their masters.

The boats were pulled onto the beach and the men waited for a sentry to come walking down the road. Once challenged, he too was out of the game and the Rangers had now infiltrated both islands. More men could now cross to the island and it was while they were doing this, that a car came along the road towards them. It was quickly surrounded as it passed and the occupants were captured – including the Naval Commander for the islands and three of his officers. He asked to be released to go about his business – which he was – and he took the opportunity to congratulate the Rangers on having captured him. It was the first time he had been captured in such a raid and he was impressed.

The bridge into Fort Pierce was to be captured at both ends to allow the unit to cross and an objective was the telephone exchange. This was done by Captain George Whittington and 1st Sergeant Grant Constable, who climbed into the building through a second floor window and scared all inside. This capture had a dual effect, not only did it stop anyone from alerting the authorities to the Rangers' presence – it also disconnected the coastal defence network and warning systems – something which went on to cause mayhem with the surrounding area.

The men captured the airport, train station, radio, police and fire stations and in effect the whole of the area was now under the Rangers' control. They succeeded where no other unit had come close previously.

Below: A further very explicit set of instructions were issued to the men leaving for the ETO regarding attempts to marry local English women while on active duty. Rumours had been circulating that men could marry an English woman and avoid being sent to France. The Army wanted to nip it in the bud before it became a problem with the men already in England.

Cir 88   Hq ETOUSA   3 Nov 1943

MARRIAGE

1. Sec I, Cir 75, 16 Sept 1943, is rescinded.

2. War Department Prohibition of Marriage Without Approval. a. Sec II, WD Cir 305, 1942, provides that: "No military personnel on duty * * * in any foreign country or possession may marry without the approval of the commanding officer of the United States army forces stationed * * * in such foreign country or possession."
b. The foregoing is not applicable to civilians who are subject to military law.

3. Delegation of Authority Within ETOUSA. a. General officers are authorized to approve or disapprove applications for permission to marry by commissioned, warrant, and flight officers under their command.
b. Regimental and corresponding commanders are authorized to approve or dis-approve applications for permission to marry by enlisted personnel under their command.
c. The authority delegated in a and b above will not be sub-delegated; however, communications relating to its exercise may be signed or transmitted by the commanders concerned either personally or as provided for official communications in general.

4. Policy to govern decision on application for permission to marry. Such an application may be approved when, in the judgment of the commander specified in Par 3, above, the marriage contemplated would not bring discredit to the military service.

5. Procedure for Handling Application for Permission to Marry. a. Application will state full name and address of the person whom applicant proposes to marry and will be accompanied by a letter from such person stating her or his acqui-escence.
b. (1) Application and accompanying papers will be signed in triplicate. All three copies will be presented by the applicant to his immediate commanding officer.
(2) Such immediate commanding officer will be responsible for advising the applicant to investigate the requirements for civil authorization to marry (the procedure prescribed in this circular has to do only with the administration of military approval; persons desiring to marry must make their own inquiries as to the requirements laid down by local civil law, as for example, the need for pre-senting to the civil authorities proof of prior divorce). Such immediate command-ing officer will, prior to forwarding the application through channels to the commander authorized to act upon the application, sign a certificate as follows: "From the official records in my custody and the information available, it does not appear that the applicant is married".
(3) Action by the commander specified in Par 3, above, will be signed in trip-licate, and authenticated by the adjutant of his headquarters; and he will re-tain on file one copy of application, accompanying letter, and action.
c. Ordinarily, approval by the commander specified in Par 3, above, will not be given until two months after the application is submitted. Such commanders may approve at an earlier date only in case of illegitimacy or pregnancy.

(Cir 88, ETOUSA, 3 Nov 1943, cont)

d. In case of approval, the approving commander will assure himself that applicant understands that: (1) When married, applicant will not be permitted any special privileges or living arrangements different from those of unmarried members of the command.
(2) Marriage to a citizen of the United States does not confer United States citizenship on an alien, under existing law, although it does facilitate the alien's later entry into the United States and naturalization after taking up residence there.
(3) Upon change of applicant's station to the United States spouse remaining in ETOUSA will not be accorded commissary or post exchange privileges, nor government quarters, nor medical or dental services.
(4) Spouse will be entitled to such allowance, allotment, insurance, and other benefits as authorized by law.
e. The original written approval of marriage and one signed copy will be delivered to applicant for presentation by applicant to the appropriate local civil or ecclesiastical official from whom the securing of civil or ecclesiastical authorization to marry is required. The original written approval will be left with said local civil or ecclesiastical official. On the copy of said approval, the applicant will obtain a notation by the appropriate local official of the date and place of marriage. The applicant will return such copy with notation of his immediate commanding officer. The immediate commanding officer will cause such copy and notation to be filed with the service or other appropriate record pertaining to the applicant and remain a permanent part thereof.
f. The fact of marriage will be entered in the applicant's service or other appropriate record, showing date of approval and by whom granted, and date of marriage and where performed.

6. Consequences of Marriage Without Approval. Marriage without approval will be dealt with as an offense under the 96th Article of War.   (AG 291.1 PerGA)

By command of Lieutenant General DEVERS:

I. H. EDWARDS,
Major General, GSC, Chief of Staff.
OFFICIAL:

Ralph Pulsifer,
RALPH PULSIFER,
Brigadier General, USA, Adjutant General.   DISTRIBUTION: "B"

Back in England with the US forces, on 15 November Lieutenant Colonel Devers wrote the following letter in praise of all those who had given up their land in the UK to allow it to be used as a training ground.

RELEASE NO. 1804   15/11/43 - No. 29

HEADQUARTERS
EUROPEAN THEATER OF OPERATIONS
UNITED STATES ARMY

GENERAL DEVERS PAYS TRIBUTE TO TRAINING-GROUND EVACUEES

HEADQUARTERS, EUROPEAN THEATER OF OPERATIONS: Tribute to the "unsung
heroes" who have sacrificed their homes and farms for all out victory was paid
today by Lieutenant General Jacob L. Devers, commanding general of the European
Theater of Operations, United States Army.

Speaking of the families who must evacuate areas which are being turned
over to the United States Army by the British government for invasion rehearsal
areas, General Devers declared:

"These property owners and residents are the unsung heroes of this
bitter all-out struggle against our common enemy. It is one of the grim
necessities of war that people must be deprived of their homes, farms and
business places. I can say this with feeling and with personal knowledge as in
the United States, several hundred camps have been constructed during the past
three years with hundreds of thousands of acres necessary for training maneuvers
and artillery ranges. Thousands of landowners made these really great contribu-
tions to the war effort uncomplainingly just as many are now doing in the United
Kingdom."

The training areas made possible by the action of the British government
which carried out the negotiations for the land will be used to further the
preparations now going forward for the invasion of the European continent.
General Devers pointed out that the present sacrifices of the people in Great
Britain come over and above that which they have already made during the five
years of war. "It is a sacrifice" he explained "requested only as a last resort
and intended, despite the demands of war, to cause the least interference to
the civilian population."

Military demands, it was made clear, have shifted and now preparations must
be made in great detail for an attack. "It should be remembered," General Devers
said, "That no military operation is more dependent on training than the landing
on a strongly-fortified hostile shore. To win a bridgehead upon the Continent

/and expend

- 2 -

and expend as few lives as possible in so doing, the training must be realistic and under actual gunfire. This requires sizeable areas free of civilians. This training is needed to develop the balance and coordination of a master plan that will set into motion what may be the greatest military undertaking of all time.

"What will be accomplished in these localities could become the difference between success and disaster for the Allied plan pf operations. Success will justify the sacrifices being made now by land-owners."

In line with their desire to retain the new training areas in their original condition for future return to the owners, American officials have issued a special order to troops that, so far as possible, historical monuments, churches and similar buildings will be "protected and preserved."

On 19 November Major General Clarence R. Huebner (1st Inf. Div.) was a guest at a training session hosted at the Assault Training Centre. The aim of his visit was to show theatre commanders the training methods and techniques being developed in preparation for the assault on Normandy.

HEADQUARTERS
U.S. ASSAULT TRAINING CENTER, ETOUSA
APO #553

DAILY ARRIVAL AND DEPARTURE REPORT

As of 2400 hours 18 November 1943

Major General L.T. Gerow and party of officers arrived singly at various times during the afternoon and evening. Party includes Major General Brown, Major General Huebner, Major General Watson, Major Genral Woodruff, Brigadier General Helmick, Brigadier General Kean, Colonel Thorson and Lieutenant Thames. SPOBS.

TITLE AND NAME	ORGANIZATION	ARRIVAL	DEPARTURE	REMARKS
Maj Gen H.J. Pfaff	Military Attaches	----------	181400 Hrs	--------------------
Maj L.J.A. Schwoonenberg	Royal Netherlands Government	----------	181400 "	--------------------
Capt Gardiner(Interperter)	U.S. Army	----------	181400 "	--------------------
Lt Col L.W. Merriam, Inf	Hq, ETOUSA	----------	181232 "	--------------------
Capt Daniel I. Dann	Aslt Tng Cen	----------	181500 "	For 3 days TD

```
                    COPY OF VEHICLE CONVOY

            VEHICLE CONVOY FOR INSPECTION TRIP
             U.S. ASSAULT TRAINING CENTER,ETOUSA
                    19 November 1943
```

Car Number	Occupants	Car Number	Occupants
00	Lt.Col. Haas	11	+Gen Whittaker
0	Lt. Olin		Gen Brown
1	Maj. Dobbins		Maj Kelly
	Radio Personnel		
		12	Gen Watson
2	MP Car		+Gen Inglis
	Lt. Henderson		Gen Lee
3	+Gen Paget	13	Gen Heubner
	Gen Devers		+Brig Pyman
	Col Thompson		Col Brewster

The attached schedule is dated 19 November and the opening page sets out the purpose of the visit.

```
                          SCHEDULE OF EVENTS

              VISIT OF THEATER COMMANDER, ETOUSA, AND PARTY

                               to the

                   U.S. ASSAULT TRAINING CENTER, ETOUSA

                           19 November 1943

                               Notes
```

Facts concerning US Assault Training Center - Established in Woolacombe-Appledore area of northwest Devon in August 1943. Mission: to train RCT's of U.S. Assault Divisions under realistic conditions in tactics and technique specifically applicable to invasion of fortified German-held coast of Europe. Composition of the Center: training staff, school (demonstration) troops, station complement (housekeeping) troops, one RCT in training, naval echelon (sufficient to lift one BCT). Characteristics of reservation: 30 square miles, 8,000 yards of beaches fronting ocean, 2500 yards of beaches within estuary, beaches very flat (slopes 1 on 50 to 1 on 200), tide range very high (18 to 24 foot), surf(on outer beaches) medium to strong, hinterlands rolling.

Facts concerning events on schedule - All events on todays program are normal training-schedule items. Troops concerned are chiefly elements of 115th RCT of 29th Infantry Division. Troops have been at Center 10 days and will remain 7 days more. First 9 days have been devoted to individual and small-unit training; today's schedule marks start of training on battalion scale. Training period ends with a regimental landing-assault exercise.

Pertinent meteorological data for 19 November 1943.- High tide, 1058 hours; low tide, 1714 hours; sunrise, 0839 hours; sunset, 1724 hours; twilight begins, 0722 hours, twilight ends, 1541 hours.

SERIAL	ARRIVAL	DEPARTURE	PLACE	EVENT	REMARKS
1	----	0800 Hrs	Barnstaple Railway Sta.	Detrain	Entruck in jeep convoy from U.S. Aslt Tng Center.
2	0830 Hrs	0840 Hrs	Est Yellow I	Waterproofing Demonstration	In this demonstration the latest methods of waterproofing have been applied to typical items of equipment (6X6 truck, recovery tractor, 57mm AT gun).
3	0840 Hrs	0910 Hrs	Beach Opposite Crow Point	Firing of 155mm gun from beached LCT(5)	This is a demonstration of technique only, indicating the practicability of firing the 155mm gun from a beached landing craft. The tactical significance of this type of fire is under study.
4	0940 Hrs	1140 Hrs	Woolacombe Beach	Bn landing-assault exercise, 2d Bn CT, 115th Inf	This landing-assault exercise involves an infantry battalion, with engineer, artillery, tank, CWS and far-shore attachments. The exercise is umpired, and enemy troops are simulated. Various training aids, including beach charges and smoke, are used; but there is no live firing. Noteworthy points are these: the use of all-infantry assault sections (not engineer) in the initial waves; and, the landing of "assault tanks" in the assault waves. From the training standpoint, this exercise complements the "Hedge-Hog assault" to be seen in the afternoon: in the one case, there is a landing and an assault without live fire; and in the other case there is an assault with full live fire but with only simulated landing.
5	(1045) Hrs	(1130) Hrs	Woolacombe Bay	Firing afloat, 155mm gun, 105mm howitzer, MK IV tank, 4.2" CW mortar, from LCT(5), LCT(5), LCM(5), LCVP, respectively.	These demonstrations involve the firing of various types of weapons (155mm gun, 105 howitzers, 75mm Mk IV tank guns, 4.2" CW mortars) from various types of landing craft (LCT, LCM, LCVP). The tactical significance of the fire from the howitzers and mortars has been demonstrated in the landing-assault exercise of this morning. The tactical significance of the other types of fire has not been determined. (Ferry service by DUKWS from Woolacombe Beach out to the landing craft is provided).

SECRET

SERIAL	ARRIVAL	DEPARTURE	PLACE	EVENT	REMARKS
6	1150 Hrs	1230 Hrs	Hq. US Aslt Tng Cen	Lunch	This must be a quick lunch.
7	1255 Hrs	1530 Hrs	Hedge-Hog Area	Bn CT assault (Live fire) 3rd Bn, 115th Infantry	This "Hedge-Hog" assault exercise is the culmination of the assault phase of the battalion's training at the Center. The exercise involves the use of live fire of many types: artillery, tank guns, anti-tank guns, infantry mortars, CW mortars, air bombs, air strafing, small arms, anti-tank rockets and grenades, etc. Each Bn of the RCT in training - in this case the 3rd Bn of the 115th RCT - goes through one live-fire Hedge-Hog assault prior to this exercise. The Bn has completed live-fire assault training on the section and company assault ranges (to be inspected later)
8	1540 Hrs	1555 Hrs	LCT Mock-up	Inspect loading training facilities.	This is a routine training exercise, involving the loading of AA Artillery into LCT(5)'s. Training on mock-ups such as these precede loading exercises on the actual craft.
9	1610 Hrs	1620 Hrs	Range 40	Inspect Assault Section training facilities.	This is a brief inspection of an "assault range", on which the individual 30-man assault section is trained under live-fire. This range - there are many more like it at the Center - is the Center's basic training aid so far as assault training goes.
10	1630 Hrs	1640 Hrs	Flamethrower Range	Demonstration, flame thrower training in use.	Throughout the area, there are many ranges and training aids devoted to basic individual training. These are necessary because the assault technique requires certain infantrymen to use weapons with which they are not familiar. A case in point is the flame thrower range, demonstrated here.
11	1645 Hrs	1700 Hrs	Shipside Obstacle	Demonstration, various training aids in use.	This is a physical conditioning area, which also provides the soldier with training in essential items: wall-climbing, net scaling, etc.

- 2 -

SECRET

SERIAL	ARRIVAL	DEPARTURE	PLACE	EVENT	REMARKS
12	1710 Hrs	1745 Hrs	Croyde Beach	Battalion landing from DUKW's w/105mm guns and 57mm guns	The DUKW was designed as a cargo-carrying vehicle. As illustrated, in this exercise, it may be put to direct tactical use, both for transporting troops and for transporting (and towing) artillery.
13	1745 Hrs	1815 Hrs	Barnstaple Railway Station.	Train party departs for Barnstaple Rail Station	Detruck from jeep convoy at rail station.

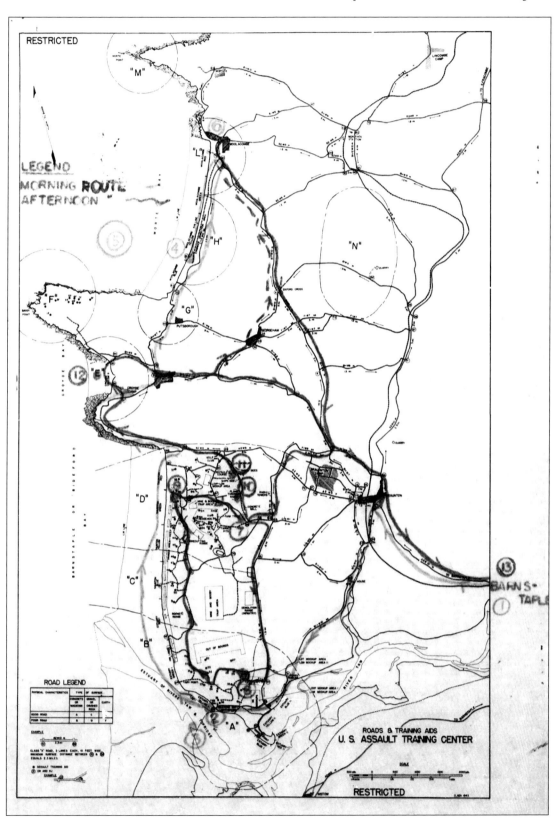

Towards the end of 1943, more intelligence was being gathered, which would affect the specific areas where the Rangers were to land. A US Army report written in October 1943 discussed the use of smoke as a screen for the landings.

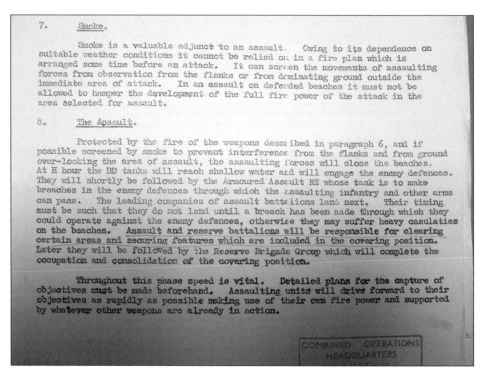

7.   Smoke.

Smoke is a valuable adjunct to an assault. Owing to its dependence on suitable weather conditions it cannot be relied on in a fire plan which is arranged some time before an attack. It can screen the movements of assaulting forces from observation from the flanks or from dominating ground outside the immediate area of attack. In an assault on defended beaches it must not be allowed to hamper the development of the full fire power of the attack in the area selected for assault.

8.   The Assault.

Protected by the fire of the weapons described in paragraph 6, and if possible screened by smoke to prevent interference from the flanks and from ground over-looking the area of assault, the assaulting forces will close the beaches. At H hour the DD tanks will reach shallow water and will engage the enemy defences. They will shortly be followed by the Armoured Assault RE whose task is to make breaches in the enemy defences through which the assaulting infantry and other arms can pass. The leading companies of assault battalions land next. Their timing must be such that they do not land until a breach has been made through which they could operate against the enemy defences, otherwise they may suffer heavy casualties on the beaches. Assault and reserve battalions will be responsible for clearing certain areas and securing features which are included in the covering position. Later they will be followed by the Reserve Brigade Group which will complete the occupation and consolidation of the covering position.

Throughout this phase speed is vital. Detailed plans for the capture of objectives must be made beforehand. Assaulting units will drive forward to their objectives as rapidly as possible making use of their own fire power and supported by whatever other weapons are already in action.

COMBINED OPERATIONS HEADQUARTERS

On 20 November the 5th Battalion moved to Fort Dix in New Jersey, where it underwent more exercises. The men were given meagre rations and told to fend for themselves from the land, as they were dropped into a small village in the middle of the night.

The battalion had been divided in half, and one group was to act as the attacking force – something which caused a stir amongst the locals, who had no idea it was going to happen. After negotiation, men would buy a chicken here, or a loaf of bread there from the inhabitants and this kept their hunger at bay. As temperatures plummeted, the various teams raced around trying to capture and avoid each other, one group managed to set up a cosy arrangement with a local bar owner, who supplied the men with drinks and hot dogs to keep them warm.

These exercises often involved taking over small villages and areas, where one unit would assault another using blank ammunition and simulated explosives, much to the amusement and often bemusement of the locals, who would not be briefed in advance.

Jack Burke, 5th Ranger recalled: *At Camp Dix we continued to weed guys out with speed marches and having unusual night problems where they would truck us out into the countryside, drop us off in small groups with no food, no directions and with orders to find our way back to camp. It was in the farming area of New Jersey and it was about 10 o'clock and cold as hell. All groups were successful. They just kept us very active and we lived in squad tents with wooden floors and it was cold. On the weekend they gave us a pass and I went to NY City with Bill Taylor and stayed at his folks' house. When we got back, I can recall that we got our orders to ship out. We were also told to remove our Ranger shoulder patches and anything that would indicate our specialty.... Secrecy in war-time, I guess.*

By November, the US Army was actively studying the whole of the Atlantic Wall, looking for weakness. They produced a Top Secret report on the German defences, covering every aspect of German defensive works. It was a large volume with many photographs and illustrations.

Thus far in Allied planning, no British or American schools existed for the study of aerial photographs. Lieutenant Colonel Harper arranged with the British War Office to have a British officer run specialised courses in the art of Aerial Photo Familiarisation and period papers defined the role:

> The purpose of this course was two-fold. First, to acquaint key personnel of combat units with the fundamentals of aerial photo reading, including elementary identification of military installations, scaling of photographs, plotting and recognition of terrain features. Secondly, the course was intended to acquaint G-2 and S-2 personnel with the capabilities and limitations of the photo interpreter teams attached to their units and also to point out the wealth of combat intelligence that could be derived from proper employment of the photo interpretation teams.

The courses were organised on a mobile basis so that the instructors could visit each unit, no matter where they were located. Each course lasted five days and all photographs and equipment such as stereoscopes, scales, maps, etc. were provided. Those attending included men from the Headquarters of the First Army.

Another issue created by preparations for D-Day was that of censorship. Orders were sent out specifically detailing what men and women subject to military law could and could not say in their correspondence. They left this sheet with each unit to be displayed on the battalion notice board.

RESTRICTED

A COPY OF THIS CIRCULAR WILL BE POSTED ON EACH HEADQUARTERS AND UNIT BULLETIN
BOARD*

Cir #65   Hq ETOUSA   26 Aug 1943

CENSORSHIP POSTAL,AND CABLE INSTRUCTIONS

1. General: a. Cir 88, Hq ETOUSA, 30 Dec 1942; Sec III, Cir 15, 16 Feb 1943;
Sec IV, Cir 32, 23 Mar 1943; Sec II, Cir 45, 21 May 1943; Sec V, Cir 49, 8 June
1943; and Sec III, Cir 56, 19 July 1943, are rescinded. Instructions therein are
superseded by this circular. No subordinate commander will publish orders at
variance with or more restrictive than the instructions contained herein.
b. The provisions of this circular apply to all persons subject to military law,
to include all civilians accompanying or serving with this command in the field
(AW 2).
c. The term "mail" as used herein applies to personal mail, cablegrams, and telegrams written by members of this command.
2. Mail of Enlisted Men: All mail written by members of this command, no matter
to whom addressed, will be subject to censorship. Mail of enlisted men will be
deposited in mail boxes in company (battery, etc.) orderly rooms only. It will be
unsealed and will be censored one hundred per cent by company officers, except
that the following classes of mail will be sealed by the writer and will not be
censored or unit stamped by company officers:
a. Blue envelopes (See Par 4).
b. Letters addressed to prisoners of war (See Par 11).
c. Mail written in foreign languages. The writer will indicate in soft pencil on
the face of the envelope, lower left hand corner, or at the top of V-mail letters
the language in which the letter is written. Such mail is subject to base censorship only. The unit censor will not countersign foreign language mail or affix
the unit censorship stamp thereto. Permission to write in a foreign language must
be obtained from either the unit commander or the theater censor.
d. Officers' mail (See Par 5).
3. Unit Censorship: a. Company officers will censor mail of enlisted men within
24 hours of the time of posting and forward, sealed, to a base censor through APC
channels. Commanders will designate as many officers as required to insure that
mail posted by troops will be censored and forwarded within 24 hours after posting.
Enlisted personnel will not be used to censor unit mail. Regimental or higher
headquarters may designate warrant officers as censors when expedient. Commanding
officers of hospitals will designate as many officers as required to censor the
mail of patients and hospital personnel. Minor violations of censorship will be
cut from letters, except that nothing will be cut from a V-mail letter. Deletions
in V-mail will be made with black ink only. Letters containing general or frequent
minor violations will be returned to the writers for educational purposes. Under
no circumstances will a letter be mutilated by excessive deleting.
- -
* Unit commanders will enter the following information on the copy posted on the
bulletin board:

APO_____is the correct address for this unit.

The code cable address of this APO is_____ _____

-1-

RESTRICTED

(Cir 65, ETOUSA, 26 Aug 43, Contd)

b. Unit censors will not repeat, discuss, make excerpts from, or additions in any form whatsoever to personal letters subjected to their censorship where censorship violations are not involved.

c. After censorship, the unit censor will countersign a letter by signing his name and rank legible in ink on the lower left hand corner of the envelope and stamp above his name with censorship stamp.

d. It will be the responsibility of unit commanders to initiate appropriate disciplinary action against members of their commands who commit major or frequent violations of censorship regulations.

e. Requests for censorship stamps will be made in accordance with FM 30-25, Par 48 b. Censorship stamp will be safeguarded against unauthorized use.

4. Blue Envelopes: a. Blue envelopes will be issued at the rate of four per month to enlisted men to enable them to write letters on purely personal or family matters. The writer's signature on a "blue envelope" certifies that the contents therein pertain strictly to personal or family matters. Each "blue envelope" will contain only one letter and will be addressed to addressee. Such letters will be censored only by base censors. Unit censors will not stamp "blue envelopes". V-mail may be inclosed in a "blue envelope", in which case it must be addressed to V-Mail Section, APO 887. Letters sent in "blue envelopes" which violate these instructions, will be returned by base censors to the senders.

b. The use of "blue envelopes" by officers is prohibited.

c. "Blue envelopes" may be requisitioned by organization commanders in the same manner as other stationery supplies.

d. No envelope will be substituted by the writer for the official US Army "blue envelope".

5. Officers' Mail: Each officer and warrant officer will censor and seal his own mail. Excepting as set forth in Par 17, his name, printed, together with full address, will appear on the upper left hand corner of the envelope. The officer will sign above his typed or printed name and such signature will constitute a certificate that he has complied with censorship regulations. Unit stamps will not be used on officers' mail. Officers' and warrant officers' mail is subject to censorship in a base censor office only.

6. Base Censorship: All mail, to include ordinary letters, letters in blue envelopes, V-mail, officers' mail, and parcel post, is subject to re-censorship by a base censor.

7. Prohibited Statements: Information useful to the enemy or affecting the security of or good relations with Great Britain or other allies will not be included in private correspondence. The items listed below are the most important and will not be mentioned in personal letters.

a. Any information or details of the trip across the Atlantic, especially the names of the transports, ports and dates of embarkation and debarkation, number of ships in convoy, naval vessels or aircraft accompanying the convoy, any action with the enemy, length of voyage, route followed, or other details of the trip.

b. Similar information or details of transatlantic or other air journeys.

c. Strength, efficiency, training, morale, or organization of military forces.

d. Location, movement, engagements, or operations of naval, military, or air force organizations, to include position or description of billets, stations, or camps.

e. Direct or inferential information linking an APO or station number with an exact geographical location. (This prohibition does not apply to general and station hospitals).

-2-

R E S T R I C T E D

f. Armament or equipment of any kind whatsoever.
g. Distinguishing signs used to identify organizations or their transportation or baggage.
h. Information or details of operations against or by the enemy on land, sea, or in the air.
i. Plans and forecasts or orders for future operations, whether known or surmised.
j. The use, condition, or probable extension of roads, railways, or transportation and signal communication facilities.
k. State of the maintenance of the services, including any reference to reserves.
l. Casualties, to include injuries or deaths by accident or natural causes, before official publication or release.
m. Information or details of any enemy action or reference to any results of enemy action.
n. Detailed reports of the weather in such form as to be helpful to the enemy.
o. Criticisms and statements that might tend to bring our armed forces or those of our allies into disrepute.
8. Prohibited Inclosures and Mail Matter: None of the following will be included in private letters: a. Classified documents of the United States or allied nations.
b. Documents captured from the enemy or containing enemy information.
c. Codes, ciphers, shorthand, maps, or blank paper.
d. Drawings, sketches, music manuscripts, and paintings will be submitted to the Theater Censor, ETOUSA, for censorship and forwarding to addressees.
e. Photographs or pictorial matters which, either alone or taken together with the letter, are censorable.
f. Letters for publication in the press, except through authorized channels.
g. Advertisements or letters for publication inviting correspondence with strangers.
h. Replies to letters or gifts from unknown persons; to advertisements or other requests inviting correspondence with unknown persons.
i. "Chain letters", "club letters", "round robin" or "news letters". Unit and base censors will return all such letters to their senders.
j. Newspaper or magazine clippings with connected or associated personal comments which disclose prohibited information.
9. Picture Post Cards which may connect a geographical location with an APO number, location of organization, or route of travel may not be sent through the mails.
10. Phonograph Records will not be mailed by personnel of this command.
11. Correspondence with Prisoners of War: a. Members of this command, regardless of rank, will exercise great caution in writing to friends or relatives held as prisoners of war to the end that no information of value is given to the enemy. No military address nor APO number will be used as a return address in mail intended for prisoners of war. Mail to friends or relatives held as prisoners of war in enemy or enemy occupied countries must be sent only through a friend or relative residing in the continental United States, which friend or relative may forward such mail using only a United States civilian return address. Nothing will be mentioned in either return address or text of such mail identifying the sender, or anyone else, as being a member of the military service.
b. All personal mail addressed to the United States and containing prisoner of war letters for re-mailing in the States will be forwarded in cover envelopes direct to the Theater Censor by the unit censors. The cover envelopes will be labeled in the lower left hand corner: "Prisoner of War Mail".

-3-

R E S T R I C T E D

Further orders came out – this time on *'Repair and reclamation'.*

Repair of clothing and equipment for return to the individual or unit. Minor repairs of clothing (including leather footwear) and equipment of individuals and organisation will be performed by QM salvage repair installations. Organisation supply officers will inspect such clothing and equipment, place like articles in separate bundles, and forward only those articles in need of repair to the nearest QM salvage repair installation. All articles will be properly tagged to ensure their return to the original owner.

Except for the repair of shoes, no provisions have been made for the repair of officers' clothing and equipment.

Officers and warrant officers having shoes in need of repair may turn them in to the sales officer of the nearest QM base depot for repair.

Charges for such repairs will be as below.

Whole soles and shoes	$2.00 a pair.	Rubber heals only	.35 per pair.
Half soles and heels	$1.25 per pair.	Re-welting (if necessary)	.25
Half soles only	.90		

<u>Control of purchase of uniforms, clothing and accessories</u>: *Rationing of uniforms. This circular prescribes the allowances and rationing system which will control the purchase by officers of uniforms, clothing and accessories in the United Kingdom.*

The initial and annual maintenance allowances for officers' uniforms, clothing, and accessories are listed below. The initial allowance represents the maximum quantities to which an officer may increase his wardrobe by purchases in the United Kingdom.

Officers and Warrant officers.	Initial allowance	Annual maintenance allowances
Headdress	2	1
Coat, service	3	2
Trousers or breeches	4	4
Overcoat, short or long	1	
Trench coat, lined	1	
Raincoat	1	1
Field jacket	1	2
Sweater	1	1
Shirt, cotton or wool	10	6
Tie	4	4
Handkerchief	10	6
Gloves	2	2
Socks, cotton or wool	12	15
Shoes or boots, pair	3	3
Leggings, canvas	2	2
Muffler	1	1
Undershirt, cotton or wool	12	6
Underdrawers, cotton or wool	12	6
Pajamas	3	2
Dressing gown	1	1
Slippers	1	1

Below: An aerial reconnaissance photograph of the Grandcamp-Maisy area – indicating the German strongpoints. F & G are the Maisy Batteries number I and II. The images are not that clear, but they proved to the Allies that coastal defence works were taking place at this location (more are shown in the RAF section).

21 November 1943
Maurice Prince: A Company 2nd Rangers:

Word had come down to us that we were to embark on our ship that day and that we were leaving our homeland to visit new and distant lands. We had been working, training, and planning for that ever-coming day of reckoning with the enemy, so that now we were ready to depart. We were confident in our abilities and we were most anxious to go forth to prove ourselves.

The train ride from Camp Shanks to the ferry-boat which awaited to bring us to the shores of New York from the banks of Jersey, was an uneventful trip. It was a rather uncomfortable journey as we were laden down with all our earthly Army possessions. We had carried full field packs, while the remainder of our equipment, which lay in duffle bags, had been thrown into a special baggage car.

Our conversations were the usual Army bull sessions, which made for a lot of slang and unfunny wise remarks, but in general provided good material for passing time. We joked and talked about our forthcoming trip as a young girl would talk to her girl friend while waiting for her best beau to arrive to take her out. We were all enthused by our coming voyage, but we didn't display too much concern or nervousness. We tried to hide our enthusiasm thru a veil of indifference.

There were no bands on hand to greet us that early morning, we set foot on the pier to board our ship. I suppose it was a bit too early for the musicians to be up and about as it was an ungodly hour to be up. Our ship was to be that great boat the 'Queen Elizabeth' which looked as gallant and as majestic as the old lady – whose name she bore. She towered so much above us and was so gigantic in size, that upon our entrance, we looked like tiny ants carrying our burdens of life on our backs, only to be swallowed up into the huge bowels of the ship.

Aboard ship one gained the impression of being in a hotel. Our surroundings were so immense and the boat so stable that one could hardly realize that he was on a movable object. The huge mess-rooms and neat staterooms, plus the immaculately clean lounge and deck rooms gave one the feeling that this boat was more suited for royalty than for the 15,000 troops that filled up every cubic inch of space on the ship. Our first day aboard (we didn't pull out, due to loading, till the third day) was one of exploration and orientation. The boat being so large was an easy place in which to get lost. The more we became acquainted with the ship, the more we marvelled at its structure and greatness. Everything was of such stature, that it was hard to believe that this huge monster could cross the ocean, and so rapidly. The giant engines and turbines which ran the ship were always a spectacle to gaze at. The huge steam pumps, the giant boilers and other equipment that were contained in this room were always interesting to behold.

There was a special recreation room where you could smoke, write letters, sing and pass away the tiresome moments while on ship. Laughter, song, and rattle of dice against the floor boards could always be heard coming from this room. The thick hazy smoke that arose from the pipes, cigars, and cigarettes gave this place the appearance of some honkey-tonk back home.

The boat being of English origin was composed of a Limey crew. These sailors were most capable and knew their jobs well. They had made more crossings over this ocean and in this ship than I have years. Then, also, there were some American personnel aboard, who were in charge of the anti-aircraft protection for the ship. These men were excellent soldiers and many an interested hour was spent watching them go through their paces in gun drill.

It wasn't 'till the third day that our boat weighed anchor and prepared to sail. The engines started to tune up their songs of life and away we went. We could experience that feeling of something new and adventurous about to happen, but what this emotion was, we never could ascertain.

The Rangers' attitude toward this new mode of traveling was one of indifference. You would think that these men had been experienced sea-goers and that this crossing was just another one they were partaking in, instead of the first they were actually making. I guess you could have noticed some difference in their conversations and jokes, as the English way of speaking became ridiculed, and slandered, not to mention imitated.

I felt proud of these men, these Rangers, proud to be amongst them and proud to be one of them, as here they were embarking on a voyage that for many was to be their last. Yet their spirit and morale was never better. They looked and acted like a bunch of kids going on a picnic cruise up the Hudson.

It was hard to visualize that we were leaving our native land, as everything seemed unreal. When the Statue of Liberty was passed, realization began to set in. Many a throat had a lump in it and some guys even had tears in their eyes. We couldn't help but think that we were departing for lands unknown, and that we were headed in a direction that led only one way — the way to Victory. A way that had many traps and pitfalls in its course, where there was no turning back until the final objective of Victory was obtained.

Our ride across the ocean was uneventful in itself, but it was novel and entertaining to us strangers of this mode of travel. We hadn't fared too well in the obtainance of our quarters. We had one large room for the entire battalion, and to say we were cramped and crowded would be putting the facts down gentle. Our bunks were arranged, or should say stacked four high, so that every time we tried to sleep, we'd have a good climb to reach our beds on top, if we were on the bottom, the odds were fairly even that we would be stepped on and trod over by someone trying to get to his den above us.

Added to this misery were the affairs at chow time. Long mess lines caused our nerves to be frayed and longer wash kit lines learned us the virtues of patience. Onboard ship we drew the assignment of being the Military Police. This was both good and bad, as although it gave us some work to do, to help pass away the monotonous hours of the journey, it greatly interfered with our hours of leisure we would have had otherwise. It greatly imposed itself on the sleeping hours we would have been able to have taken advantage of. It was ironical, I thought, to draw this job,

HEADQUARTERS FIFTH RANGER INFANTRY BATTALION
Camp Forrest, Tennessee

THE FIGHTING FIFTH BATTALION

Oh, the Fighting Fifth Battalion,
are the very sons of hell.
They'll fight for their women,
and their liberty as well.
Now we are gentlemen it's true,
But we're here to prove to you,
That we are the FIGHTING FIFTH BATTALION.

Now there's Hitler and El Tojo
and a lot of other scum
Who thought they had old glory
started on the well known run,
But we're here to call their bluff,
Cause we're made of better stuff
For we are the FIGHTING FIFTH BATTALION.

Now when we meet those yellow bastards (censored)
Don't think we'd give in.
We'll carry it right to em.
And we'll tear em limb from limb.
Now if that is not enough
Then we really will get tough,
For we are the FIGHTING FIFTH BATTALION.

Now it's us that does the fighting
when there's fighting to be done.
And it's us that wins the trenches,
When there's trenches to be won.
But we'll never get the glory
for we stand and take the blow,
We are the FIGHTING FIFTH BATTALION.

We have won our ground and held it,
while we've seen our buddies go.
And times when one is needed to
stand against the foe.
We the privates, rank and file,
We're the boys that are always sent.
For we are the FIGHTING FIFTH BATTALION.

No we will never get the glory for
the battles that we have won.
And we'll never get the medals for
the other things that we have done.
Still we got a job to do and By God
We'll see it through,
We are the FIGHTING FIFTH BATTALION.

(Sung to the tune of "WHO THREW THE OVERALLS IN MRS. MURPHY'S CHOWDER)

The 'official' Rangers' song sheet.

as after all the affairs and run-ins we have had with the M.P.'s during our infant days at Camp Forrest, and Fort Dix. Now, it was our turn to learn the headaches that this fine branch of service has to undergo.

We did our tasks to the best of our ability, giving directions, taking care of the exits and stairways during boat drill, making sure that the blackouts were on the windows during the hours of darkness, and making sure that no trouble or friction occurred on deck.

For the length of the trip, which was five days and nights, we worked on this job. These days flew by as swiftly as the waves themselves. We always managed to do something to occupy ourselves during the ride. We were most fortunate that we were hardly affected by that harsh malady of seasickness. I guess our extensive training in co-operation with our naval and amphibious forces at Ft. Pierce, Florida, had stood us in good stead.

We did have some sickness, but from another cause. This was the dreaded malady of pneumonia. We were continually subjected to a draft in our quarters, so that when one man caught a cold, it was easily spread around and several boys developed the stem illness of pneumonia. These men were well taken care of by the ship's trained medical staff, and were given the best of care and attention. They were immediately transferred and rushed to a hospital when we hit land.

Chapter 3

December 1943 – Rangers USA and UK

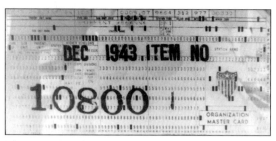

The original 2nd Battalion shipping order which accompanied the unit aboard.

The 5th Battalion shipping order.

1 December 1943
5th Rangers – Companies A – F, Medical and HQ were in Fort Dix, New Jersey.
The men of the 2nd Rangers arrived in England.
2nd Rangers – Companies A – F, Medical and HQ – En route.
All companies disembarked at 1000 hours. Entrained 1800 hours en route to a new station.

Maurice Prince: *Our ride had been a routine one, although at one time during our journey we were supposed to have been under the surveillance of a submarine. I personally never saw any signs of this menace. Our ship constantly took so many different twists and turns in its voyage, that I never knew if we were being chased or this was the usual method used in avoiding enemy craft. We had travelled unescorted as our ship was supposed to have been speedy enough to out run any German vessel. The large guns, which were on deck, stood always ready and handy, just in case there was a need to use them.*

Our ship docked in the great naval harbour of Greenock, Scotland on December 1, 1943. Once more no bands came forth to greet us on our arrival to this new continent. All we had was the view of the hustling and bustling of the dockhands and other operators, who were occupied in seeing that everything that was carried on the boat would be unloaded and put into its proper place.

It was a good feeling to walk down the gangplank and place our cramped and muscle-bound feet on solid terra firma. We marched down to a large warehouse, which was a couple of squares away; we were supposed to mess there. I guess the people of Scotland were well used to the sight of the American GIs as no curious eyes or flocks of people crowded about to view us. A couple of kids did run up to us and in a shy manner and thick Scottish accent made the famous and well-known inquiry of 'Any gum, chum?' Some were fortunate in receiving the article requested while the others had to continue their quest of gum in other parts of the column.

We entered the warehouse, unloaded, and prepared ourselves for our first feed on foreign soil. The meal was substantial and good. We ate our chow, washed our plates and returned to our places to light up and relax.

We could look back even then and dream of the happy days we had spent in the States. Those days were all behind us now, gone for the time being. So we gazed ahead and imagined ourselves already on the return trip. We had travelled 3,000 miles across a span of water that separated the evil land of Germany from the blessed land of America and we were prepared to travel that many more miles if need be, to convert that evilness into goodness, and believe me, we did.

That night we stayed in that warehouse in Scotland. When morning broke we prepared to go forth to a new destination somewhere in 'Merrie Old England'. We had come through our sea voyage in good shape. We had won our sea legs, and now we were ready to regain our land legs. What the future held in store for us then was a mystery, but I'm positive there wasn't a one of us who lacked the confidence or the courage of solving it.

Medical Detachment 2nd Rangers – Bude, Cornwall. Disembarked at 1000 hours. Entrained 1800 hours en route to a new station.

Headquarters Company 2nd Rangers Advanced Detachment
No change. Disembarked at 1000 hours. Entrained 1800 hours en route to a new station.

An Army order was distributed stating: '*It is extremely important that arrangements be made to convert all currency and coin (U.S. dollars, lire and francs) to British currency immediately upon the arrival of an organization in the United Kingdom.*'

The commanding officer (or an officer designated for the purpose) of each company collected the money from all personnel of the unit and listed the amount collected from each person on a form provided by the finance officer. This form, together with the aggregate amount collected, was to be taken to the nearest disbursing officer. '*The disbursing officer converts to sterling the amount collected from each man and furnished the proper change in Sterling to effect payment to each person.*'

WHEN YOU CABLE
DON'T
SAY OR INDICATE -

- THAT YOU HAVE *ARRIVED SAFELY*
- THAT YOU HAVE A *NEW* OR *PERMANENT* A P O NUMBER
- THAT YOU ARE *SOMEWHERE IN ENGLAND*
- THE NAME OR NUMBER OF YOUR UNIT

---

2 December 1943
5th Rangers – Companies A – F, Medical and HQ – Fort Dix, New Jersey.
2nd Rangers – Companies A – F, Medical – Bude, Cornwall.
All companies arrived in Bude, Cornwall via train at 1300 hours.

Maurice Prince: *Our first home in sunny England was to be the summer resort town of Bude, in the county of Cornwall. It had taken us approximately twenty hours of riding to bring us to our new location from our starting point in Scotland. We had travelled along the entire western sea coast of the United Kingdom. We had passed through many a village, town, and city. We had chance to see the lovely countryside and the beautiful scenery of the country that is England. It was most refreshing to view the pretty landscape and to gaze over the greenness of the hills and dales which are so remarkable and enchanting to behold.*

The quaint old villages, and towns, which our train passed through gave us the feeling of being in another world. The babbling brooks and streams were plentiful and effervescent in appearance. The monotony of the train ride was vanquished by our acquaintanceship with this new land.

Our train was small and puny looking in comparison to our huge affairs back in America. It was a wooden job, that would never have been able to stand the gaff that our trains have to. The smallness of the train gave it a more homey taste though. It had lots of speed, but due to wartime conditions, it wasn't put to the test.

On the whole, we had been fairly comfortably quartered. Each platoon had one car to itself. We made ourselves as comfortable as was possible and took advantage of going sight-seeing. There were the usual card games being played, and the same boys who never did catch up on their sleep, tried their darnest to do just that on the ride.

Our arrival into Bude was a heralded affair. A local GI band from an artillery outfit was on hand to welcome us. Also at the station were other members of our battalion who had left the States weeks before we did, as a quartering and billeting party. It was a warm affair, and a swell reception. It felt good to see more GIs about and it was nice to see those other Rangers, as some of them were old friends.

We then proceeded to march up (and in every respect of that word, as the town is on a hill with the station being at the foot of it) through the winding and spiraling streets that led from the station to the centre of the town. It was quite a climb for us, as we had all our possessions right on our persons. The heavy overcoats we wore and the steel helmets that sat on our craniums didn't add to our ease. We reached the place we were headed for, which was the battalion mess house. This hall was originally a garage which had been converted into a dining salon for us. We dropped and unloaded our equipment in the alley on the outside, and prepared to engage in our noonday dietary ritual, which was to be our first meal in England.

After chow we lined up in the street just outside the mess hall. There we were formally introduced and greeted by some English officers. We were given a few hints on matters pertaining to our new mode of living amongst our new neighbours and we were told what to expect and how to behave.

The strangest part of the session came though when we were told of the novel manner of housing we were to have. It seems like there weren't any barracks or Army camps about and being it was too cold for outdoor life, it had been decided to put us into private civilian homes, where we were to become similar to boarders in these private homes. It appears that the English government had gone out of its way to solicit these billets for us from the civilian population. The people had been requested to give up a room or two or as much space as they could spare and they had complied. When that day came to its end, we found ourselves billeted in civilian homes, living the life of Riley.

This was a fine gesture on the part of the British people and it showed the spirit and enthusiasm these people have in their pursuit of the war, but now they were actually giving up parts of their own homes, so that we could be billeted. A friendlier gesture than this could never be made by anyone, anywhere.

Bude is a peaceful small town on the southwestern coast of England. Its normal population in peacetime couldn't have run over 5,000, but then being, on the west coast and removed from the danger vicinity of air raids, its population had naturally increased a great deal. It was a lovely resort town, fairly modern and up-to-date. The main occupation of this community derived from the fact that it was a resort town. Hotels and homes for tourists did a flourishing business here.

We were all very fortunate in the securing of good billets and homes. I was most lucky as I was in a house, all by myself, while most of the other guys were grouped in homes by twos and threes. I was alone with just an old man and his wife, plus a maid. I had a swell room and I never lacked for room service as the maid was really on the ball. There wasn't anything these kind people wouldn't have done for me and the same was true with the maid.

It didn't take long for us to get over our first doses of shyness and bashfulness. At first it was a bit awkward to get friendly with the people we were living with, as we didn't want to overdo taking advantage of them; but as time wore on, these people got to know us and we to know them.

Our billets had been secured at the outskirts of town about a square above the railroad station. Our company area consisted of approximately two blocks of houses as that was as many homes as we needed to billet us. We were fairly well bunched up, so that it was possible to hold formations whenever the need for one arose.

Our mess hall was still located in the centre of town, so that every chow call was a period of road marching for us. Our Battalion headquarters was situated on the other end of town – so we always had a nice hike to get there. We could either go thru the centre of town to reach the place, or we could take a shortcut across the town's golf course, which was very hilly and appeared to be more of an obstacle course than a golf course.

Headquarters Company 2nd Rangers Advanced Detachment – Bude, Cornwall.
The following three officers from the Advanced Detachment went from detached service and returned to Duty: Major Max F. Schneider, 1st Lt. Louis A. Dahan, 2nd Lt. William G. Heaney.
Headquarters Company 2nd Rangers – Bude, Cornwall.
Major Max F. Schneider was assigned to the advanced detachment per SO#28 HQ – 1st Army DTD – 11 November 1943.
He arrived in Bude, Cornwall via train at 1300 hours.
The unit had no telephone. Their commanding officer was listed on this day as Lieutenant Colonel James E. Rudder.
The Code Shipment Number for their trip from the US to England was No. 10800 A.

Upon entering southern England, the allocated Ranger supply officer was directed to call at Headquarters, Southern Base Section, where he was told of the location of equipment for his troops. At this time, he contacted every service from which he would subsequently need supplies. Laundry, dry cleaning and shoe repairs were handled by British civilian agencies under Reciprocal Aid Agreements. Gasoline was supplied by the British and distributed from pumps which had formerly belonged to civilian companies, but had now been requisitioned for Government use for war purposes.

Bread (brown only) was baked by British soldiers and ATS girls, then supplied locally to the Rangers.

Every unit entering Southern Base Section was also given the location of its nearest hospitals, supply and evacuation maps for the area and they were also provided with administrative orders which outlined the whole supply procedure and supplemented the personnel contacts made by the supply officer. The Rangers' officers found a complete file of orders and administrative instructions awaiting them when they arrived, which included all details surrounding the maintenance and welfare of their troops.

Operation Overlord was planned jointly by British and American staff at a high level and the assault force was fifty per cent British and fifty per cent American; thus southern England was divided into two sectors, one British and one American. Southampton was the dividing line and it was to be used by both forces for launching the attack.

The 2nd Battalion set up its Headquarters in the Flexbury Lodge Hotel. The hotel described itself as: *'Exclusively and charmingly situated in spacious grounds, facing south with sea views. With hot and cold water in bedrooms, central heating, separate tables, excellent cuisine, own garden produce and a riding school attached…'* And most importantly it offered *'Special Christmas Fayre'*.

To this end, the US Southern Base Section geographically was in the American Sector and was under American control, but maintained close liaison with Southern Command, the parallel British headquarters.

While the 2nd Rangers were settling into their new home in Bude, the men of the 5th Battalion were still in Fort Dix, New Jersey, USA.

On 2 December all 2nd Battalion communications personnel were ordered to attend a four-hour class called *Orientation, Organisation and Equipment*. The Rangers were noted during the class as having a specific role to play during the invasion. The itinerary for the class was as follows.

S E C R E T

UNITED STATES ASSAULT TRAINING CENTER ETOUSA

INSTRUCTION GUIDE:

CODE NO.   A-91:   2 December 1943

ORIENTATION, ORGANIZATION & EQUIPMENT

Attendance: All communications personnel

4 Hours

SECTION ONE

ORIENTATION

Points to be covered

1. Mission of an assault division
    a. Break through beach defenses
        (1) Under-water obstacles
        (2) Barb wire
        (3) Sea Walls
        (4) Pill boxes
        (5) Open emplacements
        (6) Land mines
        (7) Coastal batteries

    b. Be prepared to meet counterattack in force.

2. Support for an assault division
    a. Air Bombardment
        (1) Strategic bombing
        (2) Supply line bombing
        (3) General invasion area bombing
        (4) Specific invasion area bombing
        (5) General support of division
        (6) Direct support of division
            (a) Air support party

    b. Naval gunfire
        (1) General tactical bombardment
        (2) General support for division
        (3) Direct support for Infantry Battalions
            (a) Shore Fire Control Party
                1 - Navy Liaison Officer
                1 - Army Gunfire Spotter
                4 - Radio Operators
                2 - Wiremen
                2 - Basics
                1 - Chief of party and assistant gunfire spotter.
                    2 - SCR-284 Radio sets
                    2 - SCR-536 Radio sets (SCR-300) sound power
                        phones or EE8A and wire.

    c. Tanks for direct support of Infantry Sections
        (1) 8 tanks per Infantry assault company
        (2) Tank Liaison Officer (equipped with SCR-509 radio) to
             accompany each assault company commander to provide
             control.

- 1 -

RESTRICTED

<u>d</u>. Artillery to fire from landing crafts
  (1) 2 Battalions of artillery to support each Regimental
      Combat Team
  (2) Each assault company to have artillery forward observer
  (3) Each assault Battalion Hq to have FA Ln Officer

<u>e</u>. Chemical Warfare Smoke
  (1) Fire 4.2" smoke mortars from landing crafts
    (a) 4 mortars in direct support of each
       assault battalion (2 per company front)
    (b) 4 mortars in general support of each
       assault battalion.
  (2) Also carry HE projectiles
  (3) Mainly pre-arranged fires although controlled by radio
     from Bn or Regtl headquarters.

<u>f</u>. Rangers and/or commandos
  (1) To protect flanks
  (2) Specially trained for landing on difficult terrain and for
     operating against coastal batteries, isolated strong points, etc.
  (3) To make initial landings in certain situations

<u>g</u>. Paratroops
  (1) To attack gun positions
  (2) To attack and prevent movement of enemy reserves
  (3) To capture airfields
  (4) To capture key road junctions
  (5) To attack beach defenses from the rear

<u>h</u>. Beach or Naval Commando's
  (1) To demolish booms, underwater obstacles, etc.

<u>i</u>. Far Shore Brigade
Mission: To organize beach area composition:
(discuss each)
    (88) Brig Hq
   (225) Signal Co Special
   (505) Medical Bn
   (135) Military Police Company
   (552) DUKW Company
   (414) Naval Beach Battalion
  (1982) Engineer Bn
   (128) QM Gasoline Company
   (223) QM Railhead Company
   (169) Ordnance Medium Maintenance Co.
   (204) Chemical Warfare Service Decontaminating Co.
   (450) 2 – Port Companies
   (186) Ordnance Company (ammunition)
   5276

<u>j</u>. The amphibious-assault technique of the army is sound.
  (1) The amphibious technique has been tried and proven:
    (a) Guadalcanal
    (b) North Africa
    (c) Attu
    (d) Solomons
    (e) Sicily
    (f) Italy
    (g) Our landing crafts are perfected, crews are trained
       and maintenance is available.

3 December 1943

5th Rangers – Companies A – F, Medical and HQ –
Fort Dix, New Jersey.

2nd Rangers – Companies A – F, Medical and HQ –
Bude, Cornwall.

COMPANY MORNING REPORT	ENDING 2400	3 December	194 3
STATION	Fort Dix, New Jersey		
ORGANIZATION	Co B 5th Ranger Inf Bn		Infantry

SERIAL NUMBER	NAME	GRADE	CODE
0403921	Whittington	Capt	
	Dy to ordinary leave of absence (4das)		
32781581	Popovics	PFC	
11184187	Cardinali	PFC	
31609527	Healy	PFC	
32569478	Devlin	PFC	
31226448	Gardner	PFC	
34455843	Carawan	PFC	
31226855	Beaton	PFC	
31617355	Brady	PVT	
33795298	Craig	PFC	
15071738	Gunnoe	TEC 5 Gr	
35551415	Liebherr	PVT	
31176674	Brunelle	PFC	
	Above 12 EM dr to fur (5 das)		

Maurice Prince: *I'll never forget the trouble we had the first time our Company had reveille formation. It looked like although we were fairly grouped together, that it was a difficult task to assemble us all at one time and at one place. Then there was also the matter of clocks and timepieces. Few of us owned individual wrist watches so that we had to depend on the clocks that were in our homes. We were to learn, strange as this might seem, that there were no two clocks which read the same. So that when morning rolled around and our formation which was scheduled for 6:45 a.m. approached, there were only a handful of men present.... This situation couldn't last long, as our first Sgt. (then 1st Sgt. Sowa) took the necessary precautions to insure that this farce wouldn't occur again. A formal statement was handed down concerning this status. The contents read we'd either be on time or else suffer consequences and it implied many an unpleasant and ugly hour to be spent on some detail. That next day at reveille found us all present and accounted for, with the exception of the 1st Sgt., who it seems was absent himself.*

Following this and other similar incidents of poor timekeeping, many of the Rangers were issued with the Army 17 Jewel Hamilton Wristwatch.

4 December 1943

5th Rangers – Companies A – F, Medical and HQ –
Fort Dix, New Jersey.

The story behind it is this. The official Ranger patch was described in a publication we had, but there were no patches in the supply stream. Our fiesty young Ranger enlisted men were ALWAYS in trouble with the Post Commander. Often the miscreants escaped because they were wearing no patches to identify their units. The Post Commander put out an order that required all military personnel to wear shoulder patches. In the case of the 5th Rangers, we would henceforth wear the SECOND Army '2' until we could obtain Ranger patches. I was one of the first to get the word, and went down to the Post exchange and bought a couple. Out of the kindness of my heart, I gave one to Sully and he blew up. 'No Ranger is ever going to wear a SECOND Army '2' said he. 'Go out to a local tailor, have patches made up according to the regulations, pay for them with company funds, and issue them to the troops.' And it was done. I think the basis of issue was two per man. Probably less than 1200 or 1300 were made.

John Raaen HQ 5th Battalion describes the history of this particular badge:

This photo was taken in New York before going overseas. From L to R: Jack Snyder, Charles Parker and Jay Mehaffay all enjoying a final drink before leaving for the European Theatre of Operations, more commonly known as the ETO or ETO-USA. (Note the very early unofficial RANGERS shoulder patch being worn in the photograph.)

5 December 1943
5th Rangers – Companies A – F, Medical and HQ –
Fort Dix, New Jersey.
2nd Rangers – Companies A – F, Medical and HQ –
Bude, Cornwall.

Maurice Prince: *It was here at Bude that not only did we become acquainted with, but we became part of the British. Such food combinations as fish and chips, cheese and jelly, tea and crumpets, etc. etc. became ritual with us.*

Then at night and during our free evenings, we learned to dance the English way. We became adept at doing the Lambeth-Walk, the Bumps-a-daisy, and other steps that are danced in the British Isles. Many an enjoyable evening was passed doing these terpsichorean steps.

We saw for ourselves from very close range the effects of the war upon these people and on their country. We began to learn the extreme hardships these people were enduring. We learned what rationing really was, the darkness of a total black-out, the shortage of petrol, and the absence of motor vehicles. We could fully appreciate the many sacrifices that were being made by these people on their home front. Added to all this, there wasn't a home that didn't have a close kin in the Armed services, or one that didn't have an active hand in some home defence organization.

During our first days here, a light training schedule was drawn up for us. This was merely to give us a chance to recuperate and get over the effects of our sea voyage and also it gave us the opportunity to fix ourselves up in our new homes. Then as the days passed by, our training increased. An arduous physical training program saw that we kept in trim and in good mental shape. The weapons training that we underwent saw that we didn't forget our basic training as far as arms were concerned. Compass and map reading courses, which were laid out for us, kept us on the beam and in constant preparedness in those subjects and the inevitable night courses we ran brought the fact home to us that we were Rangers, and as Rangers, we had to perform our missions in either daylight or darkness.

6 December 1943
5th Rangers – Companies A – F, Medical and HQ –
Fort Dix, New Jersey.
Captain Richard Sullivan went from Duty to Detached Service at Fort Hamilton NY.
Advanced Detachment HQ Company 5th Rangers –
Fort Hamilton, New York.
2nd Rangers – Companies A – F, Medical and HQ –
Bude, Cornwall.

7 December 1943
5th Rangers – Companies A – F, Medical and HQ –
Fort Dix, New Jersey.
2nd Rangers – Companies A – F, Medical and HQ –
Bude, Cornwall.

Overleaf: Dated 7 December, this US Army map shows the distribution of US Forces throughout Great Britain. The closer the time came to D-Day, each US Army unit would gradually move towards the southern ports.

8 December 1943
5th Rangers – Companies A – F, Medical and HQ –
Fort Dix, New Jersey.
2nd Rangers – Companies A – F, Medical and HQ –
Bude, Cornwall.

G-2 SECTION – PLANNING PERIOD: For seven months before D-Day, in Bristol and in London, the G-2 Section of the First US Army had one major mission: to know the enemy, his strength, dispositions, capabilities and intentions in the Cherbourg Peninsula and to put that information in the hands of those who could make use of it.

All other work – training, preparation for operations in the field – was secondary. During the planning period, the G-2 Section was made up of fifteen officers and twenty-one enlisted men. For the operation code named 'Neptune'

THE BRITISH ISLES

BASE SECTIONS
4 DECEMBER 43

SECRET
AUTH:CG EOS ETO
DATE:7 DEC 1943
INITIALS:

WESTERN

XXVI   DISTRICT

XXXVII
DISTRICT

XXXIX   XXXVI   DISTRICT
DISTRICT

XXXV   • WILMONT
DISTRICT

XXVII
DISTRICT

BASE

EASTERN

X DISTRICT

NORTHERN
IRELAND BASE
SECTION

SECTION

BASE

VII DISTRICT

CHESTER

XXVIII DISTRICT

SECTION   VIII DISTRICT

XXIX   DISTRICT

XVII

VI
DISTRICT

IX DISTRICT

WATFORD

XXXI DISTRICT

XVI   DISTRICT
DISTRICT

LONDON

EASTERN
DISTRICT

SOUTHERN BASE SECTION

XIX
DISTRICT

XVIII
DISTRICT

• SALISBURY

CENTRAL BASE SECTION

DISTRICT X)

PREPARED BY PROGRESS DIVISION
7 DECEMBER 43   28 VOLUME I

no less than sixteen intelligence teams were attached. The intelligence gathered by the G-2 Section was published in various forms – plans, estimates, overlays, defined overprints.

ASSAULT PERIOD: For Operation Neptune, the G-2 Section was broken up into smaller groups, who would all land or prepare to land separately. These groups were to be sited on LST 391, LST 392 and LST 59, the reason being, if one group was lost due to enemy action, the remaining groups could continue their work immediately.

---

9 December 1943
5th Rangers – Companies A – F, Medical and HQ – Fort Dix, New Jersey.
2nd Rangers – Companies A – F, Medical and HQ – Bude, Cornwall.

---

10 December 1943
5th Rangers – Companies A – F, Medical and HQ –
Fort Dix, New Jersey.
2nd Rangers – Companies A – F, Medical and HQ –
Bude, Cornwall.

Company Morning Reports state: *Organisation undergoing unit training. All persons in this organisation are billeted in private homes throughout Bude, Cornwall.*

Maurice Prince: *It was funny to us, this new and novel manner in which we were being billeted. We felt as though we were back in our own homes, working on a civilian job. For when our working day was ended and retreat formation over, we could do whatever we pleased. We could either go home and pass away the evening with our people we lived with, or we could go to town without a pass and spend the evening there. All that was required of us was that we remembered that we were gentlemen and that we were Rangers.*

There were many things we could do in town. There was a local movie house that was fairly up to date and which featured American films. The cafes and pubs always welcomed our entry into their establishments, and the fish and chips places were a good place to go and always satisfied our appetites. Then there were dances held quite often in the large dance hall that stood in the rear of the movie hall. Lots of girls would attend these affairs. This more than attracted us Rangers, this lured us there. We ran into competition for the hands of these fair damsels from the local artillery unit, which was still in town. This competition didn't worry us in the least, as it wasn't long before we had all the women we desired.

---

11 December 1943
5th Rangers – Companies A – F, Medical and HQ –
Fort Dix, New Jersey.
Captain Richard P. Sullivan was promoted to the rank of major as of 10 December 1943.
Advanced Detachment HQ Company 5th Rangers –
Fort Hamilton, New York.
[Author: This small unit was to go ahead of the rest of the 5th Battalion and prepare for their arrival.]
2nd Rangers – Companies A – F, Medical and HQ –
Bude, Cornwall.

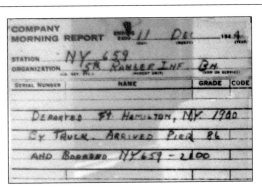

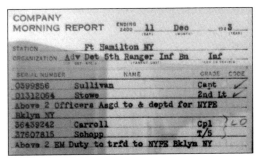

12 December 1943
5th Rangers – Companies A – F, Medical and HQ – Fort Dix, New Jersey.
2nd Rangers – Companies A – F, Medical and HQ – Bude, Cornwall.

13 December 1943
5th Rangers – Companies A – F, Medical and HQ –
Fort Dix, New Jersey.
2nd Rangers – Companies A – F, Medical and HQ –
Bude, Cornwall.
The following officers were messed with A Company:
Captain Eichnor, First Lieutenant Suchier, Second
Lieutenant Askin.

US Army regulations in relation to religious celebrations were issued: *Unit commanders are urged to take advantage of the authority contained in regulations to grant such passes and furloughs as may be necessary within the limits authorized, to permit members of the Jewish faith in their commands to be absent from their duties to observe the Seder celebrations and the observance of Passover, Good Friday and other religious celebrations.*

Commanding officers will utilise the service of the chaplains in securing the use of local facilities, churches and homes for their personnel.

14 December 1943
5th Rangers – Companies A – F, Medical and HQ – Fort Dix, New Jersey.
The following officers were messed with HQ Company: Major Owen H. Carter, Captain Edmund J. Butler, Captain William Murray, 1st Lt. William Byrne Jr., 1st Lt. John C. Raaen Jr., 1st Lt. Howe Van Riper.
2nd Rangers – Companies A – F, Medical and HQ – Bude, Cornwall.

15 December 1943
5th Rangers – Companies A – F, Medical and HQ –
Fort Dix, New Jersey.
2nd Rangers – Companies A – F, Medical and HQ –
Bude, Cornwall.

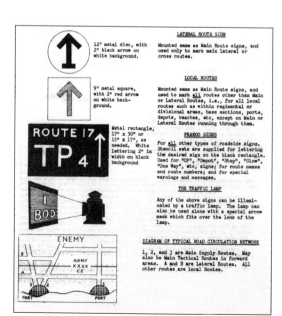

ETOUSA CIRCULAR No. 26

1. *BRITISH TYPE ROAD TRAFFIC SIGNS*

1. The British type road traffic signs prescribed in Par 3, below, are adopted for use by all forces in this theater for the control of road movement. This type of road signing equipment will be distributed to all military police units (except aviation) which engage in road traffic control. Units preparing their own signs will conform to the specifications and uses prescribed in Par 3, below. This type of sign will be the only type used for road traffic control and will be used strictly in conformity herewith and in no other way.

2. As rapidly as distribution of the signs permits, all units and organizations will allocate the necessary training time to insure familiarity with them and proficiency in their use. Military police, as the route signing agency, will make full use of them in road traffic control, both in exercises and actual operations. All units will, through use in exercises and actual operations, become fully acquainted with them.

3. A British poster showing graphically the proper use of the signs has been distributed. Full use will be made of the posters in training. The following is a further brief description of the signs :

12" metal disc, with
2" black arrow on
white background
STRAIGHT AHEAD

MAIN ROUTE SIGN

Mounted on trees, posts, etc., along roadside or on a supporting peg on the shoulder of road. Direction of arrow indicates direction to follow. e. g., if pointed to right it indicates a right turn. Used *only* on MAIN supply or tactical routes.

TURN RIGHT

12" metal disc, with
2" white arrow on red
background.

DETOUR SIGN

Mounted same as Main Route signs, and used *only* to mark a detour or " diversion " along a MAIN supply or tactical route.

Given the huge influx of US troops into England, the European Theatre of Operations USA (US Army HQ) issued a series of instructional signs and gave instructions to units to comply with British road signage at all times. Although it might seem a little obvious to point out that an arrow pointing right means 'turn right' – there were a lot of accidents occurring because the British drive on the left hand side of the road and also many units had been putting up their own more 'elaborate' signage. Therefore the more consistent and obvious the road signs, the fewer accidents and – as Circular No.26 points out – the US Army were having to use British road signs, not US ones.

---

16 December 1943
5th Rangers – Companies A – F, Medical and HQ – Fort Dix, New Jersey.
2nd Rangers – Companies A – F, Medical and HQ – Bude, Cornwall.

---

17 December 1943
5th Rangers – Companies A – F, Medical and HQ –
Fort Dix, New Jersey.
Officers messed with D Company: Captain Heffelfinger, 1st Lt. Marrow, 2nd Lt. Dunegan.
2nd Rangers – Companies A – F, Medical and HQ –
Bude, Cornwall.

Maurice Prince: *Our morale during our pleasant stay in Bude was of the highest quality. Everyone seemed happy and pleased by the way things had turned out. I never heard any complaints or saw any down hearted looks on the men. There may have been a couple cases of homesickness, but you could never tell it or notice it from the features of these soldiers.*

Yet, with all the merriment and recreation we had in Bude, we never lost sight of the reason why we were on this side of the ocean.

We continually prepared ourselves for that ever coming day of reckoning with the enemy. We put our entire efforts into our training never bitching about the most gruelling and killing of speed marches, never complaining about the tiring night problems we ran every so often and never saying a word about anything that gripes the average soldier.

---

18 December 1943
25th Rangers – Companies A – F, Medical and HQ – Fort Dix, New Jersey.
Officers messed with HQ company: Major Owen H. Carter, Captain Edmund J. Butler, 1st Lt. William P. Byrne, 1st Lt. John D. Garvik, 1st Lt. John C. Raaen, 1st Lt. Howe E. Van Riper.
2nd Rangers – Companies A – F, Medical and HQ –
Bude, Cornwall.

In one of its more bizarre orders the US Army decreed that the utmost paper on any given correspondence should be utilised:

Paper saving…
Unused margins. Unused margins of the following widths will be left in each communication:

At top: First page ½ inch. Second and succeeding pages, 1 inch.
At left: ½ inch.
At right: ½ inch
At bottom: ¾ inch excluding page number, which will be ⅜ inch from the bottom as indicated.

The use of the small size stationery will be governed by the judgement of the author of the letter. If a reply is not anticipated and it is practicable to include a subject matter on a small sheet, the latter will be used invariably. If a reply is anticipated or is likely, the larger size will be used. In case of doubt, economy demands the use of the smaller sheet.

19 December 1943

5th Rangers – Companies A – F, Medical and HQ – Fort Dix, New Jersey.
2nd Rangers – Companies A – F, Medical and HQ – Bude, Cornwall.

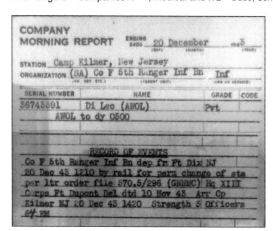

20 December 1943

5th Rangers – Companies A – F, Medical and HQ – Camp Kilmer NJ.
Advanced Detachment HQ Company 5th Rangers – Crewe, Wales.
2nd Rangers – Companies A – F, Medical and HQ – Bude, Cornwall.

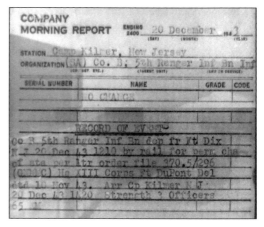

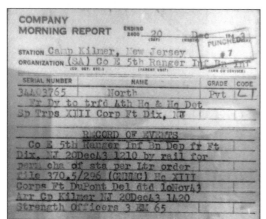

21 December 1943

5th Rangers – Companies A – F, Medical and HQ –
Camp Kilmer NJ.

Advanced Detachment HQ Company 5th Rangers –
Llangattock, Wales.

2nd Rangers – Companies A – F, Medical and HQ –
Bude, Cornwall.

Major Max F. Schneider went from Duty to Detached
Service as of 19 December 1943.

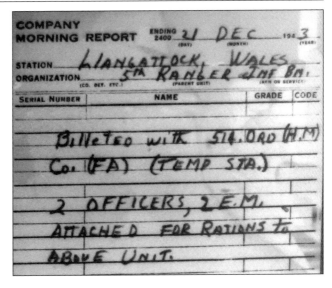

22 December 1943

5th Rangers – Companies A – F, Medical and HQ – Camp Kilmer NJ.
2nd Rangers – Companies A – F, Medical and HQ – Bude, Cornwall.

23 December 1943

5th Rangers – Companies A – F, Medical and HQ – Camp Kilmer NJ.
2nd Rangers – Companies A – F, Medical and HQ – Bude, Cornwall.

24 December 1943

5th Rangers – Companies A – F, Medical and HQ – Camp Kilmer NJ.
2nd Rangers – Companies A – F, Medical and HQ – Bude, Cornwall.

25 December 1943

5th Rangers – Companies A – F, Medical and HQ –
Camp Kilmer NJ.

2nd Rangers – Companies A – F, Medical and HQ –
Bude, Cornwall.

Maurice Prince: *Our first Christmas overseas we spent in the town of Bude. By now we had fully gained the honest respect and confidence of the townspeople. Many of us received invitations to attend family gatherings for Christmas dinners, and some gladly accepted this honor.*

Our own Christmas day meal was real affair. Turkey with all the trimmings, all the beer we could drink and such delicacies as cake and candy decorating our tables. That afternoon after we had finished eating, we arose from the table and found that we had picked up a few pounds.

That day we also threw a Xmas party for the kids of Bude, and of the surrounding towns. We had been chipping in our weekly candy rations for the past couple of weeks so as to enable the laying of a sweet table. We had fixed up and decorated the local dance hall for this affair and had a beautiful tree set up. This was a real treat for the kids. There isn't a thing in this world that pleases the youngsters of England more than candy and gum. It did our hearts good just watching them enjoying themselves.

That night for our own Xmas entertainment, we had a show and dance. We had obtained the services of a USO group that had been touring our section of the country, to perform for us. They put on a gala performance. The dance too, was a lively affair, with alcoholic beverages flowing freely. The dance didn't break up 'till early the next morning. When we went back to our homes to get a little sleep that a.m. we were all merry from an evening well spent.

26 December 1943

5th Rangers – Companies A – F, Medical and HQ – Camp Kilmer NJ.

2nd Rangers – Companies A – F, Medical and HQ – Bude, Cornwall.

The US Army issued a salvage directive: *Inedible Garbage: Other garbage which is unfit for animal food, such as coffee grounds, tea leaves, egg shells, citrus rinds, fish heads and scales and similar waste, will be placed in separate containers, and arrangements should be made through the local British Inspector of Salvage to have it turned over to a collector of garbage without charge, or in case this cannot be done, it should be incinerated in the usual manner.*

Lumber: Packing cases, boxes, crates, dunnage and other waste wood, (other than cases, boxes and crates used for subsistence) will be used to the fullest extent. Empty boxes can be advantageously used in the retail distribute of rations, clothing and so forth, or they may be knocked down and use for shelving, bins or dunnage. Similarly, crating materials may be used for packing supplies for shipment, shelving, bins, etc. Sound such material not required for use will be turned over to the British Timber Control Officer.

The opening of cases, boxes and crates containing subsistence must be carefully done to avoid unnecessary damage and breakage and after being emptied they will be returned in their entirety to the depot from which the subsistence is drawn. Under no circumstances will they be broken up or used for any other purpose. All labour and transportation required in connection with the salvaging of lumber turned over to the British Timber Control will be provided by the British.

The opening of cardboard subsistence boxes will be done carefully. They will be kept clean and dry and returned to the depot from which subsistence is drawn. The opening of all burlap, cloth and paper bags will be done by unlacing or untying; they will be protected from the weather and returned to the depot from which subsistence is drawn.

Classified Waste Paper. Wherever practicable, available adequate shredding and pulping facilities will be employed for disposing of waste paper of a confidential and secret nature. The destruction must be complete.

27 December 1943

5th Rangers – Companies A – F, Medical and HQ – Camp Kilmer NJ.
1st Lt. Anderson went from Duty to Detached Service at the New York Port of Embarkation as a loading officer.
2nd Rangers – Companies A – F, Medical and HQ – Bude, Cornwall.
Captain Cleveland A. Lytle went from Duty to Detached Service in Scotland.
1st Lt. Stanley E. White was relieved of principal Duty as platoon leader and assumed Duty as Company Commander for the duration of Cleveland Lytles' absence.1st Lt. James Eikner went from Duty to Detached Service.
1st Lt. Frederick Wilken was assigned and joined, and assumed temporary command.
2nd Lt. Frank Kennard went from Duty to Detached Service to the American School Centre, Schrivenham.
Lt. Col. James E. Rudder went from Duty to Detached Service as of 27 December 1943.

28 December 1943

5th Rangers – Companies A – F, Medical and HQ – Camp Kilmer NJ.
2nd Lt. Mehaffey returned to Duty from Detached Service at the NY Port of Embarkation, Brooklyn NY as a loading officer at 1630hrs.
A Company 2nd Rangers – Titchfield, Hampshire.
Pfc. Robert C. Lambert joined A Company from the Medical Detachment of the 2nd Battalion.
The company entrained at 0630 hours for a new station. They arrived in Southampton at 1230 hours. Then travelled by truck at 1700 for Titchfield and arrived at 1730 hours.

Maurice Prince: *We received the order to move out. We packed our belongings and prepared ourselves for the coming journey. We said our farewells and bade our dear friends of Bude adieu for a while. Hands were tightly grasped and heavily shaken. There were some tears flowing from the eyes of the weaker sex. Whoever said that the English were cold and aloof must have been in a different part of England than I had been. They took complete strangers back to their homes and cared for us tenderly. They never complained about anything we did and always went about their tasks cheerfully. No wonder these Britishers have earned the respect and admiration of the entire world. I knew then how these people had the courage to stand off their enemies in the worst days of Dunkirk and of the Blitz. I knew then which side was going to emerge victorious from this conflict.*

The next leg of our itinerary was to be the small, insignificant town of Titchfield, which is situated on the southern coast of England. Ancient Titchfield with its cobbled streets, historical Church and cemetery, the narrow lanes, worn-out buildings and the many old-fashioned pubs and hotels.

Our train ride from Bude which brought us to the city of Southampton, had taken us nearly seven hours. Hours which were spent in rapture, drinking in the wonderful endowment of Mother Nature upon the lovely English terrain. At Southampton, we boarded trucks, and after an hour's ride we reached our new area –Titchfield.

2nd Rangers – Companies B, C, E & Medical & HQ – Bude, Cornwall.

D Company 2nd Rangers – Park Gate, Hampshire.

Pfc. William A. Geitz as attached to D Company from the 2nd Battalion Medical Detachment.

D Company entrained at 0630 hours for a new station. They arrived in Southampton at 1230 hours and then mounted trucks. At 1330 hours they left for Park Gate and arrived at 1600 hours.

F Company 2nd Rangers – Botley, Hampshire.

Pfc. Charles W. Korb was attached for Duty from the Medical Detachment 2nd Battalion.

F Company entrained at 0630 hours for a new station. They arrived in Southampton at 1230 hours and then mounted trucks at 1700 bound for Botley. They arrived at 1730 hours.

While his men were moving around to new stations, Lt. Colonel Rudder was scheduled to arrive at the US Army Assault Training Centre in Devon. He was to study and learn from the operational practices that the centre provided. Moreover, these were some of the exact techniques his men would need in Normandy.

His schedule for the visit and the itinerary (similar to that of Major General Huebner some time before) was as follows:

HEADQUARTERS
U.S. ASSAULT TRAINING CENTER, ETOUSA
APO 553

ANTICIPATED ARRIVALS

Today: 28 December 1943 (Tuesday)

None

Tomorrow: 29 December 1943 (Wednesday)

Col Rudder   To arrive by car at 1030 Hours tomorrow.
Lt Moany

SERIAL	ARRIVAL	DEPARTURE	PLACE	EVENT	REMARKS
1	----	0800 Hrs	Barnstaple Railway Sta.	Detrain	Entruck in jeep convoy from U.S. Aslt Tng Center.
2	0830 Hrs	0840 Hrs	Est Yellow I	Waterproofing Demonstration	In this demonstration the latest methods of waterproofing have been applied to typical items of equipment (6x6 truck, recovery tractor, 57mm AT gun).
3	0840 Hrs	0910 Hrs	Beach Opposite Crow Point	Firing of 155mm gun from beached LCT(5)	This is a demonstration of technique only, indicating the practicability of firing the 155mm gun from a beached landing craft. The tactical significance of this type of fire is under study.
4	0940 Hrs	1140 Hrs	Woolacombe Beach	Bn landing-assault exercise, 2d Bn CT, 115th Inf	This landing-assault exercise involves an infantry battalion, with engineer, artillery, tank, CWS and far-shore attachments. The exercise is umpired, and enemy troops are simulated. Various training aids, including beach charges and smoke, are used; but there is no live firing. Noteworthy points are these: the use of all-infantry assault sections (not engineer) in the initial waves; and, the landing of "assault tanks" in the assault waves. From the training standpoint, this exercise complements the "Hedge-Hog assault" to be seen in the afternoon: in the one case, there is a landing and an assault without live fire; and in the other case there is an assault with full live fire but with only simulated landing.
5	(1045) Hrs	(1130) Hrs	Woolacombe Bay	Firing afloat, 155mm gun, 105mm howitzer, MK IV tank, 4.2" CW mortar, from LCT(5), LCT(5), LCM(3), LCVP, respectively.	These demonstrations involve the firing of various types of weapons (155mm gun, 105 howitzers, 75mm Mk IV tank guns, 4.2" CW mortars) from various types of landing craft (LCT, LCM, LCVP). The tactical significance of the fire from the howitzers and mortars has been demonstrated in the landing-assault exercise of this morning. The tactical significance of the other types of fire has not been determined. (Ferry service by DUKWs from Woolacombe Beach out to the landing craft is provided).

SECRET

SERIAL	ARRIVAL	DEPARTURE	PLACE	EVENT	REMARKS
6	1150 Hrs	1230 Hrs	Hq. US Aslt Tng Cen	Lunch	This must be a quick lunch.
7	1255 Hrs	1530 Hrs	Hedge-Hog Area	Bn CT assault (Live fire) 3rd Bn, 115th Infantry	This "Hedge-Hog" assault exercise is the culmination of the assault phase of the battalion's training at the Center. The exercise involves the use of live fire of many types: artillery, tank guns, anti-tank guns, infantry mortars, CW mortars, air bombs, air strafing, small arms, anti-tank rockets and grenades, etc. Each Bn of the RCT in training - in this case the 3rd Bn of the 115th RCT - goes through one live-fire Hedge-Hog assault prior to this exercise. The Bn has completed live-fire assault training on the section and company assault ranges (to be inspected later)
8	1540 Hrs	1555 Hrs	LCT Mock-up	Inspect loading training facilities.	This is a routine training exercise, involving the loading of AA Artillery into LCT(5)'s. Training on mock-ups such as these precedes loading exercises on the actual craft.
9	1610 Hrs	1620 Hrs	Range 40	Inspect Assault Section training facilities.	This is a brief inspection of an "assault range", on which the individual 30-man assault section is trained under live-fire. This range - there are many more like it at the Center - is the Center's basic training aid so far as assault training goes.
10	1630 Hrs	1640 Hrs	Flamethrower Range	Demonstration, flame thrower training in use.	Throughout the area, there are many ranges and training aids devoted to basic individual training. These are necessary because the assault technique requires certain infantrymen to use weapons with which they are not familiar. A case in point is the flame thrower range, demonstrated here.
11	1645 Hrs	1700 Hrs	Shipside Obstacle	Demonstration, various training aids in use.	This is a physical conditioning area, which also provides the soldier with training in essential items: wall-climbing, net scaling, etc.

SERIAL	ARRIVAL	DEPARTURE	PLACE	EVENT	REMARKS
12	1710 Hrs	1745 Hrs	Croyde Beach	Battalion landing from DUKW's w/105mm guns and 57mm guns	The DUKW was designed as a cargo-carrying vehicle. As illustrated, in this exercise, it may be put to direct tactical use, both for transporting troops and for transporting (and towing) artillery.
13	1745 Hrs	1815 Hrs	Barnstaple Railway Station.	Train party departs for Barnstaple Rail Station	Detruck from jeep convoy at rail station.

29 December 1943

5th Rangers – Companies A – F, Medical and HQ – Camp Kilmer NJ.

Advanced Detachment HQ Company 5th Rangers – Llangattock, Wales.

2nd Rangers – Companies B, C, E, Medical & HQ – Bude, Cornwall.

A Company 2nd Rangers – Titchfield, Hampshire.

D Company 2nd Rangers – Park Gate, Hampshire.

F Company 2nd Rangers – Botley, Hampshire.

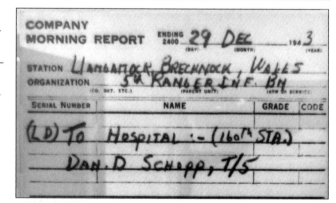

US ARMY DIRECTIVE ON THE CARRYING OF ARMS:

Unit commanders will be held strictly responsible for the security of the arms and ammunition in the possession of personnel of their respective units. Provision will be made for the safeguarding of all arms and ammunition when not being used for official duties.

Special care will be taken to insure that arms are carried only when required in the performance of duty. The carrying of weapons of any kind, including straight razors and knives other than small pocket knives (3 inch blade or less), during off-duty hours among the civilian population is forbidden. All enlisted personnel leaving station on furlough or pass will be inspected by a commissioned officer to assure that compliance is held with the foregoing. Any infraction will be severely dealt with.

The above provisions are not applicable in the case of military or civilian personnel who own private firearms, provided they are carrying such arms only for the immediate purpose of sport or target practice, and further provided that they have fully complied with the British laws as set forth in letter dated 1943 'License to Carry Gun or Hunt'.

30 December 1943

5th Rangers – Companies A – F, Medical and HQ – Camp Kilmer NJ.

Advanced Detachment HQ Company 5th Rangers – Llangattock, Wales.

2nd Rangers – Companies B, C, E, Medical & HQ – Bude, Cornwall.

A Company 2nd Rangers – Titchfield, Hampshire.

D Company 2nd Rangers – Park Gate, Hampshire.

F Company 2nd Rangers – Botley, Hampshire.

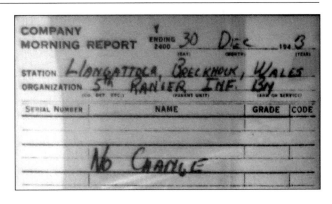

Maurice Prince: *Like many other small towns of England (Tichfield) had been built in a valley. There were many roads that led into the main street, which bisected this community and formed the main square. This main street continued until it joined the main highway that led to the city of Fareham. It was to be our misfortune to have to march over these roads in our training. Many was the time a sweating, cursing Ranger could be seen travelling through these thoroughfares at the double time pace, hell bent for election.*

To gain a fair idea of our doings in this area, I must run back the pages of our Battalion history, and relate to you a basic idea of the fundamental principle of the Ranger Battalion of its organization and of its operations.

The Ranger Battalion was organized as a small, fast, hard-hitting, and compact unit. We were patterned after the style and fashion as our brethren from England, 'the Commandos'. A lot of information had come down to us concerning the training and experiences of this famous outfit and we tried to mould ourselves into an organization similar to theirs. Our training was continually stressed and emphasized along these lines. We were especially proficient to work in small bands of squads and sections. To work independently from other units, using our own initiative, hitting hard and striking fast.

We were experts in the use of demolitions, small arms and automatic weapons. In fact, we were all familiar with every known gun and explosive which is to be found in an Infantry division, we knew how, where and when to use this equipment.

We were now in our present location because of this specialized training. Our company was operating by itself, away from our other companies of the Battalion. We were now on our own, responsible only to ourselves for our maneouvers and training.

Before we had left our last station, our Battalion Commander Colonel Rudder, then Major, had given us some inkling of our doings in this vicinity. He had informed us that the work we were about to undertake was not to be new to us, but what was to be novel, was to be the manner in which we were to operate.

31 December 1943

5th Rangers – Companies A – F, Medical and HQ – Camp Kilmer NJ.

Advanced Detachment HQ Company 5th Rangers – Llangattock, Wales.

2nd Rangers – Companies B, C, E, Medical & HQ – Bude, Cornwall.

A Company 2nd Rangers – Titchfield, Hampshire.

D Company 2nd Rangers – Park Gate, Hampshire.

1st Lt. McBride went on Detached Service in London and returned to Duty with D Company.

F Company 2nd Rangers – Botley, Hampshire.

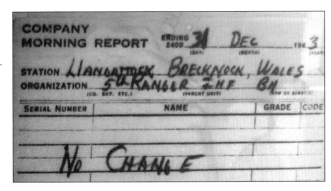

The Advanced Detachment of the 5th Battalion stayed in Wales pending the arrival of the rest of their Battalion.

Chapter 4

January 1944 – Rangers Reunited

1 January 1944

5th Rangers – Companies A – F, Medical and HQ – Camp Kilmer NJ, USA.

A Company 2nd Rangers – Titchfield, Hampshire.

B, C, E & Medical Companies 2nd Rangers – Bude, Cornwall.

D Company 2nd Rangers – Park Gate, Hampshire.

F Company 2nd Rangers – Botley, Hampshire.

Headquarters Company 2nd Rangers – Advanced Detachment Bude, Cornwall. No change.

Headquarters Company 2nd Rangers – Bude, Cornwall.

The US Army issued a booklet called 'How we look to the British': *You are going to Great Britain as part of an Allied offensive – to meet Hitler and beat him on his own ground. For the time being you will be Britain's guest. The purpose of this is to get you acquainted with the British, their country and their ways.*

America and Britain are allies. Hitler knows that they are both powerful countries, tough and resourceful. He knows that they, with the other United Nations, mean his crushing defeat in the end.

So it is only common sense to understand that the first and major duty Hitler has given his propaganda chiefs is to separate Britain and America and spread distrust between them. If he can do that, his chance of winning might return.

No Time To Fight Old Wars. *If you come from an Irish-American family, you may think of the English as persecutors of the Irish, or you may think of them as enemy Redcoats who fought against us in the American Revolution and the War of 1812. But there is no time today to fight old wars over again or bring up old grievances. We don't worry about which side our grandfathers fought on in the Civil War, because it doesn't mean anything now.*

We can defeat Hitler's propaganda with a weapon of our own. Plain, common, horse sense; understanding of evident truths.

The most evident truth of all is that in their major ways of life the British and American people are much alike. They speak the same language. They both believe in representative government, the freedom of worship, in freedom of speech. But each country has national characteristics which differ. It is by causing misunderstanding about these differences that Hitler hopes to make his propaganda effective.

British Reserved, Not Unfriendly. *You defeat enemy propaganda not by denying that these differences exist, but by admitting them openly and then trying to understand them. For instance: The British are often more reserved in conduct than we. On a small crowded island where forty-five million people live, each man learns to guard his privacy carefully – and is equally careful not to invade another man's privacy.*

So if Britons sit in trains or buses without striking up conversation with you, it doesn't mean they are being haughty and unfriendly. Probably they are paying more attention than you think. But they don't speak to you because they don't want to appear intrusive or rude.

Another difference. The British have phrases and colloquialisms of their own that may sound funny to you. You can make just as many *****s in their eyes. It isn't a good idea, for instance to say 'bloody' in mixed company in Britain – it is one of their worst swear words. To say 'I look like a bum' is offensive to their ears, for to the British this means that you look like your own backside. It isn't important – just a tip if you are trying to shine in polite society.

British money is in pound, shillings and pence. The British are used to this system and they like it, and all your arguments that the American decimal system is better won't convince them. They won't be pleased to hear you call it 'funny money', either. They sweat hard to get it (wages are much lower in Britain than America) and they won't think you smart or funny for mocking it.

2nd Battalion Narrative History.

Commando-style Raids   D-Day Preparation

1 January

By 1 January 1944, plans for Ranger participation in Commando-style raids on the coast of France were well under way. Pursuant to instructions contained in Ltr, Hq-COSSAC 14 Dec 43, file COSSAC/00/136/OPS; Subject: :use of Rangers in Raids and Reconnaissance", Lt Col James E. Rudder, Major Max D. Schneider, Captain Harvey J. Cook, and two Intelligence enlisted men were at this time in the initial stages of planning at COHQ, Whitehall, London. A detachment of Headquarters personnel was obtaining billets in the Southampton area. Both parties had departed from Bude, Cornwall, the Battalion's home station, during the latter part of December 1943.

So as to facilitate training under Commando techniques, the following measures were authorized:

(1)   The Battalion was placed on a Per-Diem basis under authority contained in Ltr, Hq-ETOUSA, 27 Dec 43, file AG 245; Subject: "Authorization for Payment of Per-Diem and/or monetary allowances, in lieu of Rations and Quarters, to U. S. Ranger Battalion".

(2)   The 2nd Indorsement to the above letter made by FUSA, 1 Jan 44, file 370/22, contained the following instructions from CG FUSA: "There is no change in the assignment or attachment of the 2nd Ranger Battalion but for the purpose of carrying out the instructions of COSSAC, you will operate under orders from COHQ".

Companies A/D/F departed from Bude by train on 28 December 1944. On 1 January, these units were billeted in the following towns; Company A - Titchfield, Company D - Park Gate; Company F - Botley; all being in the Southampton area. Headquarters personnel were billeted in Warsash. The Battalion Staff, at this time, operated from the British Naval Headquarters located near Warsash.

---

2 January 1944

5th Rangers – Companies A – F, Medical and HQ – Camp Kilmer NJ. USA.

A Company 2nd Rangers – Titchfield, Hampshire.

Maurice Prince: *It seems that not only was the company to be on its own, but every individual was to be on his own. The Army was experimenting and they were prepared to learn from experience. They had given each of us sustenance money, which amounted to four dollars per day. We were to go out and find our own billets, buy our own food and other purchases, and to pay for anything we may have a need for. To make the purchase of food legal we were issued regular civilian ration cards, so that there wouldn't be any trouble in obtaining the groceries required to exist upon.*

That meant upon our arrival, we had to seek out our own private billets, or homes, and seek for a place to shop and cook. But, thanks again to the fine cooperation and collaboration of the people and the police force, we were most fortunate in obtaining the requirements we were searching for.

Practically all of us found houses where the people did the shopping, and cooking for us. The monetary end of this deal was very profitable to us, as many of the good civilians of Titchfield refused monetary payment for the use of their houses and labours. When we did have to pay for our room and board, we found it didn't amount to one half of what the Army was paying us. So, we pocketed the extra money and went about the various pubs, and celebrated.

Most of the fellows were billeted in fine houses. All the homes had the luxuries and comforts that a soldier in the field dreams of. Radios, laundry, libraries, etc. etc. It was just like being home. Unfortunately, fifteen of us men got a dirty deal and we were stuck in a filthy house about a mile out of town. While the others were sleeping on warm feather beds, we were reclining on Army cots and trying to keep from freezing under GI blankets.

It didn't take us long to be situated and set up in our new homes. We became acquainted with the people we lived with and made their friendship. By our fine and exemplary behavior, we won the respect and plaudits of the towns folks.

B, C, E & Medical Companies 2nd Rangers – Bude, Cornwall.
D Company 2nd Rangers – Park Gate, Hampshire.
F Company 2nd Rangers – Botley, Hampshire.
Headquarters Company 2nd Rangers – Advanced Detachment Bude, Cornwall.
Headquarters Company 2nd Rangers – Bude, Cornwall.

Army Directive: Enlisted men, disposition of men physically or mentally unqualified: *When an enlisted man is considered by his immediate commanding officer to be physically or mentally unqualified to perform his assigned duties or any other appropriate duty within his unit – action will be taken as follows:*

a) *A physical examination will be made to determine whether the subject enlisted man is physically or mentally qualified to perform any duty within his unit.*

b) *In event the enlisted man is found to the physically or mentally unqualified to perform any appropriate duty within the unit, his case will be reported through channels with applicable recommendation for his reassignment within the command or his transfer to the detachment of patients of an SOS, ETOUSA, hospital. When the enlisted man is transferred to an SOS, ETOUSA hospital, the report of physical examination directed under a) above, together with his service records and allied papers, will be forwarded to the commanding officer of the hospital.*

c) *The commanding officer of the hospital will determine whether the man can be utilised in the service or is to be discharged under current regulations.*

d) *Enlisted men who are to be retained in the service will be transferred from the hospital to the 10th Replacement Control Depot, SOS, ETOUSA, if formerly assigned to the ground forces or SOS.*

At the time of the transfer, a report concerning the man, will include a statement as to physical and mental qualifications and duty limitations.

e) *The commanding officer of the replacement depot will take the necessary action to effect reassignment of such enlisted men to appropriate units.*

---

3 January 1944
5th Rangers – Companies A – F, Medical and HQ – Camp Kilmer NJ, USA.
A Company 2nd Rangers – Titchfield, Hampshire.
B, C, E & Medical Companes 2nd Rangers – Bude, Cornwall.
D Company 2nd Rangers – Park Gate, Hampshire.
F Company 2nd Rangers – Botley, Hampshire.
Headquarters Company 2nd Rangers – Advanced Detachment Bude, Cornwall.
Headquarters Company 2nd Rangers – Bude, Cornwall.

Army Directive: Prevention of waste of food and of nutrients: *All commanders will exercise close and constant supervision over the preparation of the messes in their respective commands in order to insure that unnecessary waste of food is avoided..*

They will also give attention to the storage and handling of food generally with a view to retaining its maximum nutritive value during preparation and service, prohibiting the accumulation of surplus supplies and enjoying the greatest care in the prevention of waste.

---

4 January 1944
5th Rangers – Companies A – F, Medical and HQ – Camp Kilmer NJ, USA.
A Company 2nd Rangers – Titchfield, Hampshire.
B, C, E & Medical Companies 2nd Rangers – Bude, Cornwall.
D Company 2nd Rangers – Park Gate, Hampshire.
F Company 2nd Rangers – Botley, Hampshire.
Headquarters Company 2nd Rangers – Advanced Detachment Bude, Cornwall.
Headquarters Company 2nd Rangers – Bude, Cornwall.

The Rangers were lucky to be billeted with British families. The logistics of accomodating the average US soldier in British camps was complicated as this memo explains::

Accommodation stores issued to any installation are for that camp only, and will not be taken away when the organisation moves out. Base Section Commanders will be responsible for insuring that such property is left at the camp by the vacating organisation, and that all stores are securely guarded during all periods of disuse of the installation.

Exceptional Items.

A. *The following items will be supplied to US forces as indicated:*
  (1) *Beds: A bed or cot will be furnished by the British for each officer and enlisted men in British hutted camps. US Army cots, canvas, folding, will be supplied to personnel of the US forces in permanent tented camps by the normal US Quartermaster depot for Class II supplies.*
  (2) *Sheets and Pillow Cases: All US officers will procure their own sheets and pillow cases from sales stores of QMSO's.*
  (3) *Blankets: The Quartermaster service will provide blankets for all troops.*
  (4) *Stoves, tent, M-1941: This stove will be supplied from US Quartermaster stocks for use in tented camps only, when personnel are actually being housed in tents.*
  (5) *Mess Equipment: US enlisted personnel will use their field mess equipment and will not receive tableware from British sources. An exception is made for AAF enlisted men, who will be issued earthenware drinking mugs and plates by the RAF for US use.*
  (6) *Tentage: No tentage will be provided by the British for US use; all tentage required will be supplied from Quartermaster depot stocks.*
  (7) *US units will use the British equipment while in the UK. It is not authorised for task force units. T/E equipment may be used to supplement that furnished by the British with exception of items the use of which is restricted by the Theater Commander (i.e. field ranges, etc.).*

---

5 January 1944

5th Rangers – Companies A – F, Medical and HQ – Camp Kilmer NJ, USA.

A Company 2nd Rangers – Titchfield, Hampshire. 1st Lt. Joseph A. Rafferty returned from Detached Service and assumed command of A Company. 1st Lt. Stanley E. White was relieved of his duties as A Company commander and resumed his duties as platoon leader.

Maurice Prince: *A daily training schedule was drawn up for us. Each day saw us going through the process that makes the average soldier a Ranger. Strenuous physical exercises, exhausting speed marches, compass and map courses, night problems, and amphibious work, all became a part of our labours. The most outstanding and stressed work here was our training in conjunction with the Royal Navy. Many was the evening we'd return to our respective homes, wet, cold, and miserable from our practice landings off the Isle of Wight. We'd sometimes be set to wade ashore from a point 100 yards off shore. We'd have to wade through this January, icy, waist-deep water to assault imaginary beach defences.*

Our operations with the Royal Navy gave us faith in their ability. We learned that these Limeys were on the ball and knew what they were doing. I'm also sure that we left a positive impression on these birds' minds in the way we handled our assignments, either on board ship, or in the assaulting of the beaches.

B, C, E & Medical Companies 2nd Rangers – Bude, Cornwall.

D Company 2nd Rangers – Park Gate, Hampshire.

F Company 2nd Rangers – Botley, Hampshire.

Headquarters Company 2nd Rangers – Advanced Detachment Bude, Cornwall.

Headquarters Company 2nd Rangers – Bude, Cornwall.

Classified Ordnance and Chemical Warfare items Directive: *All fired cartridge cases, empty clips and packing material pertaining thereto will be turned in or shipped to the nearest US Army ammunition depot. This material should be sorted or packed for shipment as follows.*

Small arms cartridge cases and packing material such as bandoliers, clips, metallic links, fabric belts, cartons, boxes and their tin lining, will be packed by types in boxes or sandbags. Each box or sandbag must bear a certificate signed by an officer of the organisation concerned showing that the contents are 'free from explosives'. It is important that those sorting and packing this material have sufficient supervision to insure that the salvage is free from explosives.

Artillery ammunition, cartridge cases and packing material such as fibre containers, clover leaf packs, wood boxes from which the material was removed. Fired cartridge cases may be shipped loose if boxes are not available. Other components should be sorted, packed and certified as above.

Chemical warfare. The boxes in which incendiary bombs are packed will be reassembled and returned to the continental United States for repacking and subsequent reshipment.

6 January 1944

A Company 5th Rangers – Camp Kilmer NJ.

B Company 5th Rangers – Camp Kilmer NJ, USA. 2nd Lt. Mehaffey went from Duty to Detached Service at the New York Port of Embarkation, Brooklyn NY as a loading officer. He returned to Duty the next day.

C Company 5th Rangers – Camp Kilmer NJ, USA. 2nd Lt. Gawler went from Duty to Detached Service at the New York Port of Embarkation, Brooklyn NY as a loading officer. He returned to Duty the next day.

D, E, F and Medical Companies 5th Rangers – Camp Kilmer NJ, USA.

Headquarters Company 5th Rangers – Camp Kilmer NJ, USA.

1st Lt Bryne and 1st Lt Garvik went from Duty to Detached Service at the New York Port of Embarkation, Brooklyn NY as loading officer.

A Company 2nd Rangers – Titchfield, Hampshire.

COMPANY MORNING REPORT		
Example morning report form for Camp Kilmer, New Jersey		

Maurice Prince: *Our outfit was beginning to shape up in good fashion; we were operating and functioning in a true Ranger style. Our organisation was good and our leadership was excellent. We were acting and thinking as a team. We had that confidence and cockiness that makes the Ranger the outstanding soldier that he is. With all this arduous and rough training, our morale and spirit were never higher or better. The harder we worked, the louder we sang. The more fatigued we were, the more we joked and the rougher the problem, the more we enjoyed our homes and the trips to the pubs in the evenings.*

We sang all the time we were here. 'Roll Me Over In the Clover' that famed English ballad became synonymous as our battle cry. We Rangers must have presented a queer picture in this quaint and peaceful town. We were just about the opposite, lively, noisy, and playful all the time, never once serious.

We really got ourselves familiar with beers and bitters while we were here. There were beaucoup pubs and bars and they always had drinking substances on hand. Being well heeled with dough from the sustenance deal, we could afford to indulge in alcoholic refreshment quite often. The name of 'Wheatsheaf', 'Carriers', 'Horse and Carriage' became as well known to us as Joe's beanery is back home. If you were lonely in your home, all you had needed to do was to make the rounds of these places, and you'd be sure to meet up with some of the boys.

B, C, E & Medical Companies 2nd Rangers – Bude, Cornwall.

D Company 2nd Rangers – Park Gate, Hampshire.

F Company 2nd Rangers – Botley, Hampshire.

Headquarters Company 2nd Rangers – Advanced Detachment Bude, Cornwall.

Headquarters Company 2nd Rangers – Bude, Cornwall.

The British Government issued a memo entitled 'Understanding the British': *There will be no lack of discussion among your men when you tackle the theme of this bulletin, for all of us are only too ready to air our views about 'foreigners'. And the less we know about them, the readier we are to pronounce judgment. It isn't a particularly British characteristic either, for all nations (whether they live on an island or not) are inclined to an insular outlook. They think of themselves as 'the tops' and they rather look down on all other nationalities.*

This disparagement of the 'foreigner' begins much nearer home than that. The Yorkshire lad says rude things about the Cockney; the Midlander makes fun of the Welshman. There's a lot to be said for this robust and defiant local pride, for it keeps alive a healthy sense of rivalry. Yet after many centuries of experience, we've learned to keep that rivalry in its place. We take it out for an airing to Wembley, or Old Trafford; we make it the peg for good knock-about arguments in the four-ale bar. But when it comes to serious business, we forget all these differences of local merit and custom and accent. And because we have unity under the skin, we men of all the shires march together, endure together, and win together.

It is in exactly the same spirit that we shall learn to march with the Americans.

At the moment, the soldiers of the two nations are in the position of two people who have just been introduced. Neither of them, thank heaven, is the emotional sort which falls on each other's neck. They like the look of the other fellow, but they don't intend to commit themselves yet. They're on the defensive, they're sizing each other up. Besides that, they've heard vague rumours about each other, and they've seen photographs which weren't too flattering. They want to see how the other fellow shapes, what he's like at work and play, before they let the friendship ripen. That is exactly the situation between the American and the British soldiers today – and that's good enough for a beginning. There's a bit of prejudice on both sides, a colossal ignorance of each other's attitudes and characteristics – but there's also a willingness to get together.

We need to exercise three qualities if Anglo-American friendship is to develop under the exacting conditions of war. They are Good Will, Respect, and Patience.

---

7 January 1944

5th Rangers – Companies A – F, Medical and HQ – Onboard HMS *Mauretania.*

2nd Lt. Gawler (C. Co.) returned to Duty from detached service as a loading officer with the New York Port of Embrkation.

Headquarters Company 5th Rangers – Camp Kilmer NJ
A Company 2nd Rangers – Titchfield, Hampshire.

In the evening of 7 January 1944, the men of the 5th Battalion left Camp Kilmer on a packed military train heading for the port side. There they were to board the HMS *Mauretania,* the Cunard White Star liner, which had previously been an English luxury cruise liner and then converted into a troop ship in 1939.

Maurice Prince: *For our social life, we had a local NAAFI place, in the middle of town which would attract the ATS and WRENS from the nearby English camps and airfields. These girls were really alright, and in every sense of that word. When we had to say goodbye to Titchfield, many a romance was shattered and many a heart broken.*

There was a slight hitch to these romantic affairs, though. It seems as the girls had to be back in camp quite early, and although these camps were nearby (nearby meaning anywhere from two to ten miles in England) a Ranger indulged in a bit of footwork, each time he had to take his girl back to camp. I guess a lot of the boys must have needed the exercise since they did it every night, and truthfully, if the opportunity should ever present itself again, I'm sure we would gladly, cheerfully, and willingly travel over these same courses without griping.

B, C, E & Medical Companies 2nd Rangers – Bude, Cornwall.
D Company 2nd Rangers – Park Gate, Hampshire.
F Company 2nd Rangers – Botley, Hampshire.
Headquarters Company 2nd Rangers – Advanced Detachment Bude, Cornwall. No change.
Headquarters Company 2nd Rangers – Bude, Cornwall.

On 7 January 1944 Lt. Col. Rudder requested the return to the United States of Major Max Schneider, his 2nd Battalion executive officer. The letter overleaf requests that Major Schneider would be available to be shipped home just over one month later – on 15 February. It states no reason for this request.

HEADQUARTERS SECOND RANGER INFANTRY BATTALION
APO 571   U. S. Army

Originally Submitted:
7 January 1944

SUBJECT: Rotation and Return of Military personnel as Individuals on
duty Outside Continental United States.

TO   : Commanding General, First United States Army, APO 230, U. S. ARMY

1. The following information is submitted in accordance with Memorandum
No 1, your Headquarters, dated 1 January 1944.

NAME: Max F. Schneider

GRADE: Major

ASN: 0384849

ARM: Infantry

MILITARY CLASSIFICATION NO: 2020 (Infantry Battalion Executive Officer)

AGE: 28 4/12

RACE: White

SERVICE: General

DEMONSTRATED FITNESS FOR PROMOTION: Yes

DATE ARRIVED IN ETO: 30 April 1942

PERIOD OF CONTINUOUS DUTY OVERSEAS: 30 April 1942 to present date

DATE AVAILABLE FOR SHIPMENT: 15 February 1944

REMARK AS TO REASON FOR RETURN:

Major Schneider has served in this Theater for almost two years
During that time he has been a member of the First, Fourth and Second
Ranger Battalions.

Major Schneider was with the First Ranger Battalion when they were
the first ones to land during the African Invasion. It was with that
organization that he fought the entire African Campaign. Major Schneider
was transferred to the Fourth Ranger Battalion and with that Organization
participated in the invasion of Sicily and campaign that followed.   He
was also with the Fourth Ranger Battalion when Italy was invaded. He left
Italy after fighting in that campaign on 27 October 1943 when he was
transferred to the SECOND Ranger Battalion.

While Major Schneider was engaged in the above campaigns, he earned the
Purple Heart Award and the Silver Star Award.

JAMES E. RUDDER
Lt Col Infantry
Battalion Commander

8 January 1944
5th Rangers – Companies A – F, Medical and HQ – Onboard HMS *Mauretania.*

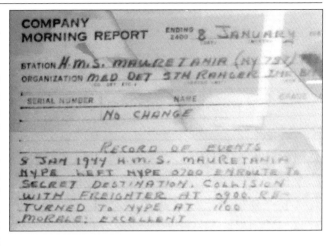

On Saturday, 8 January, 1944 the *Mauretania* was involved in a minor collision. She was still well within the harbour when she was accidentally rammed in the bow by another US ship, a USMC tanker called *Hat Creek.*

The *Mauretania* was forced to return to dock and whilst being secured, she struck the dock itself, causing further, light damage. At 4.30pm on 9 January she sailed again. William McLain of the Army 54th Replacement Battalion was onboard the *Mauretania* along with the Rangers and describes the event:

The ship departed the dock on a clear day with blue sky from horizon to horizon. It cleared the harbor with the vast sea before it, only one other ship, heading in, on the entire ocean. He was curious to see how they would pass. As they closed in, they seemed to be playing a game of 'chicken'. Then they hit, the other ship's prow striking the Mauretania *at the front port side. Both ships came to a stop, then the* Mauretania *turned about and went back into the port for inspection. She was found to be dented, but seaworthy. The fuel tanks were topped off and the eight-day voyage continued.*

The USMC tanker *Hat Creek.*

9 January 1944
5th Rangers – Companies A – F, Medical and HQ – Onboard HMS *Mauretania.*

Onboard ship the men were given a booklet from the War & Navy Departments, Washington D.C. It was a guide to how to understand the British – something which would come in handy as time went on.

A short guide to Great Britain: *Don't Be A Show Off. The British dislike bragging and showing off. American wages and soldier's pay are the highest in the world. When your payday comes, it would be sound practice to learn to spend your money according to British standards. They consider you highly paid. They won't think any better of you for throwing money around; they are more likely to think that you haven't learnt the common-sense virtues of thrift. The British 'Tommy' is apt to be specially touchy about the difference between his wages and yours. Keep this in mind. Use common sense and don't rub him the wrong way.*

You will find many things in Britain physically different from similar things in America. But there are also important similarities – our common speech, our common law, and our ideals of religious freedom were all brought from Britain when the Pilgrims landed at Plymouth Rock. Our ideas about political liberties are British and parts of our own Bill of Rights were borrowed from the great charters of British liberty.

Remember that in America you like people to conduct themselves as we do, and to respect the same things. Try to do the same for the British and respect the things they treasure.

2nd Battalion Narrative History

> During the period 1-10 January, Companies A/D/F conduct-
> ed physical conditioning and watermanship, working with Com-
> mando instructors in the Southampton Bay area. Emphasis was
> placed on the handling of motor-dories and the technique of
> disembarking from the LCI(S). During this same period, com-
> panies B/C/E conducted a four-day, small unit reconnaissance
> exercise extending from Bude to Braunton Sands, North Devon,
> a distance of approximately fifty miles. Plans for Ranger
> participation in raids were delayed due to the difficulties
> involved in obtaining the necessary special equipment not
> readily obtainable thru normal U.S. Army supply channels.

A Company 2nd Rangers – Titchfield, Hampshire.
B, C, E & Medical Companies 2nd Rangers – Bude, Cornwall.
D Company 2nd Rangers – Park Gate, Hampshire.
F Company 2nd Rangers – Botley, Hampshire.
Headquarters Company 2nd Rangers – Advanced Detachment Bude, Cornwall.
Headquarters Company 2nd Rangers – Bude, Cornwall.

In January the US Air Force was photographing the French coast area where the Rangers were due to attack. These photographs were then placed at the disposal of the army intelligence officers who would provide regular briefings to Lt. Col. Rudder.

These teams worked day and night, producing high quality photographs of the enemy coastline.

The following series of pictures were marked as being '*taken at zero feet and at right angles to the coast: Distance offshore about ¾ mile*'. They cover Omaha Beach to Pointe du Hoc and to the east of Grandcamp-les-Bains.

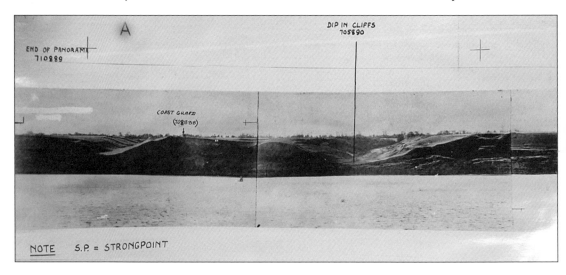

CHURCH
686882

COLVILLE-SUR-MER
(687882)

S. P.
687894
(3 LT. GUNS)

D

MOUTH OF R. RUQUET
675900

MOUTH OF THE "RUQUET"
(678900)

S. P.
678896

E

S. P.
677901

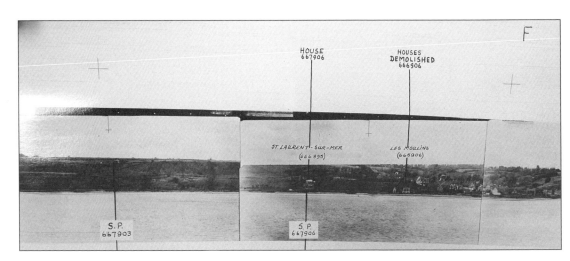

Above: Pointe du Hoc.

Below: German workers scatter on the beach as the observation plane flies low over them.

The Chaplain

The Rangers were assigned a chaplain called Joseph R. Lacy, who held the rank of captain. In the US Army there was one chaplain for approximately 1,000 men. The primary mission of the chaplain was to help their men to live well as soldiers. In order to fully understand the life of a soldier, the chaplain had to *'be a good soldier himself, understand the military thoroughly, and release the duties he had to perform.'*

The mission and functions of the chaplain was defined by the military as follows:

The mission of the chaplain is to promote religion and morality in the Army. To accomplish this mission, chaplains perform the following principle functions.
1)   Making available to military personnel opportunities for the public worship of God and instruction in religion.
2)   Administration of sacraments, rites and ordinances.
3)   Personal visitation.
4)   Counselling of individuals and groups.
5)   Character guidance instruction.
6)   Positive encouragement of military personnel to engage in organised religious fellowship and personal devotions.

In many cases the chaplains that arrived in the UK were men who had been in the service for only a few months, and were not accustomed to many of the army procedures, especially those perculiar to the European theatre. Although primarily organised for orientating new arrivals in the UK, it was the policy for all chaplains in the theatre, to attend a course of instruction at the Orientation School, which had been established at HQ Service of Supply (SOS) Cheltenham.

On 9 January 1944 quotas for each Base Section were allotted, to include chaplains of the SOS, AGF and AF units. The course of instructions was two days in length, covering almost anything that the chaplains brought up for discussion. Many technical problems were answered at once, regarding the security regulations, particularly in regard to letters of condolence, and giving information to relatives and friends concerning grave location.

Chaplains were to be acquainted with the peculiarities of the British law regarding marriage. According to British law, no US Army Chaplain was authorised to solemnise a marriage in the UK, and no US Army Chapel was approved as a place for a marriage service. Chaplains could assist in a marriage service, but had to ascertain that a Registrar was present and that the place had been approved by law.

Father Lacy, the Rangers' Chaplain, made a census of the personnel of the command by obtaining, through the personnel officer, the religious preferences entered on each individual's service record. Chaplains in general were also encouraged to establish this information directly from the men themselves through personal discussions and interviews. This information was then to be held as an ongoing and permanent record within their own office.

The Chaplain was 'morally obligated' to provide for the religious needs of the whole battalion and this was sometimes only fully obtained by using the services of civilian clergymen. This was also achieved by allowing men of varying denominations to join in with services conducted in other units or in neighbouring civilian communities.

Lt. Colonel Rudder was – as were all commanding officers – asked to permit Father Lacy to carry out his duties freely when the needs of the battalion in combat allowed. Father Lacy was also given the 'spiritual authority to teach and preach in public, to conduct religious services' and he was allowed the autonomy to conduct such services and rites as his flocks' denominations specifically required.

Equally, Army Regulation 660-20 instructed army commanders, that no attempt should be made 'to make attendance of Army personnel at religious services compulsory.' However, Lt. Col. Rudder was expected to be supportive of Father Lacy in 'encouraging and persuading individuals to attend religious services regularly on a voluntary basis.'

Athletic and recreational activities held on Sunday were scheduled so as not to interfere with attendance at services of worship under Army instruction. Lt. Col. Rudder was duty bound to adhere to this principle as far as practicably possible. The Army Regulations also positively authorised commanding officers to excuse from military duty personnel who wished to attend religious services on other days of religious importance – beyond that of the normal Sunday worship. These relaxed regulations were all based around military necessity and ordered in such a way that 'military personnel desiring to attend such services, either on the post of in adjacent communities, may be absent for such period as will enable them to be at their places of worship as publicly announced, provided no serious interference with their military training or duty is occasioned thereby.'

Father Lacy would make various services known to the men in advance, however, he could not do so without the prior approval of Lt. Col. Rudder. He was also charged with 'endeavouring to render assistance to those in need, by counselling those seeking help; by comforting the bereaved; and, where such personnel are affiliated with a religious denomination, by assisting them as necessary.'

The role of the chaplain was also given the status of a 'spiritual confidant' and discussions with Father Lacy were always treated as privileged and in confidence. Army Regulations took this a stage further and stated 'Unless this privilege is expressly waived by the individual concerned, the chaplain cannot be required to disclose information received in this manner to an investigating officer, courts martial, board of inquiry, board of officers, or in other proceedings wherein the testimony of the chaplain is otherwise competent and admissible.'

Father Lacy – as with all Army Chaplains – was encouraged to set aside certain periods of time to make informal visits to the men during work or play. Chaplains in general were encouraged to visit the men during training, in day rooms and mess halls, during manoeuvres and in mock combat situations, and use this time to make personal contact with small groups and even individuals. This was aimed at strengthening the bond between the chaplain and the men. Men could also request a private meeting with Father Lacy and he had attended counselling courses at the Chaplain School for this very purpose. It was Lt. Col. Rudder's responsibility to provide a suitable location for Father Lacy to perform his duties. Confidential and secret information was supposed to be held within a safe and all chaplains were given instruction on how to destroy confidential files in case of enemy Action.

Father Lacy was deemed under the terms of The Geneva Convention as a *'protected person'* and as such, all chaplains were defined as noncombatants and not required to bear arms. Equally, he could not be expected to do any duties which were at odds with that status. He could not be asked to perform a large number of duties, which included becoming involved in Courts Martial, acting as an investigating officer, a defence council or a member of a military court. However, because of his status within the battalion, Father Lacy was officially *'a member of the staff of the commanding officer and is the consultant of the commander and his staff in matters involving the spiritual welfare of the command.'.* This included getting involved with everything from teaching personal hygiene and sexual morality – in conjunction with the Rangers' medical officer Captain Block – to co-ordinating the moral tone and quality of entertainment provided to the men. If men were ill or hospitalised, it was part of Father Lacy's duties to visit where and whenever possible. This was especially the case when a man had a grave illness.

Combat is the final test of the preparation, practice, training, and effort of the army. The success of the Army team in combat depends to a great extent upon the spirit of teamwork which has been developed, and the proficiency with which each man does his part. As an active participant in the Army combat team, the chaplain has a contribution to make in attaining the mission of that team. His ability to fit himself into the team and its teamwork largely measures his success as a chaplain and to that extent, the success of the team.

Father Lacy was issued with a portable typewriter, a chaplain's flag of bunting; a company/regimental size field desk; and a *'hymnal chest' in which to carry the 150 copies of the Song and Service Book for Ship and Field.'*

Bude, Cornwall. A mock German bunker position was built to resemble a German blockhouse above almost vertical cliffs. It was one of the many obstacles created for the Rangers to assault and train on in Bude. This area was only a few hundred yards from where the men were staying, so it was a regular training position for them.

10 January 1944

5th Rangers – Companies A – F, Medical and HQ – Onboard HMS Mauretania.

Maurice Prince: *When the time came to move out, Co. A received a job to do. It didn't surprise me or the others in the least. We had been working hard and preparing for just that sort of mission, so when orders came down that we were scheduled to make a guerrilla raid upon the coast of France, some time near the end of the month, we were fully ready for it. So, when the day of January 10 rolled around, it saw sixty-four men and three officers prepared to go forth, once more. With regrets, we said Au Revoir to our friends of Titchfield and boarded our train for a new destination in England. We knew our days of dry running were behind us. We were now heading for pay dirt, as our Company Commander, Captain Lytle, so aptly put it. It was no wonder that the last night spent in Titchfield was one of celebration and toasting. This was to have been it!*

2nd Battalion Narrative History

Lt Col Rudder, making a special trip to SHAEF, London, was given a blanket authorization by General Eisenhower for the necessary supplies and, on 10 January, Company A moved to the Beachborough House, a Commando Training Center, near Folkestone, England. A detachment of sixteen men from Company D was sent to another Training Center at Dartmouth. The base of operations for the Battalion was moved to Titchfield.

The mission of Company A, reinforced to a strength of ninety-four men by Headquarters personnel and French guides, was to make a raid on the coast of France in the vicinity of Calais for the purpose of taking a prisoner. The detachment from Company D was to conduct a reconnaissance of the Island of Herm, one of the Channel Islands group.

As afforded by eye-witness accounts, the preparations and actions of Company A were as follows:

The plan finally selected was to divide the force into four teams, two to an Assault Craft. The Company would board the LCI(S) at Dover, transfer into LCA's for the run-in to the beach, recall the LCA's by the pre-arranged light signal upon the completion of the mission, then, using secret British direction-finding devices, locate and re-embark on the LCI(S). Ashore, the force would accomplish its' mission by either of three plans, as follows:

Plan 1 - If a prisoner was captured on the beach, the mission was considered accomplished and the Company would not proceed inland but would recall the LCA's at once.

Plan 2 - Group 1 would cut the beach wire, clear a path thru the beach mine belt, and establish a perimeter to defend the beach exit. The other three groups would pass thru Group 1, turn right just beyond the coastal road and, moving parallel to the road, would proceed 1000 yards to a known beach position consisting of 7-8 pillboxes and numerous dug in emplacements. This strongpoint was enclosed within a ten-yard wide belt of concertina and apron fences. Being that the position was semi-flooded at this time due to recent Channel storms, it was believed to be unoccupied except for possible sentrys.

Cutting the wire by stealth and blowing it by a previously inserted bangalore if discovered, the Number 2 Group would clear and search the position. The remaining two groups would cover this action in position on the landward side of the strongpoint.

A Company 2nd Rangers – Folkestone, Kent.
A Company left Titchfield at 0900 hours for Folkestone.
They arrived at 1530 hours.
The following eleven men were attached to A Company
from Headquarters Company:
T/5 Ramsey A. Turner, T/5 Oscar H. Anderson,
T/5 Paul Galloway, Pfc. Clarence L. Elsy, Sgt. William L.
Mollohan, T/4 Ted P. Smith, T/4 Virgilio V. Prebenna,
T/4 Isadore Diamond, T/5 Donald W. Bailey,
Pfc. Arthur J. Greenwood, Pfc. Charles A. Little.

Good Will: The British View was given out to British Soldiers

We must be willing to like each other – willing, because the common cause demands it. Goebbels and his gang will do all they can to produce ill will between us. Our answer to that game is persistent, determined good will: the resolution to believe the best about people we don't yet know. It should be matter of personal mental discipline to adopt this attitude.

Respect: Towards nations, as towards individuals, we must show respect for positive achievement. We may dislike a man's face or the cut of his clothes or his fashion in food – yet acknowledge him as a fine engineer or architect or musician. Respect for American achievement is one of the ways by which we shall discover the Americans. Look, for example, what they've done to refrigerators and combustion engines and acknowledge them as the world's inventive wizards.

```
    Plan 3 - No enemy having been found in the beach posit-
ion, Group 3, followed by Group 4, would proceed inland
thru  a  network of drainage  ditches,  parallel to the
main road leading  inland, to two  known enemy occupied
dwellings;  these  were CP's  for the defenders of this
area and were to the seward side of an extensive defen-
sive installation.
    Group 3, placing one squad forward as a roadblock,
would assault the left house  while Group 4 was, simul-
taneously, attacking the house to the right.  Group  4
was then to return to the beachexit  by the most direct
cross-country route  while  group 3,  with one squad as
rear-guard, would move back to the beach along the main
road.  When Group 3 had  reached the  junction with the
coastal road, Group 2 would take up the rear-guard act-
ion.   The final unit to enter the LCA's would be Group
1, which would cover the embarkation with two LMG's and
60-mm mortars.
    Training for the contemplated raid was of  two aspects;
boat-work in  Dover Bay  and rehearsals of the expected land
action at Beachborough House.  The final rehearsal, executed
on a scale exactly  that of  the area  to be covered by  the
raid,  was  witnessed by  the GOC Special Service Group, who
commended the unit on its' excellent state of readiness.

    Two important  factors governed  the execution of  the
action; the moon and the sea.  The precise timing necessary
afforded only three nights on which the "Dark Period" was of
sufficient duration to permit the carrying out of the operat-
ion under cover of complete darkness. On each of these three
nights, the  Royal Navy postponed the embarkation due to the
roughness of the waters of  the English Channel.  On 27 Jan-
uary,  the  now  insufficient "Dark Period" precluded  any
further action for the month and the raid was cancelled.  If
the weather  had  permitted,  Company A  would have been the
first complete American unit  to strike the coast of forti-
fied Europe;  the 1st Ranger Battalion had been represented
by selected individuals at the Dieppe raid.

    The detachment of Company D trained  under 4th Cammando
instructors at Dartmouth.  These sixteen men, only twelve of
whom would be selected to make the  raid, specialized in the
handling of motor-dories and movement by night.  The plan by
which they were to proceed with their mission of reconnoiter-
ing the Island of Herm was as follows:

    Dividing into  four three-man  teams,  they would cross
the Channel by British Gun-boat, disembarking into the
dory for the  silent approach  to  the beach.  Enemy
patrols being expected, one  team would return the dory
to the open sea while  the three remaining groups each
had a sector to reconnoiter.  The teams would return to
a designated point  on the beach  and would then signal
the dory in.  Proceeding ten miles out to sea, the party
would then contact the Gun-boat.
```

This raid was also cancelled due to the Royal Navy's refusal to undertake the operation in foul weather.

Along with Company A and the detachment from Company D were Headquarters Communication and Intelligence personnel. Communications training consisted of instruction by Commando personnel in secret techniques of radio transmission and direction-finding. A portion of this personnel was selected to accompany the raiding parties and participated in the rehearsals. The Battalion Staff secured the intelligence information necessary for detailed planning and also procured the necessary special equipment.

The following Communications Plan is submitted with the view of portraying the extensive planning necessary for this type of operation:

Radio was to be the primary means of communication. Alternate nets, employing different frequencies and radios, were established; to insure communications in the event of enemy jamming, interference, radio set failure, or the operator becoming a casualty.

The Primary mission of communications was to provide a means for coordinating the tactical operations. Strict radio silence was to be maintained until "Touch-down". Thereafter, all transmissions were to be made in accordance with a prearrangement, employing Code-words. In the event of an unforeseen emergency, any message necessary could be transmitted.

Blue-colored signal lamps were to be carried by all radio operators for use in event of set failure. The Beachmaster was also to employ the blue lamp to provide a beam for the LCA's on the pickup run.

An escape plan was also formulated for the purpose of picking up at a prearranged time and place any members of the Task Force who may have been stranded. Under this plan, the Beachmaster's party was to bury a SCR-536 and a signal lamp in a near-by gravel pit for use by the stranded members. A MTB was to appear off-shore at the proper time and the proper place and would transmit a certain codeword. The stranded party was to reply with the proper codeword or the proper code-letter with the signal lamp. A dory from the MTB would then evacuate the stranded party, providing that the proper return symbol was received.

(Note: Pursuant with VOGOC Special Service Force, all correspondence and files pertaining to the contemplated action were destroyed by this unit. Should additional information be desired, it is believed that the files of COHQ, Whitehall, London, would provide such information)

B, C, E & Medical Companies 2nd Rangers – Bude, Cornwall.
D Company 2nd Rangers – Park Gate, Hampshire.
Lt. David A. Baikie was attached for Duty from C.G. #4 (Commando Group).
The following five enlisted men were attached for Duty from C.G. #4 (Commando Group):
Sgt. Frank Major, L/Cpl. John Wells, L/Cpl. Anthony Irving, Pvt. William McGonnigle, Pvt. Angus Meek.
The following man was attached for Duty from HQ#1 Special Service Brigade.
Cfn Fred McMaster.
F Company 2nd Rangers – Botley, Hampshire.
Headquarters Company 2nd Rangers – Bude, Cornwall.

British Government requests were sent out to the general public for their holiday postcards and in particular, any photographs of the French coastline – and they proved to be invaluable to D-Day planners. Thousands of the pictures of the specific Rangers' target areas were handed in by the public and they were studied by Allied Intelligence.

Overleaf are some postcards showing Grandcamp Harbour, Pointe du Hoc, Omaha Beach, the beach in front of the Maisy Batteries and Maisy village. Also shown is Fort Samson – an imposing old harbour fort which sat on the coastline just to the west of the newer Grandcamp Harbour – it is shown here prior to the German occupation. (Prior to D-Day the Germans destroyed it to allow them a greater field of fire over the small port).

Fort Samson.

Grandcamp village.

A view of the Maisy church and the sleepy rural village before the war.

The main Grandcamp to Isigny road in the centre of Maisy village. Trams were a regular form of transport along the busy coastal roads before the war.

In the fields behind the coastal positions at La Casino in the direction of the Maisy Batteries – the ruins of the Chateau Duguesclin.

The inside of the Maisy church. This postcard shows much of the gothic interior.

The beach front at Grandcamp was a real tourist destination for Parisian holidaymakers pre-war.

A group of photographs showing the port of Grandcamp-les-Bains and the Vierville to Colleville beach – an area which was now known by planners by the code name 'Omaha Sector'.

On 10 January the US Army issued the Rangers with guidelines for the completion of battle casualty reports for each Battalion. It was used to instruct medical staff on the correct method of filling in their forms.

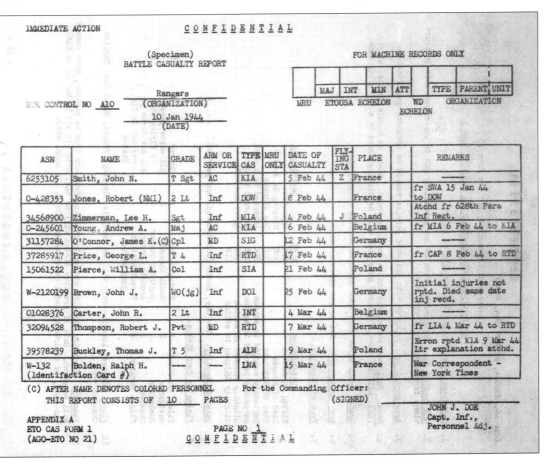

IMMEDIATE ACTION   C O N F I D E N T I A L

(Specimen)   FOR MACHINE RECORDS ONLY
BATTLE CASUALTY REPORT

                          Rangers
BCR CONTROL NO A10   (ORGANIZATION)   MRU   ETOUSA ECHELON   WD
                       10 Jan 1944   ECHELON
                          (DATE)

ASN	NAME	GRADE	ARM OR SERVICE	TYPE CAS	MRU ONLY	DATE OF CASUALTY	FLY-ING STA	PLACE	REMARKS
6253105	Smith, John N.	T Sgt	AC	KIA		5 Feb 44	Z	France	------
0-428353	Jones, Robert (NMI)	2 Lt	Inf	DOW		8 Feb 44		France	fr SWA 15 Jan 44 to DOW
34568900	Zimmerman, Lee H.	Sgt	Inf	MIA		4 Feb 44	J	Poland	Atchd fr 628th Para Inf Regt.
0-245601	Young, Andrew A.	Maj	AC	KIA		6 Feb 44		Belgium	fr MIA 6 Feb 44 to KIA
31157284	O'Connor, James K.(C)	Cpl	MD	SIG		12 Feb 44		Germany	------
37285917	Price, George L.	T 4	Inf	RTD		17 Feb 44		France	fr CAP 8 Feb 44 to RTD
15061522	Pierce, William A.	Col	Inf	SIA		21 Feb 44		Poland	------
W-2120199	Brown, John J.	WO(jg)	Inf	DOI		25 Feb 44		Germany	Initial injuries not rptd. Died same date inj recd.
01028376	Carter, John R.	2 Lt	Inf	INT		4 Mar 44		Belgium	
32094528	Thompson, Robert J.	Pvt	MD	RTD		7 Mar 44		Germany	fr LIA 4 Mar 44 to RTD
39578239	Buckley, Thomas J.	T 5	Inf	ALW		9 Mar 44		Poland	Erron rptd KIA 9 Mar 44 Ltr explanation atchd.
W-132 (Identifaction Card #)	Bolden, Ralph H.	---	----	LWA		15 Mar 44		France	War Correspondent – New York Times

(C) AFTER NAME DENOTES COLORED PERSONNEL   For the Commanding Officer:
     THIS REPORT CONSISTS OF 10   PAGES   (SIGNED) _____
                                                                 JOHN J. DOE
APPENDIX A   Capt. Inf.,
ETO CAS FORM 1   Personnel Adj.
(AGO-ETO NO 21)   PAGE NO 1
                          C O N F I D E N T I A L

11 January 1944

5th Rangers – Companies A – F, Medical and HQ – Onboard HMS *Mauretania.*
Record of events: 11 January 1944. HMS *Mauretania* day at sea. En route to destination. Morale excellent.

A Company 2nd Rangers – Folkestone, Kent.

B, C, E & Medical Companies 2nd Rangers – Bude, Cornwall.

D Company 2nd Rangers – Park Gate, Hampshire.

F Company 2nd Rangers – Botley, Hampshire.

Headquarters Company 2nd Rangers – Bude, Cornwall.

Miscellaneous Waste Materials Order:

The Inspector of Salvage, British Army will undertake to collect and dispose of all the other waste materials which are no longer required for use by the US Army.

Paper will be folded and protected from the weather; paper unprotected from the weather or crumpled has lost much of its value. Paper soiled by contact with food will be destroyed.

Glass will be rinsed of all food particles. Bottles which have contained poison, disinfectants, or oil are to be broken and buried.

The Army issued a memorandum on the importance of choosing the correct time for H-Hour and it discusses the pros and cons of the options.

~~CONFIDENTIAL~~

"H-HOUR"
(Daylight or Darkness)
MEMORANDUM ON CONFERENCE WITH BRIGADIER PYMAN

1. INTRODUCTION.

The purpose of this memorandum is to point out the factors affecting the determination of whether H-Hour for the assault of a heavily fortified coast should be in daylight or darkness.

2. ASSUMPTIONS.

a. The operation under discussion is the assault of a heavily fortified coast. The assault of a less heavily defended coast would involve different considerations.

b. Local conditions peculiar to a particular stretch of coast might introduce special considerations which, under the circumstances, would be controlling.

c. The assault division will have the mission of seizing the beachhead line (covering position), and in connection therewith will be given a limited objective from five to nine thousand yards inland.

d. We will have complete air supremacy.

e. There will be a prolonged and heavy preliminary aerial bombardment, but the effectiveness of it has not been estimated.

f. Enemy reserves are mainly Panzer divisions. We may expect a heavy armored or combined attack by day or an infantry attack by night.

g. There will be from sixteen to twenty hours of daylight on D-Day, leaving only 4 - 8 hours of darkness and twilight.

h. Naval and air considerations have been included only to the extent that they affect the military phases of the operation. Naval and air problems peculiar to those respective services have not been considered, although they are recognized as important. For example, with only a few hours of darkness available, the Navy must decide whether it prefers to have it for cover when leaving the embarkation points, when enroute, when forming up the craft in the rendezvous and assembly

~~CONFIDENTIAL~~

CONFIDENTIAL

areas or when approaching the shore.

i. This memorandum does not include a study of the availability of craft.

3. HOLDING THE FINAL OBJECTIVE.

a. Regardless of whether the assault division lands in daylight or darkness, it will not have fulfilled its mission until it has successfully held its objective against counter-attack. A counter-attack may be expected as soon after H-Hour as the following factors permit:

(1) Time when enemy can determine with confidence where the main landing will occur. (This may be several hours before or after H-Hour).

(2) Distance of enemy reserves from the objective.

(30 Terrain and road net.

(4) Extent to which we can interfere with movement of enemy reserves.

b. If our arrival upon the final objective occurs too long after the enemy has determined with reasonable certainty where the main landing is being made, we may have to meet a coordinated armored attack before we have reached the objective, or at least before it has been organized adequately. Therefore, the less time which lapses between the alerting of the defenses and our occupation of the final objective, the better. It is considered that defensive fires enroute could be overcome, road blocks and other obstacles removed and heavy support weapons advanced to the final objective more rapidly in daylight than in darkness.

c. Furthermore, we want as much time as possible for organizing the final objective before being hit by an armored counter-attack. Since the latter is not likely to occur during darkness, the following H-Hour considerations apply:

(1) If H-Hour is during the night or in the early morning hours, the enemy may be able to put in an armored counter-attack the same day, and the only time we will have for organizing the position for defense will be the amount by which we beat him to the objective.

CONFIDENTIAL
-2-

CONFIDENTIAL

(2) If H-Hour is late enough on D-Day so that insufficient time remains before dark for the enemy to launch an armored counter-attack, he probably will not make it until D/1. We would then have whatever time remains on D-Day plus all of the night D-D/1 for preparation.

(3) If H-Hour is too late on D-Day, we will arrive on the objective after dark, whereas, in order to reconnoiter and plan the organization of the objective for defense, including the siting and registering of anti-tank guns, artillery and other supporting weapons, some daylight is necessary. It is considered desirable to have about 2 hours of daylight for this purpose before darkness falls. Organization of the position could then continue throughout the night.

(4) As H-Hour is shifted earlier or later on D-Day, the above factors apply with greater or lesser force.

4. Additional consideration affecting H-Hour are as follows:

   a. Naval considerations, as they affect military operations.

   b. Air considerations, as they affect military operations.

   c. The assault and reduction of the beach fortifications.

	-D-A-Y-		N-I-G-H-T	
	For	Against	For	Against
NAVAL	Complicated craft formations are possible. Accurate navigation is facilitated Smoke may provide some of the advantages of darkness and enemy cannot counter with artificial light. Gun fire support most accurate & effective. Less craft required. *	Army's daylight assault technique requires complicated No concealment during approach to shore except smoke and that is difficult to control	Simpler craft formation are acceptable to Army. Craft approach shore under cover of darkness, or at worst under conditions of artificial light (Flares & searchlights)	Complicated craft formations are impossible. Navigational difficulties will be increased. Flares & searchlights may remove cover of darkness. Naval gun fire support is less effective and may be impossible. More craft required. *
AIR	Enemy air effort will be minimized, as our fighters cover and AA fire are more effective in daylight. Maximum air ground support is possible			Enemy air interference most difficult to prevent. (Bombing by flares as in Sicily). Minimum air ground support is possible. If

Airborne troops and rangers are most effectively landed at night and their employment must be coordinated with H-hour accordingly. If H-Hour is in daylight, such troops might be landed the night before.

CONFIDENTIAL

	D-A-Y		N-I-G-H-T	
	For	Against	For	Against
	Less affected by slight errors in point of landing. Maximum fire support from air, Navy, organic artillery and tanks possible.	All defense weapons will be at their maximum effectiveness.	Enemy weapons less effective.	Orientation difficult if landed in wrong place. Air, Naval gunfire and artillery support less effective; tanks cannot be used at all. Enemy's automatic weapons can fire on final protective lines while we must rely on aimed fire. Therefore, darkness will reduce effectiveness of our fire more than enemy's.
	Some of the advantages of night may be obtained from smoke and enemy cannot counter with artificial light.	Troops will be under observed fire during assault except as smoke is used.	Cover of darkness. (Unless removed by searchlights or flares.)	If enemy uses lights or flares, we will have neither the cover of darkness nor the fire support which we would provide for a day-light assault. Special technique required.
ASSAULT AND REDUCTION OF BEACH DEFENSES	Standard technique forreduction of fortifications applicable with minor changes. Success relatively quicker and more certain. Initial build up at maximum speed. *			Initial build up slow until dawn*

*These points are considered correct, but have not been proved.

~~CONFIDENTIAL~~

5. It has been suggested that **Infantry** be infiltrated through the enemy beach fortifications under cover of darnkess to operate against enemy rear installations, and that a landing assault be made against the fortifications later, in daylight, over the same beaches. The following factors are con-sidered controlling:

For	Against
Troops in his rear may delay and confuse enemy. May open lanes through bbstacles for daylight assault troops. May secure observation for Naval and artillery fire. May reduce enemy artilley and mortar fire before assault troops land	Paratroops or Rangers (landed on flanks) may accomplish same results, and Paratroop attack would be easier to coordinate. Troops too lightly equipped to hold objective. (Paratroops would have heavier weapons.) Surprise compromised earlier, and en-emy has better chance of counter-attacking before anti-tank weapons are in position. Troops would require a high degree of special training to operate with necessary stealth. All troops landing before daylight-as-sault troops reduce fortifications will receive full force of enemy's direct fire. Casualties will be higher than if 1st wave reduces pill-boxes. Cose of failure is high: loss of sur-prise, cluttered-up beaches, etc. Since infiltration troops must be fol-lowed by assault troops, more craft are required.

12 January 1944

5th Rangers – Companies A – F, Medical and HQ – Onboard HMS *Mauretania.*

2nd Battalion Narrative History

> Companies D/F trained under Commando instructors, working out of Warsash, Hants, in Southampton Waters. Company D specialized in motor-dory handling while Company F conducted exercises involving the LCI(S). The following exercise, offered for your information, proved the Ranger capabilities during this period:
>
> The problem given Company F was to effect a dry-landing from the LCI(S) at a point on the English coast at what was thought to be an abandoned fortress. The Company was to breach the coastal wire barriers and reconnoiter to an airfield one mile inland with emphasis placed on stealth and proper timing for the operation.
>
> The landing was made the night of 12 January, as scheduled and the reconnaissance parties moved inland according to plan under the protection of a covering party on the beach. At the appointed time, the company assembled on the beach for re-embarkation. Roll was then called and three men were found to be missing. One of these appeared shortly thereafter, in custody of two Royal Marine Shore-patrolmen. It was then discovered that the Fort had been secretly re-occupied and that the British sentrys knew nothing of our presence until they over-heard the noise of roll call. Almost sixty men had passed thru their lines twice without detection.
>
> The remaining two missing men were recovered the following morning. They had scouted to the right, entering the grounds of a secret laboratory before they were detected, only 100 feet short of a charged protective wire.

A Company 2nd Rangers – Folkestone, Kent.

B, C, & Medical Companies 2nd Rangers – Bude, Cornwall.

D Company 2nd Rangers – Park Gate, Hampshire.

E Company 2nd Rangers – Bude, Cornwall.

Pvt. George H. Crook was attached to E Company from the 2nd Battalion Medical Detachment.

F Company 2nd Rangers – Botley, Hampshire.

Headquarters Company 2nd Rangers – Bude, Cornwall.

---

13 January 1944

5th Rangers – Companies A – F, Medical and HQ –
Onboard HMS *Mauretania.*

A Company 2nd Rangers – Folkestone, Kent.
The following six men were attached for Duty with A Company from Headquarters Company: Sgt Francis J. Roach, Cpl. Charles A. Parker, T/5 Stephen A. Liscinsky, T/5 Louis Lisko, T/5 Tasker, L. Hooks, Pfc. Owen J. Paradis.

Maurice Prince: *About the most vivid and exciting moments, not to mention jolly and frivolous times, we've spent in the land of England, took place during our reign in the famous Commando house of Beachborough (known as B.B. house) which is situated on the English battle ground about four miles outside the city of Folkestone, a county of Kent.*

It was from this base that we were to set out to make that attempted Ranger raid, somewhere on the enemy-held coast of France.

Our arrival to this well-known place was one of great momentousness, since our being there marked the first time in the annals of the Commandos' history, that American troops were to be billeted in this house. It was a great honour and privilege to us, and we were enthralled by its prospects.

It was from this headquarters that all the arrangements, planning and operations of the No.4, No.10 and the Marine Commandos had been made. It was from here that these illustrious and brave men set out to make their raids and assaults upon the German defences off the coast of France. And it was to this place that these daring men returned after their exploits and adventures on the other side of the Channel. It is no wonder that we look upon our residence here with the greatest of pride. It isn't anyone that can call this place of such noble merit their home, even for the short period of time we had the delight of staying there.

Our company strength, upon our arrival, was sixty-four enlisted men and three officers, our company commander not being with us, as he had gone to some school in London. Our 1st platoon leader, (then 1st Lt. Joe Rafferty) was in charge of the outfit. In addition to our own company, we had the added personnel of the kitchen, one section of headquarters communications, and a few men from our Battalion supply.

We didn't waste any time stripping for action. We were here on business purposes only, and we meant to get down to brass tacks, as immediately as was possible. We really put in some real licks in our training. We were very fortunate that we had the capable assistance and instruction from some of the commando officers themselves, in our work.

We learned a great deal from these artists, who were skilled in the art of silent death. Strict attention was applied every time these men held classes and we tried to absorb all we could from them, since we knew that what these men told us didn't come from any field manual, but from actual experiences.

B, C, & Medical Companies 2nd Rangers – Bude, Cornwall.
D Company 2nd Rangers – Park Gate, Hampshire.
E Company 2nd Rangers – Bude, Cornwall.
Organisation engages in a tactical movement to a new station. Left Bude, Cornwall at 0915 hours. APO 571.
F Company 2nd Rangers – Botley, Hampshire.
Headquarters Company 2nd Rangers – Bude, Cornwall.

Army directive: Wearing of the Steel Helmet

When personnel are likely to be subjected to blast, the chinstrap of the steel helmet will not be fastened under the chin. Casualties in North Africa and Italy included men whose necks were broken due to the upwards thrust of concussion inside the helmet, the chinstrap having been buckled under the wearer's chin.

The chinstrap will habitually be worn buckled around the rear of the helmet, just above the rim. The headband in the helmet liner will be adjusted to the wearer's head to fit snugly and aid in holding the assembled helmet and liner in place without fastening the chinstrap under the chin.

Under no circumstances will the chinstrap be allowed to hang, unbuckled, at the sides of the helmet.

The chinstrap may be buckled under the chin if the wearer is riding in a vehicle, and there is a likelihood of losing the helmet unless buckled on. However, if there is danger of blast, the chinstrap will be worn as outlined above.

---

14 January 1944
5th Rangers – Companies A – F, Medical and HQ – Onboard HMS *Mauretania*.
A Company 2nd Rangers – Folkestone, Kent. No change.
B, C, Medical and HQ Companies 2nd Rangers – Bude, Cornwall. No change.
D Company 2nd Rangers – Park Gate, Hampshire.
E Company 2nd Rangers – APO 571. Station and record of events. Continued tactical movement to a new station.
F Company 2nd Rangers – Botley, Hampshire.

Immunisations: *In accordance with Army Regulation 40-210 each unit commander will ensure that the military personnel under his command are immunised as set forth below, and that the indicated records thereof are properly maintained.*

A) Routine Immunisations (all personnel).

Disease & Agent	Initial dose
Smallpox (vaccine)	*Vaccination on entry into service*
Typhoid-paratyphoid fevers	*3 subcutaneous injections of .5cc,*
(triple vaccine)	*1cc and 1cc, respectively, at weekly intervals*
Typhus fever	*3 subcutaneous injections of 1cc (vaccine) each at weekly intervals*

(An additional dose of 1cc of typhus vaccine should be administered every 4 – 6 months in the presence of serious danger of infection).

Tetanus	*3 subcutaneous injections of 1cc each*
(plain toxoid)	*at 3 week intervals*

(An emergency stimulating dose of 1cc of tetanus toxoid will be administered as soon as possible after injury, to individuals receiving wounds or severe burns, and, when deemed advisable by the responsible medical officer, to those undergoing secondary operations or manipulations of old wounds.)

---

15 January 1944

5th Rangers – Companies A – F, Medical and HQ – Onboard HMS *Mauretania*.

A Company 2nd Rangers – Folkestone, Kent. Pfc's William K. Doinoff and Gerard C. Rotthoff were both attached to A Company from Headquarters Company.

B and HQ Companies 2nd Rangers – Bude, Cornwall.

C Company 2nd Rangers – Bude, Cornwall. Pvt. Insko was transferred in grade to 2913th Disciplinary Training Centre, Langport, Somerset. Pfc. Frank E. South was attached from the Medical Detachment of the 2nd Rangers for Duty rations and quarters.

D Company 2nd Rangers – Park Gate, Hampshire,

E Company 2nd Rangers – APO 571. Station and record of events. Continued tactical movement to a new station.

F Company 2nd Rangers – Botley, Hampshire.

Medical Detachment 2nd Rangers – Bude, Cornwall. Pfc. South was attached and joined C Company 2nd Battalion.

Maurice Prince: *It was only natural that during our stay here we would become acquainted and friendly with the Commando personnel that still remained on the grounds. These men, for the most part, were non-operational troops which were due to certain misfortunes obtained during their fighting days. These fellows were great sports and as swell a bunch of soldiers I have ever met. They were as typically British as the grounds themselves. They were shy, modest, and quiet. A bit cool at first, but when we broke them down, they were most friendly and warm. Although the bull was thrown around quite a bit, especially after a few bitters had been downed at the local NAAFI, they were most modest in their story-telling. It was like pulling teeth to get anything from these soldiers. They, who had participated in many an action against the enemy. I learned that these fellows were by no means braggarts or show-offs, although they had done enough to spout off about.*

---

16 January 1944

5th Rangers – Companies A – F, Medical and HQ – Onboard HMS *Mauretania*.

A Company 2nd Rangers – Folkestone, Kent. No change.

Maurice Prince: *Folkestone, being a large city, had many facilities and centres for amusement and entertainment. There were several movie houses, many eating places, cabarets, nightclubs, & few movie halls and innumerable pubs. Many was the night we visited this city and enjoyed ourselves to the utmost.*

We were about the only American GIs in this area. Since Folkestone is only a stone's throw away from the enemy across the Channel. This city wasn't exactly healthy or a suitable place for soldiers to be stationed at. This had its advantages and also its setbacks. On the good side was the fact that we had the run of the city. Being there were a great many pretty girls about, we had the pleasure of sharing their leisure time without competition from other GIs.

There was also lots to drink and being the rich Americans, we were able to participate in alcoholic energies, ever so often. On the bad side of the ledger was the fact that we were so near the enemy. We were nightly subjected to air raids. This wasn't too bad, as the Luftwaffe generally passed over Folkestone to head for the inland cities, such as London, Birmingham, etc.

What was dangerous and hazardous to us was when there was allied shipping in the Channel. Every time a friendly convoy would attempt to run the gauntlet along the coast, there was bound to be enemy long range shelling and rocket firing. This shelling was very inaccurate. Many shells instead of hitting the ships in the convoy, landed on the shores and in the city proper. Many a scar and an empty lot stood in defiance to prove the ineffectiveness of this fire. Also, there were too many graves and hospitalized persons to show what a menace to the civilian population, this shelling was.

B Company 2nd Rangers – Bude, Cornwall.
C Company 2nd Rangers – Bude, Cornwall.
Record of events. Left Bude, Cornwall at 0915 hours en route to a new station.
D Company 2nd Rangers – Park Gate, Hampshire
E Company 2nd Rangers – Sandown, Isle of Wight. Station and record of events. Arrived Sandown, Isle of Wight 1400 hours. End of tactical movement.
F Company 2nd Rangers – Botley, Hampshire
Medical Detachment 2nd Rangers – Bude, Cornwall.
Headquarters Company 2nd Rangers – Bude, Cornwall.

Companies of the 2nd Battalion split up and went to various parts of the South coast. D & F Companies went to Hampshire, E Company to the Isle of Wight, while B, C and HQ remained in Bude. This allowed the Rangers to undertake varied training to strengthen the overall capabilities of the battalion. All of the locations were seaside ones – thus there was a continual theme of practice assaults and landings from landing craft, in particular using the British boat LCA (Landing Craft Assault).

D Company spent a lot of their time blowing up obstacles, understanding explosives and learning the art of destruction on static defences, straight after they had completed a beach assault. These assaults took place day and night and the men became adept at approaching, landing and destroying targets in almost pitch black – then returning to their base soaking wet and often worn out.

The positioning of D and F companies on the South Coast alongside the River Hamble Estuary allowed them to train from one of many landing points. Their LCAs and British Royal Navy crews would work with them every day and return again the next day at the agreed time.

A rifle range was built along the waterfront by mounding up soil into a huge bank and their training comprised landing assaults, shooting and explosive practice on a daily basis.

German air activity was not heavy – but aerial reconnaissance and subsequent bombing was considered an issue. The US Army produced a series of pamphlets describing how the German air force attacked its targets.

Pattern Bombing: In pattern bombing, each plane simultaneously releases one bomb as it flies over the target. Afterwards the bombers fly back along their course, or return at right angles and repeat the bombardment, which process is carried on until all the bombs are dropped or the planes are driven off by anti-aircraft gunfire.

This form of bombing can only be used when there is an almost complete absence of counter-defence. The process is deliberate, and would not be attempted where there was strong opposition. The idea is to maintain a continuous period of suspense, and accordingly pattern bombing is used against poorly defended towns in an effort to break the morale of the civilians. Pattern bombing is also employed against troops and ships in convoy.

Mass bombing: Mass bombing is employed where the target is large and fairly well defended. Planes come over suddenly (often by Silent Approach technique), release their bombs and speed away before AA batteries can come into effective action. Concussion of the simultaneous explosion of many bombs causes widespread collapse of buildings, so that mass bombing is used over crowded areas. It is also used against quite small targets of high military value, when it is considered that the dropping of many bombs will be worthwhile if only one direct hit is obtained.

Dive bombing: Dive bombing is used where accuracy of aim is essential. Plane dives – generally from 10,000 feet – straight for target. Power dive – that is, engines pulling – gives speed well in advance of 400 mph. One thousand feet above target, bomb released, and plane pulls out of dive.

Large bombs generally used in dive bombing. Targets small, of high military importance – bridges, railways, roads, ships etc. Most effective defence against dive bombing is by multiple machine gun.

On clear days, spiral power dive is often employed. Plane descends in 'steps' to spoil aim of gunners on ground. Dive bombing is highly dangerous for pilot as well as for the attacked.

Series Bombing: The object of series bombing is to cover as wide an area as possible. The title is an explanation in itself – bombs are dropped in series, one pattern after another being formed by the explosions. Series bombing is most effective, of course over a large target or a long one. (i.e. over a crowded city) where every bomb might be expected to do great damage, or say, along a line of trenches occupied by soldiers.

17 January 1944
5th Rangers – Companies A – F, Medical and HQ – Onboard HMS *Mauretania*.

2nd Battalion Narrative History

> On 17 January, Company D, less the detachment of sixteen men at Dartmouth, moved by LCA to Freshwater, IOW, for two-weeks of cliff scaling on the Needles. These were sheer chalk cliffs from 200 to 300 feet in height. Only one fall, fortunately not serious, occurred during the period. Company F continued LCI(S) training at Warsash.
>
> Companies B/C/E, together with the remainder of Headquarters Company, less the Personnel Section, moved to the Isle of Wight on 18 January. To preserve secrecy, this change of station was executed Commando-style; small groups of men traveling in any manner they chose, with 72-hours permitted for the movement. Companies B/C were billeted in Sandown. These Companies conducted training in cliff scaling, forced marches, removal of mines, and exercises involving boat-work and reconnaissance.
>
> Bude, Cornwall, remained as the official home station but the bulk of the Staff activities was carried on at the Beachborough House and in Titchfield. This condition lasted thru-out the month of January.

A Company 2nd Rangers – Folkestone, Kent.
T/Sgt. Edward Gurney was attached from Headquarters Company to A Company.
B Company 2nd Rangers – Bude, Cornwall.
1st Lt. Brice from Duty to Detached Service, School, London.
C Company 2nd Rangers – No change. Record of events. En route to a new station.
D Company 2nd Rangers – Freshwater, Isle of Wight.
E Company 2nd Rangers – Sandown, Isle of Wight.
F Company 2nd Rangers – Botley, Hampshire.
Medical Detachment 2nd Rangers – Bude, Cornwall. Record of events. The Medical Detachment left Bude, Cornwall at 1200 hours by truck en route to a new station.
Headquarters Company 2nd Rangers – Bude, Cornwall.

D Company mounted trucks at 0930 hours for a new station. They arrived at Warsash at 0945 hours and embarked at 1000 hours for Yarmouth. D Company arrived in Yarmouth, Isle of Wight at 1200 hours and marched from Yarmouth to Freshwater. They took station there and performed usual camp duties with soldiers being billeted in private homes throughout Freshwater and Freshwater Bay.

The US Army issued a report on beds:

In January 1944 England ran short of beds. To make matters worse, thousands and thousands of U.S. folding cots were already in use. U.S. soldiers were faced with sleepless nights on hard ground or draughty floors. Southern Base Section took the problem in hand. The G-4 Section procured lumber, wiring and nails and purchased power tools on the commercial market through Reciprocal Aid. The job of mass-producing over 100,000 'sack holders' was assigned to various depots… Over 50,000 double tiered bunks were produced for loading millions of tons of supplies needed in the invasion.'

Jan 17 Army orders: *"casualty information is "confidential" and will not be included in personal letters or correspondence… personnel will make no reference to casualties in their letters as it might reach the next of kin prior to notification by the War Department.*

On 17 January – as a follow-on letter to the one written on 7 January by Lt. Colonel Rudder – Battalion Doctor, Captain Walter Block wrote a letter about Major Schneider to the Rangers' superior officer Major General Huebner. There is no doubt that this letter will have been written at the express request of Colonel Rudder. Presumably because there had been no response to Col. Rudder's less direct, yet similar letter dated 7 January. This letter directly states that Major Schneider was in danger of having a complete mental 'crack up' – the implication being that he should be removed immediately.

```
                        MEDICAL DETACHMENT
                     SECOND RANGER INFANTRY BN
                       APO #571, U.S. Army

                                          17 January 1944

      SUBJECT:  Transfer of Major Max F. Schneider, 0384849, 2nd Ranger Inf Bn

      TO     :  Commanding Officer, 2nd Ranger Inf Bn, APO #571, U.S. Army

              1. It is the opinion of the undersigned that Major Max F. Schneider,
      Executive Officer of the 2nd Ranger Infantry Battalion, is suffering from
      a Neurasthenic condition brought on by overwork and mental fatigue.

              2. It is strongly recommended that application for transfer to the
      United States of Major Max F. Schneider , 2nd Ranger Infantry Battalion,
      be instituted.

              3. It is the further opinion of the undersigned that unless such
      a radical measure is resorted to, the above mentioned officer may suffer
      a complete mental "crack up."




                                    Capt W E Block M C,


                                    WALTER E. BLOCK
                                    Captain, MC
                                    Bn Surgeon
```

The reason for the rather formal second request for the removal or Major Schneider from his post is very clear. Demotion, reassignment or separation (return to the US) is outlined in the standing US Army instructions called *'Demotion of officers by commanding General, ETOUSA.'*

Under Army regulations it was only possible with the permission of the Commanding General ETOUSA, that permanently ranked officers could be removed from position for any of the reasons stated below. The regulations are as follows:

1. Authority to make necessary demotions has been granted to the Theatre Commander, ETOUSA, by the provisions of the following War Department Letter: January 9th 1943
SUBJECT: Authority to demote.
To: Commanding General – European Theatre of Operations
℅ Postmaster, New York, New York.

1. *This regulation is designed to effect the reassignment, demotion or separation of an officer when it is considered that he is performing duty for which he is not suited. The procedure prescribed therein insures justice to the individual and protects the best interests of the Government. It will be normal procedure in applicable cases.*
2. *It is recognised, however, that in contact with the enemy or when such contact is considered imminent, morale and example may require demotion equally as expeditious as promotion. Accordingly, in addition to the procedures authorised in AR 605-230, you are hereby authorised to demote officers of your command, holding temporary higher grade, to a lower grade for failure to perform satisfactorily the duty of the higher grade.*
3. a) *Each order directing demotion will include the following: "The Secretary of War has directed me to inform you that the President has terminated this date your temporary appointment as _____ , AUS".*
   b) *The Adjutant General will be informed promptly by radio of all action under this authority to include: name, rank and serial number of the officer concerned, grade held prior to demotion, grade held subsequent*

to demotion, date of demotion, the reasons therefor. This radio message will be followed by confirming air mail letter with statement of the circumstances.

A. The authority contained herein will NOT be utilised to affect the following:

1) Demotion of general officer or officers serving in permanent grades.

2) Separation from the service.

3) Punishment in lieu of courts martial proceedings.

4) Demotion of any officer where conditions and circumstances indicate that provisions of AR 605-230 would be equally effective and desirable.

B. Each officer demoted may be reassigned under your jurisdiction. This authority is granted only to you. It will not be delegated to subordinates.

By order of the Secretary of War. J.A. Grotenrath. Adjutant General.

Therefore based on this US Army legislation, without the Commanding General's approval, Major Schneider was not eligible for removal from service with the Rangers. It is not known if Major Schneider was aware of these letters at the time.

---

18 January 1944

5th Rangers – Companies A – F, Medical and HQ – Onboard HMS *Mauretania*.

A Company 2nd Rangers – Folkestone, Kent. Captain Cleveland A. Lytle returned to A Company from Detached Service in Scotland and resumed his principal Duty as Company Commander. 1st Lt. Joseph A. Rafferty was therefore relieved of his temporary command and reassumed his duties as executive officer.

B Company 2nd Rangers – En route to new station 64 enlisted men and 1 officer authorised quarters and mess separately. Departed Bude, Cornwall 0600 hours, en route to new station.

C Company 2nd Rangers – No change. Record of events. En route to a new station.

D Company 2nd Rangers – Freshwater, Isle of Wight.

E Company 2nd Rangers – Sandown, Isle of Wight.

F Company 2nd Rangers – Botley, Hampshire.

Medical Detachment 2nd Rangers – Sandown, Isle of Wight.

Captain Block went from Duty to Detached Service.

Headquarters Company 2nd Rangers – Bude, Cornwall. No change. En route to new station.

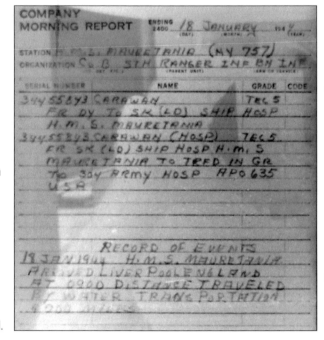

The passage of the 5th Battalion to England was uneventful, although the ship was forced far off course to escape suspected enemy submarines. No enemy was sighted and the *Mauretania* arrived in the outer harbour of Liverpool docks, where they had to wait for minesweepers to clear a path wide enough for the ship to enter.

Aerial Reconnaissance Report: Maisy Battery La Martinière – 18 January 1944 (B758): *Four sunken casemates/shelters in all have been completed among the emplacements of this battery, three of them being approximately 35' x 30' and the fourth 55' x 30'. (2054/5 of sortie RB/41, 6 January 1944, 1/10,000, quality fair).*

19 January 1944

5th Rangers – Companies A – F, Medical and HQ – Leominster, England.
Advanced Detachment HQ Company 5th Rangers – Leominster, England.
A Company 2nd Rangers – Folkestone, Kent.
Pfc. Neal B. Berke was attached to A Company from Headquarters Company.
Pvt. Andre Bourret was attached for Duty from French Troop No 10 Commando.
B Company 2nd Rangers – Shanklin, Isle of Wight.
C Company 2nd Rangers – No change. Record of events. En route to a new station.
D Company 2nd Rangers – Freshwater, Isle of Wight.
E Company 2nd Rangers – Sandown, Isle of Wight.
F Company 2nd Rangers – Botley, Hampshire.
Medical Detachment 2nd Rangers – Sandown, Isle of Wight.
Headquarters Company 2nd Rangers – Sandown, Isle of Wight.
Arrived at Sandown, Isle of Wight at 1300hrs by truck.

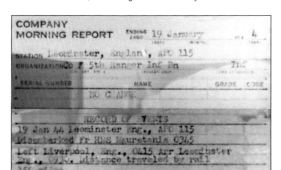
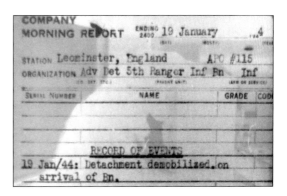

20 January 1944

5th Rangers – Companies A – F, Medical and HQ – Leominster, England.
A Company 2nd Rangers – Folkestone, Kent.
T/5 Donald F. Mentzer and T/4 Otto C. Bayer were attached for Duty with A Company from Headquarters Company. Usual Camp Duties.
B Company 2nd Rangers – Shanklin, Isle of Wight.
C Company 2nd Rangers – Sandown, Isle of Wight.
Record of events. Arrived in Sandown, Isle of Wight at 0900.
D Company 2nd Rangers – Freshwater, Isle of Wight.
E Company 2nd Rangers – Sandown, Isle of Wight.
F Company 2nd Rangers – Botley, Hampshire.
No change… Usual camp duties.
Medical Detachment 2nd Rangers – Sandown, Isle of Wight.
Elements of Headquarters Company 2nd Rangers – En route to new station.
2nd Lt. Frank C. Kennard went from Detached Service to Duty.

With the approach of D-Day, the British Government placed movement restrictions on travel, which were announced on 20 January 1944 – the changes were as follows:

> *At the request of the military authorities, the British Government has announced that, effective 1 April 1944, the restrictions are placed upon travel in certain areas, defined, in general as: An area from the coast inland for ten miles in counties of Norfolk, Suffolk, Essex, Kent, Sussex, Hampshire, Dorset, Devon and Cornwall.*
>
> *All personnel in the theatre under US military jurisdiction (including, but not limited to, Technical Observers and Representatives, accredited War Correspondents, and civilians who are members or employees of the American Red Cross, Lockheed Overseas Corporation, Army Transport Service and United Service Organisation) are prohibited from entering the areas referred to above, except on official business.*

While within the above-mentioned areas, all persons, other than those permanently stationed there, will carry with them, at all times, evidence that their presence there is in pursuance of their official duties. Such evidence will be displayed, upon demand, to proper US and British military and police authorities.

It will be the responsibility of the major subordinate commanders to ensure that their personnel, whether stationed inside or outside restricted areas, comply with the regulations laid down by the British authorities, and close co-operation with the British Regional Security Liaison Officers and local security personnel by appropriate echelons as directed. It will be borne in mind that the restrictions are placed for reasons of security, a matter with which the US forces are as vitally concerned as are the British authorities issuing the prohibitions.

The US Army issued the following order on the subject of Camouflage Nets:

a)   *The net, camouflage, twine, fabric garnished, is the authorised net for operational use in this theatre.*
b)   *The net, camouflage, cotton, shrimp, may be issued for training purposes.*

All field force units not authorised camouflage nets on current table of equipment are hereby authorised camouflage nets on the basis of one net per vehicle, crew served weapon. (calibre .30 machine gun with tripod, and larger). Such camouflage nets will be requisitioned through normal engineer supply channels, listing the vehicles, guns or liaison airplanes for which the nets are intended.

---

21 January 1944
5th Rangers – Companies A – F, Medical and HQ – Leominster, England.

Jack Burke, A Company: *In Leominster we did a lot of speed marches and working on our general conditioning – they were our main things. We also did field problems and drills etc. They were getting us in shape for Scotland.*

A Company 2nd Rangers – Folkestone, Kent.
Pfc. Paul W. French was attached to A Company from Headquarters Company.
Cpl. Gerome LeJall was attached to A Company from French Troop No.10 Commando.
B Company 2nd Rangers – Shanklin, Isle of Wight.
Pfc. Paniaha was recorded as being en route to Shanklin, Isle of Wight and then marked as being Absent Without Leave – AWOL.
0930 hours. Arrived in Shanklin, Isle of Wight 0930 hours.
C Company 2nd Rangers – Sandown, Isle of Wight.
D Company 2nd Rangers – Freshwater, Isle of Wight.
E Company 2nd Rangers – Sandown, Isle of Wight.
F Company 2nd Rangers – Botley, Hampshire.
Medical Detachment 2nd Rangers – Sandown, Isle of Wight.
Elements of Headquarters Company 2nd Rangers – Titchfield, Hampshire.

---

22 January 1944
5th Rangers – Companies A – F, Medical and HQ – Leominster, England.
A Company 2nd Rangers – Folkestone, Kent. No change.
B Company 2nd Rangers – Shanklin, Isle of Wight.
2nd Lt. Robert C. Fitzsimmons was assigned and joined this company from Headquarters Company this Battalion – as of 21 January 1944. The following five enlisted men were attached and joined for Duty from Headquarters Company of this Battalion as of 21 January 1944:
Pfc. Charles L. Davis, Pfc. George J. Frechette, Pvt. Sidney L. Isaacson, Pvt. George Lengyel, Pvt. Herbert. H. Adams.
Pfc. Paniaha was marked as returned from AWOL to Duty 1300 hours.
C Company 2nd Rangers – Sandown, Isle of Wight.
D Company 2nd Rangers – Freshwater, Isle of Wight.
E Company 2nd Rangers – Sandown, Isle of Wight.
F Company 2nd Rangers – Botley, Hampshire.
The following six enlisted men were sent on Detached Service to Folkestone, Kent:
Sgt. Otto, T/5 Roosa, Pfc. Gilhooly, Pfc. Kelly, Pfc. Taylor, Pfc. White.
Medical Detachment 2nd Rangers – Sandown, Isle of Wight.
Elements of Headquarters Company joined with Headquarters Company (Detachment)

Headquarters Company 2nd Rangers – Titchfield, Hampshire.
Captain George S. Willams returned from Detached Service and returned to Duty – and assumed command.
1st Lt. Frederick G. Wilkin transferred to HQ Company 2nd Battalion and was relieved of his role as HQ Co. Commander.

Every man in the US Army was taught how to clean, maintain and fight with a bayonet. With the exception of some specialists and officers, the bayonet was issued widely throughout the army and was to be the infantryman's weapon of choice in many combat situations. Which particular bayonet you were issued depended upon the rifle or carbine you carried, but the principles of use remained the same.

Training adopted the *esprit de corps* of bayonet use and suggested it was the way a real man went into battle. In period training films the emphasis on bayonet use was one of complete victory over your enemy. A confident man with a bayonet could conquer all before him, etc. and in period training manuals it was referred to as the 'spirit of the bayonet'.

The US Army described the use of the bayonet as follows: *The will to meet and destroy the enemy in hand-to-hand combat is the spirit of the bayonet. It springs from the fighter's confidence, courage, and grim determination, and is the result of vigorous training. Through training, the fighting instinct of the individual soldier is developed to the highest point. The will to use the bayonet first appears in the trainee when he begins to handle it with familiarity, and increases as his confidence grows. The full development of his physical prowess and complete confidence in his weapon culminates in the final expression of the spirit of the bayonet – fierce and relentless destruction of the enemy. For the enemy, demoralizing fear of the bayonet is added to the destructive power of every bomb, shell, bullet, and grenade, which supports and precedes the bayonet attack.*

Dating back to training and usage during the First World War, the Army determined that the enemy could not always be removed from his position by bombing or shelling alone. There would come a point in any battle when the enemy had to be met face to face and the use of the bayonet was an effective method for that.

There were also other factors which would instigate the use of the bayonet. Night attacks where the random firing of weapons could endanger the soldier's own men – as well as missions where the necessity for quiet precluded the immediate use of a bullet. The bayonet also served as a backup weapon, if a rifle or carbine jammed in combat, or no ammunition was available.

Primarily seen as an offensive weapon, the bayonet was taught to be used without hesitation and in particular without any degree of '*fencing*' with the enemy. '*The delay of a fraction of a second may mean death.*'

---

23 January 1944
5th Rangers – Companies A – F, Medical and HQ – Leominster, England.

A Company 2nd Rangers – Folkestone, Kent.
The following six men were attached to A Company from F Company of the 2nd Battalion: Sgt. Leon. H. Otto, T/5 Robert G. Roosa, Pfc. Joseph C. Kelly, Pfc. Bonnie M. Taylor, Pfc. Alvin E. White, Pfc. John J. Gilhooly.
T/5 Gilbert N. Gleckl was attached for Duty with A Company from Headquarters Company.

B Company 2nd Rangers – Shanklin, Isle of Wight.

C Company 2nd Rangers – Sandown, Isle of Wight.
The following 5 enlisted men were attached from Headquarters Company 2nd Btn for Duty and rations. Pvt. Stanley E. Moak, Pvt. James E. Donahue, Pvt. Fred W. Plumlee, Pfc. James K. Robison, Pfc. Wayne D. Goad.
Pfc. Noyes returned to light Duty from the American Evac Hospital in Glasgow, Scotland.

D Company 2nd Rangers – Freshwater, Isle of Wight.

E Company 2nd Rangers – Sandown, Isle of Wight.

F Company 2nd Rangers – Botley, Hampshire.

Medical Detachment 2nd Rangers – Sandown, Isle of Wight.

Headquarters Company 2nd Rangers – Titchfield, Hampshire.

5th Btn's Jack Burke talking about Leominster:

Six of us lived upstairs over a vacant store across the street from a bank. The mess hall was in a vacant garage. I would spend my evening hours in a pub and we went to the Grape Vaults where the owner's wife sang all the songs and played the piano. Our officers stayed in a hotel in the centre of town.

Below: One of the regular posters titled 'BATTLE HINTS' – these were put up onto notice boards where the men could see them.

```
                        BATTLE HINTS

        When under air bombardment or heavy shelling undo the
   chin strap of your helmet. This may save you a broken neck
   if a big one happens to fall near you.
        When falling flat on the ground or in a foxhole during
   a bombardment raise yourself slightly and rest on your elbows
   and knees. Keep your chin and head off the ground. Failure
   to do this may result in serious head or internal injuries
   possibly death, should one fall close.
        If caught in the water during air bombardment or while
   ships are dropping depth charges, roll over and swim on your
   back. This will minimize the danger of serious injury from
   underwater explosions.
        Enemy-held territory may be full of booby-traps. Cur-
   iosity and souvenir-hunting have cost many lives unneces-
   sarily. Leave things alone and you'll be safer.
```

24 January 1944
5th Rangers – Companies A – F, Medical and HQ – Leominster, England.
A Company 2nd Rangers – Folkestone, Kent.
B Company 2nd Rangers – Shanklin, Isle of Wight.
C Company 2nd Rangers – Sandown, Isle of Wight.
D Company 2nd Rangers – Freshwater, Isle of Wight.
E Company 2nd Rangers – Sandown, Isle of Wight.
F Company 2nd Rangers – Botley, Hampshire.
Medical Detachment 2nd Rangers – Sandown, Isle of Wight.
Headquarters Company 2nd Rangers – Titchfield, Hampshire.

25 January 1944
5th Rangers – Companies A – F, Medical and HQ – Leominster, England.
A Company 2nd Rangers – Folkestone, Kent.

Maurice Prince: *The day rolled around that put an end to our training. Now our work was to be operational. Our mission had come down to the company and we were to be briefed and oriented. Our task, or our mission, was quite a simple one. All we had to do was land somewhere on the coast of France and pick up one prisoner; that was all. The raid was to be essentially reconnaissance, but we were to be prepared to fight if it was necessary to complete our job of bringing back the prisoner.*

Now that we knew what we were to do, all we needed was the planning and training to put this deal on ice. Our S-2 gathered up all the available data concerning the enemy situation, and we were thoroughly briefed on this subject. Most of our information was derived from the latest aerial photos, which were obtained for us daily by the air corps. We had special ground maps prepared for us which were very skilfully made up, so, that we had a fair picture of the terrain and of the enemy's defences in the sector we were to attack.

Being our mission was of amphibious nature, a great deal of coordination and timing had to be effected between the Royal Navy, which was to bring us to the coast of France, and ourselves. We did this by drawing up time schedules and setting up a system of signalling which coordinated our efforts. It was upon these factors, that we based our battle plans.

Our plan of operations, as worked out by the staff, was a rather simple one. We took certain things for granted and if these things weren't what we supposed them to be, we sort of had an alternative plan. The master plan ran along this line. The company was to split up into four groups, with each one having a definite mission. The first group was to be the one that actually nabbed the prisoner. Whenever they got one, our job was to be completed and no matter what the other three groups were doing, they were to stop and to return to a prearranged assembly area. The second group was to act as protection for the first one. They were supposed to be the ones to do the actual fighting if it were necessary, while the other group went after the prisoner. The third group was also to be a body guard for the first group. They were supposed to protect the flanks of the other groups by taking up a defensive position. While the last section had the task of defending the beach landing to keep the escape route open and to make certain enemy infiltrations didn't endanger the other groups. They were also responsible for signalling and other bits of information we were to bring with us concerning the enemy beach defences and also of the ocean tides.

There was also included in this master plan our co-ordination and timing with the Royal Navy. We had to be well versed in knowing about the administrative details, such as what we were to do in case we incurred casualties, and what we should do if perchance one of us was cut off and couldn't effect an escape. These and a million and one other minor details were taken care of in our planning.

The job was to be run off in the following manner: we were to have two LCAs (landing craft assault) carry the company. The boat carrying groups one and two were to be the first to touch down on the field with one man carrying a mine detector and another man equipped with a roll of white tape in the lead. To follow behind and in single file, were to come the two groups. They were to come to a path that ran parallel to the ocean, follow the path until it led into a road that ran perpendicular to this path, and which led into the community where a known garrison of enemy troops were stationed.

Meanwhile No.3 group was to come in right behind the other two groups, but instead of going up the main road – as the other section had supposed to have done, they were to cross it and take up a defensive position in this sector, covering this road junction and protecting the rear and flanks of the other groups. While No.4 group was to remain at the beach where they had originally landed and take up a defensive position; send out a couple of men to study the enemy's set up, and send out a couple of men to widen the tape path in the minefield. This was so as to facilitate matters in case there was a need for a hasty retreat. We wanted to make sure that more than one man at a time could get back through the mine field without getting blown up. How the first group was to capture the prisoner was left up to the leader's initiative and to the situation – which might present itself.

Now that all that had been taken care of, we had to do some training on this score. We studied all the available data we had on the enemy defences. We built a course on our grounds and made it as similar in terrain and appearance as was possible to that which we had seen in the aerial photos and ground maps. Many a daylight hour and evening were spent on this course. We got ourselves so well familiarized that each man could have gone through these dry runs blindfolded. Our timing meanwhile was being synchronized and our teamwork coordinated.

Besides our training on our built-up course, we had to undergo more training in conjunction with the Royal Navy. Although we were considered experts in the field of amphibious work, we still needed the practice. Also, our operation called for something a bit different than that what we had gone through previously. In the past, we had worked with LCAs and L.C.I.s that made the run into the beaches directly, but now we were to operate with a mother ship. We had to sail out into the channel on this ship and to transfer to our assault crafts from this boat, then, we were to make the run onto the shore. That transferring at sea business was the part that was a bit different to us.

Added to this training, we got special instructions from the Commandos in enemy mines and booby traps. We learned their nomenclature and we were taught how to neutralise them. We were shown how to safe them under various combat conditions and we were versed in the art of avoiding wires and booby traps. Very ticklish and nerve-racking studies.

B Company 2nd Rangers – Shanklin, Isle of Wight.
C Company 2nd Rangers – Sandown, Isle of Wight.
D Company 2nd Rangers – Freshwater, Isle of Wight.
E Company 2nd Rangers – Sandown, Isle of Wight.
F Company 2nd Rangers – Botley, Hampshire.
Medical Detachment 2nd Rangers – Sandown, Isle of Wight.
Headquarters Company 2nd Rangers – Titchfield, Hampshire.

Mines and booby traps were a problem the Rangers were expected to come across on a regular basis. There were varying types used by German forces and the men had to train with them all – Land Mines, Anti-Tank Mines, Anti-Personnel Mines, etc.

26 January 1944

5th Rangers – Companies A – F, Medical and HQ – Leominster, England.

A Company 2nd Rangers – Folkestone, Kent.

B Company 2nd Rangers – Shanklin, Isle of Wight.

C Company 2nd Rangers – Sandown, Isle of Wight.

D Company 2nd Rangers – Freshwater, Isle of Wight.

E Company 2nd Rangers – Sandown, Isle of Wight.

F Company 2nd Rangers – Botley, Hampshire.

Medical Detachment 2nd Rangers – Sandown, Isle of Wight.

Headquarters Company 2nd Rangers – Titchfield, Hampshire.

Jack Burke: *I was in a Leominster pub when Red O'Hare told me the latrine was outside. 'Just go out, turn left, kick the wall, and take a leak'... I did what he said and the next thing I knew a flash light was shining in my face and the Boston accent demanding my name. I said 'for God sake O'Hare turn off the light'. The guy holding the light said 'I'll show you who O'Hare is' – it was Major Sullivan. It was lights out for me. The next day I had to report to Major Sullivan. I said 'Corporal Burke reporting sir' ... he said 'you were Corporal. Now you are a Private.' ... After that we went to Scotland for commando training and when we completed it, Major Sullivan gave me my stripes back. The Major was one great guy!*

---

27 January 1944

5th Rangers – Companies A – F, Medical and HQ – Leominster, England.

A Company 2nd Rangers – Folkestone, Kent.

B Company 2nd Rangers – Shanklin, Isle of Wight.

C Company 2nd Rangers – Sandown, Isle of Wight.

D Company 2nd Rangers – Freshwater, Isle of Wight.

E Company 2nd Rangers – Sandown, Isle of Wight.

F Company 2nd Rangers – Botley, Hampshire.

Medical Detachment 2nd Rangers – Sandown, Isle of Wight.

Headquarters Company 2nd Rangers – Titchfield, Hampshire.

---

28 January 1944

5th Rangers – Companies A – F, Medical and HQ – Leominster, England.

A Company 2nd Rangers – Folkestone, Kent.

Pfc. Bonnie M. Taylor went from being sick in Hospital to arrest in his quarters.

Maurice Prince: *Our raid was to be pulled off at night, so we underwent night firing problems, night compass courses and other night exercises. We'd been made proficient at this kind of work. We all realized and knew that this was it. We wanted to make sure that we'd put on a good show, so we toiled hard and long putting our best into our dry runs.*

All the while our morale and spirits were never better. I never saw such a happy and carefree bunch of guys in all my days. More playful and babyish than a hatful of kittens. About the place we had lots of small firing devices which were used to set off charges. They were harmless gadgets, but when set off, made a loud bang. Well, to make a long story short, you couldn't touch anything or take an unwary step, as these do-dads were planted all over the place. Many a grey hair was added to our heads because of the pranking of some of the boys.

We underwent a couple of dry runs off the coast of Dover with our mother ship and LCAs. We functioned smoothly and performed our jobs without mishaps. It was an experience to be operating in these waters, as this part of the channel was an integral part of no-man's-land.

While we were undergoing these runs, off Dover, we got the opportunity to view for ourselves the famed chalk cliffs of this city. We also saw at close range the damage wrought by the German Luftwaffe during the hectic days of the Blighty. Although a great deal of the ruined structures had been repaired, too many scars and bare places existed to escape our attention.

A couple days before the date set for the raid, we had to go through our paces before an inspecting general and his staff. It seems as though we needed the approval and permission of these high officials before we would be allowed to participate in the assault of the German-held coast.

It was a cold, crisp, and starry night when we reached our starting point. We were now on alien terrain as they wanted to see how we could operate in an area that wasn't familiar to us. Our task was to be similar to that of our coming raid, so that all in all it was a fair trial.

We went through our paces in a manner which gained us the wanted permission, besides winning the plaudits and the praises of the general. He was well pleased with our showing and he wasn't the least backwards in his fine opinion of us. We were proud and happy Rangers that evening.

The problem hadn't taken long to run so that it was a fairly early in the night. The skies were clear and the light given off by the stars radiated the area, making it an ideal night for an air raid; and an air raid is what we did get. We were just about organized and prepared to move back to our awaiting vehicles when the heavy drone of bombers was heard. Inquisitive searchlights turned the skies into day. The planes were immediately identified as enemy and all hell broke loose. Ack-Ack and machine gun tracers filled the air, putting on as brilliant a display of fireworks I've ever seen. We could distinctly ascertain a direct hit on one of the bombers and we could see it burst into flames and watch this flaming pyre twisting and spiralling earthward. We could feel the earth shake under us as the bombs released by the Heinies hit the ground, the large flashes which arose told us that incendiaries were being used.

Being in the midst of an open field we felt fairly safe and immune from the danger of being bombed, as no enemy objective or target was anywhere nearby. We casually watched the ensuing battle as interested spectators at some sporting event. Another huge flash, plus more flames told the story of another plane lost to the Heinies. The searchlight continued to form weird patterns as they criss-crossed and searched the skies. Ack-Ack and machine gun fire were increasing in crescendo. Falling pieces of shrapnel made us seek cover. More incendiary bombs were dropped and we could see the bonfires arising from this sort of bombing. This was an unforgettable experience for us. Although we had undergone air raid warnings and had gazed at the Luftwaffe aircraft as it passed over our heads, this was our first taste of actual aerial warfare.

The scope of the battlefield was immense, as at one time the flak and tracer fire would seem to our front, then this would cease and now the firing could be seen in the skies to our rear, then to our left, and then to our right. No matter how or where we turned, the battle seemed to be raging.

The best part of this show came when the beams of two criss-crossing searchlights caught an enemy plane in its midst. We could so plainly see the Heiny plane doing its fantastic dance of death. The pilot was using all his ability and manouevering skill to escape from this trap, but was unsuccessful. The work on the part of the batteries operating the giant rays were brilliant, they never once lost track of the Jerry with all its diving, climbing, rolling, and twisting. This looked so unreal like being home at a vaudeville show watching the star actor going through his paces as the spotlight accents his every movement. I felt a same thrill as I did when viewing that actor.

We were all waiting to see the flashes of the Ack-Ack and ground machine gun fire blast this plane from the sky. But we were to be rudely shaken from our trances, as from out of the dark skies above the light beams came the clear traces and flashes of machine gun fire from the wings of an English night fighter which shattered the large bomber into nothingness. Before the plane fell to earth we could see the enemy crew bailing out in the far distance. The heavy rumbling sound and the quaking of the earth about us gave evidence that the pilot had ridden the plane of its bombs, which had fallen into an empty field in our near vicinity. The paratroopers were falling away from our positions, so that there was nothing we could do about them. I'm certain that other persons took good care of them.

The entire air raid hadn't taken long and it ended as quickly as it had begun. We boarded our respective trucks and returned to B.B. House where we turned in to get a good night's sleep, which we had well earned for ourselves.

B Company 2nd Rangers – Shanklin, Isle of Wight.
The following two men were reduced to the grade of Private as of 15 January 1944: T/Sgt. Kobylinski, S/Sgt. Dolinsky.
Cpl. Thomas was appointed Sgt. as of 25 January 1944.
Pfc. DeCapp was appointed Cpl. as of 25 January 1944.
Pfc. Henwood was appointed T/5 as of 25 January.
C Company 2nd Rangers – Sandown, Isle of Wight.
D Company 2nd Rangers – Freshwater, Isle of Wight.
No change… Prepared for movement to new station.
E Company 2nd Rangers – Sandown, Isle of Wight
F Company 2nd Rangers – Botley, Hampshire.
Pfc. McMullin went from Duty to Detached Service to the American School Centre, Shrivenham.
Medical Detachment 2nd Rangers – Sandown, Isle of Wight.
Headquarters Company 2nd Rangers – Titchfield, Hampshire.

_____

29 January 1944

5th Rangers – Companies A – F, Medical and HQ – Leominster, England.
A Company 2nd Rangers – Folkestone, Kent.
Sgt. Francis J. Roach was attached to A Company from Headquarters Company and appointed S/Sgt as of 25 January 1944.
B Company 2nd Rangers – Shanklin, Isle of Wight.
2nd Lt. Robert C. Fitzsimmons was attached and joined this company from Headquarters Company 2nd Btn as of 21 January 1944.
C Company 2nd Rangers – Sandown, Isle of Wight.
D Company 2nd Rangers – Shanklin, Isle of Wight.
No change. Company entrained at 0900 hours for new station. Arrived at Shanklin, Isle of Wight at 1100 hours.

E Company 2nd Rangers – Sandown, Isle of Wight.
F Company 2nd Rangers – Botley, Hampshire.
Medical Detachment 2nd Rangers – Sandown, Isle of Wight.
Headquarters Company 2nd Rangers – Titchfield, Hampshire.

Maurice Prince: *The next day's account of the air raid said that of an approximate fifty planes, sixteen had been lost to the enemy with no losses to us. Damage had been light due to the ineffectiveness of the bombing and due a great deal to the skills of the men operating the air defences of England. They really had given a good exhibition and had gotten a good toll for their work. It is no wonder that England managed to best the Luftwaffe in the great German aerial offensive of 1941.*

---

30 January 1944
5th Rangers – Companies A – F, Medical and HQ – Leominster, England.
A Company 2nd Rangers – Folkestone, Kent.
T/5 Gilbert N. Gleckl was returned to his position in Headquarters Company.
B Company 2nd Rangers – Shanklin, Isle of Wight.
1st Lt. Brice returned to Duty from Detached Service, School, London.
C Company 2nd Rangers – Sandown, Isle of Wight.
Sgt. William Lindsay went from Duty to Detached Service to the American School Centre, Shrivenham, England.
D Company 2nd Rangers – Shanklin, Isle of Wight.
E Company 2nd Rangers – Sandown, Isle of Wight.
F Company 2nd Rangers – Botley, Hampshire. Usual camp duties.
Medical Detachment 2nd Rangers – Sandown, Isle of Wight.
Headquarters Company 2nd Rangers – Titchfield, Hampshire.

---

31 January 1944
5th Rangers – Companies A – F, Medical and HQ – Leominster, England.
Privates Gabaree and Pavey were both appointed to the rank of Pfc.
A Company 2nd Rangers – Folkestone, Kent.
T/5 Gilbert N. Gleckl was returned to his position in Headquarters Company.
B Company 2nd Rangers – Shanklin, Isle of Wight.
C Company 2nd Rangers – Sandown, Isle of Wight.
D Company 2nd Rangers – Shanklin, Isle of Wight.
E Company 2nd Rangers – Sandown, Isle of Wight.
F Company 2nd Rangers – Botley, Hampshire.
Medical Detachment 2nd Rangers – Sandown, Isle of Wight.

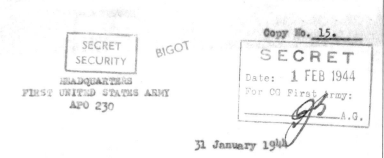

Copy No. 15.

SECRET
SECURITY

BIGOT

SECRET

Date: 1 FEB 1944

For CG First Army:

_____A.G.

HEADQUARTERS
FIRST UNITED STATES ARMY
APO 230

31 January 1944

SUBJECT: Planning Directive for OVERLORD.

TO   : CG, V Corps.
         CG, VII Corps.
         CG, 1st Inf Div.
         CG, 4th Inf. Div.
         CG, 29th Inf. Div.
         CG, 101st Airborne Div.

1. General.

        For detailed schedule of Planning see par. 5 below. Corps and
Divisions indicated above will initiate preliminary planning without delay.
Information requested in par. 6, will be forwarded so as to reach Hq, First
U.S. Army (London Planning Group) by 10 February 1944.

2. General Army Plan for OVERLORD.

        (For Enemy information see G-2 Annex 1 and 4 attached).

        The First Army will assault Beach 46 and Beach 49 (see overlay)
simultaneously on D Day and capture CHERBURG with the least possible delay.
The British 2nd Army will attack on the left of the First Army as indicated
on overlay. For the initial assault the 1st Infantry Division with 2 CTs
in the assault will capture Beach 46, and the 4th Infantry Division attacking
in columns of CTs will capture Beach 49. The 101st Air Borne Division will
assist the attack on Beach 49 as indicated on overlay. Successive objectives
for Corps and Divisions are as indicated on overlay. One follow-up Division
(29th Inf Div) in craft will reinforce Beach 46 at the completion of unloading of Assault Division. Two additional Divisions (the 28th Inf Div and
one Division from Third Army) will sail from the Bristol Channel, (The 28th
Division for Beach 46 and other division for Beach 49), so as to arrive on
far shore on D $\neq$ 1 and D $\neq$ 2. A shuttle service (LST's, LCT's and MT ships)
will ferry units from Southampton and Portland to the far shore. These units
will begin to arrive on far shore on 2nd tide of D $\neq$ 2. Expected order of
arrival on Beach 46 is: 2nd Armored Division, 30th Infantry Division and 3rd
Armored Division by D $\neq$ 8 (this will make a total of four (4) Infantry and
two (2) Armored Divisions on Beach 46). On Beach 49 the 9th Infantry Division
should arrive by D $\neq$ 4 (this will make a total of three (3) Infantry and one
(1) Air Borne Division). The 82nd Air Borne Division may be dropped north of
LA HAYE DU PUITS on D $\neq$ 1.

SECRET
SECURITY

- 1 -

BIGOT

This document, with the highest security rating BIGOT stamp, gives details of the general army plan for Operation
Overlord.

Chapter 5

February 1944 – Planning for D-Day

---

1 February 1944
5th Rangers – Companies A – F, Medical and HQ –
Leominster, England

Jack Burke: *We loved the British pubs. We really enjoyed them, as they gave us the opportunity to meet the locals and have pleasant conversations whilst drinking beer – followed by fish and chips. It was very relaxing and we would sing songs, etc. We also converted all our dollars at the British bank for pounds and shillings.*

For training we wore our field fatigues, a cartridge belt, skin packs, helmets and carried our rifles. We suffered in training with many blisters on our feet from the speed marches to places like Abergavenny, but we recovered quickly as we were young and strong. We were also given a lot of field problems, we worked on general conditioning and drills on a daily basis.

2nd Battalion Narrative History

```
     During the period 1-10 February, all Companies remained
in location and continued training.  Companies B/C/E rehear-
sed but were unable to carry out,  a  three-company exercise
against the IOW Home Guard.  Battalion  Staff Officers,  dur-
ing the period 2-4 February,  interviewed prospective Ranger
applicants from the 28th Division under  authority contained
in Ltr, Hq-FUSA,  27 Jan 44,  file 200.3/39 (AGCL);  Subject:
"Overstrength Fillers for 2nd Ranger Battalion".
```

A Company 2nd Rangers – Folkestone, Kent.
The following six men were all returned to their original units:
T/Sgt Edward Gurney, Sgt. Leon H. Otto, T/5 Robert C. Roosa, Pfc. Joseph C. Kelly, Pfc. Alvin E. White, Pfc. John J. Gilhooly.
B Company 2nd Rangers – Shanklin, Isle of Wight.
C Company 2nd Rangers – Sandown, Isle of Wight.
D Company 2nd Rangers – Shanklin, Isle of Wight.
E Company 2nd Rangers – Sandown, Isle of Wight.
F Company 2nd Rangers – Botley, Hampshire.
The following men returned to Duty with F Company from Detached Service in Folkestone, Kent: Sgt. Leon H. Otto, T/5 Robert C. Roosa, Pfc. Joseph C. Kelly, Pfc. Alvin E. White, Pfc. John J. Gilhooly.
Medical Detachment 2nd Rangers – Sandown, Isle of Wight.
Captain Block went from Detached Service to Duty.
Elements of Headquarters Company 2nd Rangers – Bude, Cornwall and Titchfield, Hampshire.

The US Army 'GENERAL PLANS' were issued on 1 February 1944

1. *The purpose of this Initial Joint Plan is to provide a basis for planning by subordinate commanders. Modifications may be found necessary in the course of planning, but no major alterations will be made without reference to the Joint Commanders-in-Chief. A serial of detailed instructions on various aspects of the operation will be issued in due course.*

2. *The object of 'Neptune' is to secure a lodgment on the Continent from which further offensive operations can be developed. It is not an isolated operation, but is part of a large strategic plan designed to bring about the total defeat of Germany by means of heavy and concerted assaults upon German occupied Europe from the United Kingdom, the Mediterranean, and Russia.*

Target Date: The target date for the operation in respect of which all preparations will be completed is 31 May.

H-Hour: H-Hour, which is defined as the time at which the first wave of landing craft should hit the beach, will be about 1½ hours after nautical twilight, and approximately 3 hours before high water, so as to allow a minimum period of thirty minutes daylight for observed bombardment before H-Hour and to enable the maximum number of vehicles to be landed on the first tide. Should the operation be postponed from D-Day, the time of H-Hour on successive days may be extended to about 2½ hours after nautical twilight.

Bombardment of Coast Artillery Batteries and Beach defences: Coast artillery and field batteries will be engaged by Naval and Air action, starting before H-Hour. A Joint Plan is under preparation and will be issued later.

The assault will be immediately preceded by pre-arranged Naval and Air bombardment of selected points in beach defences. Close support will be provided at call by Naval and Air Forces. Detailed instructions concerning these forms of co-operation and spotting for Naval gunfire, will be issued later.

RANGERS AND COMMANDOS: In the 'Neptune' area Rangers and Commandos will make landings approximately simultaneously with the main assault. Their action will be co-ordinated with the Fire Support Plan.

THE MAIN ASSAULT The object will be to capture the towns of St. Mere-Eglise 3495, Carentan 3984, Isigny 5085, Bayeux 7879 and Caen 0368 by the evening of D-Day.

EMBARKATION FACILITIES: The United States formation and Ninth United States Air Force, will move through Southampton and Portland sectors and the South West.

POSTPONEMENT ARRANGEMENTS
a) *Postponement of D-Day may be from day to day up to two days in each suitable tidal and lunar period, or for up to twenty-eight days between suitable tidal and lunar periods.*
b) *For day to day postponement troops will remain on board LSI/APA and LST. Troops in LCT and LCI secured alongside may be disembarked into adjacent accommodation. Troops in LCI not secured alongside may also be disembarked, if conditions permit, but those in certain LCT not alongside, will not be disembarked.*
c) *For the longer type of postponement, i.e. to the next suitable period troops will be disembarked and will return to Marshalling Areas, vehicles remaining embarked.*

OUTLINE ASSAULT PLAN
Armies in conjunction with their associated Naval and Air Forces and after consultation with subordinate Commanders if required, will submit an Outline Assault Plan to the Joint Commanders-in-Chief by 15 February showing:
a) *Brigade or regimental combat team frontages and objectives: Ranger, Commando and Airborne tasks.*
b) *Provisional list of breach defence targets for pre-arranged Naval and Air fire support, and approximate timings in relation to H-Hour.*
c) *Approximate numbers of men and vehicles to be landed on each brigade, or regimental combat team beach on each of the first four tides; and the numbers and types of landing ships and craft involved in each case.*
d) *Tentative list, by types of units, showing the number of men and vehicles allocated to the initial list of landing ships and craft.*

LANDING TABLES
Landing Tables, by beaches and embarkation sectors, will be prepared by Armies and associated Air forces in respect of the initial lift of landing ships and craft, and of the pre-loaded shipping lift, and will be forwarded to Headquarters 21st Army Group by 7 April for transmission to War Office/ETOUSA.

REHEARSALS
Rehearsals as distinct from Combined Exercises cannot take place until detailed Landing Tables have been worked out. This will not be before the end of March. The month of May will be required by the Navy for passage to Assembly Areas and servicing craft, and by the Army for concentration and waterproofing.

Owing to moves of Naval Assault Forces it appears that the only areas in which rehearsals with firing can take place during the month of April are Slapton Sands (for First United States Army) and Studland Bay (for Second British Army), except for the early part of the month when training can be continued in the Scottish Area.

The significant town to be captured by the Rangers in these orders was Isigny to the south west of Omaha Beach.

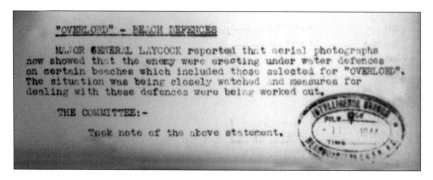

The coastline was divided up and photographed section by section.

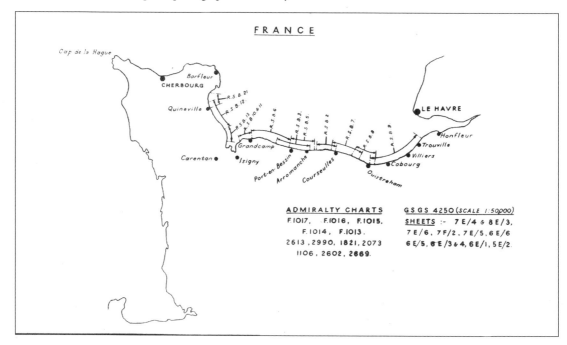

Once again the area between Grandcamp-les-Bains and Maisy was photographed from *'zero feet and at right angles to the coast: distance to shore about ¾ of a mile.'*

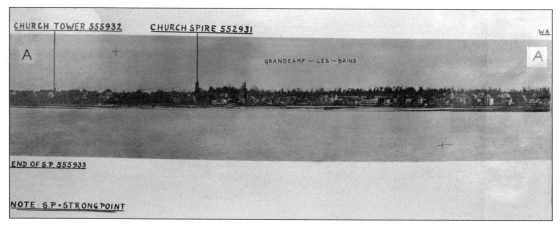

WATER TOWER 546929

ENTRANCE
TO PORT

GRANDCAMP – LES – BAINS

NOTE : S.P. = STRONGPOINT

541934   LARGE S.P.   537935

CHURCH TOWER 555932   CHURCH SPIRE 552931

GRANDCAMP — LES — BAINS

END OF S.P. 555933   NOTE : S.P. = STRONGPOINT

GRANDCAMP LES BAINS

As well as harbour photographs of Grandcamp-les-Bains, an engineer's illustration was produced, one assumes to discuss the feasibility of capturing it for use as an operational landing port.

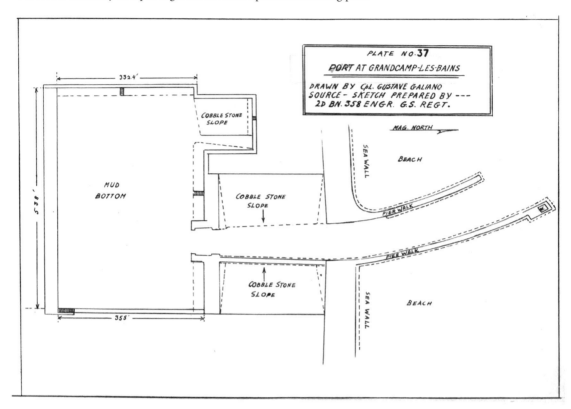

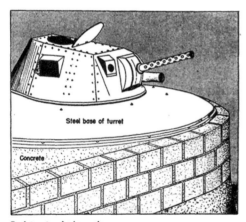

Tank turret on harbor mole.

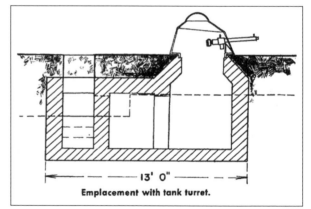

Emplacement with tank turret.

Line drawings were also produced to indicate the type of machine gun position on the quayside.

2 February 1944

5th Rangers – Companies A – F, Medical and HQ – Leominster, England.

A Company 2nd Rangers – Folkestone, Kent.

B Company 2nd Rangers – Shanklin, Isle of Wight.

C Company 2nd Rangers – Sandown, Isle of Wight.
1st Lt. Saloman returned to Duty from Detached Service in London.

D Company 2nd Rangers – Shanklin, Isle of Wight.

E Company 2nd Rangers – Sandown, Isle of Wight.
1st Lt. Majane returned to Duty from Detached Service in Folkestone, Kent.

F Company 2nd Rangers – Botley, Hampshire.

Medical Detachment 2nd Rangers – Sandown, Isle of Wight.

Elements of Headquarters Company 2nd Rangers – Bude, Cornwall and Titchfield, Hampshire.

A US Army report stated the following: *In February 1944, corps commanders were brought to London, briefed on the 'Neptune' plan and instructed to prepare detailed plans for their portions of the operation. After a certain amount of preliminary work at their own stations, these corps commanders established small planning groups of their own in London – so that their plans would be drawn with the constant opportunity of adjustment to fit details and adjustments of the First U.S. Army plan. The peculiar character of the operation i.e. assaults on separate beaches, separated by flooded areas in the neighbourhood of Carentan, and the fact that First Army Headquarters would in the initial stages not be able to bring much influence to bear upon the operation, placed a great deal of responsibility upon these corps commanders.*

They were accordingly given a great deal of independence in their planning: *Troops which would follow the assault waves onto the beaches, were to be phased so far as practicable according to priorities desired by those corps commanders. Each corps therefore prepared a priority build-up list. At first these lists were prepared for the units designated to go in with the assault force on the first four tides, and other units according to the days following D-Day.*

Lieutenant Colonel Trevor was attached to the Rangers from the British Army. He describes the discussions being held about the Pointe du Hoc battery assault. [This was written Post D-Day but it is still relevant here. The report is shown in full in its original form in the Conclusion – Volume II].

ASSAULT ON POINTE DU HOE BATTERY

The Battery dominated the OMAHA and UTAH beaches and shipping. It was essential, therefore, that the guns be destroyed at the earliest possible moment.

The outline plan at the time that I started to work on the project was to land the Rangers on OMAHA beach in the second wave, pass them through the forward troop and then for them to advance along the coast line for 4-5 miles and attack the Battery from the landward (South-East) side. This plan was identical with the plan used to attack the POINTE MATIFOU battery at ALGIERS. There it was demonstrated that even against light opposition it is impossible to reach and reduce the Battery quickly enough to prevent it engaging our shipping to considerable effect. The plan was, therefore, partially abandoned and a landing was sought nearer the objective.

The search for a nearer landing was complicated by the topography of the coast – which, Westward of OMAHA to POINTE DU HOE and on to GRANDCAMP, consists of 90-100ft high cliffs.

The second plan consisted of a landing at GRANDCAMP, some two miles to the East* of the Battery, and then attacking the Battery from the East. Here, however, there was a large artificial innundation which restricted the line of advance and forced the attack over open country up hill on ground dominated by prepared positions on commanding ground. A careful study of photographs convinced everyone that not only had the enemy foreseen this attack, but that he had made very elaborate preparations to meet it, and had prepared a 'killing ground'. The object of the inundation being solely to canalise the attackers' advance over this prepared ground. This plan was abandoned.

The right and left attacks having been ruled out, if the battery was to be quickly silenced, there remained only the centre which, as already mentioned, consisted of high vertical cliffs. A plan was produced to scale the cliffs to the East and West of the battery at selected places between the strong points, which were sited at regular intervals along the cliff top, and then attack the battery from the East and West by means of a pincer movement. This plan offered every prospect of success, if the assault could scale the cliffs under fire. However, when they had done so – no easy task – the defences of the battery still had to be reduced, and these in themselves were formidable.

A study of these defences showed that they all faced inland and that the enemy were relying for defence of the battery to seaward on the sheer cliffs. If the assault force had to climb the cliffs under fire it was obviously better to do so and get right into the objective without having to overcome any additional obstacles, rather than climb the cliffs and then have to deal with the prepared defences. An additional inducement was the vital importance of obtaining a quick decision, coupled with the economy of supporting fire which resulted from combining the supporting fire for the attack, with the neutralizing fire necessary to keep the battery silent during the approach. The final deciding factor was that it was a very bold conception and it is an old dictum that 'bold conception and cautious execution leads to quick and favourable decisions'. This plan was adopted.

[*Author: I think he meant to say "West" and not East].

---

3 February 1944

5th Rangers – Companies A – F, Medical and HQ – Leominster, England.

A Company 2nd Rangers – Folkestone, Kent.

T/5 Donald F. Mentzer was returned to his original unit.

B Company 2nd Rangers – Shanklin, Isle of Wight.

C Company 2nd Rangers – Sandown, Isle of Wight.

D Company 2nd Rangers – Shanklin, Isle of Wight.

Captain Slater went from Detached Service in Dartmouth, Devon to Duty as of 2 February 1944.

1st Lt. McBride went from Detached Service in Dartmouth, Devon to Duty as of 2 February 1944.

The following fourteen enlisted men went from Detached Service in Dartmouth, Devon to Duty as of 2 February 1944: 1st Sgt. Lomell, T/Sgt. Coxon (illegible), S/Sgt. Kuhn, S/Sgt. Stevens, S/Sgt. McCrone, S/Sgt. Johnson, S/Sgt. Miller, Sgt. Bernard Szewczuk, Sgt. Branley, T/5 Graham, T/5 Schneller, Pfc. Hoffman, Pfc. Fruhling, Pfc. D. Sparaco.

Lt. Baikie was relieved from attached and returned to C.G. #4 as of 1 February 1944.

The following five enlisted men were relieved from attached and returned to C.G. #4 as of 2 February 1944: Sgt. Frank Major, L/Cpl. John Wells, L/Cpl. Anthony Irving, Pvt. William McGonnigle, Pvt. Angus Meek.

Cfn Fred McMaster was relieved from attached and returned to HQ#1 SS Brigade as of 2nd February 1944.

E Company 2nd Rangers – Sandown, Isle of Wight.

F Company 2nd Rangers – Botley, Hampshire.

Medical Detachment 2nd Rangers – Sandown, Isle of Wight.

Headquarters Company 2nd Rangers – Titchfield, Hampshire.

---

4 February 1944

5th Rangers – Companies A – F, Medical and HQ – Leominster, England.

A Company 2nd Rangers – Folkestone, Kent.

B Company 2nd Rangers – Shanklin, Isle of Wight.

C Company 2nd Rangers – Sandown, Isle of Wight.

D Company 2nd Rangers – Shanklin, Isle of Wight.

E Company 2nd Rangers – Sandown, Isle of Wight.

F Company 2nd Rangers – Botley, Hampshire.

Medical Detachment 2nd Rangers – Sandown, Isle of Wight.

Headquarters Company 2nd Rangers – Titchfield, Hampshire.

The Army issued orders and restrictions about the Ownership and Use of Cameras.

Individual members of this command are authorised to possess a camera and to take photographs of subjects having no military significance. Such photographs will be restricted to scenery, buildings, individuals, or groups of individuals, provided that the photographs do not show recognisable landmarks, signs, or signposts which might indicate the location of identity of any United States or Allied military unit or organisation.

No photograph that reveals secret or classified United States or Allied Military information or that would aid the enemy will be taken by an individual in this command. It is difficult to define these prohibitions exactly, and often individual common sense will discern the restriction. The following points are to be noted especially:

No photograph will be taken of any piece of military equipment of a specialised or secret nature, such as guns, searchlights, tanks, fire control instruments, military aircraft, or new types of transportation.

No photograph which might give a clue to new tactical methods will be taken of any form of training.

No photograph will be taken of any aerodrome, seaplane station, fortification, or other defined works if the photograph might disclose the position of such works, or the method of constructing or concealing such works.

No photograph will be taken of any munitions factory, dockyard, harbour, shipbuilding, or naval vessel.

No photograph will be taken showing damage done to civilian or military buildings or installations by enemy air attack.

5 February 1944

5th Rangers – Companies A – F, Medical and HQ – Leominster, England.

A Company 2nd Rangers – Folkestone, Kent.
Captain Cleveland A. Lytle was sent from Duty to Special Duties.

Maurice Prince: *Before the scheduled day of the raid, our Captain returned to us. It was good seeing him back. It gave us added faith and confidence. He took over the company and found himself a role in the raid with no actual change being made in the original plan.*

The eventful day of the raid finally rolled around. A heavily clouded sky forewarned us of nasty and stormy weather conditions. We were all prepared and ready. Our morale and spirits were excellent and there wasn't the least sign of nervousness to be seen. We were all confident – and had all the faith in the world, in ourselves, and in our leaders. We were set to show the world that the American Rangers didn't believe in the Nazi myth of supermen and we were ready to prove that fact.

The skies still hung heavy when we prepared to board our vehicles, which were to take us to Dover. A last minute cancellation put an abrupt stop to that, so we stayed in and sweated it out till the morrow. Reports of turbulent conditions in the channel the following morning put a conclusive crimp in our operations in that body of water for the rest of the month. This marked a finish to our hopes of ever making the raid.

It was sort of a let down to us as we had planned and put our everything into the making of this assault. We had set our hearts and minds on making this attack and now it was all over, ended, and in no way our fault. Oh well, maybe it was for the better, we hadn't lost anything by our labours, in fact we had gained, we had benefitted from our contacts with the Commandos. Our friendship with these men never slackened, and in fact, were tightened now that we had more time and opportunity to go out together.

We received many commendations from the commander of B.B. House for our fine behaviour and sportsman-like spirit while we were there. So, although, we didn't do the job that time, fate saw that we weren't to be let down again.

We really went to town after this failure. Three day passes were issued, and daily passes were continually in effect. So, we went to town, drank bitters and ale, and danced away our troubles.

B Company 2nd Rangers – Shanklin, Isle of Wight.
C Company 2nd Rangers – Sandown, Isle of Wight.
D Company 2nd Rangers – Shanklin, Isle of Wight.
E Company 2nd Rangers – Sandown, Isle of Wight.
F Company 2nd Rangers – Botley, Hampshire.
Medical Detachment 2nd Rangers – Sandown, Isle of Wight.
Headquarters Company 2nd Rangers – Titchfield, Hampshire.

On 5 February a direction for the Establishment of Organisation of a Military Intelligence Course, American School Centre was issued from ETO Headquarters. It stated that the *object of the course is to raise the professional standard of student officers and enlisted men by providing instruction in combat intelligence, as it will be used in this theatre.*

By March 1944 it aimed to be giving students a four-week combat intelligence course for up to 105 students at a time.

The course was to include the following:

1) *Recognition of enemy uniforms, branches of service, ranks and grades.*
2) *Identification, tactical employment, capabilities and functioning of enemy weapons, particularly small arms, and how to use them to good advantage in the event of the U.S. troops' own equipment becoming lost or ammunition exhausted.*
3) *Familiarisation of enemy equipment, i.e. equipment other than weapons, so that the average soldier could evaluate his own equipment with that of the enemy.*
4) *Interpretation of minor tactics and organisation of the German Army Units.*

6 February 1944

5th Rangers – Companies A – F, Medical and HQ – Leominster, England.
A Company 2nd Rangers – Folkestone, Kent.
B Company 2nd Rangers – Shanklin, Isle of Wight.
C Company 2nd Rangers – Sandown, Isle of Wight.
D Company 2nd Rangers – Shanklin, Isle of Wight.
E Company 2nd Rangers – Sandown, Isle of Wight.
F Company 2nd Rangers – Botley, Hampshire.
Medical Detachment 2nd Rangers – Sandown, Isle of Wight.
Headquarters Company 2nd Rangers – Titchfield, Hampshire.

Taken on 6 February this series of low-level aerial reconnaissance photographs shows Omaha Beach. The intelligence services were trying to determine its profile.

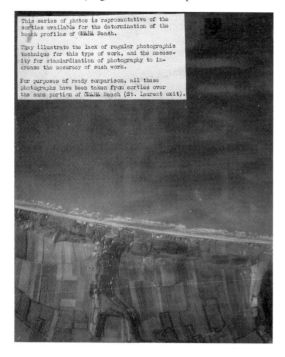

This series of photos is representative of the sorties available for the determination of the beach profiles of OMAHA Beach.

They illustrate the lack of regular photographic technique for this type of work, and the necessity for standardization of photography to increase the accuracy of such work.

For purposes of ready comparison, all these photographs have been taken from sorties over the same portion of OMAHA Beach (St. Laurent exit).

8.

Light reflection from surface of water, spoiling transparency, caused by high angle of sun at time of photography. Compare VT.

Tide 2½-6 feet water at base of sea wall

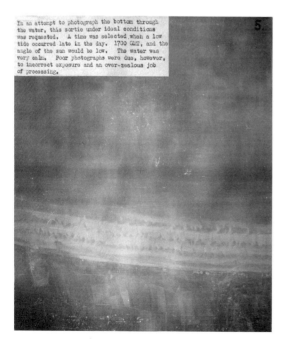

5.

In an attempt to photograph the bottom through the water, this sortie under ideal conditions was requested. A time was selected when a low tide occurred late in the day, 1700 GMT, and the angle of the sun would be low. The water was very calm. Poor photographs were due, however, to incorrect exposure and an over-zealous job of processing.

4.

Obstacles began to appear on this beach in April.

Port

Four distinct bars (here indicated by numbers) and four runnels (A, B, C and D) extend nearly the full length of OMAHA Beach.

Compare with VT. If the same conditions of photography as found in Photo No.1 could have been obtained at this low tide-level, the foreshore bottom would be revealed.

Within the Omaha Sector, each piece of coastline was also given a name relating to its 6-figure grid reference. These names were the same for the Army, Navy and Air Force personnel. Omaha area starts to the west of the Maisy Batteries and continues east to the breakwater at Port-en-Bessin.

TOP SECRET   2

OPERATION NEPTUNE—NAVAL ORDERS
(Short Title : ON)

ON 1.—General Outline of the Operation—*continued*

Appendix VIII.—Division of Enemy Coast into Sectors—*continued*

Annexe B.—Schedule of Sectors

Sector Letter.	Brief Description.	Co-ords.	Length (yards).
	OMAHA AREA (O)		
ABLE	Mouth of River VIRE to PTE DU MAISY	491878–527935	7600
BAKER	A to PTE DU HOE (PTE ST. PIERRE)	527935–587940	6500
CHARLIE	B to rd	587940–648917	8000
DOG	C to mouth of stream	648917–667907	2400
EASY	D to rd	667907–688897	2900
FOX	E to rd	688897–723886	3900
GEORGE	F to PORT EN BESSIN (West breakwater)	723886–751882	3200

The sectors then become part of a much bigger landing schedule with multiple beaches, and then each of those groups were then the responsibility of either the British or American forces.

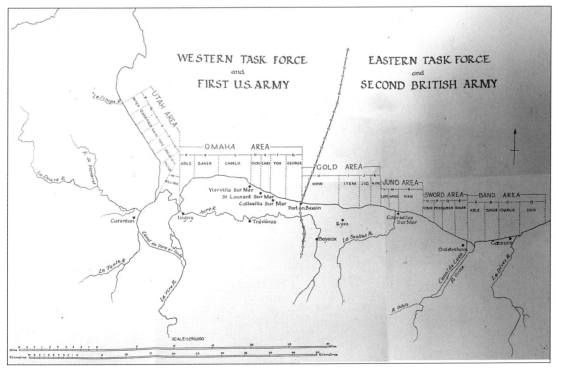

7 February 1944

5th Rangers – Companies A – F, Medical and HQ – Leominster, England.
A Company 2nd Rangers – Folkestone, Kent.
B Company 2nd Rangers – Shanklin, Isle of Wight.
C Company 2nd Rangers – Sandown, Isle of Wight.
D Company 2nd Rangers – Shanklin, Isle of Wight.
E Company 2nd Rangers – Sandown, Isle of Wight.
F Company 2nd Rangers – Botley, Hampshire.
Medical Detachment 2nd Rangers – Sandown, Isle of Wight.
Headquarters Company 2nd Rangers – Titchfield, Hampshire.

SECRET - SECURITY

HEADQUARTERS, V CORPS
APO 305, U. S. ARMY

7 February 1944.

SUBJECT: V Corps Amphibious Training Exercise "FOX".

TO   : The Commanding General, First United States Army, APO 230.

1. This letter is intended to rescind and to replace letter this subject, dated 21 January 1944, to permit more full compliance with the First US Army Planning Directive for OVERLORD, 31 January 1944. Reference is likewise made to letter 4 February 1944, "Amphibious Training Exercises", from Commanding General, FUSA, to Commanding General, V Corps.

2. General. In further preparation for the assault on the continent of Europe, it is desired to conduct an amphibious training exercise involving the V Corps, the Navy, and the Air Force. This exercise to be held on the SLAPTON SANDS Assault Training Area during the first half of March 1944, and to be known as Exercise "FOX".

3. Object. The object of Exercise "FOX" is to train the 1st and 29th Divisions for the forthcoming attack on the continent of Europe, using the troops scheduled to take part in the actual assault, together with the types of weapons and formations contemplated for the actual operations under as nearly real conditions as can be duplicated with the facilities available.

4. Scope. It will be a V Corps combined exercise involving the initial assault by the 1st Infantry Division (less 1 RCT) plus 1 RCT from the 29th Division with other troops attached, followed by the 29th Division (less 1 RCT) plus 1 RCT 1st Division with other troops attached, to seize and hold a beachhead and cover the landing of follow-up forces (assumed). It will involve the Air Force and the Navy in the performance of their normal functions as may be determined by proper authority. It is further desired that the exercise include the establishment and operation of a beach maintenance area of a size to fully develop the capabilities of the Far Shore Brigades and Naval Beach Parties, the extent of such operation,

- 1 -

SECRET - SECURITY

C O P Y

Planning documents for Operation Fox which was to involve the 1st Inf. Division.

beyond support of the landing of the combat forces, to be indicated by
the Commanding General, First US Army.

    5. <u>Troops</u>.

        a. Ground Forces.
        (1) V Corps troops consisting of the 1st and 29th Infantry
Divisions, reinforced by Corps and Army troops indicated in
Forces "O" and "B", First US Army Planning Directive for
OVERLORD, 31 January 1944, subject to availability of lift.

        b. Air Force. Such air support and air force landing personnel
as may be designated by competent authority.

        c. S.O.S. Such S.O.S. forces and facilities as may be required.

        d. U. S. and/or Royal Navy. Such U. S. and/or Royal Navy per-
sonnel and facilities as may be designated by competent authority.

    6. <u>Areas</u>.

        a. Concentration and Embarkation. Concentration and Embarkation
to be in areas to be used for mounting Forces "O" and "B" for the forthcoming overseas operations.

        b. Assault. The entire SLAPTON SANDS Assault Training Area will
be utilized. Live ammunition of all sizes will be used subject to availability of weapons and safety restrictions. (Steps are already being
taken to provide the necessary exits across Higher and Lower Leys to
accommodate the numbers of troops and equipment involved in an operation
of this magnitude.)

        7. <u>Target Date</u>. a. The target date for this exercise is the first half
of March 1944. The exact date of touchdown will be determined as the planning
progresses, but the present thought is that the participating troops should
be out of the area by 15 March.

        b. Because of the limited time available for the planning and con-
duct of this exercise without detriment to the actual operations, the V Corps
is proceeding with the preparations of plans for this exercise as outlined
herein.

    8. <u>Approvals and Assistance Desired</u>.

        a. It is requested that Exercise "FOX" be approved as herein in-
dicated, and that the following essential action be taken by the First U. S.
Army to facilitate the conduct of the exercise:

        (1) Designate the Engineer Special Brigades who will participate.

        (2) Obtain the necessary authority and directives for Air

- 2 -

Force participation, with especial reference to air support prior to and during the assault (See Par. 5 b).

      (3) Obtain the necessary authority and directives for the SOS to perform the services required to supply and mount this exercise.

      (4) Take the necessary action to obtain Naval participation up to the limit of available lift.

      (5) Obtain authority for the use of the hards and docks to be used in the embarkation of Forces "O" and "B" in Operation "OVERLORD".

      (6) Designate to V Corps those Army and G.H.Q. units listed in Forces "O" and "B" which will be available for participation.

      (7) Indicate to V Corps those agencies with whom direct contact is authorized. (At present, direct contact is limited to Admiral HALL and his Staff.) Direct contact with the participating agencies on Corps level is essential.

   9. For your information, it is necessary to commence the assembly of the participating troops on or about 1 March if the exercise is to be conducted in the time allocated; viz., the first half of March. Much preparatory work is necessary before that time, particularly by the SOS, for which reason it is necessary that V Corps know very early the action of the First United States Army on the points raised in paragraph 8 above.

L. T. GEROW,
Major General, U. S. Army,
Commanding.

8 February 1944
5th Rangers – Companies A – F, Medical and HQ – Leominster, England.
A Company 2nd Rangers – Folkestone, Kent.
B Company 2nd Rangers – Shanklin, Isle of Wight.
C Company 2nd Rangers – Sandown, Isle of Wight.
D Company 2nd Rangers – Shanklin, Isle of Wight.
E Company 2nd Rangers – Sandown, Isle of Wight.
F Company 2nd Rangers – Botley, Hampshire.
Medical Detachment 2nd Rangers – Sandown, Isle of Wight.
Headquarters Company 2nd Rangers – Titchfield, Hampshire.

9 February 1944

5th Rangers – Companies A – F, Medical and HQ – Leominster, England.

A Company 2nd Rangers – Folkestone, Kent.

B Company 2nd Rangers – Shanklin, Isle of Wight.

C Company 2nd Rangers – Sandown, Isle of Wight.

D Company 2nd Rangers – Shanklin, Isle of Wight.

E Company 2nd Rangers – Sandown, Isle of Wight.

F Company 2nd Rangers – Botley, Hampshire.

Medical Detachment 2nd Rangers – Sandown, Isle of Wight.

Headquarters Company 2nd Rangers – Titchfield, Hampshire.

9 February a letter from Admiral Kirk giving more details of the Slapton Sands Training Exercise.

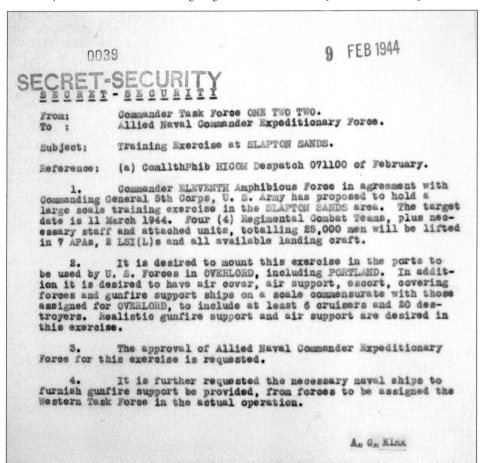

Regular studies were made of the German tactics and once provided to HQ of each command, these were to be discussed with the men. One such report released in February talked about the German deployment of Artillery:

> *Artillery in the defense is organized the same way as in the attack. The only difference in dispositions is that the direct support weapons (light howitzers) are located slightly farther to the rear, and the general support guns (medium howitzers) are in a central location where they can interdict at long ranges to force an early deployment of approaching enemy formations.*

CO-OPERATION WITH INFANTRY

Time and space must be carefully coordinated by both the infantry and the artillery. It is essential that the artillery observers be at all times alert, not only to locate targets and hostile forces but, to follow closely the movements of friendly troops, particularly the infantry. To facilitate this close contact, it devolves upon the infantry to seize and hold terrain which offers excellent observation for the artillery. Communication is effectively maintained. Close contact between infantry and artillery officers is absolutely essential. The division commander indicates, as promptly as possible, the plan of manoeuver to the artillery commander – so as to permit the latter the maximum freedom in planning the role for the artillery.

In the advance the artillery renders immediate support to the infantry when contact with the enemy is gained. This is accomplished by the artillery observers, who accompany the foremost infantry elements, or observe from balloon or airplane. In the attack the artillery must neutralize the hostile resistance and open the way for the advance of the infantry. Rapid reconnaissance and prompt deployment for action contribute to the success of this mission. It is generally advantageous for the infantry to wait for the support of the artillery. It is also important for the infantry to understand the limitations and capabilities of the artillery.

---

10 February 1944
5th Rangers – Companies A – F, Medical and HQ – Leominster, England.
A Company 2nd Rangers – Folkestone, Kent.
B Company 2nd Rangers – Shanklin, Isle of Wight.
1st Lt. Smudin went from Duty to Detached Service, School, London.
C Company 2nd Rangers – Sandown, Isle of Wight.
D Company 2nd Rangers – Shanklin, Isle of Wight.
E Company 2nd Rangers – Sandown, Isle of Wight.
F Company 2nd Rangers – Botley, Hampshire.
Medical Detachment 2nd Rangers – Sandown, Isle of Wight.
Headquarters Company 2nd Rangers – Titchfield, Hampshire.

A series of photographs were produced and dated 10 February looking at underwater detail and the sea bottom on the Omaha Beach approaches. The area of Omaha Sector covered is illustrated on the first diagram.

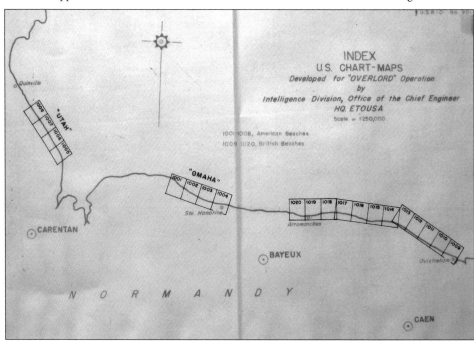

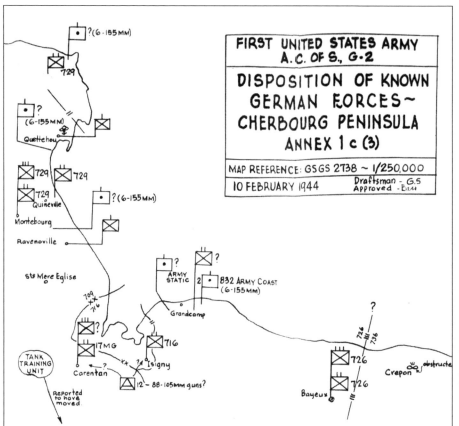

One of the regular troop evaluation updates produced to keep commanders updated about the units they would face.

Dated 10 February Allied intelligence produced and distributed a complete list of major German positions.

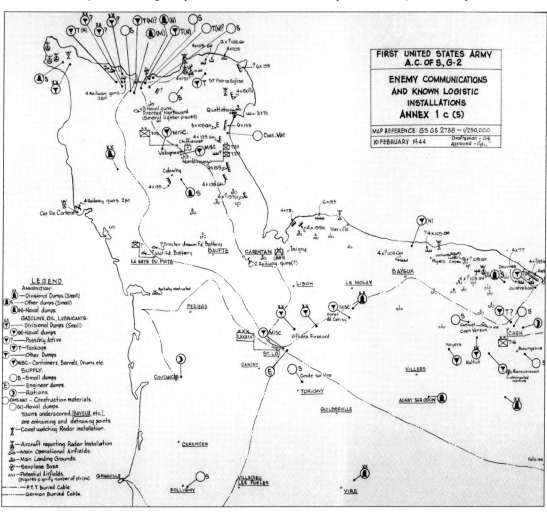

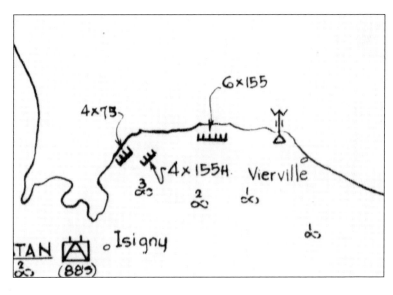

In the Rangers' scope of operations – shown are the Radar Station, the gun position at Pointe du Hoc and the two batteries at Maisy. Pointe du Hoc is represented by the 6 x 155 and the Maisy Batteries by the 4 x 75mm and 4 x 155H (howitzers).

The study also includes a comprehensive list of artillery positions with the range of each group of weapons being shown by the arcs as distances out to sea.

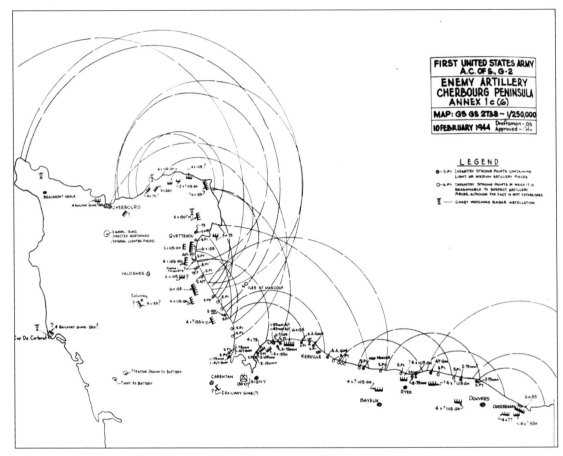

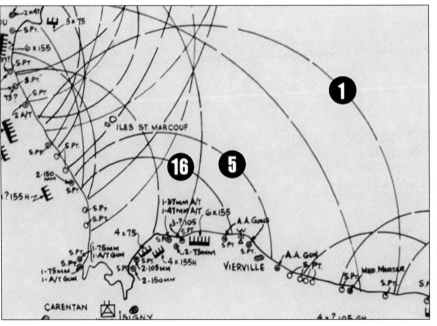

This is a blow up of the section showing the battery ranges and I have numbered their arcs of fire. Positions number 1 (Pointe du Hoc). No 5 Maisy Les Perruques & No 16 La Martinière.

11 February 1944

5th Rangers – Companies A – F, Medical and HQ – Leominster, England.

A Company 2nd Rangers – Folkestone, Kent.

B Company 2nd Rangers – Shanklin, Isle of Wight.

C Company 2nd Rangers – Sandown, Isle of Wight.

D Company 2nd Rangers – Shanklin, Isle of Wight.

E Company 2nd Rangers – Sandown, Isle of Wight.

F Company 2nd Rangers – Botley, Hampshire.

Medical Detachment 2nd Rangers – Sandown, Isle of Wight.

Headquarters Company 2nd Rangers – Titchfield, Hampshire.

Obviously still a problem – the US Army issued further instructions to their men concerning 'Interaction with the British.'

Keep Out of Arguments. *You can rub a Britisher the wrong way by telling him 'we came over and won the last one'. Each nation did its share. But Britain remembers that nearly a million of her best manhood died in the last war. America lost 60,000 in action.*

Such arguments and the war debts along with them are dead issues. Nazi propaganda now is pounding away day and night asking the British people why they fight 'to save Uncle Shylock and his silver dollar.' Don't play into Hitler's hands by mentioning war debts.

Neither do the British need to be told that their armies lost the first couple of rounds in the present war. We've lost a couple, ourselves, so do not start off by being critical and saying what the Yanks are going to do. Use your head before you sound off, and remember how long the British alone held Hitler off without any help from anyone.

In the pubs you will hear a lot of Britons openly criticizing their government and the conduct of the war. That isn't an occasion for you to put in your two-cents worth. It's their business, not yours. You sometimes criticize members of your own family – but just let an outsider start doing the same, and you know how you feel!

The Briton is just as outspoken and independent as we are. But don't get him wrong. He is also the most law-abiding citizen in the world, because the British system of justice is just about the best there is. There are fewer murders, robberies and burglaries in the whole of Great Britain in a year than in a single large American city.

Once again, look, listen, and learn before you start telling the British how much better we do things. They will be interested to hear about life in America and you have a great chance to overcome the picture many of them have gotten from movies of an America made up of wild Indians and gangsters. When you find differences between British and American ways of doing things, there is usually a good reason for them.

British railways have ****y freight cars (which they call 'goods wagons') not because they don't know any better. Small cars allow quicker handling of freight at the thousands and thousands of small stations.

British automobiles are little and low-powered. That's because all the gasoline has to be imported over thousands of miles of ocean.

British taxicabs have comic-looking front wheel structures. Watch them turn around in a 12-foot street and you'll understand why.

The British don't know how to make a good cup of coffee. You don't know how to make a good cup of tea. It's an even swap.

12 February 1944

5th Rangers – Companies A – F, Medical and HQ – Leominster, England.

A Company 2nd Rangers – Folkestone, Kent.

Sgt. William L. Mullohan was sent back to his original unit.

B Company 2nd Rangers – Shanklin, Isle of Wight.

C Company 2nd Rangers – Sandown, Isle of Wight.

1st Lt. Moody went from Duty to Detached Service in London.

Sgt. Hendrickson went from Duty to Detached Service in London.

D Company 2nd Rangers – Shanklin, Isle of Wight.

E Company 2nd Rangers – Sandown, Isle of Wight.

1st Lt. Lapres went from Duty to Detached Service, London.

F Company 2nd Rangers – Botley, Hampshire.

Medical Detachment 2nd Rangers – Sandown, Isle of Wight.

Headquarters Company 2nd Rangers – Titchfield, Hampshire.

2nd Battalion Narrative History.

> On 12 February, the Battalion Commander received the
> following Ltr, Hq-SHAEF, 2 Feb 44, file SHAEF/21306/SD;
> Subject: "Cancellation of Raids and Reconnaissance for oper-
> ation OVERLORD" and, in accordance with instructions con-
> tained therein, directed all Companies to re-assemble at
> Bude. Movement was primarily by rail with the Supply in-
> stallation at Titchfield returning by organic transportation.

Field Marshal Rommel touring the battery at Pointe du Hoc with his general staff. This film footage was released to the public in February 1944 as part of a Nazi propaganda film (shown are stills from that film).

13 February 1944

5th Rangers – Companies A – F, Medical and HQ – Leominster, England.

Tec Sgt. V. Fast went from Duty to Detached Service with the Intelligence School, London.

A Company 2nd Rangers – Folkestone, Kent.

Pvt. Andrew Bourret and Cpl. Gerome LeJall were both returned to their original unit.

B Company 2nd Rangers – Shanklin, Isle of Wight.

C Company 2nd Rangers – Sandown, Isle of Wight.

D Company 2nd Rangers – Shanklin, Isle of Wight.

E Company 2nd Rangers – Sandown, Isle of Wight.

F Company 2nd Rangers – Botley, Hampshire.

Medical Detachment 2nd Rangers – Sandown, Isle of Wight.

Record of events. The Medical Detachment 2nd Btn left Sandown, Isle of Wight at 1500 hours by truck and ferry en route to another station.

Headquarters Company 2nd Rangers – Titchfield, Hampshire.

1st Lt. James V. Eikner returned to Duty from Detached Service.

Sgt. William L. Mollohan Jr returned to Duty from Detached Service.

Maurice Prince: *When February 13 rolled around, we received our moving orders. We packed our equipment, and said our farewells. We headed for the station to catch a train which was to bring us back to Bude. We departed with a load of memories, while we left behind the firm and already established reputation of us Rangers as being fighting soldiers and gentlemen.*

US Army Meterological Report dated 13 February 1944 stated: *H-Hour to be timed to permit a second high water in daylight on D-Day to permit the maximum discharge during this period. The only dates on which all these factors are available are May 21st, 22nd and 23rd, June 5th, 6th and 7th, June 19th, 20th and 21st or July 3rd, 4th or 5th.*

---

14 February 1944

5th Rangers – Companies A, B, C, D & F, Medical and HQ – Leominster, England.

E Company 5th Rangers – Acton Court, Wrexham, England. [Author: The section of Morning Report for E Company 5th Battalion indicates that they were in Acton Court in Wrexham. As yet, I have no explanation as to why they were there for some days.]

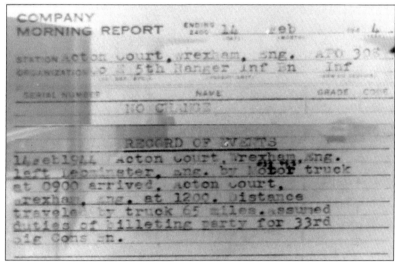

A Company 2nd Rangers – Folkestone, Kent.

Pfc. Paul French was returned to Headquarters Company.

Captain Cleveland A. Lytle returned from Detached Service to Duty with A Company.

The following twenty men were returned to their duties with Headquarters Company: Pfc. Robert C. Lambert, T/5 Ramsey A. Turner, T/5 Oscar H. Anderson, T/5 Paul Galloway, Pfc. Clarence L. Elsy, T/4 Ted P. Smith, T/4 Virgilio V. Prebenna, T/4 Isadore Diamond, T/5 Donald W. Bailey, Pfc. Arthur J. Greenwood, Pfc. Charles A. Little, Sgt. Francis J. Roach, Cpl. Charles A. Parker, T/5 Stephen A. Liscinsky, T/5 Louis Lisko, T/5 Tasker L. Hooks, Pfc. Owen J. Paradis, Pfc. William K. Doinoff, Pfc. Gerard C. Rotthoff, T/4 Otto C. Bayer.

Pfc. Bonnie M. Taylor was returned to Duty from his placement under arrest in quarters.

At 0630 hours A Company left Folkestone train station in Kent and arrived at Bude in Cornwall at 1745 hours.

B Company 2nd Rangers – Shanklin, Isle of Wight.

Sgt. Shave and Pfc. Carpenter went from Duty to Detached Service. 1st Lt. McCullers assumed temporary command as of 10 Feb 1944.

C Company 2nd Rangers – Sandown, Isle of Wight.

D Company 2nd Rangers – Shanklin, Isle of Wight.

1st Lt. Baugh went from Duty to Detached Service in London as of 12 February 1944.

E Company 2nd Rangers – Sandown, Isle of Wight.

S/Sgt. Cleaves went from Duty to Detached Service in London. 1st Lt. Merrill was promoted to the rank of Captain as of 1 February 1944.

F Company 2nd Rangers – Botley, Hampshire.

Captain Otto Masny went from Duty to Detached Service. 1st Lt. Robert C. Arman assumed temporary Duty as Company Commander.

Medical Detachment 2nd Rangers – Bude, Cornwall.

The Medical Detachment 2nd Btn arrived in Bude, Cornwall at 1700 hours by truck.

Headquarters Company 2nd Rangers – Bude, Cornwall.

Twenty-one enlisted men returned to Duty from Detached Service. 1st Lt. Frederick G. Wilkin and 2nd Lt. Frank Kennard both returned from Detached Service in Titchfield to Duty in Bude, Cornwall.

Captain George S. Williams was appointed S-4 in addition to his present Duty as Company Commander. S/Sgt. John S. Walker was appointed to T/Sgt.

Record of Events: Left Titchfield, Hampshire at 1100 hrs and arrived at Bude, Cornwall at 1800 hours by truck.

Maurice Prince: *Our return entry into Bude on the 14th day of February was one of mixed feelings and emotions. We were disappointed in a minor sort of way because we had once said goodbye to these good people of this community, and now, we were returning like bad relatives that had no other place to go. While on the other hand, we were happy to be back, happy to pick up the shreds and bonds of friendship we had knitted the first time we were here.*

It took us no time to get back into the swing of things. Most of the boys, including myself, got their old billets back and took up their living habits as though they had never left in the first place. The people were as jovial and cordial as ever, and they were only too happy to have us back. In fact, it became so that we got to know these civilians so well and became so familiar with them that the names of Mom, Pop, Aunt and Uncle were bestowed on them.

Photo: 2nd Lt. Frank Kennard on his way to collect the battalion payroll from Barnstaple, a task he undertook regularly – but it was only done under the authority as sanctioned below. This movement order applied to all motorised movement for the battalion:

Army Regulations Regarding Road Route Information

1. *The Intelligence Division, Engineer Service, HQ SOS, ETOUSA, APO 871, is prepared to furnish road routes consisting of strip maps, and detailed directions between any two or more points in the British Isles, upon application, to any authorised personnel making journeys with motor transportation. Insofar as possible, requests for routings should be submitted at least 24 hours in advance, in person, by telephone or in writing.*
2. *Requests for routings should include information as to the following:*
   a. *Starting point and destination.*
   b. *Intermediate points to be visited en route.*
   c. *Date and time of departure and approximate date of return of maps.*
   d. *Name, address, telephone number, and official capacity of person requesting information.*
3. *Failure of any individual to return maps will be reported without delay to the Chief Engineer this headquarters.*

Every opportunity was taken to educate and inform US servicemen of the hardships being suffered by the British.

BRITAIN IS AT WAR: At home in America you were in a country at war. Since your ship left port, however, you have been in a war zone. You will find that all Britain is a war zone and has been since September 1939. All this has meant great changes in the British way of life.

Every light in England is blacked out every night and all night. Every highway sign has come down and barrage balloons have gone up. Grazing land is now ploughed for wheat and flower beds turned into vegetable gardens. Britain's peacetime army of a couple of hundred thousand men has expanded to over two million men. Everything from the biggest factory to the smallest village workshop is turning out something for the war, so that Britain can supply arms for herself, for Libya, India, Russia, and every front. Hundreds of thousands of women have gone to work in factories or joined the many military auxiliary forces. Old-time social distinctions are being forgotten as the sons of factory workers rise to be officers in the forces and the daughters of noblemen get jobs in munitions factories.

But more important than this is the effect of the war itself. The British have been bombed, night after night and month after month. Thousands of them have lost their houses, their possessions, their families. Gasoline, clothes and railroad travel are hard to come by and incomes are cut by taxes to an extent that we Americans have not even approached. One of the things the English always had enough of in the past was soap. Now it is so scarce that girls working in the factories often cannot get the grease off their hands or out of their hair. And food is more strictly rationed than anything else.

---

15 February 1944

5th Rangers – Companies A, B, C, D & F, Medical and HQ – Leominster, England.

E Company 5th Rangers – Acton Court, Wrexham, England.

A Company 2nd Rangers – Bude, Cornwall.

B Company 2nd Rangers – Shanklin, Isle of Wight.

C Company 2nd Rangers – Sandown, Isle of Wight.

D Company 2nd Rangers – Shanklin, Isle of Wight. D Company boarded a train in Shanklin at 0815 hours and arrived in Bude, Cornwall at 1900 hours.

E Company 2nd Rangers – Sandown, Isle of Wight.

F Company 2nd Rangers – Botley, Hampshire.

Medical Detachment 2nd Rangers – Bude, Cornwall. T/4 Clark was appointed to the rank of S/Sgt. T/5 Mentzer was appointed to the rank of T/4. Pfc. South was appointed to the rank of T/5.

Headquarters Company 2nd Rangers – Titchfield, Hampshire. Lt. Colonel James E. Rudder and 2nd Lt. Harry Weinman both returned to Duty from Detached Service. Major Max F. Schneider and 1st Lt. Harvey J. Cook both returned to Duty from Detached Service.

Headquarters Company 2nd Rangers – Bude, Cornwall.

The following US Army report was produced on 25 February entitled *'Smoke… considerations for employment*. Although it may not have seemed relevant to the Rangers at this time – it was to prove an important aid and sometimes hindrance in their 6 June attempts to climb the bluffs at Omaha Beach.

Decisions as to whether smoke will be used at the time of landing will depend upon the existing weather conditions. It follows that no definite decision or plan can be made prior to the time of assault as to the use of smoke, although adequate means for its production and various plans applicable to meet varying conditions must be prepared and available for instant use. This will require complete understanding and co-operation between respective Naval and Landing Force Commanders or their representatives as to appropriate methods and means of employing smoke under all possible conditions or weather and anticipated emergencies.

First consideration in the use of smoke should be that it does not hinder or prevent observation of supporting air, naval, and army bombardment fires.

As a rule, no screening of tactical smoke will be placed on or along landing beaches. The exception to the above, however, may be that under certain circumstance with an on-shore wind, smoke may be of temporary greater value placed on or along the landing beaches, than the supporting fires which the smoke hinders or prevents.

One smoke requirement which is anticipated at this time is the provision of a flank smoke screen on the eastern flank of Utah beach for the protection of those troops landing thereon, against enemy fire from shore batteries through D-Day. Such a screen would also afford protection for naval landing craft, which will be subjected to the same shore fire prior to and at the time of landing.

A second requirement will be the anticipated call for smoke screening of designated targets on or in the rear of beach areas at the time of landing, when fire support including smoke support will be at a minimum. During this critical period, it is believed that naval gunfire employing 'P' shell may be the most effective means of screening such targets.

Detailed plans and methods of execution involving smoke support tactical during landing operations will be prepared and finally concluded by Commanders of Operating Forces "O" and 'U' in direct collaboration with appropriate Corps and Division Commanders of the First US Army.

The following map shows a simulated laying of smoke along the higher ground behind Omaha Beach.

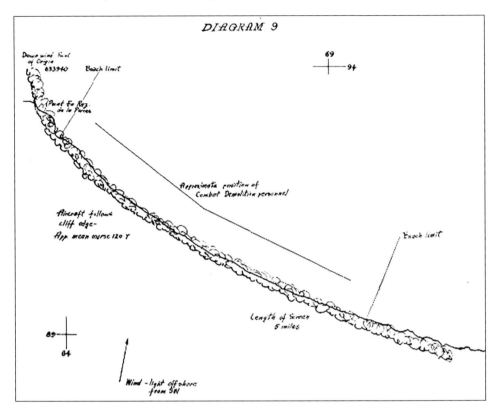

On 15 February the Rangers' commanders were provided with GSGS Intelligence maps of the areas in which they were going to be fighting. This map shows the Pointe du Hoc battery with the symbol for 6 x 155mm cannon on emplacements.

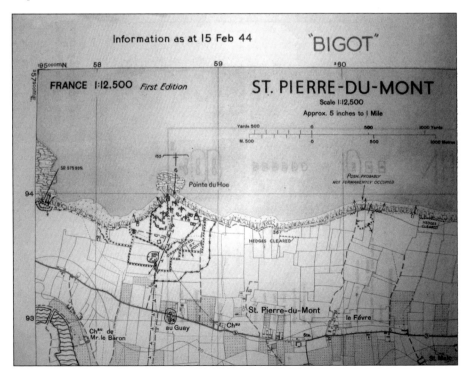

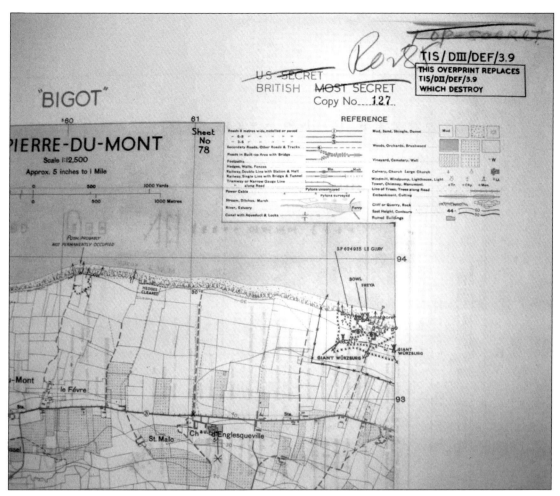

'GSGS maps', as they are known, were provided by the Geographical Section, General Staff operated under the Director of Military Operations and Intelligence. Its role was to supply maps to the forces, collect data on foreign survey networks, provide training, and prepare survey data for Expeditionary Force mobilization.

---

16 February 1944

5th Rangers – Companies A, B, C, D & F, Medical and HQ – Leominster, England.
E Company 5th Rangers – Acton Court, Wrexham, England.
A Company 2nd Rangers – Bude, Cornwall.

2nd Battalion Narrative History.

> By 16 February, all Companies occupied their original billets in Bude. Training was resumed; this consisted of small unit assault exercises employing demolitions and live ammunition. Cliff climbing was also stressed. Volunteer-interviewing parties continued to be dispatched, some going to the 8th Division while others contacted the Armored units in the area. Various officers and enlisted men were sent to Army Specialist Schools under existing quotas.

Maurice Prince: *It was nearly two months now since Able Company had been put on its own to operate as a separate organization away from battalion. Now we were back again under the folds of Battalion. It was nice to be back as this gave us a chance to acquaint ourselves with the other guys in the unit and to renew our friendship with our buddies in the other companies. Inter-company bull sessions were held frequently, with members from each company trying to relate a better story of their company's doing than the others.*

A vigorous training schedule was drawn up for us here. This was to make certain that we kept in condition and that we didn't forget all that we had learned. Hikes, speed marches, and physical training made sure that our bodies didn't become soft and lumpy. While squad, section and platoon firing problems saw that we knew how to use our weapons in cooperation and coordination with our buddies. Night problems, map and compass courses kept our mental facilities alerted. Also it gave us the needed skill and adeptness for the battle we were endlessly preparing for.

To further prepare us for the coming invasion, we were given a specialized course in overcoming hilly and mountainous obstacles. This came to us under the cognomen of cliff scaling. Many was the afternoon that saw us Rangers weary and tired, going up and down the hilly cliffs that bordered the ocean at Bude.

We had done this sort of training before in our infant days back at Camp Forrest. We had been given certain practical demonstrations on the usage of ropes entwined about the body to overcome an over-hanging cliff obstacle. Then we also had been taught certain other principles in ascending and descending the sides of steep hills. We had been given the opportunity to test our skills on the sheer cliffs (60 to 100 feet high), which were situated in the vicinity of Tullahoma, Tennessee.

We had come thru this rough training with flying colours, so that now we stood ready to tackle the cliffs of England or anywhere else on the European continent, for that matter.

In Bude due to the facilities and different kinds of cliffs we had nearby, we could experiment with many different ways of surmounting this kind of obstacle. We would climb certain cliffs without the use of rope, some with and then for others we used little steel ladders which were 4 feet in length and which had ends which could be connected to one another. We built up ladders which extended in length to 80 to 100 feet. With these all we had to do was place the ladder against the cliff, and walk up. Very simple, all you had to do was just hope and pray that the ladder wouldn't break or that the construction rods weren't loose and could give way while you were going up or down.

The Rangers' physical training, although considered much more thorough than the 'average' US infantry man, was in fact in line with US Army policy at the time which stated:

B Company 2nd Rangers – Shanklin, Isle of Wight.
Company entrained from Shanklin, Isle of Wight at 0815 hours en route to new station. Arrived in Bude, Cornwall at 1900.
C Company 2nd Rangers – Sandown, Isle of Wight.
Record of events. Entrained Sandown, Isle of Wight at 0820. hours en route to new station. Arrived Bude, Cornwall at 1900 hours. All members of this company were billeted in private homes.
D Company 2nd Rangers – Bude, Cornwall.
E Company 2nd Rangers – Bude, Cornwall.
S/Sgt. Cleaves returned from Detached Service in London to Duty.
Pvt. Crook was relieved of his attachment to E Company and returned to the Medical Detachment. Record of events. Entrained Sandown, Isle of Wight at 0820 hours en route to new station. Arrived Bude, Cornwall at 1900 hours. All members of this company were billeted in private homes.
F Company 2nd Rangers – Botley, Hampshire.
Record of events: F Company left Botley by truck at 0011 hours and arrived at Fareham at 1215 hours. There they took a train at 1230 hours and arrived in Bude, Cornwall at 1900 hours.
Medical Detachment 2nd Rangers – Bude, Cornwall.
Headquarters Company 2nd Rangers – Bude, Cornwall.

To perform his duties satisfactorily, the soldier must possess great organic vigor, muscular and nervous strength, endurance, and agility. The average recruit does not possess the degree of physical fitness required of a trained soldier. The required degree of physical fitness can be acquired only through physical training. The performance (of purely military exercises, that is, drill, marching, etc), is not alone sufficient to correct the deficiencies and incorrect postures too often acquired before becoming a soldier. Further, the complexities of modern warfare require so much technical training for the soldier that all too frequently no time is allotted for physical training; yet the soldier who possesses great technical skill, but is unable to withstand the rigorous life demanded is of questionable value. Hence, physical training must be an integral part of every training program. There is no more justification for failure to allow time in the training program for physical training on the grounds that the soldier will attain satisfactory physical development through performing his daily duties, than there is for failure to allow time for training in marksmanship on the grounds that the soldier will learn to shoot by being taken to the range, issued a weapon and ammunition, and left to his own devices.

The primary purpose of military physical training is the production of a state of health and general physical fitness which will permit the soldier to perform the arduous duties required of him.

The disciplinary and setting-up exercises prepare the soldier mentally and physically for training in such basic skills as marching and running, jumping and vaulting, climbing, crawling, lifting and carrying, and throwing and kicking. Superiority in these basic skills becomes the soldier's immediate objective and gives him a definite goal for which to strive. From the effort the soldier puts forward to become proficient in these simple skills, he develops endurance and agility. The soldier is among the first to become aware of his own physical development. This knowledge of improvement results in confidence, courage, alertness, initiative, pride, discipline, and posture. The development of these many desirable qualities during the conduct of the physical training program is a certainty and may equal, if not surpass, the purely physiological value of the training. The final result of all of this training is physical efficiency, which, as stated before, is an essential to military effectiveness.

The US Army issued a letter entitled '*Indoor Amusements*'. Both it and similar publications were aimed at better informing the US serviceman to help him integrate and further understand the British way of life.

The British have theatres and movies (which they call 'cinemas') as we do. But the great place of recreation is the 'pub'. A pub, or public house, is what we would call a bar or tavern. The usual drink is beer, which is not an imitation of German beer as ours is, but ale. (But they usually call it beer or 'bitter'.) Not much whiskey is now being drunk. Wartime taxes have shot the price of a bottle up to about $4.50. The British are beer-drinkers – and can hold it. The beer is now below peacetime strength, but can still make a man's tongue wag at both ends.

You will be welcome in the British pubs as long as you remember one thing. The pub is 'the poor man's club', the neighbourhood or village gathering place, where the men have come to see their friends, not strangers. If you want to join a darts game, let them ask you first (as they probably will.) And if you are beaten, it is the custom to stand aside and let someone else play.

The British make much of Sunday. All the shops are closed, most of the restaurants are closed, and in the small towns there is not much to do. You had better follow the example of the British people and try to spend Sunday afternoon in the country.

British churches, particularly the little village churches, are often very beautiful inside and out. Most of them are always open and if you feel like it, do not hesitate to walk in. But do not walk around if a service is going on.

You will naturally be interested in getting to know your opposite number, the British soldier, the 'Tommy' you have heard and read about. You can understand that two actions on your part will slow up the friendship – swiping his girl, and not appreciating what his army has been up against. Yes, and rubbing it in that you are better paid than he is.

Children the world over are easy to get along with. British children are much like our own. The British have reserved much of the food that gets through solely for their children. To the British children you as an American will be 'something special'. For they have been fed at their schools and impressed with the fact that the food they ate was sent to them by Uncle Sam. You don't have to tell the British about lend-lease food. They know about it and appreciate it.

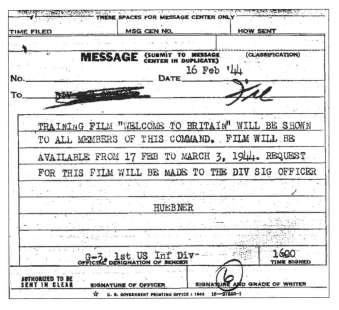

17 February 1944

5th Rangers – Companies A, B, C, D & F, Medical and HQ – Leominster, England.

E Company 5th Rangers – Acton Court, Wrexham, England.

A Company 2nd Rangers – Bude, Cornwall.
Rangers T/5 Earl W. Shireman and Arvin L. Duncan were put under arrest in their quarters.
Pfc. Bonnie M. Taylor was relieved from his attachment with A Company and returned to his unit.

B Company 2nd Rangers – Bude, Cornwall.
Pfc. Carpenter and Pfc. O'Neal were relieved from attached.
1st Lt. McCullers was relieved of temporary command and assumed his duties as platoon leader.
1st Lt. Smudin went from Detached Service, School, London to Duty and assumed command.

C Company 2nd Rangers – Bude, Cornwall.
1st Lt. Moody and Sgt. Hendrickson returned from Detached Service in London to Duty.
The following six enlisted men returned to Duty from attached: Pvt. Moar, Pvt. Donahue, Pvt. Plumlee, Pfc. Robison, Pfc. Goad, Pvt. Rorpomen. Pfc. Frank South was relieved from attached as of 16 February 1944.

Maurice Prince: *While we were here, we had the good fortune, socially speaking, to have the Red Cross open up a Donut Dugout. The place was situated right in the midst of our company area, so the Able Co. had almost a complete monopoly of the place. It was a treat and pleasure to go visit the Donut Dugout to drink down a coke or engage in the art of dunking donuts in coffee. Besides, there were other facilities handy such as writing tables, reading material, checker boards, a large ping pong table, a good radio with phonograph attached, and many other things that can be found in such places. Then, also the pretty hostesses that took care of the Dugout were an added attraction that lured the Rangers into coming.*

At this time many of the officers started to be sent off to various establishments for specific training. Army instructions for students being sent to the Army Training School were as follows: *'bring full field equipment including two blankets, fatigue clothes and overshoes. The School Centre will supply mattress, pillow and one additional blanket. Students will eat at the student officers' mess which will be paid for by deductions on pay vouchers at the rate of sixty cents per day. Students will report to the Commandant, American School Centre, two days in advance of the opening date of the course.'*

Men of B Company 2nd Battalion. T/5 Charles J. Bramkamp cuts the hair of T/5 Elmer Olander. Others present, Sgt. Joseph Shedaker, Pfc. Robert Herlihy, Pfc. James Roush, Pfc. William Gower, Pfc. Charles Davis and S/Sgt. Paul Shave.

Photographs of Bude coastline and town where the Rangers were training and lived. The small house shown was occupied by Lt. Col. Rudder for some time and the training bunker can be seen clearly on the cliff top.

D Company 2nd Rangers – Bude, Cornwall.
Captain Slater went from Duty to Detached Service as directed.
1st Lt. McBride assumed the responsibility of Company Commander.
Pfc. Roberson was appointed to the rank of T/5 as of 25 January.
E Company 2nd Rangers – Bude, Cornwall.
1st Lt. Lapres returned to Duty from Detached Service in London.
F Company 2nd Rangers – Bude Cornwall.
Pfc. Taylor returned to Detached Service in Folkestone, Kent to Duty.
Pfc. Charles W. Korb was relieved from his attachment to F Company as of 16 February 1944.
Medical Detachment 2nd Rangers – Bude, Cornwall.
Headquarters Company 2nd Rangers – Bude, Cornwall.

UNITED STATES ASSAULT TRAINING CENTER ETOUSA

TRAINING MEMORANDUM: 17 February 1944

THE COMPANY AID MAN

    The company aid man is one of modern warfare's unsung and unpublicized heroes. He is the only unarmed combat soldier in our army who must face all the dangers, suffer all the hardships and yet be denied the opportunity to carry the fight to the enemy.

    He must remain with his combat group at all times. He must provide good first aid in the heat of battle, disregarding often his own safety to perform these duties.

    On maneuvers and pre-combat training his duties and relationships with his platoon or section are simple. He merely attaches himself to his unit, tags along at the rear, often disdaining to wear his Geneva brassard and treats the different minor cuts or foot conditions which arise. His job is seemingly a "cinch".

    How different it is when the chips are down and live ammunition makes a body dig foxholes. The company aid man becomes an important character. Upon him rests the efficiency of medical care. Upon him rests the entire medical service. Upon him falls the responsibility of going out to administer the initial medical treatment to a wounded man. Does he know how to control hemorrhage, apply a tourniquet, administer morphine, put on a firm dressing that will not slip off, improvise splints out of twigs, boards, rifles, bayonets or whatever he has at hand or doesn't he? Do you men know all this? If you don't you better learn. As the aid man becomes more experienced and proficient he must develop judgment — the ability, the "hunch", the feeling that a man is lightly or severely wounded. Such knowledge cannot be taught. It must be acquired. It's acquisition depends upon good basic training of the sort mentioned above. In addition to his knowledge about first aid a good company aid man must know the things every combat soldier knows — security and cover, scouting and patrolling, map and compass reading. He must be a bit smarter than the average buck private in the rear rank, especially in his knowledge about things in general. For instance he should know the location of the aid station, not as a point on the map but where it is on the ground, he should know where his company headquarters is and something about the local war. He should be a cool, calm messenger with definite information. Once, in Africa, a company aid man came back with the lurid story that an entire battalion had been captured. What actually happened was that he lost his company and imagined the rest of the story to compensate for his bad performance.

In land warfare a company aid man stays with his platoon or section. In this type of amphibious operation that you now are being trained in, some of you company aid men will find yourselves in a company headquarters boat. Don't stay with the company commander. Your place is to join up with your platoon or section as the case may be. By this time you should be assigned to a definite platoon and know your platoon leader and platoon sergeant by face or name. You ought to know the face at least and if possible the name of every dogface in the platoon. When you land with company headquarters many of your buddies in the platoon expect you to be with them. It's against a company aid man's code to stay behind once his platoon is up there fighting. Stay with your platoon. Treat patients on the beach only if your platoon remains on the beach. Otherwise get off the beach quickly. It's an unhealthy spot. If your company commander doesn't know that fact then you should very politely and courteously explain that fact to him. Start now and learn that fact. It might be wise now to begin to know that a company aid man without his equipment is of no value. In recent battalion landing team operations company aid men were questioned about their kits. Some were fully equipped. One fellow didn't even have one roll of bandage to care for an injured soldier. It so happened that the injured man (and this man was definitely hurt) had his first aid packet with him. That didn't speak well of that particular company aid man.

Aside from these two points: (1) Join up with your platoon as soon after you land as possible and (2) Be fully equipped when you do land, amphibious operations are just the same as any maneuver. There may be more confusion at first but after everything quiets down and you've gotten over the queazy feeling in your stomach remember your job and do it.

Your job is to keep the soldier fit and give the best first aid treatment you are capable of, at the earliest moment, to a wounded soldier.

To do this job you must be physically fit, well trained and aware of your responsibilities.

Jack Burke was the A Company 5th Battalion Medic: *We had just one pouch, one canteen (carried on the right side of the cartridge belt). We did not have a harness. The pouch contained a lot of bandages, gauze pads, adhesive tape, tags to describe what treatment you gave, with string to tie on the Rangers' shirt, scissors, antibiotic sulfa powder and morphine syrettes. No safety pins.*

My training was as a rifleman, but the officers knew I was a pre-med major in college and they asked me to fill in as a medic. The battalion surgeon trained me in rest camp and I became a medic. All medics had to qualify on all physical requirements as a Ranger as well as any other on rifle, grenade, gas, live fire, speed marches etc.

At night in town we would wear our dress uniforms and overseas cap.

Another US Army information letter on the British:

For many months the people of Britain have been doing without things which Americans take for granted. But you will find that shortages, discomforts, blackouts and bombings have not made the British depressed. They have a new cheerfulness and a new determination born out of hard times and tough luck. After going through what they have been through it's only human nature that they should be more determined than ever to win.

You are coming to Britain from a country where your home is still safe, food is still plentiful, and lights are still burning. So it is doubly important for you to remember that the British soldiers and civilians have been living under a tremendous strain. It is always impolite to criticise your hosts. It is militarily stupid to criticise your allies. So stop and think before you sound off about lukewarm beer, or cold or boiled potatoes, or the way English cigarettes taste.

If British civilians look dowdy and badly dressed, it is not because they do not like good clothes or know how to wear them. All clothing is rationed and the British know that they help war production by wearing an old suit or dress until it cannot be patched any longer. Old clothes are 'good form'.

One thing to be careful about – if you are invited into a British home and the host exhorts you to 'eat up – there's plenty on the table', go easy. It may be the rations for the whole week spread out to show their hospitality.

18 February 1944

5th Rangers – Companies A, B, C, D & F, Medical and HQ – Leominster, England.
E Company 5th Rangers – Acton Court, Wrexham, England.
2nd Rangers – Companies A, B, C, D & F, Medical and HQ – Bude, Cornwall.

The following extracts are taken from letters which were read by US Army censors and intercepted. They indicate well some of the issues that had been occurring between black troops with both white soldiers and civilians.

Written by a white officer: '*The coloured boys seem to be doing quite well with the local belles, so you can well assume that we are steering clear. The MPs have quite a job keeping them out of their tent area.*'

Written by a black Sergeant: '*The English people mingle with our fellows freely in a big way, the only trouble we have is from the American sailors and soldiers, and since our fellows have been knocking them down every time they are insulted, we have about eliminated that.*'

19 February 1944

5th Rangers – Companies A, B, C, D & F, Medical and HQ – Leominster, England.
Major John D. Parish, Major Charles Porter, Tec 4 George Thompson and Tec 5 Carl Mullings were attached to HQ Co. from the 196th Field Artillery Group. 2nd Lt. William Adams, C.W.O. Homer Fogleman, T/Sgt. Ray Andes and Corporal John Taylor were attached from the 12th Field Artillery Observation Battalion.
E Company 5th Rangers – Acton Court, Wrexham, England.
2nd Rangers – Companies A–F, Medical and HQ – Bude, Cornwall.

More instructions from Army HQ on dealing with the British: *THE BEST WAY to get on in Britain is very much the same as the best way to get on in America. The same sort of courtesy and decency and friendliness that go over big in America will go over big in Britain. The British have seen a good many Americans and they like Americans. They will like your frankness as long as it is friendly. They will expect you to be generous. They are not given to back-slapping and they are shy about showing their affections. But once they get to like you they make the best friends in the world.*

In 'getting along' the first important thing to remember is that the British are like the Americans in many ways – but not in all ways. You will quickly discover differences that seem confusing and even wrong. Like driving on the left side of the road, and having money based on an 'impossible' accounting system, and drinking warm beer. But once you get used to that you will realise that they belong to England just as baseball and jazz and Coca-Cola belong to us.

Below: confirmation that Major General Huebner was due to attend a meeting at the Assault Training Centre.

HEADQUARTERS
U.S. ASSAULT TRAINING CENTER, ETOUSA
APO 553

DAILY ARRIVAL AND DEPARTURE REPORT

ANTICIPATED ARRIVALS

Today: 19 February 1944 (Saturday)

Maj Gen J S Wood, CG, 4th Armd Div.   To arrive by car this afternoon and will remain
Col L J Storck Lt. Col Watt   until Feb. 21, 1944.
Maj Gen Huebner   To arrive by car this morning.
Lt Crowley and 3 EM.

20 February 1944

5th Rangers – Companies A, B, C, D & F, Medical and HQ – Leominster, England.
E Company 5th Rangers – Acton Court, Wrexham, England.
2nd Rangers – Companies A – F, Medical and HQ – Bude, Cornwall.

Dated 20 Feb this GSGS map shows the enemy positions from Omaha Beach towards Pointe du Hoc and the sluice gates to the east of Grandcamp-les-Bains.

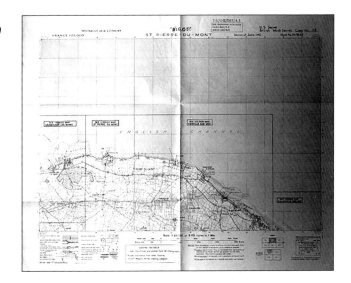

The area shown below is the portion of the coastline including the positions at Maisy and Gefosse-Fontenay. The x lines represent barbed wire entanglements and defences.

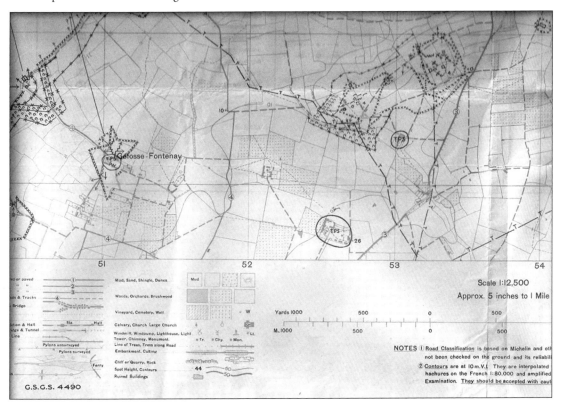

On 20 February the US Army Training Centre issued the following memorandum to its staff. The Rangers were one of the units who would be attending courses there in the near future.

HEADQUARTERS
U. S. ASSAULT TRAINING CENTER, ETOUSA
APO   553

20 February 1944

TRAINING MEMORANDUM)
)   TRAINING DIRECTIVE FOR UNITS OF THE
NO. 2   )   U. S. ASSAULT TRAINING CENTER

FOR THE PERIOD 1 MARCH to 31 MARCH 1944

1. GENERAL:

Training of all units of this command will be directed toward increased efficiency in achieving the mission of the U. S. Assault Training Center, which is to train combat teams in assault and amphibious operations.

2. TRAINING OBJECTIVES:

(1) To attain and maintain proficiency in the subjects demonstrated at the U.S. Assault Training Center, so that every individual will be thoroughly familiar with his assignment, and be able to carry it out in a superior manner.

(2) To attain and maintain a high state of discipline, so that every officer and enlisted man, in individual assignments or in collective assignments, will exemplify the highest standards of alertness, military bearing and soldierly appearance.

(3) To complete all training prescribed by higher headquarters without delay, and to maintain proficiency in these subjects.

(4) To undertake such additional training in technical and tactical subjects as may be feasible after the objectives indicated above have been accomplished.

3. RESPONSIBILITY:

Training is a function of command. All unit commanders are directly responsible for the state of training of their units. They are responsible for every subordinate leader being qualified to assume the duties of the next higher unit leader. All instructors under their control will be thoroughly familiar with the provisions of FM 21-5 and TM 21-250, and will present instructions as outlined therein.

4. TRAINING WEEK:

Six days a week, Monday through Saturday, will be devoted to training, with a minimum of 48 hours per week to be devoted to training, demonstrations, and work or administrative details. If necessary unit commanders will exceed this

- 1 -

minimum time to accomplish the training program set forth in this directive. Each Sunday will be devoted to religious and recreational activities.

5.   TRAINING PROCEDURE AND SUBJECTS:

   (a)   GENERAL: Training must be progressive. Subjects once satisfactorily covered will not be disregarded, but will be reviewed, not as isolated items, but by introducing them into other training situations. Instruction should be so integrated that the soldier receives a complete picture of the relationship that each subject bears to the others.

   (b)   BASIC SUBJECTS: Military courtesy will be emphasized, with particular attention to saluting and general conduct. Instruction will not be limited to instruction periods, but will be given at any time or place that high standards do not appear. Instruction in Interior Guard Duty will be carried on concurrently with each tour of guard duty.

   (c)   TRAINING IN SECURITY MEASURES: Safety of all members of his command is the responsibility of every unit commander. Every individual must be thoroughly familiar with local security measures as they affect him as an individual, and with the general security measures for the command as a whole. A high degree of proficiency must be attained in the security measures listed below:

      (1)   Defense against air attack:

         It is essential that the highest possible standard of proficiency in recognition of aircraft be attained by all personnel. Aircraft recognition training should not be restricted to indoor instruction, but should be closely linked with other training and practiced daily wherever possible. No opportunity should be lost to take full advantage of aircraft seen in flight. Every individual will be thoroughly familiar with his part in the unit plan for defense against air attack.

      (2)   Defense against Chemical attack:

         Individual gas protective equipment will be carried in accordance with the provisions of Training Memorandum No. 4, ETOUSA, dated 27 Jan. 1944, which rescinds Tr Memo No. 22, dated 27 July 1943. Every individual must be thoroughly familiar with methods of personal decontamination, First Aid against Chemical attack (TM 42, ETOUSA, dated 23 Dec 43), and the general provisions of the unit plan for Defense against Chemical attack.

      (4)   Firefighting training:

         Firefighting training will be carried out in accordance with the provisions of the unit fire plan, and Training Memo, No. 20, Hq SOS.

      (5)   Defense against ground attack:

         Area plan for defense against ground attack will be practiced as often as possible without interfering with operational requirements. The nature

---

of these plans are such that practice can be held in the form of a unit problem, thereby affording valuable training as well as ensuring that the plan is practical, and will afford the necessary protection in any emergency.

(d) ADDITIONAL SUBJECTS:

See annex No. 1 to 5 attached.

6. TRAINING SCHEDULES AND RECORDS:

(a) Two copies of training schedules for each company and detachment will be submitted to this headquarters not later than Saturday of the week prior to which the training is to be held.

(b) Training attendance and progress charts will be maintained by all units.

By order of Colonel THOMPSON:

---

21 February 1944
5th Rangers – Companies A, B, C, D & F, Medical and HQ – Leominster, England.
Tec 5 Fast returned to Duty from Detached Service from the Intelligence School, London, England.
1st Lt. Norbert Schmidt, 1st Lt. William Purndrett, Tec 4 George Magurean, Tec 5 Nicolas Gallo were all attached from the 312th Ordnanace Battalion as of 1000hrs 20 February.
E Company 5th Rangers – Acton Court, Wrexham, England.

Jack Burke talking about Leominster: *I liked the town, the people were nice and we had a lot of dances with the Women's Land Army girls. But later we were restricted to barracks every other night because of the fights we were having with the black quartermaster outfit stationed nearby. One of them hit a Ranger over the head with a shovel. Put him in hospital to the point where he was sent home to the States.*

James Gabaree, A Co, 5th Rangers: *One of our own had been done in. Revenge! Headquarters closed its eyes as the Rangers armed themselves. Armed men with blackened faces spread out and slipped through the sentries that were guarding our compound and then through the guards at the ordnance compound. Rangers waited in the darkness until the targeted men were in their sleeping cots. On command, the Rangers cut the ropes holding the tents up and then proceeded to beat the hell out of anything that moved.*

Before the guards could respond to the situation, the Rangers slipped back to their own quarters. By the time the investigating forces arrived, the Rangers were back in their cots. The Rangers couldn't figure what all the fuss was about. Our stay in this town was cut short and we were soon on our way!

2nd Rangers – Companies A – F, Medical and HQ – Bude, Cornwall.

On 21 February General Huebner is confirmed as attending the Assault Training Centre as part of a group tour in preparation for the D-Day training of the men under his command.

HEADQUARTERS
U.S. ASSAULT TRAINING CENTER, ETOUSA
APO 553

PRE-ARRANGED MESSAGE CODE FOR 20 FEB. AND 21 FEB. 1944

1.   Tour of visiting officers will be known as "BRANDY".

2.   Geographical locations will be designated by the Serial Number indicated on "Schedule of Events".

3.   Members of the visiting Officers Party and the Assault Training Center Staff will be identified by the letter "O" followed by a code number as shown below.

VISITORS		STAFF OFFICERS	
Code No.	NAME & RANK	Code No.	NAME & RANK
O-13	GORBATOV, Col.	O-63	FINN, Col.
O-14	HOUGHTON, Lt.	O-64	HAAS, Lt. Col.
O-15	HUEBNER, Maj. Gen.	O-65	HORTON, Col.
O-16	KEUSSEFF, Lt.	O-66	KUNZIG, Lt. Col.
O-17	KHARLAMOV, Rear Admiral	O-67	LEARNARD, Lt. Col.

22 February 1944

5th Rangers – Companies A–F, Medical and HQ – Leominster, England.

F Company 5th Rangers – Leominster, England.

Medical Detachment 5th Rangers – Leominster, England.

Headquarters Company 5th Rangers – Leominster, England.

2nd Rangers – Companies A – E, Medical and HQ – Bude, Cornwall.

F Company 2nd Rangers – Bude, Cornwall.

Captain Otto Masny returned from Detached Service as of 17 February 1944 and assumed principal Duty as Company Commander of F Company.

1st Lt. Robert C. Arman was relieved of his temporary Duty as Company Commander and assumed his principal Duty as platoon leader.

23 February 1944

5th Rangers – Companies A – F, Medical and HQ – Leominster, England.
One officer (1st Lt. J. Raaen) and nineteen enlisted men were sent on Detached Service to a temporary station at Tighnabruaich, Scotland.
2nd Rangers – Companies A – F, Medical and HQ – Bude, Cornwall.

```
                        C-O-P-Y
                 SECRET-SECURITY-BIGOT                    BIGOT

                      HEADQUARTERS
                 FIRST UNITED STATES ARMY
                      APO 230
                                        23 February 1944.

    SUBJECT:      Joint Exercises and Rehearsals

    TO    :       Commander, CTF 122.

         1.       In order to complete the necessary coordination for
    joint exercises and rehearsals required in preparation for NEPTUNE,
    it is highly desirable to confirm as early as possible the date on
    which these exercises and rehearsals will be held.

         2.       The minimum essential number of exercises and re-
    hearsals together with the dates suggested by Admiral Hall or agreed
    to by you are as follows:

         EXERCISES                                   SUGGESTED DATE

    1st Division (Two Assault CTs of Force "O").
         To be loaded out of Portland-Weymouth Area    11 - 15 March

    4th Division (Assault CT of Force "U"). To
         be loaded out of Dartsmouth Area.             28 - 31 March

         REHEARSALS

    FORCE "O" (load out of Portland-Weymouth Area)     12 - 14 April

    FORCE "U" (load out of Dartsmouth & Plymouth East) 26 - 28 April
                                              Area
         3.       Your comments concerning the scope and dates of
    exercises as outlined above are requested.  In connection with
    proposed dates, your attention is invited to the periods of radio
    silence as published in Joint NEPTUNE Plan.

         4.       Reference 21st Army Group's request dated 17 Feb to
    load Force "O" out of Portland for rehearsal 2 - 9 May, this head-
    quarters believes it inadvisable to schedule a rehearsal at so late
    a date.  Troops can be made available, however, during this period
    for a dry shod test of BUCO and processing of build-up units, if
    desired.

         For the Commanding General:


                            W.B. KEAN
                      Brigadier General, G.S.C.
                         Chief of Staff


         SECRET-SECURITY-BIGOT

                              ENCLOSURE (A). 0070
                                    24 FEB 1944
```

The set of divisional orders for the assault practice with the code name Operation Fox. It was intended that the Rangers would be available to take part in this rehearsal.

S E C R E T

Hq 1st US Inf Div
APO #1, US Army
23 February 1944

COPY No. 29

: By Auth of CG :
: 1st US Inf Div:
: Initials AB :
: 23 February 44:

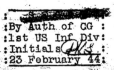

G-2 ESTIMATE OF THE ENEMY SITUATION
EXERCISE "FOX"

MAPS: GSGS 3957, scale 1:253,440, sheet 10; GSGS 3906, scale 1:25,000 sheets 32/4 NW & 32/6 SW, 32/6 NW, 29/6 NE, and 29/6 SE.

NOTE: The DARTMOUTH--START POINT area of the Devon coast of England represents a sector of the western coast of France along the English Channel. The enemy situation outlined herein is based on the enemy situation as it might exist in a similar area of the French coast.

1. SUMMARY OF THE ENEMY SITUATION.
   a. Enemy Ground Forces.
      (1) The coastal sector between the KINGSBRIDGE Estuary and a point between TEIGNMOUTH and EXMOUTH is held by the 719th Infantry Division. For location of other divisions in the vicinity of the assault area, see Overlay No. 1.
      (2) The 719th Division is disposed, with the 723rd Infantry Regiment south of the River DART and the 743rd Infantry Regiment north of the River DART; both are holding coastal sectors. A third (CROATIAN) Regiment, composed of former Yugoslav troops, is located in the vicinity of ASHPRINGTON (Y2478). The location of the reserve battalion of the 723rd Infantry is shown on Overlay No. 2; the location of the reserve battalion of the 743rd Infantry is unknown.
      (3) The SS Panzergrenadier Division HITLER JUGEND is located in the vicinity of BODMIN (X5089), and although it is composed mostly of unseasoned troops, it is considered an effective division. It is thought probable that a regimental combat team has been detached, and if so, the present strength is about 11,500. Other than this division, the nearest mobile reinforcements available are in the vicinity of BRISTOL, where SS Panzergrenadier Division HOHENSTAUFEN is located.
      (4) For additional information concerning enemy ground forces and order of battle, see Appendix I.
   b. Enemy defenses in the assault area (STOKES FLEMING-BEESANDS).
      (1) It is impossible, on the basis of present information, to determine the organization of the defending forces, but all known defenses are shown on Overlay No. 2. The various defended localities are divided into two classes:. those that will probably be defended by about a squad, and those that will probably be defended by about a platoon. The only conclusion that can be drawn is that the coastal front between the DART River and the KINGSBRIDGE Estuary is held by about two battalions, with no organized positions more than about a thousand yards in rear of the beach.
      (2) The only artillery believed to be in the assault area and immediate vicinity is as follows:
         (a) Four-gun battery of 155-mm howitzers at (248590).
         (b) Two 75-mm light infantry guns at 262674.
         (c) Three 75-mm gun-howitzers at (255666).
         (d) Four-gun battery of 150-mm howitzers at (219681).

- 1 -

S E C R E T

(3) Antiaircraft weapons include two three-gun 88-mm batteries and about fifteen light AA weapons, all located in the vicinity of the PASTURE CROSS Airfield.

(4) There is one 81-mm mortar located at (250654), and there are twelve pillboxes between BLACKPOOL and BEESANDS, as shown on Overlay No. 2. The ROYAL SANDS HOTEL at (257659) is fortified, as are the villages of SOMPUIS (256680), VAILLY (240660), and ST. ELOI (248674). Pillboxes are known to be concrete and of standard 6'6" thickness.

> Note: The villages will be simulated for the purpose of the exercise, and will be designated by white panels.

(5) Much of the beach is protected by barbed wire, and all defended localities are protected on exposed sides by wire entanglements.

(6) Minefields exist throughout the landing area; their exact extent is unknown, but are reported to be more densely laid in the vicinity of MANOR HOUSE and just north of TORCROSS.

(7) A concrete road block is located at (265678), blocking the secondary road that runs northward from MANOR HOUSE parallel to the beach. A number of temporary road blocks are reported to be located throughout the assault area, and practically all are defended by at least a squad.

c. Enemy air force.

(1) Enemy air strength within 250 miles of the assault area was reported on 22 January 1944 to have consisted of the following:

> (a)   Long range bombers, 252.
> (b)   Dive bombers, none.
> (c)   Fighter bombers, 30.
> (d)   Single engine fighters, 308 day and 11 night.
> (e)   Twin engine fighters, 40 day and 240 night.
> (f)   Long range reconnaissance, 70.
> (g)   Tactical reconnaissance, 20.
> (h)   Coastal, 20.
> NOTE: The air strength as it will be considered for this exercise will be the actual enemy air strength shown in the ETO G-2 Weekly Report for France, Belgium, and Holland.

(2) Enemy airfields within a 25-mile radius of the assault area are located at PASTURE CROSS (simulated), TEIGNMOUTH, PLYMOUTH, OKEHAMPTON, and EXETER.

d. Naval forces. Approximately ten submarines and 13 to 15 motor torpedo boats have been operating in the TEIGNMOUTH--SALCOMBE area in recent weeks, but no larger craft are at present in a position to intervene immediately. A submarine base is located at PLYMOUTH, and torpedo boat bases are located at DARTMOUTH and SALCOMBE.

e. Terrain and the weather.

(1) The area of operations is rolling country, with abrupt hills rising to more than 600 feet in places.

(2) There is an excellent landing beach, some 7,000 yards in length, which extends from BEESANDS northward to PILCHARD COVE, but is backed by steep cliffs some 250 feet high near TORCROSS, a marsh less than 200 yards behind the waterfront from TORCROSS to SLAPTON Road that is impassable except for three causeways and a marshy ley some 200 yards behind the waterfront from SLAPTON Road to STRETE GATE.

> NOTE: For the purpose of this exercise, LOWER LEY (the body of water behind the beach between TORCROSS and SLAPTON Road) will be considered marshland that cannot be crossed except by the three causeways that will be simulated by two foot bridges and one ponton bridge previously prepared by Corps Engineers. It will be assumed

- 2 -

that none of these will be destroyed prior to or during
the exercise. Location of these bridges is shown on
Overlay No. 2. The trail leading to STOKELEY FARM
(243646) from these bridges has been made into a usable
road by the Corps Engineers.
      (a) The stretch of beach from STRETE GATE to
PILCHARD COVE is about 1,400 yards long and 50 to 60 yards wide, and
is reasonably good. The upper part is backed by high, steep, but
scaleable cliffs.
      (3) There are only four reasonably good roads leading
from the beach into the interior. Two of these, in the vicinity of
TORCROSS, cross each other about a mile inland. The road running
northwest from SLAPTON SANDS is quite narrow in the village of
SLAPTON, and the road leading northwest from STRETE is so narrow in
places that two-way traffic is difficult. Secondary roads lead from
the beach at BEESANDS and SUNNYDALE, with a road (prepared by the
Corps Engineers; see note following Par. 1 e. (2), above) leading to
STOKENHAM from the bridges crossing LOWER LEY, and two roads leading
into the interior from BLACKPOOL beach. A lateral road runs parallel
to the beach from TORCROSS northward to STOKE FLEMING, and thence to
DARTMOUTH, while two other lateral roads run parallel to the beach
approximately three and five miles inland, respectively.
      (4) The nearest railroads in this sector are at KINGS-
WEAR (3273), TOTNES (2382) and KINGSBRIDGE (1666). Wire communication is negligible.
      (5) The terrain inland is characterized by valleys that
run generally at right angles with the beach and are broken by many
ridges. The main ridge in the general area runs west from DARTMOUTH
through MORLEIGH (195746), with numerous ridges branching out from
it. The country is broken into numerous small fields by high massive
rock and brush hedges.
      (6) Many of the roads are sunken, with high hedges on
either side and steep banks; deployment and movement of vehicles
across country will be difficult. Tracked vehicles may operate
across country on the higher ground, if the routes are carefully
chosen.
      (7) The weather is quite changeable, and much rain may
be expected during the spring months. Temperature may be expected
from 35 to 55 degrees fahrenheit. For hours of daylight and darkness, see Appendix II.
      (8) Although prevailing winds are from the southwest,
causing offshore winds, they are subject to quick change. A landing
with an on-shore wind along this coast would be difficult and coastly.
      (9) For additional terrain information, see Tactical
Terrain Study of SLAPTON SANDS.
   f. Civilian population.
      (1) The coastal area for a distance of approximately
five miles inland has been evacuated of all civilians other than
those workers necessary to the war effort. The few civilians remaining in the coastal area are mostly Germans and mixed nationalities.
      (2) The economic condition of the civilian population
in the interior is believed to be extremely poor, and the success of
Allied espionage has been improving during recent months.

  2. CONCLUSIONS.

    a. Enemy capabilities.
      (1) Limited air action against convoys and landing
troops and harassing of concentration and embarkation areas.
      (2) Limited submarine and motor torpedo boat action
against all types of naval craft.
      (3) Defend at all costs the beach itself by utilizing
prepared strongpoints until rendered useless by naval gunfire and
assault units.

(4) Fight a stubborn delaying action withdrawing to the fortified towns of SOMPUIS (256680) and ST. ELOI (248674), and counterattacking with major infantry elements, including armored elements by H plus 10, until strength and weight of our main effort has been determined.

(5) Reinforcement with additional units prior to D-day if tactical surprise is lost or by H plus 10 if tactical surprise is gained.

b. Discussion.

(1) Five enemy airdromes are located within 25 mile radius of the area of operations. If these fields are operating, the enemy will be capable of bombing and strafing our convoys as they approach the coast. Friendly fighter cover is not possible and cannot be expected.

(2) It is unlikely that the enemy will be able to bring more than a few submarines and motor torpedo boats into action, but some attacks on the convoys may be expected.

(3) The enemy's defense of the area is built around the employment of a maximum effort on the beach line. Because of the disadvantage imposed by the terrain on the attacking forces, the attackers will be most vulnerable in securing the initial beach-head. When the beach defenses are overcome, enemy forces will probably defend from successive positions inland and the nature of the terrain will permit defense at numerous places in the hills. Because of the abrupt rise of the land, commanding ground will be availble for the defenders during the initial stages of withdrawal.

(4) If tactical surprise is gained, the reserve battalion of the 723rd Infantry Regiment can be committed by H plus 2, the reserve regiment of the division by H plus 5, elements of the SS Panzergrenadier Division HITLER JUGEND by H plus 10, and one battalion of the 16th Luftwaffe Field Division by H plus 11. SS Panzergrenadier Division HITLER JUGEND could stage a coordinated attack by H plus 14, and leading elements of the SS Panzergrenadier Division HOHENSTAUFEN could arrive by H plus 24, with the entire division by H plus 30. The maximum number of additional infantry or Luftwaffe Field Divisions that could be employed would not exceed one by D plus 3 and another by D plus 5.

(5) If tactical surprise is lost, a total of five battalions could be committed at any time after H-hour, the HITLER JUGEND Division by H plus 4, the HOHENSTAUFEN Division by H plus 12, and one infantry or Luftwaffe Field Division late on D-day, with others on D plus 1 and D plus 2. The rate of reinforcement if tactical surprise is gained, is set forth above.

HUEBNER
Maj Gen

OFFICIAL: *Evans*
EVANS
G-2

The sketch accompanying the report indicates three gun batteries – one on the coast on the headland then a further two – 75mm and 150mm marked inland. In real terms representing the batteries at Pointe du Hoc and then the two together at Maisy.

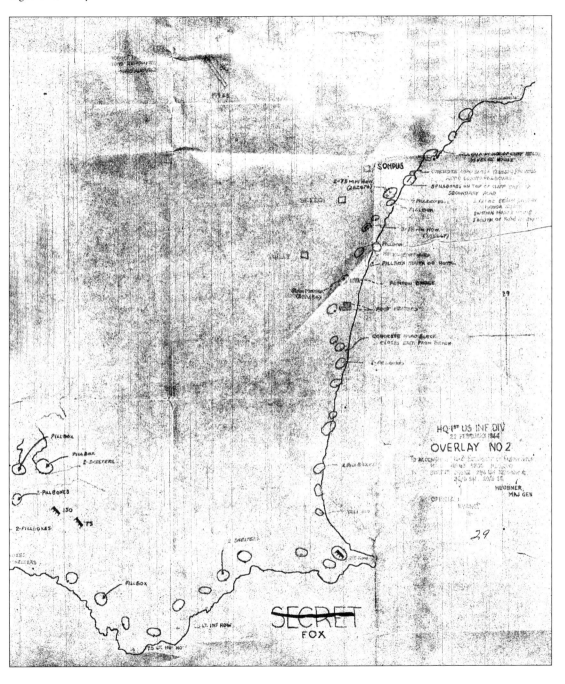

24 February 1944
5th Rangers – Companies A – F, Medical and HQ
– Leominster, England.
2nd Rangers – Companies A – F, Medical and
HQ – Bude, Cornwall.

The 24th brings more detail for the Operation Fox training exercise. CT116 stands for Combat Team 116 – on Page 2 of these documents it indicates the necessity to *'secure first phase line 2 hours prior before dark on D-Day.'*

"FOX"

```
:  ~~SECRET~~  :                          Hq 1st US Inf Div
:By authority of  :                       APO #1, U.S. Army
:CG, 1st US Inf Div:                      24 February 1944.
:24 February 1944 :
:Initials: AUG  :                         Copy No. [    029
```

<u>RECONNAISSANCE INSTRUCTIONS</u>

1. ESSENTIAL ELEMENTS OF INFORMATION.

    See Intelligence Annex to FO #33.

2. SPECIFIC MISSIONS.

    a. <u>CT 16</u>

        (1) Reconnoiter and report condition of bridges and fords crossing the GARA RIVER.

        (2) Reconnoiter routes of approach to airdrome north of Hr WALLATON CROSS (221700) and report most practicable route for night movement.

        (3) Reconnoiter N from SLAPTON (249667) to STRETE (2768) and report the location of mine fields, road blocks, strong points, and demolitions.

    b. <u>CT 116</u>

        (1) Reconnoiter routes west from SLAPTON (249667) and report mine fields, road blocks, strong points, stream crossings, and demolitions effected by the enemy as well as the location, strength, and composition, of any enemy forces encountered.

        (2) Reconnoiter roads S from SLAPTON and report the location of mine fields, road blocks, strong points, and demolitions.

    c. <u>Aviation</u>

        First light)   Location, strength, mobility, of enemy movements along
        Midday   )   roads: DARTMOUTH, HALLWELL, MODBURY, PLYMOUTH; EXETER,
        Last Light)   MARETON-HAMPSTEAD, PLYMOUTH; TORCROSS, KINGSBRIDGE,
                        HALLWELL, TOTNES, NEWTON ABBOT; PLYMOUTH, LISKEARD,
                        BODMIM, LAUNCESTON.

OFFICIAL: G.H.   HUEBNER
           GIBB   Maj Gen
           G-3

<u>DISTRIBUTION</u>:
    Same as FO #33

"FOX"

:By authority of :
:CG, 1st US Inf Div:
:24 February 19 :
:Initials: R   :

Hq 1st US Inf Div
APO #1, U.S. Army
24 February 1944.

Copy No. 029

FO #33

Maps: Gt Britain, GSGS 3906, 1/25,000:
Sheets 29/6 NE, 29/6 SE, 32/6 NW, 32/6 SW.

1. a. For information of the enemy see G-2 Annex (Annex 2).

   b. (1) The 102d Brit Corps and V US Corps land simultaneously on
          SLAPTON SANDS with the mission of securing beach heads for
          the landing of follow-up trs, and establishing a bridgehead
          as a base for future opns.

      (2) US Navy will provide escort, clear underwater minefields (off-
          shore), protect the transport area, be prepared to assist
          landings with gunfire on call from this hq. (Annex 6).

      (3) US 9th Air Force will support the atk and opns subsequent to
          landings. (Annex 7).

2. a. The 1st US Inf Div (rein) with 116 RCT atchd assault SLAPTON SANDS
       with two RCTs abreast, 116 RCT on the left; clear the shore line
       of enemy resistance in Corps zone of action, secure first phase
       line two hours prior to dark on D-day prepared to adv to the NW.

   b. Ship assignments and tr list (Annex 3).

   c. Beach assignments and designations, boundaries, zones of action,
      contact points, see Opn overlay (Annex 1).

3. a. CT 16 (REIN)

      (1) Land two BLTs simultaneously at H-hour on D-day on ABLE beach.
          Res Bn to follow as directed by CT Comdr.

      (2) Clear the beaches in the 1st US Inf Div zone of action (Opn
          overlay).

      (3) Capture SOMPUIS, ST ELOI, and airport at WALLATON CROSS, seize
          and hold obj designated, initiate rcn to first phase line.
          Establish defensive position along IBL.

      (4) Gain and maintain contact with 102d Brit Corps on rt, and 29th
          US Inf Div on the left.

      (5) Protect rt flank of the Div.

      (6) See Opns overlay (Annex 1).

- 1 -

FO #33, Hq 1st US Inf Div, 24 Feb 44 contd.

  b. CT 116 (REIN)

    (1) Land two BLTs simultaneously at H-hour on D-day on BAKER beach. Res Bn to follow as directed by CT Comdr.

    (2) Clear the beaches, 29th US Inf Div zone of action (Opn overlay).

    (3) Capture VAILLY, seize and hold obj designated, initiate rcn to first phase line, establish defensive positions along IBL.

    (4) Protect left flank of 1st US Inf Div.

    (5) See Opn overlay (Annex 1).

  c. CT 18 (REIN)

    (1) Land H plus 2 on ABLE Green beach and secure first phase line two hours prior to dark D-day. (Opns overlay, Annex 1)

    (2) Make immediate rcn to 2d phase line. Prepare for continuation of atk to the NW in 1st US Inf Div zone of action. (Adv rcn elements to accompany CT 16).

  d. CT 26

    Land D plus 1, move to assembly area as Div res. (Opn overlay, Annex 1).

  e. Engr plan (Annex 8).

  f. Arty plan - initially CT atchmts as shown:

                CT 16   - 7th FA Bn
                            62d FA Bn

                CT 116   - 111th FA Bn
                            58th FA Bn

                CT 18   - 32d FA Bn

                CT 26   - 33d FA Bn

            Gen support   - 5th FA Bn

  x. (1) Watches synchronized with ship's time prior to debarkation and daily thereafter with CP 1st US Inf Div.

    (2) Request for air support to CP of RCT.

    (3) H-hour and D-day to be announced later.

4. See Adm O (Annex 4).

5. a. Communications (Annex 5).

Regimental Combat Team 116 were to be supported by the 58th Field Artillery Battalion during the exercise.

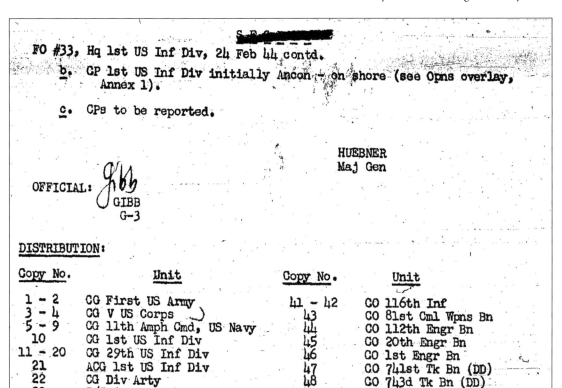

FO #33, Hq 1st US Inf Div, 24 Feb 44 contd.

    b. CP 1st US Inf Div initially Ancon – on shore (see Opns overlay, Annex 1).

    c. CPs to be reported.

                                                 HUEBNER
                                             Maj Gen

OFFICIAL: Gibb
            GIBB
            G-3

DISTRIBUTION:

Copy No.	Unit	Copy No.	Unit
1 - 2	CG First US Army	41 - 42	CO 116th Inf
3 - 4	CG V US Corps	43	CO 81st Cml Wpns Bn
5 - 9	CG 11th Amph Cmd, US Navy	44	CO 112th Engr Bn
10	CG 1st US Inf Div	45	CO 20th Engr Bn
11 - 20	CG 29th US Inf Div	46	CO 1st Engr Bn
21	ACG 1st US Inf Div	47	CO 741st Tk Bn (DD)
22	CG Div Arty	48	CO 743d Tk Bn (DD)

A number of copies of the above brief were sent to the 1st Infantry Division for distribution within their sub-units.

---

25 February 1944
5th Rangers – companies A – F, Medical and HQ – Leominster, England.
2nd Rangers – Companies A – F, Medical and HQ – Bude, Cornwall.

'Secret' US Army papers dated 25 February confirmed the area of French coast to be attacked. They stated the following: *'This plan was complete except for minor modifications to meet the changing situation. The general plan of attack called for a simultaneous landing on two main beaches. The VII Corps, with the 4th Infantry Division making the assault by sea and assisted by the 82nd Airborne Division and the 101st Airborne Division landing in the rear of the German coastal defences, was to establish a beachhead in the neighbourhood of Varreville, near the southern portion of the east coast of the Cotentin Peninsula. The V Corps, with one combat team of the 29th Infantry Division on the right and one combat team of the 1st Infantry Division on the left, all under the command of the 1st Division was to establish a beachhead on the northern coast of Calvados near St. Laurent-sur-Mer.'*

Overleaf: Alert Orders dated 25 February gave instructions to the Rangers that they were to be ready to move at a moment's notice. The orders were to be accompanied with the relevant paperwork on where to load – as well as papers to be completed by the unit once exact personnel numbers were known. When movement was imminent, it was marked on the bottom of each company's Morning Report as 'Alerted for Departure'.

███████████████ BIGOT

PROPOSED WARNING ORDER

HEADQUARTERS
FIRST UNITED STATES ARMY
APO 230

(Date)

SUBJECT: Alert Order.

TO   : (Commanding Officer, Unit)

1. Your organization is alerted effective this date.

2. On or after ____(date)____ you will receive a movement warning from the Transportation Corps. This movement warning will allow five or more days before actual movement.

3. You will comply with instructions as issued by SOS during the period of movement and processing from Concentration Areas through the Marshalling Areas to the Embarkation Points.

4. You will move with strength of personnel and vehicles as indicated in Inclosure No. 1.

5. You will comply with the provisions of "European Theater of Operations, Preparation for Overseas Movement, United States Army, Short Sea Voyage," dated 10 January 1944 (corrected). Forms SOSTC 8, 8a, 9 and 10 will be completed based on the strengths listed in Inclosure No. 1. (Following the word "Remarks" near the bottom of Form SOSTC No. 8, the unit commander will insert the number officers and men, respectively, that can travel in the unit vehicles reported on FORM SOSTC No. 10. Such personnel are included in those reported in the body of Form SOSTC No. 8). Forms will be delivered to HQ, SOS, ETO, Office of the Chief of Transportation, Traffic Division, APO 887, by ____(date)____. These forms may be obtained from the local RTO who will also be available for assistance and advice in completing and delivering forms. It is prescribed that the above forms be delivered by officer courier. Where several units are located in the same area or when battalion or larger unit is involved, Commanding Officers may assemble such reports and forward by one courier if delivery is not delayed.

6. Paragraphs 70 & 72, ETO, POM, SSV are interpreted as follows: Residues, including overstrength in personnel and organizational equipment not carried on vehicles, will be formed as a separate detachment and will complete all preparations prescribed for the parent unit. At an appropriate time the residual detachment will be separated from the parent unit for concentration in an area to be designated by SOS until time for its movement to the marshalling and embarkation areas, as prescribed by Combined Headquarters. Detachments that are not self-sustaining will be grouped so that they can be mutually sustaining. SOS will furnish necessary assistance. Forms SOSTC No. 8, 8a, 9 and 10 will be completed for each residual detachment and delivered to the Transportation Corps as prescribed for the parent unit.

7. Administrative details necessary for your information are attached as Inclosure No. 2.

By command of the ARMY COMMANDER.

2 Incls.
Incl 1--Unit Strength for Overseas Movement.
Incl 2--Administrative Details (sample not attached).

- 1 -
██████████████ BIGOT

BIGOT

HEADQUARTERS
(Unit)

LANDING TABLE

Page No. _____ of _____ Pages .

Landing Table Index No.	Craft ready to beach.	Unit/Craft or Ship Serial	Unit or Portion of Unit (Indicate unit designating the CO Troops by "Ø")	Personnel		Vehicles or Supplies			Embark-ation Sector or Fort	Landing Ship or Craft		Landing Sector and Beach	Remarks
				March-ing	Veh-icle	Sup-plies-Tons	Veh-icles-No.	Type-Supplies or vehs.		Craft Serial	Type & Mark		
(a)	(b)	(c)	(d)	(e)	(f)	(g)	(h)	(j)	(k)	(l)	(m)	(n)	(o)

BIGOT

ANNEX NO. 22 c.
Page No. 1 of 2 pages.

BIGOT

FINAL ASSEMBLY AND LOADING POINTS FOR ASSAULT AND FOLLOW-UP FORCES

FORCE "O"

FINAL ASSEMBLY		SHIP OR CRAFT			Pers	Veh	LOADING	
LOCATION								
Quay	Anchorage	Type	Flo-tillas	Nos.			Points	Time
a	b	c	d	e	f	g	j	k
	Portland & Weymouth Bay	(APA	--	7(1)	10010	(560)(2)	) Weymouth	36 to 48 hrs (3)
		(LSI(L)	--	2	2800		)	
	Portland	LCI(L)	--	18	3600	--	)	
	Portland	LCH	--	3(4)	600	--	)	
	Poole	LCT(A)	--	8(5)	80	16	) Poole	36 hrs.
	Poole	LCT(HE)	--	8(6)	440	88	)	
	Portland	LCT	11	110(7)	5780	1024	Portland Hards	43 hrs.
	Portland & Weymouth Bay	LST	--	22	6600	1320	Portland Hards	48 hrs.
	Poole	Support Craft	--	24	--	--		
	TOTAL FORCE "O"				29910	2448		

REMARKS: (1) APA can carry up to 1430 personnel.
(2) Light vehicles, as agreed to by Navy, may be carried. Not included in total.
(3) Marching personnel ferried to APA and LSI(L) by tender.
(4) Each LCH embarked with 200 personnel.
(5) Each LCT(A) loaded with two tanks and ten personnel.
(6) Each LCT(HE) loaded with 11 vehicles and 55 personnel.
(7) Includes 6 LCT's slightly armored, carrying minimum of two tanks and 10 personnel each and twelve LCT(5 & 6) preloaded with supplies and personnel only – no vehicles.
(8) Note that present land capacities are 23,590 personnel and 2,530 vehicles.

BIGOT

FINAL ASSEMBLY AND LANDING POINTS FOR ASSAULT AND FOLLOW-UP FORCES

FORCE "O"

FINAL ASSEMBLY						LOADING	
LOCATION	SHIP OR CRAFT			ARMY LIFT			
Anchorage	Type	Flotillas	Nos. Net Gross	Pers	Veh	Points	Remarks
a	b	c	d	e	f	g	j
Portland & Weymouth Bay	LSH	-	1 1	-	-	Weymouth	All ships & craft Force B to load within 48 hours (2).
	LST(S)	-	3 3	260	-	"	
	LSI(H)	-	3 3	350	-	"	
	APA	-	7 7	10010	(560)(1)	"	
	LSI(L)	-	2 2	2800	-	"	
	LCI(L)	-	18 21	3600	-	"	
	LCH	-	4 4	600	-	"	
	LCT(5)	))	98 36	5390	1078	Portland Hards	16 LCT(6) Sp load DD at Torcross, anchor at Portland
	LCT(6)	) 11)	64				
	LCT(6)	)	7 7	385	-	Plymouth	Each loaded with 200 tons supplies.
Portland	LCI(L)	-	10 12	2000	-	Plymouth	
	LCT(4)	-	2 2	110	22	Portland Hards	
	LST(2)		22 24	6600	1320	" "	
	LSD		1 1	100	20	" "	Loaded with 20 LCM's each of which carry one M-4 Medium Tank. 16 lifted on APA's.
	LCVP		220 220				
	LCM(3)		81 81				
Poole	LCT(A)	-	8 8	80	16		Loaded with three tanks (1 Armored Bulldozer) and 15 personnel each.
	LCT(HE)		8 8	170	34	6 Poole, 2 Portland	2 ordinary LCT(5)'s; 6 slightly armored LCT(5)'s carrying minimum 2 tanks and 10 personnel each.
	LCT(CB)		2 2	110	22	Portland	Ordinary LCT(5).
TOTAL ARMY LIFT FORCE "O"				32565	2512		

Remarks: (1) Light vehicles, as agreed to by Navy, may be carried. Not included in total.
(2) Marching personnel ferried to APA and LSI(L) by tender.
(3) Minor adjustments may be made in the above by agreement between CG, V Corps, Naval Comdr, Force "O" & CG, XIX Dist, SBS.
(4) Figures for personnel and vehicles in most cases are planning figures only. Exact number to be determined by prestowage.

BIGOT

INITIAL MOVEMENT - LOADING OF LCT AND LST

LOADING POINTS	D - 5 LST	D - 4 LCT	D - 4 LST	D - 3 LCT	D - 3 LST	D - 2 LCT	D - 2 LST
Portland	-	-	-	66(Force O)	10(Force O)	60(Force O)	12(Force O)
Dartmouth East and Brixham	-	28(Force U)	-	60(Force U)	-	-	-
Dartmouth West	-	-	2(Force U)	35(Force U)	7(Force U)	-	-
Plymouth East	-	-	8(Force U)	-	4(Force U) (complete noon)	-	-
Plymouth West	-	-	10(Force B)	60(Force B)	4(Force B)	-	-
Falmouth East and West	12(Force B)	-	24(Force B)	-	-	-	-

Also issued on 25 February was the 'ASSAULT PLAN' and the following overlay for the GSGS maps. It shows the Ranger force of two Ranger battalions landing at Pointe du Hoc – advancing inland in a westerly direction along the coast with the aim of reaching the *'PM D-Day'* line. It is clear from this point in February that the landing beaches and the Rangers' objectives had been decided upon.

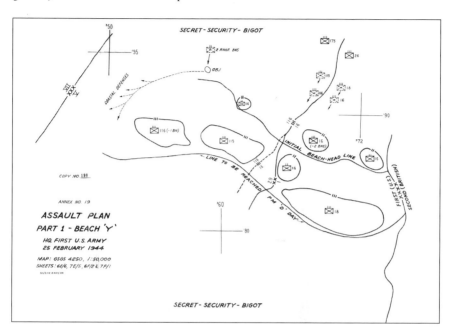

Below is the same overlay but this time shown in place on a period map.

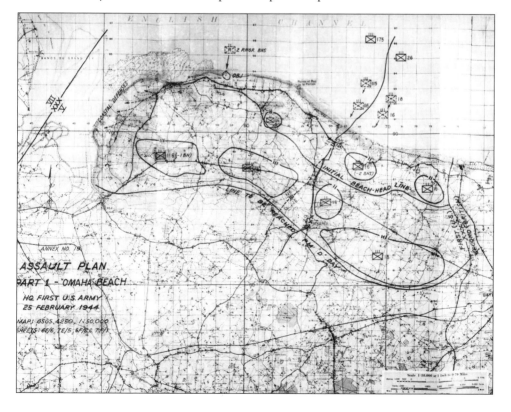

Below the same type of map with overlay shown underneath it, but this time covering the landing areas on Utah Beach. This was provided to the Rangers so that they were made aware of the other US elements who were landing opposite them. It also amplified that their mission to attack the Batteries at Maisy could have a profound effect on these troops landing directly across the water, if it was not carried out quickly.

The almost vertical line towards the right of the overlay below indicates the boundary between the Utah Sector and the Omaha Sector. The batteries at Maisy are on the far left of the V Corps / Omaha Sector of operations.

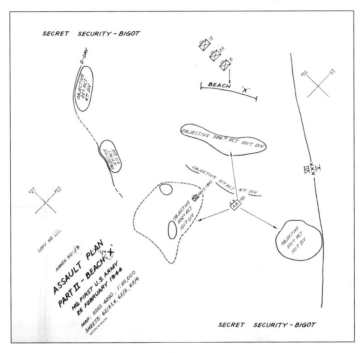

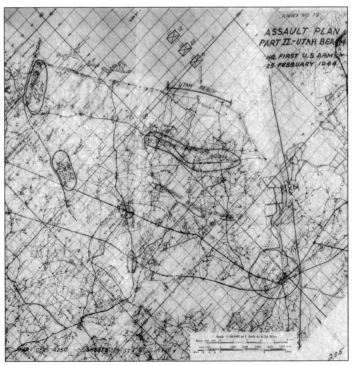

V Corps report on Naval Gunfire Support being made available to the Rangers. The liaison between the Navy and the Rangers would be co-ordinated by men of the 293rd Joint Assault Signal Company who would accompany them when they landed. These men were called Naval Shore Fire Control Parties (NSFCP).

B_I_G_O_T

4. Missions:

a. Field Artillery – As assigned by Division and Corps Commanders.

b. Naval Fire Support Ships – To protect shipping from attack by surface forces and submarines, and to support by bombardment, the initial amphibious and airborne landings and subsequent coastwise advance inland.

c. Fire Support Craft – To furnish during the approach to the beaches and prior to touchdown, area fire on and in rear of the beaches, fire on strong points, beach defenses and to take part in the beach drenching.

5. Employment and Coordination of Field Artillery:

a. Upon the arrival of field artillery units ashore, the employment will be normal, except initially direct support units will be doubled whenever the availability of assigned craft will permit. Prior to landing, organic and attached 105mm How M7 units will fire from craft as outlined in paragraph 7 j below.

b. It is imperative that some medium and heavy artillery units be brought ashore early by both V and VII Corps in order to effectively execute counterbattery. In this connection, one battery of 155mm Guns M12 will be available to V Corps and one battery to VII Corps if pre-stowage discloses that these units can be transported.

c. Early artillery support will be provided by the V Corps for the Ranger units operating on the right of the Corps Sector.

6. Employment and Coordination of Naval Fire Support:

a. The Western Naval Task Force will support the assault, follow up, and build up of the First Army. Initially, the heavier gunfire support ships (battleships and cruisers) will participate in the prearranged bombardment upon coast defense batteries (See Annex No. 12). When the coast defense batteries have been silenced, these ships will continue to furnish general support to First Army within their capabilities of range. Destroyers will be assigned to deliver close support fire for the initial assault. This support will include fire on strong points, beach defenses, and flanks of beaches and participation in the beach drenching during the approach to the beaches of the assault wave of troops.

d. (1) Twenty-seven (27) Naval Shore Fire Control Parties will be available for the adjustment of naval gunfire. Nine (9) such parties from the 294th Joint Assault Signal Company will operate with the 1st Infantry Division, nine (9) from the 286th Joint Assault Signal Company with the 4th Infantry Division, and nine (9) from the 293rd Joint Assault Signal Company with the 29th Infantry Division. The necessary number of parties from the last named group will operate with the Ranger Battalions landing in the V Corps Sector.

ALLOCATION OF CRAFT

TO

FIRST 3 TIDES

		FORCE								
		"O"		"B"		"U"			RANGER	
ITEM	TYPE	1st Tide	2nd Tide	2nd Tide	3rd Tide	1st Tide	2nd Tide	3rd Tide		TOTAL
1	LSH	1	–	–	–	1	–	–	–	2
2	APA & XAP	g7	–	–	–	h3	–	–	–	10
3	LSI(L)	2	–	–	–	1	–	–	–	3
4	LST	a10	12	15	27	i5	16	d8	–	93
5	LCT	c128	–	60	–	f123	–	–	–	311
6	LCI(L)	b22	–	15	–	e29	–	–	–	66
7	LSI(S)	–	–	–	–	–	–	–	3	3
8	LSI(H)	–	–	–	–	–	–	–	3	3

26 February 1944
5th Rangers – Companies A – F, Medical and HQ –
Leominster, England.
2nd Rangers – Companies A – F, Medical and HQ –
Bude, Cornwall.

Instructions were given to chaplains to file a monthly report to their unit commander *on the first of each calendar month, and to be promptly forwarded, through channels, so as to reach this headquarters not later than the sixteenth day of the month.*

The reports will not be classified, unless such action is deemed necessary by the officer accomplishing the first endorsement. When both the unit's APO number and geographical location are indicated in the report, it will be classified as "Confidential" or higher.

Letters of condolence may be written by chaplains only in special cases and only when directed by the chaplain's commanding officer. In preparing such letters, strict compliance will be had with the following:

In the case of a letter reporting a battle casualty, particular care will be taken to see that the letter contains the same categorical description of the casualty's condition – as does the official report. These categories are:

1) *Killed in Action.*
2) *Seriously Wounded in Action.*
3) *Slightly Wounded in Action.*
4) *Missing in Action.*
5) *Captured by the enemy.*

The letter will clearly state the subject's full name and serial number. Care will be taken in a case of sickness or injury not to magnify the subject's condition and not to indicate that there is no possibility of return to duty.

Security and censorship regulations will be strictly observed. Information concerning locations of graves, disposal of remains and effects etc. will not be included and photographs of graves will not be enclosed.

If letters are written to relatives or friends they should be advised to communicate directly with The Quartermaster General, ASF, Washington, DC for information concerning such matters.

On 26 February the British 21st Army Group Headquarters released a larger scale forecast map. It shows how the US D-Day line corresponds to the Canadian and British lines beyond Bayeux and Caen. The continuance of this line along all the fronts would in theory ensure that no gaps appeared between the different Allied units and this would stop any German incursion between the Allies.

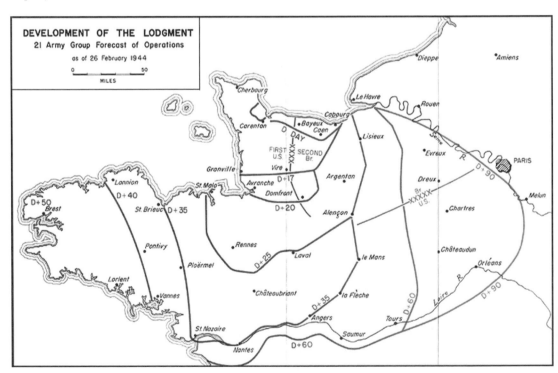

27 February 1944

5th Rangers – Companies A – F, Medical and HQ – Leominster, England.
2nd Rangers – Companies A – F, Medical and HQ – Bude, Cornwall.

On 27 February 1944 an Aerial Reconnaissance Report entitled – Maisy La Martinière (B798) stated the following: '*This is now considered to be a 4 gun light battery. (5004/5 of sortie AA/725, 24 February 1944, 1/16,000, quality good).*'

Paperwork issued on 27 February shows that the Rangers had the ability to promote officers as they saw fit. This became a regularly used piece of army paperwork.

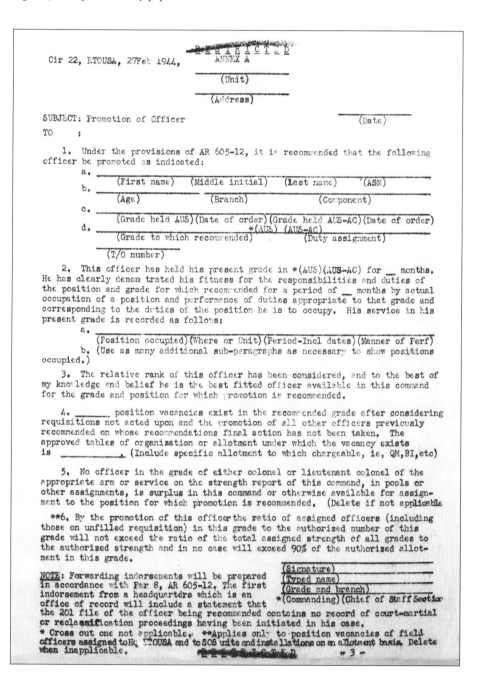

28 February 1944
5th Rangers – Companies A – F, Medical and HQ – Leominster, England.
Captain William F. Murray was sent on Detached Service to a temporary station at Tighnabruaich, Scotland.
2nd Rangers – Companies A – F, Medical and HQ – Bude, Cornwall.

2nd Rangers Narrative History.

> During the last week of the month, all troops participated in a thirty-mile, light equipment march; the last nine miles of which were cross-country along the hilly coast.

Continuing with the education of its men, the US Army released a paper entitled 'Britain, The Cradle of Democracy'

Today the old power of the King has been shifted to Parliament, the Prime Minister and his Cabinet. The British Parliament has been called the mother of parliaments, because almost all the representative bodies in the world have been copied from it. It is made up of two houses, the House of Commons and the House of Lords. The House of Commons is the most powerful group and is elected by all adult men and women in the country, much like our Congress. Today the House of Lords can do little more than add its approval to laws passed by the House of Commons. Many of the titles held by the lords (such as 'baron' and 'duke' and 'earl') have been passed from father to son for hundreds of years. Others are granted for outstanding achievement, much as American colleges and universities give honorary degrees to famous men and women. These customs may seem strange and old-fashioned but they give the British the same feeling of security and comfort that many of us get from the familiar ritual of a church service.

The important thing to remember is that within the apparently old-fashioned framework, the British enjoy a practical, working twentieth century democracy which is in some ways even more flexible and sensitive to the will of the people than our own.

A photograph taken on 28 February 1944 shows the 80th Smoke Generating Company testing beach covering mobile smoke dispensers. These were considered vital in the run up to D-Day. If the Germans were to fly reconnaissance flights over the embarkation areas, it could prove essential for the area to be covered in smoke, thus depriving the Germans of any aerial intelligence photographs.

29 February 1944

5th Rangers – Companies A – F, Medical and HQ – Thornhill, Dunfrieshire, Scotland.

2nd Rangers – Companies A – F, Medical and HQ – Bude, Cornwall.

Captain Merrill went from Detached Service to London and returned to Duty.

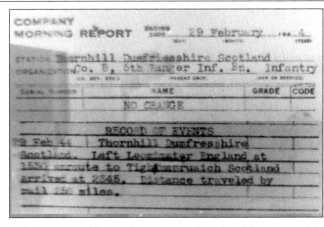

James W. Gabaree: *The small ship was overloaded with men and equipment. One could hardly breathe. We were on our way to a secret commando training base in Achnacarry, Scotland. This would be our home as we commenced the gruelling training to prepare us for landing somewhere in France. This would be as close as you could get to being in actual combat. The purpose of the training was to push us to the breaking point. If you couldn't take it, you were out. The coming invasion depended, in a great measure, on us knocking out the big guns on Pointe du Hoc.*

On 29 February 1944 the US Army issued a Table of Organisation and list of Equipment specifically designed for a Ranger Battalion. Known in the military as a T/O & E. It shows all the quantities of each item that was needed and should be issued to them.

TABLE OF ORGANIZATION
AND EQUIPMENT
No. 7–87

WAR DEPARTMENT,
WASHINGTON 25, D. C., 29 February 1944.

RANGER COMPANY, RANGER INFANTRY BATTALION

	Page
SECTION I. Organization	2
II. Equipment:	
General	4
Army Air Forces	5
Chemical	5
Engineer	5
Ordnance:	
Weapons and miscellaneous	5
Quartermaster:	
Organizational clothing	6
Individual equipment	6
Organizational equipment	7
Signal	8

*This table supersedes all prior tables and equipment lists on the organization of this unit.

SECTION I

ORGANIZATION

Designation: Company †__, ‡__ Ranger Infantry Battalion

	Unit	Specification serial No.	Technician grade	Company headquarters	Platoon headquarters	Section headquarters	Assault squad	Light machine gun squad	Total section	Special weapons section	Total platoon	Total company	Enlisted cadre	Remarks
						2 platoons (each)								
						2 assault sections (each)								
2	Captain, including			1								1		† Insert letter of company.
3	Company commander	1542		(ᵃ 1)								(1)		‡ Insert number of battalion.
4	First lieutenant, including	1542									1	2		ᵃ Armed with rifle, antitank, cal. .55, if required.
5	Platoon leader	1542			(ᵃ 1)						(1)	(2)		ᵇ Armed with rifle, cal. .30, M1903A4.
6	Total commissioned			1	1						1	3		ᶜ British equipment.
7	First sergeant	585		ᵇ 1								1	1	ᵈ Armed with pistol, automatic, cal. .45.
8	Technical sergeant, including				1						1	2	2	ᵉ Armed with rifle, cal. .30, M1.
9	Platoon	651			(ᵇ 1)						(1)	(2)	(2)	ᶠ Armed with gun, submachine, cal. .45.
10	Staff sergeant, including				1		1	2			5	10	5	For specification serial numbers for enlisted men shown in column 2, see AR 615-26. For officers, see TM 12-406 and 12-407.
11	Section leader	652				(ᶜ 1)			(ᶜ 1)		(3)	(6)	(3)	
12	Squad leader	653					(ᶜ 1)				(2)	(4)	(2)	
13	Sergeant, including					1		1	1		3	6		
14	Section leader, assistant	652							(ᵃᵇ 1)		(1)	(2)		
15	Squad leader	653				(ᶜ 1)			(1)		(2)	(4)		
16	Clerk, company	405		1								1	1	
17	Corporal, including			(ᶜ 1)							(ᶜ 1)	(1)		
18	Private, first class, including			1	2		4	4	8	4	22	45		
19	Ammunition carrier	504					(ᶜ 2)	(2)		(ᶜ 2)	(6)	(12)		
20	Gunner, machine gun	604					(ᶜ 1)	(1)			(2)	(4)		
21	Gunner, machine gun, assistant	604					(ᶜ 1)	(1)			(2)	(4)		
22	Gunner, mortar	607							(ᶜ 1)		(1)	(2)		
23	Gunner, mortar, assistant	607							(ᶜ 1)		(1)	(2)		
24	Messenger	675		(ᶜ 1)	(ᶜ 1)						(1)	(3)		
25	Rifleman	745					(ᶜ 4)		(4)		(8)	(16)		
26	Rifleman, sniper	745				(ᵉ 1)						(1)	(2)	
27	Total enlisted			3	3	1	5	5	11	6	31	65	9	
28	Aggregate			4	4	1	5	5	11	6	32	68	9	
29	O Gun, machine, cal. .30, light, flexible							1	1		2	4		
30	O Gun, submachine, cal. .45			2	2						2	6		
31	O Launcher, rocket, at, 2.36-inch									1	1	2		
32	O Mortar, 60-mm									1	1	2		
33	O Pistol, automatic, cal. .45			1	1					2	2	3	8	17	
34	O Rifle, antitank, cal. .55ᵉ									1	1	2		
35	O Rifle, cal. .30, M1			2	1	1	5		3	9	3	22	46		
36	O Rifle, cal. .30, M1903A4					1					1	2		

AGO 273

T/O & E 7-87

RANGER COMPANY, RANGER INFANTRY BATTALION

T/O & E 7-87   29 February 1944

RANGER COMPANY, RANGER INFANTRY BATTALION
Section II
EQUIPMENT
GENERAL

1. This table is in accordance with AR 310–60, and it will be the authority for requisition in accordance with AR 35–6540, and for the issue of all items of equipment listed herein unless otherwise indicated. This table rescinds all Tables of Basic Allowances and Tables of Equipment heretofore published except T/E No. 21, Clothing and Individual Equipment, so far as they pertain to the allowances of equipment for the organization and individuals covered by this table.

2. When there appears a discrepancy between the allowances shown in column 2, "Allowances," and column 3, "Basis of distribution and remarks," the amount shown in column 2 will govern.

3. Items of clothing and individual equipment, components of sets and kits, spare parts, accessories, special equipment, special tools, and allowances of expendable items are contained in the following publications:

Army Air Forces.
   Air Corps Stock List.
   Technical Orders of the 00–30–series.
Chemical Warfare Service.
   Standard Nomenclature and Price List.
   Chemical Warfare Series, Army Service Forces Catalogs.
Corps of Engineers.
   Engineer Series, Army Service Forces Catalogs.
Medical Department.
   Medical Department Supply Catalog.
   Army Service Forces Catalog, Medical 4.
Ordnance Department.
   Standard Nomenclature Lists (SNL), index to which is the index to Ordnance
      Publications, Volume 1, OFSB 1–1.
   T/A for Cleaning, Preserving and Lubricating Materials, Recoil Fluids,
      Special Oils and Similar Items of Issue.
   T/A 23, Targets and Target Equipment.
Quartermaster Corps.
   Table of Clothing and Individual Equipment, T/E 21.
   Quartermaster Series, Army Service Forces Catalogs.
   AR 30–3010, Items and Price Lists of Regular Supplies Controlled by
      Budget Credits and Price List of Other Miscellaneous Supplies.
Signal Corps.
   Signal Corps Catalog (T/BA items).
   Signal Corps Series, Army Service Forces Catalogs.
AR 310–200, Military Publications, Allowance and Distribution.
AR 775–10, Qualification in Arms and Ammunition Training Allowances.

4   AGO 273

RANGER COMPANY, RANGER INFANTRY BATTALION

ARMY AIR FORCES

1	2	3
Item	Allow-ances	Basis of distribution and remarks
Raft, Pneumatic life, A-2, complete w/CO$_2$ cylinders and hand pump.	6	
Vest, life, preserver, type B-4_____	68	1 per indiv (10 percent overage incl in and asgd to hq co).

CHEMICAL

Alarm, gas_____	1	
Flame thrower, portable, M1A1_____	1	
Kit, chemical agent detector, M9___	1	In T of Opns.
Mask, gas, service, lightweight, M3-10A1-6.	68	1 per indiv (mask, gas, sv will be issued as directed by the WD until exhausted).

ENGINEER

Board, drawing, machine gun_____	2	1 per plat.
Compass:		
Lensatic, luminous dial, w/case___	20	1 per off; 1st sgt; s sgt; sgt.
Wrist, liquid filled_____	48	1 per indiv not issued compass, lensatic. Pending availability subsitute compass, watch.
Demolition equipment, Set No. 5, individual.	8	1 per sqd.
Protractor, plastic, semi-circular, MG, 10-inch graduated in mils.	4	1 per MG sqd.

ORDNANCE

Weapons and miscellaneous

Binocular, M13_____	22	1 per off; 1st sgt; t sgt; s sgt; sgt.
Gun:		
Machine, Browning, cal. .30, M1919A6, flexible.	4	1 per LMG sqd. See SNL A-6.
Submachine, cal. .45, M3_____	6	2 per co hq; 2 per plat hq. See SNL A-58.
Knife, trench, M3, w/scabbard, M8_	68	1 per indiv. See SNL B-37.
Launcher:		
Grenade, M7_____	46	1 per rifle, cal. .30, M1. See SNL B-39.
Rocket, 2.36-in, M9_____	2	See SNL B-36.
Mortar, 60-mm, M2 w/mount M2__	2	1 per sp wpns sec. See SNL A-43.
Mount, tripod, machine gun, cal. 30, M2.	2	1 per sp wpns sec. See SNL A-6.
Pistol, automatic, cal. .45, M1911A1_	17	1 per indiv armed w/pistol as shown in sec I. See SNL B-6

5

RANGER COMPANY, RANGER INFANTRY BATTALION

1	2	3
Item	Allowances	Basis of distribution and remarks
Projector:		
Pyrotechnic, hand, M9_____	8	1 per sqd (see SNL B–38). (Pending availability of projector, pyrotechnic, hand, M9, issue pistol, pyrotechnic, AN–M8, see SNL B–33.)
Signal, ground, M4_____	4	Limited standard item. (See SNL B–24.)
Rifle, U S cal. .30:		
Antitank, cal. .55, Boy's_____	2	1 per indiv armed w/rifle, anti-tank, cal. .55 as shown in sec I nonstandard item).
M1_____	46	1 per indiv armed w/rifle cal. .30, M1 as shown in sec I (each rifle to be equipped w/bayonet, M1905 and scabbard bayonet, M3, see SNL B–21).
M1903A4, (Sniper's) _____	2	1 per indiv armed w/rifle cal. .30. M1903A4 as shown in sec I. See SNL B–3.
Watch, wrist:		
7 jewel_____	65	1 per EM
15 or more jewels_____	3	1 per off (in T of Opns outside continental limits of US).

QUARTERMASTER

Organizational clothing

Brassard, arm, gas_____	3	
Gloves, protective, impermeable_____	2	1 per 40 EM outside continental US (to be stored in nearest available dep for issue as determined by T of Opns comdr).
Mittens, asbestos, M1942_____	12	2 per MG; mort.
Suit, protective, one-piece impermeable.	2	1 per 40 EM outside continental US (to be stored in nearest available dep for issue as determined by T of Opns comdr).

Individual equipment

Bag, canvas, field, od, M1936_____	3	1 per off, except in Alaska.
Belt:		
Cartridge, cal. .30 dismounted, M1923.	48	1 per indiv armed w/rifle cal. .30 as shown as in sec I.
Pistol or revolver, M1936_____	20	1 per indiv not atzd belt, cartridge, cal. .30, dismounted, M1923.
Carrier, pack, M1928_____	65	1 per EM, except in Alaska.
Cover, canteen, dismounted, M1910_	68	1 per indiv.
Haversack, M1928_____	65	1 per EM, except in Alaska.
Pocket, magazine, double web, EM, M1923.	17	1 per indiv armed w/pistol, auto, cal. .45.

6

RANGER COMPANY, RANGER INFANTRY BATTALION

1	2	3
Item	Allow-ances	Basis of distribution and remarks
Strap, carrying, general purpose.....	3	1 per bag, canvas, fld (strap, carrying, od, bag, canvas, fld, will be issued in lieu thereof until exhausted).
Suspenders, belt, M1936............	3	1 per off.

Organizational equipment

Axe:		
Handled, chopping, single-bit, standard grade, weight 4-lb.	1	
Intrenching, M1910.............	7	1 per 10 EM.
Bag:		
Canvas, water, sterilizing, complete w/cover and hanger.	1	
Carrying:		
Ammunition.................	86	
Rocket, M6.................	4	2 per launcher, rocket.
Delousing...................	2	1 per 35 indiv or maj fraction thereof in areas where louse-borne typhus is low when atzd by WD.
	or	
	3	1 per 20 indiv or maj fraction thereof in areas where louse-borne typhus is high when atzd by WD.
Bucket, canvas, water, 18-qt........	10	1 per sec; 4 per co.
Can, water, 5-gal.................	14	1 per 5 indiv.
Carrier:		
Axe, intrenching, M1910..........	7	1 per axe, intrenching, M1910.
Cutter, wire, M1938............	68	1 per cutter, wire, M1938.
Pickmattock, intrenching, M1910.	14	1 per pickmattock, intrenching, M1910.
Shovel, intrenching, M1943........	47	1 per shovel, intrenching, M1943 (carr, shovel, intrenching, M1910 will be issued when shovel, intrenching, M1910 is issued).
Case, canvas, dispatch.............	6	1 per off; msgr.
Chest, record, fiber...............	1	
Clipper, hair.....................	2	1 per 30 indiv or maj fraction thereof operating in extremely cold areas when atzd by army or T of Opns comdr.
Cutter, wire, M1938...............	68	1 per indiv.
Desk, field, empty, fiber, company.	1	
Flag, guidon, bunting.............	1	
Kit:		
Barber, w/case.................	1	In T of Opns outside continental US.
Sewing.......................	6	1 per 12 indiv or maj fraction thereof.
Lantern, gasoline, 2 mantle, commercial.	1	
Machete, 18-in blade, M1942.......	8	1 per sqd.
Pick, handled, railroad, 6–7 lbs.....	2	
Pickmattock, intrenching, M1910..	14	2 per 10 EM.

RANGER COMPANY, RANGER INFANTRY BATTALION

1	2	3
Item	Allow-ances	Basis of distribution and remarks
Ropes, climbing set_____	12	6 per plat (non-standard item).
Screen, latrine, complete (with-pins-and-poles).	1	
Sheath, machete, leather, 18-in blade, M1942.	8	1 per machete.
Shovel, intrenching, M1943_____	47	1 per off; 7 per 10 EM (shovel, intrenching, M1910 will be issued in lieu thereof until exhausted).
Typewriter, portable, w/carrying case.	1	Per desk, fld.
Whistle, thunderer_____	22	1 per off; 1st sgt; t sgt; s sgt; sgt.

SIGNAL

Chest BC–5_____	1	
Flag:		
Kit MC–44_____	2	
Set M–133_____	2	
Flashlight TL–122–( )_____	22	1 per off; 1st sgt; t sgt; s sgt; sgt.
Lantern, electric, portable, hand____	2	
Reel Equipment CE–11_____	4	
Telephone, EE–8–( )_____	1	
Wire W–130–( ) on mile Spool DR–8.	1	For use w/reel equipment CE–11.

[A. G. 320.3 (11 Feb 44).]

By order of the Secretary of War:

> G. C. MARSHALL,
> *Chief of Staff.*

Official:

> J. A. ULIO,
> *Major General,*
> *The Adjutant General.*

More US Army information on 'dealing with the British':

ALTHOUGH you'll read in the papers about 'lords' and 'sirs', England is still one of the great democracies and the cradle of many American liberties. Personal rule by the King has been dead in England for nearly a thousand years. Today, the King reigns, but does not govern. The British people have great affection for their monarch, but they have stripped him of practically all political-power. It is well to remember this in your comings and goings about England. Be careful not to criticise the King. The British feel about that the way you would if anyone spoke against our country or our flag. Today's King and Queen stuck with the people through the blitz and had their home bombed just like anyone else, and the people are proud of them.

A revised overlay version of the Slapton Sands – Operation Fox objectives were released with different objectives. It shows troops going along the coast – as well as attacking a position on the cliffs. Again there is the objective indicated by the words: *'1st Phase Line – to be reached by PM D-Day*.

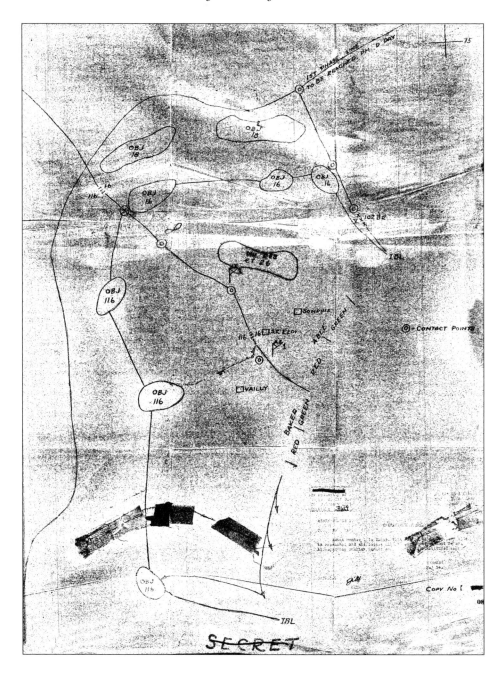

Chapter 6

March 1944 – Commando Training

The arrival at the Commando Training Centre in Scotland for the 5th Battalion was to be a memorable one. The 'trainees' were to be taught military tactics, war techniques and often they devised a good many new ones. The Rangers used the latest weapons and equipment and trained to be experts in handling captured enemy weapons. They were also taught unarmed combat and survival skills in the unpredictable mountain climate of Lochaber, near Fort William. Not only were they trained in physical fitness, personal survival, orienteering over very hostile terrain by day and night, their training also included close quarters combat, the art of silent killing, signalling using various pieces of military equipment, amphibious and cliff assaults, vehicle operation of all types, weapons (including those of the enemy) and demolition.

Henry S. Glassman, HQ Company 5th Battalion: *On 1 March 1944, the Rangers (5th Btn) left Leominster, England for a month of training in Scotland – site of the British Commando Training. A month that the Rangers have never stopped discussing, a month of the most difficult marches and problems, the most firing training that any solider has ever experienced. It was this training in Scotland that the Rangers believe brought them through the Invasion of France and all of the difficult assignments that followed. The hills of Scotland proved to be more than anything that had been encountered in former Ranger training, and here Rangers were made or lost. On the coastlines of Scotland, Amphibious landing operations were practised daily. Assault landings on beaches specially prepared with barbed wire, beach obstacles and every type of anti-assault landing device that our Air Corps had been able to photograph on the beaches of Normandy, plus every device that G-2 could conceive. Upon completion of infiltration of this maze of defenses, the battalion practised the art of reassembling at rallying points, for the continuation of the attack. Too much cannot be said for the Scotland training. To it, many of the Rangers owe their lives and their success.*

John Raaen – Captain 5th Battalion: *The 5th was scattered throughout the three villages. At that time, I believe that Hathaway was in Headquarters and HQ of the 5th was in Tighnabruaich – others were based in Kanes nearby.*

The US Army Intelligence Service produced a document on the subject of the Training Centre.

The Special Training Center was located in extremely rough terrain in the Scottish Highlands, on a lake connecting with the sea. The surrounding country is mountainous, reaching altitudes up to 4,000 feet, and the rainfall is the heaviest in the British Isles. In such terrain it was possible to conduct training that required the greatest physical exertion.

At this Center full recognition was given to the imperative need for physical efficiency in war. On many occasions, students were exposed to conditions in which the noise, the extreme fatigue, and the mental strain of battle were simulated in a very realistic manner. Such training tested the relation between fatigue and mental efficiency, for students were required to consider and render tactical decisions when the going was seemingly unbearable.

Training Programme

Opening Address	2	Training Films	4
Physical Training	17	Forced Marches	19
Unarmed Combat	8	Cross Country Marches	33
Rope Work	10	Range Work	37
Drill	15	Demolitions	15
Weapon Training	50	Commando Day	11
Fieldcraft	40	Make and Mend	55
Boating	28	Preparing for Course	33
Climbing	10	Interior Economy	9
Map Reading	30	Competitions	11
Assault Courses	5	Spare	11
Woodcraft	3		
Medical Lecture	6	Total No of 40 minute periods	462

Maps: Practical and theoretical instruction in map problems was stressed. French, German, and Russian, as well as English, maps were used. Students were taught to make hasty sketches, perspective drawings of shore-lines and overlays.

Day and night, practical map problems that required mountain-craft and considerable physical exertion were worked out in the field. The average distance covered in these map problems was approximately 40 miles. The students had to contend with poor visibility, sleep in the rain, build fires with wet fuel, cross swift mountain streams and move rapidly over exceedingly difficult terrain. In the beginning some students unfamiliar with the terrain and training were lost in the Highlands for as many as 3 days.

The use of ground and cover was taught practically in progressive stages. At first the students were required to move toward given objectives over terrain affording good cover; and when they exposed themselves unnecessarily, this fact was brought to their attention. In the later training, the facilities for cover were much more limited. In the middle stages of this work, blank cartridges were fired from an Enfield rifle when a student exposed himself unnecessarily. In the final stage, ball cartridges from rifles and Bren guns were fired so that the bullets fell 3 to 5 feet from such a student. This method produced excellent results, compelling the men to take cover naturally and quickly.

The first 2-day exercise was in mountainous country; the second in closely wooded country.

Saturday was the only day on which the students could get to the nearest town; hence this was a free day and Sunday was a work day.

The practical map-reading periods included the following subjects:

- *Route finding*
- *Keeping direction with and without map and compass*
- *Long-range observation*
- *Panoramic drawing*
- *Field sketching*
- *Visualization of ground from map*

The periods on stalking were intended to teach use of ground and cover, silent and unobserved movement, and the ability to find the way to an objective which is visible only from a distance. The periods on bridging dealt with a method of constructing a quick and serviceable bridge over an obstacle without calling on the engineers.

Boats: Another phase of training involved the use of canvas assault boats and reconnaissance boats. Practice in the use of this equipment was conducted in swift streams as well as in the sea. This training was further developed in the form of opposed landings, usually made before dawn, the students being required to fight their way to objectives situated from a few hundred yards to several miles inland. These objectives were usually high up the side of a mountain. During the attack the men were subjected to very close fire from Bren guns and rifles as well as to the bursts of the Mills grenade, the bakelite grenade and 2-inch-mortar smoke shells. This realistic instruction occasionally produced casualties. In one exercise one man lost an eye and another was cut severely in the leg by grenade splinters. On another occasion one man was killed. A combination of confusion and a strong desire to take cover quickly when under fire caused a number of sprained ankles and twisted knees. It was emphasized that these casualties were generally a result of carelessness.

Many hours were devoted to unarmed combat, involving ju-jitsu, wrestling and general brawling tactics. This training improved the individual's self-confidence and developed a keen desire to fight. Close combat proved highly interesting to both officers and noncommissioned officers. It was an excellent means of physical training, requiring the use of all the muscles and improving bodily coordination. The methods learned were actually employed in tank-hunting exercises and in taking fortified points.

A short course was given on the subject of tank hunting. Men were informed that determined individuals had been able to stalk and destroy tanks effectively in Africa, Norway, and Greece. Highly skilled stalkers are required, who must be aggressive to the point of recklessness.

In a typical problem at the Special Training Center, reconnaissance units located a park of dummy tanks before darkness. Although the park was guarded, the raiders were required to approach the tanks and destroy them without being seen. Usually the results were highly successful. Many parties reached their objectives either without being seen or after having quietly removed the guards in their path. The exercise demonstrated that soft-soled shoes must be worn, that helmets and any equipment which rattles must be left behind, and that knife fighting is effective against sentries. Men were taught that methods of hunting tanks must be varied to meet widely different concrete situations, and common sense was stressed as the basic rule in these exercises.

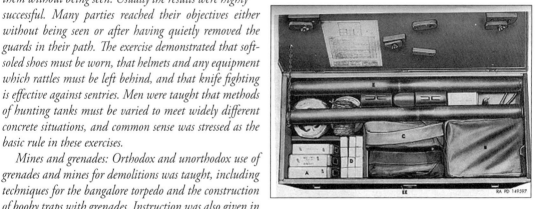

Mines and grenades: Orthodox and unorthodox use of grenades and mines for demolitions was taught, including techniques for the bangalore torpedo and the construction of booby traps with grenades. Instruction was also given in the employment of demolitions and explosives in conjunction with ambushes. Several accounts of actual ambushes contrived by commandos were studied and discussed, and a number of ambushes were set up in practice for the instruction of students.

Another subject in the course was the negotiation of obstacles. This included the crossing of barbed-wire barriers set up in German fashion, the crossing of mine fields, and the passing of booby traps and of natural and man-made obstacles of other types. The bangalore torpedo was employed to blast a path through wire.

Other methods of crossing, such as the use of logs, gunny sacks and blankets placed over wire, were demonstrated. A lecturer suggested that bodies of dead men might be employed effectively for bridging wire obstacles, and also that men wearing overcoats for protection against the wire could lie across entanglements so that other men could pass over them.

Two methods of crossing minefields were taught. In one, students used bayonets to prod the ground until a mine was discovered. These were then dug out or exploded with guncotton. The other method was to use the cup projector in conjunction with an Enfield rifle and a Mills grenade. A 30-yard length of cordtex (explosive cord ¼ inch in diameter) was coiled with one end tied to the Mills grenade (detonator removed). The grenade was fired across the minefield, dragging the cordtex approximately 30 yards. The cordtex was then detonated, causing all mines in a path

8 inches wide to explode. Ten feet to one side a similar exercise was carried out. Two men followed the paths of the exploded cordtex, dragging a net of cordtex with an 8-inch mesh, 10 feet wide, across the minefield. When the net was detonated, a 10-foot path was cleared. In a practice crossing in which a U.S. observer participated, every mine within the 10-foot path was exploded. The mines were the British Mark IV anti-tank mines.

Small tactical exercises were conducted during the course in order to give the students practical work in the subjects covered. The individual's ability to participate in offensive operations, after enduring hardships and forced marches through strange country at night, was tested in exercises of 1 to 3 days' duration. But even when he had reached his objective, he was not allowed to rest, for then he had to practise a rapid withdrawal. These operations usually involved demolitions or sabotage of vital points and utilities; they were often carried out in conjunction with small landing operations in which naval forces participated.

The men were taught to live on concentrated rations during these exercises, to take care of themselves in the field under all conditions of weather and climate, and to maintain themselves in a 'fighting condition'.

Each man wore battle dress, carried his own arms, and kept all his rations and ammunition in his rucksack. Every effort was made to keep the weight of the load down to a minimum; the pack usually averaged about 35 pounds. As one instructor expressed it: 'I tell them the job to be done; the number of days we will be out; the arms and ammunition required; and leave it to the individual to decide what he will carry for his own personal comfort. As each man carries his own load, only the bare necessities are taken along.'

Two former sergeants of the Shanghai police force, commissioned as captains in the British Army, gave the instruction in unarmed combat, the use of the fighting knife and self-defence. The fighting knife was developed at the school as a weapon to be carried by all members of a raiding party, and was carried in the side pocket of the trousers of the battle dress.

Instruction was given in firing single shots from the submachine gun while it was set for full automatic operation; this was to conserve ammunition and yet have the gun immediately ready for full automatic fire if necessary.

Considerable time was spent in teaching students to fire the rifle and Bren gun from the hip.

A very difficult pistol course was arranged which required the student to fire from various angles at unexpected targets.

ADVANCE TRAINING	Days allocated	Night
Boatwork	1	1
Embarking and disembarking from boats for both beach and rock landings; loading of craft.		
Battle Patrol Formations	1	
Suitable formations for raiding parties by day and night.	2	
Landing Exercises	2	1
Simple company exercises involving a landing, a formation of beachhead party, and limited move to objective. The second exercise was preparation for night-landing training.		
Seamanship	2½	
Pulling cutters and dinghies; bends and hitches; embarking and disembarking from drifters at sea; compass work; rope ladder climbing.		
Assault	2½	
Firing from boats; crossing and clearing obstacles; firing from hip; use of grenades; close combat.		
Daylight Raids	2	
Company exercises in raids by day; elaborating and extending the scope of earlier landing exercises.		
Night Raids		1
Exercises involving landing in darkness with objective some distance from beach; object of raid to be achieved and troops withdrawn to boats in darkness.		

ADVANCE TRAINING	Days allocated	Night
Field Firing – Preparation	1	
Field Firing – Exercise	2	
Each company to prepare exercise on field-firing range and subsequently carry it out with ball ammunition; preparation by day, but exercise to involve landing before dawn to secure beachhead, and offensive after first light; mortars to be in support of company on at least one occasion during course.		
Discussion	1	
On return from field-firing exercise; other discussions and lectures to be arranged by group staffs.		
Demonstration	2	
By Royal Engineers – to include demolitions, booby-trap torpedoes, and booby-traps.		
Battle Exercise	2	2
Commanded by battalion commander.		
Probable hours 0500 to 2100, which will involve landing and disembarking in darkness.	2	2
Total	24	6

Type	Assault landing craft (A.L.C.). Also known as the LCA:
Draught:	1ft 7in loaded.
Speed in knots:	10½ loaded.
Length:	38ft 9in.
Beam:	10ft
Opening Load:	4ft 5in.

35 men plus naval crew of 5 men or a subsec. 3.7 lt. (how.) btry.
Armoured against small-arms ammunition.
Rate of discharge one platoon 9 sec.
Weight: loaded. 10½ tons; unloaded, 7½ tons.
Range: 70 miles.
Low silhouette. Silent engine.

The British LCA (Landing Craft Assault) boat was to be the method of delivery onto the beaches for the Rangers.

<u>List of topics covered</u>
Offensive demolitions

Close combat, comprising:

Unarmed combat	Pistol
Thompson submachine gun	Grenade
Bren firing from hip and shoulder	Rifle firing from hip
Use of the fighting knife	Bayonet fighting
Stalking	Fighting in closely wooded country
Street fighting and house clearance	

Assault, comprising:

Assault course	Opposed landings
Field firings	Surmounting obstacles
Destruction of antitank mines	Elementary bridging
Use of assault boats	Use of scaling ladders
Tactical schemes (exercises) involving:	Endurance

Living on concentrated rations
Automatic battle drill
Night operations
Fieldcraft
Necessity for rapid decisions.

Subordinate leadership
Ambushes
Road blocks
Quick reactions

Some of the weapons used and illustrated during training.

Below: Some of the many areas of training undertaken were also shown to the men on film. The use of an enemy dressed in German uniform was considered appropriate and the various ways in which he could be assaulted in close quarter fighting were discussed in detail.

Below: The assault course.

1 March 1944

5th Rangers – Companies A – F, Medical and HQ – Tighnabruaich, Scotland (the original report is blurred, so the timings are illegible).

Companies A, B, C & D 2nd Rangers – Bude, Cornwall.

E Company 2nd Rangers – Bude, Cornwall.
1st Lt. Lapres went from Duty to Detached Service with Headquarters Company 'Detachment A', 2nd Btn at Saunton Sands, North Devon.

F Company 2nd Rangers – Bude, Cornwall.
Captain Otty Masny and T/Sgt. John Franklin went from Duty to Detached Service with 'Detachment A' Headquarters Company 2nd Battalion at Saunton Sands, North Devon and Captain Masny is relieved of principal Duty as Company Commander of F Company.
1st Lt. Robert Arman assumed temporary Duty as Company Commander.

Medical Detachment 2nd Rangers – Bude, Cornwall.

HQ Company 'Detachment A' 2nd Rangers – Saunton Sands, N. Devon.
Captain Otto Masny was attached from F Company 2nd Battalion with principal Duty as Detachment Commander.
1st Lt. Louis A. Dahan was attached from Headquarters Company 2nd Battalion with principal Duty as Supply Officer.
1st Lt. Theodore E. Lapres Jr was attached from E Company 2nd Battalion with the principal Duty of Instructor.
14 enlisted men from units of the 2nd Btn were attached for Duty, rations and quarters. (see list).

2nd Battalion Narrative History.

> Selected officers and NCO's under the command of Major Schneider, set up a Ranger Replacement Training Center located at Braunton Camp, North Devon. Volunteers, selected by the interviewing teams from the 8th and 28th Divisions, commenced to arrive on 1 March. The course consisted of cliff scaling, weapons instruction and firing, and other intensified technical and physical training. Those replacements who satisfactorily completed the course were assigned to the Companies on 22 March. Another new addition to the Battalion at this time was the Cannon Platoon, consisting of twenty-six volunteers from Armored units and four half-tracks mounting 75-mm Assault Guns. The Battalion now had its' authorized over-strength of 25% officers and 15% enlisted men.

Headquarters Company 2nd Rangers – Bude, Cornwall

Record of Events. Detachment 'A' Headquarters Company 2nd Ranger Infantry Battalion was formed and made a part of Headquarters Company for training replacements for this battalion as per Circular 66 HQ SOS ETOUSA April 1943.

DET "A" HQ CO
2ND RNGR INFANTRY BATTALION
APO 308   US ARMY

1 March 1944

R O S T E R

RANK	NAME	ASN	ATCHD FROM
Tsg	John W. Franklin	6974460	Co F 2d Rngr Inf Bn
Tsg	John S. Walker	33446631	Hq Co 2d Rngr Inf Bn
Sgt	Joseph R. Devoli	19066135	Co D 2d Rngr Inf Bn
Tec4	Isadore NMI Diamond	31049014	Hq Co 2d Rngr Inf Bn
Tec4	Otto C. Bayer	33355053	Med Det 2d Rngr Inf Bn
Tec5	Oscar H. Anderson	35330347	Hq Co 2d Rngr Inf Bn
Tec5	Fred NMI Slager	15078965	Hq Co 2d Rngr Inf Bn
Pfc	Walter O. Akridge	35496679	Hq Co 2d Rngr Inf Bn
Pfc	Donald NMI Hicks	35359014	Hq Co 2d Rngr Inf Bn
Pfc	Charles W. Korb	33248275	Med Det 2d Rngr Inf Bn
Pfc	James W. Willis	33214154	Hq Co 2d Rngr Inf Bn
Pvt	George H. Crook	11131236	Med Det 2d Rngr Inf Bn
Pvt	Raymond H. Hubert	31355543	Hq Co 2d Rngr Inf Bn
Pvt	Alfonso NMI Singleton	15061516	Hq Co 2d Rngr Inf Bn

*Otto Masny
capt Inf*

---

2 March 1944
5th Rangers – Companies A – F, Medical and HQ – Tighnabruaich, Scotland.

James W. Gabaree: *I remember disembarking from a landing craft and jumping into the frigid water up to my shoulders while carrying heavy equipment. We pushed our way through moors, heavy brush and up steep hills. Exhausted, we arrived at an obstacle course, stripped to the waist, and charged at a full run. There were dummies with extended rifles, bayonets attached. Explosions were going off all around us. Stab the dummies, shoot the simulated enemy. Bob and weave, faster, faster. Dive into the gully filled with mud. Things were happening every second. There were barricades to climb. Streams to be forded.*

The grand finale was having to crawl on our stomachs under barbed wire while live machine gun bullets were fired just inches over our bodies. At the end we had to make a fifty-yard dash at full speed while screaming at the top of our lungs. It was all in a day's work. I felt like a spent bullet, but elated that I had completed the exercise. The Rangers took everything that English commandos could dish out. This type of training went on for most of the month.

2nd Rangers – Companies A – F, Medical and HQ – Bude, Cornwall.
HQ Company 'Detachment A' 2nd Rangers – Saunton Sands, N. Devon.

Orders were given for internal transfers within the Ranger Battalions and also for leave.

RESTRICTED

HEADQUARTERS
SECOND RANGER INFANTRY BATTALION   RPM/pfm
APO 308 US Army

SPECIAL ORDER)
                :
NUMBER 20   )

1. MAJOR MAX F. SCHNEIDER, 0384349, Hdqs., 2nd Ranger Infantry Battalion is granted five (5) days leave of absence on or about 13th of March 1944.

2. UP of AR 615-5, the following reductions are announced:

TO BE PRIVATE

T/5	James W. Eaton	18217459	Co F
T/5	Gerald O. Sejba	16024982	Hqs Co

3. UP Par 11g, AR 615-200 the following named EM are trfd in grade to organizations indicated:

			FROM	TO
Pfc	James K Robison	37342359	Hqs Co	Co "C"
Pfc	Wayne D. Goad	38403468	Hqs Co	Co "C"
Pvt	Fred W. Plumlee	34764014	Hqs Co	Co "C"
Pvt	James E. Donahue	11104243	Hqs Co	Co "C"
Pvt	Stanley E. Moak	32853621	Hqs Co	Co "C"
Pvt	Sidney L. Isaacson	32714447	Hqs Co	Co "B"
Pvt	Herbert N. Adams	38425004	Hqs Co	Co "B"
Pfc	George J. Frechette	36807180	Hqs Co	Co "B"
Pfc	Charles L. Davis	39931299	Hqs Co	Co "B"
Pfc	George NMI Langyal Jr.,	35230082	Hqs Co	Co "B"
Pvt	John M Hanlon	36029176	Co "B"	Med. Detachment

4. 2ND LT FRANK L. KENNARD, 0514714, 2nd Ranger Infantry Battalion is granted five (5) days leave on or about 3 March 1944.

By Order of Lt Col RUDDER:

R. P. MERRILL
Capt., Infantry
Adjutant

OFFICIAL: *R.P. Merrill*
R. P. MERRILL
Capt., Infantry
Adjutant

---

3 March 1944
5th Rangers – Companies A – F, Medical and HQ – Tighnabruaich, Scotland.
2nd Rangers – Companies A – F, Medical and HQ – Bude, Cornwall.
HQ Company 'Detachment A' 2nd Rangers – Saunton Sands, N. Devon.
1st Lt. Morton L. McBride was attached from D Company 2nd Battalion with the principal Duty of instructor.

The US Army released a study called 'The German defensive rules for retaining possession of a town or village': *As a rule, if the Germans believe that a town or village in their possession is likely to be attacked, they prepare it for all-around defence. In the outskirts of the populated area, they generally construct a belt of field defences around the town, with ditches, minefields, and other anti-tank obstacles protecting all approaches, and with every obstacle covered by fire according to a well co-ordinated plan.*

Within the populated centre itself, the German defence plan is based on the theory that in all street fighting, the element of surprise is important. Certain buildings are transformed into fortified strongholds, and several such buildings, capable of mutual fire support, become a centre of resistance. Streets and houses which are outside these zones are covered by small-arms fire.

The ground floor of a fortified point is usually reserved for such heavy weapons as guns, anti-tank guns and mortars. Artillery and mortars are also emplaced in parks, gardens, and courtyards where the Germans believe that they can be especially effective in repelling tanks. Tanks may be placed in ambush inside barns or other buildings; also, they may be cleverly dug-in around the outskirts of the town to cover possible avenues of tank approach.

Heavy and light automatic weapons, snipers, and grenade throwers are dispersed throughout the upper floors of buildings and on roofs.

If one or two buildings of a fortified zone are lost, the Germans try to counter-attack vigorously before the opposition has had time to consolidate its gains.

The Germans now include, as part of their normal equipment, means of destroying anything which should not be allowed to fall into our hands. In addition to their regular ammunition, guns are allotted charges to be placed in the barrels so that the equipment may be thoroughly demolished. Drivers are equipped with grenades to destroy their own vehicles. Company headquarters keep on hand a bottle of gasoline to pour over all classified documents. They also have another incendiary bottle, not unlike the phosphorous bomb used in close combat against tanks. Just in case this does not function, a box of matches is kept in reserve. The German theory is that if they allow us to capture anything intact, their loss is double – we gain a tank, for example, while they must call for a replacement.

Below: A letter was sent from Major General Gerow to Major General Huebner confirming that he had ordered the Army Training Centre to allow the Rangers to have extra training.

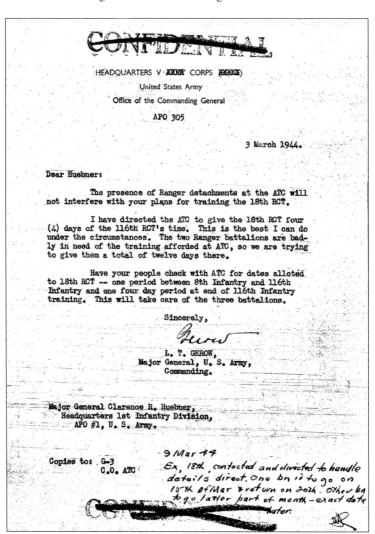

4 March 1944

5th Rangers – Companies A – F, Medical and HQ – Tighnabruaich, Scotland.
2nd Rangers – Companies A – F, Medical and HQ – Bude, Cornwall.
HQ Company 'Detachment A' 2nd Rangers – Saunton Sands, N. Devon.
Three officers and 57 enlisted men were assigned and joined from the units indicated here. [apologies for the quality of the copy.]

DET "A" HQ CO
2ND RANGER INF BATTALION
APO 230   U. ARMY

A March 1944

ROSTER

NAME	RANK	ASN	ASGD FROM	
...Y. ADLER	1st Lt Inf	01293387	110th Inf Regt	
... L. ...	1st Lt Inf	0662340	110th Inf Regt	
... A. WISE	1st Lt Inf	01015197	126th Ord Maint Bn	
... ... VINSON	1st Lt CE	01103450	2d Engr Bn	
ENLISTED MEN				
Charles C. Flanagan	Cpl	34132826	36th Armd Inf Bn	653
Harley R. Sampson	Cpl	37120562	36th Armd Inf Bn	675
Rudford L. Riddle	Tec5	18015009	2d Engr Bn	345
William E. Gower	Tec5	20301487	10th Armd Inf Bn	745
Robert S. Koffman	Pfc	37273776	23d Inf Regt	744
Virgil ... White	Pfc	6958249	9th Inf Regt	504
Chester S. Walczak	Pfc	15014594	10th Armd Inf Regt	504
Kenneth ... Sharff	Pfc	36567766	10th Armd Inf Regt	675
Willie B. Richardson	Pfc	34185779	11th Inf Regt	745
Roy R. Stanley	Pfc	15055378	10th Inf Regt	604
Joseph ... Van Hassel	Pfc	16012479	10th Inf Regt	745
Joseph ... Trainor	Pfc	36227819	11th Inf Regt	607
Durene J. Sielke	Pfc	36257523	11th Inf Regt	177
William ... Bruce	Pfc	35727584	112th Inf Regt	060
Donald L. McCreery	Pfc	36457530	110th Inf Regt	767
Robert K. Roe	Pfc	32588257	110th Inf Regt	604
Alfred F. Elsie	Pfc	36581093	109th Inf Regt	745
...lace ... Young	Pfc	33299717	109th Inf Regt	745
William A. McKitrick	Pfc	15324421	109th Inf Regt	746
Donald C. Pechacek	Pfc	36265454	109th Inf Regt	745
Madison ... Cobb	Pfc	32547548	112th Inf Regt	745
James B. Rudnell	Pfc	34761449	112th Inf Regt	746
Jack ... LaVere	Pfc	39264129	112th Inf Regt	675
Foy E. Latham	Pfc	34608049	110th Inf Regt	604
Arthur J. Dienkel	Pfc	36266590	112th Inf Regt	604
John D. Oehlberg	Pfc	16127068	112th Inf Regt	675
Thomas B. Caudle	Pfc	34607990	110th Inf Regt	345
George ... Seburg	Pfc	36379572	112th Inf Regt	504
Alvin B. Bustebakker	Pfc	39600002	110th Inf Regt	405
William J. Horvath	Pfc	35255073	33rd Armd Regt	835
John V. Keating	Pfc	31076213	36th Armd Inf Regt	745
Robert B. Cooley	Pfc	17051924	36th Armd Inf Regt	405
Charles J. Semchuck	Pfc	35565704	121st Inf Regt	746
Nathan C. Reed	Pfc	35643427	13th Inf Regt	745
George B. Sinbine	Pfc	12050576	121st Inf Regt	014
Joseph A. Cournoyer	Pvt	6145859	37th Tank Bn	345
Charles A. Faris Jr.	Pvt	35802011	4th Armd Div	745
Martin D. Maikin	Pvt	32790566	110th Inf Regt	504
Edison ... Crull	Pvt	36379412	110th Inf Regt	504
Joseph R. Chrane	Pvt	32588236	110th Inf Regt	504
Robert D. Schmitt	Pvt	36415386	110th Inf Regt	345
Gilbert ... Strassburger	Pvt	35697791	112th Inf Regt	675
George ... Ostrowski	Pvt	36576861	112th Inf Regt	604
Wayne ... Beseron	Pvt	32583023	112th Inf Regt	504
John ... Terselove	Pvt	36372151	109th Inf Regt	604
Louis J. Franczek	Pvt	32587594	112th Inf Regt	607
Robert ... King	Pvt	31299584	112th Inf Regt	745
Mark ... Keefer, Jr.	Pvt	35548468	112th Inf Regt	745
Albert ... Parker	Pvt	35727794	109th Inf Regt	745
William ... McDonough	Pvt	39320199	110th Inf Regt	675
Seymour ... Molnik	Pvt	12355479	54th Armd Fd Bn	861
John J. Kilburne	Pvt	36311534	32nd Armd Regt	...
William D. Gregory	Pvt	37013760	36th Armd Inf Regt	745
William H. Bevan	Pvt	34133761	13th Inf Regt	060
Oliver R. Cowlents	Pvt	32063177	13th Inf Regt	504
Andrew F. McCorckle	Pvt	35999537	13th Inf Regt	345
	Pvt	34306331	121st Inf Regt	405

5 March 1944

5th Rangers – Companies A – F, Medical and HQ – Tighnabruaich, Scotland.

2nd Rangers – Companies A – F, Medical and HQ – Bude, Cornwall.

HQ Company 'Detachment A' 2nd Rangers – Saunton Sands, N. Devon.

US Army Memo: Waste Means Lives

It is always said that the Americans throw more food into their garbage cans than any country eats. It is true. We have always been a 'producer' nation. Most British food is imported even in peacetimes, and for the last two years the British have been taught not to waste the things that their ships bring in from abroad. British seamen die getting those convoys through. The British have been taught this so thoroughly that they know that food and gasoline represent the lives of merchant sailors. And when you burn gasoline needlessly, it will seem to them as if you are wasting the lives of those seamen – and when you destroy or waste food you have wasted the life of another sailor.

Below: One of the regular personnel update reports detailing the number of men in each battalion and how many vehicles they were using.

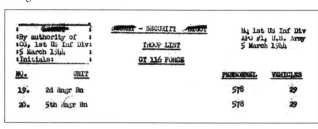

Dated 5 March a letter was sent from Major General Huebner regarding the term 'Assumed Troops'.

The term 'Assumed Troops' is used to indicate the operations of troops during an exercise – but their positions on the map and stated objectives are in reality false. The units 'Assumed' for Operation Fox (a Slapton Sands practice) would not actually be taking part in the exercise, but their movements and objectives would be recorded on the maps and given to other units for them to fully understand the whole campaign. The 1st Inf. Div. *assumed troops lands in 16th RCT (Regimental Combat Team) Sector. 18th RCT (-1 Bt) seized and secures the first phase line prior to dark on D-Day.* etc.

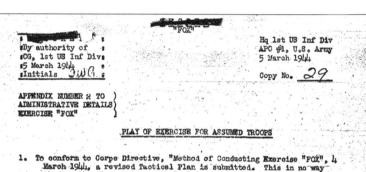

A map overlay dated 5 March is entitled *HQ 1st US Inf. Div. Administrative details for exercise FOX Assumed Troops.* It shows companies of Rangers attacking a rocky outcrop at the far bottom right of the plan.

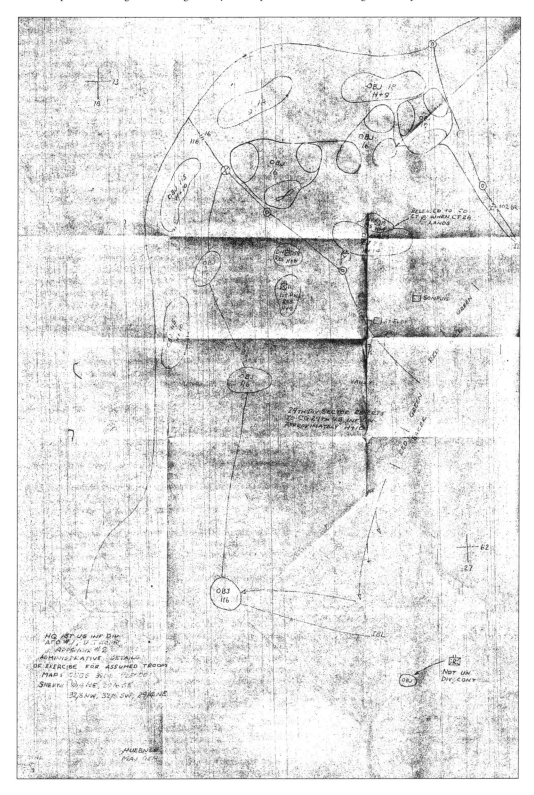

For orientation purposes, the same overlay has been imposed onto a plan of the area. The originals of these overlays are far from perfect quality, but their historical importance cannot be overstated. These are the original versions of the Rangers orders being placed onto paper in geographic terms. These were done for 'assumed' purposes so that the surrounding units could understand the whole D-Day operation and who else was fighting around them.

A Ranger unit marked as a letter 'R' in a square is to attack an objective at the bottom of the map on this overlay (bottom right). When placed over the actual area view it becomes clear that this is a cliff top out crop position, which juts into the sea. Another unit of Rangers are to land on the beach and advance along to the same position – then advance inland to other objectives.

Taking the gun battery targets from the intelligence document/briefing for Operation Fox – published on 23 February, the four gun positions/objectives along with a grid have been marked on the map.

It is worth noting at this stage that there is a gun battery on the cliff top. Two gun batteries near the coastline and one further inland. (I have added the grid lines to aid the reader's understanding of the overlay, and have also added the dots to indicate the gun positions).

248590 4 x 155mm   255666 3 x 75mm
262674 2 x 75mm   219681 4 x 150mm

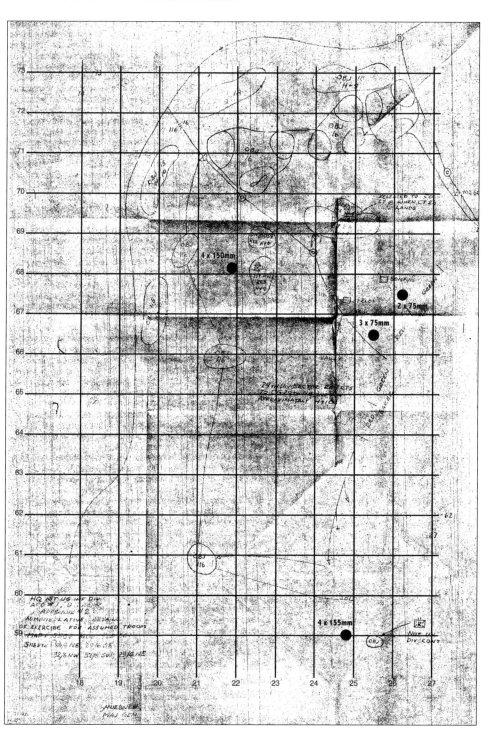

6 March 1944

5th Rangers – Companies A – F, Medical and HQ – Tighnabruaich, Scotland.

A Company 2nd Rangers – Bude, Cornwall.

B Company 2nd Rangers – Bude, Cornwall.

1st Lt. Smudin was relieved of command and transferred to Headquarters Company 2nd Btn as of 5 March 1944. Captain Edgar L. Arnold was assigned and joined from Headquarters 28th Inf. Division APO 28 and assumes command as of 5 March 1944.

C Company 2nd Rangers – Bude, Cornwall.

D Company 2nd Rangers – Bude, Cornwall.

E Company 2nd Rangers – Bude, Cornwall.

F Company 2nd Rangers – Bude, Cornwall.

Medical Detachment 2nd Rangers – Bude, Cornwall.

HQ Company 'Detachment A' 2nd Rangers – Saunton Sands, N. Devon.

Headquarters Company 2nd Rangers – Bude, Cornwall.

Captain George S. Williams was assigned and joined from HQ Co. 2nd Btn and assumed principal Duty as Btn. S-4. Captain Williams was relieved of his duties with HQ Company.

1st Lt. Joseph Smudin was assigned to HQ Company and assumed command.

2nd Lt. Conway Epperson was assigned and joined this command with HQ Company.

T/5 Lick and Cpl. Worman went from Duty to Detached Service in Woolacombe.

Below: A British produced intelligence map shows the Grandcamp-les-Bains port and the Maisy Batteries. Of particular note is the addition of another gun battery of four guns to the rear of the La Martinière and the Les Perruques positions. (the map has an arrival date of 6 March for the additional guns).

This map was printed and backed up by low level aerial reconnaissance photographs showing the area in greater detail. Also shown on the photographs are dummy gun positions in the fields to the north of the batteries.

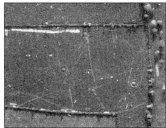

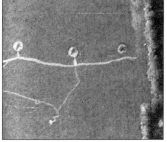

Above and Right: Low-level reconnaissance photographs of the dummy battery in front of Maisy 1.

Left: From the same date, an aerial view of the land and road junction just behind Pointe du Hoc.

7 March 1944

5th Rangers – Companies A – F, Medical and HQ – Tighnabruaich, Scotland.
2nd Rangers – Companies A – F, Medical and HQ – Bude, Cornwall.
HQ Company 'Detachment A' 2nd Rangers – Saunton Sands, N. Devon.
Headquarters Company 2nd Rangers (less Detachment A) – Bude, Cornwall.

Below is the training information for Ranger Replacements who were being built up at the same time as the main 2nd and 5th Battalion men. This was necessitated by the assumption that each battalion would suffer heavy losses on D-Day.

HEADQUARTERS
U. S. ASSAULT TRAINING CENTER, ETOUSA
APO   553

7 March 1944

Subject: Range Assignments.

To   : C.O. Ranger Replacements.

    1. Range Assignment for Ranger Replacements stationed at the U. S. Assault Training Center, the Week of March 12-18 is as follows:

        March 13-14
        Ranges 37,38, & 39 Area "D"
        Hours Available 0830-1130

        March 15, 16, 17, & 18
        Ranges 37, 38, & 39 Area "D"
        Hours Available 0830-1230, 1330-1730

        March 18
        Rocket Range Area "C"
        Hours Available 0830-1230, 1330-1730

    2. Weapons to be fired, Rifle M-1 Cal. .30, Pistol Cal. .45, Thompson Sub-Machine Gun, BAR Cal. .30, 60-mm Mortar, 81-mm Mortar, Light Machine Gun & Rockets.

    3. The safety regulations pertaining to individual weapons and safety regulations of the U. S. Assault Training Center will be strictly complied with.

                    For the Commanding Officer:

                                    H. A. MILLER
                                    Lt Col, FA
                                    Tng, Plans

DISTRIBUTION:
    Staff Sections (2) each
    Training Branch - 3
    Range Officer - 3
    C.O. Ranger Repl - 15

8 March 1944

5th Rangers – Companies A – F, Medical and HQ – Tighnabruaich, Scotland.
2nd Rangers – Companies A – F, Medical and HQ – Bude, Cornwall.
HQ Company 'Detachment A' 2nd Rangers – Saunton Sands, N. Devon.
Headquarters Company 2nd Rangers (less Detachment A) – Bude, Cornwall.

All Rangers were to be issued with clothing, which had been impregnated with anti-gas agents. The aim was to prevent gas seeping into their clothing and then onto the skin.

The clothing was issued as follows:

1 suit, one-piece, herringbone twill, protective, or   *1 pair socks, wool, light, protective*
1 jacket, herringbone twill, protective, and   *1 pair leggings, dismounted, canvas, protective*
1 trousers, herringbone twill, protective   *1 hood, wool, protective*
1 drawers, cotton, protective   *1 pair gloves, cotton, protective*
1 undershirt, cotton, protective   *2 covers, protective, individual (cellophane type).*

The orders stated that the clothing was to be stored by various organisations and to be made available to the troops without delay in the event of an emergency or, as required, for training purposes.

One-piece herringbone could only be issued to people who were 'authorised to wear one-piece herringbone suits' and any units which had been previously issued with the British anti-gas capes had to return them.

On 8 March 1944 orders were issued that all other impregnated clothing had to be returned to the nearest quartermasters' depot for reimpregnation. It was the responsibility of the Chemical Warfare Service to then inspect the clothing, relaunder it and then reissue it.

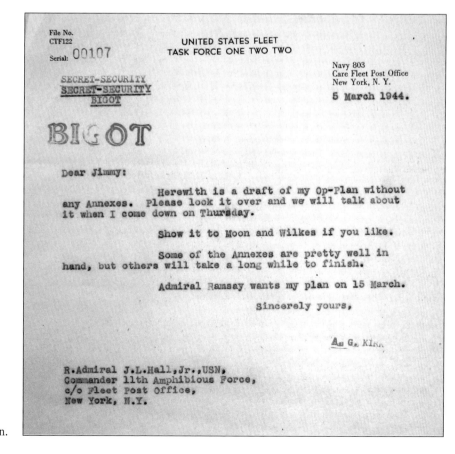

A series of papers starting with a date of March 5 and continuing on the 8th, which contain instructions in the event of a postponement of D-Day for any reason.

Second Draft (3-8-44)
SECRET-SECURITY-BIGOT
ANNEX M TO OPERATION PLAN NEPTUNE

No. 1-44

POSTPONEMENT PLAN MIKE ONE (24 hours).

1. Postponement of D-day may be from day to day, up to two days in each suitable tidal and lunar period.

2. Arrangements as follows will be made for ships which have not yet sailed.

(a) For day to day postponement the troops will remain embarked on LSI, APA and LST. Troops in LCI and LCT still secured alongside may be disembarked and distributed into adjacent accommodations. Troops in LCI not secured alongside may also be disembarked if conditions permit. Those in certain LCT not alongside will not be disembarked.

3. For Forces already at sea the following arrangements will be made.

(a) For day to day postponement ships which have sailed within the previous seven hours will return to their staging points. Ships which have been underway more than seven hours and which by returning would not gain any rest period will (a) back-track a sufficient distance to absorb the twenty-four hour period or (b) if shelter and anchorages are available enroute, plans will be made for these ships to rest in them

POSTPONEMENT PLAN MIKE TWO (To next lunar period)

(1. For the longer postponement i. e. to the next suitable tidal and lunar period, troops will be disembarked and returned

---

Second Draft (3-8-44)
SECRET-SECURITY-BIGOT
ANNEX M TO OPERATION PLAN NEPTUNE

No. 1-44

to Marshalling Areas. Vehicles, however will remain embarked.

2. For the longer type postponement, i.e., to the next suitable period ships which have sailed will return to their staging and loading points and their troops will be disembarked and return to Marshalling Areas. Vehicles will remain embarked.

GENERAL

1. Assault Force commanders will implement detailed plans within the frame work of the above instructions.

2. The signal of execution of postponement is as follows:

(a) POST MIKE ONE . . . . 24 hours

(b) POST MIKE TWO . . . . longer period
(about 14 days)

Below shows a map produced by General Huebner's office indicating much of the Pointe du Hoc position. This was used as a planning assault map and given to Lt. Col. Rudder.

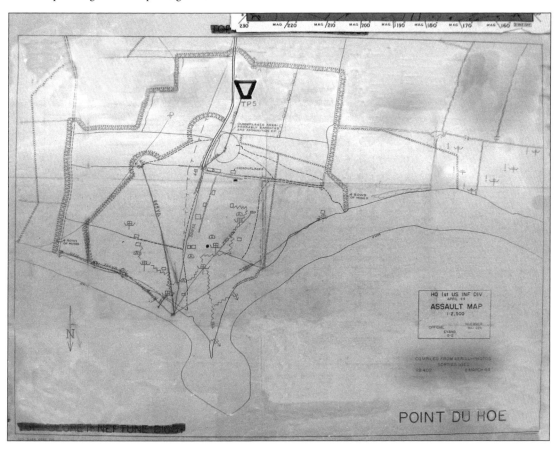

The standard issuing of maps required detailed instruction. Army orders were issued in March to clarify from whom and to whom specific maps could be issued [highlights shown below]:

Issuing of maps.
Distribution.
1. *Operational Maps (United Kingdom).*
    a. *The stock levels for the marshalling area map depots were determined by requisition selection, and the relevant depots stocked. Unit map requisitions were grouped according to 'sealed area camps' and the map depot in each camp was stocked accordingly from the marshalling area map depots. Maps were issued to the units from the camp map depots as follows:*
Advance Requirements
1. *Preliminary estimates of map requirements were submitted to ETOUSA several months prior to the operations. As soon as it was possible, at least three months prior to the operations, more accurate estimates of map requirements were submitted to ETOUSA.*
2. *Map requisitions for shipment of maps to the continent were submitted by First Army to ETOUSA. The maps of the various scales were 'phased in' for shipment according to planned tactical phase lines.*
3. *Prior to the operation each of the assault, follow-up and build-up divisions was required to submit requisitions for maps for each battalion and separate company.*
4. *Long range bulk map requirements on the continent were submitted as far ahead as possible. However, the optimum time of sixty days in advance of delivery date was seldom attained.*
5. *Planning for map supply on the continent involved an intimate knowledge of the tactical plan, troop disposition, stocks of maps on hand and issue figures compiled from actual experience.*

PREPARATIONS FOR OPERATIONS AGAINST THE CONTINENT
Planning in London for operations 'Neptune'
1. *In order to be in close proximity to the following headquarters, a Planning Group from Headquarters First US Army, consisting of several officers and enlisted men from practically all general and special staff sections assembled in London with the Army Commander and Chief of Staff in January of 1944.*
1. *In accordance with Plan 'Neptune', the field artillery and tank destroyer organisation for the beach assault was as follows.*
    a. *Force 'O' (V Corps Beach).*
       58th Armd FA Bn – direct support of 116 RCT (29th Inf Div).
       1st In. Div Arty (-33rd FA Bn 105mm How) with 11th FA Bn 105mm How (29th Inf Div) attached.

JOINT FIRE PLAN
1. *The mission of the Joint Fire Plan was to destroy the enemy artillery and strong point positions, which were capable of firing on the transport areas and assault beaches. If this destruction was not accomplished, it was believed that effective neutralisation would be maintained by continuing some of the air bombardment and naval gunfire on the targets up to H-5 minutes before lifting to flanking or more distant inland targets.*
2. *No doubt, one of the most effective parts of the plan was the pre-Y day bombardment. Included in this project were five battery positions which were (to be) bombed at least once before 1 June.*
3. *A second important part of the Fire Plan was the employment of heavy and medium bombers on the assault beach defence positions immediately prior to H-Hour.*
4. *A third task of co-ordination was accomplished with relation to the Airborne Divisions and the Rangers' efforts. Several conferences were held, at which both the 82nd and 101st Airborne Division Commanders or their Artillery Commanders attended. Areas to be attacked in relation with landing and dropping zones and time of attack had to be most carefully adjusted. Provisions for employment of naval gunfire support on call were also planned.*

On the next page is a map showing the lanes from where the Navy were to provide fire support. [The Kansas lane runs right up in front of the Maisy Battery positions].

The information relating more specifically to the Rangers' areas of attack is covered by the next paragraphs; also of note is this paragraph '*b. Maps will only be issued for area coverage of immediate and primary interest,*' thus ensuring that each unit commander and his men obtained only the maps relative to *their* area of the assault.

THE OPERATION OF THE NAVAL SHORE FIRE CONTROL PARTIES

1. *Organisation for combat. 2nd and 5th Ranger Battalions – 1 NSFCP each.*
Basis for issue.
    a. *Map requisitions will be approved by Engineer Headquarters, First Army for corps (for corps headquarters only), corps, troop units, divisions and separate units for training purposes up to the total quantities indicated on the Map Allowances Table attached hereto.*
       The maps will be used with care and with the understanding that quantities in excess of the allowances will not be forthcoming. If, however, organisational variations from standard type units represented in the Map Allowances Table justify additional allotments, requisitions submitted should so indicate.
    b. *Maps will only be issued for area coverage of immediate and primary interest.*
    c. *Maps covering areas of future operations will also be automatically issued by Engineer Headquarters, First Army, to all units at the proper time (see paragraph 3b) in the quantities indicated on the attached Map Allowances Table. Prior to this distribution of operational maps, issue will be rigidly limited to higher headquarters only when, and in quantity and coverage required for planning purposes.*
    d. *Corps headquarters will be provided with and will maintain a stock of a limited number of training maps covering their sector and adjacent areas above their immediate needs. Corps headquarters will submit requisitions monthly on the 15th day of each month for the necessary maps to maintain their stock of training maps, but will distribute those received with a view to their complete utilisation for training.*
    e. *Stocks of operational maps covering areas of primary interest will be maintained by corps and divisions for emergency use in quantities indicated on the Map Allowance Table attached.*

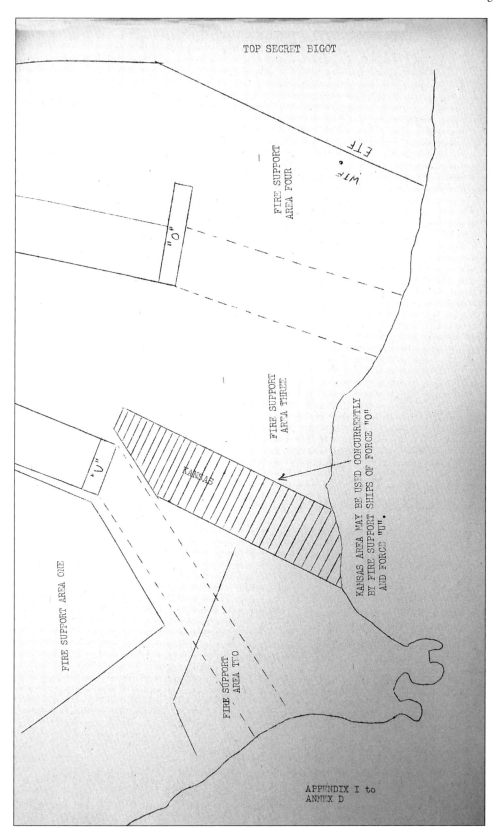

TOP SECRET BIGOT

FIRE SUPPORT AREA FOUR

ETF

WTF

"O"

FIRE SUPPORT AREA THREE

KANSAS

"U"

KANSAS AREA MAY BE USED CONCURRENTLY BY FIRE SUPPORT SHIPS OF FORCE "O" AND FORCE "U".

FIRE SUPPORT AREA ONE

FIRE SUPPORT AREA TWO

APPENDIX I to ANNEX D

Map Security

    a) *All operational maps of scales larger than 1:500,000 (Topographical or Photo) issued to units of this command which cover the general area of perspective operations will be classified immediately as "Confidential" prior to issue to planning or operational agencies.*

    b. *For issues of operational maps of limited area coverage, or if information of tactical or strategical nature is added to any operation map, said map will immediately be given an appropriate classification and will be handled under security control procedure or the map security instructions pertinent to the operation.*

DISTRIBUTION

    a. *Distribution of maps will be made by Engineer Headquarters, First Army to corps. All division and separate unit commanders will be responsible for the distribution of maps to their subordinate units.*

    b. *Upon assignment of units to this command, an initial requisition covering basic requirements of the unit consisting of 40% of the quantities of training maps, strategical and tactical, given in the Map Allowances Table attached hereto will be submitted by Engineer Headquarters First Army, to Headquarters Services of Supply ETOUSA, specifying delivery direct to the unit concerned. A copy of this requisition will be furnished to the unit concerned. Delivery may be expected within a week after submission of the requisition.*

       Maps to scale of 1:25,000 are usually not included in initial distribution because of lack of information as to exact location of training areas. These maps may be requisitioned as required as hereinafter prescribed. Delivery of operations maps will be made after security control measures and orientation in an operation have been accomplished.

    c. *All requests for maps not covered by the Map Allowances Table or covered by the initial allotment referred to above will be submitted through channels, in quintuplicate, to Engineer Headquarters, First Army.*

    d. *Insofar as practicable, requests for maps not covered by the Map Allowances Table or the initial automatic allotment will be consolidated by the corps (for corps headquarters), the divisions and separate units and submitted to Engineer Headquarters, First Army, in quintuplicate, on the 15th day of each month. Special requisitions other than the above monthly requisition will be kept to a minimum and will cover emergency requirements only.*

    e. *No requests for maps or other material will be made direct to S.O.S. ETOUSA, by units of this command.*

    f. *All maps no longer required for use because of obsolete area coverage or for other reasons will be returned direct to the Headquarters.*

---

9 March 1944

5th Rangers – Companies A – F, Medical and HQ – Tighnabruaich, Scotland.

HQ Company "Detachment A" 5th Rangers – Saunton Sands, N. Devon.

A Company 2nd Rangers – Bude, Cornwall.

Captain Cleveland A. Lytle was sent from normal duties to Detached Service.

Companies B, C, D & E 2nd Rangers – Bude, Cornwall.

F Company 2nd Rangers – Bude, Cornwall.

Pvt. Holly transferred to the 2913th Disciplinary Training Centre, Langport, Somerset.

Medical Detachment 2nd Rangers – Bude, Cornwall.

HQ Company 'Detachment A' 2nd Rangers – Saunton Sands, N. Devon.

T/Sgt Walker and Pfc. Willis were both relieved from their attachment to 'Detachment A' and returned to Headquarters Company 2nd Battalion.

Sgt. Devoli relieved from attachment to 'Detachment A' and returned to D Company 2nd Battalion.

Headquarters Company 2nd Rangers (less Detachment A) – Bude, Cornwall.

The US Army issued a letter to all of its men entitled:

British Women at War

    A British woman officer or non-commissioned officer can – and often does – give orders to a man private. The men obey smartly and know it is no shame. For British women have proven themselves in this war. They have stuck to their posts near burning ammunition dumps, delivered messages afoot after their motorcycles have been blasted from under them. They have pulled aviators from burning planes. They have died at the gun posts and as they fell another girl has stepped directly into the position and "carried on." There is not a single record of any British woman in uniformed service quitting her post or failing in her duty under fire.

Now you know why British soldiers respect their women in uniform. They have won the right to the utmost respect. When you see a girl in khaki or air-force blue with a bit of ribbon on her tunic – remember she didn't get it for knitting more socks than anyone else in Ipswich.

On 9 March the Army released the following TOP SECRET Operations Plan for Operation 'NEPTUNE' – it was called ANNEX No. 24 (and it was revised as of 9 March 1944). It is a concise countdown of the days in the run up to D-Day.

PLANNING TIME SCHEDULE
TIME (days)

Y – 92	First US Army issues Operations Plan 'NEPTUNE'.
Y – 90	Final Planning starts on Corps and Divisional level.
Y – 82 to 81	V Corps Amphibious Training Exercise for Force 'O'.
Y – 80	Corps submit to First US Army final list of Beach defences for pre-arranged Naval and Air Fire Support.
Y – 75	First US Army submits to 21st Army Group final list of Beach Defence Targets for pre-arranged Naval and Air Fire Support.
Y – 66	Corps submit to Army final Landing Tables for Forces 'O', 'U' and 'B', and Build-up Priority Tables for reminder First US Army. Army and Corps issue Alert Order, including administrative instructions to all organic and attached units.
Y – 65 to 63	VII Corps Amphibious Training Exercise for Force 'U'.
Y – 58	Detailed and final stores tables from First US Army to 21st Army Group.
Y – 55	Army submits to 21st Army Group final Landing Tables and Build-up Priority Tables for Army units and on behalf of 9th Air Force and CTF122.
Y – 50	Army submit to First US Army advance requisitions for estimated personnel losses as prescribed in Annex No 3.
Y – 46	All alerted units return to T/C, ETOUSA completed forms prescribed in ETO POM SSV.
Y – 45 to 15	Units move to concentration and marshalling areas in conformity with movement orders issued through T/C, ETOUSA.
Y – 45	Army receives from Joint C-in-C's Final Fire Support Plan.
Y – 38 to 34	Dress Rehearsal for Force 'U'.
Y – 30	Army issues to Corps final Fire Support Plan.
Y – 30 to 28	Dress Rehearsal for Force 'O'.
Y – 21	Concentration of Assault and Follow-up, and early Build-up units completed.
Y – 15	Final instructions issued by Army to subordinate commanders.
	CG, First US Army holds final conference with assault Corps and Division Commanders.
Y – 15 to Y	Assault, Follow-up, and Preloaded Build-up complete waterproofing, briefing and marshalling. Units embark in accordance with orders received through T/C, ETOUSA.

Early Build-up units receive final Army administrative order of instructions just prior to marshalling.

---

10 March 1944

5th Rangers – Companies A – F, Medical and HQ – Tighnabruaich, Scotland.

2nd Rangers – Companies A – F, Medical – Bude, Cornwall.

HQ Company "Detachment A" 2nd Rangers – Saunton Sands, N. Devon.

Headquarters Company 2nd Rangers (less Detachment A) – Bude, Cornwall.

The next page shows an overview of where the assault convoys were to meet up and then build together for the simultaneous attack on Normandy.

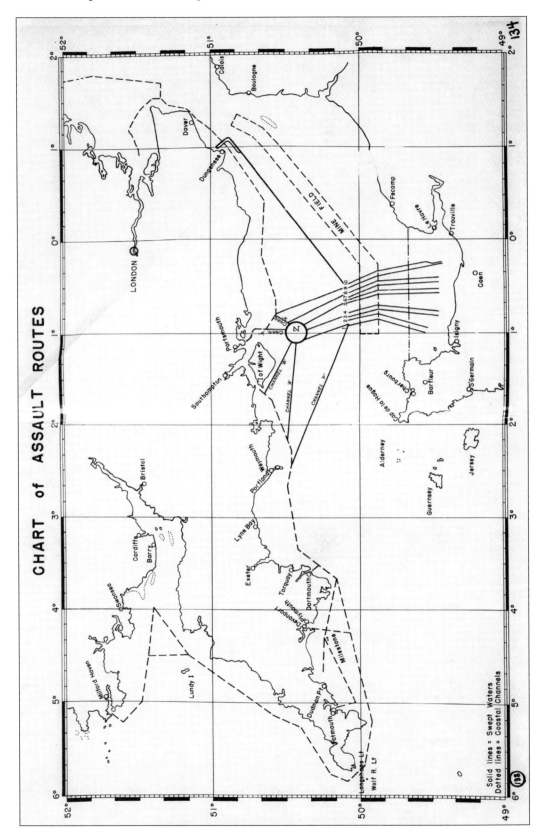

11 March 1944

5th Rangers – Companies A – F, Medical and HQ –
Tighnabruaich, Scotland.
2nd Rangers – Companies A – F, Medical – Bude,
Cornwall.
HQ Company "Detachment A" 2nd Rangers –
Saunton Sands, N. Devon.
*Headquarters Company 2nd Rangers (less
Detachment A)* – Bude, Cornwall.

Below is a G-3 Report produced for the 1st Infantry Division during their training for Operation Fox. Reports involving the Rangers are marked *(for procedure only)* – so that they are included in these practice landings on paper – but not in reality. In a similar way to the 'Assumed' word used previously.

HEADQUARTERS 1ST INFANTRY DIVISION
APO #1, U. S. Army

G-3 (JOURNAL*
~~REPORT~~

Time

(From   0001

(To   2400

Date   11 March 1944   CP Location   USS ANCON

TIME	NO.	FROM	SYNOPSIS	REC'D VIA	DISPOSITION#
0001	1		JOURNAL OPENED		
0745	2	ACG	Gen Wyman requests that H-hour be delayed It appeares that LCT with tanks will be late. REQUEST GRANTED	Mgr	J
0750	3	Navy	36 B26's due at 0815	Mgr	J
0815	4	Navy	Order given to cease fire. Shells falling on craft.	Mgr	J
0915	5	Br Ln O	Assault elements 102d Br Corps cleared beach at 0910.	Mgr	J
0945	6	Army	CO 16 CT landed on beach	Mgr	J
1003	7	G-3	Report your location	Mgr	CO 16th CT
1026	8	Navy	LCT's 510, 147, 163 and LCI's 90 and 84 unloaded.	Mgr	J
1040	9	Navy	743d Tk Bn reported landed	Mgr	J
1110	10	Navy	LST & LCI landed (See msg #10)	Mgr	J
1120	11	Army	Radio communication with 16CT & 116CT	Mgr	J
1125	12	Navy	Five waves have landed on Red Beach and 6th wave touched beach 1045	Victor Ln	J

NOTES:
        *Delete one.
        "Rec'd Via" column will indicate how message was transmitted, i.e., Tp - tele-
phone; Rad - radio; Tgp - telegraph; Tpe - teletype.
        #Following abbreviations only will be used in this column, other information will
be written out: M - Noted on situation map; J - Appended to journal (applies to Overlays, Msg blanks, written orders, etc.); CG, C/S, etc. - indicates information passed
on to Officer indicated; T- indicates information disseminated to units or troops, as
indicated in text of message.
(Revised 3 Jan. '44)

- 1 -

G-3 Journal* ~~Diaryx~~ for 11 Mar 44 ~~SECRET~~ Cont'd.

TIME	NO.	FROM	SYNOPSIS	REC'D VIA	DISPOSITION#
		(Col Pickett)			
1130	13	Army	Adv Div CP landed - not set up	Mgr	J
1133	14	G-3	Report your location immediately		CO's 16CT & 116CT
1204	15	G-3	Mortar fire landing at 265714 - cease firing		CO 16 CT
1214	16	G-3	Contact Rn Bn on your (For procedure only) left. Report your location.		CO 116 CT
1242	17	V Corps	115 RCT landing at H⁄8 hrs. Comes under Div control upon landing.		J
1305	18	G-3	Assume effective 1145 all 18CT complete landed.		J
1305	19	G-3	Adv CP opened 1115 at 251667.		

HEADQUARTERS 1ST INFANTRY DIVISION
APO #1, U. S. Army

ADVANCE G-3 (JOURNAL*
(~~DIARY~~

(From 1200
Time :
(To

Date 11 March   CP Location Slapton Wood

TIME	NO.	FROM	SYNOPSIS	REC'D VIA	DISPOSITION#
	1	G-3	JOURNAL OPENED		
1142	2	G-3	Advance CP, with Gen. Wyman, landed		CG, 1st Div
1145	3	ACG	18th CT assembled rear beaches		J
1210	4	Rr CP	Desire info from Adv CP		J
1230	5	G-3	CP moved from CR to Slapton Wood		J
1320	6	ACG	Obj taken 1st Bn 116th at 1110		J
			2d Bn 116th at 1230		
			3d Bn moving on their obj		
1325	7	LtColGara	CP 1st Engr Bn - 245672	Pers	J
1345	8	Div Arty	CP established at 1225 hrs at 25320 67290	Rad	J
1345	9	Rr CP	Report location.	Rad	J
1345	10	AT Co 16	Present location 942705	Rad	J
1350	11	Inter	M 2 on final obj (3d Bn 16th)	Rad	J
1400	12	Div Atry	Front lines at 1310 hrs. Moving forward	Rad	J
			to atch strong point at 245687 at 1315 hrs	~~Pers~~	
			7th FA Bn at 269687 - 62d FA Bn at 25106660		
1400	13	Adv CP G-3	Air missions between Blackawton & Ashpring-ton during period 1530 and 1600.		J
1352	14	CO 16th	White 970719 - 977710. Blue 957797 CP 941794. 1105.	Rad	J

NOTES:
    *Delete one.
    "Rec'd Via" column will indicate how message was transmitted, i.e., Tp - tele-phone; Rad - radio; Tgp - telegraph; Tpe - teletype.
    #Following abbreviations only will be used in this column, other information will be written out: M - Noted on situation map; J - Appended to journal (applies to Over-lays, Msg blanks, written orders, etc.); CG, C/S, etc. - indicates information passed on to Officer indicated; T- indicates information disseminated to units or troops, as indicated in text of message.
(Revised 3 Jan. '44)
                                - 1 -

G-3 Journal* ~~Report~~ for 11 Mar '44   Cont'd.

TIME	NO.	FROM	SYNOPSIS	REC'D VIA	DISPOSITION
1412	15	2d-16th	Forward element at 25 grid moving forward	Inter	J
1445	16	Adv CP G-3	Sit Rep		CG, V Corps
1450	17	16th Inf	1st Bn in reserve at 265685.	Rad	J
1500	18	Lt Kam	3d 116th on objective on 1330 hrs		J
1508	19	Adv CP G-3	Request bombing and strafing mission – between Blackawton and Ashprington		Air Support O Ancon
1510	20	Adv CP "G-3	116th CT have contacted Rangers on L flank		CG V Corps
1120	21	16 CT	IBL 1030. Resistance at 248673. P-temporary 267682. 3d Bn seized initial objs 1050	Rad	J
1512	22	I116th	CP closed at 1413	Rad	J
1515	23	2d – 16CT	A Co pushed enemy back and now moving forward	Inter	J
1515	24	S2 16 CT	3d on objs. 2d Bn ---G Co 230698, E Co 238697, F Co back 244688 1st Bn at 247724.	G2	J
1530	25	S2 16 CT	Auto wpns at 222700. Co C stopped by Co enemy inf at 241711. Enemy plat 251726	G2	J
1530	26	16th CT	CP AT 368089. A Co stopped by plat of enemy with automatic weapons at 979670. C Co stopped by Co. of enemy inf at 355095. B Co moving	Inter	J
1530	27	Adv CP G-3	Sit Rep		CG V Corps
1537	28	16th CT	A Co has reached their obj (no time)	Inter	J
1545	29	Adv CP G3	Sit Rep		CG V Corps
1235	30	AC G	Seized St. Eloi – Atck still progressing Radio contact established with both CTs.	Mgr	J
1545	31	CP 16th	CP located at 271687		None
1545	32	116th CP	116th In by radio 1545.		None
1325	33	CG V Cops	Info CG Engr Spec Brig Up time coaster unloading begins paren PD will be reported without delay	Rad	J

Overleaf is one of the 'fake' radio reports which were sent out at the time. The importance of these messages was to maintain the appearance of the Rangers' participation in the exercise to the other units. Major General Huebner signed these fake radio messages himself as Commanding General (CG) 1st Inf. Div.

CG 1st Div
CO CT 116   CnE P.

Contact Ranger Bn on your (for C.P.
Procedure only) left. Report your
location.

                              Andrus

THESE SPACES FOR MESSAGE CENTER ONLY

TIME FILED	MSG CEN NO.	HOW SENT

MESSAGE (SUBMIT TO MESSAGE CENTER IN DUPLICATE)   (CLASSIFICATION)

No. _____   DATE 11 MARCH 1944

To C.G. V CORPS

·116TH CT HAVE CONTACTED
RANGERS ON LEFT FLANK.

HUEBNER

CG 1st Inf Div.   1510
OFFICIAL DESIGNATION OF SENDER   TIME SIGNED

AUTHORIZED TO BE SENT IN CLEAR   SIGNATURE OF OFFICER   SIGNATURE AND GRADE OF WRITER

☆ U. S. GOVERNMENT PRINTING OFFICE : 1942   16—27880-1

THESE SPACES FOR MESSAGE CENTER ONLY

TIME FILED	MSG CEN NO.	HOW SENT

MESSAGE (SUBMIT TO MESSAGE CENTER IN DUPLICATE)   (CLASSIFICATION)

No. _____   DATE 11 MAR 1944

To _____

115TH LANDED AT 1630 – MOVING
FORWARD 1715 TO Obj 1ST PHASE LINE.
RANGERS HAVE CLEARED OUT SOUTH
FLANK DEFENSIVES

OFFICIAL DESIGNATION OF SENDER   TIME SIGNED

AUTHORIZED TO BE SENT IN CLEAR   SIGNATURE OF OFFICER   SIGNATURE AND GRADE OF WRITER

☆ U. S. GOVERNMENT PRINTING OFFICE : 1942   16—27880-1

12 March 1944

5th Rangers – Companies A – F, Medical and HQ – Tighnabruaich, Scotland.

A Company 2nd Rangers – Bude, Cornwall.
Captain Cleveland A. Lytle returned to the unit from Detached Service.

B Company 2nd Rangers – Bude, Cornwall.

C Company 2nd Rangers – Bude, Cornwall.
Alerted for departure.

D Company 2nd Rangers – Bude, Cornwall.
No change.

E Company 2nd Rangers – Bude, Cornwall.
1st Lt. Lapres returned from Detached Service with Headquarters Company 'Detachment A', 2nd Btn at Saunton Sands, North Devon to Duty.

F Company 2nd Rangers – Bude, Cornwall.

Medical Detachment 2nd Rangers – Bude, Cornwall.

HQ Company 'Detachment A' 2nd Rangers – Saunton Sands, N. Devon.

Headquarters Company 2nd Rangers (less Detachment A) – Bude, Cornwall.
Major Max F. Schneider went from Duty to 5 days ordered leave.
2nd Lt. Robert Fitsimmons was relieved of his duties with HQ Company and transferred to B Company 2nd Battalion.

A US Army directive was issued with the title: Leaves, Furloughs and Passes.

The photograph shows 2nd Lt. Frank Kennard taken whilst he was on leave in Clovelly, Devon.

Leaves, furloughs and passes involving rail or bus travel will not be granted on Saturdays or Sundays. This prohibition will be construed not to apply to informal leaves or passes involving travel to nearby cities or towns, or to personnel authorised to attend educational courses of British Universities while in a leave or furlough status. When travel by rail or water is involved in any leave, furlough or pass, twenty-four hours' notice will be given to the nearest rail transportation officer.

The carrying of weapons of any kind, including razors and knives, other than pocket knives (three-inch blade or less) on leave, furlough or pass is prohibited.

On 12 March the US Army via the office of General Eisenhower issued clarification of the procedures surrounding the various levels of Secrecy.

 BIGOT

        All BIGOT communications will be classified TOP SECRET and handled by TOP SECRET Control Procedure.

        Each addressee of this letter is responsible for advising all concerned in his command of the contents of this letter. The information concerning subjects falling under BIGOT Procedure will necessarily be disseminated only to individuals entitled to it.

                By command of General EISENHOWER:

                                /s/ R. B. LOVETT
                                    R. B. LOVETT
                            Brigadier General, USA
                                Adjutant General

Incl: No. 1.   ▃▃▃▃▃ ⸺ BIGOT   NEPTUNE

                                                    AUTH: CG ETOUSA
                                                    INIT: RBL
                                                    Date: 12 March 1944.

                    HEADQUARTERS
            EUROPEAN THEATER OF OPERATIONS   COPY NO. 20
                 UNITED STATES ARMY
                                                        6.27-3

AG 311.5 SCD   12 March 1944.

SUBJECT: Operational Codeword Plans and BIGOT Procedure – Instruction No. 1.

TO   : See distribution.

    1. Reference letter this Headquarters, Subject: Security Classification and Changes in AR 380-5, 5 March 1944, and letter this Headquarters Subject: TOP SECRET Control Procedure, 12 March 1944.

    2. Documents concerning particulars of the following Operational Codeword Plans which disclose the Plans Proper, their code names, contemplated areas of action, dates, certain special equipment, and all matters which tend to reveal the foregoing will be handled under TOP SECRET Control Procedure:

        a. ATLANTIS
        b. FORTITUDE
        c. MULBERRIES
        d. NEPTUNE
        e. OVERLORD
        f. PLUTO
        g. RANKIN
        h. CROSSBOW

    3. Documents pertaining to all of the above-named plans with the exception of NEPTUNE and FORTITUDE (NEPTUNE) which do not disclose directly or by inference the particulars listed in paragraph 2 above, can be classified SECRET although the codeword is mentioned therein.

    4. The following specific information pertaining to the use of Codewords OVERLORD, NEPTUNE and FORTITUDE is furnished for the guidance of all concerned:

        a. Any document or map which contains any information concerning the target area or precise date of the assault of OVERLORD will NOT be issued under the codeword OVERLORD but under the codeword NEPTUNE.

        b. The codeword FORTITUDE has been allotted for the cover and deception policy for NW Europe from 1st January 1944, until OVERLORD D-21. Any FORTITUDE document which contains NEPTUNE information should be headed FORTITUDE (NEPTUNE) and will be subject to the BIGOT Procedure. The word NEPTUNE need not be repeated in the body of the document.

        c. Any document which reveals, directly or by inference, the cover target area of OVERLORD will be issued under the codeword NEPTUNE, or FORTITUDE (NEPTUNE) according to the contents of the document.

                            -1-   BIGOT

 - BIGOT

d. No OVERLORD document will be subject to the BIGOT Procedure. However, all documents marked OVERLORD-BIGOT in your possession prior to the receipt of this directive will be subject to the BIGOT Procedure. All NEPTUNE documents will be subject to the BIGOT Procedure.

e. The codeword OVERLORD may be used in the body of a NEPTUNE Document. Great care must be exercised in the use of NEPTUNE and extreme efforts will be made to issue documents under the codeword OVERLORD rather than NEPTUNE by omitting reference to the target area or date of assault or inferences thereto. If an originator of a document is in any doubt as to the codeword under which that document should be issued, he should communicate with the TOP SECRET Control Officer of the Section or Headquarters concerned. It remains the responsibility of the Headquarters or Section concerned to insure that TOP SECRET Control Procedure is followed in all appropriate cases.

5. For the information of all concerned BIGOT Procedure mentioned in paragraph 1 above is outlined below to establish uniformity in U. S. and British marking, and will be rigidly adhered to.

a. The object of the BIGOT Procedure is to ensure that BIGOT communications are opened only by the person to whom they are addressed, or by the person authorized by him in writing to do so.

b. Documents received from British or other sources marked BIGOT will be automatically handled by TOP SECRET Control Procedure. The codeword BIGOT is a British designation and will not be originally applied to any papers by U. S. Forces until the British have designated the subject matter as receiving BIGOT Procedure.

c. Marking and Transmitting BIGOT Documents.

(1) Documents will be marked BIGOT in large letters on the top righthand corner. The codeword BIGOT will be buried in the text of cables and other messages as near the beginning as practicable.

(2) BIGOT documents will be transmitted only by hand of officer and in double envelopes, each addressed to a named person, and the codeword BIGOT will be clearly marked in large letters adjacent to the address on the inner envelope only.

(3) When transmission is by Officer Courier, the outer envelope will be marked "Handle by Officer Courier Only" to assure proper handling at all times.

d. It is the responsibility of the initiator of any BIGOT communication to ensure that the addressee is authorized to receive the information which it contains.

e. Initiators who require guidance as to the correct addressee for any BIGOT communication should refer to the appropriate TOP SECRET Control Officer or comparable officially designated officer for the handling of BIGOT documents in his Headquarters.

-2-

- BIGOT

Details of FAKE missions being undertaken by the Rangers were also recorded in After Action Reports. They are again marked as 'ASSUMED' to have been there. On the overlay the Rangers are indicated by the black circle.

Hq. 29 US Inf Div
APO #29, US Army
12 March 1944

Copy No _5_

Cmth: Cg, 29 Inf Div
Init: S.S.W.
Date: 12 March 44

FO #1.

Maps: Gt Britain, GSGS 3 36, 1/25000
Photo Map, Sheets and 2, Eng: Slapton Sands and Vicinity

1. For enemy situation see G-2 Annex.

2. 29th Inf Div (reinf) will defend and hold first phase line in its sector, (see Ops overlay,) and actively patrol to front.

3. a. 115th Infantry (assumed)

  (1) 1st and 2nd Bns will prepare defensive positions in depth in present positions.

  (2) 3rd Bn in Div reserve.

  (3) Maintain contact with 1st Div on right and 116th Inf to rear and left.

  (4) Protect right flank of Div.

 b. 116th Infantry

  (1) Prepare defensive positions in depth in present position.

  (2) 2nd Bn establish strong point in vicinity of Frogmore (see Ops overlay).

  (3) Cannon Co be prepared to deliver reinforcing fires in support of strong point, vicinity Frogmore.

  (4) Maintain contact with 115th Inf on right, and Ranger Bn on left.

  (5) Co C, 81st Chem Bn, attached to 116th Inf.

 c. 175th Infantry

  (1) Designated as Corps reserve.

  (2) Will reconnoiter routes and possible assembly areas for counterattack in sectors of 1st and 29th Divs, to first phase line, with particular emphasis on boundary between Divs. Submit overlays to this Hq prior to 0500 hours 12 March 1944.

 d. Division Artillery

  (1) All artillery to under Div arty control.

  (2) Div Arty prepared to deliver mass of fire in sector of 115th Inf. Majority of bns to and left sector of 1st Div. Two bns to be prepared to reach approaches from west through Frogmore.

 e. 121st Engrs (with 112th Engrs attached)

  (1) Carry out

(2) Be prepared on two hours' notice to assemble in area, (see Ops overlay,) as Div reserve.

f. 29th Cav Ren Troop (Mecz) (-)

(1) Move to vicinity EAST ALLINGTON (Y 198702). Reconnoiter N to River AVON and N to Road GARABRIDGE (Y 158753) - MORELEIGH (Y 195746).

(2) CO, Rcn Tr, coordinate with elements 1st Cav Rcn Tr at HALWELL (Y 205749).

g. 803rd TD Bn

(1) On landing, will move to assembly areas, (see Ops overlay,) reconnoiter routes of approach, and be prepared to resist armored attacks from northwest and west.

h. 459th AAA AWpns Bn

(1) Be prepared to defend beach organizations and dumps in Div sector.

i. 743rd Tank Bn

(1) Reconnoiter routes to west and northwest, and be prepared in present assembly area to counterattack any armored attack in Div sector, with particular emphasis on Div right flank.

j. Ranger Bn (assumed)
    (1) Prepare defensive positions (see Ops overlay).
    (2) Maintain contact with 116th Inf on right.
    (3) Protect left flank of Div.

k. Co C, 81st Chem Bn - Attached to 116th Infantry

4. a. Supply
        Water point: 220644 now open. Engrs DP (219646) now open.

    b. Evacuation
        (1) Casualties: By Collecting Cos to Div Clearing Stations.
        (2) Cemeteries: MATTISCOMBE TROSS (233639). START (237668).

    c. Personnel
        Straggler line: WHITE STONE CROSS (239685); FRITTSCOMBE (231655); KELLATON (229610).

    d. Other administrative details - No change.

Division CP (See Ops overlay)

Axis of Signal Communications: STOKENHAM (235648)
                                 COLERIDGE CROSS (229652)
                                 DEERBRIDGE (241663)
                                 ALSTON CROSS (229680)
                                 COLE'S CROSS (206686)

OFFICIAL: GERHARDT
        Watts   Maj Gen
        WATTS
        Asst G-3

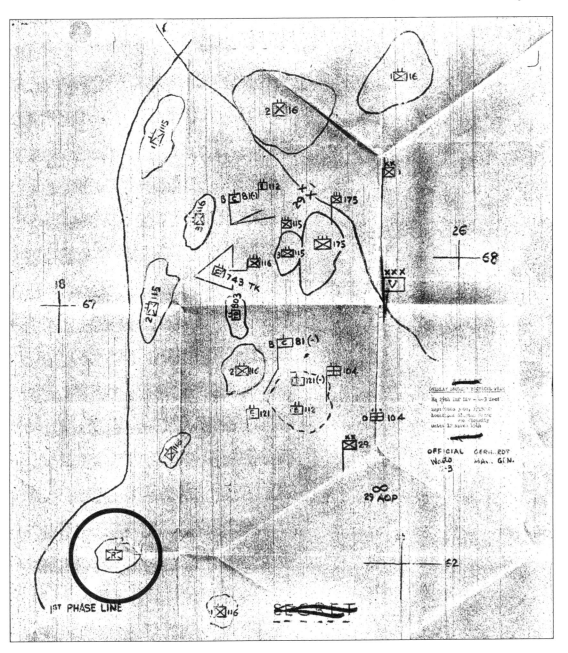

13 March 1944
5th Rangers – Companies A – F, Medical and HQ – Tighnabruaich, Scotland.

2nd Rangers – Companies A – F, Medical – Bude, Cornwall.

HQ Company 'Detachment A' 2nd Rangers – Saunton Sands, N. Devon.

1st Lt. Theodore Lapres Jr was relieved from his principal Duty as Instructor attached to 'Detachment A' and returned to E Co. 2nd Btn.

1st Lt. Joseph C. Smudin was attached from HQ Company 2nd Btn for Duty, rations and quarters with the principal Duty of Instructor.

Headquarters Company 2nd Rangers (less Detachment A) – Bude, Cornwall.

1st Lt. James Eikner went from Duty to 5 days ordinary leave.

1st Lt. William Heavey went from Duty to 5 days leave.

The following sixteen enlisted men were assigned and joined HQ Company on 4 March 1944 and were carried on the Morning Report of 4 March. This corrected Morning Report gives the men's prior organisations.

Cpl. Harvey E. Robertson Jr. was assigned and joined HQ Company from Cannon Company, 23rd Inf. APO#2 US Army.
T/5 William J. Gottel Jr. was assigned and joined from Battery A 391st Armoured Field Artillery Battalion APO 253 US Army.
T/5 Peter A. Ruta was assigned and joined from Service Battery 67th Armoured Field Artillery Battalion APO 253 US Army.
T/5 Earl W. Sorger was assigned and joined from Service Battery 67th Armoured Field Artillery Battalion APO 253 US Army.
Pfc. Edmond A. Sworsky was assigned and joined from HQ Company 3rd Battalion 320th Armoured Regiment APO 253 US Army.
Pfc. Colin J. Lowe was assigned and joined from HQ 110th Infantry APO#28 US Army.
Pfc. Joseph J. Duffy was assigned and joined from B Company 109th Infantry APO 28 US Army.
Pfc. Roy M. Wilson was assigned and joined from A Company 112th Infantry APO 28 US Army.
Pfc. Ray H. Ogle was assigned and joined from A Company 11th Infantry APO #5 US Army.
Pfc. Lloyd Burns was assigned and joined from G Company 10th Infantry Division APO#5 US Army.
Pfc. Leonary E. Coley was assigned and joined from HQ Battery 94th Armoured Field Artillery Battalion APO 254 US Army.
Pvt. William L. Graham was assigned and joined from I Company 32nd Armoured Regiment, APO 253 US Army.
Pvt. Bill M. Mooneyham was assigned and joined from Service Company 32nd Armoured Regiment APO 253 US Army.
Pvt. Albert A. McFadden was assigned and joined from E Company 23rd Armoured Engineer Battalion APO 253 US Army.
Pvt. Frank J. Kosina was assigned and joined from C Company 112th Infantry APO 28th US Army.
Pvt. William H. McWhirter was assigned and joined from HQ 25th Cavalry Reconnaissance Squadron HEC2 APO 254 US Army.

These experienced artillery and armoured trained men became the basis for the 2nd Battalion cannon company, rocket squads and defensive infantry. An adaption was made to the standard M3 half-track which included adding a 75mm cannon mounted on the back, which fired over the driver's cab.

2nd Lt. Frank Kennard standing beside his two 75mm half-tracks in Bude.

Second Lt. Kennard and 1st Lt. Conway Epperson from the 2nd Battalion were each given command of two half tracks and newly supplied infantrymen were taken from the 2nd Battalion men above, as crew. Each vehicle was fitted with a 75mm gun and they both formed what was to be known as a Cannon Platoon. Epperson and Kennard's group had in total 33 men taken from the 2nd Battalion.

Frank Kennard, 2nd Rangers:

Our half tracks were essentially a big box (on tracks) with a 75mm gun (WWI vintage). Its floor had a number of ammunition lockers (for 75mm shells). On the outside of the box were tools, pick and shovel, a bangalore torpedo and 5gal gas cans. Personal gear was 'hung' on the outside otherwise the items would block access to the ammo lockers!

Like everyone else the cannon platoon was 'expendable' and I am unaware of any plan for the cannon platoon to continue after D-Day.

The 75-mm Gun Motor Carriages, as they were officially designated, were to be employed chiefly as tank destroyers and the gun was to be used in direct fire mode only. The gun was mounted in the approximate centre of the vehicle and was only designed to fire forwards. These were a new addition to increase the firepower of the Ranger Battalions.

An armour-plate gun shield was mounted in front of the gun. This supplemented the protection given to the gun and crew by the armour-plate windshield and door shields, and by the armoured hull. Therefore the movement of the gun was limited by the halftrack and it was the vehicle which would position itself on the target with only limited movement from the actual weapon.

---

14 March 1944
5th Rangers – Companies A – F, Medical and HQ – Tighnabruaich, Scotland.
HQ Company 'Detachment A' 5th Rangers – Saunton Sands, N. Devon.
2nd Rangers – Companies A – F, Medical – Bude, Cornwall.
HQ Company 'Detachment A' 2nd Rangers – Saunton Sands, N. Devon.
Headquarters Company 2nd Rangers (less Detachment A) – Bude, Cornwall.

---

15 March 1944
5th Rangers – Companies A – F, Medical and HQ – Tighnabruaich, Scotland.
2nd Rangers – Companies A – F, Medical – Bude, Cornwall.
HQ Company "Detachment A" 2nd Rangers – Saunton Sands, N. Devon.
Headquarters Company 2nd Rangers (less Detachment A) – Bude, Cornwall.

2nd Battalion Narrative History.

> Information of the D-Day mission was received during the first week of March and, on 15 March, the Battalion Commander, the S-2, and one enlisted man departed for Plymouth, England, to obtain the available information and initiate planning for the assigned mission.

---

16 March 1944
5th Rangers – Companies A – F, Medical and HQ – Tighnabruaich, Scotland.
2nd Rangers – Companies A – F, Medical – Bude, Cornwall.
HQ Company 'Detachment A' 2nd Rangers – Saunton Sands, N. Devon.
Headquarters Company 2nd Rangers (less Detachment A) – Bude, Cornwall.

Overleaf: The A Company 2nd Battalion roster for 16 March. [Apologies for the quality].

---

17 March 1944
5th Rangers – Companies A – F, Medical and HQ – Tighnabruaich, Scotland.
2nd Rangers – Companies A – F, Medical – Bude, Cornwall.
HQ Company 'Detachment A' 2nd Rangers – Saunton Sands, N. Devon.
Headquarters Company 2nd Rangers (less Detachment A) – Bude, Cornwall.

One by one each company started to send their men on identical training courses – and others received temporary changes of rank or company to accommodate them. This rotation of men to specialist training centres would continue for some time.

16 March 1944

REGISTER

MASTER SERGEANT

..., Robert ...   36362677

TECHNICAL SERGEANTS

Gunther, Harold ...   20605263
Mairs, Clifton ...   20306365

STAFF SERGEANTS

Anderson, Christopher M.   36127525
Cleaves, Joseph J.   36428501
Denbo, Charles H.   36025912
Hayden, Millard W.   33066939
Pyles, Robert S.   6667402
Robinson, Frank B.   20530005
Rupinski, Frank A.   13097753
Simmons, Curtis A.   32251141

SERGEANTS

Boggetto, Domenick B.   36330165
Fritchman Jr, Harry G.   13129178
Meccia, Alban NMI   32772980
Rosal, Aloysius S.   33170436
Robey, Hayward A.   35386313
Yardley, Andrew J.   20927510

CORPORALS

Lare, Lawrence NMI   35408976

TECHNICIANS GRADE 5

Burnett, John S.   20457332
Catelani, Anthony P.   39011279
Colvard Jr, E. G. (IO)   34708304
Honhart, Robert A.   20311626
La Brundt, Frank J.   32073436
McCalvin, Charles G.   15091484
Milalas, Theodore M.   31235920
Putses, George J.   35380446
..., Harold ...   ...
..., Albert J.   ...
..., LeRoy ...   ...
..., Glenn ...   36455241
..., ...   1197...

PRIVATES FIRST CLASS

Aguzzi, Victor J.   34625130
Bargmann, Kenneth H.   33562066
Bell, William D.   35604873
Bellows Jr, Charles H.   31299814
Bowens, Howard NMI   32772897
Clark, Rex D.   39378566
Connolly, Francis J.   31300634
Crook, George H.   11131236
Daugherty, Duncan N.   36578082
Davis, Raymond G.   15323647
Dunlap, Charles M.   13053850
Gaydos Jr, Joseph P.   33345744
Hubbard, Richard NMI   35791278
Knor, Paul P.   13089855
Lawson Jr, Jack NMI   35435736
Lock, Joseph J.   16141165
Mackey, George W.   35604231
Maimone, Salva P.   34188123
Main, Harold D.   39183669
Medeiros, Paul I.   33320351
Miller, William J.   31340914
Palmer, Roy L.   33128996
Peterson, Frank H.   11096301
Roberts, Harry W.   33422943
Sillmon, John J.   34607717
Sooy, Ralph B.   13112554
Talkington, Woodrow NMI   35738031
Theobald, Earl A.   36477655
Wadsworth, Loring L.   31231880
Welmer, Martin R.   36378405
Wood, Henry A.   32772425

PRIVATES

Bachleda, Anton NMI   32808036
Pachman Jr, Clarence F.   13135758
Ferris, Wilfred E.   39013424

W.C. Mefane

---

18 March 1944

5th Rangers – Companies A – F, Medical and HQ – Tighnabruaich, Scotland.

2nd Rangers – Companies A – F, Medical – Bude, Cornwall.

HQ Company 'Detachment A' 2nd Rangers – Saunton Sands, N. Devon.

1st Lt. Dahan was relieved from attached and returned to Headquarters Company 2nd Btn and was relieved from his primary Duty as Supply Officer. 1st Lt. Smudin was relieved from attached and returned to Headquarters Company 2nd Btn and was relieved from his primary Duty as Instructor.

Headquarters Company 2nd Rangers (less Detachment A) – Bude, Cornwall.

2nd Battalion Narrative History.

> *All Companies were rotated on five-day furloughs during the month of March. Training was continued with emphasis on cliff scaling and Company-size firing problems. A typical enemy beach strongpoint was constructed with enemy artillery represented by emplaced explosives. The Company assault team, using hand-placed charges, Bangalores, Bazookas, and 81-mm mortar screening smoke, became quite adept at this type of assault.*

---

19 March 1944

5th Rangers – Companies A – F, Medical and HQ – Tighnabruaich, Scotland.

A Company 2nd Rangers – Bude, Cornwall.
The following men were sent on Detached Service to the Army Training Centre at Woolacombe: 1st Lt. Stanley E. White, S/Sgt. Elmer C. Carr, Sgt. Robert P. Gary.

B Company 2nd Rangers – Bude, Cornwall.
2nd Lt. Fitzsimmons went from Duty to Detached Service – Army Training Centre at Saunton Sands, North Devon.
S/Sgt. Dorchak and Sgt. DeCapp went from Duty to Army Training Centre at Saunton Sands, North Devon.

C Company 2nd Rangers – Bude, Cornwall.
1st Lt. Salomon and S/Sgts Kennedy and Maynard Priesman went from Duty to Detached Service – Army Training Centre at Saunton Sands, North Devon.

D Company 2nd Rangers – Bude, Cornwall.

E Company 2nd Rangers – Bude, Cornwall.
1st Lt. Lapres went from Duty to Detached Service at the Amphibious Training Centre, Woolacombe.
S/Sgt. Pyles and S/Sgt. Simmons went from Duty to Detached Service at the Amphibious Training Centre, Wollacombe.

F Company 2nd Rangers – Bude, Cornwall.
1st Lt. Hill went from Duty to Detached Service at the Amphibious Training Centre, Saunton Sands, North Devon.
S/Sgt. Fulton and S/Sgt. Stivison both went from Duty to Detached Service at the Amphibious Training Centre, Saunton Sands, North Devon.

Medical Detachment 2nd Rangers – Bude, Cornwall. No change.

HQ Company 'Detachment A' 2nd Rangers – Saunton Sands, N. Devon.
T/5 Anderson was relieved from his attachment with 'Detachment A' and returned to Headquarters Company 2nd Btn.

Headquarters Company 2nd Rangers (less Detachment A) – Bude, Cornwall.

---

20 March 1944

5th Rangers – Companies A – F, Medical and HQ – Tighnabruaich, Scotland.

2nd Rangers – Companies A – F, Medical – Bude, Cornwall.

HQ Company – 'Detachment A' 2nd Rangers – Saunton Sands, N. Devon.

Headquarters Company 2nd Rangers (less Detachment A) – Bude, Cornwall.

---

21 March 1944

5th Rangers – Companies A – F, Medical and HQ – Tighnabruaich, Scotland.

'Detachment A' HQ Company 5th Rangers – London, England.
3-20th March. Usual Camp Duties. 21 March: Left Saunton Sands, N. Devon. 1200 hrs. Arrived London, England 2350 hrs. 172 miles travelled by rail.

A Company 2nd Rangers – Bude, Cornwall.
1st Lt. Richard L. Cook was relieved of Duty and transferred to the 4th Infantry Division.
Pvt. Arvin L. Duncan was transferred to the 4th Infantry Division. Two enlisted men were transferred to the 30th Infantry Division (names unclear).

B, C, D, & E Companies 2nd Rangers – Bude, Cornwall.
Captain Otto Masny returned to Duty from ATC, Saunton Sands, North Devon and assumed principal Duty as Company Commander of F Company. T/Sgt. John. W. Franklin and Pfc. Walter T. Bialkowski returned from Detached Service with 'Detachment A' at Saunton Sands, North Devon to Duty.

Medical Detachment 2nd Rangers – Bude, Cornwall.
HQ Company 'Detachment A' 2nd Rangers – Saunton Sands, N. Devon.
Headquarters Company 2nd Rangers (less Detachment A) – Bude, Cornwall.
1st Lt. Willian G. Heaney went from Duty to Detached Service at Woolacombe as of 19 March 1944.
1st Lt. Louis Dahan was relieved from his assignment and transferred to the 1st Infantry Division APO 1, US Army.
1st Lt. Joseph C. Smudin was relieved of command and transferred to the 113th Cavalry Reconnaissance Squadron, US Army.

CENSORSHIP

Dated 21 March 1944 the guidelines regarding censorship had been redrawn and were thoroughly explained to the Rangers as follows:

> *Prohibited Items.*
> *Statements prohibited in private correspondence are those which in general:*
> 1) *Give information useful to the enemy.*
> 2) *Affect the security of the US or its armed forces.*
> 3) *Affect the security of Great Britain or other allies.*
> 4) a) *Are likely to embarrass the US in its relations with Great Britain or other allies.*
>   b) *Specific items which will give aid and comfort to the enemy and which will not be mentioned, directly or by inference, in personal mail are:*
> 1) *Any details of movement to or from this theatre; especially the names or types of aircraft or transports; the designation of airports or ports of embarkation or debarkation; the exact dates of arrival or departure; the number of ships in convoy; naval vessels or aircraft accompanying the convoy; any action with the enemy EN ROUTE; the length of voyage, or the route followed.*
> 2) *Military armament, equipment or supplies of any kind whatsoever.*
> 3) *Strength, efficiency, training, morale or organisation of US or allied military forces.*
> 4) *Location, movement, engagements or operations of naval, military or air force organisations; to include location of billets, stations or camps in any theatre of operation.*
> 5) *Direct or inferential information linking an APO or station number or unit with an exact geographical location. (This prohibition applies equally to station and general hospitals).*
>   a) *The expressions 'Somewhere in England, North Ireland, or Iceland' are permitted in mail – but not in cables. No more specific geographical location of unit or APO is permitted.*
>   b) *As the sole exception to this rule, personnel authorised to use APO 887 are permitted to reveal their presence in London. Similarly, personnel using APO 860 may reveal their presence in Reykjavik, Iceland.*
> 6) *Distinguishing signs used to identify organisations or their transportation or badges.*
> 7) *Information or details of operations against or by the enemy on land, sea or in the air. This will include references to any results of enemy action.*
> 8) *Plans and forecasts or orders for future operations, whether known or surmised.*
> 9) *The use or probable extension of roads, transport facilities or signal communication facilities.*
> 10) *Casualties, before official notification of next of kin or release.*
> 11) *Detailed reports of the weather in such form as to be helpful to the enemy.*
> 12) *Criticisms and statements of a disparaging nature which would bring our armed forces or those of our allies into disrepute.*
>   c) *The following items will not be included in personal letters or packages.*
> 1) *Classified documents of the US or allied nations.*
> 2) *Documents captured from the enemy or containing information about the enemy. Any such material will be sent to Theatre Censor, HQ ETOUSA, APO 887.*
> 3) *Codes, ciphers or any other secret writing.*
> 4) *Games, puzzles, riddles, maps or blank paper.*
> 5) *Photographs or other picture matter which, when taken alone or together with written information in the communication, violate the instructions contained in this circular.*
> 6) *Newspaper or magazine clippings which are accompanied by comments causing a disclosure of prohibited information.*

22 March 1944

5th Rangers – Companies A – F, Medical and HQ – Tighnabruaich, Scotland.

HQ Company 'Detachment A' 5th Rangers – Glasgow, Scotland.

22nd March: Left London, England 0200hrs. Arrived Glasgow, Scotland 2345. 344 miles travelled by rail.

A Company 2nd Rangers – Bude, Cornwall.

Captain Cleveland A. Lytle was assigned to 2nd Battalion Headquarters, in his place 1st Lt. Joseph A. Rafferty was relieved of his principal Duty as platoon leader and he assumed the role of Company Commander to cover for Captain Lytle. 1st Lt. Robert T. Edlin was assigned and joined A Company from the 28th Infantry Division as of 21 March 1944 and assumed the principal Duty as platoon leader.

Maurice Prince: *Our Battalion underwent a reorganization while at Bude. A few men and some officers were released and transferred to other outfits. It appears that although these men had put out to the best of their ability, it didn't quite meet the rigid standards and morale requirements of the Rangers, in exchange, new men and new life were added to the Battalion. Our company was fairly well affected by this move as we lost a couple of men and an officer. But, in return we got Lt. Edlin and several other swell soldiers.*

B Company 2nd Rangers – Bude, Cornwall.

C Company 2nd Rangers – Bude, Cornwall.

Pfc. Fulford went from Duty to being confined to the Guardhouse.

D Company 2nd Rangers – Bude, Cornwall.

E Company 2nd Rangers – Bude, Cornwall.

Capt. Richard P. Merrill was relieved from being assigned to E Company and re-assigned to HQ 2nd Btn as of 3rd March 1944. 1st Lt. Wilfred C. Majane was relieved of principal Duty as platoon leader and assumed Duty as Company Commander whilst Captain Merrill was away. 1st Lt. Joseph E. Legans was assigned and joined from 'Detachment A' of the 2nd Btn and assumed principal responsibility as platoon leader.

F Company 2nd Rangers – Bude, Cornwall.

Medical Detachment 2nd Rangers – Bude, Cornwall.

HQ Company 'Detachment A' 2nd Rangers – Saunton Sands, N. Devon.

[Report not legible.]

Headquarters Company 2nd Rangers (less Detachment A) – Bude, Cornwall.

2nd Lt. Harry J. Heinman was relieved from this assignment and transferred to the 37th Engineers C. Battalion.

Sgt. Richard P. Merrill was assigned and joined from Company E this battalion. Principal Duty as S-1 as of 3 March 1944.

Captain Cleveland A. Lytle was assigned and joined from A Company 2nd Btn with principal Duty as S-3.

1st Lt. Frederick G. Wilkens was relieved from being assigned and transferred to HQ Company this Battalion.

1st Lt. Elmer M. Vermeer was assigned and joined from Detachment A 2nd Btn. with principal Duty as S-2.

1st Lt. James A. Malaney was assigned and joined from Detachment A 2nd Btn with principal Duty as Btn S-4.

1st Lt. Frederick G. Wilkin was assigned and joined from HQ Company this battalion and assumes principal Duty of Company Commander.

2nd Lt. Frank L. Kennard was assigned and joined from HQ Company this battalion.

(S-1 handles personnel actions; S-2 is intelligence; S-3 is the operations and mission planning; S-4 is supply and logistics).

The US Army issued a letter entitled: Co-operation and Liaison with British Civil Police

For the purpose of implementing the USA (Visiting Forces) Act of 1942, each base section commander is charged with the responsibility for maintaining effective co-operation and liaison with the civil police within his base section.

In all cases of arrest of, or alleged offences by members of the US forces occurring in their respective jurisdictions, the British civil police authorities have been instructed to notify the Provost Marshal of the base section within which such civil police authorities are located. Each base section commander will co-ordinate civil police liaison for all US forces activities within his base section.

Various wartime offences punishable under defence regulations are:

Communication without authority with any person in enemy or enemy-occupied territory.

Trespassing on or loitering near any government premises used for important war purposes.

Black market offences, i.e. evasions of any control imposed by the government on the acquisition of any article or on the price at which it may be sold.

Obstructing or endeavoring to persuade from their duty any members of the UK forces or public servants, or inciting anyone to evade duties of national service to which he may become liable.

Trespassing on agricultural land on which there is growing any crop other than grass.

Lighting restrictions: Lights on service vehicles will be fitted as prescribed by the military authorities.

During blackout hours no light will be displayed in the open, except that flash lights may be used provided that: the aperture does not exceed one inch in diameter. The light is white and dimmed and the beam is directed downward at all times.

Postal Restrictions: It is unlawful to mail packages containing food-stuffs out of the British Isles.

It is unlawful to send any package through the mail which contains articles of a dangerous nature such as explosives, matches, corrosives, etc.

Organisation commanders will continually impress all military personnel within their commands with the importance of observing all laws and defined regulations in force in the UK.

---

23 March 1944

5th Rangers – Companies A – F, Medical and HQ – Tighnabruaich, Scotland.
Thirteen enlisted men were assigned from 'Detachment A' HQ 5th Btn to A Company.

'Detachment A' HQ Company 5th Rangers – Tighnabruaich, Scotland.
23rd March: Left Glasgow, Scotland 0825hrs. Arrived Wemyss Bay 0930hrs. Left Wemyss Bay 1000hrs. Arrived Tighnabruaich Scotland 1100. 22 miles travelled by rail, 30 miles travelled by water. Detachment demobilised.

2nd Rangers – Companies A – F, Medical – Bude, Cornwall.

HQ Company 'Detachment A' 2nd Rangers – Saunton Sands, N. Devon.
1st Lt. Joseph E. Legans was relieved of his assignment to 'Detachment A' and re-joined E Company 2nd Btn.
1st Lt. James. A. Malaney returned to Duty with Headquarters Company 2nd Btn.
1st Lt. Elmer K. Vermeer returned to Duty with Headquarters Company 2nd Btn.
Fifty-three enlisted men transferred in grade from Detachment A Headquarters 2nd Btn to the Companies indicated on the following roster. 'Detachment A' Headquarters Company was inactivated as of this date and all personnel assigned and attached were returned to their Companies of origin and re-attached.

Headquarters Company 2nd Rangers – Bude, Cornwall.

Overleaf: Dated 23 March, this is an Army Alert Order telling Lt. Col. Rudder that his unit is subject to a change of location at any minute and for them to be ready.

US Army HQ issued the following orders under the title of: *Preparation for Short Sea Voyage.*
As part of the Alert Order process, the Army produced and issued to the Rangers headquarters the following very exacting set of instructions:

Units will move into the Concentration Area at full War Establishment without First Reinforcements. Units already located in the Concentration Area will shed their reinforcements some time before briefing and moving to the Marshalling Areas.

These over strength replacements will, in so far as practicable, be earmarked for forwarding to the same division to meet combat losses.

Briefing and Issue of Operational Maps. Units of the Assault and Follow-up will be briefed and operational maps issued after residues and First Reinforcement over-strengths have been detached and immediate units proceed to Marshalling Area. In the case of the Build-up and above will take place immediately before the units move into the Marshalling Area, except in the case of certain units of the early Build-up, who will receive their maps etc. immediately on arrival in the Marshalling Area.

Vehicles will leave Concentration Areas and, except for motorcycles, will be embarked with petrol tanks full, unless orders to the contrary are issued. Arrangements will be made for final filling up of vehicles in Marshalling Areas. Where necessary, armoured fighting vehicles may be filled up in Embarkation Areas or in the vicinity of hards.

Copy No. 5

HEADQUARTERS V CORPS
APO 305,   U. S. ARMY

```
: Auth:  CG, V Corps :
: Date:  23 March 44 :
: Initials:    /R    :
```

23 March 1944 (211)

SUBJECT: Alert Order.

TO   :   See Distribution.

1.   Your unit is alerted effective this date.

2.   You will be notified without delay of any attachments involving your unit.

3.   On or after 2 April 1944, your unit will receive a movement warning direct from the Commanding General, Transportation Corps.   This movement warning will allow five or more days before actual movement.

4.   You will comply with instructions as issued by SOS during the period of movement and processing from Concentration Areas through the Marshalling Areas to the Embarkation Points.

5.   Units (as differentiated from detachments) will move to Concentration Areas at T/O & E strength plus currently authorized overstrength in personnel and vehicles.   A unit may be concentrated in more than one area.   Detachments will move at the strengths directed by the headquarters to which attached (see Par. 2 above)

6.   a.   Units will comply with the provisions of "European Theater of Operations, Preparation for Overseas Movement, United States Army, Short Sea Voyage", dated 10 January 1944 (corrected).   Forms SOSTC 8, 8a, 9 and 10 will be submitted in duplicate based on the strengths indicated in Par. 5 above.   (Following the word "Remarks" near the bottom of Form SOSTC No. 8, the unit commander will insert the number of officers and men, respectively, that can travel in the unit vehicles reported on Form SOSTC No. 10.   Such personnel are included in those reported in the body of Form SOSTC No. 9.)   Forms may be obtained from the local RTO.   Completed forms, in duplicate, will be submitted by the units or detachments concerned through the Commanders to whom this order is addressed, so as to reach the Commanding General, V Corps at the Plymouth Headquarters, V Corps Detachment by 1200 hours, 29 March 1944.   (Telephone: Plymouth 2841, Ext 7, or MILESTONE, Ext 7.)

b.   Commanders to whom this order is addressed will notify the Commanding General, V Corps, at Plymouth Headquarters, V Corps Detachment, by officer courier, as soon as all units or detachments with whom he is concerned have been alerted, furnishing a list showing the date the units or detachments were alerted.

By Command of Major General GEROW:

Irwin J. Degnan

IRWIN J. DEGNAN,
2nd Lt., A. G. D.,
Asst. Adj. General.

2 Incls:
    Incl 1 – (omitted)
    Incl 2 – Administrative Instructions.

DISTRIBUTION: Copy Nos.
    CG, First U.S. Army   1 – 3
    CG, V Corps   4 – 8
    CG, 1st Inf Div   9 – 164
    CG, 29th Inf Div   165 – 268
    CG, V Corps Arty   269 – 285

Organisational equipment will be marked with the serial number of the case, the unit serial number, the unit colour stripes, cubic feet and weight in pounds. Ammunition, inflammables, corrosives and other dangerous articles must be distinctly marked as such.

Personal baggage and organisational equipment will be marked with colour stripes stencilled horizontally, approximately 1" by 4" in size, in the colours allocated to the numbers as follows:

1) *Buff*
2) *Olive Drab*
3) *Yellow, bright*
4) *Green, bright*
5) *Gray*

6) *Blue, dark*
7) *Maroon*
8) *Red, bright*
9) *White, lead*
0) *Brown, dark*

The colour representing the last figure of the unit serial number is used for the middle stripe. The colour representing the next to the last figure will be used for the top and bottom stripes.

The unit serial number will be stencilled above the colour stripes. The name of the unit will not appear on any personal or organisational equipment. At least two complete markings, preferably on one side and one end, will be stencilled on each piece of personal baggage or organisational equipment.

EMBARKATION DOCUMENTS

Immediately on receipt of the alert order, the commanding officer of each unit will prepare SOSTC Forms 8, 8a, 9 and 10. Copies of the forms may be secured upon application to the nearest RTO. The local RTO will render all possible assistance in connection with the preparation of these forms. The forms will be completed, classified SECRET and delivered in duplicate, to the Office of the Chief of Transportation, Movements, Division, Operational Branch by Unit Officer Courier on or before the date specified in the alert order.

After being alerted, each organisation will note in capital letters under 'Record of Events' on

each day's Morning Report the phrase 'ALERTED FOR DEPARTURE'. These reports will be dispatched by the most expeditious means to the servicing Machine Records Unit by 1100 hours on the day following the effective day of the report.

Prior to departure from the home station, all units will request their servicing MRU, to whom the Morning Report is sent, to prepare and furnish 8 copies of the Embarkation Personnel Roster. In any event, these 8 copies will be taken with the unit when it departs from its home station.

Upon receipt of the Unit Sheet in the Marshalling Area, unit commanders will prepare Unit Party Embarkation Personnel Rosters for each Unit Party by merely ruling out the names of personnel on the original roster, not part of the Unit Party, and adding names not shown on the original roster.

Unit Party Embarkation Personnel Rosters will be prepared with 8 copies and turned over to the officer or NCO in charge of each such Unit Party. Upon the formation of Craft or Ship Loads in the Marshalling Area, each Unit Party CO or NCO will deliver to the CO Craft or Ship Load the 8 copies of the Unit Party Roster.

The CO Craft or Ship Load will securely fasten all of the Unit Party Rosters so that he will have five complete sets, which will then constitute complete craft or ship rosters (i.e. Passenger lists).

The distribution of the Personnel Embarkation Roster is as follows:

Three copies will be handed to the ESO at the Embarkation Point. The ESO will insure that Embarkation Personnel Rosters are collected for all Craft or Ship Loads embarking. The ESO will indorse on those Rosters the date and place of embarkation and the name or number of the craft or ship.

Two of these copies were to be dispatched to the Central Machine Records Unit, HQ, SOS, ETOUSA, and one copy to the AG at the Base Section in which the port is located.

The Fourth copy was to be retained by the CO Craft or Ship Load and was to be corrected to reflect casualties, etc., en route.

Upon debarkation, the copy of the Embarkation Personnel Roster was to be turned over to the first available personnel administration section for forwarding to the servicing MRU.

Three copies were to be handed to the Commanding Officer of the ship.

Units will hold themselves in readiness to move at six hours' notice.

Movement to the Marshalling Area. Assault and follow-up formations will normally be concentrated in, or adjacent to Marshalling Areas. Their first movement will then be into their Marshalling Camps in accordance with a predetermined allocation to craft or ships. This will be short movement by march route and there will have been ample time for reconnaissance and for the provision of any necessary advance parties and guides.

(To be classified)

SECRET

U.S. ARMY

EMBARKATION PERSONNEL ROSTER

ORGANIZATION NAME	UNIT SERIAL NUMBER	LOCATION HOME STATION

SERIAL No. NAME AND GRADE

Captains
O-1289999 Doe, John N.
O-1289993 James, Roger NMI

1st Lieutenants
O-1369984 Smith, John S.
O-1399999 Trown, Philip R.

M/Sgt.
15999988 McClure, Robert R.

NOTE : List names alphabetically by grade.

AUTHORIZING SIGNATURE........................ GRADE............... ORGANIZATION......................

(To be classified)

SECRET

SECRET

SHIP SHEET

SHIP / CRAFT SERIAL NUMBER...........................

ISSUED AT MARSHALLING CAMP..............................

DATE........................

Unit Craft or Unit Ship Serial Number	Unit Name	Per-sonnel	* Vehicles		Move to Embarkation Area						Remarks
			No.	Type	Marshalling Area SP	Depart		Route	RCRP	Arrive	
						Date	Time			Time	
(a)	(b)	(c)	(d)	(e)	(f)	(g)	(h)	(i)	(j)	(k)	(l)

* Include in this column Bicycles, Handcarts and Motor-Cycles not carried in other vehicles. Only the vehicles shown in columns (d) and (e) will be embarked.

Distribution :—

(To be classified)

SECRET

Instructions for movement and marshalling, in accordance with the Assault Plan, will be issued to units with copy to formation/division or higher echelon HQ. Responsibility for the smooth execution of the move rests primarily on formation or unit commanders.

Movement will normally be as follows: Vehicle parties (including units wholly mobile) by road, except that heavy tanks or slow mechanical equipment may be moved by rail or transporter when distance exceeds 25 miles.

Marching parties by march route of troop-carrying transport or rail.

Road movement from Concentration to Marshalling Areas will usually be by day. Vehicle parties will, as far as possible, be grouped in convoys of convenient size. Convoy commanders will conform to normal road movements practice. Route timing, spacing, speed and halts will be specified in the Movement Instruction.

Arrangements will be made for traffic control on certain routes and the civil police will be warned of the movement, but convoy commanders will at all times be responsible for guiding their convoys and maintaining prescribed timings.

Convoys will not be delayed for individual vehicles that are late or break down. Every driver must know his destination. Provost Marshal will provide necessary escort for US Convoys.

(To be classified)

SECRET

UNIT SHEET

MOBILIZATION/UNIT SERIAL NUMBER .... DATE........................

UNIT NAME........................

Craft or Sh'p Serial Number	Allocation to Craft				Marshalling Camp Location		Remarks
	Personnel	Vehicles			Personnel Camp	Vehicle Park	
		No.	Type				
(a)	(b)	(c)	(d)		(e)	(f)	(g)

IMPORTANT: The craft or ship serial number in column (a) will be added to the mobilization/unit serial number on right front side mudguard or similar place of each vehicle

(To be classified)

SECRET

During air raid warnings, road movement was to continue. If a convoy was directly attacked, the convoy commander was to use his discretion whether to continue the move or whether to halt and engage the enemy aircraft. In the latter case every available weapon was to be employed.

(To be classified)

SECRET

ROAD OR RAIL MOVEMENT TABLE

DATE ISSUED........................

Phone No. (for inquiry)............

Unit Serial No.	Unit Name	Unit Location	Strength		Depart from Concentration Area SP or Entraining Stn			Arrival at Marshalling Area RCRP or Detraining Stn			REMARKS
			Per-sonnel	Veh-icle	Location	Date	Time	Location	Date	Time	
(a)	(b)	(c)	(d)	(e)	(f)	(g)	(h)	(i)	(j)	(k)	(l)

For Details of vehicles see overleaf

Highway Route to Marshalling Area ....

Speed .... Density .... Lighting ....

Halts :—

(To be classified)

SECRET

Convoy commanders will send forward an Officer with full details of the convoy, accompanied by unit representative, to report at the Marshalling Area one hour before the convoy is due to arrive. On arrival, convoys will close up to two yards between vehicles and 20 yards between units in order to facilitate control. Marching parties will normally be conveyed by troop-carrying vehicles or rail, should the distance involved, during any phase of movement, exceed five miles.

Movement procedure. On arrival in the Marshalling Area, Commanding Officers of units receive detailed instructions for marshalling into Unit Parties and for the move of their units into the appropriate Marshalling Camps. Commanding officers units will detail the individual personnel and vehicles to compose these Unit Parties, at the same time appointing an officer or NCO in charge of each. Each Unit Party will add the craft or ship serial number, as shown on the Unit Sheet, to the mobilisation / unit serial number, already painted on the front of its vehicles.

i.e. 12478/46 LST. This composite number then becomes the Unit Craft Serial or Unit Ship Serial number.

The Unit Sheet is part of the embarkation programme, but shows only the information which is required by one particular unit. The embarkation programme is governed by the Field Force Commander's movement priorities and the naval forecast of the craft and ships available.

The officer or NCO in charge of each Unit Party will ensure that each officer and other rank/enlisted man knows his full unit craft or unit ship serial number.

Every Officer Commanding troop will be given, in the Marahalling Area, a copy of Standing Orders for OC Troops of Craft or Ships. These orders will include the following points:

Discipline and Adminstration.	Co-operation with ESO.
Security.	Embarkation details.
Checking emergency and landing rations, lifebelts, etc.	Passage details.
Embarkation documentation.	Disembarkation arrangements.
AA protection.	

Officer Commanding Troops will, on appointment in the Marshalling Area, assume command of the several unit parties which constitute his craft or ship load and will remain in command until relieved of his responsibilities on arrival at the far side.

Special security restrictions will be imposed on troops passing through the Marshalling Area, and it will be the responsibility of unit commanders to impress on all personnel the importance and necessity of the restrictions.

Documentation. All Marching Party and Vehicle Party documentation will be completed before leaving the Marshalling Area. The principle underlying all embarkation documentation is that no man (or vehicle) shall sail without a record being kept of the craft or ship in which he sails, so that in the event of the vessel being lost at sea, an accurate list will be available of those on board.

Movement. Routes will be clearly marked by direction signs, and traffic control assistance will be provided where necessary.

Procedure in Embarkation Areas.

On arrival at the Embarkation Area, craft or ship serial Commanders will report and will return all maps, movement orders, movement instructions and pamphlets except those required for use overseas. Their documents will be checked and arrival reported to Embarkation Area HQ. If embarkation cannot take place immediately, marching personnel and vehicle parties will be guided to the ERP.

A halt up to about three hours may be required in the ERP. Where necessary, a hot drink will be issued by the Static Staff. A small medical staff will be in each Embarkation Area to deal with casualties.

Marching personnel will be embarked, under the instructions of the ESO, either to personnel ships or craft. Embarkation on some personnel ships may be by tender and scrambling nets.

(US) Lifebelts and vomit bags will be issued at the Embarkation Point by the ESO on the basis of one each for all personnel embarking on craft or ships.

At hards, vehicles will be called forward for loading by the ESO after consultation with the Naval Hardmaster.

At hards, Officers and NCO's in charge of craft or ship parties remain responsible for the safe custody of their vehicles and loads; any damage or loss must be reported to the ESO.

During an air raid warning, embarkation will continue. In the event of an actual attack, the senior military officer at the point of embarkation, after consultation with the ESO and Naval representative, will exercise his discretion whether embarkation shall continue or be temporarily suspended. The ESO will indicate the nearest shelters, medical aid posts and gas cleansing and treatment centres.

Relation of Military to Naval Personnel.

Whatever the rank of the senior Military or Air Force Officer on board, Naval Commanding Officers and Masters of Merchant vessels are always in command of the vessels and loads, and they are solely responsible for the control and safety of their vessels. They will, however, keep OC Troops, who is their military adviser, informed of any signals received affecting him.

OC Troops is responsible to the Naval Commanding Officer or Master for the discipline and administration of all military and RAF personnel from the moment they embark.

Feeding. On moving from the Concentration Area to the Marshalling Areas, when the length of the journey warrants, units will take with them a haversack ration or bag lunch.

Marshalling Area. In the Marshalling Area, all cooking and feeding will be arranged by the Static Organisation.

Embarkation Area. Where necessary, a hot drink (and in case of delay, a bag ration) will be provided for all personnel in the Embarkation Area for consumption prior to embarkation.

Passage. 'Sea Passage Rations' will be placed on board for consumption during the voyage.

Every craft or ship will hold 'Voyage (Ship's Reserve) Rations' on board for consumption only in emergency.

Landing. For 24 hours after completion of voyage, personnel will consume the landing ration which was issued to them in the Marshalling Area.

Medical. The treatment and evacuation of casualties and sick in Concentration Areas will be carried out under formation or unit arrangements in conformity with Command/Base Section arrangements.

Personnel who are in hospitals or convalescent depots when their unit moves to the Marshalling Area will be sent on discharge from hospital to the Reinforcement Holding Unit/Replacement Centre.

It is the responsibility of the CO unit to insure that personnel under his command are medically inspected and passed as free from infection – before departure from Concentration Areas.

Light medical equipment will accompany units by road, rail or sea. Units must be prepared to render first aid to casualties occurring at any stage of the journey from Concentration Areas to Embarkation. Stretchers/Litters and essential first aid outfits will, therefore, be available for both rail and road parties.

On the larger ships which carry an establishment of medical personnel, OC Troops will co-operate with the Naval Commanding Officer or Master in the establishment of first-aid posts to deal with casualties.

All small ships and craft will be equipped with medical facilities, which will include first-aid equipment and shell dressings. Medical orderlies will be available only on certain of those ships and craft, and OC units should, therefore, insure that each sub-unit includes at least one man trained in first-aid duties.

In the Marshalling Area will normally be the last place in which personnel casualties will be replaced before embarkation.

In the Embarkation Area. No replacement will be made. Casualties incurred in this area will be replaced in the overseas theatre of war.

Replacements

a.   Normal replacement procedures will cease when units enter the concentration area, after which replacements will only be furnished in limited quantities and based on the following considerations:

(1)   Prior to entering the Marshalling Area, residues, representing the difference between reduced scales and T/O strengths, will be detached from units and sent to special camps designated by SOS. Any unit overstrength existing at the time of these movements will accompany unit residues. Unit overstrengths will be considered as initial replacements and will be forwarded as early as possible in accordance with prearranged schedule.

(2)   Casualties in the Concentration Areas, including those caused by enemy attack, will be replaced from permanent depots of the Field Force Replacement System.

(3)   Casualties in the Marshalling Area, including those caused by enemy attack, will be replaced immediately from overstrengths or from replacements in the Field Force Replacement System installations.

(4)   Units will not receive replacements in the Embarkation Area.

b.   Normal requisitioning will be resumed on a date to be announced later.

Postal

a.   General

(1)   The delivery and posting of letter mail and packages in concentration areas will follow normal procedure. Commanders will warn personnel that all mail must be routed through the U. S. Army Postal Service and cannot be deposited in civilian post offices or post boxes, Red Cross facilities, or relayed to civilians for mailing.

(2)   No letters will be carried on the operation. A collection of these will be made by battalions and separate units prior to briefing in accordance with Field Manual 30-25.

b.   Incoming Mail - Normal mail deliveries cease upon departure of units from the concentration areas, or, in the case of units in a concentration status in a marshalling area, prior to the time of briefing, but will be resumed at an early date.

c.   Outgoing Mail

(1)   All correspondence and packages will be routed through Army Postal Service channels and will be subject to censorship.

(2)   Letters written in Marshalling Areas will be unit censored and placed in bags labelled: "Base Censor No. 2, APO 887". All letters will be collected prior to embarkation.

(3)   Personnel will be forbidden to write letters after embarkation unless there is a provision for the collection of such mail enroute.

For transit all enlisted men were instructed to mark their baggage as follows:

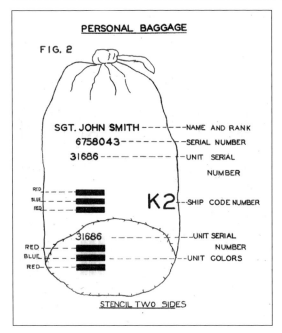

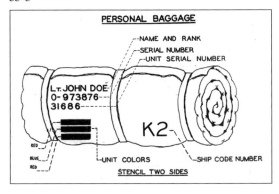

Officers were instructed to mark their baggage as follows:

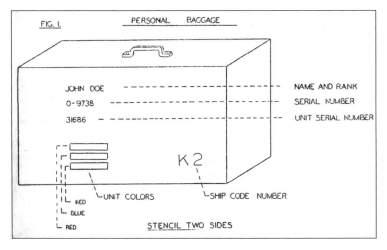

Upon receiving the Alert Order additional medical supplies were issued to the Rangers:

```
                    HEADQUARTERS, V CORPS
                    APO 305, U.S.ARMY

ANNEX NO 3

TO ADMINISTRATIVE INSTRUCTIONS- ALERT ORDER

                         MEDICAL

                        SECTION I

                      IMMUNIZATIONS

     1.  All immunizations required by the following schedule will be completed at
once:
          a.  Individuals who have no record of a vaccination against smallpox or of an
initial series of inoculations against typhoid-paratyphoid fever, tetanus and typhus fever
will be appropriately immunized.

          b.  Individuals who have no record of vaccination or revaccination against
smallpox, typhoid-paratyphoid fever, or typhus fever since 1 July 1943 will be appro-
priately immunized.

          c.  Individuals who have no record of immunization or reimmunization against
tetanus since 1 February 1944 will be reimmunized.

                        SECTION II

                         SUPPLY

     1.  Supplemental Equipment and Supplies - The following supplemental items will
be requisitioned at once by the following units:

          Medical Department Units of 1st Infantry Division ) and
          Medical Department Units of 29th Infantry Division.) Att. Troops.

Requisitions will be submitted to the Chief Surgeon, ETOUSA, through the Surgeon, First
U. S. Army.

          a.  Litter, Straight, Steel.

              12 - per Inf. Bn; Arty. Bn; Chem Bn; Engr Bn.
              24 - per Ranger Bn.
              180 - per Med Bn (Inf); Med Bn (Engr Spec Brig).

          b.  Chest, M.D., No. 1

              2 - per Coll. Co.
              4 - per Clr. Co.
              6 - per Med Bn (Engr Spec Brig)

          c.  Splint Set

              1 - per Inf Bn; Arty Bn; Chem Bn; Engr Bn; Ranger Bn.
              5 - per Coll. Co.
              10 - per Med Bn (Engr Spec Brig).

          d.  Blanket Set, Small

              3 - per Inf Bn; Arty Bn; Chem Bn; Engr Bn; Ranger. Bn.
              4 - per Coll Co; Clr Co.
              10 - per Med Bn (Engr Spec Brig).

     2.  Special Waterproof Medical Supply Units - Special waterproof medical supply
units in containers (packed in 60mm mortar shell packing cases - approximately eight
(8) cases per unit) are to be issued on the following basis to units listed in paragraph
1 above.
          a.  Special Waterproof Medical Supply Units

              1 Unit - per Inf Bn; Arty Bn; Chem Bn; Engr Bn; Ranger Bn.
              2 Units - per Coll Co., Division.
              4 Units - per Clr Co., Division.)
              6 Units - per Med Bn (Engr Spec Brig).
```

On 23 March one of the regular updates of vehicles and personnel numbers expected to leave for the Omaha landings were recorded.

```
Copy No. 5

                        HEADQUARTERS  V CORPS
                        APO 305,   U. S. ARMY

                            TROOP LIST
                    BEACH OMAHA - FORCE "O"

Inclosure No. 1 to letter, subject:
Alert Order, dated 23 March 1944.

  ITEM              UNIT                        VEHICLES      PERSONNE

  1st Infantry Division Troops

   18.      2nd and 5th Ranger Bns                 58            64
                                                              (1062 Spe
                                                               ial Lift
   19.      Air Support Party, 116th CT             4            11

   20.      Air Support Party (with Rangers)        4            11
```

---

24 March 1944

5th Rangers – Companies A – F, Medical and HQ – Tighnabruaich, Scotland.

2nd Rangers – Companies A – F, Medical and HQ – Bude, Cornwall.

On 24 March a statement of both Naval bombardment and Air Force bombing targets was drawn up. These covered Coastal Gun Battery targets to be attacked by the Rangers. Note: Pointe du Hoc is now listed as containing *'casements under construction.'*

BIGOT

SUBJECT: Fire Plan.

BIGOT
TOP SECRET
Copy No. 22......

First United States Army. (3)
Second British Army   (3)

21 A Gp/00/74/38/G(Plans)

1.   The First Draft of the Naval and Army requirements for the joint pre-arranged fire plan for the assault are set out in the attached Appendices as under:-

        Appendix 'A' - Targets for pre D day bombing.
        Appendix 'B' - Targets and timings for the night heavy bombers.
        Appendix 'C' - Targets and timings for the medium Oboe bombers.
        Appendix 'D' - Targets for Naval bombardment.
        Appendix 'E' - Allotment of day bomber effort.
        Appendix 'F' - Fighter bomber targets.

2.   The provisional efforts allotted in Appendices 'C', 'E' and 'F' leave the following reserve until the first turn round of aircraft :-

        1 box heavy day bombers.
        4 boxes medium bombers.
        6 squadrons of light bombers.
        18 squadrons of fighter bombers, of which two will be on
            call in the initial stages of the assault.

3.   The provisional turn round times of aircraft are as follows :-

        Fighter bombers   2 hours
        Medium bombers   4½ hours
        Heavy bombers   6 hours.

        The efforts in the first turn round will be considerably reduced.

4.   It is emphasised that the selection of targets cannot be considered as firm until near D Day.   The factors which will affect the final selection of targets are as follows :-

        (a) Pre D day bombing results will affect the selection of targets
            for night heavy bombing.

        (b) Changes as a result of (a) above may affect the selection of
            targets for medium Oboe bombing.

        (c) Fresh intelligence may affect the selection of all types of Naval
            and Air bombardment.

5.   As a general principle batteries covering the sea approaches and the beaches should be regarded as primary targets for the night and medium Oboe bombers, whilst beach defences should normally be dealt with by daylight heavy and medium bombers and Naval bombardment by ships and close support craft. Subject to this principle Armies, in consultation with their associated Naval and Air forces will :-

        (a) Examine the lists of targets and timings with a view to confirmation
            or amendment so far as is practicable at the present time.

        (b) Indicate the desired sub-allotment of the day bomber effort to beach
            targets.

-2-

Serial	Priority	Location	Type	Map Ref	Remarks
23	4	ETAPLES	6 x 155 mm	644371	
24	4	ETRETAT	6 x 105 mm	565452	

Notes:

1.   The selected targets in the NEPTUNE area are as follows:-

Target	Map Ref	Remarks
CARNEVILLE	265267	In turrets.
POINTE DU HOE	586958	Casemates under construction.
OUISTREHAM	117797	
HOULGATE	256809	Casemates under construction.
BENERVILLE	422107	In concrete.
VILLERVILLE	486156	In concrete.
LE HAVRE	(468311 (464314	Emplacements under construction.
LE HAVRE	486252	Emplacements under construction.

The priority for attack of these targets will be indicated to AEAF by 21 Army Group from time to time according to the state of construction and its suitability for attack.

2.   The basis on which the selection of the above targets has been made was as follows:-

(a) Eight targets have been selected in the NEPTUNE area.

(b) To provide cover for their bombardment a further eight battery targets in the DIEPPE and PAS DE CALAIS areas respectively have been selected.

3. (a) In the PAS DE CALAIS targets have been selected with the object stated in paragraph (b) above and also to ease the problem of passing convoys through the STRAITS OF DOVER immediately before, during and after D Day and safeguard shipping in DOVER Harbour.

(b) Batteries in the PAS DE CALAIS capable of interfering with the movement of convoys are numerous.   Inquiries from the Naval and Military authorities at DOVER supplied four principal batteries:-

Location	Type	Map Ref
NOIRE MOTTES	3 x 406 mm	786758
CAP GRISNEZ	4 x 280 mm	687698
ANDRESSELLES	3 x 380 mm	681665
WISSANT	4 x 170 mm	743726

(c) The above batteries are all known to be very heavily protected by concrete. If AEAF therefore consider that they are impervious to bombing it will be more profitable to attack other batteries, which are known to be a menace, but less heavily protected.   Alternatives have, therefore, been suggested. These batteries have been considered as alternatives rather than additions on the assumption that the air effort will not be sufficient to do both without denuding other areas.

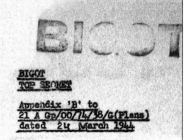

BIGOT
TOP SECRET

Appendix 'B' to
21 A Gp/00/714/38/G(Plans)
dated 24 March 1944

NIGHT HEAVY BOMBING TARGETS

1.

Ser-ial	Target Name	Location	Timing
1	POINTE DU HOE	586938	Civil Twilight – 2 hours to Civil Twilight – 1 hour
2	LA PERNELLE	365200	Civil Twilight – 3 hours to Civil Twilight – 2 hours
3	CARREVILLE	265267	Civil Twilight – 1 hour to Civil Twilight
4	FONTENAY SUR MER	368044	Civil Twilight – 1 hour to Civil Twilight
5	MORSALINES	354139	Civil Twilight – 1 hour to Civil Twilight
6	ST MARTIN DE VARREVILLE	405980	Civil Twilight – 4½ hours to Civil Twilight – 3½ hours
7	HOULGATE	256809	Civil Twilight – 2 hours to Civil Twilight – 1 hour
8	BENERVILLE	422107	Civil Twilight – 1 hour to Civil Twilight
9	VILLERVILLE	486156	Civil Twilight – 2 hours to Civil Twilight – 1 hour
10	OUISTREHAM	117797	Civil Twilight – 2 hours to Civil Twilight – 1 hour

2.   In the event of intelligence reporting that any of the above batteries have been destroyed by pre-D Day bombing alternative targets will be selected on ANCXF/21 Army Group level in consultation with their lower formations.   Possible targets might be the following batteries :–

Serial	Target Name	Location	Remarks
1	EMONDVILLE	359023	In casemates
2	MAISY	533918	
3	LONGUES	798872	Casemates under construction
4	VER SUR MER	914844	ditto
5	COLLEVILLE SUR ORNE	076782	ditto
6	OUISTREHAM II	104781	ditto
7	SALENNELLES	155776	ditto

NOTES

1.   The Naval Assault Forces will reach the Lowering Position (at about H – 2 hours) during the middle period of the night bombing, i.e. between Civil Twilight – 2 hours and Civil Twilight – 1 hour. Therefore, the four batteries selected for bombing in this period are those which are the greatest menace to the Lowering Positions.

2.   The minimum number of batteries have been engaged in the early period in order to compress the maximum amount of bombing into the period nearest to H Hour.   ST MARTIN DE VARREVILLE must be bombed in the early period to avoid interference with the airborne troops.   LA PERNELLE has been selected as the other target for this period because of its long range.

3.   The remainder are, therefore, engaged in the late period.

4.   Timings given in paragraph 1 are provisional.

BIGOT

FIRST DRAFT

BIGOT
TOP SECRET

Appendix 'C' to
21 A Gp/00/74/58/G(Plans)
dated 14 March 1944

MEDIUM OBOE BOMBERS

Batteries at:-

Serial	Target Name	Location	Timings	Remarks
1	OZEVILLE	343057	H hr	
2	MAISY	533918	Civil Twilight	
3	ARROMANCHES	848853	Civil Twilight	
4	ARROMANCHES	860863	Civil Twilight	
5	MOULINEUX	972808	H hr	
6	OUISTREHAM I	117797	Civil Twilight	

Notes

1.   The effort per "box" of medium oboe bombers is the equivalent of about 36 tons, which is inadequate for dealing with batteries under concrete.   In consequence batteries in open emplacements have been selected.

2.   The timings given above are provisional pending more information from AEAF.

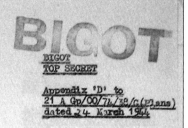

FIRST DRAFT

BIGOT
TOP SECRET

Appendix 'D' to
21 A Gp/00/74/38/G(Plans)
dated 24 March 1944

NAVAL BOMBARDMENT

The following batteries will be engaged by naval gunfire from about
H – 30 mins i.e. the time at which Naval spotting can begin:-

Serial	Target Name	Location	Remarks
1	GATTEVILLE	392277	
2	LA PERNELLE	365200	
3	MORSALINES	354139	
4	OZEVILLE	343057	
5	FONTENAY SUR MER	368044	
6	EMONDVILLE	359023	
7	MAISY	533918	
8	POINTE DU HOE	586938	
9	PIERRE DU MONT	599934 ?	Calibre unknown
10	LONGUES	798872	
11	BEAUVAIS	792831	
12	MANVIEUX	815866 ?	Calibre unknown
13	ARROMANCHES II	846849	
14	ARROMANCHES I	848853	
15	VER SUR MER	914844	
16	MOULINEUX	972808	
17	COLVILLE SUR ORNE	076782	
18	OUISTREHAM II	104781	
19	OUISTREHAM I	117797	
20	SALENNELLES	155776	
21	HOULGATE	256809	
22	BENERVILLE	422107	

NOTES
1. ST MARTIN DE VARREVILLE will only be a Naval bombardment task
   if called for by a shore observer.

2. Where the calibre of the guns is unknown, battery positions
   have been marked with a query, and the allotment of a warship
   is provisional.

FIRST DRAFT

BIGOT
TOP SECRET

Appendix 'F' to
21 A Gp/00/74/38/G (Plans)
dated 24 March 1944

FIGHTER BOMBERS

The following batteries in open emplacements will be attacked at H hour:-

Serial	Target Name	Location	Remarks
1	FONTENAY SUR MER	368044	
2	OZEVILLE	343057	
3	GEFOSSE FONTENAY	531914	
4	PIERRE DU MONT	599934 ?	Calibre unknown
5	BEAUVAIS	792831	
6	ARROMANCHES II	846849	
7	MANVIEUX	815866 ?	Calibre unknown
8	MOULINEUX	972808	
9	PERIERS-EN-AUGE	248780	
10	CONNEVILLE-SUR-MER	254784	

NOTES

1.   Batteries in open emplacements have been selected.   The results will
be more effective than against batteries in concrete:

2.   Some of these targets may prove difficult to find in which case the
pilots will attack any active battery they can see.

3.   Serials 4 and 7 are included provisionally until it is established
that batteries do exist at these points.

Below: A more detailed naval bombardment schedule was also produced.

APPENDIX NO. 1
to
ANNEX NO. 12

NEPTUNE
Appendix No. 1
in 4 pages
Page No. 1

NAVAL FIRE PLAN

SHIP	ARMAMENT	TOTAL ROUNDS	RANGE IN THOUSANDS OF YARDS	FIRE SUPT AREA	TARGET	TIME	NO OF ROUNDS	REMARKS	BALANCE OF AMMUNITION
1	2	3	4	5	6	7	8	9	10
1. Battleships USS Texas (BB)	10x14"	1000	18	3 Anchored Position	T1,T86	H-40 to H-5	up to 250	14" Air Spot 65% AP, 35% HC	738x14"
					T88,T89	H-25 to H-10	100	5"	
	6x5"	1800	18		T88,T89	H-4 to H hour	12	14" Air Spot HC	1700x5"
USS Arkansas (BB)	12x12"	1356	18	4 Anchored Position	T60,T63,T65	H-40 to H-5	385	12" Air Spot Rock Salvos 30% AP, 70% HC	921x12"
	6x5"	1800	18		T166	H to H/1 Hr	50	12" Air Spot Harassing	1550x5"
					T43	H-40 to H-7	250	5"	
2. Cruisers HMS Glasgow (CL)	12x6"	2400	24	3 Anchored Position	T59,T61	H-36 to H-3	400	Rock Salvos Air Spot	2000
FS Montcalm (CL)	6x152mm	1020	28	4 Anchored Position	Port-En-Bessin T22,T23,T24, T25 T27,T28,T29	H-40 to H/30	300	Cover Area Air Spot	720
FS Georges Leyques (CL)	6x152mm	1020	28	4 Anchored Position	T53	H-40 to H-3	250	Rock Salvos	770
3. Destroyers USS Endicott (DD)	4x5"	1600	18	4 inshore	T47 T49	H-40 to H-5 H-hour to H / 20	300 50	Rock Salvos Air Bursts	1250
USS Doyle (DD)	4x5"	1600	18	4 inshore	T41,T40 T55	H-40 to H-5 H-hour to H / 20	300 50	Rock Salvos	1250

Overleaf: Targets No 1, 5 and 16 were the Rangers' interest. But all other targets within the scope of V Corps operations area are also listed.

Nos 2, 3 & 4 were outside the Rangers' area of operations. Thus the two top priority targets in the Omaha Sector are T1 = Pointe du Hoc and T5 = Maisy I.

 BIGOT

NEPTUNE
Appendix 2
to Annex 12
In _3_ pages
Page No. 1

APPENDIX 2
TO
ANNEX NO. 12

V CORPS TARGET LIST

TARGET NO.	CO-ORDINATES	DESCRIPTION
T1	58609390	6 Guns, 155mm
T5	53309180	4 Guns, 155mm, 5 concrete shelters, 3 MGs, 1 Hut
T10	79268316	4 Guns, 105mm
T16	52159150	4 Guns, 75mm, 2 MGs, 1 Pillbox, 3 Shelters
T20	77008600	Strongpoint with possible 75 Cal Guns
T21	76708775	7 MGs, 1 Pillbox
T22	76008780	2 MGs, 1 Hut, 1 Shelter
T23	75808785	4 MGs, 1 AT Gun
T24	75508790	1 Pillbox
T25	75308795	1 Pillbox, 1 MG
T26	75308838	1 Pillbox
T27	75008805	1 4.7 Gun, 3 AA Guns, 6 Pillboxes
T28	75008790	5 MGs, 3 Shelters
T29	74908710	9 MGs, Road block, Troops in houses
T30	74508815	Strongpoint, 2 Arty Guns, 2 Shelters
T31	73238843	Pillbox
T32	72698850	3 MGs
T33	72208860	2 Concrete shelters, 16 MGs, Road blocks
T34	72108780	4 Houses
T35	72098740	Houses
T36	71808800	Houses
T37	71198810	Houses
T38	71218880	C/D Gun in concrete
T39	70498820	Houses
T40	69908910	5 Pillboxes, 2 MGs, 2 Concrete shelters
T41	69558930	3 Pillboxes
T42	69508830	Houses
T43	69308940	3 Pillboxes, 1 Concrete shelter, 4 MGs, AT Ditch
T44	69408910	Beach Exit
T45	69308883	Beach Exit, 1 Camouflaged position
T46	69108820	Troops in Houses
T47	68808950)	(4 Casemates, 3 Concrete Shelters, 5 MGs, 1 AT
T50	68708943)	(Gun, 3 Pillboxes, 1 Med Gun, 1 Casemate u/c
T48	68808910	Beach Exit
T49	68608870	Beach Exit
T51	68368970	Construction Activity
T52	68128978	AT Ditch
T53	67808970	AA Gun, 4 Concrete Shelters, 2 Pillboxes, 5 MGs
T54	67609010	4 Guns in concrete, 6 MGs, 4 Inf weapons
T55	67558930	Beach Exit
T56	67458780	Troops
T57	67109010	4 Emplacements unoccupied
T58	67148932	Troops
T59	66809030	1 AA/MG, 8 Concrete Shelters, Concrete OP, 3 Pillboxes, 2 Concrete Shelters under construction
T60	66739060	Fortified house, 1 Pillbox, 2 Concrete Shelters
T61	66609030	11 MGs, 3 weapon emplacements, 3 Pillboxes
T62	66258960	2 MGs, possible CP
T63	66459073	6 MGs, 1 Pillbox
T64	66309020	Beach Exit
T65	66149075	Radar Station
T66	65689100	1 Pillbox, 3 MGs
T67	65509120	Fortified House

-1-

BIGOT

NEPTUNE
Appendix 2
to Annex 12
In _3_ pages
Page No. 2

TARGET NO.	CO-ORDINATES	DESCRIPTION
T68	65389120	5 Concrete Shelters, 1 Pillbox, 10 MGs, 1 AA Gun, Infantry weapons unspecified
T69	65109150	3 MGs, 1 AT Gun
T70	64809120	Possible AT Gun, possible fortified houses
T71	64809170	4 Pillboxes, 6 MGs, 3 Concrete Shelters, 1 AA/MG, 1 AT Gun
T72	64509190	2 Pillboxes, 4 Mortars, 2 Emplacements, 11 MGs, 1 Casemate
T73	64808660	Cross Roads
T74	63709273)	(4 Concrete Shelters, 1 OP, 4 Pillboxes, 14 MGs,
T75	63629302)	(AT weapons, Hutted Camp
T76	62479350)	(13 MGs, 2 Pillboxes, 10 Concrete Shelters, 6 Con-
T77	62229350)	(crete Shelters u/c, Würzburg Radar Station, Battery of 4 AA Guns, 1 Searchlight, 1 Hutted Camp
T78	62209060	Troops
T79	62208870	2 MGs, Supply Depot
T80	61179165	2 MGs, Houses
T81	61229270	Strongpoint
T82	60609380	1 MG
T83	60209380	10 MGs, 2 Concrete Shelters
T84	59409288	Road Junction, Houses
T85	58609307	Troops in houses
T86	58509345	1 AT Gun
T87	58409155	Possible CP, Cable trench junction
T88	57609390	3 MGs, 2 Pillboxes, 2 Shelters
T89	57409390	1 MG
T90	57359335	2 Gun positions, Troops
T91	56559365	12 MGs, 1 Pillbox, 2 Shelters
T92	56208926	Strongpoint, Troops in Houses, 7 MGs
T93	55809330	29 MGs, 3 Pillboxes, 4 Shelters, 2 Flak Guns
T94	55409260	Houses with Troops
T95	55279327	Houses, 1 MG, 1 Pillbox
T96	54609100	Cable trench junction, Possible CP
T97	54459335	7 MGs, 1 Pillbox, 1 Flak Gun, 4 Road Blocks
T98	54459290	Strongpoint with 9 MGs, possible CP
T99	54309353	1 Light Gun
T100	54159235	Houses with Troops
T101	54309190	Houses with Troops
T102	54009205	Strongpoint
T103	53909230	4 Possible Gun Positions, Troops in Houses
T104	53809340	Road Block, Houses, 14 MGs, 3 Pillboxes
T105	53609240	Houses
T106	53309350	2 MGs
T107	53159050	Possible CP, Cable trench junction
T108	53029130	Houses with Troops
T109	52709350	4 Pillboxes, 4 MGs, 4 Concrete Shelters
T110	52609070	Troops in Houses
T111	52159330	13 MGs, 2 Concrete Shelters
T112	51708670	Troops in Houses, 1 MG
T113	51109240	11 MGs, 2 Pillboxes
T114	51109120	Strongpoint, 7 MGs
T115	50909215	2 MGs
T116	50728824	2 MGs, 1 Shelter under construction
T117	50509160	2 MGs, 1 Pillbox
T118	50359080	Strongpoint, 4 Pillboxes, 1 MG
T119	50208570	Strongpoint, 1 Concrete Shelter
T120	49709060	1 AT Gun, 1 Pillbox, 1 MG
T121	49708840	4 MGs
T122	49309040	5 Pillboxes, 1 AT Gun, 3 MGs
T123	49208780	Bridge, 4 Pillboxes, 3 AT Guns, 2 Flak Guns, 2 MGs

- 2 -

▆▆▆▆▆ BIGOT

NEPTUNE
Appendix 2
to Annex 12
In __3_ pages
Page No. 3

TARGET NO.	CO-ORDINATES	DESCRIPTION
T124	59909340	Ammunition Depot
T125	57959370	6 Flak Guns
T127	61609370	4 MGs, 1 Pillbox
T128	67508995	2 Pillboxes, C/D casemate, 3 MGs, 1 Concrete Shelter
T129	79708710	Casemating under construction
T130	66309058	4 MGs, 2 Pillboxes, 1 AT Gun
T150	76218090	Road junctions in town
T151	76108210	Houses with Troops
T152	75917876	Bridge and Road Junction
T153	75178457	Troops, 5 MGs, CP, Cable trench junction
T154	75107765	Road and Railroad Crossing
T155	74488066	4 MGs, Houses
T156	73708320	Bridge over Canal, Road Junction
T157	73348213	Road Junction in Town
T158	72417800	Road and Railroad Crossing
T159	71908283	Road Crossing
T160	71408490	Troops
T161	71318280	4 Possible Arty Emplacements
T162	69768393	Road Junction
T163	69267752	Bridge and Road Junction
T164	65788134	Road Junction
T165	64667700	Railroad Underpass
T166	64308390	Troops in Town
T167	64308441	Bridge
T168	61508360	Road Junction
T169	60308158	2 Road Crossings
T170	55218424	Road Junction
T18●	58408240	6 MGs

An objective map overlay was issued showing where each unit must reach on D-Day. The sea and landing beaches are at the top of this overlay. Even at this early stage of briefing the 'D-Day Objective' line is being marked well inland away from the coast.

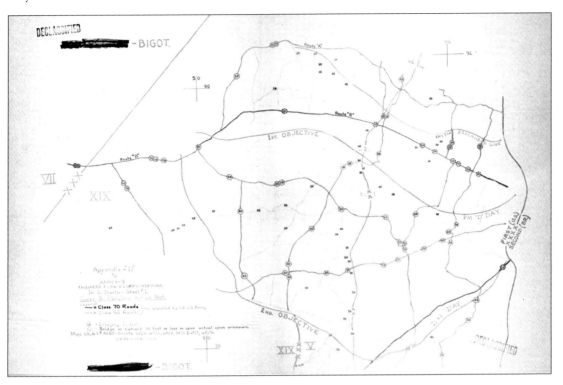

For illustrative purposes shown below is the same overlay – but this time it is placed over a modern map. The placement of the D-DAY PHASE LINE some miles inland was deliberate and it allowed the Allies to block any of the routes to the coast by the German units stationed in Isigny-sur-Mer.

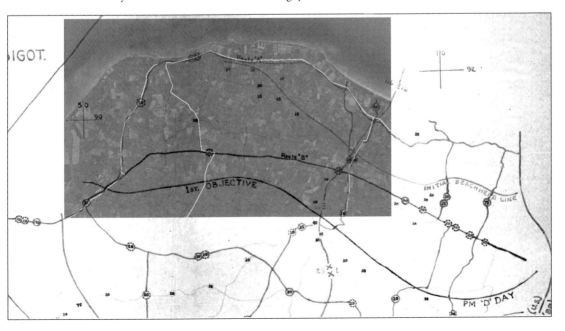

Below is a list of maps being made available for each area and below that is the specific map allocation for the Rangers.

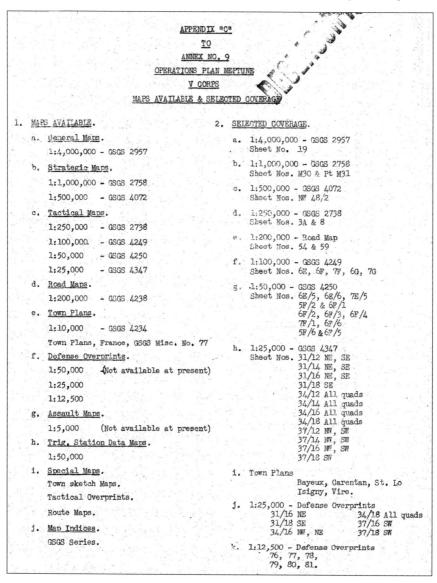

All levels of map could be obtained and the quantities shown should allow all senior members of each platoon to have at least one copy.

MAP ALLOWANCE TABLE

CONFIDENTIAL — REVI

UNIT	EACH OF (5)	TRAINING STRATEGICAL				TRAINING TACTICAL			OPERATIONS STRATEGICAL			OPERATIONS TACTICAL											
RANGER BATTALION	1	1	1	0	35	10	50	50	0	1	0	35	10	10	50	50	5	5	0	50	50	50	0

25 March 1944

5th Rangers – Companies A – F, Medical and HQ – Tighnabruaich, Scotland.
2nd Rangers – Companies A – F, Medical – Bude, Cornwall.
Headquarters Company 2nd Rangers – Bude, Cornwall.
Record of Events –'Detachment A' Headquarters Company was absorbed into HQ Company and other companies of this Battalion as of 23 March 1944.

On 25 March the US Army released a 'Ridge and Stream Map' as part of a Tactical Terrain Study. It shows water-courses and heights of land for the Omaha Sector – and all high and low points within the Rangers' assault area.

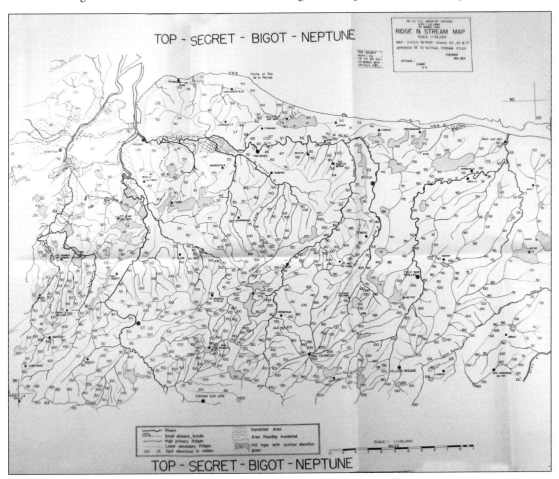

Once again, the Army felt it necessary to continue to restate to their men the finer points of dealing with the British – this may have been to accommodate replacements to the armed services, who had recently arrived in England.

> *NEVER criticize the King or Queen.*
> *Don't criticize the food, beer, or cigarettes to the British. Remember they have been at war since 1939.*
> *Use common sense on all occasions. By your conduct you have great power to bring about a better understanding between the two countries after the war is over.*
> *You will soon find yourself among a kindly, quiet, hard-working people who have been living under a strain such as few people in the world have ever known. In your dealings with them, let this be your slogan:*
> *It is impolite to criticize your hosts; It is militarily stupid to criticize your allies.*

On the next page: dated 25 March the Army via Major General Huebner's office released the following Tactical Study of Terrain in the 1st Infantry Division assault area. [It has been shown in full, and Beach 46 is in the Omaha Sector].

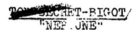

~~TOP SECRET-BIGOT/~~
"NEPTUNE"

Hq 1st US Inf Div
APO 1, US Army
25 March 1944

Copy N°. ___

```
:TOP SECRET      :
:Authority:  CG:
:1st US Inf Div:
:25 March 1944 :
:Initials:/𝐴𝐸 :
```

TACTICAL STUDY OF TERRAIN

Maps: GSGS 4250 (1/50,000) - Sheets 6E/5, 6E/6, 7E/5, 5F/2, 6F/1,
                                             6F/2, 7F/1.
                   GSGS 4249 (1/100,000)- Sheets 6E, 6F, 7F.
                   GSGS 2738 (1/250,000)- Sheets 3A & 8.
                   GSGS 4347 (1/25,000) - Sheets 34/18 NW, NE, SW, SE.
                                             34/16 NW, NE, SW, SE.
                                             37/16 NW, SW.
                                             37/18 SW.

1.   PURPOSE AND OTHER LIMITING CONSIDERATIONS.

     The purpose of this study is to give a brief general descrip-
tion of the area of the NEPTUNE Operation, and detailed analysis
of Beach 46 and the area behind it from the assault viewpoint.
The area considered in detail includes the probable zone of action
of V Corps through D ≠ 9.

2.   GENERAL TOPOGRAPHY OF THE CHERBOURG PENINSULA.

     a.   The Cherbourg Peninsula may be roughly divided into three
geographical regions: the Cotentin to the North, the Bessin to
the East and the Bocage to the South.

     (1)   Cotentin.   This is the area north of the Taute River,
a well-marked geographical region forming the seaward projection
of the Peninsula.   Its irregular coastline has numerous inlets,
bays and high cliffs.   The highest elevation is approximately 500
feet, and there are frequent precipitous valleys.   The southeast
section of Cotentin consists of low marshy plain.   This is the area
of the VII Corps assault.

     (2)   The Bessin.   This lies to the east of the Taute River
and extends to Bayeux and includes the 1st Div. assault sector.
The western portion of the area is low and marshy, but towards the
east rolling hills predominate.   Although the country is generally
open, between St. Lo and Bayeux numerous wooded areas exist.   The
country is extensively cultivated and consists principally of
rectangular pastures and orchards bordered by hedges.

(3) Due to the steepness of the slope directly in rear of the beach west of Le Ruquet River (665905), tanks accompanying troops in the assault will have to use the two corridors in this sector as exits from the beach. Since these corridors are narrow and are provided with concrete road blocks, enemy tank defense in this sector is greatly facilitated.

(4) The terrain in rear of the beach permits the employment of howitzer or mortar fire from defiladed positions. Excellent observation is afforded the enemy for the control of this fire. Houses and hedges that interfere with observation generally have been removed.

d. (1) After withdrawal from the first positions in rear of the beach, the next high ground available to the enemy for a line of defense will be the ridge generally about 2,000 yards in rear of the beach, using the small villages on the forward slope as fortified localities. Except for the hindering effects of intervening hedges, excellent fields of fire for flat trajectory weapons will be afforded from these positions.

(2) Until such time as the enemy has been driven from this high ground, the valley of the Aure and its tributaries will afford some defilade for the movement of mobile troops to positions from which counter-attacks may be launched.

(3) The defense of the Grandcamp-Isigny area by enemy forces will be facilitated by basing a defensive line on the flooded area 1½ miles to the east of Grandcamp.

e. (1) After withdrawal from the principal ridge north of the Aure, the next position suitable to the enemy for prolonged defense is the ridge running east-southeast of Trevieres and, in view of the flooded condition of the lower Aure, withdrawal by the hostile main force will have to be made east of Trevieres. For those forces caught in the Isigny-Grandcamp area it will have to be made through the Isigny corridor. The enemy can cause some delay to our forces by blowing all bridges across the Aure and it may be expected that this will be done.

(2) During this phase of the operation the only suitable terrain available to the enemy for armored operations will be in the area between Trevieres and Bayeux and even in this area armored deployment will be difficult due to narrow sunken roads and stout tree-hedges. Likewise, the enemy will be protected from our armor along that section of his line based on the flooded Aure Valley.

f. (1) Having been driven from the Trevieres Ridge, the enemy can pivot his line on the flooded Aure Valley and form a defensive line on the first ridges behind La Tortonne River. From this position he will have fair observation and will still be able to use the Aure Valley for the protection of his left.

"NEPTUNE"

b. **Assault Beach.** Beach 46 runs from 699894 to 638930. The gradient from the back of the beach to the high water level varies between 1/10 - 1/20. From the high water line to the low water line the gradient varies between 1/55 and 1/70; it generally flattens out seaward from the low water mark. Mean level of the water is 13 ft above Admiralty Chart Datum, with a neap rise of 19 ft and springs 23 ft. The beach is of firm sand below HWL and of coarse shingle above this line to the back of the beach. Beach roadway expedients will be necessary above HWL. The beach is 7,900 yards long. Runnels exits sporadically along this beach and though they are never more than 2½ ft deep they will cause difficulty at certain stages of the tide at various points on the beach. Landing of LCT and smaller craft can begin 5 hours before HW and continue to about 5 hours after HW. LST must be dried out for unloading, as gradients will not permit the craft to approach the shore close enough for vehicular wading. Tidal streams are a maximum of 3 knots at springs and run east to west. A series of low pile-type groynes are placed along the sea wall between Vierville-sur-Mer and Les Moulin (649916-665905). The distance from the back of the beach to HW is not great, averaging 25 yards. The eastern portion of beach is backed by a low grassy bank 4 to 6 ft high, slope 1:4 (696894 and 673902). The remaining portion of the beach has a rought stone seawall 6 to 12 ft high, slope 1:1, back of which is a 10 ft promenade road (673902 and 648917). At the western end of Beach 46 there are cliffs 120 ft high, slope 1:1 to 1:2 (648917 and 637930). It is possible that at HW springs with an onshore wind, the seawall may be awash. The cliffs between Vierville and Ponte de la Percee are not scaleable without apparatus; thus, the portion of the beach backed by these is not useful and the effective length of the beach is reduced to 5,000 yards. Since the beach is slightly concave, the heights on either end command its entire length, and considerable sections are subject to observed fire from high ground immediately to the rear.

c. **Beach Exits.** Initially, five exits can be made off the beach; these have been designated as D1, D3, E1, E3 and F1, and are so indicated on Appendix "A". They are all up short narrow valleys and run from 648917 to Vierville-sur-Mer (647912), 665906 to St. Laurent-sur-Mer (664897), 677901 to near St. Laurent-sur-Mer (671896), 688896 to Colleville-sur-Mer (687882) and from 697893 to Cabourg (694884) respectively. Each of the five principal exits is discussed separately below. In general, although the beach is narrow at HW, a narrow bench runs parallel to the beach and between it and the slopes that front on the sea. This bench will aid in lateral traffic between beach roadways and exits.

(1) **Exit D1.** At 649918 a triangular groyne has, under the effect of the westerly tidal currents, piled sand along the seawall to its west until the effective height of this wall is reduced to not over four feet. Hence from the west of this groyne an easy approach is possible to the promenade road. From this road a 15 ft tarmac road runs to Vierville, through a narrow valley that will not permit deployment.

(2)   Exit D3.   By ramping over the low seawall near the valley's mouth, access is had to a small net of roads which lead to a 15 ft tarmac road that runs to St. Laurent. The village of Les Moulins, at the foot of the exit, constricts traffic to a track that may be full of rubble.

(3)   Exit E1.   By building about 100 yards of roadway to the road that parallels the beach, access can be had to a rought 8-10 ft gravel road that runs up on the west side of a narrow valley, across an open field into the St. Laurent road net. Except for some 200 yards on the road, as it climbs over the valley rim, wheeled vehicles can negotiate the exit off the road at will.

(4)   Exit E3.   A 10 ft tarmac road runs from back of the beach to Colleville. This exit is narrow and winding, but is adequate. About 100 yards of roadway will be necessary over the dune sand between the beach and the road. Wheeled vehicles will be restricted to the road; tracked vehicles will be able only to deploy between extensive shubbery along the road.

(5)   Exit F1.   At 697893 sandy track - not more than 6 ft wide - leads from beach over rising ground at 698891; then it joins rough road 8 ft wide at 698887 leading to Colleville. Track would need to be made good over 500 yards before carrying anything other than light M/T in wet weather.

(6)   Other Exits:

(a)   A trail which runs up from 678900 to 682895.
(b)   693895. Track, little more than a footpath, leads from beach over meadows and scrub on rising ground to 694891 where it joins the same 8 foot wide road to Colleville. Track would need to be made good over 500 yards before carrying anything other than light M/T in wet weather.

(c)   692895. Sandy track, not more than 6 ft wide, leads from beach over level ground for 300 yards to 689894 where it joins 10 - 12 ft metalled road leading inland to Colleville.

(d)   Anywhere between 678900 and beginning of seawall at 673902, over 50 yards sandy scrub to track 6 - 8 ft wide leading west along coast. This track becomes a metalled road 10 ft wide at 673902.

d.   Avenues of Approach - (see Paragraph 3 d.).

(1)   Approach from the coast inland is difficult throughout the area and particularly in the westerly portions. Here the inundated areas and marshlands, together with numerous drainage ditches and small streams, will confine all movement to the roads. Enemy demolitions in the form of road craters and demolished bridges,

augmented by well-placed antitank mines and road blocks will make
movement slow and laborious. In the easterly half of the area
conditions are not so difficult although cross-country movement
will not be easy.

(2) Even the principal roads must be considered one-way
in most cases because of numerous bottlenecks, usually in the form
of narrow bridges. Inasmuch as the principal roads are those connecting Cherbourg with the interior, we will find our laterals
better than our axials. Hence, many axial roads will be "dead-
ends" until they are improved or intersect the main roads.

(3) Gradients, in general, are not excessive but curves
are numerous and frequently sharp.

(4) Communications will not improve appreciably until St.
Lo has been taken.

e. Observacles. The most important obstacles in the area are
the inundated regions near Grandcamp, in the lower Aure Valley,
along the River Vire and the River Taute. These areas are flooded
by fresh water held back by weirs (dam) or "control stations"
located at suitable points along the streams. The Grandcamp and
the lower Aure areas are now permanently flooded and other areas
could be inundated. (For details, see Appendix "A"). The soil
underlying these inundated areas is composed of soft clay and some
saturated peat and therefore has tendency to retain water. The
depth of the water varies from six inches to about three feet. If
the weirs (dam) or "control points" were opened it would require
about 10 days to six weeks for the water to subside and the ground
would probably never dry out completely.

(1) Roads running through the inundated areas are either
completely under water or are so saturated as to be useless, with
a few possible exceptions.

(2) Infantry can cross most of the inundated areas only
with great difficulty. Vehicles cannot cross.

(3) Other obstacles in the area are in the form of narrow
roads, sometimes sunken, and almost always flanked by thick earth
fences, hedges or embanked fields.

(4) Scattered woods, increasing in density to the south,
will add to the difficulty of cross-country movement.

(5) With exceptions already noted, streams are fordable by
infantry.

f. Observation. Observation, in general, favors the defender
throughout the area under study. Observation, however, will be
severely limited throughout the area behind the beaches as the

elevations are not high and the numerous orchards and tree-lined fields will tend to conceal activity from most ground observation except within the immediate vicinity of the observer. Certain observation vantage points for the attacker to secure include:

(1)   The high ground immediately along the coast. Observation from cliffs in the vicinity of St. Pierre (5993) and St. Honorine-des-Pertes (7288) enables the defender to overlook all operations that may take place on Beach 46 and the water before it. The high ground behind Grandcamp (5593) enables him to observe the entrance to the River Vire. Seizure of these areas and the two east-west ridges between the coast and the River Aure places the attacker in position to overlook the valley of the Aure.

(2)   The most favorable observation from the attacker's standpoint can be found on Mt. Cauvin (705853) and on the high ground to the north of Trevieres (645853). These two vantage points if held by the attacking forces, give good observation of the main routes of approach which must be used by the defending forces when they launch their counter-offensives.

(3)   Limited observation of the Aure Valley south of Grandcamp can be obtained from the ridge in the vicinity of Longueville (605876) and the high ground east of Osmanville at 550880 may give observation on the town of Isigny.

(4)   The high ground lying in the triangle formed by the Rivers Aure, Tortonne and Drome. This offers good vantage point and should be secured as early as possible to deny enemy observation close to the beachhead.

(5)   The high ground in the general areas: Foret de Cerisy, Le Soultaire (5765) and La Luzerne (5266).

(6)   The high ground south of Isigny. This gives fair observation of the Carentan Lowlands.

g.   Fields of Fire. Fields of fire for the attacker are poor in the early stages of the advance for weapons of all types. After crossing the Aure and moving into the north-south valleys the fields of fire continue to be limited. Small arms and machine guns will be limited to short ranges. The low areas between the Rivers Vire and Taute offer excellent fields of fire for all weapons.

(2)   During this phase of the operation, the corridor on the east formed by the valley of the Drome will be available to the enemy for the launching of counter-attacks against our left flank. On the western flank the enemy will be protected by the River Vire and its marshy lowlands.

(3)   The defense of the Grandcamp-Isigny area by enemy forces will be facilitated by basing a defensive line on the flooded area 1½ miles to the east of Grandcamp.

e. (1) After withdrawal from the principal ridge north of the
Aure, the next position suitable to the enemy for prolonged defense
is the ridge running east-southeast of Trevieres and, in view of
the flooded condition of the lower Aure, withdrawal by the hostile
main force will have to be made east of Trevieres. For these
forces caught in the Isigny-Grandcamp area it will have to be made
through the Isigny corridor. The enemy can cause some delay to our
forces by blowing all bridges across the Aure and it may be expected
that this will be done.

(2) During this phase of the operation the only suitable
terrain available to the enemy for armored operations will be in the
area between Trevieres and Bayeux and even in this area armored
deployment will be difficult due to narrow sunken roads and stout
tree-hedges. Likewise, the enemy will be protected from our armor
along that section of his line based on the flooded Aure Valley.

f. (1) Having been driven from the Trevieres Ridge, the enemy
can pivot his line on the flooded Aure Valley and form a defensive
line on the first ridges behind La Tortonne River. From this position he will have fair observation and will still be able to use
the Aure Valley for the protection of his left.

g. When the enemy is driven from the Trevieres Ridge-- Aure
River line, a good defensive line will be afforded by the dominating
Lison-Baynes-Foret de Cerisy Ridge. Although the eastern flank is
broken by the spreading corridors of the River Drome and several
small corridors lead well into the forward slopes, this position
dominates the valleys to the north, its western flank is fairly
secure, and its front and flanks are not suitable for extensive
tank attacks.

h. The main rail line running parallel to the coast from Bayeux
to Carentan is double track, but it is so close to the initial
assault area that it is unlikely that this line will be used for the
detrainment of mobile reserves. The next line, which also runs
parallel to the coast between Folligny-Vire-Fiers, is 30 miles away
and involves at least a 2-hour motor movement or a forced march of
some 15-20 hours on foot to reach the assault area. The main rail
lines into the area are sufficient for the transport and detrainment of two full-strength divisions in a period of 24 hours.

i. The road net leading into the area is sufficient to carry
all available reserves which may be brought into the area either
by rail or motor. Since the principal through routes center on
Bayeux in the East and Isigny in the West, major motor movements
may be expected to come into the assault area through or near these
points. Minor roads leading into the assault area are narrow,
frequently sunken and usually lined with strong hedges. Deployment
from these roads will be difficult for motors and tanks.

j. The telephone and cable net is ample to permit prompt warning and the issuance of orders to mobile reserves.

HUEBNER
Maj Gen

OFFICIAL:

EVANS
G-2

26 March 1944

5th Rangers – Companies A – F, Medical and HQ –
Tighnabruaich, Scotland.

Below: This paragraph comes from a letter dated 16 July (see Conclusion in Vol. 2) – it confirms that Lieutenant Colonel Rudder's request to remove Major Schneider from his post on 26 March 1944 was officially denied. Thus Major Schneider could not be removed from his position at this time. General Eisenhower considered that Major Schneider was an asset and of value – at least until after the invasion had taken place.

> Request was submitted by cable E-20672, this headquarters, 26 March 1944, to withdraw his name from the rotation report, this being approved by cable WAR 16751 March 311657Z. This request was made in order that officer's services could be utilized in initial invasion of the continent.

On the same day Lt. Col. Rudder transferred Major Schneider to the 5th Battalion and placed Captain Cleveland A. Lytle in his place at the top of the 2nd Battalion.

> On 26 March, Major Schneider was relieved of assignment as Executive Officer and assumed command of the 5th Ranger Battalion. Captain Cleveland A. Lytle was appointed Executive Officer on this day.

2nd Rangers – Companies A – E, Medical – Bude, Cornwall.

F Company 2nd Rangers – Bude, Cornwall.
Captain Otto Masny went from 5 days leave back to Duty as Company Commander F Company.
1st Lt. Arman went from 5 days leave and returned to Duty and is relieved of temporary Duty as Company Commander F Company – and assumes principal Duty as platoon leader.

Headquarters Company 2nd Rangers – Bude, Cornwall.
Major Max. S. Schneider was relieved assigned and transferred to 5th Ranger Infantry Battalion. US Army.

On 26 March 1944 the Ranger battalion command were given the following documents, and their inclusion in the distribution list specifically states the 'CO' Ranger Battalion. The orders include instructions for the Rangers to attack Pointe du Hoc and the batteries at Maisy. In the later pages it also records the calibres, grid references and positions of all the Coastal Artillery weapons in the area.

- BIGOT

HEADQUARTERS
V CORPS

O P E R A T I O N   P L A N

NEPTUNE

Distribution

	Copy No.
Commanding General, First US Army	4 - 15.
Commander Eleventh Amphibious Force, USN	16 - 17.
Commanding General, V Corps	18.
Commanding General, VII Corps	19 - 20.
Commanding General, XX Corps, British Army	21 - 22.
Commanding General, 1st Infantry Division	23 - 30.
Commanding General, 28th Infantry Division	31 - 33.
Commanding General, 29th Infantry Division	39 - 46.
Commanding General, Provisional Engineer Special Brigade Group	47 - 49.
Commanding General, Southern Base Section, SOS, ETOUSA	50.
Commanding General, V Corps Artillery	51 - 55.
Commanding General, 49th AAA Brigade	56 - 59.
Commander Landing Craft and Bases, USN	60 - 61.
Commanding Officer, XIII District, SBS	62.
Commanding Officer, 3rd Armored Group	63.
Commanding Officer, 3rd Tank Destroyer Group	64.
Commanding Officer, 102nd Cavalry Group	65.
Commanding Officer, 1115th AA Group	66.
Commanding Officer, 1121st Engineer Group	67.
Commanding Officer, 1171st Engineer Group	68.
Commanding Officer, 2nd Ranger Battalion	69.
Commanding Officer, 5th Ranger Battalion	70.
Commanding Officer, 53rd Signal Battalion	71.
Commanding Officer, 53rd Signal Battalion	72.
Commanding Officer, 67th AA Battalion	73.
Commanding Officer, 67th AA Battalion	74.
Commanding Officer, 109th Ordnance Ammunition Battalion	75.
Commanding Officer, 177th Ordnance Battalion	76.
General and Special Staff, V Corps	77 - 96.
Spares	97 - 125.

HEADQUARTERS

V CORPS

APO 305

O P E R A T I O N S   P L A N

N E P T U N E

26 March 1944

APPROVED:

By Direction of Major General GEROW:

H. J. MATCHETT,
Colonel, G.S.C.,
Chief of Staff.

BIGOT

HEADQUARTERS
V CORPS

OPERATIONS PLAN
NEPTUNE

SECTION 1 - GENERAL

1. a. PURPOSE. The purpose of V Corps Operational Plan NEPTUNE is to provide a basis for the V Corps participation in an amphibious attack of the continent of Europe. The instructions contained herein will be complied with by subordinate commanders. Planning must run concurrently with training to the end that maximum efficiency of operation may be attained.

   b. SCOPE
       (1) The scope of the V Corps Operational Plan NEPTUNE covers:
            (a) Time Schedule for the completion of the necessary plans, exercises, rehearsals and mounting of the overseas operation.
            (b) V Corps Tactical Plan.
            (c) V Corps Mounting Plan, together with the necessary Annexes to such plans.
       (2) The V Corps Operational Plan NEPTUNE is applicable to all units and personnel assigned or attached to the V Corps for this operation. Should modifications be found necessary or desirable, commanders will make appropriate requests to Commanding General, V Corps.

2. TIME SCHEDULE.

    a. The following plans, as called for by First United States Army, have been completed:

        3 March - Final Planning Commenced.
        13 March -List of Beach Defense Targets for prearranged Naval and Air Fire Support.
        15 March - Amphibious Training Exercise "FOX" terminated.
        23 March - Alert order issued by V Corps, including administrative instructions to all organic and attached units.
        27 March - Final Landing and Loading Tables for Forces "O" and "B" and Build-Up-Priority Tables for remainder of Corps and attached units.

    b. The following plans will be completed as stated below:

        1 April - V Corps Operational Plan NEPTUNE issued.
        6 April - Advance requisitions for estimated personnel losses as prescribed in Annex No. 3, submitted by Corps Troop units to Corps.
        8 April - Directive for Dress Rehearsal issued by V Corps.
        11 April - Corps submits advance requisitions for estimated personnel losses to First U. S. Army. Divisions submit similar requests direct to First U. S. Army
        16 April - Forces "O" and "B" submit Final Operational Plan to V Corps.
        21 to 26 April - Units move to concentration for Dress Rehearsal.
        2 to 4 May - Dress Rehearsal.
        7 May - Commanding General, First United States Army, holds final conference with Corps and Division Commanders.
        11 May - Concentration for overseas movement completed for assault, follow-up and early build-up units.
        17 May - a. Units complete waterproofing, briefing and marshalling and embark as ordered.
                 b. Build-up units receive final instructions.

- 1 -

SECTION II - TACTICAL PLAN

Reference, NEPTUNE Plan - PG 492.
Map - 1:50,000, GSGS, Sheets 6E5, 6E6, 7E5, 5F2, 6F1, 6F2, 7F1.

1.   SITUATION.   a.   See G-2 Estimate of the Situation. Annex No. 1).

b.   (1)   The First United States Army, consisting of the V and VII Corps
           associated U.S. and Allied Naval and Air Forces and the British
           Second Army will conduct a simultaneous assault on the continent
           of Europe.

     (2)   The British Second Army on the left of the First United States
           Army will assault the beaches in its sector and capture BAYEUX
           and CAEN on D-day. The 50th British Division, part of the XXX
           British Corps, will be on the left of the V Corps.

     (3)   The VII Corps, with the 4th Division in the initial assault and
           supported by the 101st Airborne Division, will assault Beach
           "UTAH" on D-day at H-hour, advance rapidly, and capture CHER-
           BOURG.

     (4)   The assault will be supported by U.S. and Allied Naval gunfire
           and aerial bombardment commencing at H minus 40 minutes or
           earlier. (See Fire Support Plan - Annex No. 12).

     (5)   Air support will be continuous during D-day. It will consist of
           all classes of aircraft and in addition squadrons will be on air
           alert and on call from the United Kingdom to support ground force
           operations. (See Air Plan - to be furnished).

     (6)   A Provisional Engineer Special Brigade Group, consisting of the
           5th and 6th Engineer Special Brigades (reinforced) will support
           the landing of the V Corps. It will, under the senior U.S. Army
           Commander ashore, organize and operate all shore installations
           necessary for debarkation, supply, evacuation and local security
           in order to insure the continuous movement of personnel, vehicles
           and supplies across the beaches. The senior commander ashore
           will not divert equipment or personnel of the Engineer Special
           Brigade Group from assigned mission as prescribed by First U.S.
           Army except in a grave emergency. The responsibility of such
           diversions, if any are made, will rest with the senior commander
           ashore.

2.   MISSIONS.   a. The V Corps, consisting of the 1st, 28th and 29th Infantry
Divisions, with the 2nd and 5th Ranger Battalions and other forces attached, will
assault Beach "OMAHA", reduce enemy resistance, secure VIERVILLE-SUR-MER -- COLLE-
VILLE-SUR-MER beachhead and advance southward towards ST. LO to cover the landing
of other troops and supplies of the First United States Army. The rate of advance
will be in conformity with the advance of the Second British Army and instructions
issued by Headquarters, V Corps, at the time. (See Operations Overlay - Annex No.
21).

b.   Boundaries.

     (1)   Left boundary (between V Corps and Second British Army) the line
           (incl to Second British Army) PORT EN BESSIN 7587--River DROME
           from ESCURES 7585 to ENGLESQUEVILLE 7587 thence (excl Second
           British Army) road AGY -- ST. PAUL DU VERNAY 7470 -- STE HONORINE
           DE DUC 7365--LA VITARDIERE 7262--thence to LE REPAS 7159--LA LONDE
           7157--ST. MARTIN-DES-BESACES 6750--CATHEOLLES 7044--ST. CHARLES-
           DE-PERCY 6941--BEAULIEU 6839.

     (2)   Right boundary -- See overlay, Annex No. 21A.
     (3)   Boundary between divisions -- See overlay, Annex 21.
     (4)   Time: D-day, H-hour to be announced.

a.   1st Division. The 1st Infantry Division (less 26 RCT) with 116 RCT
of the 29th Division and other troops attached (Force "O") will make the initial
assault with two RCTs abreast, the 116th RCT on the right. It will clear the

- 2 -

shoreline of enemy resistance in the Corps Zone of Action and secure the ~~D-day~~
phase line two hours before dark. It will contact the VII U. S. Corps on the
right and the 50th Division of the British Second Army on the left. It will patrol
strongly to the D-plus one phase line.

Rangers. The 2nd and 5th Ranger Battalions are attached to 1st Division. They will destroy coast defense batteries at POINT-DU-HOE by simultaneous
direct assault up the Cliffs between POINT-DU-HOE and POINT de la PERCEE and by
flanking action from Beach "OMAHA". They will then, assisted by elements of the
assault force, capture enemy batteries at GRANDCAMP and MAISY. Thereafter to
operate against enemy positions along the coast between GRANDCAMP and ISIGNY. (See
Ranger Plan - Annex No. 19).

b. 29th Division. The 29th Infantry Division (less 116 RCT) with 26 RCT
of the 1st Division and other troops attached (Force "B") will land on Beach
"OMAHA" behind the initial assault force on orders of Commanding General, V Corps.
(For Corps plan on landing schedule, see Annex 2). Prior to assumption of command
ashore by the Commanding General, V Corps, it will operate under control of the
Commanding General, 1st Division. It will complete the mopping up of enemy resistance and defend the D-day phase line in the right half of the Corps Zone of Action.
It will continue active patrolling to the D plus one phase line. The 175th Infan-
try will be in Corps Reserve and will not be employed except on orders of the Corps
Commander. The attached RCT of the 1st Division (26 RCT) will pass to the command
of the Commanding General, 1st Division, on landing.

c. 28th Division. The 29th Infantry Division (Build-Up) will arrive in
the Transport Area early on D plus one and will be prepared to commence landing by
combat teams on Beach "OMAHA" immediately. (For assembly areas see Overlay No.
21B). It will be prepared to extend the bridgehead to the SOUTH and SOUTHEAST or
to assist in the defense of the beachhead position. Upon landing, artillery of
28th Division will be prepared to furnish general support to the Corps. Upon commitment of the division, the artillery will revert to division control.

d. Artillery. Prior to assumption of command ashore by Commanding
General, V Corps, Corps Artillery units, upon landing, will be attached to 1st
Division. Upon assumption of command by Commanding General, V Corps, Corps Artillery units will revert to Corps control. Missions of Corps Artillery, counter--
battery, distant interdiction, general support. See Corps Artillery Annex No. 16.

e. The 635th Tank Destroyer Battalion upon landing is attached to the 1st
Division. It will be disposed initially in depth to protect the front and left
flank of the division. (See Overlay 21B).

f. Antiaircraft. The 49 AAA Brigade will provide antiaircraft defense
of the beaches, beached craft, beach exits and airfields. The operations of Corps
and divisional AA units will be coordinated by the Corps. (See Antiaircraft Plan -
Annex No. 15).

g. Chemical Warfare. Gas will not be employed except on orders from
Supreme Headquarters and no gas offensive ammunition will be taken overseas. All
personnel will wear protective clothing and carry gas masks. (See Chemical Warfare
Plan - Annex No. 10).

h. Civil Affairs. Civil Affairs operations will be through Command
Channels. (See Civil Affairs Annex - No. 18).

i. Corps Reserve. The 115th Infantry (29th Division), the 102nd Cavalry
Rcn Squadron and the 747th Tank Battalion will upon landing be assembled in the
vicinity of the boundary between divisions. (See Overlay No. 21B).

x. (1) Upon landing units of Force "B" will operate under command of the
Commanding General, Force "O", until the D-day line is secured, or
until otherwise directed by the Commanding General, V Corps. The

9th Division and attached units will be employed in the right half of the Corps Zone of Action, if in the opinion of the Commanding General, Force "O", the tactical situation at the time will permit.

(2) Concurrent with or shortly after the landing of the initial RCT of the 29th Division (Force "B") or on Corps order, the Corps Zone of Action will be divided into division sectors, whereupon the Commanding General, V Corps, will assume command ashore. The responsibility for the right sector and the troops operating therein (including the 2nd and 5th Ranger Battalions) will be at that time transferred to the Commanding General, 29th Division.

(3) An information detachment consisting of four (4) officers and eight (8) enlisted men of Headquarters, V Corps, equipped with three (3) vehicles and two (2) radio sets will land behind the assault CTs. Upon landing the detachment commander will contact the Senior Army Commander ashore for information, will observe the progress of operations and keep the Commanding General, V Corps, informed of the tactical and supply situation in the Corps Zone of Action. He will furnish to the Senior Army Commander ashore copies of messages sent by him to the Commanding General, V Corps. This additional means of obtaining information does not relieve appropriate commanders of their responsibility for keeping higher commanders informed of the situation in accordance with normal procedures.

(4) For forecast of future operations see Forecast of Operations - Annex No. 20.

BIGOT
NEPTUNE
Annex No. 2 to
V CORPS OPERATIONS
PLAN NEPTUNE

BUILD-UP FERRY SERVICE
(SOUTHAMPTON - PORTLAND - SOUTHWEST PORTS)

ITEM	UNIT	VEHICLES	PERSONNEL
92.	Ranger Bns	10	30

BIGOT
NEPTUNE

Annex No. 2 to
V CORPS OPERATIONS
PLAN NEPTUNE

TROOP LIST

BEACH OMAHA - FORCE "O"

ITEM	UNIT	VEHICLES	PERSONNEL
1.	1st Inf Div (- 26 CT)(+ 116 CT)	1472	16141
19.	2nd and 5th Ranger Bns	58	64 (860 sp lift
20.	Air Support Party (w/Rangers)	4	11

27 March 1944
5th Rangers – Companies A – F, Medical and HQ – Tighnabruaich, Scotland
2nd Rangers – Companies A – F, Medical and HQ – Bude, Cornwall.

Overleaf: The Army issued clarification of its policy on handling Top Secret information – and in particular who was able to do so.

HEADQUARTERS
FIRST UNITED STATES ARMY
APO 230

AUTH: CG, First US Army
INIT:
DATE: 27 March 1944

COPY NO 20

27 March 1944

SUBJECT: Classification of Personnel.   5-27-3

TO   : Corps, Division and Separate Unit Commanders.

1. Reference is made to:

    a. Letter ETOUSA file AG 311.5 OpGB, subject: TOP SECRET Control Procedure, 12 March 1944.

    b. Letter ETOUSA file AG 311.5 SCD, subject: "Operational Codeword Plans and BIGOT procedure - Instruction No. 1", 12 March 1944, copy transmitted separately because of higher classification.

    c. Letter this Headquarters file AG 311.5/150 (B), subject: "TOP SECRET Control Procedure", 27 March 1944.

2. <u>Classifications for Operational Codeword Plans</u>.

    a. The following classification of officers and enlisted men who are given access to documents or information concerning Operational Codeword Plans is established for use within this command:

        (1) Those who have knowledge of RANKIN "C" will be classified TOP SECRET-RANKIN "C".

        (2) Those who have a general knowledge of OVERLORD exclusive of target area or date of assault will be classified TOP SECRET-OVERLORD.

        (3) Those who have a knowledge of specific target area or date of assault of OVERLORD will be classified BIGOT-NEPTUNE. This last classification permits access to all OVERLORD and NEPTUNE material.

    b. Classification of personnel thus corresponds with the classification of documents which they are authorized to handle.

    c. Personnel formerly classified as BIGOT-OVERLORD will be considered BIGOT-NEPTUNE personnel; SECRET-SECURITY-OVERLORD personnel now becomes TOP SECRET-OVERLORD. Personnel formerly classified BIGOT-RANKIN or SECRET-SECURITY-RANKIN will be considered TOP SECRET-RANKIN.

3. <u>Classification Authority</u>.

    Authority to classify officers and enlisted men who are to be given access to documents and information covered by Operational Codeword Plans is delegated to Corps and Division Commanders. Personnel of Army units, other than Divisions, will be classified by the Commanding General

First Army. Corps, Division and separate Army unit Commanders are responsible that such personnel is of unquestioned loyalty and discretion and that the number so classified is held to the minimum.

4. Classification Procedure.

a. Requests for personnel to be classified will specify the operation and classification when submitted to the appropriate Commander for approval.

b. Numbered passes will be issued by Corps, Divisions and Brigades showing headquarters of origin, classification, first two letters of the code word of the operation for which classified, signature of the bearer and signature of the TOP SECRET Control Officer and the Chief of Staff Section or Commander. Separate passes, preferably of different colors, will be provided for each separate operation for which personnel is classified.

c. Each individual classified will read this letter, letters referred to in paragraphs 1 a and 1 c above relative to TOP SECRET Control Procedure and, in the case of BIGOT-NEPTUNE personnel, letter referred to in paragraph 1 b. He will sign a statement that he has read and understands the provisions of these letters. This provision applies to all personnel classified, including those classified under provisions of previous directives.

d. Classified personnel will be oriented in the particular plan for which classified, to the extent necessary for their work, before access is given to any documents or information classified TOP SECRET or BIGOT.

e. Name, rank, serial number, assignment and type of classification will be submitted to the Commanding General, First Army by Corps and Division Commanders immediately upon the classification of any officer or enlisted man. Names of personnel previously classified and submitted to this Headquarters do not have to be resubmitted unless a higher classification is authorized (see paragraph 2 c above).

f. In the event of any person being removed from the classified list, his card will be turned in to the TOP SECRET Control Officer and voided and all headquarters furnished lists will be notified without delay.

5. Lists of Classified Personnel.

a. Lists of classified personnel for all First Army units will be exchanged by this Headquarters with major U.S. and British commands.

b. Corps and Divisions will furnish such lists upon request as provided by paragraph 7 (3) (c) of letter referred to in paragraph 1 a above. Lists should be requested by Corps and Division from Base Section Commanders, SOS and U. S. Army Air Force and U.S. Naval Commands with which joint planning is being done.

c. Lists of classified personnel will omit any information
which may disclose directly or by inference the meaning of the operational
codeword and will be classified SECRET. These lists should be readily
available to all classified personnel.

6. Safeguarding of TOP SECRET Information.

a. TOP SECRET information will not be discussed with another
officer until that officer's classification with respect to the particular
operation has been verified from a list or by an inspection of his pass
and WD AGO Form 65-1.

b. TOP SECRET documents will be safeguarded at all times in
such a way as to preclude access to them by unauthorized persons. BIGOT
officers and enlisted men will be isolated from personnel with lower
classifications while working on BIGOT papers so that it is impossible
to reach them without being challenged as to classification.

c. BIGOT and TOP SECRET maps will be kept covered when not
in actual use even in rooms restricted to classified personnel.

d. Any compromise of TOP SECRET or BIGOT information will be
reported through intelligence channels to the AC of S, G-2, First U.S.
Army without delay.

By command of the ARMY COMMANDER:

/s/ S. A. MACKENZIE
S. A. MACKENZIE
Captain, A.G.D.,
Asst. Adj. Gen.

28 March 1944

5th Rangers – Companies A – F, Medical and HQ –
Tighnabruaich, Scotland.
2nd Rangers – Companies A – F, Medical and HQ –
Bude, Cornwall.

The US Army kept a keen eye on any Axis powers change in weapons and in particular the development of its armoured vehicles. By August 1943 they had a fairly up-to-date description of each armoured vehicle in service with the German, Japanese and Italian armies.

The general doctrine employed was to educate the men on whichever types of vehicle they would encounter in their particular field of deployment. For example the Rangers were not shown photographs or silhouettes of Italian or Japanese tanks, but they were given a comprehensive training of the German military vehicles in operation at that time.

The basis behind it was to train the soldier until he was capable of recognising instantly the country of origin of the vehicles he was potentially going to come into contact with during combat. And if and when new adaptations or types came into the battlefield, he would be competent enough to know whose vehicles they were.

The training was devised to enable the soldier to recognise them in varying conditions such as terrain, weather and with varying degrees of light. Also when the vehicles were stationery, moving, viewed from the front, side, top, rear and at varying angles. Training was to be spaced out, as it was considered that it was a subject that could not be easily learnt in a few sessions. Therefore vehicle recognition was spread throughout the training schedule.

In addition to the shape and type of vehicles being studied, a working knowledge of the vulnerable areas of the vehicles was taught, along with their approximate speed, probable armament and a study of their deployment – certainly in terms of its potential future actions when spotted.

29 March 1944
5th Rangers – Companies A – F, Medical and HQ – Tighnabruaich, Scotland.
2nd Rangers – Companies A – F, Medical and HQ – Bude, Cornwall.

2nd Battalion Narrative History.

> *A Battalion exercise with the view of testing Supply activities and inter-Company cooperation under field conditions was held from 29-31 March. The Battalion marched approximately forty miles during this exercise, under full combat load, overcoming innumerable rear-guard actions by the detchment simulating "enemy" forces.*

Maurice Prince: *It was during our stay here that our Battalion issued out five day passes. We could go wherever we wished to go as long as we didn't become A.W.O.L. doing so. The boys took advantage of the break and took off. (The passes were issued so that an entire company would be on leave at one time.) Some went traveling over the land of England and some even went as far as Scotland. Many were attracted by the glamour of London, so they went there, while others, including myself, went to look up buddies of ours who happened to be stationed in the British Isles.*

There were a few men who never even left Bude. These few were content to just loaf around, relax and catch up on their sleep, and do a bit of sightseeing in the immediate vicinity, which was full of historic views.

We came back from our leave with new vigour and added energy. We tackled our training schedule with fresh life, and we clambered up and down the cliffs like a handful of monkeys.

---

30 March 1944
5th Rangers – Companies A – F, Medical and HQ – Tighnabruaich, Scotland.
2nd Rangers – Companies A – F, Medical and HQ – Bude, Cornwall.
Record of events: Alerted for departure.

On 30 March the US Army Photo Interpretation Unit released a series of maps showing enemy defences along the Omaha Sector of coastline. All of the Ranger objectives were included on these maps. The first one shows the Omaha Beach landing area with all known enemy positions from Pointe et Raz de la Percée (top left) and along the actual beach itself.

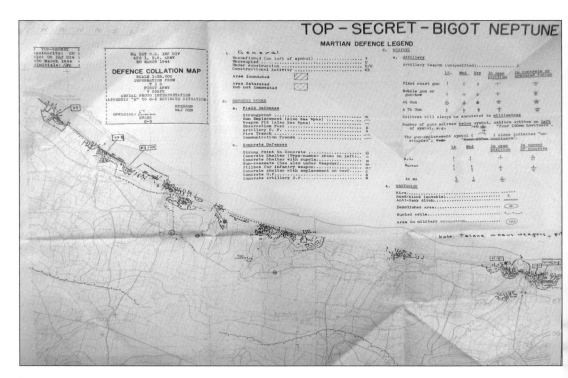

Close up of the Pointe et Raz de la Percée and the beach area.

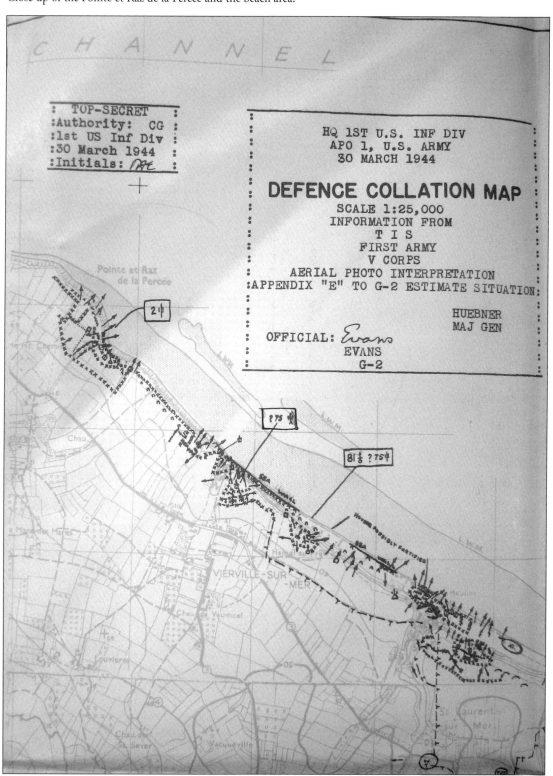

Right to left: The coastline along past Pointe du Hoc, the sluice gate, Grandcamp-les-Bains and Maisy – then along the coast to Isigny, covering the western end of the Omaha sector.

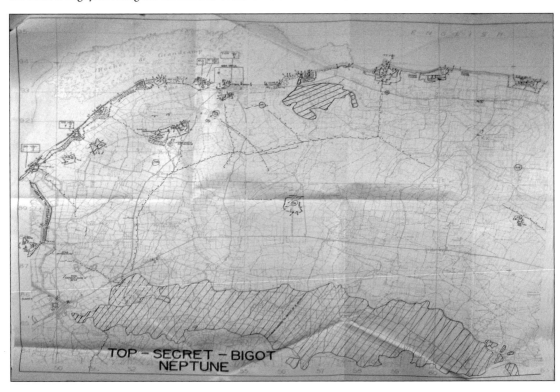

Enlarged area from the same map.

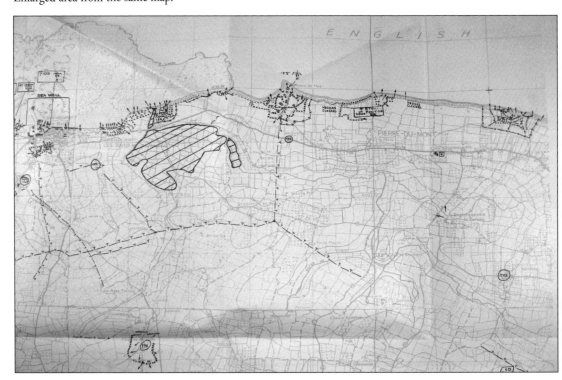

Blow up of the Grandcamp-les-Bains – Maisy Battery and Gefosse coastal area. The positions at Foucher's Farm (Target 16A) are marked as 4 x 75mm guns in open emplacements. It also indicates that the positions at Target 16 as abandoned. It is not clear if this refers to the original open emplacements in the field positions in front of Target 16, or if it refers to the casements which were under construction at Target 16. Originally Target 16 started life as 4 open gun pits in the fields and latterly behind them concrete casements were being built. The map key indicates a dotted square and a No.4 – which means that the 4 casements were thought to be under construction at the point when the intelligence was gathered.

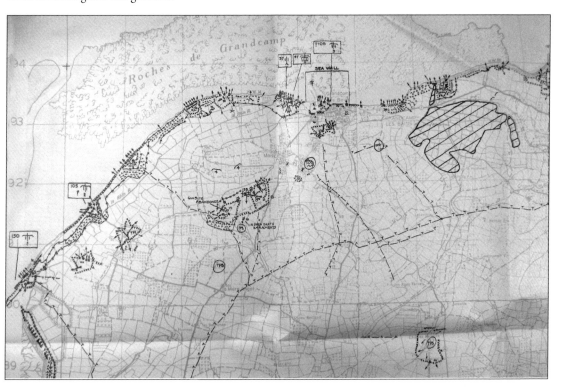

A photograph of the Giant Wurtzburg Radar and part of the Radar control building at Pointe et Raz de la Percée.

The last map in this series shows the Rangers' D-Day objective line inland just north of Osmanville. Note the three guns in field positions shown at this point.

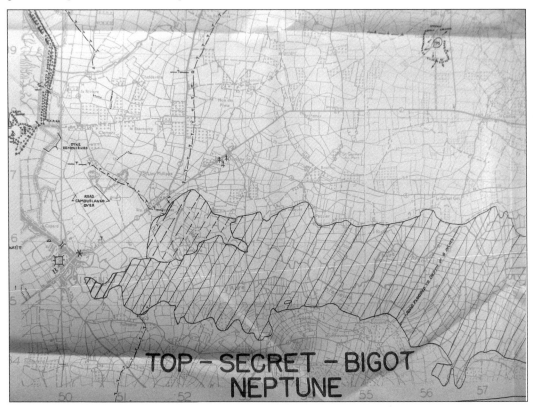

The key for the above plans.

31 March 1944
5th Rangers – Companies A – F, Medical and HQ – Tighnabruaich, Scotland.
2nd Rangers – Companies A – F, Medical and HQ – Bude, Cornwall.

The US Army issued a set of orders on Policing: *Upon the request of a British civil police officer, when in uniform or displaying other lawful sign of authority, each member of the command will show his identification card or identification tags, and promptly give his name, rank, and serial number.*

All members of the command will be informed immediately of the provisions of the paragraphs above. In all cases where British civil police authorities request information concerning disciplinary action taken against members of the command for alleged violations of UK laws, such request will be complied with when the final disciplinary action has been taken.

When a person subject to military discipline is in the custody of the British civil police, the appropriate base section commander will co-operate with such police in establishing such person's identity and, upon US jurisdiction being established, will take the offender into US military custody within forty-eight hours.

Arrests by Military Police. Arrests by the members of the US Army are to be limited to the members of the US forces in uniform and those not in uniform who at the time may be unmistakably identified. In no case will the search of, or entry into or upon, a private dwelling or vehicle be made unless the co-operation of the British civil police has first been secured.

In all cases where it is desired to arrest or detain persons not in uniform who are not unmistakably identified at the time as members of the US forces, assistance of the British civil police will be requested.

In the case of semi-public places such as hotels and places of amusement for which an entrance fee is charged, entry will be made only at the invitation or with the consent of the management, or in case of a commotion in which members of the US armed forces are believed to be involved.

Military police will resort to the use of firearms only when in imminent danger of death or great bodily harm, and then only when all other means of self-defence have failed.

Chapter 7

April 1944 – Operation Neptune and Ranger Training

1 April 1944

5th Rangers – Companies A – F, Medical and HQ –
Tighnabruaich, Scotland.
Major Max S. Schneider (Detached Service) assigned (Detached Service 2nd Ranger Inf. Battalion APG No.308 US Army) as Commanding Officer.

A Company 2nd Rangers – Bude, Cornwall.
No change. Alerted for departure.

B Company 2nd Rangers – Bude, Cornwall.
Pfc. Roush went from Duty to Detached Service to the Army Training Centre, Braunton Camp. North Devon. Alerted for departure.

C Company 2nd Rangers – Bude, Cornwall.
No change. Alerted for departure.

D Company 2nd Rangers – Bude, Cornwall.
S/Sgt. Kuhn went from Duty to Detached Service. Alerted for departure.

E Company 2nd Rangers – Bude, Cornwall.
No change. Alerted for departure.

F Company 2nd Rangers – Bude, Cornwall.
T/5 Jackson went from Duty to Detached Service, ATC Saunton Sands. North Devon.
Alerted for departure.

Medical Detachment 2nd Rangers – Bude, Cornwall.
Alerted for departure.

Headquarters Company 2nd Rangers – Bude, Cornwall.
Alerted for departure.

Maurice Prince: *The Ranger Btn celebrated its first anniversary while we were at Bude on April 1. A party was thrown for us to commemorate this occasion. It was a grand affair and a huge success as each company put on command performances on certain subjects and persons who have or have not been the butt of numerous jokes ever since the Battalion's activation.*

This was all done in a sportsmanlike manner, and in the spirit of good humour. Everything and everyone was ridiculed and satired from our Battalion Commander down to the lowly mess sergeant; no officers escaped a dirty dig, and no sergeant got away un-punned about. It was lots of fun and everyone had a swell time. Even our Colonel who was the butt of many a witty remark, gave out with mighty guffaw every time he was slandered. A swell sport and a swell leader was our Bn. CO., Lt. Colonel Rudder.

After these skits came a few speeches from various officers of the staff and of the companies. Nothing new or great was said, but all that was spoken came from the bottom of these men's hearts. It's no wonder we hold our officers in such high esteem.

It was here that our own Co., Capt. Lytle, gave birth to the name of the Ranger as a character. I plainly remember his famous words distinctly, I quote him, 'You fellows have about broken every rule and law that there are in the Army regulations manual, and not only that, when you ran out of rules, you made up your own and then went out and broke them. You men are a bunch of characters and it's these characters that I can't help but like and admire. Their manner, their willingness, and their fighting spirit. That is why I'm so proud to be amongst you and to be one of you.'

From then out, the Rangers became Characters with no two individuals the same. What a fine bunch of soldiers these characters were. I can't help myself when I think of their loyalty, courage, and gumption. It was just two days later that we were packed and prepared to move.

The area of Grandcamp-les-Bains harbour and to the bottom left the three sets of Maisy Batteries are indicated.

EMBARKATION.

a. Forces will embark from ports, hards or docks as follows:

FORCE "O" - PORTLAND AREA

Type Ship or Craft	Number	Port, Hard or Dock	Remarks
LSH	1	Great Western Railway Pier	Hq Ship of Naval Commander Force "O", CG, V Corps and CG, Army Force "O".
APA	7	Great Western Railway Pier	Note: Light vehicles will load at R-1, in craft from APA.
LSI(L)	2	Great Western Railway Pier	
LCI(L)	18	Great Western Railway Pier	
LCH	4	Great Western Railway Pier	
LST	22	R-2	
LCT(5&6)	110	40 at R-1 70 at R-3	12 LCTs will be used for Supplies and be loaded by First US Army.
LCT(A))	8)	R-3	To carry 2 M4 Tanks each plus
LCT(HE))	8)	R-3	a 3rd vehicle to be designated by Force Commander.
LCT(CB)	2	R-3	To be considered as LCTs.
LSI(S)	3	Great Western Railway Pier	For Ranger Bns
LSI(H)	3	Great Western Railway Pier	For Ranger Bns

FORCE "B" - PLYMOUTH WEST AND FALMOUTH

Type of Craft	Number	Port, Hard or Dock	Remarks
LSH	1*	Harvey's Wharf, Plymouth	*To be designated by US Navy. Plymouth West
LCT	60	40 TP-3 20 Ps	Plymouth West

Embarkation locations were issued and the Rangers were to embark from the Great Western Railway Pier in Weymouth.

UNCLASSIFIED   - NEPTUNE - BIGOT

HEADQUARTERS V CORPS

Annex No. 1
in 23 pages
Page No. 3.
1 April 1944.

G-2 ESTIMATE OF THE ENEMY
SITUATION - OPERATION "NEPTUNE".

DECLASSIFIED

I. SUMMARY OF THE ENEMY SITUATION.

1. STATIC DIVISIONS IN THE ASSAULT AREA.

a. 716th Infantry Division, located in the ISIGNY - CAEN area.
(1) Defensive division, thought to be composed of three infantry regiments, two artillery battalions or possibly three, and other ancillary units. A battalion of Russian troops, located at CAEN, is believed to belong to this division, and probably forms a part of the Third Infantry Regiment.
(2) Quality of troops reported as poor, with at least 30% foreigners, mostly Poles.
(3) Division is disposed on a 50-mile front, from the mouth of the ORNE River (East of CAEN), to the mouth of the DOUVE River, but not including CARENTAN.
(4) One RCT, covering a 21-mile front, is in the CAEN - RYES area (east of the U.S. assault area). The other RCT covers a 29-mile front from BAYEUX to the mouth of the DOUVE River; this RCT (which is in the U.S. assault area) has battalions disposed as follows:
(a) A battalion (with CP at ISIGNY) in the area around the mouth of the DOUVE River.
(b) A battalion (with CP thought to be East of GRANDCAMP) holding the 21-mile coastal front between LONGUES and a point 4,000 yards west of GRANDCAMP. (This battalion is holding approximately the same frontage as the entire RCT on its east flank).
(c) The third battalion (with CP in BAYEUX) is probably the reserve battalion of the regiment, and is thought to be located in the vicinity of BAYEUX.
(5) The location of the reserve RCT is unknown, but in addition to the battalion at CAEN, Russians (Georgians) in German uniform have been observed in TREVIERES. It is possible that the reserve RCT is distributed throughout this general area.
(6) Artillery battalions, antiaircraft units, infantry gun companies, heavy weapons companies, and other supporting elements of this division are almost completely integrated into the small strongpoints along the fifty-mile division coastal sector.

b. 709th Infantry Division, covering the CHERBOURG Peninsula.
(1) Defensive division, composed of three infantry regiments, and two or three battalions of light artillery.
(2) Two regiments have a high proportion of non-Germans, and the third, with the exception of the officers and non-coms, is composed of Georgians.
(3) Quality of troops believed to be low; the Georgian troops are most certainly of low quality. The morale of the German element has frequently been reported to be low.
(4) Disposed with all three regiments holding coastal sectors, one on the east side of the peninsula and about a third of the north side, another regiment covering the remainder of the north side, and at last reports the Georgian regiment covering the west side of the peninsula. There is a possibility that the 243rd Infantry Division, with headquarters at LA HAYE DU PUITS, is now holding part of the western coastal sector.

c. 711th Infantry Division, holding a sector beginning just east of CAEN, and extending eastward to the SEINE River.
(1) Defensive division, composed of two infantry regimental combat teams; the addition of Russian troops to this division has recently been reported, which may mean that the organization of the division has expanded.
(2) Quality of troops considered as low; is thought to consist of a German cadre, with a considerable proportion of foreigners, including Russians, Flemings, and Dutch.

UNCLASSIFIED   NEPTUNE BIGOT

-3-

V Corps produced a summary of the German military forces in their area of assault.

- NEPTUNE - BIGOT

Annex No. 1
in 29 pages
Page No. 4.

(3) Three of the four forward battalions of this division are thought to be covering the 13-mile coastal front West of TROUVILLE; assuming that each of the forward regiments has a battalion in reserve, this would mean that one battalion is holding the coastal front of approximately 17 miles between TROUVILLE and the SEINE. Since some protection is afforded this battalion by the peninsula to its North, with the defenses of LE HAVRE, this is probable.

d. 243rd Infantry Division, located on the CHERBOURG Peninsula with headquarters at LA HAYE DE PUITS. Identification not definitely confirmed; may be the 245th Infantry Division.
(1) Defensive division, thought to be composed of three regimental combat teams.
(2) Has only recently been identified in the area, and little is known concerning combat value or dispositions.
(3) May be holding a portion of the West coast of the CHERBOURG Peninsula. There is a possibility that it may be employed as a local reserve.

2. MINOR GROUND FORCE ELEMENTS.

a. A cavalry regimental headquarters has been reported at COUTANCES, some 34 miles from the assault area; it is therefore probable that a regiment or less of cavalry is located in this area.

b. A battalion of the 193rd Local Defense Regiment is at CAEN, probably providing local security for the 716th Division CP at that place, and a battalion of the same regiment at ST. LO, probably has a similar mission to protect the LXXXIV Corps CP there.

3. ENEMY DEFENSES IN ASSAULT AREA.

a. General. The general scheme of hostile defenses in the assault area is shown on Map 2. It will be noted that practically all of the organized defenses are either on the beach or are on the plateau immediately behind the beach. There is no evidence that any definite defensive lines in the way of pillboxes and infantry positions have been constructed or are under construction inland from the coast.

b. Artillery.
(1) The location of all hostile field artillery, infantry guns, antitank guns and mortars within the assault area or adjacent thereto and the effective fields of fire of each battery or single piece are shown on Map No. 3. The following is a summary of the weapons in this area:

Artillery: 2 - 75-mm guns or howitzers, 200 yds SE of PORT EN BESSIN.
2 - Light coast guns, PORT EN BESSIN.
1 - 75-mm gun or howitzer, PORT EN BESSIN.
2 - Medium guns or howitzers, PORT EN BESSIN.
6 - 155-mm coast guns, POINTE DU HOE.
3 - 105-mm howitzers, GRANDCAMP.
4 - 155-mm howitzers, in fixed positions, 1,750 yds SW of GRANDCAMP.
2 - 105-mm howitzers, 5,000 yds W of GRANDCAMP.
1 - 150-mm gun or howitzer, 7,000 yds N of ISIGNY.

Infantry: 1 - 80-mm mortar, PORT EN BESSIN.
3 - Infantry guns, 1,500 yds N of COLLEVILLE.
1 - 75-mm infantry gun, VIERVILLE.
1 - 81-mm mortar, VIERVILLE.
2 - Infantry guns, POINTE ET RAZ DE LA PERCEE.
1 - Infantry gun, GRANDCAMP.

A.tank: 1 - 47-mm gun, PORT EN BESSIN.
1 - 75-mm gun, VIERVILLE.
1 - 47-mm gun, GRANDCAMP.

- NEPTUNE - BIGOT

NEPTUNE - BIGOT

Annex No. 1
Page No.

1 - 37-mm gun, GRANDCAMP.
1 - Light gun, 7,000 yds N of ISIGNY.
2 - Light guns, 1,000 yds NW of ISIGNY.
    (2) New emplacements for artillery have recently been located at MONTIGNY (623887), ST. PIERRE-DU-MONT (598934), and at (530913), Southwest of MAISY. All of these positions were first discovered on air cover of March 1944, and all appear to be for four-gun batteries. It is possible that the new position Southwest of MAISY is for the 75-mm battery recently removed from emplacements 500 yards Northwest of this position.

    c. Antiaircraft Artillery. The disposition of antiaircraft artillery weapons is shown on Map No. 4. Since all of these weapons are probably capable of being used against surface targets, the effective ground range for each battery or individual gun is indicated on the map. The following is a tabulation of the antiaircraft weapons in the assault area:
        2 - Machine guns, along coast E of PORT EN BESSIN.
        1 - Machine gun, PORT EN BESSIN.
        1 - Machine gun, on coast N of COLLEVILLE.
        2 - Machine guns, on coast NE of ST. LAURENT.
        1 - Machine gun, LES MOULINS.
        2 - Machine guns, HAMEL AU PRETRE.
        3 - Light guns, at Radar Station (623937).
        4 - Light guns, at the 155-mm btry at PTE DU HOE.
        2 - Machine guns, GRANDCAMP.
        3 - Light guns, at Arty position SW of GRANDCAMP.
        3 - Light guns, 3 miles S of ISIGNY (unconfirmed).
        2 - Light machine guns, at (481846), (unconfirmed).
        8 to 12 - Mobile 88-mm dual purpose guns in vicinity of HALT (unconfirmed).
        4 - Heavy guns, 8 miles South of TREVIERES, (unconfirmed).
        Unknown number of guns 2½ miles South of TREVIERES.

    d. Field Fortifications. (1) For detailed information as to the location of entrenchments, pillboxes, wire entanglements and mine fields, see TIS Map 1/12,500, Defense Overprint (Sheets 3 - 10 incl.).
        (2) There are a total of eleven entrenched positions covering Beach 46. These positions are small, in most cases accomodating less than a platoon, and are usually placed on elevated points covering corridors and exits from the beach. Nine of these positions are now occupied by units of squad strength or less and two are occupied by units not larger than a platoon. They are usually prepared for all around defense and with ample communicating trenches to the fire trenches on front and flanks. They are protected by wire entanglements and in some cases land mines. Most of them contain concrete pillboxes and concrete shelters within their limits. Houses and hedges interfering with fields of fire have been removed.
        (3) There are eighteen concrete pillboxes covering Beach 46. Eight of these are located on the flat area between the beach and the plateau and are apparently sited so as to permit bands of grazing fire on the beach. The remaining ten pillboxes are located on the first high ground in rear of the beach and are sited to deliver plunging fire on the beach, on craft approaching the beach, and to cover corridors leading inland from the beach. Many of the houses on the beach are reported to be fortified with concrete pillboxes. There are eleven pillboxes in the vicinity of PORT-EN-BESSIN. There are three (possibly four) covering the beach east of GRANDCAMP, three on the beach at GRANDCAMP and six along the coast from GRANDCAMP to PTE DU GROWN. Some of these pillboxes are probably old construction with walls 3 feet thick; those of more recent construction have walls of 6' 6" thickness.
        (4) There are no continuous bands of wire entanglements on or in rear of the major portion of Beach 46. There is a continuous band tending across the entrance to the corridor at VIERVILLE-SUR-MER and the extending Westward along the escarpment to POINTE EN RAZ DE LA PERCE. the exception of the strong-point Northeast of CABOURG (69-88), all strong-points in rear of the beach are completely surrounded by wire, usually single bands. The excepted strong-point is protected by a single band on flanks

NEPTUNE - BIGOT

NEPTUNE - BIGOT

and near. Strong-points in the vicinity of PORT-EN-BESSIN and in the GRAND-CAMP area are completely surrounded with wire. Beginning just West of GRAND-CAMP a continuous band (double along the coast Northwest of GEFOSSE-FONTENAI) extends along the coast as far as PTE DU GROWN. The artillery positions Southwest of MAISY are surrounded by double bands. Some of these bands are reported to be electrified.

(5) From the evidence available, Beach 46 area is only lightly mined. Between COLLEVILLE SUR MER and LES MOULINS no mines have been reported; however, a few have been reported and confirmed from airplane photographs in rear of the strong-points North of COLLEVILLE-SUR-MER. Beginning at LES MOULINS, an almost continuous belt has been reported to extend Westward for approximately 3,000 yards, with a small break at the corridor exit North of VIERVILLE; however, this report has not been confirmed by airplane photographs. The strong-points East and West of PORT EN BESSIN are strongly protected with mines. Beginning at PTE DU HOE, there is an almost continuous belt extending to the West along the coast as far as ST. CLEMENT (near ISIGNY), with the heaviest belts in the vicinity of the sluice East of GRANDCAMP and along the coast Northwest of FONTENAY and a gap of 2,000 yards centered on the town of GRANDCAMP-LES-BAINS. The 75-mm artillery position Southwest of MAISY is well protected on the Western flank.

e. Obstacles. (1) For the location of obstacles, in the assault area, see Map No. 5.

(2) Information available at the present time indicates that there are no underwater obstacles along the principal part of Beach 46. Recent photo coverage has indicated that the enemy is placing underwater obstacles along many beaches in the West, however, and February 1944 coverage indicates newly placed underwater obstacles in the BERNIERES--COURSEULLES beach area, about 17 miles East of Beach 46. More recent information has indicated that these obstacles in some cases are breaking up and becoming displaced, probably due to the action of the surf against them. As a general rule, underwater obstacles constructed on other beaches in the OVERLORD area have been placed some 75 to 150 yards from the high water line. If so placed on Beach 46, they would be exposed until about three hours before high water.

(3) The two sandbars off the beach northwest of VIERVILLE-SUR-MER are covered by 24 feet of water at high tide and by about one or two feet of water at lowest tide. There are three runnels extending parallel to the beach for its entire length. At low tide these runnels are exposed and are filled with water varying in depth from 9" in the upper one to 2' 6" in the lower.

(4) There is a strip of shingle, about 15 yards wide, extending along the entire beach near the high water mark. It is composed of stone about 2" in diameter and forms a ridge with a gradient on the lower side of 1/8 to 1/10.

(5) A sea wall 8 feet in height extends from the exit at 649917 to a point 500 yards to the Southeast at 654914. At the latter point there is a break of 200 yards and then a wall 2 feet six inches high (reduced to this height by drifting sands) extending 2,000 yards to the Southeast to 673903. A series of few wooden groynes extend at right angles to the sea wall between 664912 - 661909.

(6) The following miscellaneous obstacles are indicated on Map No. 5.

PORT EN BESSIN Area: 7 fixed road blocks, 1 movable road block at (753879).
Fixed road block at (753872).
Small antitank wall at (755879).

Beach 46 Area: Movable road block at (723886).
Movable road block at (698889).
Antitank ditch at (680899).
Wall road block, (677900) to (676899), with 12 ft gap; road block is 8 ft high and 6 ft thick.

NEPTUNE - BIGOT

NEPTUNE – BIGOT

	3 Movable road blocks at (664906), of wire, probably knife rests. Antitank ditch at (665906).
VIERVILLE Area:	Seawall extends from (662909) to (658911) and (655913) to (648917). Tank trap reported on road at (648917); trench 5 ft 6 in wide covered with tarpaulin. Round-topped wall 5 ft thick and 7 ft high diagonally across road in two staggered 18 ft sections at (648917); gap 3 ft wide reported.
POINTE DU HOE:	Post obstructions protecting Arty position on SE side at (587936).
GRANDCAMP Area:	Sluice at (563936) forms antitank wall. Wall blocking road at (555933). Vertical masonry seawall 6 ft high extends from (551933) to (546933) with gap at (548933). Seawall 6 ft high extends West of the harbor, (544933) to (543934) with gap at (543932); and (543933) to (543934). Walls 10 ft 6 in thick block all exits from sea-front (5493). Steel obstacle on West side of harbor, part Element "C" and part hedgehog. Movable roadblocks on almost all roads S and W of GRANDCAMP.

(7) East of TREVIERES the AURE River constitutes a minor obstacle. Its average width in this area is 15 - 20 feet, its maximum depth in summer is 2' 6", and its banks are 2 - 3 feet high. Its bottom is silt, with gravel in some places. It is crossed by several bridges and fords. West of TREVIERES the AURE constitutes a considerable obstacle, especially so since its valley is now flooded to a depth of about three feet and the highway North of DOUET is awash for a distance of 600 yards. There is also a flooded area East of GRANDCAMP-LES-BAINS with all roads covered except Highway No. G.C. 32 (GRAND-CAMP- ARROMANCHES).

(8) Although not listed as obstacles, the hindering effects of hedges and walls should not be overlooked. The cultivated fields which lie inland from the coastal cliffs are bordered by low hedges and earth banks. In the more fertile lowland these banks are several feet high and are frequently crowned with beech or hawthorn hedges. Almost all roads leading from Beach 46 are bordered by low tree-hedges and banks and in some places stone walls. These hedges and banks are fairly old and probably sufficiently resistant to constitute definite obstacles to deployment and cross-country movement of motor vehicles and tanks.

4. MOBILE RESERVES.

a. There are 56 divisions in France and the Low Countries. Of these 42 are defensive divisions and 14 are offensive divisions. Twenty-six of the defensive divisions are holding coastal sectors and, since they are not provided with transportation and are definitely tied down to coastal defenses, these divisions do not constitute mobile reserves for early employment against an invading force. The other defensive divisions are either in the interior of France or are unlocated.

b. Divisions in reserve are not held centrally, but disposed at fairly regular intervals some twenty miles inland from the coast, around centers of communications. During the past few weeks, several infantry divisions have been identified immediately behind static coastal divisions along the ENGLISH CHANNEL; these include three static divisions in the CALAIS

UNCLASSIFIED   NEPTUNE - BIGOT

NEPTUNE – BIGOT

Annex No. 1
in 2? pages
Page No. 8.

DIEPPE area, a static division and an unidentified division (believed offensive infantry) in the CHERBOURG – ST. LO. area, and an offensive infantry division on the BREST Peninsula. It may be expected that in an emergency the two divisions nearest the area assaulted will move toward it at once, preferably by road. Every effort will be made to bring at least one division into counterattack on the afternoon of the day of the assault.

c. Of the offensive divisions in the West, nine are located in the Interior within 350 miles of the assault area and hence may be used against the invading forces within the first three or four days. Two others, unlocated, may also be used, but their availability is extremely doubtful; a mobile division on the Mediterranean Coast and an offensive division holding the LORIENT coastal sector are not considered as available during the early stages of the attack. The following is an estimate of the optimum time, giving no consideration to air or resistance-group action, for these divisions to be committed to action against V Corps:

Division	Location	Distance
1. SS Pz Div FRUNDSBERG	LISIEUX	53 miles; 9 hours (by highway)
2. SS Pz Gr Div GOETZ VON BERLICHINGEN	ALENCON	85 miles; 11 hours (by highway)
3. 352nd Inf Div	ST. LO	28 miles; 25 hours (foot movement)
4. 21st Pz Div	PARIS	160 miles; 15 hours (by highway) or 40 hours (by rail)
5. SS Pz Div DAS REICH	BORDEAUX	390 miles; 46 hours (by rail)
6. 353rd Inf Div	HUELGOAT	212 miles; 46 hours (by rail with highway movement to railhead)
7. 2nd Pz Div (Identification unconfirmed)	AMIENS	178 miles; 43 hours (by rail)
8. SS Pz Div HITLER JUGEND	TURNHOUT	573 miles; 69 hours (by rail)
9. 3rd Parachute Div	RHEIMS	245 miles; D plus 1 (by air)

d. Due to limited rail net and the small number of detraining stations near the assault area, it is estimated that only two full-strength divisions can be brought into the area in any 24-hour period; hence the extra time indicated for some of the divisions listed above.

e. In addition to the divisions listed above, there are three Panzer Training Divisions in the West. Although listed as divisions, the maximum force that they could muster is believed to be less than a battalion of tanks, and probably not more than four to six battalions of infantry. Probably not more than about one-third of each division could move by its own organic transportation. These divisions are as follows:

Division	Location	Distance
1. 155th Pz Training Div	FOUGERES	85 miles; 11 hours (by highway)
2. 179th Pz Training Div	RENNES	109 miles; 12 hours (by highway)
3. 273rd Pz Training Div	ANGOULEME	309 miles; 42 hours (by rail)

f. For detailed information on the movement of mobile reserves into the assault area, see Appendix I – Table of Reinforcements.

g. The 3rd Parachute Division has been reported in the vicinity of MELUN, South of PARIS. It is estimated that sufficient lift can be assembled to drop 2,400 men at one time, but unless advance warning is given this lift could not be assembled earlier than D plus 1. The time from embarkation fields to dropping areas is negligible.

h. The following is an estimate of the minimum time required to move divisions from other theatres to the U.S. assault area.

Northern Italy – D plus 5
Russia   – D plus 10
Norway   – D plus 8
Balkans   – D plus 10

– BIGOT – NEPTUNE

UNCLASSIFIED

██████ – NEPTUNE – BIGOT

i. Although there is a considerable amount of coast artillery (both Army and Navy) in the LE HAVRE and CHERBOURG areas, there is only one battery in the V Corps sector of the assault area. This consists of 6 – 155-mm guns located at PTE DU HOE, 2½ miles east of GRANDCAMP. Its range of 22,000 yards extends well across the entire V Corps assault area.

5. AIR STRENGTH.

a. Estimated strength of the German Air Force on the Western Front in aircraft of combat units, as reported on 10 March 1944, was as follows:

	France West of the SEINE	Eastern France and Belgium	Holland	Northwest Germany	Total
Long Range Bombers	60	150	0	210	420
Dive Bombers	0	0	0	0	0
Fighter Bombers	0	30	0	0	30
Single Engine Fighters (day)	60	60	80	390	590
Single Engine Fighters (night)	10	0	0	130	140
Twin Engine Fighters (day)	30	0	0	170	200
Twin Engine Fighters (night)	0	110	110	330	550
Long Range Reconnaissance	70	0	0	0	70
Tactical Reconnaissance	10	0	0	0	10
Coastal	10	0	0	0	10
Total	250	350	190	1230	2020

b. All fighters may be converted into fighter-bombers and when so converted can carry a 500-lb. bomb load. It may be expected that at least some of the fighters listed above will be converted prior to D-day.

6. ENEMY NAVAL FORCES. The major units of the German Navy are located in Baltic or Norwegian waters, but during recent weeks an average of five destroyers, 40 to 45 motor torpedo boats, 25 submarines and 8 to 10 TB's have been operating in the BAY OF BISCAY and ENGLISH CHANNEL waters. No submarines have been sited in the ENGLISH CHANNEL for a number of weeks.

7. EFFICIENCY.

a. The morale of coast defense divisions, of which the 709th, 711th and 716th are typical, is not good. They contain a good 25% of non-Germans and a further 50% of men who in varying degrees are elderly, juvenile, tired or unfit. In view of the length of time they have been at it, training for their static defense roles should be reasonably good. Their equipment is generally second rate, motor transport is non-existant, and supporting elements and services are very inadequate. It is estimated that the value for war of these defensive divisions ("700", "300 static", Training and GAF Field) averages not more than 50% of that of a first class infantry division, even in static coast defense, and not more than 25% in open warfare.

b. The morale of troops in offensive divisions is usually much better than that of troops in static divisions. Their value for war will depend upon their strength, the status of their equipment, and the length of time they have been in process of reformation. Heretofore, they have rarely remained long in the West after they have reached full efficiency, but present indications are that this policy is being changed and that at least some fully trained divisions, with full fighting efficiency, will be kept in mobile reserve behind the Channel Coast.

17. EFFECT OF TERRAIN ON ENEMY.

a. The rapid rise and fall of the tide and the strong tidal current make it difficult for the enemy to maintain underwater obstacles on Beach 46. Furthermore, the width of the beach at low tide presents difficulties in the siting of underwater obstacles to prevent landing at various stages of the tide. The shingle strip along Beach 46 is a definite obstacle to movement of motor transport and tanks.

b. The concave shape of Beach 46 permits grazing fire by flat trajectory weapons sited anywhere along the beach or on the flat strip directly to the rear.

c. (1) The rapid rise of the terrain directly behind the beach favors plunging fire by flat trajectory weapons placed on the steep slope in rear of the beach or on the forward border of the plateau. On the other hand, flat trajectory weapons to be used for the defense of the beach will have to be placed well forward. If placed further in the interior, troops on the narrow land strip bordering the beach will have protection from the fire of these weapons.

(2) The enemy will have difficulty in covering the winding corridors and narrow draws leading from the beach with effective flat trajectory fire. Unless all of these are effectively covered, our forces will be able to find protection in them from flat trajectory weapons and to infiltrate through them to the rear of pillboxes on the beach.

(3) Due to the steepness of the slope directly in rear of the beach West of LE RUQUET River (665905), tanks accompanying troops in the assault will have to use the two corridors in this sector as exits from the beach. Since these corridors are narrow and are provided with concrete road blocks, enemy tank defense in this sector is greatly facilitated.

(4) The terrain in rear of the beach permits the employment of howitzer or mortar fire from defiladed positions. Excellent observation is afforded the enemy for the control of this fire. Houses and hedges that interfere with observation generally have been removed.

d. (1) After withdrawal from the first positions in rear of the beach, the next high ground available to the enemy for a line of defense will be the ridge generally about 2,000 yards in rear of the beach, using the small villages on the forward slope as fortified localities. Except for the hindering effects of intervening hedges, excellent fields of fire for flat trajectory weapons will be afforded from these positions.

(2) Until such time as the enemy has been driven from this high ground, the valley of the AURE and its tributaries will afford some defilade for the movement of mobile troops to positions from which counterattacks may be launched.

(3) The defense of the GRANDCAMP - ISIGNY area by enemy forces will be facilitated by basing a defensive line on the flooded area 1½ miles to the east of GRANDCAMP.

e. (1) After withdrawal from the principal ridge North of the AURE, the next position suitable to the enemy for prolonged defense is the ridge running East-South-East of TREVIERES and in view of the flooded condition of the lower AURE, withdrawal by the hostile main force will have to be made East of TREVIERES. For those forces caught in the ISIGNY - GRANDCAMP area, it will have to be made through the ISIGNY corridor. The enemy can cause some delay to our forces by blowing all bridges across the AURE and it may be expected that he will do this.

- NEPTUNE - BIGOT

- NEPTUNE - BIGOT

Annex No. 1
in **21** pages
Page No. 14.

(2) During this phase of the operation the only suitable terrain available to the enemy for armored operations will be in the area between TREVIERES and BAYEUX and even in this area armored deployment will be difficult due to narrow sunken roads and stout tree hedges. Likewise, the enemy will be protected from our armor along the section of his line based on the flooded AURE Valley.

f. (1) Having been driven from the TREVIERES Ridge, the enemy can pivot his line on the flooded AURE Valley and form a defensive line on the first ridges behind LA TORTONNE River. From this position he will have fair observation and will still be able to use the AURE Valley for the protection of his left.

(2) During this phase of the operation, the corridor on the East formed by the Valley of the DROME will be available to the enemy for the launching of counterattacks against our left flank. On the Western flank the enemy will be protected by the River VIRE and its marshy lowlands.

g. When the enemy is driven from the AURE River - LA TORTONNE line, a good defensive line will be afforded by the dominating LISON - BAYNES - FORE DE CERISY Ridge. Although the Eastern flank is broken by the spreading corridors of the River DROME and several small corridors lead well into the forward slopes, this position dominates the valleys to the North, its Western flank is fairly secure, and its front and flanks are not suitable for extensive tank attacks.

h. The main rail line running parallel to the coast from BAYEUX to CARENTAN is double track, but it is so close to the initial assault area that it is unlikely that this line will be used for the detrainment of mobile reserves. The next line, which also runs parallel to the coast between FOLLIGNY-VIRE-FIERS, is 30 miles away and involves at least a 2-hour motor movement or a forced march of some 15 - 20 hours on foot to reach the assault area. The main rail lines into the area are sufficient for the transport and detrainment of only two full strength divisions in a period of 24 hours.

i. The road net leading into the area is sufficient to carry all available reserves which may be brought into the area either by rail or motor. Since the principal through routes center on BAYEUX in the East and ISIGNY in the West, major motor movements may be expected to come into the assault area through or near these points. Minor roads leading into the assault area are narrow, frequently sunken, and usually lined with strong hedges. Deployment from these roads will be difficult for motors and tanks.

j. The telephone and cable net is ample to permit prompt warning and the issuance of orders to mobile reserves.

IV. CONCLUSIONS.

18. ENEMY CAPABILITIES. In operations against this Corps prior to and during the initial stages of the assault the enemy has the following capabilities:

a. Limited air action against concentration and embarkation areas and possibly strong action against convoys and landing troops.

b. Limited submarine and motor torpedo boat action against convoys.

c. Reinforcement of existing defenses in the V Corps assault area prior to D-day.

d. Rigid defense of the beaches with static troops in existing prepared defenses.

e. Counterattacks with reserve elements of coastal divisions or with mobile reserves either piecemeal or coordinated.

f. Defense in successive positions in rear of the landing area.

g. Attack with chemicals.

- NEPTUNE - BIGOT

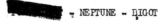

19. DISCUSSION.

a. In recent months the German Air Force has shown very little inclination to engage Allied Forces beyond the coastal frontier or to make other than tip-and-run raids on the United Kingdom. The bomber strength of the German Air Force is small and its fighter strength, due to continual bombing of coastal bases has withdrawn to considerable extent into the interior. On the other hand, when it can fight over its own territory or the defense of a vital area is involved, it has fought strongly and has been willing to sacrifice large numbers of planes. The German Air Force is capable of making 1,500 sorties per day in the Channel area and although this will largely be defensive (fighter operations), the employment of available bombers and fighter bombers (including converted fighters) may be expected. Although enemy air attacks against the United Kingdom have been increasing in recent weeks, it is not likely that heavy commitments will be made against strongly protected concentration and embarkation areas, but when the cross-channel movement is detected the German Air Force may be expected to employ its maximum strength against convoys and against the actual landing operations.

b. German naval strength in the Channel and in Bay of Biscay waters is limited to E-boats, TB's, submarines and destroyers. The operation of submarines in the Channel has become so dangerous that apparently none has operated in these waters in recent months and German destroyers have not been inclined to operate in waters frequented by strong Allied naval units. E-boats and TB's have been fairly active and may be expected to exert their maximum efforts against invasion convoys.

c. The number of German divisions in the West has increased from forty to fifty-six in the past five months, and although Western France is still being used for the organization of new divisions and reorganization of those returning from other fronts, such divisions are remaining in the West longer than heretofore. The Atlantic coastline of some 1,600 miles is still held by only twenty-three divisions, or an average of almost seventy miles per division. The 716th Division is defending a 53 mile front, of which 20 miles of the coastal defenses in the V Corps assault area is being held by a single battalion. This is not much for a strong coastal defense and there are only nine defensive divisions in rear coastal sectors available for use to reinforce coastal sectors. Defensive divisions cannot be moved from other theaters or from other sectors of the invasion coast without weakening the defense in those areas. If the enemy gets advance information of the location of the assault area he may be expected greatly to strengthen the defenses in this area or if he is able to draw definite conclusions as to the general area of the assault he may feel justified in withdrawing some strength from other areas and in reinforcing the defenses along the channel coast. In view of the many indications that will be available to the enemy as to the general zone of the invasion, some strengthening of defenses in the V Corps assault area may be expected prior to D-day.

d. (1) The German plan of defense contemplates maximum effort at the beach. The coast defense line is not in great depth; in the V Corps assault area there is no evidence of the construction of any pillboxes or the organization of any ground in rear of the beach crust. Labor is not available to construct strong defense lines in the interior and besides it would be difficult to decide before the battle develops where to place them. Hence, the German command considers it better to expend their energy and material on strengthening the one really good defense line available to them - the coast. In the V Corps assault area the defending battalion is disposed with three rifle companies holding coastal sectors and with the fourth company (heavy weapons) completely broken up and integrated into forward combat groups of the rifle companies. Artillery units are similarly disposed and the weapons of both infantry and artillery units are positioned to bring maximum frontal and enfilading fire on the beaches at the moment which is most critical for

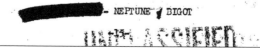

- NEPTUNE BIGOT

- NEPTUNE - BIGOT

the attack i.e., at the instant of landing. Local reserves in rear of
Beach 46 consist of one infantry battalion at BAYEUX and perhaps part of a
Georgian regiment which is believed to be the reserve for the whole 50-mile
divisional front. About one-third of the German forces along the channel
coast are mobile and these are well disposed behind the coastal crust for
rapid concentration at any threatened point. All of these things indicate
that the enemy intends to defend the coast line as strongly as possible in
an effort to hold the attackers until mobile reserves can arrive.
        (2)   The 716th Division has two regiments forward and probably
has one (Georgian) in reserve. Each of the forward regiments has a battalion
in reserve. Two battalions of light artillery and one medium are disposed in
coastal positions in the divisional sector. Thus, in the sector held by the
716th Division, two battalions and one regiment are available as local reserves
and these reserves must suffice until the arrival of elements of mobile divisions. Since one of these battalions is disposed in rear of beach defenses in
the British sector, it will not be available for employment against V Corps
troops. It is estimated that the battalion at BAYEUX can be brought into
action against the Eastern flank of the V Corps assault by H plus 2 and the
Georgian regiment, the location of which is not definitely known, not earlier
than H plus 3. It is not likely that reserve elements of other coastal divisions will be employed against V Corps.

        e.   (1)   As stated above the German plan of defense contemplates
holding the attacker at the beach until mobile reserves can arrive. At the
present time about one-third of the identified divisions on the Western Front
are either of the panzer or panzergrenadier type and the majority of these are
located behind the channel coast. In recent months there has been no tendency
to reduce the number of these mobile divisions or to place them in static
positions on the coast. As indications of invasion become more evident to the
enemy the German High Command will undoubtedly try to increase the number of
these mobile reserves. However, this will be difficult because all available
offensive divisions are engaged elsewhere and his defensive divisions are so
lacking in mobility and supporting elements that their employment in mobile
operations is impossible without radical reorganization.
        (2)   In his defense plans, the enemy has given primary con-
sideration to the defense of ports. Surveying the situation from this viewpoint, it might be expected that he will concentrate his efforts on the attack
of forces nearest to the ports of CHERBOURG and LE HAVRE. On the other hand,
due to the restricted nature of the terrain in the CHERBOURG area, he will
probably commit the major portion of his panzer and panzergrenadier strength
in the BAYEUX - CAEN area. Since the front in the V Corps sector (TREVIERES
to BAYEUX) favorable for panzer and panzergrenadier operations is small, it
may be expected that the enemy will employ only a small proportion of his
mobile reserves against this Corps. Nevertheless, extra precautions should be
taken to protect the left flank of V Corps against panzer and panzergrenadier
penetrations.
        (3)   In view of his desire to limit the penetration of the
hostile forces and the difficulties to be expected in their rapid deployment,
initially the enemy will undoubtedly commit his panzer and panzergrenadier
combat teams as they arrive. As other elements appear on the scene and time
becomes available for regrouping, coordinated attacks will be the general rule.

        f.   It has already been stated that the 716th Division is defending
a 53-mile front, and that its reserve regiment is of relatively low combat
value. Therefore, a major counterattack will not be possible until the
arrival of mobile forces which are at least nine hours away. Since these
mobile forces cannot arrive until the evening of D-day, and are not likely to
stage a coordinated counterattack until the morning of D plus 1 (they will
probably not begin movement to the area until some indication is received as
to the location of the main assault), the defending forces in the coastal
sector will most likely seek to prevent our establishment and expansion of a
beachhead by defense in successive positions. If counterattacks by initial
mobile reserves do not succeed in driving our forces from the beachhead,

- NEPTUNE - BIGOT

 - NEPTUNE - BIGOT

Annex No. 1.
in 23 pages.
Page No. 17.

further defensive operations in successive positions will undoubtedly be under-taken in order to hold our forces until additional mobile reserves can be brought up.

g. In the early years of the war, the enemy manufactured and stored large quantities of toxic chemicals on the channel coast. In recent months there has been no evidence from the West that the enemy intends to resort to chemical warfare. If he ever intends to use toxic chemicals, his best oppor-tunity will be in the early phases of our invasion. On the other hand, the enemy is poorly equipped to wage large-scale gas warfare and he must know that the capabilities of the Allies in this respect are far greater than his own. Portable flame-throwers are known to be available to the enemy on the invasion coast and their employment in defense of the beach may be expected.

20. PROBABLE ENEMY ACTION.

a. Strong air attacks against our convoys and landing troops, prin-cipally with fighter and fighter bombers.

b. E-boat attacks against convoys.

c. Limited reinforcement of coastal defenses prior to D-day.

d. Rigid defense of the coast line.

e. Attacks of V Corps Assault Forces with mobile reserves beginning piecemeal on the afternoon of D-day and becoming coordinated by D plus 1.

f. Defense in successive positions in rear of the beach to limit V Corps penetration until adequate mobile reserves can be disposed for large scale counterattacks.

g. The use of non-toxic chemicals only.

To fully understand the German Army's capability for counter-attack, each mobile German division in the area was evaluated.

▬▬▬▬▬ - NEPTUNE - BIGOT

APPENDIX TO G-2 ESTIMATE OF THE ENEMY SITUATION

TABLE OF REINFORCEMENTS

SECTION I - MOBILE DIVISIONS IN THE WEST.

1.   10th SS Panzer Division FRUNDSBERG

     a.   Composition - Probably has one tank regiment, two infantry regiments, an artillery regiment, and ancillary units.

     b.   Quality - Good.

     c.   Location - LISIEUX and vicinity to the south and east.

     d.   Movement by railroad - Would not be feasible because of short distance.

     e.   Movement by highway - 53 miles, with three good routes available.
        (1) Leading elements could arrive by H plus 5.
        (2) Entire division could arrive by H plus 9.

     f.   Earliest probable time of employment - H plus 9.
        NOTES: (1) Probably would operate in the British area.
              (2) A portion of this division is believed to be at FALAISE, about 37 miles from the assault area; it is therefore believed that these troops could arrive by H plus 5.

2.   17th SS Panzergrenadier Division GOETZ VON BERLICHINGEN.

     a.   Composition - Probably has one tank regiment, two infantry regiments, one artillery regiment, two reconnaissance units, and ancillary units.

     b.   Quality - Unknown; probably good.

     c.   Location - Vicinity of ALENCON.

     d.   Movement by railroad - 89 miles, double-tracked; alternate route is single-tracked and 50% farther. Movement by rail unlikely because detraining stations are far in rear, and only 65% of the 189 miles could be covered by rail.

     e.   Movement by highway - 85 miles, with two main routes available, but no other alternate routes.
        (1) Leading elements could arrive by H plus 8.
        (2) Entire division could arrive by H plus 11.

     f.   Earliest probable time of employment - H plus 11.

3.   352nd Infantry Division.

     a.   Composition - Probably has three regimental combat teams.

     b.   Quality - Unknown, but classified as an Offensive division.

     c.   Location - ST. LO - TORIGNY area.

     d.   Movement by railroad - Because of short distance, rail movement would not be feasible.

     e.   Movement by highway - 28 miles, with three good routes available.

- NEPTUNE - BIGOT

Annex No. 1
in   23 pages
Page No. 19.

(1) Since the division is not believed to be mobile, it would probably arrive in the area after a forced march on foot. Most probable place of employment is V Corps assault area.

(2) Considering time to be alerted and begin movement, 19 hours for the forced march, and an hour for reconnaissance and deployment, the division could arrive by H plus 25.

f. Earliest probable time of employment - Morning of D plus 1.
  NOTE: (1) Recently arrived from the Russian Front.
         (2) If motors can be commandeered, a portion of the division might arrive by H plus 8, but to commandeer motors for the entire division would probably require longer than movement by foot.

4. 21st Panzer Division.

a. Composition - One tank regiment, (or possibly a brigade of four battalions), two infantry regiments, one artillery regiment, reconnaissance battalion, and ancillary units.

b. Quality - Good.

c. Location - East, north, and west of PARIS.

d. Movement by railroad - 169 miles, double-tracked; alternate route, mostly double-tracked, is 30% farther.
  (1) Leading elements could arrive by H plus 17.
  (2) Entire division could arrive by H plus 40.

e. Movement by highway - 160 miles; two main routes and one secondary route available.
  (1) Leading elements could arrive by H plus 12.
  (2) Entire division could arrive by H plus 15.

f. Earliest probable time of employment - Afternoon of D plus 1.
  NOTES: (1) Being reorganized after destruction in TUNISIA.
          (2) Movement by highway unlikely.
          (3) Probably would operate against the British.

5. 2nd SS Panzer Division DAS REICH.

a. Composition - Probably one tank regiment, three infantry regiments, an artillery regiment, and ancillary units.

b. Quality - Unknown, but believed up to strength.

c. Location - East of BORDEAUX.

d. Movement by railroad - 390 miles, double-tracked; alternate route, single-tracked is 20% farther.
  (1) Leading elements could arrive by H plus 28.
  (2) Entire division could arrive by H plus 46.

e. Movement by highway - 495 miles, two main routes. Movement by highway unlikely because of distance.

f. Earliest probable time of employment - Morning of D plus 3.
  NOTE: (1) This division and 273rd Panzer Training Division will have to use the same route, so if the 273rd Division moves first, this division cannot arrive until H plus 60.

- NEPTUNE - BIGOT

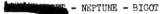 - NEPTUNE - BIGOT

Annex No. 1
in 23 pages.
Page No. 20.

6. 353rd Infantry Division.

   a. Composition - Probably has 3 regimental combat teams.

   b. Quality - Unknown; classified as Offensive.

   c. Location - HUELGOAT area of BREST Peninsula.

   d. Movement by railroad - 212 miles, 80% double-tracked; alternate
route almost twice as far.
         (1) Leading elements could arrive by H plus 19.
         (2) Entire division could arrive by H plus 46.

   e. Movement by highway - 195 miles; two main routes available. Movement by highway unlikely because of distance.

   f. Earliest probable time of employment - Morning of D plus 2.
         NOTES: (1) Formed late in 1943.
                 (2) Division is about eighteen miles from railhead
                      at MORLAIX.

7. 2nd Panzer Division.

   a. Composition - Probably has a tank regiment, two infantry regiments, an artillery regiment, and ancillary units.

   b. Quality - Unknown.

   c. Location - AMIENS area.

   d. Movement by railroad - 178 miles, double-tracked; alternate route,
double-tracked, is 65% farther.
         (1) Leading elements could arrive by H plus 18 or 22.
         (2) Entire division could arrive by H plus 39 or 43.

   e. Movement by highway - 176 miles; two main routes and one alternate route available.
         (1) Leading elements could arrive by H plus 12.
         (2) Entire division could arrive by H plus 15.

   f. Earliest probable time of employment - Afternoon of D plus 1.
         NOTE: Time of arrival by rail considers a four hour delay
                caused by the 21st Panzer Division.

8. 12th SS Panzer Division HITLER JUGEND.

   a. Composition - Probably has a tank regiment, two infantry regiments,
an artillery regiment, and ancillary units.

   b. Quality - Good; fully up to strength.

   c. Location - TURNHOUT area, Belgium.

   d. Movement by railroad - 573 miles, double-tracked; no suitable
alternate route in Belgium.
         (1) Leading elements could arrive by H plus 27.
         (2) Entire division could arrive by H plus 69.

   e. Movement by highway - Considered unlikely because of distance.

   f. Earliest probable time of employment - Late on D plus 2, or
morning of D plus 3, (latter most probable).
         NOTE: Movement of entire division considers a twelve hour
                delay; 3 hours caused by delay in LISIEUX-EVEREUX area, and
                9 hours caused by inadequacy of railroads in Belgium.

 - NEPTUNE - BIGOT

UNCLASSIFIED

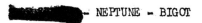 – NEPTUNE – BIGOT

Annex No. 1
in 23 pages
Page No. 21.

9.   3rd Parachute Division.

 a.   Composition - Unknown; classified as 3 regiment - offensive.

 b.   Quality - Unknown.

 c.   Location - Vicinity of RHEIMS.

 d.   Movement by railroad - 245 miles, double-tracked; alternate route, double-tracked, is 20% farther.
        (1)   Leading elements could arrive by H plus 36.
        (2)   Entire divisions could arrive by H plus 48.

 e.   Movement by highway - Considered unlikely because of distance.

 f.   Earliest probable time of employment - D plus 1.
        NOTES: (1)   Movement by rail might be delayed by the 21st Panzer Division. If so, the entire division could not arrive until H plus 58.
               (2)   It is estimated that sufficient lift can be assembled to drop 2,400 men at one time, but unless advanced warning is given, this lift could not be assembled earlier than D plus 1. The time from embarkation fields to dropping areas is negligible.

Shown below: low-level aerial reconnaissance photographs of Pointe du Hoc with additional interpretation of the cliffs. Then followed by V Corps Operations plan and Neptune Fire support plan.

ANNEX NO. 12   NEPTUNE

BIGOT   TO

                 V CORPS OPERATIONS PLAN

                         NEPTUNE

                      FIRE SUPPORT PLAN

    1. Naval gunfire support ships and craft, tactical airforce units, field
artillery, and tank units will support the initial assault and subsequent advance inland of the 1st U. S. Division.

    2. Initial Organization for Combat.

        a. Naval Support Ships.

            1 - Battleship
                RAMILLIES   4 x 15 in. guns@ 106 rpg.
                                   6 x 6 in. guns @ 180 rpg.

            3 - Cruisers
                BELLONA   8 x 5.25 in. guns @ 200 rpg.
                BLACK PRINCE   8 x 5.25 in. guns @ 200 rpg.
                GLASGOW   12 x 6 in. guns @ 200 rpg.

            10 - Destroyers
                8 Fleet type - 6 ships - 4 x 4.7 in. guns @ 250 rpg.
                              2 ships - 6 x 4.7 in. guns @ 250 rpg.

                2 Hunt type - 4 x 4 in. guns @ 250 rpg.

        b. Fire Support Craft.

            5 LCG (L)   - 2 x 4.7 in. guns @ 240 rpg.
            8 LCT (R)   - 1000 x 29 lb. rockets.
           24 LCS (S)   - 2 x .50 cal. MG and 48 x 29 lb. rockets.
           16 LCT (A&HE)- 32, M-4 tanks - 1 x 3 in. gun each @ 200 rpg.
            9 LCT (5)   - 36 x 105mm SP Mk 7 @ 100 rpg.

        c. Air Support Controlled by First U.S. Army, Targets Allotted in V
Corps Area.

            (1) Night Heavy Bomber Force: 1 mission of 250 tons.

            (2) Night Medium Bomber Force: 2 missions, amount to be announced.

        d. Air Support Controlled by V Corps.

            (1) Day Heavy Bomber Force: 4 missions, 180 tons per mission.

            (2) Day Medium Bomber Force: 5 missions, 36 tons per mission.

            (3) Day Fighter-Bomber Force: 4 missions, 12 planes each 6 x
                                           60 lb. rockets per plane.

    3. Missions.

        a. Naval Fire Support Ships: To protect shipping from attack by
enemy aircraft, surface forces and submarines, and to support by bombardment
the initial assault and subsequent advance inland.

                         BIGOT

BIGOT

b. Night Medium Bomber Force: Between H-80 and H-40, on battery No. 1, Pointe du Hoe (586938), and No. 5, Maisy (533918).

c. Day Heavy Bomber Force: H-25 to H-hour, on strongpoints commanding the beach, by prior arrangement with 1st Division. Tentative targets, (637926), (648916), (666903) and (688895).

d. Day Medium Bomber Force: H-25 to H-hour. Breach lanes in wire and minefields, by prior arrangement with 1st Division. Tentative locations, (649916), (665907), (677901), (688895) and (691898).

e. Day Fighter-Bomber Force: H-25 to H-hour. On strongpoints commanding beach, by prior arrangement with 1st Division. Tentative targets, (653912), (664908), (667906) and (678897).

6. Target Designation.

a. The Lambert grid will be used for Naval target designation. Supporting ships and shore fire control parties will be furnished 1/50,000 scale map charts and 1/25,000 vertical mosaics gridded with the Lambert grid.

b. Gridded obliques will be furnished naval gunfire spotters to facilitate target identification, but Merton coordinates will not be used for target designation.

c. Obliques marked to show locations of known targets will be furnished to all craft firing on point targets in order to facilitate target identification.

7. Visual Signals. Smoke signal of colors to be designated later will be used to lift naval gunfire in case of radio failure. Its meaning will be "Cease fire, gunfire falling too close to friendly troops".

8. Navy Shore Fire Control Parties.

a. Attached to 1st Division: Nine parties, 294th Joint Assault Signal Company.

b. Attached to 29th Division: Nine parties, 293d Joint Assault Signal Company, two of which will be allotted to Ranger units.

c. Artillery Air OP's used to adjust naval gun fire will operate through battalion fire direction centers and attached naval liaison officers.

9. Liaison.

a. One Navy liaison officer will accompany each FA battalion and each division artillery and corps artillery headquarters.

b. One corps artillery liaison officer will accompany each division artillery headquarters.

10. Ammunition. Commanding officers, 58th and 62nd Armored Field Artillery Battalions (SP) and 745th Tank Battalion (Med), will requisition and load on craft ammunition to be expended during support firing afloat. This will be in addition to basic load.

SP Battalion - 100 rounds per Howitzer.

Tank, M-4 - 150 rounds HE Shell per tank firing.

BIGOT

A map overlay was sent to commanding officers stating that aerial photographs had been taken of these areas and were available for their use.

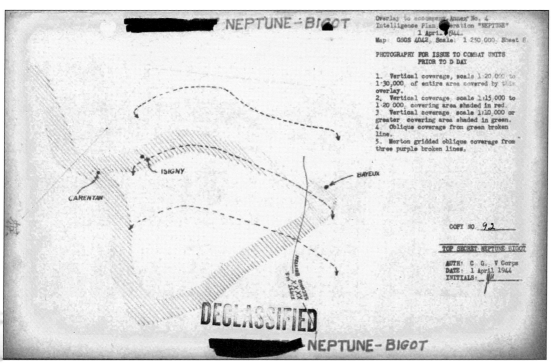

BIGOT   ANNEX NO. 16   NEPTUNE

TO

V CORPS OPERATIONS PLAN

NEPTUNE

ARTILLERY PLAN

MAPS: G.S.G.S. 4250, Sheet No's 6F/6, 6F/2, 7E/5, 7F/1, Scale 1:50,000.

1. See V Corps Plan Operation "NEPTUNE".

2. The Arty with the Corps will support the attack.

3. a. Organization of the FA
    (1) V Corps Arty   Estimated Arrival
    (2) 1st Inf Div
        5th FA Bn (155mm How)   D
        7th FA Bn (105mm How)   D
        32nd FA Bn (105mm How)   D
        33d FA Bn (105mm How)   D
        58th Arm'd FA Bn (105mm How SP)   D   (attached - will revert
                                                    later to 29th Inf Div)
        62nd Arm'd FA Bn (105mm How SP)   D   (attached)
        Det Btry "A" 17th FA Obsn Bn   D ≠ 1 (attached after landing)

    (3) 29th Inf Div
        110th FA Bn (105mm How)   D
        111th FA Bn (105mm How)   D
        224th FA Bn (105mm How)   D
        227th FA Bn (155mm How)   D
        Det Btry "B" 17th FA Obsn Bn   D ≠ 1 (attached after landing)

Arty with the Corps.
(1) Missions:
    (a) Div Arty direct and general support in assigned zone of action.
        Early support will be provided ranger units operating on right
        of sector. Support will be provided to British 50th Div as far
        east as grid line 80.

    (b) Corps Arty: Early support will be provided ranger units opera-
        ting on right of sector. Support will be provided to British
        50th Div as far east as grid line 80.

    (10) Shore Fire Control Parties: Nine (9) Naval Shore Control Parties,
         294th Joint Signal Assault Company, are attached to 1st Inf Div.
         Nine (9) parties, 293d Joint Signal Assault Company, are attached
         to 29th Inf Div. Two (2) parties from 29th Inf Div will be al-
         located to Ranger Units.

    (11) Naval Liaison Officers: One (1) Naval Liaison Officer is attach-
         ed to each of the following units: Hq V Corps Arty; Hq 1st Inf
         Div Arty; Hq 29th Inf Div Arty; each FA Bn, 1st and 29th Div
         Artys.

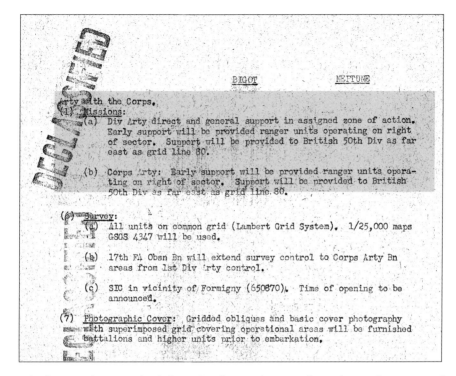

BIGOT   NEPTUNE

rty with the Corps.
(1) Missions:
    (a) Div Arty direct and general support in assigned zone of action.
        Early support will be provided ranger units operating on right
        of sector. Support will be provided to British 50th Div as far
        east as grid line 80.

    (b) Corps Arty: Early support will be provided ranger units opera-
        ting on right of sector. Support will be provided to British
        50th Div as far east as grid line 80.

(6) Survey:
    (a) All units on common grid (Lambert Grid System). 1/25,000 maps
        GSGS 4347 will be used.

    (b) 17th FA Obsn Bn will extend survey control to Corps Arty Bn
        areas from 1st Div Arty control.

    (c) SIC in vicinity of Formigny (650870). Time of opening to be
        announced.

(7) Photographic Cover: Gridded obliques and basic cover photography
    with superimposed grid covering operational areas will be furnished
    battalions and higher units prior to embarkation.

Once occupied, the coastal areas inland from Omaha Beach were allocated uses for troop and equipment concentrations, storage areas and ammunition dumps.

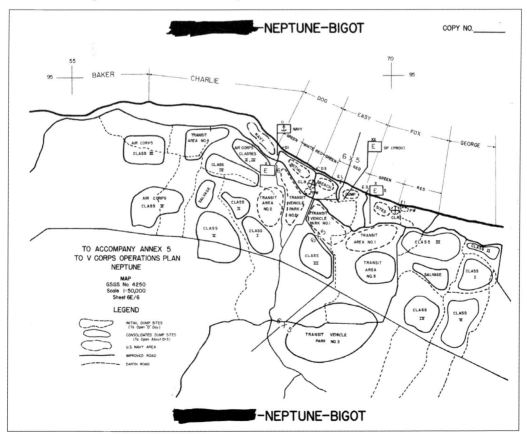

An assessment and breakdown of German units expected in the Overlord landing area was undertaken in April. (Of note – the indication that the 352nd Infantry Division were in the area. It is often wrongly stated that they were not known to have been in the area before D-Day. They are marked on this map two months before landing started.)

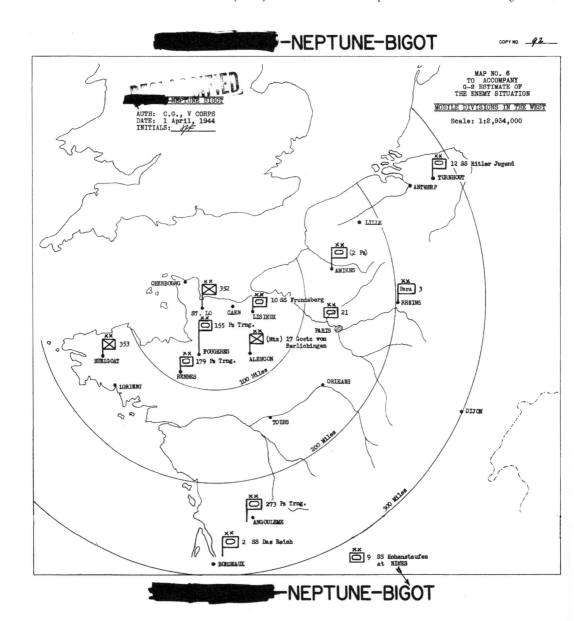

A map articulating the expected reaction times to the landings by German units in France. Speed and advancement was of the utmost importance to ensure these units could not attack the beaches.

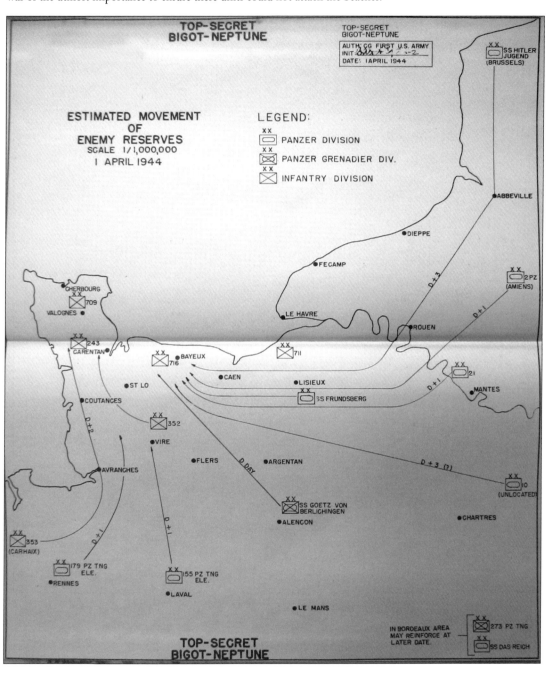

A study was produced indicating the static German units already positioned in the invasion area.

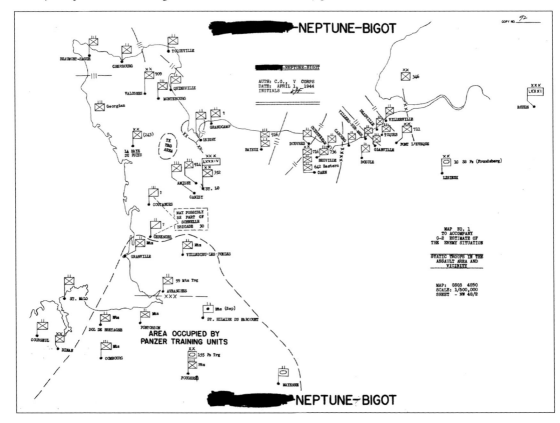

A study showing all of the German strongpoints and gun positions along the Rangers' line of attack. They are listed by calibre.

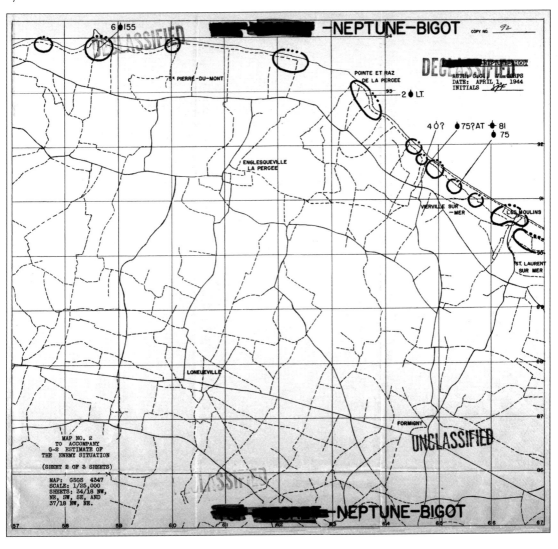

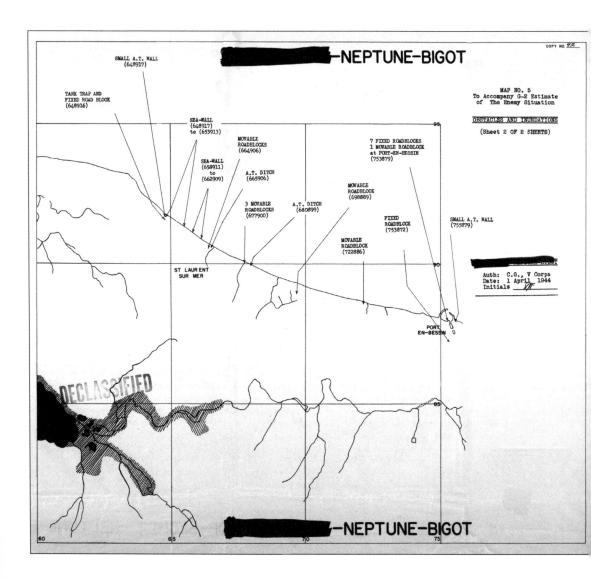

The range of each series of guns was calculated and plotted.

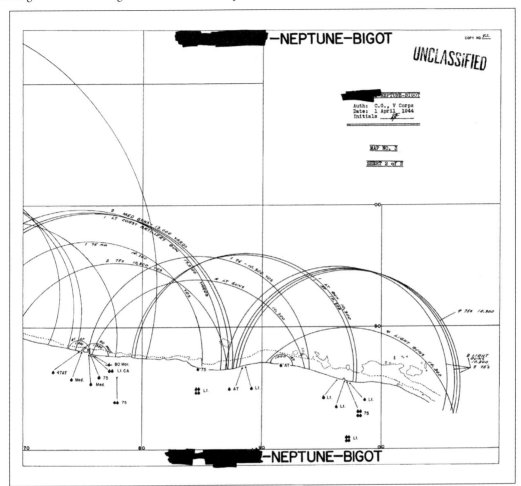

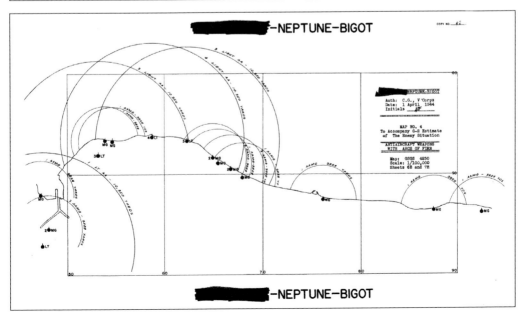

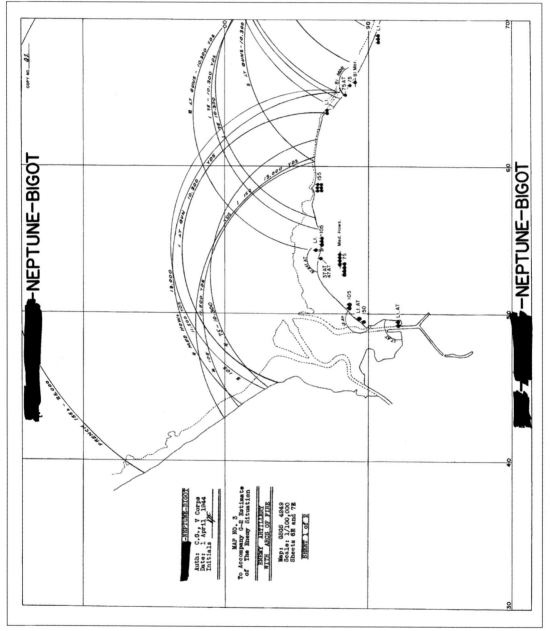

This portion contains all of the Ranger objectives on one map.

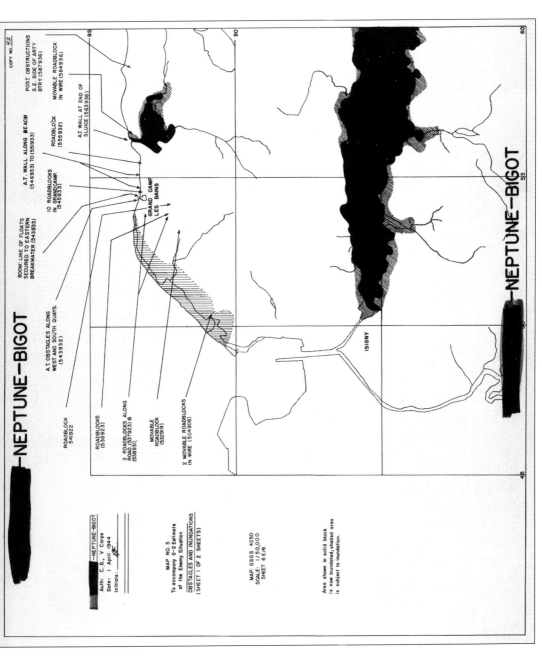

A list of roadblocks placed by the Germans was also provided.

Below shows the coastal defences around Grandcamp – including the two static batteries at Maisy.

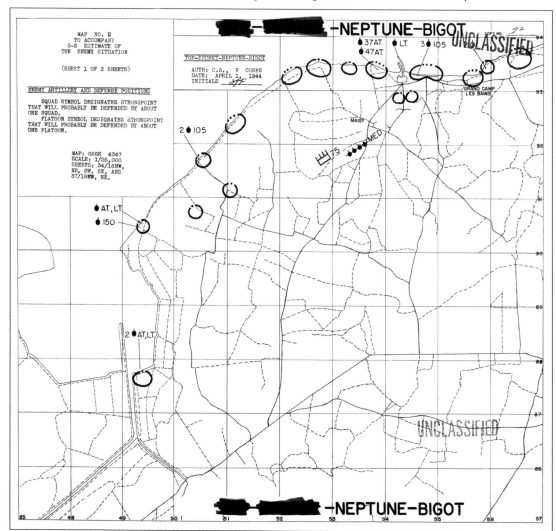

Strict written orders were again issued as to who was and who was not able to see NEPTUNE – BIGOT classified information.

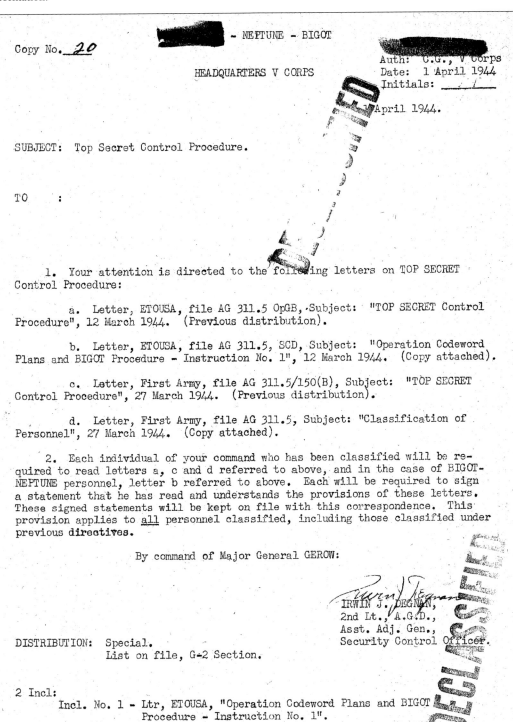

Copy No. **20**

— NEPTUNE – BIGOT

HEADQUARTERS V CORPS

Auth: C.G., V Corps
Date: 1 April 1944
Initials: _____

1 April 1944.

SUBJECT: Top Secret Control Procedure.

TO   :

    1. Your attention is directed to the following letters on TOP SECRET Control Procedure:

        a. Letter, ETOUSA, file AG 311.5 OpGB, Subject: "TOP SECRET Control Procedure", 12 March 1944. (Previous distribution).

        b. Letter, ETOUSA, file AG 311.5, SCD, Subject: "Operation Codeword Plans and BIGOT Procedure – Instruction No. 1", 12 March 1944. (Copy attached).

        c. Letter, First Army, file AG 311.5/150(B), Subject: "TOP SECRET Control Procedure", 27 March 1944. (Previous distribution).

        d. Letter, First Army, file AG 311.5, Subject: "Classification of Personnel", 27 March 1944. (Copy attached).

    2. Each individual of your command who has been classified will be required to read letters a, c and d referred to above, and in the case of BIGOT-NEPTUNE personnel, letter b referred to above. Each will be required to sign a statement that he has read and understands the provisions of these letters. These signed statements will be kept on file with this correspondence. This provision applies to all personnel classified, including those classified under previous directives.

            By command of Major General GEROW:

                                IRWIN J. DEGNAN,
                                2nd Lt., A.G.D.,
                                Asst. Adj. Gen.,
DISTRIBUTION: Special.   Security Control Officer.
               List on file, G-2 Section.

2 Incl:
       Incl. No. 1 – Ltr, ETOUSA, "Operation Codeword Plans and BIGOT
                     Procedure – Instruction No. 1".
       Incl. No. 2 – Ltr, First Army, "Classification of Personnel".

                          NEPTUNE – BIGOT

Dated 1st April a BIGOT map overlay. The Rangers' D-Day objective line is marked, as is Pointe du Hoc, Grandcamp-les-Bains and the Batteries at Maisy. The Rangers are then to advance to the line indicated on the map. This revised map now more clearly shows a precise set of orders with the 2nd and 5th Rangers attacking in different places, the beach, the Radar Station, Pointe du Hoc, Grandcamp, Maisy Batteries and then inland.

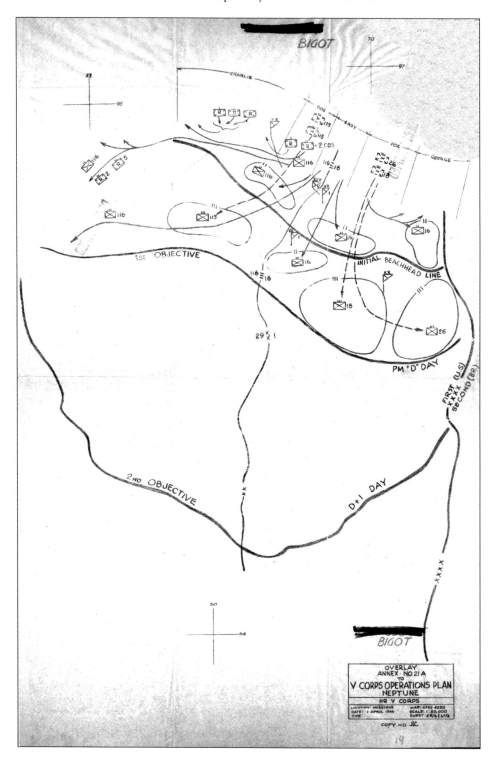

Below shows the same overlay placed over a modern aerial photograph of the coast to aid the reader. It also shows both the 2nd and 5th Btn's at Maisy.

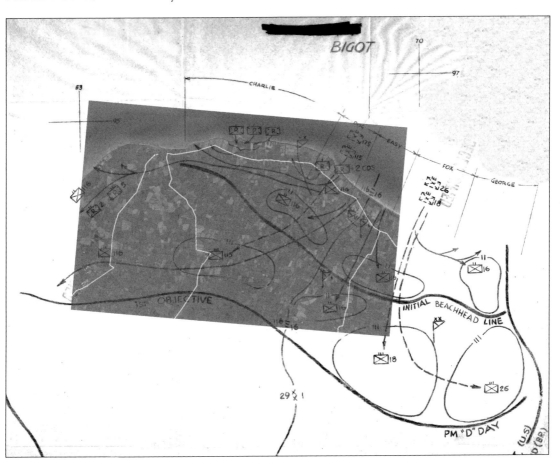

James W. Gabaree: *Our dress for battle consisted of a field jacket, smelly impregnated clothing to protect us in the event the Germans used chemical weapons, parachute jump boots and a steel helmet. We carried two bandoleers of ammunition, an M-1 rifle, a first aid kit, a gas mask, four or five hand grenades and three days of food rations. I also carried three 4ft cylinders filled with dynamite to blow a path through the barbed wire fortifications. Even with the two Mae West life preservers wrapped around each man, I was convinced I would sink after disembarking the landing craft.*

Issued on 1 April was a comprehensive set of uniform instructions. In particular the use of impregnated clothing in case of enemy gas attack is mentioned.

NEPTUNE

BIGOT

Annex 3

UNIFORM AND PERSONAL EQUIPMENT.

a. Reference:

(2) Annex 10, Chemical Warfare Plan.

b. Protective (impregnated) Field Uniform. Effective on the date indicated in Annex 10, Chemical Warfare Plan, protective clothing (outer layer) will be worn by all US personnel until such time as the Field Uniform, paragraph c, below, the Work Uniform, paragraph e, below, or the Service Uniform, paragraph h, below, is authorized. Initially, all troops of any one division; group, separate brigade, regiment, battalion, company or similar unit will be uniformed either as prescribed in sub-paragraph (1) below or as prescribed in sub-paragraph (2) below.

(1) For troops issued protective (impregnated) suits, herring-bone twill, the following uniform is prescribed:

(a) Belt, web, with full field equipment.

(b) Boots, army russet, leather, legging top pattern, with three (3) buckles or with laces, or officers' tank boots; when authorized by commanders in lieu of leggings, canvas, and shoes; service.

(c) Gas mask and gas protective equipment as prescribed in Annex 10, Chemical Warfare Plan.

(d) Gloves, protective (impregnated), when issued.

(e) Headgear: Steel helmet and liner, with combat identification markings in accordance with Circular No. 41, Headquarters First U.S. Army, 27 December 1943, or such headgear issued for special purposes, as is authorized.

(f) Hood, protective (impregnated) when issued.

(g) Jacket, field, or jacket, combat.

(h) Leggings, canvas, protective (impregnated).

(i) Raincoat, optional.

(j) Shirt, wool, olive drab.

(k) Shoes, service, high, russet

(l) Socks, protective, impregnated.

(m) Tags, identification, with heat resistant necklace.

(n) Trousers, wool, olive drab.

(o) Underwear: Drawers, woolen and undershirt, woolen.

(2) For troops issued protective (impregnated) shirts, wool, olive drab and trousers, wool, olive drab and not issued protective (impregnated) suit, herring-bone twill, the following uniform is prescribed:

(a) Belt, waist.

(b) Belt, web, with full field equipment.

(c) Boots, army russet, leather, legging top pattern, with three (3) buckles or with laces, or officers' tank boots, when authorized by commanders in lieu of leggings, canvas and shoes, service.

(d) Gas mask and gas protective equipment as prescribed in Annex 10, Chemical Warfare Plan.

(e) Gloves, protective (impregnated), when issued.

(f) Headgear: Steel helmet and liner, with combat identification markings in accordance with Circular No. 41, First U.S. Army, 27 December 1943, or such headgear issued for special purposes, as is authorized.

(g) Hood, protective, (impregnated), when issued.

(h) Jacket, field, or jacket, combat.

(i) Leggings, canvas, protective (impregnated).

(j) Raincoat, optional.

(k) Shirt, wool, olive drab, protective (impregnated).

(l) Shoes, service, high russet.

(m) Socks, protective (impregnated).

(n) Tags, identification with resistant necklace.

(o) Trousers, wool, olive drab, protective (impregnated).

(p) Underwear: Drawers, woolen and undershirt, woolen.

c. Officers Field Uniform. At such time as directed in administrative orders of this headquarters, personnel will be authorized to wear the Field Uniform, which is prescribed as follows:

(1) Belt, waist.

(2) Belt, web, with full field equipment.

(3) Boots, army russet, leather, legging top pattern, with three (3) buckles or with laces, or officers' tank boots, when authorized by commanders in lieu of leggings, canvas, and shoes, service.

(4) Breeches, service, may be worn by officers who are required to be mounted as specified in AR 605-130 when on mounted duty. Personnel of animal mounted, animal drawn, or pack organizations (except pack units of Field Artillery) may wear breeches at all times. Officers of such units as have been issued breeches for all their personnel are authorized to wear breeches.

(5) Gas mask and gas protective equipment as prescribed in Chemical Warfare Annex.

(6) Gloves, optional.

(7) Headgear:
   (a) Steel helmet and liner, with combat identification markings in accordance with Circular No. 41, Headquarters First U.S. Army, 27 December 1943.
   (b) Headgear issued for special purposes, as authorized.

(8) Jacket, field or jacket combat. The jacket, flying, winter, medium or heavy, may be worn by personnel required to make frequent aerial flights while enroute to, engaging in, or returning from such flights.

(9) Leggings, canvas.

(10) Raincoat, trench coat, or officer's field coat, optional.

(11) Shirt, wool, olive drab.

(12) Shoes, service, high russet. Shoes, flying winter may be worn by personnel required to make frequent aerial flights while enroute to, engaging in, or returning from such flights.

(13) Socks.

(14) Tags, identification, with heat resistant necklace.

(15) Trousers, wool, olive drab.

(16) Underwear: Drawers, woolen and undershirt, woolen.

d. Enlisted Mens' Field Uniform. Articles listed in sub-paragraph c., above, as issued except that, at formations, the wearing of the raincoat and gloves will be as prescribed by unit commanders.

e. Work Uniform:
   (1) At such time as is authorized in administrative orders, the work uniform as prescribed in paragraph (2) below may be worn by troops while actually engaged in combat or physical labor such as demolition work, construction road repair or normal fatigue and maintenance duties within the quartering area.
   (2) The work uniform will consist of the suit, herringbone twill, leggings, canvas, belt web with field equipment and such outer garments as may be required by weather conditions. The fatigue hat or cap will not be worn.

f. Shoulder Sleeve Insignia. Shoulder sleeve insignia will be worn by personnel of all units authorized to wear such insignia by Circular No. 28, Headquarters ETOUSA, 13 March 1943, and current War Department directives.

The Army distributed a paper on the issue of intelligence maps and the restrictions on who was able to procure them as well as aerial photographs.

MAPS. a. Maps available for the operation will be of the following scales: 1:4,000,000; 1:1,000,000; 1:500,000; 1:250,000; 1:100,000; 1:50,000; 1:25,000; 1:5,000 and a 1:200,000 road map. The 1:5,000 issue is now in process of printing.

b. During the planning phase, all maps of the area of operations will be issued through intelligence channels. A maximum of one set of the 1:4,000,000 maps, three sets of the 1:1,000,000 maps and ten sets each of all other maps will be available for issue to each division. Map requirements for briefing will also be issued through intelligence channels.

c. Maps to be issued to subordinate units for operational purposes will be as set forth in letter from Headquarters, First U. S. Army, dated 7 March 1944, subject: "Map Supply and Distribution", file 061.05/44 (ENGR). Map depots will be established by ETOUSA in or near sealed assembly areas and maps will be issued therefrom directly to battalions and separate units of equal or smaller size located in sealed areas. The issue will be made at a time to be specified by this Headquarters and will be made under the supervision of the division headquarters (division engineer) concerned for divisional units and under the supervision of the Corps Engineer for nondivisional units. The supervising officers will insure that issues are made on the basis of the tactical groupings in effect at the time. Special precautions will be taken by all concerned to safeguard all maps of the invasion area and to prevent the dissemination of information concerning map requisitions and issues.

d. Operational plans of divisions and higher units will be prepared on the 1:50,000 map.

AERIAL PHOTOGRAPHS.

a. Planning Requirements. For coverage to be provided prior to D-day, see attached Overlay. One (1) copy of each sortie will be distributed to Corps Artillery and each division for the use of Planning Staffs.

b. Combat Requirements. Distribution will be made on the following basis:
(1) Basic coverage 1:20,000 - 1:30,000.
      20 per Corps Artillery.
      25 per Division.
(2) Beach coverage 1:10,000 or larger, vertical, and oblique beach strips.
      25 per Assault Division.
(3) Artillery Obliques (Merton gridded).
      7 per Field Artillery Battalion.
      1 per Division Artillery Headquarters.
      1 per Artillery Regimental Headquarters.
      1 per Division Headquarters.

c. Special Combat Coverage. For coverage on D-day and D plus 1, see paragraph 4 c (3). Requests for special photographic coverage will be submitted through intelligence channels to the A. C. of S., G-2, First U.S. Army, giving area (preferably by map or overlay), scale desired, number of prints needed and purpose. In the absence of a specific request, only one copy of each special combat photograph normally will be supplied to an interested unit. In such case, requests for additional prints will be made through intelligence channels to the A. C. of S., G-2, First U.S. Army.

Special orders on the conduct of personnel within the Embarkation areas and Marshalling areas were issued. In effect everyone was under lock-down and all communication with the outside world was to cease or at least be heavily censored.

<u>During Concentration and Embarkation</u>.

(1) Adequate guard will be maintained in all concentration, marshalling and embarkation areas after briefing begins to prevent un-authorized entry into such restricted areas and to prevent any contact whatsoever between troops and civilians or other unauthorized persons.

(2) All military personnel will be restricted from movement outside camps in which they are located within concentration, marshalling or other restricted areas after briefing begins except where such movement is necessary in the transaction of official business, in which case a pass will be provided by the camp commander (SOS). Passes will be issued to members of tactical units only upon the approval of the unit commander concerned.

(3) Rigid censorship, in accordance with ETO Circular #65, as amended, will be maintained by unit censors after concentration begins. After unit censorship is completed all outgoing mail will be placed in bags and forwarded to the THEATRE CENSOR, ETOUSA. Only official telephone calls and telegrams, approved by the Camp Commander, will be permitted after briefing begins.

(4) Prior to briefing, all personal diaries, letters, and effects giving information of possible value to the enemy will be collected from all military personnel, placed in individual containers, marked with owners name and shipped to the Commanding General, SOS for Central Records, AGO, APO 871, U. S. Army. Upon embarkation, military personnel will be searched and personal effects containing information of possible value to the enemy found on board craft will be collected and destroyed. The number of operational orders, marked maps and classified documents carried will be limited to the minimum essential to the execution of assigned tasks. All military personnel will be prohibited from taking personal cameras and radios.

(5) All tactical personnel not embarking with their units will be segregated before briefing begins and will be kept in restricted areas until after H-hour. Personnel sent to hospitals after briefing begins will be admonished regarding security precautions.

(6) Briefing of command and staff personnel will be in accordance with the following schedule: (a) Y-60, Regimental and Separate Battalion Staffs; (b) Y-30, Battalion and Separate unit Staffs; (c) Immediately prior to processing through marshalling areas, all personnel of assault forces ("O" and "B") except residues.

(7) During all movements from concentration to marshalling to embarkation areas all unit commanders and craft-load commanders will take necessary precautions to prevent contact of any nature between the troops and civilians or other unauthorized persons.

(8) Corps and Divisional patches may be worn on uniforms by individuals. Vehicle markings will remain as now authorized.

(9) Effective Y-30, daily countersigns and paroles for all elements of this command will be issued by Headquarters, V Corps.

(10) Complete radio silence will be maintained by all units from the time their concentration begins until lifted by competent authority or until the initiation of the assault.

On 1 April orders were re-issued to all battalion HQs in relation to the handling of prisoners of war.

ANNEX 3d   NEPTUNE
TO
V CORPS
1 April 1944.   OPERATIONS PLAN
NEPTUNE

G-1 PLAN

PRISONERS OF WAR AND CIVILIAN SUSPECTS

2. <u>Prisoners of War.</u> All members of the hostile armed forces captured in uniform in the front lines or behind the front lines and
all enemy civilians forming part of a levee en masse, high civil
functionaries, civil officials and diplomatic agents attached to
the armed forces, persons whose services are of particular use to
the hostile army or its government, and hostages have a right to be
treated as prisoners of war and will be handled accordingly. Although
members of sanitary formations, members of voluntary aid societies
(officially recognized and authorized by their government) and chaplains may be detained, they will be respected and protected but shall
not be treated as prisoners of war.

348-353, 396-400.

   a. Evacuation of prisoners will not interfere with the circulation, movement or tactical employment of our own troops.

   b. Provisions of FM 27-10, Rules of Land Warfare and inter-
pretations thereof issued by higher headquarters will be adhered
to in spirit and letter. Prisoners of war (except those who, because of wounds or sickness would run greater risks by being evacuated than by remaining where they are) shall be evacuated within
the shortest possible period after their capture to locations far
enough from the zone of combat for them to be reasonably safe.

Further fine tuning of the orders relating to follow up troops, replacements and casualties were issued.

BIGOT

ANNEX 3
TO
V CORPS
OPERATIONS PLAN
NEPTUNE

G-1 PLAN

SECTION I – PERSONNEL PROCEDURES

1.   INITIAL STRENGTH.

   a.   Reference.

      (1)   Annex 2, Organization of Assault and Follow-up.

   b.   Scale of Entrance. Units of the Assault, Follow-up and certain
units of the Build-up will enter this operation in accordance with Troop
list shown in Annex 2. In the absence of specific instructions to the
contrary, all other units will enter the operation at T/O plus any overstrength existing at the time.

   c.   Residues.

      (1)   Residues, representing the difference between reduced
            scales and T/O strengths, will be detached from units
            and sent to special camps designated by SOS. Any unit
            overstrength existing at the time of these movements
            will accompany unit residues, except in the case of
            certain units of Force "O" which have been specifically
            authorized to have their overstrength accompany and
            embark with the units.

      (2)   Division and other unit residues and overstrengths which
            are self sustaining will provide for their own house-
            keeping. Small residual detachments which are not
            self sustaining will be grouped by SOS to provide for
            mutual housekeeping assistance. Additional assistance
            as may be required by groups of small residues and over-
            strengths will be furnished by SOS upon request. Re-
            quests for such assistance will be made by divisions
            direct to Army headquarters. Units of Corps Troops will
            request such assistance through this headquarters.

      (3)   Residues and overstrengths will remain in the special
            camps referred to in sub-paragraph c., (1), above,
            until ordered to Marshalling or Embarkation Areas in
            accordance with Army priority list.

2.   UNIT CASUALTY ESTIMATES.

   a.   Reference: Annex 3a, Casualty Estimate Forms.

   b.   Casualty estimates will be based on the considerations and
rates indicated in paragraph 3, Army Casualty Estimates, Annex 3 to
First United States Army Operations Plan, Neptune, (G-1 Plan), dated
25 February 1944.

-5-

1 April 1944

BIGOT   NEPTUNE

This headquarters will furnish each division with a
casualty estimate for the division as a whole, for the
period up to D plus 14, inclusive. This estimate will
control the sum total of the separate casualty estimates
of the division's component elements.

(2) In general, casualty estimates for units of Corps Troops
(other than divisions), and for other units operating in
the zone of action of this Corps, will be developed by
this headquarters, and advance requisitions as prescribed
in paragraph 3 b, below, for such units will be prepared
by this headquarters.

3. REQUISITIONS FOR REPLACEMENTS.

a. Reference: Annex 3b, Personnel Replacement System.

b. Advance Requisitions. Units of the Assault, Follow-up and
certain units of the Build-up attached to this Corps or operating in
its zone of action will submit advance requisitions for estimated
initial loss replacements up to D plus 14, inclusive, as directed by
this headquarters. Unit overstrengths will be considered as initial replacements. Advance requisitions will be submitted for subsequent replacements required to maintain units at T/O strength.

c. Normal Requisitioning.

(1) Normal requisitioning will be resumed by all units on D
plus 9 to allow time for flow of normally requisitioned
replacements to begin at D plus 15.

(2) Corps units will requisition on WD AGO Form 211. Divisions will requisition on WD AGO Form 212. Insofar
as circumstances permit, units in combat will requisition
replacements by type of training desired, such as rifle,
heavy weapons, armored infantry, etc., and whenever
practicable, by military specification serial numbers.
Under combat conditions which prevent compliance with the
minimum requirements above, reports of casualties received at the rear echelons of major commands will be
made the basis of requisitions for subordinate units.

(3) Armored vehicle crews will be requisitioned as individuals.

4. FLOW OF REPLACEMENTS.

a. Reference: Annex 3b, Personnel Replacement System.

b. Preparation for Assault.

(1) Overstrengths detached from units as indicated in sub-
paragraph 1., c., "Initial Strength", above, will be
organised into detachments for shipment in accordance
with priorities determined by the operational plan.

(2) Casualties in the Concentration Areas, including those
caused by enemy attack, will be replaced from permanent depots of the Field Force Replacement Systems.

The Army Training Centre provided the Rangers with tide tables for their forthcoming training period. These were vital to ensure that timings of landings could be organised to mimic the actual landings in France.

TIDE TABLE

BRITISH SUMMER TIME   APRIL, 1944.

DATE. DAY		TIDES (Appledore)				DEPTHS (Bideford)		SUNRISE	SUNSET
		HIGH		LOW		a.m.	p.m.		
1st Saturday		–	1300	0633	1911	–	9.0	0655	1950
2nd Sunday	0136	1425	0804	2043	8.11	8.10	0653	1952
3rd Monday	0306	1547	0937	2159	9.8	10.1	0650	1954
4th Tuesday	0412	1657	1034	2252	11.2	11.8	0647	1955
5th Wednesday	0519	1743	1120	2336	13.0	13.4	0646	1957
6th Thursday	0602	1821	1200	–	14.6	14.6	0644	1959
7th Friday	0639	1855	0016	1236	15.5	15.7	0642	2000
8th Saturday	0712	1927	0051	1258	16.6	16.8	0640	2002 Full Moon
9th Sunday	0743	1958	0121	1338	17.1	17.1	0637	2004
10th Monday	0813	2028	0148	1407	17.5	16.11	0635	2005
11th Tuesday	0843	2059	0215	1435	17.0	16.7	0633	2007
12th Wednesday	0915	2132	0244	1504	16.1	15.6	0631	2008
13th Thursday	0950	2217	0317	1538	15.0	14.5	0629	2010
14th Friday	1027	2247	0354	1619	13.7	12.11	0626	2011
15th Saturday	1111	2339	0442	1717	11.10	11.4	0624	2013
16th Sunday	–	1227	0545	1819	–	10.5	0622	2015 Last Qtr
17th Monday	0051	1339	0712	1954	10.6	9.7	0620	2016
18th Tuesday	0226	1513	0855	2128	10.4	10.7	0618	2018
19th Wednesday	0346	1627	1008	2231	12.6	13.0	0616	2020
20th Thursday	0456	1728	1104	2328	14.11	15.5	0614	2022
21st Friday	0554	1818	1155	–	16.11	17.0	0611	2023
22nd Saturday	0642	1901	0018	1242	18.1	18.5	0610	2025 New Moon
23rd Sunday	0724	1942	0101	1325	18.11	18.11	0608	2027
24th Monday	0804	2025	0144	1406	18.8	18.4	0606	2028
25th Tuesday	0843	2104	0224	1445	17.11	17.5	0604	2030
26th Wednesday	0922	2143	0259	1519	16.10	15.7	0602	2032
27th Thursday	1001	2232	0335	1554	14.10	14.0	0600	2034
28th Friday	1040	2302	0413	1629	12.10	11.11	0558	2035
29th Saturday	1123	2348	0455	1716	10.8	10.1	0556	2036
30th Sunday	–	1221	0556	1830	–	9.5	0554	2037 1st Qtr

Note :- All times are British Summer Time; for Double British Summer Time add
one hour.

Opposite: On 1 April the Rangers were also given a Training Schedule prior to arrival at the ATC, breaking down into sections all of their activities (for both battalions) and covering all of their time at the Centre. Sundays were not allocated as working days.

Accompanying the Training Schedule were two 'Code Sheets' which further broke down the details of the classes to be undertaken. They also allot hours per task, appropriate uniform information and importantly where within the ATC the activity was going to take place.

U. S. ASSAULT TRAINING CENTER

2nd & 5th Bn "RANGERS" Training Schedule

5 - 22 APRIL, incl., 1944.

1 April 1944.

WEEK		MONDAY	TUESDAY	WEDNESDAY	THURSDAY	FRIDAY	SATURDAY
5 Apr to 9 Apr Incl 1944	AM			A-4 * 2nd & 5th INDIVIDUAL ASSAULT	A-6 2nd & 5th INDIVIDUAL ASSAULT	A-3X * 2nd Bn ** PLATOON ASSAULT (Dry) "D" Rngs 25-36. Dem Rng 51 for 2nd & 5th at 0830	A-9X 2nd Bn ** PLATOON ASSAULT (Ball) "C" & "D" BOOBY TRAPS Rear of Range #47
	Area			"C", "D" & "F"	"C", "D" & "F"		
	PM			A-5 2nd & 5th INDIVIDUAL ASSAULT	A-7 2nd & 5th INDIVIDUAL ASSAULT	A-10X * 5th Bn ** PLATOON ASSAULT (Dry) "B" Rngs 25-36	A-11X 5th Bn ** PLATOON ASSAULT (Ball) "C" & "D" BOOBY TRAPS Rear of Range #47
	Area			"C", "D" & "F"	"C", "D" & "F"		
10 Apr to 16 Apr Incl 1944	AM	A-23X * 2nd Bn ** COMPANY ASSAULT (Ball) "F" Baggy Point	A-23X * 5th Bn ** COMPANY ASSAULT (Ball) "F" Baggy Point	A-17X 2nd & 5th Bn PREPARATION FOR EMBARKATION	A-20X 2nd & 5th LANDING EXERCISE #1 (Ball) "A" Red 2, land at Woolacombe Red, Hl	A-24X 2nd Bn ** COMPANY ASSAULT (Dry) "F" Baggy Point	A-15X 2nd Bn ** EN HEDGE-HOG (Ball) "D" Hedge-Hog
	Area			Bn Area			
	PM	A-24X 2nd Bn ** COMPANY ASSAULT (Dry) Hedge-Hog "D" Hedge-Hog	A-24X 5th Bn ** COMPANY ASSAULT (Dry) "D" Hedge-Hog	A-17X 2nd & 5th Bn PREPARATION FOR EMBARKATION	A-21X 2nd & 5th CLEANUP & CRITIQUE of landing Exer #1	A-24X 5th Bn ** COMPANY ASSAULT (Dry) "F" Baggy Point	A-15X 5th Bn ** EN HEDGE-HOG (Ball) "D" Hedge-Hog
	Area			Bn Area	Battalion Area		
17 Apr to 22 Apr Incl 1944	AM	A-22X 2nd & 5th LANDING EXERCISE #2 (Ball) "A" Green 2, land at Woolacombe Red Hl	A-22X 2nd & 5th CONTINUATION OF LANDING EXERCISE #2	A-22X 2nd & 5th CONTINUATION OF LANDING EXER #2	R E S E R V E D F O R C. O.		
	PM	A-22X 2nd & 5th CONTINUATION OF LANDING EXERCISE #2	A-22X 2nd & 5th CONTINUATION OF LANDING EXERCISE #2	A-22X 2nd & 5th CONTINUATION OF LANDING EXERCISE #2	R E S E R V E D F O R C. O.		

Dist: "F", & 100 to Rangers

*75mm Guns firing on Woolacombe Beach to Morte Point

**One Battalion only, other Bn released to Bn C.O.

U.S. ASSAULT TRAINING CENTER
"RANGERS" Code Sheet

Code	Hours	Method	Description of Training	Uniform	Place	References	Supervisors
A-4	4	D & P	Individual Assault	Field w/eye-shields or goggles.	Mortar, MG's, BAR, report to "D" Rng #45. All others to respective Ranges. Aslt Group Tng Assignment:	Tng Memo Aslt-6 (Inf) Ch #2, Indiv Assault, Tng Memo #Aslt-12	
			1. Flame Thrower		1. Flame Thrower. Rng "D"	Instr Guides	Moore, Co Ofrs
			2. Demolitions		2. Demolition Area "D"	Instr Guides	Elliott, " "
			3. Rocket		3. Rocket Rng, "F"	Instr Guides	Lewis, " "
			4. Rifle		4. Baggy Point, "C"	Instr Guides	Co Officers
			5. MG		5. Ranges 47-48, "C"	Instr Guides	Co Officers
			6. BAR		6. Ranges 44-46, "C" & "D"	Instr Guides	Co Officers
			7. 60mm Mortar		7. Ranges 50-51, "C"	Instr Guides	Co Officers
			8. 81mm Mortar		8. Ranges 49, "C"	Instr Guides	Co Officers
			9. Wire Cutters		9. Rest of Aslt Run 15.	"D" Instr Guides	Hicker, Co Ofrs
A-5	4	P	Individual Assault (Cont'd) A-4 (Prog)	Field w/eye-shields or goggles.	Same as A-4 except report to Group Ranges.	Tng Memo # Aslt 6 (Inf) Ch #2. Instr Guides	Same as A-4
A-6	4	P	Individual Assault (Cont'd)	Field w/eye-shields or goggles.	Same as A-5	Same as A-5	Same as A-4
A-7	4	P	Individual Assault (Cont'd)	Field w/eye-shields or goggles.	Same as A-5	Same as A-5	Same as A-4
A-8X	4	P	Platoon Assault. (Dry) 2nd Battalion only.	Field w/eye-shields or goggles.	Ranges 25-36. Assemble "C" Rng #51 for demonstration. 5th Bn attend demonstration 0830 only.	Tng Memo Aslt-5 (Inf) Ch #2. Tng Memo # Aslt-4 (Tanks) Tng Memo # aslt 12 Team Aslt Codes A-3X - A-11X.	Co Officers
A-9X	2	P	Platoon Assault. (Ball) (Change to Booby Traps #1 and #2 at 1000)	Field w/eye-shields or goggles.	Aslt Co's - 37,38,39,41,45,50,51 Support Co's 46,47,48,49. "C", Rear of Range #47	Same as A-8X	Co Officers
	2	P	Booby Traps				
A-10X	4	P	Platoon Assault. (Dry) 5th Battalion only.	Field w/eye-shields or goggles.	"B" Ranges 25-36	Same as A-8X	Co Officers

U. S. ASSAULT TRAINING CENTER
"RANGERS" Code Sheet

1 April, 1944
Page 2

Code	Hours	Method	Description of Training	Uniform	Place	References	Supervisors
A-11X	2	P	Platoon Assault. (Ball)	Field w/eye-shields or goggles.	Aslt Cos - 37,38,39,41, 45,50,51. Support Cos - 46,47,48,49.	Same as A-8X	Co Officers
	2		(Change to Booby Traps #3 & #4 at 1500) Booby Traps		"C", Rear of Range #47		
A-15X	4	P	Battalion Hedge-Hog Exercise (Ball) 75mm Gun in Support.	Field w/eye-shields or goggles.	"D" Hedge-Hog		Bn Officers
A-17A	8	P	Preparation for embarkation	Field	En Area		Bn Officers
A-20A	4	P	Landing Exercise #1. (Ball) 75mm Gun in Support.	Field & life belts	"A" Red 2, & land at Woolacombe Red & Blue & "F" Baggy Point.		Bn Officers
A-21A	4	C	Critique & Cleanup	Field	Battalion Area		Bn Officers
A-22A	10	P	Landing Exercise #2 (Ball) 75mm Gun in Support.	Field & life belts	"A" Red 2, & land at Woolacombe Red & Blue & "F" Baggy Point.		Bn Officers
A-23X	4	P	Company Assault of Fortified Beach. (Ball) 75mm Gun in Support.	Field w/eye-shields or goggles.	"F", Baggy Point	Tng Memos #Aslt-4, & #5, Code A-23.	Co Officers
A-24A	4	P	Company Assault (Dry)	Field w/eye-shields or goggles.	"F" Baggy Point		Bn Officers

LEGEND: C - Conference, D - Demonstration, P - Practical.

Normal Training hours: 0830-1230. 1330-1730.

Waterproofing Signal Equipment on 7 April 0830-1730. Conference Room #5.

Waterproofing Vehicles - By groups attached to Adm Bn in training.

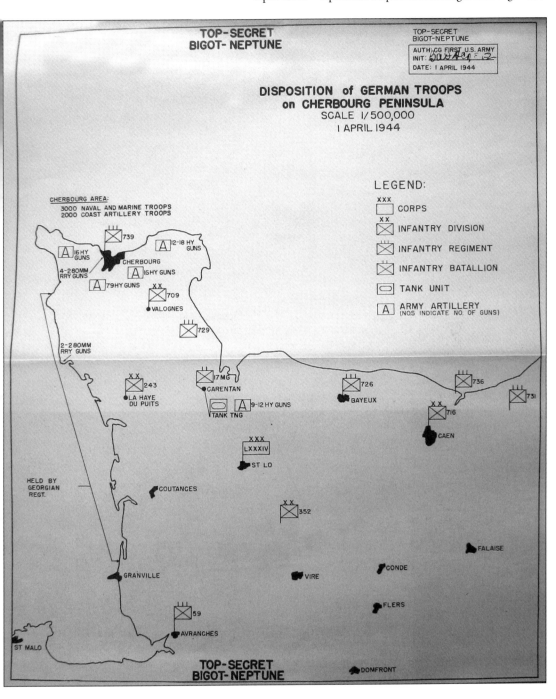

TOP-SECRET
BIGOT- NEPTUNE

TOP-SECRET
BIGOT-NEPTUNE
AUTH: CG FIRST U.S. ARMY
INIT:
DATE: 1 APRIL 1944

DISPOSITION of GERMAN TROOPS
on CHERBOURG PENINSULA
SCALE 1/500,000
1 APRIL 1944

LEGEND:
XXX ☐ CORPS
XX ⊠ INFANTRY DIVISION
⊠ INFANTRY REGIMENT
⊠ INFANTRY BATALLION
☐ TANK UNIT
A ARMY ARTILLERY
(NOS INDICATE NO. OF GUNS)

CHERBOURG AREA:
3000 NAVAL AND MARINE TROOPS
2000 COAST ARTILLERY TROOPS

739
A 12-18 HY GUNS
A 16 HY GUNS
CHERBOURG
4-280MM RRY GUNS
A 16 HY GUNS
A 79 HY GUNS
XX 709
VALOGNES
729

2-280MM RRY GUNS

XX 243
LA HAYE DU PUITS

17 MG
CARENTAN
☐ A 9-12 HY GUNS
TANK TNG

726
BAYEUX

736
731
XX 716
CAEN

XXX LXXXIV
ST LO

HELD BY GEORGIAN REGT.

COUTANCES

XX 352

FALAISE

GRANVILLE

VIRE

CONDE

FLERS

59
AVRANCHES

ST MALO

TOP-SECRET
BIGOT-NEPTUNE

DOMFRONT

2 April 1944

5th Rangers – Companies A – F, Medical and HQ –
Preston, England.
Record of events. All companies: Preston, England.
Left Tighnabruaich, Scotland 1145 by motorboat, arrived
Rothsay, Scotland 1300. 14 miles travelled by water.
Left Rothsay, Scotland 1300 on board TSS Sussex,
arrived Wemyss Bay, Scotland 1925, 25 miles travelled
by water. Left Wemyss Bay, Scotland 2130, arrived
Preston, England 2359, 100 miles travelled by rail.
2nd Rangers – Companies A – F, Medical and HQ
– Bude, Cornwall.
No change. Alerted for departure.

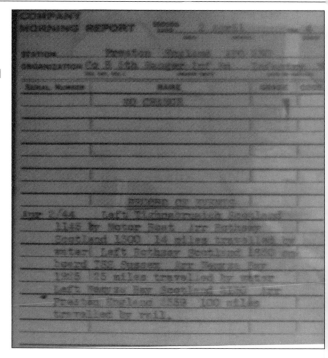

Information and guidance on the issuing of sea sickness tablets for medics was issued to units going overseas – as well as a plan of evacuation for casualties.

-- BIGOT

Sea Sickness Prevention.

a.   All troops will be supplied with Sea Sickness Prevention Capsules prior to embarkation. These capsules are safe when given as prescribed below and their efficacy has been well proven.

b.   These capsules will be issued to the Commanding Officer of troops for each craft. Such issue will be made in the marshalling area, on the basis of ten (10) capsules for each person on the troop list.

c.   The capsules will be administered on the following schedule:

(1)   One (1) capsule, by mouth, one-half hour before embarkation.

(2)   One (1) capsule, by mouth, when the ship or craft leaves the harbor, and is exposed to motion.

(3)   One (1) capsule, by mouth, every four (4) hours night and day thereafter, for the duration of the voyage (or until the entire ten (10) capsules have been taken).

d.   When a medical officer is included in the troop list of a craft, he will be responsible for the supervision of the administration of the sea sickness capsules. When no medical officer is included in the troop list, the capsules will be administered under supervision of the Commanding Officer of troops in accordance with the schedule given in par. c (3) supra.

PLAN OF EVACUATION

Policies.

a. Methods of Estimating Casualties.

(1) Sick and Non-Battle Injuries - The rate of 0.17% per day will be used in estimating hospital admissions for sick and non-battle injuries.

(2) Battle Casualties - The following rates will be used in estimating battle casualties:

TYPE OF UNIT	"LIGHT" BATTLE DAY %	"SEVERE" BATTLE DAY %	"MAXIMUM" BATTLE DAY %
Division	1	8	15
Brigade or Regiment	2.5	15	25
Corps	0.5	3	5
Army	0.35	1	2.5
Miscellaneous troops including SOS	0.25	0.6	1

Page 8

Categories of Battle Casualties

(a) "D" Day and D ≠ 1;

Killed, captured and missing ----------- 30%
Wounded -------------------------------- 70%

(b) D ≠ 2 and thereafter:

Killed, captured and missing ----------- 25%
Wounded -------------------------------- 75%

(c) Of the wounded, 50% will be litter cases and 50% will be walking cases.

b. Evacuation.

(1) Initial -- On "D" Day, and continuing until sufficient hospitals are ashore and in operation to permit retention of sick and wounded with a short hospitalization expectancy, a total evacuation policy will be in effect. This will call for the evacuation to the United Kingdom of all sick and wounded not able to return directly to duty after treatment at first and second echelon medical installations. The only exception to this policy will be the non-transportable cases.

(2) Avoidance of Unnecessary Evacuation -- Every effort will be made to prevent the UNNECESSARY evacuation of sick and wounded personnel from the continent. Medical officers of all echelons will habitually return casualties to duty as soon as their condition permits.

(3) Non-Transportables -- Cases falling into this category will be retained in units designated for the reception of this type of case until such time as their condition warrants further evacuation.

3 April 1944

5th Rangers – Companies A – F, Medical and HQ –
Braunton Camp, England APO 230.
Major Max S. Schneider (Detached Service) 2nd Ranger Inf.
Battalion APG No.308 US Army to Duty. Assumed command.
2nd Lt. Mehaffey and 2 enlisted men (Thornhill and McIlwain
returned from Detached Service at the US Assault Training
Centre, Bude, England to Duty.
Record of events. 3 April 44. Braunton Camp England.
Left Preston, England 0001, arrived US Assault Training
Centre 1530, 400 miles travelled by rail.
Telephone Number Braunton 263.

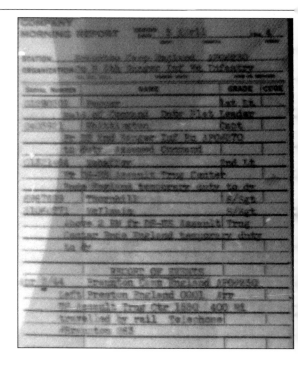

2nd Battalion Historical Narrative

> On 3 April, the Battalion moved by rail to the Assault
> Training Center, Braunton Camp, for a seven-day course in
> the technique of beach and fortification assault. Here, the
> Battalion was joined by, and worked with, the 5th Ranger Bat-
> talion. The Companies were divided into two thirty-man as-
> sault teams under A.T.C. guidance. The course consisted of
> methods of breaching wire defenses, handling of shaped
> charges and flame-throwers, and practical work in destroying
> installations. The final test of the course was held on
> Baggy Point, a promontory on which was built a replica of
> the fortification system existing on the French coast. Here,
> the Cannon Platoon proved its' effectiveness by placing pin-
> point fire on pillbox apertures at 1000 yards.

2nd Rangers – Companies A – F, Medical and HQ –
Braunton Camp, England APO 230.
All companies left Bude, Cornwall at 1030 hours by
train and arrived at Braunton Camp, North Devon at
1430 hours.

Maurice Prince: *Of all the training, manoeuvers, and operations we Rangers have undergone, about the most interesting and radical we have ever encountered was done at the Army's assault training school, which was situated outside the village of Braunton...*

It was here that we learned the most modern of techniques and plans of conducting warfare against a stable enemy's defensive position. It was here that we furthered our acquaintances with such up-to-date firing devices and weapons as the bazooka, flame thrower, Bangalore torpedoes, beehive charges, rifle grenades, etc. It was here too, that we had many practical demonstrations in the use of demolitions and where we took part in problems with the mission of destroying huge fortified pillboxes. The work was most instructive and educational, not to mention exciting and interesting. The school thoroughly felt that when a soldier had completed the course at this school, that he was more prepared for actual combat than at any other time of his Army career.

The majority of vehicle related training was also given to the men of both Ranger battalions at the US Army Assault Training Centre at Braunton, Devon.

The two Ranger battalions' full complement of vehicles for D-Day would consist of the following.

2nd Ranger Bn.	4	DUKW		5th Ranger Bn.	3	1-½T Car
2nd Ranger Bn	4	Half Tracks		5th Ranger Bn.	1	¾T Car
2nd Ranger Bn.	11	¼T Jeep		5th Ranger Bn.	1	2-½T Truck
2nd Ranger Bn.	1	1-½T Car		5th Ranger Bn.	11	¼T Jeep
2nd Ranger Bn.	1	¾T Ambulance		5th Ranger Bn.	5	¾T Weapons Carrier
2nd Ranger Bn.	1	2-½T Cargo		5th Ranger Bn.	2	1-½T Cargo
2nd Ranger Bn.	5	¼T Trailer		5th Ranger Bn.	2	1T Trailer
2nd Ranger Bn.	1	1-½T Truck		NSFCP	3	¼T Jeep
2nd Ranger Bn.	3	2-½T Cargo				
2nd Ranger Bn.	2	1T Trailer		Ranger Air Support	2	¼T Jeep
2nd Ranger Bn.	5	¾T Weapons Carrier		Ranger Air Support	2	¼T Trailer
				Ranger Air Support	1	Half Track
5th Ranger Bn.	4	¼T Trailer		Ranger Air Support	1	1T Trailer
5th Ranger Bn.	1	¾T Ambulance				

The half tracks from the 2nd Battalion were given their own loading diagram for their LCT (Landing Craft Tank) as they were to land independently to the rest of the battalion.

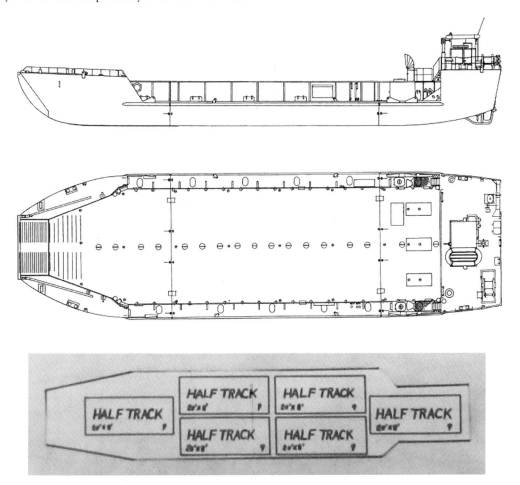

4 April 1944

5th Rangers – Companies A – F, Medical and HQ – Braunton Camp, North Devon. Alerted for departure.

A, B & C Companies 2nd Rangers – Braunton Camp, North Devon. No change. Alerted for departure.

D Company 2nd Rangers – Braunton Camp, North Devon.

1st Lt. McBride was relieved of temporary Duty as Company Commander.

1st Lt. Baugh assumed temporary Duty as Commander while 1st Lt. McBride was relieved. Alerted for departure.

E, F & Medical Companies 2nd Rangers – Braunton Camp. North Devon.

Headquarters Company 2nd Rangers – Braunton Camp, North Devon.

1st Lt. Frederick G. Wilkin was appointed to the rank of Captain as of 1 April.

In a report dated 4 April the Royal Navy were given their orders and these included an overview of what the Rangers and other land forces were expected to be doing.

TOP SECRET

OPERATION NEPTUNE—NAVAL ORDERS
(Short Title : ON)

ON 1.—General Outline of the Operation—*continued*

The Attack

34. The assaults are to be executed in accordance with the orders of the Task Force and Assault Force Commanders and are to be pressed home with relentless vigour regardless of loss or difficulty. Further instructions are given in ON 7.

The statement above is very exact. The assaults *'are to be pressed home with relentless vigour regardless of loss or difficulty.*

The Assaults

32. The following simultaneous main assaults will be made at H hour :—

Approximate Location.	Division.	Naval Force.	No. of Brigades or R.C.T. Assaulting.
OUISTREHAM ..	.. 3 Div.	S	1
COURSEULLES ..	.. 3 Canadian Div. ..	J	2
ASNELLES ..	.. 50 Div.	G	2
ST. LAURENT ..	.. 1 Div. (U.S.) .. .. 29 Div. (U.S.).	O	2
VARREVILLE ..	.. 4 Div. (U.S.)	U	1

Assaults will also be made by Commandos and Rangers as follows at or shortly after H hour.

Approximate Location.	Unit.	Associated Naval Force.	Task.
OUISTREHAM ..	One Commando ..	S	Occupation of town and capture of C.D. battery.
LANGRUNE ..	One Commando ..	S	Mopping up.
LANGRUNE ..	Three Commandos ..	S	Advance across river ORNE.
BERNIERS ..	One Commando ..	J	Mopping Up.
GRANDCAMP ..	Two Ranger Battalions	O	Capture C.D. batteries and protect flank.

Further assaults may also be made by Rangers and Commandos on the night of D/D + 1 as follows :—

Approximate Location.	Unit.	Task.
HOULGATE ..	.. One Commando ..	Destruction of C.D. battery.
BENERVILLE ..	.. One Commando ..	Destruction of C.D. battery.

The document on the previous page is from the same folder that states that the Rangers were to be in Grandcamp and *'Capture CD* [Coastal Defence] *batteries and protect flank.'* [Author: Note the use of the term in the plural – 'batteries'.]

An Aerial Reconnaissance report dated 4 April 1944 for Maisy Les Perruques Battery (AIR 34/157, 'Interpretation Report No. Y.264, Coastal Battery List of the Isigny area): Stated the following:

Four-gun medium or heavy battery. Circular emplacements 30' in diameter sited to fire NNW. Four sunken shelters, three approximately 35' x 30', one 55' x 30' have been built on the site. Guns are camouflaged. 600 yards in front there is a dummy battery.

Now considered to be a 4-gun light battery. (5004/5 of AA/725).

---

5 April 1944
Both Battalions undergoing ATC Training as per 'RANGERS' Training Schedule"

A Company 5th Rangers – Braunton Camp, North Devon. The following enlisted men went from Duty to AWOL 0600:. Pfc. Bellacome, Pfc. Farrall, Pfc. Gabaree, Pfc. McGuire. Alerted for departure.

5th Rangers – Companies B – F, Medical and HQ – Braunton Camp, North Devon.

A Company 2nd Rangers – Braunton Camp, North Devon. Alerted for departure.

Maurice Prince: *Our new homes here were to be Nissen huts on the Army grounds, on the outskirts of Braunton. This was to be our first time since we came to England that we were to be actually billeted in a real Army camp. It almost felt strange to be among all the Army personnel that was housed at this base.*

Our new homes were dirigible-shaped affairs, with tinning all around, except for the front and rear, which was of a wooden construction. These affairs were supposed to hold approximately twenty men and that was about the number of men we had in ours. We had concrete floors and we slept on Army cots. To provide the heat for these shacks, we had two pot-bellied stoves that were supposed – with emphasis on 'supposed' – to keep the hut warm.

Our company strength at our arrival was sixty-four men and three officers. Our Co., Capt Lytle had gotten himself a job at Battalion as executive officer, so Lt. Rafferty became the old man of the outfit, while Lt. White had the 2nd platoon and Lt. Edlin took over the 1st. First Sgt. Sowa was the head-boss as far as the enlisted men were concerned.

It didn't take us long to buckle down and to get our teeth into things. We got ourselves straightened out in our huts and we started to fraternize with the nearby towns and with the females that inhabited them.

B Company 2nd Rangers – Braunton Camp, North Devon.
1st Lt. William L. Sharp was assigned and joined from Headquarters F.F.R.D. (*Field Force Replacement Depot*) No 3 APO873 as of 4th April 1944, per Par 3 SO83, HFF Depot No 3 APO873 US Army. Alerted for departure.
C, D, E, F & Medical Companies 2nd Rangers – Braunton Camp, North Devon. Alerted for departure.
Headquarters Company 2nd Rangers – Braunton Camp, North Devon.
1st Lt. Harvey J. Cook was appointed to the rank of Captain. 1st Lt. Anthony Bazzocchi was assigned and joined from Replacement Depot as of 2nd April 1944.

Ranger Training Schedule at Braunton

U.S. ASSAULT TRAINING CENTER, ETOUSA   R-E-S-T-R-I-C-T-E-D

PROPOSED ASSAULT SECTION RIFLE CO (ASSAULT) BN LNGD TEAM (ASLT)	Personnel	Pistol	Rifle M-1	Carbine	Clrd Smoke	Smoke	Fragment	Launcher, Grnde	Bangalore	Wire Cutters	MG, cal.30, light	Amm, MG, boxes	Mortar, 60mm	Amm, 60mm, rds	Launcher, rocket	Rocket; AT	Pole Charge	Pack Charge	Grapnel	Flame Thrower	Signal Equip	Weight per man
					(Grenades)																	
Officer	1	1		4		2																12
Assistant Leader	1		1				8															27
Support Team	9																					29
Riflemen	(5)		5			14	12	1	2	2									3			33
Wire Cutters	(4)		4		4				8	4									2			53
LMG Team	4																					46
Gunner	(1)	1									1											46
Bearers	(3)			3								6										50
60mm Mortar Team	4																					46
Gunner	(1)	1											1									46
Bearers	(3)			3										36								45
Rocket Team	4																					
Rocketeer	(2)	2													2	16						47
Assistants	(2)			2												20						42
Flame Thrower	2	1	1			4	6													1		72 / 29
Demolition Team	5			5		5	10										5	5				40
TOTALS	30	6	11	13	4	27	38	1	10	6	1	6	1	36	2	36	5	5	5	1		

Ammunition: 96 rds per M1 Rifle = 1056
             60 rds per Carbine = 780
             21 rds per Pistol = 126

U. S. Assault Training Center
18 Sept 1943

The ATC produced a memo stating who would be responsible for undertaking the various types of training.

TRAINING PROCEDURE FOR ASSAULT AND SUPPORT SECTIONS

1   *Responsibility for Training.*
   a)   Individual Assault.
Since the weapons of the assault sections are divided into two groups – supporting weapons and co-ordinated weapons – and since the first are weapons familiar to the Infantry organisation, while the second are new and highly technical, the responsibility of training in the assault technique naturally falls into two categories.

(1)   *The responsibility for training in individual assault for supporting weapons – rifles, BARs, machine guns, and mortars lies upon the company officers, for whom instruction guides, advisers from the Assault Training Centre Staff, and training aids are furnished. Company officer instructors not only should prepare daily training in accordance with instruction guides, but also should bring the instruction guides on their persons for consultation when necessary. It is expected that team and individuals armed with the infantry weapons will be proficient in their use and well-instructed in their care.*

(2)   *The responsibility for the training in individual assault of the co-ordinated weapons – rocket launchers, wire cutters, flame-throwers, and demolition charges – lies upon the instructors of the Assault Training Centre Staff. All Officers, NCOs, and the training cadre will assist in this training.*

2   *Organisation for Training.*
   a)   Individual Assault.

(1)   *General – In organising for individual assault, qualified officers within each company will be assigned to accompany the consolidated parties of the company to the rifle, mortar, automatic rifle or machine gun, and demolition ranges. Other officers, if available, may be sent to the rocket, flame thrower, or wire cutting range. Experience has shown it is advisable that the weapons platoon leader of each company be placed in charge of the mortar party, as it is essential that an instructor with previous experience in mortars be responsible for the instruction in that weapon.*

UNITED STATES ASSAULT TRAINING CENTER ETOUSA

TRAINING MEMORANDUM:

INDIVIDUAL EQUIPMENT

1. The following equipments and method of wearing said equipments are recommended while undergoing training at the U.S. Assault Training Center:

```
Undershirt,  cotton
Shorts,      cotton
Sox,         wool
Shoes
Shirt,       W.O.D.
Trousers,    W.O.D.
Leggins,     canvas, dismounted
Belt,        web waist
Helmet,      steel, w/liner
Belt,        cartridge (or pistol)
Pack,        field, less bed roll, meat can, knife, fork.
3 pkts "I" rations, to be carried in field pack.
3 Bars "D"   "     "   "    "    "    "    "    "
5 (or 6) grenades, fragmentation and smoke.
*96 rounds, M-1 ammunition to be carried in belt and bandoleer.
First Aid Packet, to be carried on belt.
Canteen, cup, cover, on belt.
Rifle, M-1
Bayonet and Scabbard.
Gas Mask to be carried as prescribed below:
  Cover, protective, gas, to be carried in gas mask.
  Ointment   "        "    "   "    "    "    "    "
```

2. These articles are carried in the following manner until soldier reaches the beach:

   a. The life belt is worn under the equipment. The pack is slung in the usual manner, with the exception that the cartridge belt is left unbuckled. The rifle is then slung over the left shoulder, sling to the front and muzzle up. The sling is then slipped over the bayonet hilt and around the canteen bottle. The gas mask is then placed on the top of the pack with long strap to the left. The strap is wrapped around the muzzle of the rifle and hooked onto the left front side of the cartridge belt. The short strap is brought directly over the right shoulder and fastened to the right side of the cartridge belt. The equipment is now secured to the belt and can be readily disposed of by a shrug of the shoulders in case of a fall into the water. The chin strap of the helmet is buckled at all times.

   b. Equipment is readjusted as soon as possible after entering the landing craft.

   * When carbine is carried in place of M-1, only 75 rounds carbine ammunition is carried.

R I F L E M E N

1. Organization - General. Each company will detail an officer to be in charge of the 30 riflemen from the company. Each party of riflemen from a section will have a party leader. Groups will report to designated ranges by battalions. The officer in charge of a company's riflemen will instruct his group under supervision of an officer from the Assault Training Center. To assist the company instructor, the party leader of each party from a section will maintain control of his riflemen and will carry out the indicated instructions. Every effort will be made to prevent bunching of groups and to permit each party leader to exercise full control over his party. This is extremely necessary in all phases of the Riflemen's Individual Assault Training in order to teach group coordination and movement.

2. These Instruction Guides will be followed closely by company instructors in training company riflemen.

UNITED STATES ASSAULT TRAINING CENTER ETOUSA

INSTRUCTION GUIDE:

CODE NO.   A-4:   R I F L E M E N

Subject   : Zeroing of Rifles, Rifle Marksmanship, and Individual Movement.

Ranges   : Riflemen of _____ report to Chief Instructor at
                 Range 39 at _____ hours at completion of lecture at Range #40.

Uniform   : Field, with helmets and arms.

Training Aids : Silhouette targets; 8 rounds tracer ammunition each rifleman;
                 24 rounds ball ammunition each rifleman; field glasses.

Objective   : To zero rifles and observe and record percentage of hits on
                 silhouette targets at unknown distances; to increase pro-
                 ficiency in Individual Movement.

Text References: FM 23-5, Chapter 3 and 5; FM 23-30, Chapter 5.

Plan of Instruction:

     Each rifleman will zero his piece, utilizing 8 rounds of Ball ammunition
and type A targets provided on each range. When rifles are zeroed marksmanship
will begin using silhouette targets. Party leader will exercise full control of
his group. Each party of five riflemen will have five silhouette targets assigned
to them. Party leader will designate targets and have party place their fire on
the targets. Targets will then be picked up and percentage of hits recorded on
the form provided. Two groups of riflemen will be on the line firing while member
of the other groups act as coaches. Parties not firing, under the direction of
the Number One Rifleman, will review technique of Rifle fire, and carry out
instruction outlined under 5b below. When Company has completed firing, Company
Instructors should select at least one target from each party and Critique same.
Targets will be placed under direction of Company Officers who will receive their
instructions from supervisors.

Procedure: 1. Explanation of type of work to be covered in the four training
               periods of Individual Assault - Riflemen.

            2. Assignment of Ranges.

            3. Issuing of Ammunition.

            4. Practical Work.

               a. For groups firing.
                  (1) Zeroing of rifles with "A" targets provided on each
                      range, using coach and pupil method.
                  (2) Marksmanship at unknown distances.
                      (a) Each party leader under direction of Company
                          Officer assumes active control of his party.
                      (b) Sets up coach and pupil method.
                      (c) Designates target. (Silhouette)
                      (d) Recording of hits on form provided. (Sample
                          reverse hereof)

---

b)   Team Assault.

(1) Dry Runs – Perhaps the most important phase of all training is the initial 'dry run' in which the section leader trains his section in co-ordination of fire and movement. Normally, there will be one member of the Assault Training Centre Staff at every third 'dry run' range. Usually, a section can perform three 'dry runs' in four hours. Therefore, each company should rotate its six sections among the 'dry runs' assigned it in order that each section may receive the benefit of suggestions from the Staff member of the Assault Training Centre, assault over different runs, and be scored on its performance.

(2) Ball Runs – The assignment to ranges for the runs with ball ammunition will be in accordance with the following schedule in order that suitable ranges for this support sections' fire may be available. Thus a company will have two sections firing and two sections receiving instruction in mines and booby traps at any given time.

RANGES.
Assault Company   Ranges 38 & 39
Assault Company   Ranges 41 & 42

Assault Company	Ranges 45 & 46
Support Company	Ranges 47, 48 & 49
Cadre	Range 50 (Dry)
Cadre	Range 51 (Ball)

(Note: Ranges 47, 48 and 49 permit the 81mm mortar to be fired on visible targets, so that the burst can be observed and still be sufficiently far away that safety requirements can be met).

(3) Ranges for both Dry and Ball Team Assaults will be assigned by battalion and company, so that sections know exactly what they are to do prior to the day and which ranges are to be used.

3. Supply.
    a. Individual Assault.
(1) Ammunition will be delivered to the supply points for Serials A-4, A-5, A-6, and A-7 by the Regimental Munitions Officer; Training Aids will be delivered to the supply points by Area Maintenance Engineers.
    b. Team Assault.
(1) For the ball runs, the ammunition and other aids will be delivered to the battalion bivouac areas at least twenty-four hours prior to the time of the exercise. A breakdown will be given to the battalion S-4s, showing the allotment of supplies for each assault and support section for each exercise. The ammunition should be issued to each section in the battalion area. (Ammunition includes loading and charging of flame throwers).
    Each section should report properly equipped and supplied to its designated range at the time specified by schedule.
(2) Crimpers and wire-cutters will be distributed through Regimental S-4 on or before Serial A-1, Organisation and Equipment. Each section will draw two crimpers, one each to be in possession of the leader of the wire cutting party and the leader of the demolition party at all assault training. Each section will draw four wire-cutters to be carried by members of the wire-cutting party.
(3) Dummy Bangalore will be drawn from Training Aid DP by battalions.
(4) SOME COMMON ERRORS. Loss of training time has been occasioned in the past by errors and omissions, among which are the following:
    a. Training aids and ammunition were not delivered to the proper place or at the proper time.
    b. Ranges had not been assigned down to the section prior to the actual time of use.
    c. Demolition charges had not been prepared prior to the time of use.
    d. Flame-thrower cylinders had not been obtained from the Flame-thrower range or fuel tanks had not been filled.
    e. Weapons sent out by motor failed to arrive or went to the wrong place.
    f. Weapons arrived at ranges in unserviceable condition.
    g. Insufficient number of BAR magazines were provided.
    h. Rifle grenade launchers were not provided.

The work being done at the ATC was not without risks to those involved. The following is an extract from a letter written by 1st Lt. Gordon S. Ierardi: *The training undertaken at the Assault Training Centre is undertaken most seriously and at times is definitely hazardous. Training with live ammunition presents a real problem. The problems must be intense enough to acquaint the participating troops with actual battle conditions and indicate to them proper methods of self-defence – but on the other hand, they must not be so intense as to frighten the individual soldier and injure his fighting spirit. The Centre makes every effort to achieve this goal and I believe that they achieve their aim. However, occasional violent accidents are unavoidable.*

In the week prior to our arrival a most unfortunate accident occurred. While troops were being trained to advance under machine gun fire, one of the guns either went out of control or lost the correct range, firing into a group of men, killing five and wounding fourteen. On Saturday's Hedgehog, another couple were hurt. An inexperienced 57mm gun crew went completely haywire and fired a shot into one of the houses of the little village of Croyde from the training area. In every week there are several casualties, but this is the price which must be paid, for this most valuable training.

The enthusiasm of the staff and faculty at the Centre is most infectious. I have only the highest praise for everyone that I met. All were most co-operative and oozed a pride that they were a part of such important work. The results of their enthusiasm will be seen in the next few months.

6 April 1944

Both Battalions were undergoing ATC Training as per the Rangers' Training Schedule.

A Company 5th Rangers – Braunton Camp, North Devon.

The following 4 enlisted men returned to Duty from AWOL 1100: Pfc. Bellacome, Pfc. Farrall, Pfc. Gabaree, Pfc. McGuire.

Pfc James Gabaree, 5th Rangers: *The battalion was moved closer to the invasion staging area. We were quartered in a secured area surrounded by barbed wire – it was rather boring and the food rations were terrible. A group of us decided that it would be great to have some fish and chips. We slipped under the wire, eluded the guards and were on our way. Our plan was to get some greasy food and return, but we met some ladies and embarked on a two-day frolic.*

Panic happened at army headquarters, as we knew some of the invasion plans. All US Troops were told to return to quarters, anyone absent without leave would be arrested. That was us. The MPs picked us up and took us to the military police headquarters, where we were confined on the second floor. All personnel were out to lunch, leaving one not-so-bright private to guard us. My buddy had great powers of persuasion and convinced the guard that the colonel said it was OK for us to go out to eat.

We hailed a cab, overpaid the driver and were lying on the floor of the cab when we arrived at our compound. We surrendered and were promptly arrested. It wasn't such a joke when it sank in that we might miss the invasion and be sent to jail. I was seated in the middle of a room with bare concrete walls and accused of every crime committed in the last six months. Reality was setting in.

[Author – It also didn't help that Pfc McGuire decided to punch a cocky MP whilst in the process of being arrested.]

Gabaree: *The courts martial took place. The judges were from Army headquarters and were not too happy to be embarrassed by the escapees. The problem was that we knew too many secrets. My captain intervened, saying he needed us, because we were highly trained and could not be replaced. The judges, not too pleased about letting us off the hook, fined us $105 and confined us to quarters for three months. That $105-dollar fine really hurt.*

5th Rangers – Companies B – F, Medical and HQ – Braunton Camp, North Devon.

Headquarters Company 5th Rangers – Braunton Camp, North Devon. John C. Raaen Jr. appointed to the rank of Captain as of 1 April 1944.

A, B, C, D, E & F Companies 2nd Rangers – Braunton Camp, North Devon. No change. Alerted for departure.

Medical Detachment 2nd Rangers – Braunton Camp, North Devon. No change. Alerted for departure.

Headquarters Company 2nd Rangers – Braunton Camp, North Devon.

The following 4 officers were attached for Duty, rations and quarters from the 293rd Joint Signal Co. APO#553 US Army.

1st Lt. Sylvester J. Vauruska. 1st Lt. Jonathan H. Harwood. Lt Bennie Berger (USN). Kenneth S. Norton (USN).

23 enlisted men were attached for Duty, rations and quarters from the 293rd Joint Assault Signal Company, APO#553 US Army.

Sgt. Joseph J. Groth, T/4 Theodore F. Stebbins, Pfc. William J. Skelley, Pfc. Jerome O. Abare, Pvt. Francis Jakowski, Pvt. Lawrence M. McKeever, Pvt. Wallace M. Crank, Pvt. Kenneth Miller, Pvt. Henry W. Genther, T/5 Herman W. Calmes, Pvt. Irvin H. Ferriera, Pvt. Peter P Simundich, T/5 Edward G. Heineck, Pvt. Howard J. Erickson, Pvt. Ramon G. Rolande, Pfc. Albert Kamente, Pvt. Harold F. Plank, Pvt. Mitchell H. Goldenstein, Pvt. Paul Rascon, Pvt. John Gallagher, Pvt. Carles C. Arvizu, Pvt. Arthur E. Gable, Pvt. Paul E. Kimbrough. Alerted for departure.

The following maps show the Rangers' training area around Braunton, Devon.

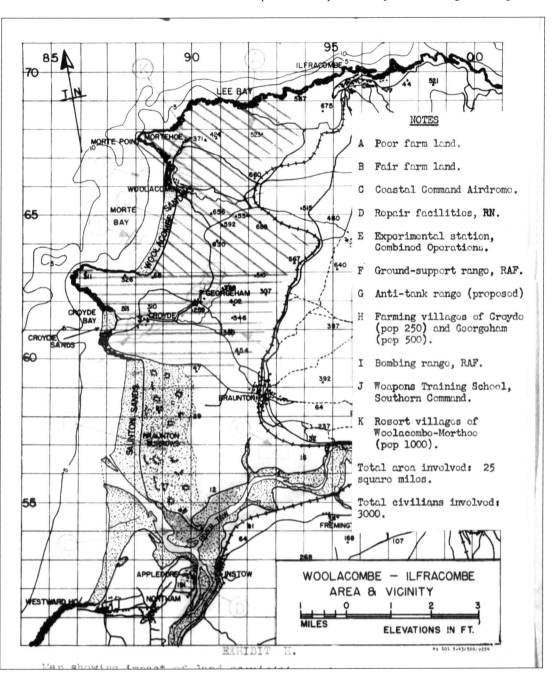

NOTES

A   Poor farm land.

B   Fair farm land.

C   Coastal Command Airdrome.

D   Repair facilities, RN.

E   Experimental station,
    Combined Operations.

F   Ground-support range, RAF.

G   Anti-tank range (proposed)

H   Farming villages of Croyde
    (pop 250) and Georgeham
    (pop 500).

I   Bombing range, RAF.

J   Weapons Training School,
    Southern Command.

K   Resort villages of
    Woolacombe-Morthoe
    (pop 1000).

Total area involved: 25
square miles.

Total civilians involved:
3000.

WOOLACOMBE — ILFRACOMBE
AREA & VICINITY

MILES

ELEVATIONS IN FT.

EXHIBIT K.

Map showing impact of land acquisiti

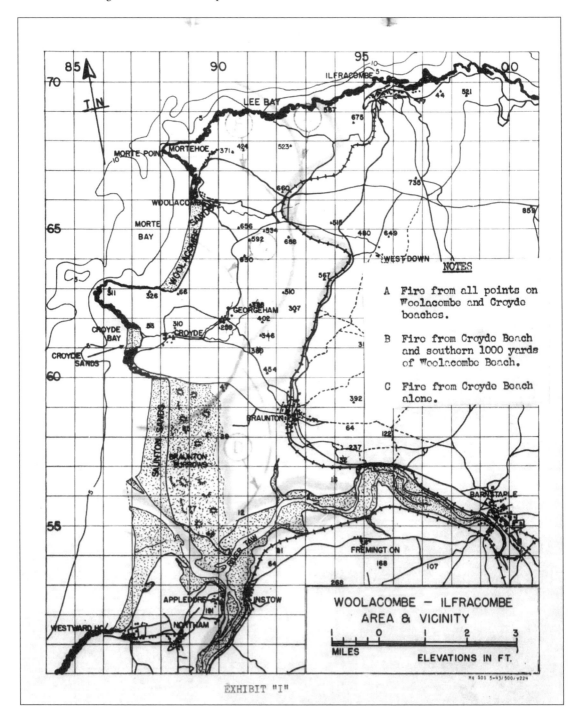

NOTES

A   Fire from all points on
Woolacombe and Croyde
beaches.

B   Fire from Croyde Beach
and southern 1000 yards
of Woolacombe Beach.

C   Fire from Croyde Beach
alone.

WOOLACOMBE — ILFRACOMBE
AREA & VICINITY

MILES

ELEVATIONS IN FT.

EXHIBIT "I"

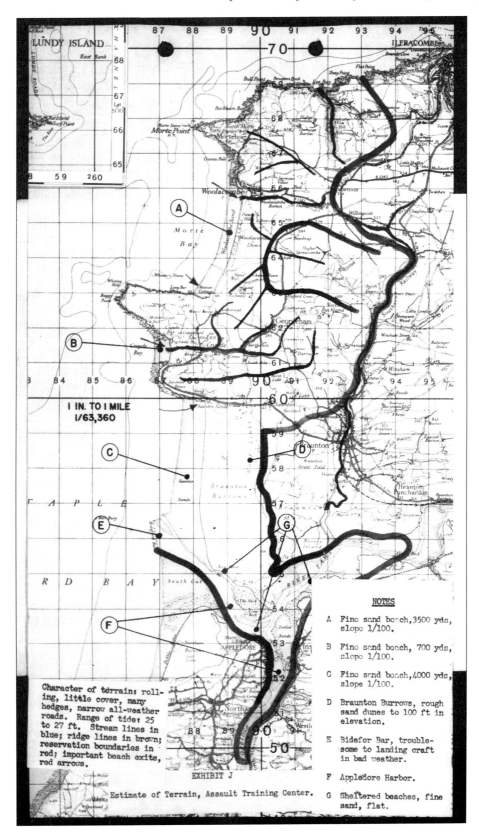

NOTES

A   Fine sand beach, 3500 yds, slope 1/100.

B   Fine sand beach, 700 yds, slope 1/100.

C   Fine sand beach, 4000 yds, slope 1/100.

D   Braunton Burrows, rough sand dunes to 100 ft in elevation.

E   Bidefor Bar, troublesome to landing craft in bad weather.

F   Appledore Harbor.

G   Sheltered beaches, fine sand, flat.

Character of terrain: rolling, little cover, many hedges, narrow all-weather roads. Range of tide: 25 to 27 ft. Stream lines in blue; ridge lines in brown; reservation boundaries in red; important beach exits, red arrows.

EXHIBIT J

Estimate of Terrain, Assault Training Center.

On 6 April the G-2 section released what they called an *'Estimate of the Enemy Situation No 1'* Of special note to the Rangers are the areas highlighted in grey. (The report has been shortened).

Page 2 of 25 Pages   TOP-SECRET   BIGOT
                            "NEPTUNE"

1. SUMMARY OF THE ENEMY SITUATION.

    a. Enemy Order of Battle.

        (1) Forces in the Assault Area.

            (a) The 716th Infantry Division with headquarters at
CAEN holds the coast line from the ORNE River to the mouth of the
DOUVE. This division was formed in April, 1941, and has had no
combat experience. Most of the personnel fall in the age bracket
32-40. 30% are reported to be Poles and not more than 50% Germans.
Equipment includes British, French, and Polish weapons. The division is composed of the 726th Infantry Regiment, holding the coast
from the mouth of the DOUVE to LONGUES, and the 736th Infantry Regiment, holding the coast from ARROMANCHES to the ORNE. There are
indications that a third infantry regiment may have been added.
Although its location is unknown, it is reported that it is made up
of Georgians under German Officers and NCOs. The Division's artillery is the 656th Regiment, probably three battalions.

            (b) The 726th Infantry Regiment with headquarters at
BAYEUX, has three battalions. One battalion, with headquarters at
ISIGNY is believed to be responsible for the defenses around the
mouth of the DOUVE, exclusive of CARENTAN. Its sector includes the
positions on the VIRE estuary and those along Beach 46 on the eastern approach to ISIGNY. Another battalion is thought to have its
headquarters at GRANDCAMP-LES-BAINS and is believed to be responsible for the defense of the coast from a point 4000 yards west of
GRANDCAMP to LONGUES. It is possible, however, that the third battalion, with headquarters in BAYEUX, may hold the coastal sector
PORT-EN-BESSIN - LONGUES. The primary function of this battalion
is believed to be that of regimental reserve.

            (c) The 726th Infantry Regiment is supported by four
batteries of artillery in addition to a considerable number of
close support infantry and anti-tank guns in the coastal strongpoints. Three of these are field artillery batteries, two located
about 1500 yards southwest of MAISY, and one at VAUX-SUR-AURE north
of BAYEUX. The fourth is the 2nd Battery, 832d Army Coastal Artillery Battalion at POINTE DU HOE. Two new artillery battery positions are now believed being constructed in the 726th Infantry area,
one at 1000 yards east of POINTE DU HOE, the other 2000 yards northeast of LONGUEVILLE. No guns are reported in these positions at
present.

        (2) Adjacent Units.

            (a) The 709th Infantry Division holds the CHERBOURG
PENINSULA. It is a three regiment static division, with two or
three battalions of light artillery. Two regiments, the 729th and
739th have a high proportion of foreigners; the third is composed
of Georgians under German officers and NCOs. Quality of troops is

believed to be low. All three regiments hold coastal sectors.
There is a possibility that the 243d Infantry Division with headquarters at LA HAYE DU PUITS is now holding part of the western
coastal sector.

(b) The 711th Infantry Division holds the sector beginning just east of CAEN and extending to the SEINE River. It is
a defensive division consisting of two regimental combat teams.
There have been reports that Russian troops have been added to this
division. The quality of the troops is considered low. The division contains a large number of non-Germans.

(c) The 243d Infantry Division is thought to be in the
CHERBOURG PENINSULA with headquarters at LA HAYE DU PUITS, although
confirmation is still lacking. It is a static type division with
three regiments, the 920th, the 921st and 922d. One of the regiments may have its headquarters in CARENTAN. The Division may be
holding a sector of the west coast of the peninsula. It may be employed as a local reserve in the upper peninsula.

(3) Enemy Reserves.

(a) Local Reserves.

1. The possible third regiment of 716th Infantry
Division may have some elements in the BAYEUX-ISIGNY area. No positive identifications have been made to date in the sector of the
726th Infantry Regiment or of the 716th Infantry Division, although
a few Russians in German uniforms have been reported in TREVIERS and
FORMIGNY.

2. At CARENTAN has been reported the headquarters
of an infantry regiment which may be part of the 243d Infantry Division reported at LA HAYE DU PUITS. Also at CARENTAN is reported
the 17th Machine Gun Battalion and a battery of two 280mm railway
guns, range 40,000 yards. At HALT west of ISIGNY is a battery of
twelve 88mm dual purpose guns.

3. Principal local reserve for this area is the
352d Infantry Division with headquarters at ST LO. It is a recently
organized division with a large proportion of men from units destroyed on the Russian front. It is made up of the 914th, 915th,
and 916th Infantry Regiments, and is believed to be at nearly full
strength. 914th Infantry Regimental headquarters is reported at
AMIGNY northwest of ST LO; another regimental headquarters is reported at CANISY west of ST LO. Also reported at ST LO is a battalion of Local Defense Regiment 193.

4. At TORIGNI-SUR-VIRE southeast of ST LO is
reported a battery of two to five railway guns, cal 280mm, range
40,000 yards.

- 3 -

          5. See Appendix "A" - "Detailed Order of Battle,
CHERBOURG Peninsula".

     (b) Mobile Reserves.

          1. The defense of northern France between the
LOIRE and the FRANCO-BELGIAN frontier is based on a firm coastal defense by static coastal divisions supported by a counterattack force
of armored, motorized, and infantry divisions. The principle of the
defense apparently does not envisage the coastal defense divisions
operating outside their own areas in the initial phase of an invasion. The armored, motorized, or infantry divisions in the counter-
attack force may be expected, however, to strike against allied
assault units with maximum speed and force.

          2. The counter-attack divisions are listed below
with an estimate of the time required for them to be committed to
action as divisions in the assault area. No allowance has been
made for the effect of our air action on troop movements, resistance-group action, or a delay in movement resulting from an incorrect estimate of our situation by the enemy.

Division	Location	Miles	Hours By Road	Hours By Rail	Hours By Air
1. SS Pz Div FRUNDSBERG	LISIEUX	53	9		
2. 21st Pz Div(reported moving to or via Germany)	PARIS	160	15	40	
3. SS Pz Gr Div GOETZ VON BERLICHINGEN	THOUARS	220		40	
4. SS Pz Div DAS REICH	BORDEAUX	390		46	
5. 353d Inf Div	HUELGOAT	212			46(with road movement to railhead)
6. 2nd Pz Div	AMIENS	178		43	
7. SS Pz Div HITLER JUGEND	TURNHOUT	573		69	
8. 3rd Parachute Div	MELUN	190			D/1

          3. In addition to the divisions listed above,
there are three Panzer Training Divisions in the West. Although
listed as divisions, the maximum force that they could muster is
believed to be a battalion of tanks, and probably four to six battalions of infantry. Probably not more than about one-third of each
division could move by its own organic transportation. These divisions are as follows:

Division	Location	Miles	Hours By Road	Hours By Rail
1. 155th Pz Training Div	FOUGERES	85	11	
2. 179th Pz Training Div	RENNES	109	12	
3. 273rd Pz Training Div	ANGOULEME	309		42

                          - 4 -

b. Enemy Defenses.

   (1) General.

      (a) Known enemy defenses PORT-EN-BESSIN - ISIGNY consist of a series of strongpoints on the coast or slightly inland.

Most of them are reinforced infantry positions guarding exits from the beaches. Others furnish local protection to enemy coastal batteries and other special installations such as the radar station west of POINTE ET RAZ DE LA PERCEE.

      (b) Strongpoints consist of pillboxes, concrete personnel shelters and ordinary field emplacements. Some tank turrets mounted on concrete structures have been reported. In addition to heavy weapons such as machine guns and mortars, many strongpoints contain light guns, AT guns and AA guns, which are mounted either in open emplacements or in concrete casemates. Older type pillboxes, personnel shelters and casemates are three feet thick, the newer type six feet six inches thick. Anti-tank ditches have been constructed across most of the important beach exits. Nearly all strongpoints are extensively wired and mined.

      (c) There is no definite evidence of any enemy defensive lines having been organized on the high ground north or south of the AURE in the BAYEUX-FORMIGNY area or on the commanding terrain CERISY FOREST-ST LO. There have been no reports of any extensive prepared defenses in either COLLEVILLE, ST.LAURENT, VIERVILLE or any of the small towns between the AURE and the BAYEUX-ST LO road. It is probable, however, that a few prepared positions and pillboxes have been erected around the enemy headquarters, troop bivouacs and key communication centers in some towns. Around BAYEUX anti-tank ditches are reported being prepared.

      (d) Photographs taken in March 1944 show that much work has been done since December 1943 in the beach defense areas. The construction of the anti-tank ditches across the beach exits North of COLLEVILLE and ST. LAURENT, and the erection of new pillboxes and shelters in beach strongpoints are examples. From other sources, there are indications that the enemy is hastening his defense construction program along the entire channel coast, and that for the first time all-around defenses of larger inland towns, such as CAUMONT and BAYEUX are being prepared.

   (2) Beach Defenses.

      (a) For detailed study of enemy defenses see Appendix "E", "Defense Collation Map".

      (b) Infantry Positions.

         From PORT-EN-BESSIN to GRANDCAMP there are thirty occupied positions including the radar station and the coastal battery. These are manned by an estimated five and one-half to six companies exclusive of the coastal battery and specialist personnel of the radar station. From the position northwest of MAISY to that on the dykes overlooking the estuary of the VIRE at 472830, are fifteen defended areas holding an estimated two to two and one-half companies. In addition there are the two field artillery batteries SW of MAISY.

Garrisons of the individual strongpoints are listed below; these are estimated on the basis of size and installations of each position.

1. PONT-EN-BESSIN.

3. COLLEVILLE-SUR-MER.

a. 698890 (Defended Locality). Infantry position on the coast in open country northeast of COLLEVILLE-SUR-MER: two pillboxes and four shelters, two rows of wire are on flanks and rear with mines between on south and east. There are

- 7 -

---

mines on beach to the north. The garrison is approximately two squads.

b. 693894 (Defended Locality). Infantry position on the coast in open country north of COLLEVILLE-SUR-MER: one pillbox; houses have been demolished in the area. Garrison is approximately one squad.

c. 687895 (Defended Locality). Infantry position on the coast north of COLLEVILLE-SUR-MER; three light infantry guns, probably 75mm; one artillery OP; four shelters; one pillbox; one casemate for light gun; position surrounded by wire. Garrison is approximately one platoon.

4. ST. LAURENT-SUR-MER.

a. 678896 (Defended Post). Small infantry position slightly inland from the coast: one AAMG; one searchlight; one pillbox; two shelters, surrounded by wire. Garrison is approximately one squad.

b. 677900 (Defended Locality). Infantry position on coast near ST. LAURENT-SUR-MER: position surrounded by wire, with mines to southeast; one pillbox; one shelter; one AT gun reported, but unconfirmed. *garrison one squad.*

c. 674899 (Defended Locality under construction. Not shown on Appendix E). Three pillboxes or gun casemates under construction of edge of plateau. Two shelters under construction on the plateau. One small ammunition depot under construction. Future garrison is estimated at two squads.

d. 668903 (Defended Locality). Infantry position 200 yards inland from the coast near ST. LAURENT-SUR-MER: two pillboxes; one concrete OP; three shelters completed; one large shelter being constructed; one AAMG; position is surrounded by wire with mines to front and possibly rear. Garrison is approximately a platoon.

e. 665906 (Defended Locality). Infantry position on coast in built-up area of ST. LAURENT-SUR-MER; one AAMG; three pillboxes; two shelters; the beach is reported possibly mined; position is surrounded by wire. Garrison is approximately two squads

f. 663907 (Defended Post). Small infantry position on coast in built-up area of ST. LAURENT-SUR-MER; one pillbox. Garrison is approximately one squad.

5. VIERVILLE-SUR-MER.

a. 655913 (Defended Locality). Infantry position on coast near VIERVILLE-SUR-MER: two shelters; one pillbox; one 81mm mortar; one AAMG; possibly one 75mm infantry gun; position is surrounded by wire. Garrison is approximately one squad.

- 8 -

b. 648915 (Defended Locality). Infantry position on coast in VIERVILLE-SUR-MER; two pillboxes; one shelter; anti-tank gun, possibly 75mm reported; one AAMG; anti-tank ditch is reported across road at approximately 648916; this is not confirmed by air photographs; position is surrounded by wire on flanks and rear; mine belt on south and east. Garrison is approximately one platoon.

c. 645918 (Defended Locality). Infantry position on coast immediately west of VIERVILLE-SUR-MER: one pill-box; one gun casemate for light gun; position is surrounded by wire. Garrison is approximately one squad.

d. 635928 (Defended Locality). Infantry position on coast in open country at POINTE ET RAZ DE LA PERCEE; two light guns; three pillboxes; one shelter; mobile flak is often present in this area; artillery OP has been reported; position is surrounded by wire. Garrison is approximately one platoon.

6. ST. PIERRE DU MONT.

a. 622935 (Defended Locality). Radar station on coast defended by infantry weapons; one pillbox; seven shelters; two under construction; wire to flanks and rear. Garrison is approximately one platoon.

b. 611927 (Defended Post). Probably a company headquarters is located at the CHATEAU D'ENGLESQUEVILLE in the wood: three pillboxes are reported here; four large huts; this position is probably defended by light automatic weapons, although details cannot be seen on air photographs.

c. 602937 (Defended Locality). Infantry position on the coast north of ST. PIERRE DU MONT; probably not permanently occupied.

d. 586939 (Battery Position). See Para 1 b. (3), Artillery.

e. 575938 (Defended Locality). Infantry position on coast in open country west of POINTE DU HOE; Two pill-boxes; three shelters completed; one under construction; one beachlight; position is surrounded by wire to flanks and rear. Garrison is approximately one squad.

7. GRANDCAMP-LES-BAINS.

a. 564936 (Defended Locality). Infantry position on coast east of GRANDCAMP; three pillboxes; one adjacent to sluice; two shelters; position is surrounded by wire and partially by mines. Garrison is approximately one platoon.

b. 562892 (Defended Post). Probably a head-quarters in the CHATEAU DE JUCOVILLE.

c. 558933 (Defended Locality). Infantry position on coast at east edge of GRANDCAMP: two pillboxes; three shelters; there were formerly two infantry guns in vicinity of this strongpoint; it is not known whether they are still present; there is wire to flanks and rear. Garrison is approximately one platoon

d. 552933 (Defended Locality). Infantry position on coast in built-up area of GRANDCAMP: details unknown; two pillboxes; road blocks blocking some exits. Garrison is approximately one squad.

e. 545932 (Defended Locality). Infantry position on coast in built-up area of GRANDCAMP: one pillbox; one AAMG; road blocks obstructing exits; possibly one light gun at the end of the eastern mole; three guns, possibly 105mm reported in area. Garrison is approximately one platoon.

f. 545928 (Defended Locality). Wire and weapons pits.

g. 538934 (Defended Locality). Infantry position on the open coast west of GRANDCAMP: three pillboxes; one shelter; one AAMG; one 37mm AT gun and one 47mm anti-tank gun in a light turret; wire to flanks and rear. Garrison is approximately one platoon.

8. MAISY

a. 533918 (Battery Position). See 1 b (3), Artillery.

b. 528915 (Battery Position). See 1 b (3), Artillery.

c. 526934 (Defended Locality) Infantry position on the coast in open country northwest of MAISY: three pillboxes; one shelter; one light gun casemate; wire to flanks and rear. Garrison is approximately two squads.

d. 521933 (Defended Locality). Infantry position on the coast in open country: two shelters; position surrounded by wire. Garrison is approximately one squad.

9. GEFOSSE-FONTENAY.

a. 511924 (Defended Locality). Infantry position on the coast in open country north of GEFOSSE-FONTENAY: two pillboxes; the position is surrounded by wire and a belt of mines protects its rear. Garrison is approximately two squads.

b. 511912 (Defended Post). Small infantry position defending a probable company headquarters. The position is surrounded by wire.

TOP-SECRET
"NEPTUNE"   BIGOT

        c.   505916 (Defended Locality). Infantry
position on the coast in open country, northwest of GEFOSSE-FONT-
ENAY; two 105mm gun-hows in open emplacements reported here; one
light gun casemate; one shelter; the rear of the position is protected by a belt of mines between wire. Garrison is approximately
one platoon.

        d.   503907 ? (Defended Locality ?) Small in-
fantry position inland near GEFOSSE-FONTENAY; three, possibly four
pillboxes; position is surrounded by wire. Garrison is approximately one squad.

        e.   493904 (Defended Locality). Infantry
position on the coast in open country covering the PASSE D'ISIGNY;
At least one 150mm infantry gun and one light anti-tank gun in open
emplacements; two concrete casemates for light guns; four pillboxes;
one searchlight. Garrison is approximately one platoon.

Page 12 of 25 Pages   TOP-SECRET   BIGOT
                           "NEPTUNE"

    (c) Pillboxes.

        There are possibly twenty-one concrete pillboxes
covering Beach 46. About ten of these are located on the flat area
between the beach and the plateau and are apparently sited to provide bands of grazing fire on the beach. The remainder are on the
high ground immediately to the rear of the beach. They are placed
to deliver plunging fire on the beach and on approaching craft.
They also cover corridors leading inland from the beach. In addition, many of the houses on the beach have been reported fortified
and converted into pillboxes. There are about eight pillboxes in
the vicinity of PORT-EN-BESSIN, four covering the beach east of
GRANDCAMP, three on the beach at GRANDCAMP and three in the strongpoint west of GRANDCAMP. Twelve or possibly thirteen are located
along the coast from the position northwest of MAISY to POINTE DU
GROWN. Two are at the strongpoint protecting the footbridge at the
mouth of the VIRE, and two in the strongpoint on the dykes west of
the mouth of the VIRE. The number in ISIGNY is unknown. Pillboxes of old construction are three feet thick; pillboxes of newer
type six feet six inches thick.

    (d) Wire.

        There are no continuous bands of wire entangle-
ments covering the length of Beach 46. There is, however, a band
on the beach from the strongpoint at 687895 north of COLLEVILLE to
about two hundred yards east of the strongpoint at 677900 north of
ST. LAURENT, and another band from the corridor at VIERVILLE-SUR-
MER along the escarpment to POINTE ET RAZ DE LA PERCEE. With the
exception of the strongpoints northeast of COLLEVILLE at 698890 and
that at VIERVILLE at 648915, all strongpoints in rear of the beach
are completely surrounded by wire, usually single bands. The ex-
cepted strongpoints are protected by a band on flanks and rear.
Strongpoints in the vicinity of STE HONORINE-DES-PERTES, PORT-EN-
BESSIN, the radar station, POINTE DU HOE, and GRANDCAMP are protected by wire to flanks and rear. Only inland strongpoints are
completely surrounded. Beginning just west of GRANDCAMP a
continuous band extends along the coast as far as POINTE DU GROWN.
The artillery positions southwest of MAISY are surrounded by double
bands. Some of these bands are reported electrified. All positions at the crossings over the VIRE and the strongpoint on the
dykes west of the mouth of the VIRE are completely surrounded by
wire.

    (e) Mines.

        No continuous belt of mines has been reported

- 12 -
TOP-SECRET

round near the entrance to ST. LAURENT along the RUQUET River from 680899 - 679899. This ditch is still under construction. A third ditch blocks the exit from LES MOULINS at 665906.

   6. The ramp to the beach at STE. HONORINE has been blown.

    c. VIERVILLE

      648917 - Tank trap reported on road trench
        5 feet, 6 inches wide covered with tar-
        paulin.

      648917 - Round-topped wall 5 feet thick
        and 7 feet high diagonally across road
        in two staggered 18 feet sections; gap
        3 feet wide reported.

    d. POINTE DU HOE

      587936 - Post obstructions protecting
        artillery position on southeast side.

    e. GRANDCAMP

      563936 - Sluice forms anti-tank wall.

      555933 - Wall blocking road.

      551933 - 546933 - Vertical masonry sea-
        wall 6 feet high with gap at 548933;

543933 + 536936 The seawall continues
(6 feet high) West of harbor.
5493 Walls 10 feet high and 6 feet thick
block all exits from sea-front.
543931 Steel obstacle on West side of harbor, part Element 'C'; part ?hedgehog.
Movable roadblocks on almost all roads
south and west of GRANDCAMP.

(3) Artillery.

(a) There are twenty light guns or gun howitzers of
75mm or 105mm calibre and seven anti-tank guns, the largest of
which is a 75mm anti-tank gun, in the coastal strongpoints PORT-EN-
BESSIN - ISIGNY.

1. PORT-EN-BESSIN.

a. 770860 - Two 75mm guns or howitzers.
Further details lacking.

b. 759877 - 75mm gun or howitzer and two
light coastal guns.

c. 756879 - Medium gun or howitzer in strongpoint in built-up area.

d. 750879 - Medium gun or howitzer in
built-up area. Also 47mm anti-tank
gun

- 16 -
TOP-SECRET
"NEPTUNE"

2. COLLEVILLE

a. 687895 - Three light infantry guns, probably 75mm in strongpoint on hill.

3. VIERVILLE

a. 655913 - One light infantry gun, probably
75mm in strongpoint on plateau.

b. 648915 - One 75mm AT gun guarding beach
exit road.

c. 635928 - Two light infantry guns, 75mm in
strongpoint on bluff.

4. GRANDCAMP-LES-BAINS.

a. 545934 - Three 105mm gun-howitzers in built-
up area with a light gun, 75mm, at the end
of the eastern mole.

b. 538934 - One 37mm and one 47mm anti-tank
guns in beach strongpoint.

5. GEFOSSE-FONTENAY.

a. 505916 - Two 105mm gun-howitzers in beach
strongpoint.

b. 493904 - At least one 150mm infantry gun
and one light anti-tank gun in beach
strongpoint.

2. POINTE DU HOE

a. 586937 - Six 155mm (6.1 inches) French
    guns, probably type GPF. Range 22,000
    yards or more (possibly 25,000 yards).
    Guns on wheel mountings, the wheels be-
    ing secured to the central pivot of a
    concrete emplacement about 40 feet in
    diameter. Each gun is camouflaged with
    netting; there is no turret or gun
    shield. B.O.P. reinforced concrete
    shelter on headland in front of gun
    position. Flank OPs - locations unknown;
    presumably near PTE. ET RAZ DE LA PERCEE
    and east of GRANDCAMP. Shelters and mag-
    azines: underground; reinforced concrete,
    3 feet, 3 inches to 6 feet, 6 inches
    thick. Connected with gun emplacements
    by trenches partly covered over. Huts
    for off-duty personnel and administra-
    tive personnel in rear of gun position.
    Secondary armament: three (?) 20mm guns
    in emplacements on roofs of concrete
    shelters (still under construction).
    Communications: telephone (buried cable);
    presumably also radio. Identification:
    2nd Battery, 832d Army Coastal Battalion.

3. SOUTHWEST MAISY

a. 528915 - Four field guns; 75mm caliber (?)
    (2.95 inches). Range (?) 10,300 yards.
    Guns mounted in open circular pits about
    25 feet in diameter. Battery faces VIRE
    estuary. Accommodation and storage:
    underground concrete shelters and maga-
    zines still under construction. Observa-
    tion Posts: unknown. There is some evi-
    dence that one or two additional batter-
    ies have practiced going into action in
    fields to west of this position. Posi-
    tion now reported abandoned: see sub-
    paragraph (c) below.

b. 533918 - Four 155mm (6.1 inches) howitzers.
    Range (?) 13,000 yards. Howitzers
    mounted in open circular pits, 35 feet in
    diameter, probably with concrete beds.
    Battery faces VIRE estuary. Accommoda-
    tion and stores: underground concrete
    shelter centrally situated in rear of

TOP-SECRET   BIGOT
"NEPTUNE"

emplacements. Observation Post: unknown, presumably on the coast west of GRANDCAMP. Communications: buried cable, presumably also radio. Secondary armaments: one (or two) 20mm AA guns.

(c) New emplacements for artillery have recently been located at MONTIGNY northeast of LONGUEVILLE (623887), east of POINTE DU HOE near ST. PIERRE-DU-MONT (598934), and at (530913) southwest of MAISY. All appear to be four-gun battery positions; the first two are not reported manned as yet. It is possible that the new position southwest of MAISY is for the 75mm battery recently removed from the emplacements 500 yards to the northwest.

(d) Two railway guns, 280mm, range 40,000 yards, are believed to be in the vicinity of CARENTAN; and at least two and perhaps as many as five railway guns of the same type and calibre have been reported as recently as January, 1944, at TORIGNI (5854).

(e) Only major unit of antiaircraft artillery in the assault area is the twelve-gun battery of 88mm dual-purpose guns which has been reported but not confirmed in the vicinity of HALT (4882) west of ISIGNY. The battery on POINTE DU HOE, the radar station, and the strongpoint on the hill east of PORT EN BESSIN; each have three light AA guns; there is one or two light AA guns at the 155mm battery position southwest of MAISY. Each of the strongpoints at the following coordinates on Beach 46 now contains one AA MG: 678896, 665906, 655913, 648915. Light AA guns on self-propelled mountings have often been reported on POINTE ET RAZ DE LA PERCEE.

Page 20 of 25 Pages   TOP-SECRET   BIGOT
"NEPTUNE"

(5) Radar Installations.

Only one enemy radar station is located between PORT-EN-BESSIN and ISIGNY. This is a coast watching station 1500 yards west of POINTE ET RAZ DE LA PERCEE. It contains one frame, two Giant Wurzburgs and possibly one standard Wurzburg. The range of this station is from 10 to 35 miles.

c. Enemy Morale.

(1) The morale of the coast defense divisions, of which the 709th, 711th and 716th are typical, is not good. They contain a good 25% of non-Germans and a further 50% of men who, in varying degrees, are elderly, juvenile, tired or unfit. In view of the length of time they have been at it, training for static defense roles, they should be reasonably good. Their equipment is generally second rate, motor transport is almost non-existent, and supporting elements and services are very inadequate. It is believed that the value for war of these defensive divisions is materially less than that of first-class infantry divisions.

(2) The morale of troops in offensive divisions is usually better than that of troops in static divisions. Their value for war will depend upon their strength, the status of their equipment, and the length of time they have been in process of reformation.

a. Enemy Capabilities

(1) The enemy may defend Beach 46 using approximately a battalion of the 726th Infantry Regiment for manning strong points.

(2) The enemy may use counter-attacking elements of approximately company size from the 726 Infantry Regiment and the possible reserve regiment to retake strong points.

(3) The enemy defense may be strongly supported by air attack, artillery, and rocket weapons.

(4) Anytime after the beach crust of defenses has been breached the enemy may counter-attack with battalion size forces; a battalion from ISIGNY northeast against elements of the 116 RCT, a battalion from TREVIERS north against the 16th and 18th RCTs, and a battalion from BAYEUX west against the 16th and 18th RCTs. A few tanks might be available to support one or more of these counter-attacks.

(5) Anytime after noon of D-day the enemy may counter-attack in the TREVIERS-ETREHAM area with one regiment of the 352d Infantry Division.

(6) During the night of D-day to D / 1 the enemy may employ elements of one regiment of the 352d Infantry Division to infiltrate our positions in the TREVIERES-ETREHAM area.

(7) During the night of D-day - D / 1 the enemy may drop parachute troops anywhere within the beachhead to disorganize the area preparatory to a dawn counter-attack.

(8) Anytime after dawn of D / 1 the enemy may launch a coordinated counter-attack against the positions of the 18th and

- 21 -

TOP-SECRET
"NEPTUNE"

26th RCT with the 352d Infantry Division supported by a battalion
of tanks and other elements of the 155th Panzer Training Division.

  b. Discussion.

      (1) Enemy doctrine indicates that the strongest possible
defense of the beach will be made. There is estimated to be not
more than one battalion in the defenses at the present time.

      (2) It is believed that the enemy will utilize counter-
attacking forces of up to company size promptly upon the breaching
of any of the key defenses, particularly the four main exits. It
is believed that the enemy will have adequate time to move these
small forces into desirable assembly areas and alert them prior to
the breaching of the beach defenses.

      (3) It is believed that the enemy will use all available
air immediately to attack our forces during the landing. Our own
air forces should diminish the effectiveness of these attacks during
daylight hours. Enemy artillery could easily be brought into the
area just prior to the assault. Rocket launching weapons may be
set up in a matter of minutes, and it is anticipated that the enemy
may have such weapons concealed in the CERISY Forest or similar
areas. It may be anticipated that positions have already been
selected for these weapons to fire upon the beach and that the
enemy will put them in position during the night of D-1 - D-day or
at dawn of D-day.

      (4) The battalion of the 726 Infantry stationed at ISIGNY
probably has elements committed to the prepared defenses between
ISIGNY and CARENTAN, but there may be sufficient forces available
to permit a battalion to move from ISIGNY at dawn. This battalion
might move to meet the assault on POINTE DU HOE or to seize the
strategically important terrain in the general LONGUEVILLE area.
TREVIERES is a likely area for either a battalion from the Division
reserve or a battalion from the 352nd Infantry Division. It is
anticipated that in all probability there will be a battalion in
this area on D-day and that it will counter-attack generally north-
wards against our forces. The enemy battalion at BAYEUX will
probably be more concerned with the British on our left than with
our own assault, but it remains a capability for this battalion to
counter-attack into our area. Support of this unit by up to a
company of tanks is possible as BAYEUX is a likely location for
such a unit. There is, however, as yet no report of tanks in the
area.

      (5) The 352d Infantry Division located in the general area
south of the AURE will be, in all probability, the immediate main
counter-attacking force against our assault. One regiment might be
in position to attack in the TREVIERES-ETREHAM area by noon. It is
believed, however, that capability (8) is slightly to be favored

- 22 -

and that an entire regiment will not be committed to an attack on
D-day. It is believed more likely that the first regiment on the
scene will attempt to contain our forces during the organization of
the division for a dawn attack on D ≠ 1.

(6) Although night infiltrations in strength are not normal German tactics, the situation that will exist on the night following D-day will be highly suitable for such tactics and this capability should not be ignored. There will be available elements of
the 352d Infantry Division which could infiltrate in the general
TREVIERES-ETREHAM area.

c. Probable Enemy Action.

(1) Strong defense of Beach 46 by one battalion of the 726th
Infantry Regiment.

(2) Company-size counter-attacks to reestablish beach
defenses.

(3) Rocket and artillery fire on our forces on the beaches
from units not yet identified in the area with air bombing.

(4) A battalion-size counter-attack against the 116th in
the LONGUEVILLE area and a battalion-size counter-attack north of
TREVIERES, both taking place about midday of D-day.

(5) Minor infiltration of our positions during the night
following D-day.

(6) A coordinated counter-attack at dawn of D ≠ 1 against
the 18th and 26th RCT positions by the 352d Infantry Division supported by up to a battalion of tanks and additional minor elements
of the 155th Panzer Training Division.

ROBERT F. EVANS,
Lt. Col., G.S.C.,
A.C. of S., G-2.

- 23 -
TOP-SECRET
"NEPTUNE"

DISTRIBUTION:

	No. Copies	Copy Nos.
CO, Ranger Force	5	157 - 161
CO, 1st Engr Bn	1	162

O.N.1. APPENDIX VII. ANNEXE A.

O M A H A   A R E A

DESCRIPTION OF BEACH DEFENCES. (incl. COLLEVILLE - excl. ST PIERRE DU MONT).

1. **On the Beach.**

   (a) **Strongpoints.**

   The beach in this area is backed by low cliffs or steep slopes. The high ground is broken at intervals by re-entrants through which a road or track leads down to the beach. There are, therefore, two types of fortified beach strongpoint: (i) positions on the beach at re-entrants and (ii) positions on the high ground overlooking the beach.

   Strongpoints are of platoon size or less: an average of 25 to 35 men is likely. They are relatively widely spaced owing to the nature of the terrain: on an average they are about 1,000 yards apart. Fortifications are NOT so heavy as on beaches further to the East; many concrete works are 3ft 3ins thick or less (although some will be of the standard type 6ft 6ins thick).

   The layout is as follows:-

   699890 - Strongpoint on high ground. The next strongpoint to the East is over 1 mile away at STE HONORINE des PERTES 720886. Between these strongpoints there may be two or three very small posts.

   692893 - Small post on the beach; connected with the next position.

   688894 - Strongpoints on high ground overlooking the outlet of a small stream; weapons are sited mainly to cover the beach in front and to the East.

   678897 - Strongpoint on high ground covering the outlet of the RUQUET stream; connected with the next position.

   677902 - Strongpoint on the beach.

   668904 - Strongpoint on high ground, commanding the beach between 677902 (above) and LES MOULINS 664907; connected with the next position.

   667905 - Small post on the beach; backed by an anti-tank ditch at the foot of the slope.

   664907 - Strongpoint on the beach.

   663905 - Small post on high ground overlooking 667905 and 664907. Consists mainly of field works.

   654912 - Strongpoint on high ground, commanding the beach LES MOULINS and VIERVILLE beach 648916.

   648916 - Strongpoint on high ground overlooking VIERVILLE beach. There are two small posts on the beach below at 647917.

   616918 - Strongpoint at top of low cliff, facing the sea; connected with the other positions on the VIERVILLE beach mentioned above.

   637917 - Extensive position on cliff top from 639916 to 636920, but probably NOT strongly held; may include a flank OP of the medium coast battery at POINTE du HOE 537938.

   623934 - Large Radar strongpoint. West of this position there are two small posts on the cliff top at 616937 and 602938; otherwise there are no defences till the battery at 586938 is reached.

2. **Fortified Strongpoints inland.**

   There is probably a lightly fortified strongpoint at COLLEVILLE 687881 - possibly the headquarters controlling beach strong-points North of COLLEVILLE. Similar positions may exist at ST LAURENT 663893 and the Chateau d'ENGLESQUEVILLE 612928. Otherwise no fortifications are known.

3. **A line of field works** (revetted dug-outs and weapon-pits) is being developed between 500 and 1,500 yards from the coast. This is so far of a very sketchy nature: small isolated localities in rear of the coastal fortifications. It could, however, be quickly developed at the last minute.

4. Artillery positions are, so far as is known, non-existent between the medium coast-battery at 586938 (six guns in Casemates) and the field battery at VAUX-sur-AURE 792831 (four field gun howitzers in field position). Both batteries could be brought to bear on OMAHA Beach, although this is NOT their main task. The coast battery is chiefly anti-shipping: to fire effectively on OMAHA Beach the guns would have to be moved out of the Casemates. VAUX-sur-AURE battery is sited to fire on the area of PORT-en-BESSIN.

   It is possible that field batteries may be brought up to meet an assault on OMAHA Beach, either from positions in other areas or from reserve units inland.

   (b) **Obstacles.**

   Steel underwater obstacles have been laid along the whole beach. They consist largely of steel tetrahedra (pyramids).

   There is probably a belt of wire along the back of the beach or on the seawall, where this exists, but the wire can seldom be seen on photographs, except round strongpoints and in their immediate vicinity. Similarly there is thought to be continuous wire along the top of the cliffs and slopes behind the beach.

   At VIERVILLE there are steel obstacles behind the sea-wall. Roads leading from the beach are blocked by walls and will probably also be cratered.

   Mines.

   Mines are probably laid along the low ground at the foot of the cliffs and slopes; anti-tank and anti-personnel mines are certain to be laid, probably irregularly, near beach exits.

   There are extensive minefields, mainly anti-personnel, on the edge of the high ground: these are laid in staggered belts up to 200 yds. deep. Minefields are found in considerable depth up to 1,000 yds. inland in the VIERVILLE and COLLEVILLE areas: these are probably anti-tank to prevent deployment off roads leading from the beach exits. Strongpoints are protected by belts of anti-personnel mines along their perimeter.

A revised description of the beach defences in the Omaha Sector was issued.

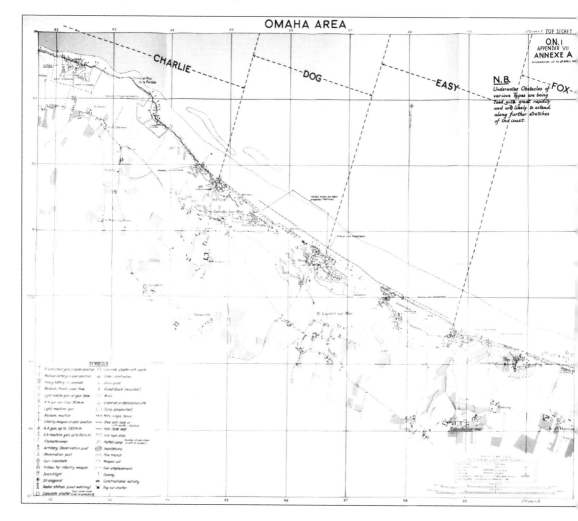

7 April 1944

A Company 5th Rangers – Braunton Camp, North Devon.
The following two men were reduced to the rank of Private: Sgt. Bellows, Sgt. Wittels.
The following men were appointed Sergeant: Cpl. Bakos, Cpl. Drish, T/5 Mazullo.
Pfc. Battice was appointed T/5.

5th Rangers – Companies B – F, Medical and HQ – Braunton Camp, North Devon.

A Company 2nd Rangers – Braunton Camp, North Devon.
The following two men were returned to the grade of Private as of 6 April 1944: T/5 McCann, T/5 Gillhamer.
Pvt. Gillhamer was then appointed Pfc. as of 6 April.
Pfc. Ewaska was appointed to the grade of T/5 as of 6 April 1944.
S/Sgt. Belmont was transferred out sick to the 313th Station Hospital Barnstaple, North Devon as of 6 April.

Maurice Prince: *All the while we were here, we toiled hard at day, but when evening rolled around and passes were issued out, we Rangers went to town and played harder. The cities of Ilfracombe and Barnstaple were places of paradise as far as we were concerned, and we took the greatest of advantage of these havens.*

Our home town, Braunton, wasn't much of a place, although it did have a cinema, several pubs and a few fish and chip joints. About the best thing that the town could boast of was the railroad and the highway that linked this village to the cities of Ilfracombe and Barnstaple. It was these transportation facilities that gave us an outlet to these cities where merriment and entertainment via wine, women and song could be obtained.

Our training program for the first couple of days consisted of elementary fundamentals and basic principles. After that came the actual school courses which began by breaking the company down into individual groups with each group a different class of instruction. The sections were placed in the following categories – demolition and explosive group; mine and booby-trap class; barbed wire obstacles; and a weapons group that combined the bazooka, flame thrower, anti-tank grenades and individual arms into one class.

These specialized groups were coached and instructed by experts in these subjects. More was learned from these qualified teachers than in all our previous training put together.

The barbed wire group learned every known way of breaching and crossing that obstacle. The demolitions and explosive group were taught formulas and were shown how to formulate them. The mine and booby-trap class got the latest and most up-to-date information of laying, blowing, safe-ing and neutralizing minefields. They were shown how to use mine detectors and became versed in the job of probing and seeking by eye and hand for enemy booby-traps, while the weapons groups absorbed all the knowledge and data these experienced teachers could throw at them concerning firearms. They learned how to use their weapons and when to use them. They got to know the functioning of their arms and they were made experts on the firing of all guns.

B, C, D & E Companies 2nd Rangers – Braunton Camp, North Devon. No change. Alerted for departure.

F Company 2nd Rangers – Braunton Camp, North Devon.
Officers 1st Lt. Jonathan H. Harwood and Lt jg (Navy) Kenneth S. Norton were both attached for Duty, rations and quarters from the 293rd Joint Signal Company. APO 553 US Army. As were the following 12 enlisted men: Pvt. Ramon G. Rolande, Pvt. Paul Rascon, Pvt. Pete P. Simich, T/5 Edward G. Heineck, Pvt. Harold F. Plank, Pvt. Mitchell Goldenstein, Pfc. Albert Kamento, Pvt. Howard J. Erickson, Pvt. Carlos C. Arvizu, Pvt. Paul E. Kimborough, Pvt. John Gallacher, Pvt. Aurhur E. Gable.

Medical Detachment 2nd Rangers – Braunton Camp, North Devon. No change. Alerted for departure.

Headquarters Company 2nd Rangers – Braunton Camp, North Devon.
The following two officers were relieved from attached for Duty, rations and quarters.
1st Lt. Jonathan H. Harwood, Lt. Kenneth S. Norton.
The following 12 enlisted men were relieved from attached for Duty, rations and quarters: Pvt. Peter P Simundich, T/5 Edward G. Heineck, Pvt. Howard J. Erickson, Pvt. Ramon G. Rolande, Pfc. Albert Kamente, Pvt. Harold F. Plank, Pvt. Mitchell H. Goldenstein, Pvt. Paul Rascon, Pvt. John Gallagher, Pvt. Carles C. Arvizu, Pvt. Arthur E. Gable, Pvt. Paul E. Kimbrough.
Alerted for departure.

BEACH OBSTACLE DEMOLITION

From the water's edge to the seawall on Omaha Beach the Rangers were expected to encounter a number of varied beach obstacles, and once inland, they would come upon stronger and more complex German concrete positions. It was therefore necessary for them to be taught all the variations of explosives and their capabilities in both a classroom environment and during exercises.

As assault troops, their mission would involve attacking difficult enemy positions, often operating behind enemy lines and they would not always have the luxury of being able to call in Engineers to do the work for them.

On the beach they were to ignore the beach obstacles on D-Day. Within three minutes of the Rangers landing on the beach, the Naval Combat Demolition units would land behind them and destroy the beach obstacles for the other men and vehicles that followed.

The Germans employed many similar obstacles inland to those on the beach and there would be situations where it would become necessary for the Rangers to destroy them.

For the beach obstacles, the Rangers were first shown enlarged photographs and diagrams detailing the latest German defences being deployed along the French coast. Some of these were intelligence photographs gathered by spies along the seafronts and others were taken by low flying aircraft using side-mounted cameras. They all combined to develop a picture of the many and varied styles of obstacles the German army was using to prevent the invasion being successful. A detailed set of diagrams were created to study these obstacles. These 'targets' not only consisted of beach obstacles, but concrete pillboxes (a generic term used by the men to describe anything of any shape and size that resembled a lump of concrete), tobruks for machineguns, anti-tank walls and bunkers of all types. These were all objects that the Rangers ultimately would encounter – so training had to be given.

The Omaha Beach defences were designed using a number of differing types of man-made items placed in such a way as to intercept and deflect a landing craft from its intended path to the beach.

One such item was called Element C – or more commonly known as the 'Belgian Gate' and consisted of a very heavy steel gate mounted upright, with a rear supporting frame. Weighing around 1,200kg, they were often mounted on concrete rollers and could be pushed out onto the beach. Variations could have steel cables tied between multiples of them across roads and then they became a most formidable roadblock for vehicles. Most of these obstacles had been

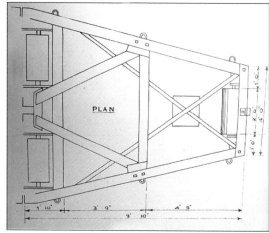

captured by the Germans during the invasion of France through Belgium. They were a readily available defensive item and one of the few obstacles which were sufficiently large, and heavy enough not to be simply pushed aside by the tanks and landing vehicles on the beach. They had to be blown up where they stood or bulldozed and pushed out of the way where possible.

A variation to the Belgian Gate was the curved static obstacle. These were not expected to be encountered by the Rangers on D-Day – but they would be found elsewhere in Europe. They were often deployed in long lines to cover wide open spaces. They would stop vehicles from crossing whilst infantry and artillery could target them.

Aerial reconnaissance photographs were displayed, and showed beach workers diving for cover as an Allied reconnaissance plane took photographs of their activities.

Mixed in along Omaha Beach were thick wooden poles used to create ramps, these were placed in groups across the sand. Rising to a height of approximately 8ft, the early construction techniques employed by the Germans' forced labourers from foreign countries – along with conscripted French locals – found them difficult to dig into the sand. After a little while in the waterlogged sand, the obstacles would collapse or sink. The next and more robust method that was actively being employed nearer to D-Day was the use of a water jet to blow a hole in the sand, which allowed the post to be

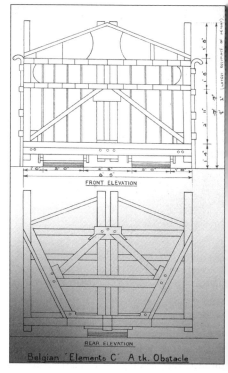

quickly inserted to a deeper level. Once this method was adopted, the whole process was sped up and this created a more solid post on the tidal beach.

There were variations constructed, with one log sloping upwards at one end from the beach level to the apex of a triangular frame at the other. The angled beam could sit on a single vertical log with the logs having an 10-18in diameter – heavy enough to support the angled beam. These could reach a height of 10-12ft with the sloping member 15-18ft long. Some of the sloping logs were also supported by 1, 2, or 3 legs and these ramps were some 20-30ft apart, in rough bands, either with pilings or Element C. The aim of them was to all allow the landing craft to run up onto them and either topple over – or to run the craft onto an attached Teller mine or explosive device. The idea was to cover the beach approaches and trap any landing craft and, with the force of the waves behind it, hopefully drive the craft onto a mine.

Mock-up Belgian gates at the ATC.

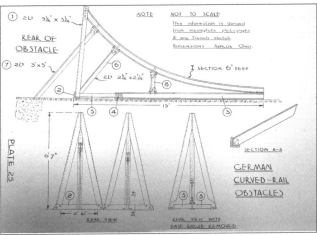

Another obstacle was the single log piling measuring 10-18in in diameter set into the sand vertically or angled at 15-25ft intervals, and these were positioned in single rows or in staggered bands. Once the tide came in, these became very difficult to spot and an unsuspecting landing craft could easily run onto one.

When inland, these were often created using varying lengths of railway track concreted into the ground. Intelligence photographs gathered covertly by the French underground before D-Day and sent back to England, showed these obstacles in use widely in French towns and cities as well as along the beaches.

It was virtually impossible for a tank or other vehicle to cross such a defence without it first having been blown up. But the steel hedgehogs could be eliminated by undoing bolts from their central gusset plates, allowing the obstacle to collapse – without an explosion which may alert enemy units in the area to the Rangers' presence. However it was impractical to achieve that whilst under fire on a beach.

The coastline at Grandcamp in front of Maisy – La Casino positions. This low-level reconnaissance aircraft photograph shows posts fitted with Teller mines.

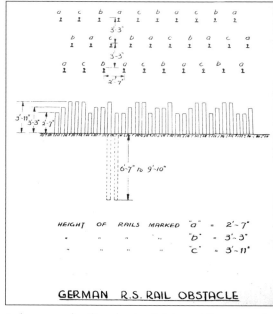

A document detailing the size, height and frequency of these type of obstacles.

Cement cones and steel pyramids were manufactured in a similar style. These and the hedgehogs (often called 'Rommel's Asparagus' by the French) were also used widely in coastal inland areas. They were particularly effective at rendering fields and outlying coastal areas useless to any glider or aeroplane landings. When mixed together, combinations of these obstacles could present a major stumbling block to the Rangers' advance and they would have to be blown up.

Behind Omaha Beach on the aerial reconnaissance photographs and drawn on maps based from these photographs were a number of anti-tank ditches and walls. Large solid walls of concrete and steel were used by the Germans as a deterrent to the invasion and as a blockage for beach exits.

Most of these obstacles were not going to interfere with the Rangers' advance as foot soldiers off the beach. Inland they were expected to be encountered frequently in various guises. In particular, the use of the anti-vehicle and anti-tank weapon, the Teller mine was expected to be the most prevalent.

Hedgehogs on Grandcamp beach.

THE BANGALORE TORPEDO

A Bangalore torpedo is removed from its transit box.

Shown here during training, the Bangalore is pushed – one attached to another – under the wire before firing.

One obstacle guaranteed to get in the way of the Rangers, as first wave landing troops was barbed wire. Studies of the German defences on Omaha beach had shown that above the sea wall along the coastal roadway, there was a large quantity of circular rings of barbed wire laid along the surface of the road. Barbed wire was particularly difficult to cut by aerial bombardment, so another more hands-on method was to be used.

The photograph shows assault engineers carrying Bangalore torpedoes to their boats. Notice the white binding rope on the Bangalores and the roll of detonation cord in the man's right hand.

A number of men in each company were to carry 1, 2 or 3 Bangalore torpedoes. These steel tubes were filled with explosives and strapped by heavy white rope either together or to the man's rifle and then carried ashore. One end was fitted with a nose cone, which allowed the Bangalore to be pushed through wire or, in the case of the Omaha roadway, underneath the barbed wire. Once one section had gone through, another was slotted onto it from the back and twisted to lock it in place. The two were then pushed forwards with the process being repeated by adding more lengths until the wire was crossed. Once the lengths of Bangalores had been pushed sufficiently under the target wire, a fuze was inserted into the rear and ignited using a pull fuze with a few seconds delay. The instruction

'Fire in the Hole' was to be yelled to announce to anyone near that something was about to explode… and hopefully the resultant explosion would create a hole in the wire.

Effective as it was, the Bangalore only created a small narrow passage through wire entanglements, and instructions were given to the effect that any breach in the wire was to be exploited immediately by the men in a column. The man who fired the Bangalore was to go through first and if any part of the wire remained uncut by the explosion, he was to lie over the wire and his comrades would use his back to walk on. He was to get up only when everyone had gone through.

During combat training and under simulated enemy fire, men are putting together two lengths of Bangalore torpedo.

A man stops to insert the fuze into the back of the Bangalore.

It was expected that multiple teams would be able to breach the German wire and advance up the bluffs at Omaha at the same time in different places.

These men are preparing the demolition charges placed onto a pole. These could be positioned more accurately against a concrete target than by simply throwing it at the emplacement.

The Army issued what they called Code Jingles to be relayed if identification needed to be verified by units between themselves once they had landed. The idea was that these would be things that either most US servicemen would already know – or they were designed specifically to be difficult for German speakers to copy.

2nd and 5th Ranger Battalion Group

A group from the 2nd and 5th Ranger Battalions underwent a training period here of three and a half weeks, apparently slightly longer than was planned. Part of this was special purpose or rehearsal work. As the Assault Training Center is not involved in the higher levels of planning, it was necessary for the Rangers to tell us what they had to do and what was needed.

All received the same individual training as the RCT's, but their team, company, and battalion exercises were modified as required.

Like the Airborne troops, the Rangers were full of enthusiasm and were very proficient with their weapons. They were not as methodical and serious as some other units we have had and there was a tendency to horseplay. Their attitude resulted in improvising and opportunism, but this is fitting for the type of unit and they were alert and keen.

TOP SECRET   NOT TO BE TAKEN ASHORE

OPERATION NEPTUNE—NAVAL COMMUNICATION ORDERS
(Short Title : ONCO)

Section XVIII

ORDERS FOR BOMBARDMENT—*continued*

APPENDIX A—JINGLES TO BE MEMORISED BY S.F.C.Ps.

Force " O "

S.F.C.P. No.

1   Pepsi Cola hits the spot,
      A pint for a nickel that is a lot.

2   Zazu Pitts is a crazy name,
      But its owner is not at all insane.

3   Would a woodchuck chuck
      If a woodchuck would chuck wood.

4   Reading writing arithmetic,
      Taught to the tune of a hickory stick.

5   Jack be nimble, Jack be quick,
      Jack jump over his candlestick.

6   Pretty little blue bird
      Flys so high that he nearly touches the sky.

7   Ride a cock horse to Banberry Cross
      To see a fair lady upon a white horse.

8   Now is the time for all good men
      To come to the aid of their country.

9   Can you remember that thirty days
      Has September, April, June and November.

10   Blue sparrows use Barclay Square
      As trysting ground and thoroughfare.

11   Nothing would be finer than to be
      In Carolina in the morning.

12   When the moon comes over the mountain
      I'll be waiting there for you.

13   Zero hour struck the clock,
      All the ships are at our dock.

14   If I were only young and fair
      And upon my bald spot had some hair.

15   Sticks and stones will break my bones,
      But names will never hurt me.

ELEVENTH AMPHIBIOUS FORCE

S-E-C-R-E-T

ELEVENTH AMPHIBIOUS FORCE, UNITED STATES FLEET
WAR DIARY - APRIL 1944

7 April 1944 - Rear Admiral HALL left the ship for a conference in London
with Commander Task Force ONE TWO TWO.
Commander Transport Division 97 in the U.S.S. ANNE ARUNDEL,
with U.S.S. DORTHEA L. DIX and U.S.S. THURSTON, reported
for duty in accordance with dispatch orders of the Chief of
Naval Operations dated 7 March 1944, and assigned to
Transports, Eleventh Amphibious Force for duty. HMS PRINCE
CHARLES, Commander S.H. DENNIS, R.N., reported for temporary
duty in connection with the training of Ranger Battalions.

[Author: The Battalion doctor – Walter Block wrote an account of events on 7 April later in December 1944. Although it is retrospective, it is still relevant to the chronology of events and thus I have included it here. It is interesting that he adjusted what he had said in terms of the number of guns in casements, etc. This is the information gleaned *after* the battle and expressed with the benefit of hindsight.]

"It was about 5:30 PM on April 7th, 1944, when Major Schneider called me in the Operations Room at the Assault training Center near Braunton, Devon, and first showed me the Pointe. 'That's it!, Doc, that's the spot where we are going to operate. Pointe du Hoe'. On the map, it actually looks insignificant, merely a tiny protuderance jutting out from the beachline, approximately mid-way between the towns of Grandcamp and Vierville-sur-Mer on the coast of Normandy. I don't think I was particularly impressed because it looked like any one of a hundred similar protuberances on the invasion coast and my face evidently showed this for, after looking up, the Major continued, 'Now, take a look at this', slowly rolling up a thick cloth covering hanging on the further wall of the room. 'This' was a series of photographs taken at every possible angle by airplanes of a coastline. Closer inspection showed this to be no ordinary coastline with smooth beaches, fine grained sand, and a gentle sloping inward. What I saw was a panorama of many air photos linked together to form an unbroken line. Carefully looking thru a lens, I saw what appeared to be an unbroken line of cliffs, for the most part sheer, stretching out on either side of a sharp spear-pointed outcropping. This outcropping was Pointe du Hoe. The beach was covered with boulders, broken-off portions of the cliff and, in outline, was irregular.

"'That's going to be a pretty hard climb, Major. Why such a tough spot to make an assault landing?' I asked. 'Good question, Doc. Come over here and I'll show you some more pictures',

"So off we went to another wall in the room and another cloth was rolled up. Here, on a 'blow-up', was an aerial photo of the Pointe and the adjacent terrain. Whereas the large over-all photos had showed only the coastline, a few houses, hedgerows, paths, and roads, this photo showed the Pointe itself and the land extending for about 1500 yards to either side and about 2000 yards inland. On the extreme tip of the Pointe, at the top of the cliff, was a square whitish-gray outline. On each side of this were three round whitish-gray masses, approximately 30-35 feet in diameter, judging from the scale of the map. The Major went on to explain that these were six 155-mm gun emplacements, two of them casemated and the others open. By casemated, he meant that the guns were encased in a protective covering of concrete on the top as well as on the outer walls. The square mass on the tip of the Pointe was an observation post.

"Each of the emplacements was linked to the others by a series of camouflaged paths and underground tunnels. Such gun emplacements were protected by coverings varying anywhere from six to ten feet of solid concrete. Most of the concrete had been poured in the past year but some of it was at least three years old and had become harder with each succeeding month. Extending back from the cliff and encompassing all six guns was row upon row of wire, single and multiple apron. Our G-2 information revealed that interspaced between the protective wire and on both sides of the position were extensive minefields. Truly a formidible setup! But that was not all! Extending along the cliffs on both sides of the Pointe were open and closed machine gun positions. There were four that could readily be seen on the left flank of the Pointe and three on the right flank. These were the ones that were visible; how many more there were that were well camouflaged was anyone's guess. Off to the upper left of the photo was a series of small buildings, the village of St. Pierre du Mont.

"The landing on this beach, the climbing up the cliffs, and the destroying of these six large guns was to be the mission of the Rangers. For many months, the men of the Battalion had been undergoing hard, intensive training; including rope climbing, cliff scaling, and physical exercises far harder than the usual infantryman undergoes.

"But there was more training in store for the men. In order to make sure that the operation would be successful, no stone was left unturned. The German mind, working on the premise that the sea and the high, steep cliffs would prove to be obstacles no human could master, had built their defenses on the assumption that any attack on this strongpoint would have to be made from inland, assuming that a bridgehead had previously been established elsewhere. Their perimeter defense clearly proved this.

"Nevertheless, this bastion could not be permitted to stand by any invading army because these guns could command and control a vast area to each flank and out to sea. If the main assault on the continent were to be made anywhere near this area, these guns must be silenced. There was one way to do it - an audacious and bold plan: To attack the position from the rear, that is, the sea side. For this attack, the 2nd Ranger Battalion, under the command of Lt Col James E. Rudder, was selected.

---

8 April 1944

5th Rangers – Companies A – F, Medical and HQ – Braunton Camp, North Devon.

No change. Alerted for departure.

A, B, C, D, E & F Companies 2nd Rangers – Braunton Camp, North Devon.

Maurice Prince: *During our courses we found time to improve our physical bodies and to build up excess stamina. The hilly and sandy terrain which bordered the beach at Braunton was an excellent route to hike and speed march over (our officers thought) so we Rangers carried our tired and weary bodies over this prescribed route while our rears dragged the ground and our tongues hung down to our toes. After we completed our individual group courses, we re-organized and started to run problems where we could combine our skills and trades we had picked up, so as to run platoon and company problems.*

Many was the morning you could see our company hiking up the hilly road that led to Baggy Point fully loaded down with weapons and equipment, sweating, cursing, and singing, but ready to run through these dry runs and wet run problems.

Generally, we'd have a defensive position set up on this hill called Baggy Point. The defence was a simulated affair, but which had several pillboxes controlling all the entrances to this point. Dummy targets represented the dug-in emplacements which were protecting the pillboxes and actual barbed wire surrounded the entire defence.

There was also more wire between the positions, themselves, so that gave us more than one wire obstacle to breach. There were no mine fields or booby-traps involved in these problems.

Our mission would be to take, destroy, and hold this position, to re-organize and either hold or prepare to move out to a new objective or else to be prepared – if the case need be – to beat off an enemy counter attack.

The plan we used to carry out our attack was plain. The wire cutting team (barbed wire breaching) was to lead off. Following and covering their movements by fire was to come from a squad of riflemen. Then spread out and further in the rear came the bazooka team, flame thrower team, demolition team and anti-tank grenadiers, in that order.

Our initial advance was to be aided by an artillery and mortar barrage plus the direct fires of our own 75s (which we had mounted on half-tracks) upon the enemy position. These fires were supposed to neutralize, and knock out some of the open emplacements which covered the enemy positions while making the defenders of the pillboxes button up.

We were to advance forward to the first line of wire. Here the wire cutting party was to breach the wire in any manner they saw fit, either cutting, blowing, or bridging while being covered by our riflemen. As soon as the wire was taken care of, the bazooka team and anti-tank grenadiers were to take up positions covering the slits in the pillbox, making sure they kept them buttoned up. Meanwhile, the flame throwers and demolitions teams were to advance under the protective fire of the bazooka. The wire party by this time would be breaching the last wire obstacle in front of the pillbox. Riflemen would be pinning down the enemy in the open emplacements. Our own mortars, artillery and s.p. guns would quit firing as they were then masked by us, and start to displace forward. By now the assault of the pillbox would begin. With the riflemen still covering, plus the bazooka and anti-tank grenadiers, the flame throwers would come forth and squirt the openings of the box. These bursts of flame didn't last longer than thirty seconds.

When the last flash burned out, the demolition team was to run forward and place a pole charge in the same slits, retreat a distance and await the big blowoff. When the explosion came, our job was nearly over. A bayonet charge plus the throwing of hand grenades made sure that any enemy playing dead would stop acting. We would overrun the position and take up a defensive position. Generally the problem ended here and we would reassemble and get ready for the critique that was sure to follow.

We won all honours in the running of these problems. The commendations and praises heaped upon us by the school's officers were most gratifying and more than atoned for the honest and arduous labours we exerted in the undertaking of these exercises.

Medical Detachment 2nd Rangers – Braunton Camp, North Devon.
Pvt. Hanlon and Pvt. McDonough were both appointed to the rank of Pfc. Medical Detachment Order No 3.
Alerted for departure.

Headquarters Company 2nd Rangers –
Braunton Camp, North Devon.
Alerted for departure.

The US Army issued instructions on water conservation.

In view of the serious drought conditions now prevailing, the utmost economy in the use of domestic water supplies will be observed in installations occupied by the US forces. All commanding officers will take proper measures to enforce water discipline and reduce water consumption to minimum requirements.

An order dated 8 April confirms that the Rangers' attachment to the 1st Infantry Division was to continue.

 - OVERLORD

HEADQUARTERS, V CORPS
APO 305, U. S. ARMY

:::::::::::::::::::::::::
:AUTH: CG, V CORPS :
:DATE: 8 April 1944:
:INIT: *SFV*   :
:::::::::::::::::::::::::

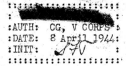

8 April 1944
Copy No. *17* of 50 Copies.

SUBJECT: Troop Assignment.

TO   : See Distribution.

     1. Inclosure No. 3 (subject: Attachment Order, 23 March 1944) to
letter, subject: Alert Order, dated 23 March 1944, and Amendment (subject:
Attachment Orders, 26 March 1944) to inclosure Number 3 to letter, subject:
Alert Order, dated 23 March 1944, are rescinded.

     2. The assignment and attachment orders issued by this headquarters
prior to the issuance of the orders referred to in paragraph 1, above, remain
in effect until 20 April 1944, on which date the provisions of paragraph 4,
following, become effective, except the 635th T.D. Battalion which is relieved
from attachment to the 28th Infantry Division and attached to the 3rd T.D.
Group, effective 8 April 1944. The present status of the _further_ attachment
within this Corps of units assigned and attached to V Corps is summarized below:

                                                    PERSONNEL VEHICLES

     b. To 1st Infantry Division for operations only:
         (1) 2nd Ranger Bn (-Det)
         (2) 5th Ranger Bn (-Det)
         (3) 1 Bridge Plat, 996th Engr Treadway Bridge Co.   24   12
         (4) 16th AAA Group, consisting of
             (a) Hq & Hq Btry, 16th AAA Gp
             (b) 413th AAA Gun Bn (M)
             (c) 197th AAA AW Bn (SP)
             (d) 467th AAA AW Bn (SP)
             (e) 320th AAA Bar Bln Bn (-1 Btry)(VLA)
             (f) 3 Provisional AAA Btrys (MG)(when attached to V Corps)
         (5) Btry "A", 17th FA Obsn (in Bristol Channel Build-up)

     f. To the 29th Infantry Division for movement overseas only effec-
tive April 8, 1944. Upon arrival in the far shore assembly areas, units are
released to their normal attachments. (Par. 4, following)
                                              PERSONNEL VEHICLES
         (4) Det, 2nd Ranger Bn) To be moved with division
         (5) Det, 5th Ranger Bn)   residue   30   10

     Orders previously issued to certain units attaching them to certain
other units for courts-martial jurisdiction remain in effect until otherwise
directed.

     Division, Brigade and Group Commanders and separate Battalion Com-
manders will notify the units within their respective commands of the provisions of this directive as pertain to those units.

          By command of Major General GEROW:

                                        Irwin J. Degnan
                                   IRWIN J. DEGNAN,
                                   2nd Lt., A.G.D.,
                                   Asst. Adjutant General.

DISTRIBUTION: Copy Numbers
CG, First U. S. Army   1,2,3
CG, V Corps   4 to 25, Incl.
CG, 1st Inf Div   26

Also on 8 April a report was issued regarding the dissemination of intelligence. In particular it describes the process under which all intelligence updates would be provided to unit commanders once their unit reached their Marshalling areas. This was particularly relevant to the Rangers as it meant that Lt. Colonel Rudder could be briefed on a daily basis in-camp and he would be in a position to re-brief his men accordingly.

TOP SECRET

OVERLORD – EASTERN COMMAND OPERATION INSTRUCTION   IA 31/1
NO 54 – INTELLIGENCE

8 Apr 44

Copy No. ~~33~~ 26

1. REPORTING OF INFORMATION:

(a)   It has been agreed by HQ 21 Army Gp that all infm of enemy action on land will be passed by 21 Army Gp Tps to the HQ of the Dist in which they are located.

(b)   Tps other than those of 21 Army Gp will report to the HQ of the Dist in which they are situated.

(c)   Dists will report to HQ Eastern Comd, repeating to the Information Room at HQ Marshalling Area and where necessary to neighbouring Dists.

(d)   HQ Eastern Comd will report to GHQ Home Forces and to ~~Joint~~ *COMBINED* HQ for the infm of Second Army and to the Naval and Air HQ associated with them.

(e)   Any urgent infm will be passed direct by HQ of Dists to ~~Joint~~ *COMBINED* HQ and repeated to Eastern Comd.

2. SITUATION REPORTS:

Situation reports will be originated by Dists in time to reach HQ Eastern Comd at 0730 hrs and 1800 hrs daily, but important infm will be forwarded immediately received. The date when these situation reports will start will be notified later.

Situation reports issued by HQ Eastern Comd will be distributed to branches of Comd HQ as necessary.

3. INFORMATION ROOMS AT HQ MARSHALLING AREA:

(a)   Information Rooms will be set up at HQ Marshalling Areas S and R, and will function on a 24 hr basis.

(b)   The object of the Information Rooms is to provide infm for fmn comds and their staffs concerning :-

(i)   The tactical situation overseas.

(ii)   The area movement situation within the Comd.

(c)   Staff.

The staff for manning the Information Rooms at HQ Marshalling Areas S and R will be found from static personnel and will be allocated by the Marshalling Area Comds. As the Information Rooms will be functioning on a 24 hr basis, the suggested minimum staff required will be 3 offrs and 6 OR.

```
                                    -2-

    (d)        Channels of infm to Information Rooms will be :-
    (i)  "The tactical situation overseas   DUCO will inform
         Marshalling Area Information Rooms direct, by means
         of COSITINTREPS, of the tactical situation overseas.
         Such infm will NOT be distributed outside Marshalling
         Area HQ Information Rooms.   Comd HQ will pass infm
         contained in GHQ Summary of Ops to HQ Dists and
         branches at Comd HQ for distribution".

              (ii) Movements.   From the MC staff at the
                   Marshalling Area HQ where the Information
                   Room is situated.  A close liaison will
                   be maintained between MC staff and the
                   Information Room staff.

4.   COMMAND INFORMATION ROOM:

              In order to illustrate the gen tactical situation
    overseas, a map will be kept up to date in the present Comd HQ
    Information Room, security considerations permitting.

              Copies of situation reports issued by Comd HQ will
    be displayed in the Information Room.
```

9 April 1944

Sunday. Both Battalions undergoing ATC Training as per 'RANGERS Training Schedule' but there were no allocated classes today.

5th Rangers – Companies A – F, Medical and HQ – Braunton Camp, North Devon.

A, B & C Companies 2nd Rangers – Braunton Camp, North Devon.

No change. Alerted for departure.

2nd Battalion Historical Narrative

On 9 April, Companies D/E/F, commanded by Captain Harold K. Slater, moved by rail to Swanage, Dorset, for instruction in the newest methods of cliff assault. All types of climbing was practised; these included free-hand, smooth rope, toggle rope, rope ladder, and steel ladders in four foot sections which could be assembled to any height desired. All manners of cliff formations were mastered; sand, chalk, solid rock, loose rock, and combinations of these. An innovation at this stage was the method of anchoring the rope at the top of the cliff by the use of naval rockets; this method had been tested and proved by the British Commandos. A rocket-type mortar was employed which could hurl a rope 200 feet into the air, the special grapnel attached to the leading end of the rope digging into the ground and providing an anchor so that the rope could be safely ascended.

Companies A/B/C underwent instruction in the technique of transferring from the LSI(S) to the LCA. Exercises were then conducted in conjunction with the 5th Ranger Battalion in the beach-assault and movement overland along a route similar to that expected on D-Day. The missions allotted to the Companies on this exercise were based on those expected on the actual D-Day mission. Another combined exercise culminated in a dawn attack on a near-by airfield with British soldiers providing the opposition.

Maurice Prince: *After this course was completed, we began a new phase of training. Already the big dealers at Battalion headquarters knew the part that we Rangers were to play in the coming assault on Fortress Europa, so that we started to undergo problems that were to be similar to those to the coming invasion plans.*

D Company 2nd Rangers – Swanage, Dorset.
Captain Slater went from Detached Service to principal Duty as Company Commander.
S/Sgt Kuhn, Pfc. Cruz and Pfc. Hudnell went from Detached Service to Duty.
1st Lt. Baugh was relieved of temporary Duty as Company Commander.
D Company departed for Swanage by train at 0500 hours. They arrived in Swanage, Dorset at 1310 hours.
Alerted for departure.

E Company 2nd Rangers – Swanage, Dorset.
E Company departed for Swanage by train at 0500 hours. They arrived in Swanage, Dorset at 1310 hours.
Alerted for departure.

F Company 2nd Rangers – Swanage, Dorset.
F Company departed for Swanage by train at 0500 hours. They arrived in Swanage, Dorset at 1310 hours.
Alerted for departure.

Medical Detachment 2nd Rangers – Braunton Camp, North Devon.
Captain Block went from Duty to Detached Service.
S/Sgt. Clark and T/5 Hillis both went from Duty to Detached Service in Cambridge.
Alerted for departure.

Headquarters Company 2nd Rangers – Braunton Camp, North Devon.
Alerted for departure.

The quiet Swanage seafront in 1944.

10 April 1944
Both Battalions undergoing ATC Training as per 'RANGERS Training Schedule'.
5th Rangers – Companies A – F, Medical and HQ – Braunton Camp, North Devon.
A & B Companies 2nd Rangers – Braunton Camp, North Devon.
No change. Alerted for departure.
C Company 2nd Rangers – Braunton Camp, North Devon.
1st Lt. Goranson was appointed to the rank of Captain as of 15 March 1944.
Alerted for departure.
D, E & F Companies 2nd Rangers – Swanage, Dorset.
No change. Alerted for departure.
Medical Detachment 2nd Rangers – Braunton Camp, North Devon.
No change. Alerted for departure.
Headquarters Company 2nd Rangers – Braunton Camp, North Devon.

On 10 April the US Air Force undertook a series of aerial reconnaissance over flights producing photographs of the Normandy coastline which included the Pointe et Raz de la Percée radar station and Pointe du Hoc.

10 April – OPERATION NEPTUNE – NAVAL ORDERS were amended and re-issued.

Counter Battery Fire.

   Ships are to be ready to open fire at their pre-arranged battery targets either from the time when assaulting convoys come within range of them, or from the time when it is light enough for the enemy to spot his fall of shot visually, whichever is the later. The latter time will be at about civil twilight – 30 mins, which is earlier than the time at which it will be possible for spotting aircraft to start operating.

   Owing, however, to the probable inaccuracy of unobserved shoots on pin-point targets, fire is not to be opened until observation from the air is possible, unless accurate fire is opened by the enemy. In this event, fire must be opened without observation, uneconomical expenditure of ammunition being accepted. In such cases, Assault Force Commanders should, if the situation permits, order a short concentration of two or more ships on the battery in order to spread out the expenditure of ammunition and to make more certain that, by a combination of probable errors, the battery area is covered.

Whilst it is still dark, radio counter measures should impede enemy fire which is, therefore, unlikely to be effective; the presence of bombarding ships during this period would increase the risk of casualties without any corresponding advantage to be gained.

Neutralisation of pre-arranged counter battery targets is to be carried out until each battery is captured or rendered sufficiently unserviceable no longer to constitute a menace to our forces. Whilst the flashes of guns sited close to the shore may indicate the degree of activity of the battery, it will be impossible for firing ships and difficult for spotting aircraft to judge this when the battery is sited inland. It is important, therefore, that neutralising fire should only cease as a result of definite information, and fire is to be continued in case of doubt.

An attempt to neutralise coast defence and field batteries without observation is unlikely to succeed, and should only be undertaken as an emergency measure.

Continuous spotting during an engagement is not essential, once range and line have been found, a ship at anchor or stopped can legitimately continue an engagement for a reasonable period without further spotting; in the case of ships making way, this period is to be kept as short as possible, as errors in estimation of ships' speed, tide, etc and alterations of course by the firing ship, will cause the fall of shot to wander off the target. Unobserved shoots should, therefore, only be carried out against larger areas such as towns and villages to prohibit their use to the enemy, rather than to destroy pin-point targets in the area.

Drenching of Beach Defences.

The object of close supporting fire during the final approach is to assist in putting down sufficient density of high explosive to neutralise the defences and demoralise the defenders preparatory to the final assault.

Warships and gun support craft are to open fire at the times laid down in the pre-arranged fire plan. A high rate of fire is to be maintained during this period, even though continuous spotting is likely to be impracticable. Ships and craft detailed to engage specific strong points are to close to as short a range as is possible and engage their targets with A.P. Shell.

~~━━━━━~~ ̶G̶O̶T̶   NEPTUNE

Page 1 of 3 pages

REVISED
ANNEX 12
TO
OPERATIONS PLAN   10 April 1944
NEPTUNE

UNCLASSIFIED

<u>PREARRANGED AIR AND NAVAL BOMBARDMENT PLAN</u>

1. <u>Air Bombardment Plan</u> – The air support for Operations Plan NEPTUNE, is based upon the attack of coast defense battery positions and neutralization of beach defense localities which are of immediate importance to the assaulting forces. Coordinates of coast defense batteries and localities are listed in Appendix 1. Also included in this plan is the air support for airborne divisions. Three phases of the prearranged air support plan are outlined below:

a. Pre Y Day Bombardment:

Air effort has been allocated for two missions in the First Army sector. Battery positions 1 and 3 have been requested. These positions are either casemated or being casemated. They are included in a plan to bomb other key defense batteries along the entire coast.

b. Night Bombardment:

(1) Time: H-314 minutes to H-44 minutes, D day.

Heavy bombers will attack battery positions 1, 1A, 3, 4, and 6. Battery position 6 will be bombed prior to daylight – 4 hours since airborne troops will be near this target at that time. Two alternate targets in order of priority are battery positions 2 and 8A.

(2) Time: H-34 minutes to H hour, D day.

Medium bombers will attack battery positions 1, 8A, and 5. If battery position 1 has been destroyed prior to Y day, then its alternate target is battery position 9.

c. Day Bombardment:

(1) Time: H-30 minutes to H hour.

(a) Heavy and medium bomber missions will attack beach defense localities with 860 short tons of bombs per beach. Co-ordinates and weight of effort for targets are listed in paragraph 2, Appendix 1.

(b) Fighter bombers will attack five battery positions with double missions. These battery positions are 1, 1A, 4, 5, and 8A. A sixth double mission will bomb ILE DU LARGE (4705) if future reports disclose that it is occupied. If not occupied, then the mission will attack road and rail centers at CARENTAN (3984). In case battery position 1 has been destroyed prior to Y day, then its alternate target is battery position 14.

(2) Time: D day, commencing at H hour.

Each Corps will have available on call one fighter-bomber squadron on air alert.

(3) Time: H/6 hours.

The following bombing missions for first turn around have been requested:

– 1 –

~~━━━━━~~ B I G O T

(a) Coastal defense battery positions 2, 7, 8, 11, and 12.

3. Naval Bombardment Plan – The naval gunfire support for Operations Plan NEPTUNE will assist the landing and subsequent advance inland and along the coast, initially by fire on prearranged targets and later on call. Previously published allocation to the Western Naval Task Force of support ships will be augmented. Definite allocation is not known at this time. Three phases of naval gunfire support are outlined below:

a. Counterbattery:

Time: H-30 minutes until silenced.

The heavier gunfire support ships will attack coast defense battery positions 1, 1A, 3, 4, 5, 6, 9, 14, and 16, which are shown in paragraph 1, Appendix 1. These battery positions are listed numerically in order of importance. Battery position 6 will be attacked only upon call, since it is in airborne troop landing area. Ships, that complete their counterbattery tasks prior to H hour, may assist in the attack of beach defense targets.

b. Attack of Beach Defenses:

Time: H-20 minutes to H hour.

2. Requests, for reassignment of air support on beach defense localities and missions scheduled after H hour, D day, will be submitted by Corps to this Headquarters on Y-45 and Y-15 days.

This drenching fire will be delivered by close support destroyers and support craft. Details concerning allotment and use of support craft are included in Annex 2, Organization of Assault and Follow Up, and Annex 21, Artillery and Naval Fire Support Plan. Heavier gunfire support ships, that finish assigned counterbattery missions will augment this phase of the fire plan. High angle fire, fire with reduced charge, and enfilade fire from flank firing positions should be utilized in order to reduce ricochets when firing on targets on beach UTAH, and the area between the beach and inundated area in the front of the 101st Airborne Division after it has dropped. Beach defense localities to be neutralized are shown in paragraph 3, Appendix 1. At H hour, close support fires will be lifted to targets further inland or on the flanks. A list of such defenses is included in paragraph 4, Appendix 1.

c. Close Support Fires on Call:

Time: After H hour.

Close support fires will be delivered on call from Shore Fire Control Parties with assault battalions by battleships, cruisers, and destroyers. Some of the targets that will require neutralizing are indicated in paragraph 5, Appendix 1.

 I_G_O_T   NEPTUNE

APPENDIX 1
TO
REVISED ANNEX 12

BEACH DEFENSE TARGETS

The following list of beach defense targets will be revised as additional batteries and defense localities are reported through intelligence channels.

1. Coast Defense Battery Positions:

First Army Number	Coordinates	Description	Location
1	586939	6-155 G	Pointe Du Hoe
1A	365201	4-170 G	La Pernelle
2	264266	4-240 G	Fermanville
3	368044	6-155 G	Crisbecq
4	354137	6-155 G	Morsalines
5	533918	6-155 H	Maisy
6	405980	4-155 H	St. Martin De Varreville
7	246264	4-170 G	Fermanville
8	392277	6-155 G	Gatteville
8A	394227	4-Med or Hy	Gatteville
9	359023	4-105 GH	Azeville
10	793832	4-105 GH	Vaux-sur-Aure
11	354291	4-105 GH	Pte de Neville
12	378204	4-150 H	Aigremont
13	848853	4?-105 GH	Arromanches
14	343057	4?-105 GH	Ozeville
15	344102	4-105 GH	Lester
16	528915	4?-77 G?	Massey
17	339138	3-105 GH	La Fosse
18	413160	3-75 G?	Tatihou

2. Defense Localities to be Bombarded by Air:

    a. Beach OMAHA:

        (1) 60 ton mission localities: 623935, 637927, 645918, 648915, 655912, 664907, 666906, 668903, 677900, 673896, 688895, and 698890.

        (2) 70 ton mission localities: 750880.

        (3) 35 ton mission localities: 755878 and 758877.

    b. Beach UTAH:

        (1) 120 ton mission localities: 451969, 442982, and 435992.

        (2) 60 ton mission localities: 456953, 448958, 442972, 429000, 418017, and 447975.

        (3) 35 ton mission localities: 493904, 505916, 538934, and 545932.

3. Defense Localities on Assault Beaches:

    a. Beach OMAHA: 722886, 698890, 694893, 688895, 678896, 677900, 668903, 666906, 664907, 655912, 657911, 652915, 648915, 645918, 637927, 635928, 623935, and 622935.

OPERATION NEPTUNE - NAVAL ORDERS
(Short Title : ON)

ON 8. - INSTRUCTIONS FOR BOMBARDING FORCES.

Amendment No. 3. (Continued).

Effect of Pre D day bombing on the D day Fire Plan.

4.   Batteries in the NEPTUNE area (See Table A) selected for pre
D day bombing have all already been attacked once, with a limited degree
of success. Although it is intended to bomb them again before D day, it
is unlikely that there will be sufficient positive evidence of damage
done to justify their withdrawal from the D day fire plan. If, however,
certain batteries are known to have been destroyed or very severely damaged,
alternative targets for bombers prior to H hour will be selected by the
Joint Commanders-in-Chief, and Task and Assault Force Commanders will be
kept informed.

5.   Similarly, should the effect of pre D day bombing be sufficient
to justify amendment to the list of targets for naval bombardment (Table C),
the list will be amended after consultation with Task Force Commanders.

Summary of Tables to this Appendix.

6.   Table A. - Battery targets for pre D day bombing.

Table B. - Battery targets for night Heavy and Medium bombers
prior to H hour.

Table C. - Battery targets for naval bombardment.

Table D. - Spotting aircraft: programme of Sorties and
pre-arranged briefing.

Table E. - Beach targets for day heavy and medium bombers
during the assault.

-4-

OPERATION NEPTUNE - NAVAL ORDERS
(Short Title : ON)

ON 8. - INSTRUCTIONS FOR BOMBARDING FORCES.

Table A. - Battery Targets for Pre D day Bombing.

The following batteries in the NEPTUNE area have already been
bombed once. See Appendix II, para. 4.

	Target	Map Reference
(a)	LE GRAND CLOS (LE HAVRE)	468311
(b)	FONTENAY SUR MER	368044
(c)	BENERVILLE	422107
(d)	HOULGATE	256938
(e)	POINTE DU HOE	586938
(f)	OUISTREHAM	117797
(g)	LA PERNELLE	365200
(h)	SALENNELLES	155776
(i)	MORSALINES	354139

<u>TOP SECRET</u>   -5-

OPERATION NEPTUNE - NAVAL ORDERS
(Short Title : ON)

<u>ON 8. - INSTRUCTIONS FOR BOMBARDING FORCES.</u>

<u>Table B. - Battery Targets for Light, Heavy and Medium Bombers
prior to H hour</u>

<u>Night Heavy Bombers (up till Civil Twilight)</u>

Target	Map Reference
POINTE DU HOE	586937
LA PERNELLE	365200
FONTENAY SUR MER	368044
MORSALINES	354139
ST. MARTIN DE VARREVILLE	405980
SALENNELLES	155776
HOULGATE	256809
BENERVILLE	422107
BARFLEUR	394228
OUISTREHAM I	117797

2.   Timing will be arranged so that those batteries which are the
greatest menace to the Assault Forces are bombed during the period when
Assault Forces reach the lowering position, subject to the necessity for
bombing certain batteries early in the night in order to avoid endangering
airborne troops.

<u>Medium Bombers (between Civil Twilight + ten minutes and H hour)</u>

	Target	Map Reference
3.	LA PERNELLE	365200
	POINTE DU HOE	586937
	MAISY	533918
	OUISTREHAM I	117797
	OUISTREHAM II	103779
	MONT FLEURY	918861

[N.B. There are dozens more bombing mission timings for the RAF and USAF for Pointe du Hoc and the Maisy Batteries. They are listed in equal number and they were to be bombed regularly in the days and hours leading up to D-Day. It would be impractical to show them all here.]

Both the US and Royal Navy were given re-confirmation of the Army landing areas as defined for the Omaha Sector. The Sector is again marked as starting to the west beyond the batteries at Maisy and goes to the east stopping at Port-en-Bessin.

TOP SECRET   OPERATION NEPTUNE—NAVAL ORDERS
                                   (Short Title : ON)

ON 1.—General Outline of the Operation—*continued*

Appendix VIII.—Division of Enemy Coast into Sectors—*continued*

Annexe B.—Schedule of Sectors

Sector Letter.	Brief Description.	Co-ords.	Length (yards).
	OMAHA AREA (O)		
ABLE	Mouth of River VIRE to PTE DU MAISY	491878–527935	7600
BAKER	A to PTE DU HOE (PTE ST. PIERRE)	527935–587940	6500
CHARLIE	B to rd	587940–648917	8000
DOG	C to mouth of stream	648917–667907	2400
EASY	D to rd	667907–688897	2900
FOX	E to rd	688897–723886	3900
GEORGE	F to PORT EN BESSIN (West breakwater)	723886–751882	3200

Overleaf: The same division of beaches is shown here on a larger scale Navy plan.

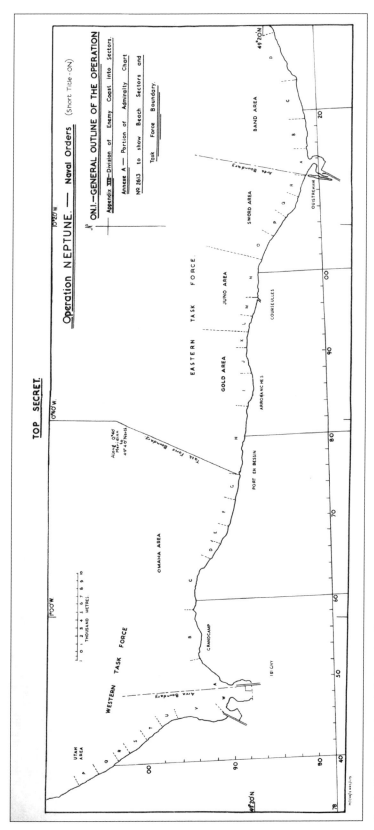

Beach divisions for the whole invasion front.

Naval Orders again restated the necessity of carrying on regardless of '*loss or difficulty*'.

OPERATION NEPTUNE—NAVAL ORDERS
(Short Title : ON)

ON 7.—Instructions to Task Forces and Assault Forces Prior to H Hour—*continued*

The Assault

30. The Assault is to be executed in accordance with the orders of the Task Force Commanders and is to be pressed home with relentless vigour and determination, regardless of loss or difficulty.

31. The following simultaneous assaults are to be made at H hour :—

Location	Division	Naval Force	No. of Brigades or R.C.T. Assaulting
ST. LAURENT (650917 to 692895)	1 Div. (U.S.) 29 Div. (U.S.)	O	2
VARREVILLE (430000 to 454960)	4 Div. (U.S.)	U	1

Timetable of the Assault

32. An approximate timetable of the Assault is given hereunder. Full details will be included in the Assault Force Commanders' Orders.

Prior to H hour	Bombardment by supporting warships, S.P. artillery and L.C.T.(R).
H – 5 to H hour	D.D. tanks beach.
H hour	L.C.T. carrying AVRE and L.C.A.(H.R.) beach.
H to H + 30 mins. ..	Assaulting infantry in L.C.A. land.

10.4.44.

The same report goes further and details the embarkation and sailing schedule for the '*Force O*' (Omaha) group.

TOP SECRET   1

OPERATION NEPTUNE—NAVAL ORDERS
(Short Title : ON)

ON 7.—Instructions to Task Forces and Assault Forces Prior to H Hour

Sailing

(*b*) Group 3 of Force O consisting of 13 L.S.T., is to rendezvous with 12 stores coasters sailing from the ISLE OF WIGHT area in Area Z and form one convoy to the assault area. *See* ON 10, para. 16 and ON.7, Appendix I.

Opposite: Naval timings were worked out using rendezvous points at intervals of 12 hours, 6 hours and H-Hour. These were called 'Mickey Mouse' Diagrams.

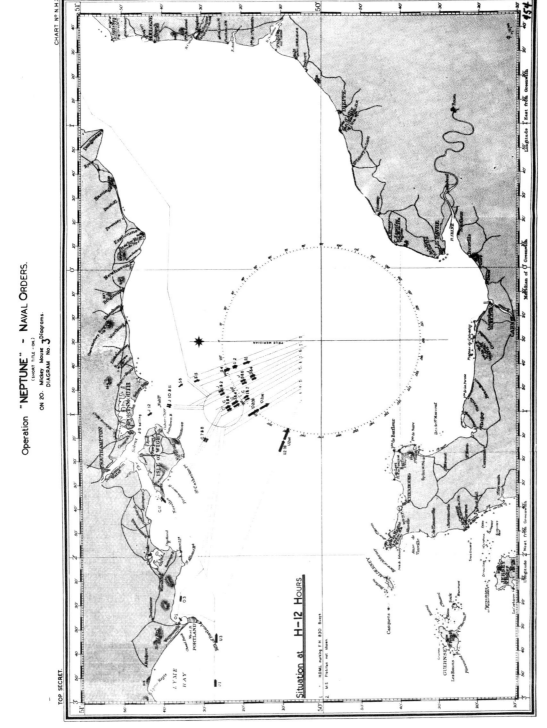

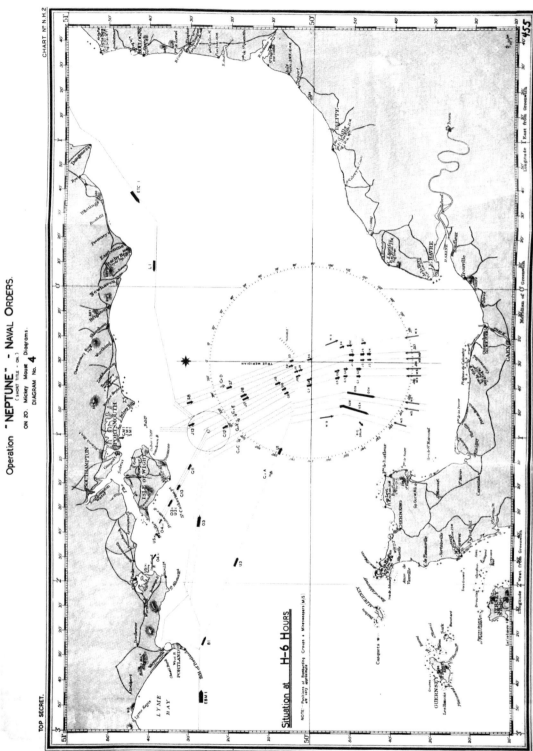

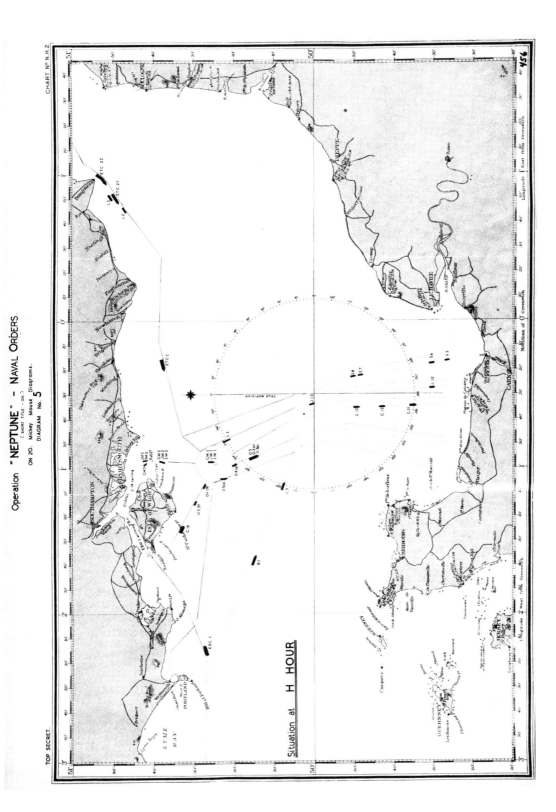

11 April 1944

Both Battalions undergoing ATC Training as per 'RANGERS Training Schedule'.

A Company 5th Rangers – Braunton Camp, North Devon.

Pfc. McGuire went from Duty to being confined (6 days) in the Battalion Guard house. Alerted for departure.

5th Rangers – Companies B – F, Medical and HQ – Braunton Camp, North Devon.

A Company 2nd Rangers – Braunton Camp, North Devon. No change. Alerted for departure.

B Company 2nd Rangers – Braunton Camp, North Devon.

1st Lt. Andrew D. Hanley was assigned and joined from 52nd Replacement Battalion. F.F.R.D. No 3 APO 873. Alerted for departure.

C Company 2nd Rangers – Braunton Camp, North Devon.

1st Lt. George F. Sarasin was assigned and joined C Company. Replacement Btn F.F.P.D. with the principle Duty of platoon leader. Alerted for departure.

D, E & F Companies 2nd Rangers – Swanage, Dorset. No change. Alerted for departure.

Medical Detachment 2nd Rangers – Braunton Camp, North Devon.

S/Sgt. Clark and T/5 Hillis both returned from Detached Service in Cambridge to Duty. Alerted for departure.

Headquarters Company 2nd Rangers – Braunton Camp, North Devon. No change. Alerted for departure.

11 April Major General Huebner met with his Naval counterpart to discuss details of the forthcoming landings.

```
                    ELEVENTH AMPHIBIOUS FORCE          SECRET

    S-E-C-R-E-T

                    ELEVENTH AMPHIBIOUS FORCE, UNITED STATES FLEET
                         WAR DIARY - APRIL 1944

    11 April 1944 - Major General HEUBNER, U. S. Army, Commanding General, First
                    Infantry Division and Brigadier General HOGE, U. S. Army,
                    Commanding General, Provisional Engineer Special Brigade
                    Group, aboard for conference.
                    U.S.S. ATLAS reported for duty in accordance with Commander
                    Twelfth Fleet dispatch orders of 3 April.
```

12 April 1944

Both Battalions undergoing ATC Training as per 'RANGERS Training Schedule.'

A Company 5th Rangers – Braunton Camp, North Devon.

The following four men were reduced to the rank of Private: Pfc. Bellacome, Pfc. Farrall, Pfc. Gabaree, Pfc. McGuire. Alerted for departure.

5th Rangers – Companies B – F, Medical and HQ – Braunton Camp, North Devon.

A Company 2nd Rangers – Braunton Camp, North Devon.

1st Lt. Morris A. Stoffer was appointed and joined from the 41st replacement battalion F.F.R.D. as of the 11th of April 1944 and assumed the principal Duty as platoon leader. Alerted for departure.

B Company 2nd Rangers – Braunton Camp, North Devon. Alerted for departure.

C Company 2nd Rangers – Braunton Camp, North Devon. Alerted for departure.

D, E & F Companies 2nd Rangers – Swanage, Dorset. No change. Alerted for departure.

Medical Detachment 2nd Rangers – Braunton Camp, North Devon. No change. Alerted for departure.

Headquarters Company 2nd Rangers – Braunton Camp, North Devon.

13 April 1944

Both Battalions undergoing ATC Training as per 'RANGERS Training Schedule'.

5th Rangers – Companies A – F, Medical and HQ – Braunton Camp, North Devon.

A, B & C Companies 2nd Rangers – Braunton Camp, North Devon. Alerted for departure.

D, E & F Companies 2nd Rangers – Swanage, Dorset. Alerted for departure.

Medical Detachment 2nd Rangers – Braunton Camp, North Devon. Alerted for departure.

Headquarters Company 2nd Rangers – Braunton Camp, North Devon. Alerted for departure.

13 April Army instruction confirming the procedures to be undertaken if anyone was found to be 'Absent Without Leave'.

No. of Copies 225

Copy No. 167

HEADQUARTERS V CORPS   Authority CG, V Corps.
APO #305, U.S. ARMY.   Date   13 April 1944.
                       Initials _____

ADDENDA
to
Inclosure No. 2
to
Alert Order
23 March 1944.

SUPPLEMENTAL ADMINISTRATIVE INSTRUCTIONS

SECTION I - GENERAL

These instructions amplify and extend those contained in Inclosure No. 2 to Alert Order, this headquarters, 23 March 1944.

1. Application of POM-ETO-SSV. The general procedure for movement of forces will be as prescribed by the pamphlet, "Preparation for Overseas Movement, European Theater of Operations, United States Army, Short Sea Voyage" (Short Title - POM, ETO, SSV), dated 10 Jan 1944 (corrected), except where this may conflict with administrative instructions published in Alert Order, this headquarters, 23 March 1944 or this Addenda, in which case instructions contained in the Alert Order or this Addenda will govern.

2. Object and Scope of These Instructions. The purpose of these instructions is to provide commanders of all echelons the essential information required by them preliminary to mounting. For clarification or interpretation of any matters appearing in these instructions, the next higher headquarters should be contacted without delay.

SECTION II - PERSONNEL PROCEDURES

3. Action to be Taken on Receipt of Alert Order.

a. Warning - AW 28.

(1) Every individual of the unit will be advised of the last sentence of the 28th Article of War, reading as follows:

"Any person subject to military law who quits his organization or place of duty with the intent to avoid hazardous duty or to shirk important service shall be deemed a deserter."

(2) It will then be explained that combat duty is considered important service within the terms of the 28th Article of War and that any person absenting himself without leave is guilty of desertion in time of war, the extreme penalty for which is death, and all lesser penalties for which are severe and involve forfeiture of rights of citizenship.

<u>Personnel Absent Without Leave or In Desertion.</u>

    The following action is prescribed in the case of personnel absent with-out authority <u>on the date of departure of the unit from its concentration area or status</u> to its marshalling area or status:

(1)   Automatic transfer in grade to the 10th Replacement Depot for all army personnel other than Air Force citing unit alert orders as authority.

(2)   If absence occurs prior to final packing of personnel records, the following records will be forwarded to the 10th Replacement Depot:

    (a)   Extract copies of Morning Report (WD AGO Form #44) certified by the unit commander, showing the change in status and citing the fact of the soldier's transfer to appropriate Replacement Depot.

    (b)   Service record with transfer indorsed therein.

    (c)   Other pertinent records (see par. 9 AR 615-300).

    (d)   Personal effects, if any.

    (e)   Letter explaining fully the circumstances.

(3)   If absence occurs any time after final packing of personnel records, the following records will be forwarded to the 10th Replacement Depot:

    (a)   Extract copies of Morning Report (WD AGO Form #44) certified by the unit commander, showing the change in status and citing the fact of the soldier's transfer to appropriate Replacement Depot.

    (b)   Letter stating fact and date of absence, all pertinent cir-cumstances and unit commander's statement that other necess-ary records will be forwarded upon receipt of organizational baggage on completion of movement.

(4)   Absentees reported under provisions of this paragraph who rejoin their units prior to departure from UK will be picked up in the strength of the unit, necessary disciplinary action taken, and the records of the individual will be obtained from the Replacement Depot as soon as practicable.

14 April 1944

Both Battalions undergoing ATC Training as per 'RANGERS Training Schedule'.

5th Rangers – Companies A – F, Medical and HQ – Braunton Camp, North Devon.

A, B & C Companies 2nd Rangers – Braunton Camp, North Devon. No change. Alerted for departure.

D, E & F Companies 2nd Rangers – Swanage, Dorset. No change. Alerted for departure.

Medical Detachment 2nd Rangers – Braunton Camp, North Devon. No change. Alerted for departure.

Headquarters Company 2nd Rangers – Braunton Camp, North Devon.

The following two officers went on Detached Service to Plymouth as of 13 April 1944.

1st Lt. Sylvester J. Vauruska. Lt. Bennie Berger (USN).

The following eleven enlisted men went on Detached Service to Plymouth as of 13 April 1944: Sgt. Joseph J. Groth, T/4 Theodore F. Stebbins, Pfc. William J. Skelley, Pfc. Jerome O. Abare, Pvt. Francis Jakowski, Pvt. Lawrence M. McKeever, Pvt Wallace M. Crank, Pvt. Kenneth L. Miller, Pvt. Henry W. Genther, T/5 Harman Calmes, Pvt. Irvin H. Ferriera.

Alerted for departure.

Overleaf: An intelligence map drawn up to show the grid references and calibres of guns in US sector and it includes all of the guns in the Rangers' area of operations.

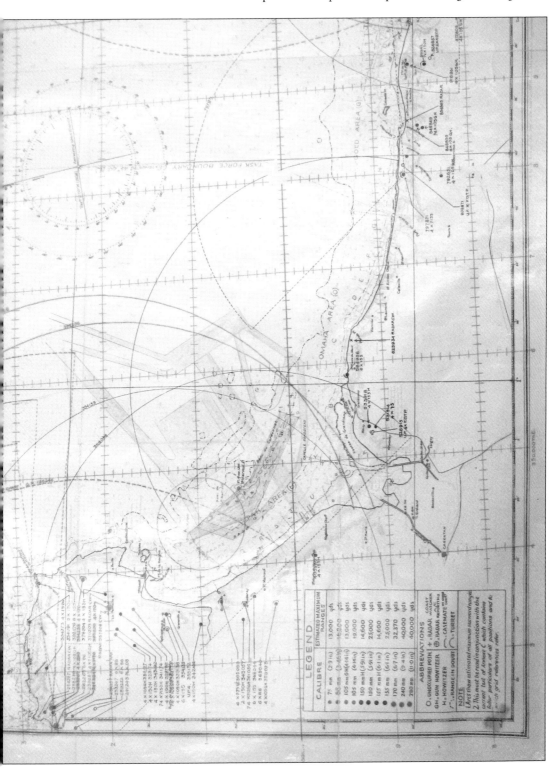

A blow up of the area showing the Radar Station, Pointe du Hoc and Maisy, all with gun quantities, calibres and 6 figure grid references.

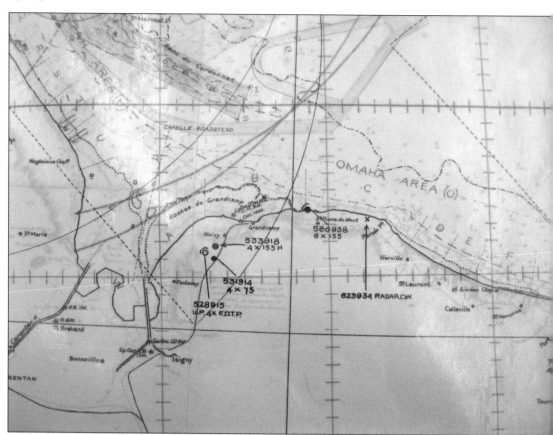

Opposite: An overlay for the GSGS intelligence maps was also produced showing the Rangers all the fixed emplacements in their area of assault. The 3 gun batteries shown at Maisy as well as Pointe du Hoc and the Radar position are again clearly marked.

[Author: It is perhaps appropriate at this point to include the Key for the Artillery – as described on the Allied Intelligence Maps. This version contains slightly more detail.]

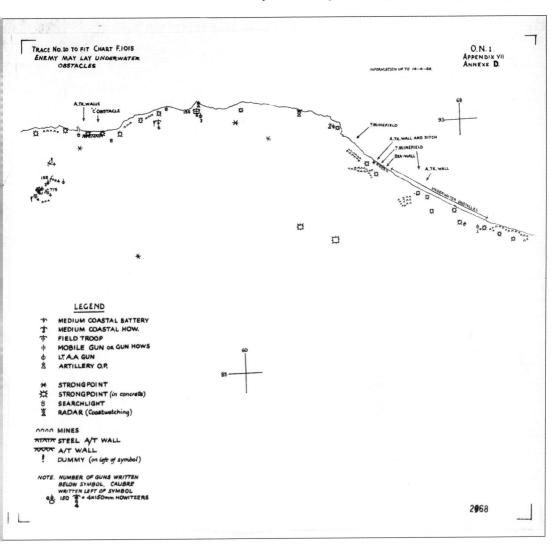

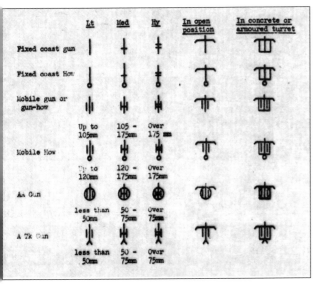

Below: A blow up from the above chart. Pointe du Hoc is centre right. Grandcamp-les-Bains is indicated by the Anti-Tank Walls and 'C-obstacles'. Maisy is represented by the quantity of guns shown in the bottom left. The dummy battery in front is also indicated by the "!" symbol.

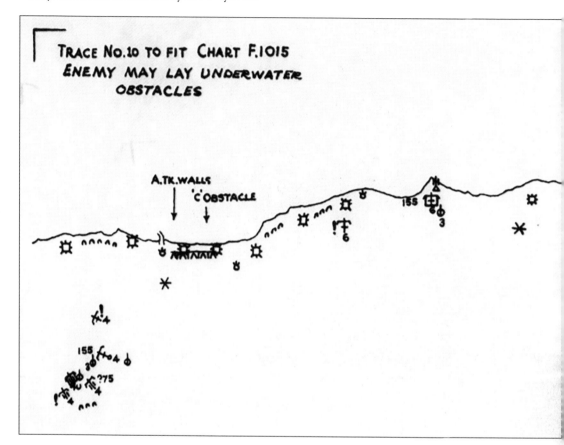

An Intelligence aerial photograph and interpretation taken from the most up-to-date developments at Pointe du Hoc.

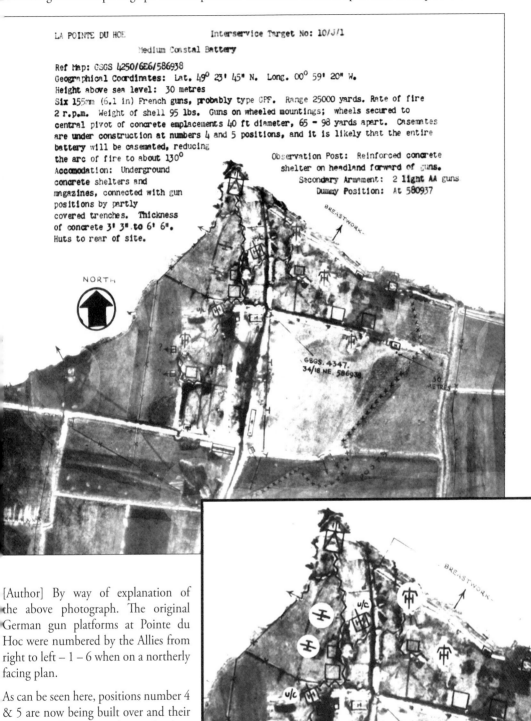

LA POINTE DU HOE   Interservice Target No: 10/J/1
                    Medium Coastal Battery

Ref Map: CSGS 4250/6E6/586938
Geographical Coordinates: Lat. 49° 23' 45" N. Long. 00° 59' 20" W.
Height above sea level: 30 metres
Six 155mm (6.1 in) French guns, probably type GPF. Range 25000 yards. Rate of fire
2 r.p.m. Weight of shell 95 lbs. Guns on wheeled mountings; wheels secured to
central pivot of concrete emplacements 40 ft diameter, 65 - 98 yards apart. Casemates
are under construction at numbers 4 and 5 positions, and it is likely that the entire
battery will be casemated, reducing
the arc of fire to about 130°   Observation Post: Reinforced concrete
Accomodation: Underground   shelter on headland forward of guns.
concrete shelters and   Secondary Armament: 2 light AA guns
magazines, connected with gun   Dummy Position: At 580937
positions by partly
covered trenches. Thickness
of concrete 3' 3" to 6' 6".
Huts to rear of site.

NORTH

[Author] By way of explanation of the above photograph. The original German gun platforms at Pointe du Hoc were numbered by the Allies from right to left – 1 – 6 when on a northerly facing plan.

As can be seen here, positions number 4 & 5 are now being built over and their guns have been moved outside their original positions and they now sit to the left of those positions. We can tell they are now in open field positions because they no longer have the arch symbol around their front – it is the arch on these plans which signifies that the guns are on concrete platforms. These have had their arch removed on this plan – thus they are in the open.

In their place are two concrete blockhouses (above ground) marked here as A & B which are under construction. This is indicated by the blockhouse/howitzer symbol (a box) – accompanied by the letters U/C (under construction) – and no arch.

Therefore, Pointe du Hoc – on 14 April or slightly before – consisted of four guns on their original gun pits, two in open fields in front of their original pits and two casements under construction.

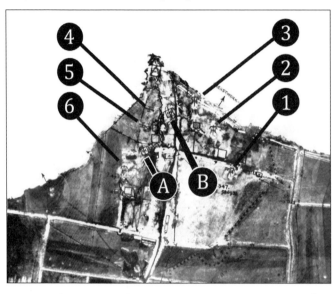

The explanation on the reconnaissance photograph, that when finished, the four casements would have a 130 degree arc of fire is noteworthy. This is better explained on a pre-D-Day distance map for coastal battery ranges. I have taken the liberty of inserting my own protracted arc directly over the arc on the map for Target No. 1 below – showing those degrees and what area 130 degrees would actually cover. It matches exactly the curve of range as estimated by US intelligence. Therefore the comment on the previous aerial photograph stating that the guns at Pointe du Hoc would cover a section over a 130 degree curve is correct. This had been worked out by someone in Military Intelligence at the time based on the direction each casement was facing and capable of firing. On this basis – when built and operational – the four casements would not have been able to fire at Omaha Beach and only the two remaining guns (if retained) in open emplacements could have done that.

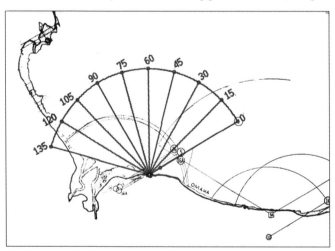

This is further highlighted in the text shown below and it confirms that the Rangers were informed on 14 April 1944 that the number of guns and their positions at Pointe du Hoc had changed. By default, the site could not have been fully operational on D-Day. If the Germans only intended to install four guns at Pointe du Hoc, then the arc of fire from the next battery to the East (Longues-sur-Mer) would have covered the remaining coastline to PdH's right. As it is shown to do on the Range Map (portion of) shown here. But it does not have the ability to hit the actual beach area to the east beyond the range of the Maisy guns.

Included in the following resumé of gun positions from the same documents are:

528915 Maisy – La Martinière
531914 Maisy – Foucher's Farm
533918 Maisy – Les Perruques
586938 Pointe du Hoc
623934 Pointe et Raz de la Percée – Radar Station.
All of the Rangers' D-Day objectives.
The text for PdH also confirms the removal of the guns being known at this time.

TOP SECRET

Grid.	Lat. N.	Long.	Category.	No. of Guns.	Particulars.
529915	49 22' 24"	01 04' 06"W.	Fd.Tp. Dummy		Unocc, possibly only a temporary posn for 4-gun Fd. Tp. Open circular pits about 25' diam; 45-55x apart. Staggered arc layout. Bty faces VIRE estuary. Accommodation and storage; underground concrete shelters and magazines still u/c. CASEMATES 35'x 40' u/c facing NNW; spaced 44x apart. O.P. - unknown. Ident: ? Div.Fd.Tp. There is some evidence that one or two additional troops have practised going into action in fields to the N. of this posn. Dummy at 527923.
531914	49 22' 14"	01 03' 47"W.	Fd. Tp.	4	? 75 mm (2.95") Fd. guns. Range 13,000x. Practical rate of fire 6-8 r.p.m. Wt. of shell 13 lbs. Centre line NW. Staggered layout. Rough open earthen emps 20-25' diam; 32-35x apart, sited in an open field. Probably only a temporary posn.
533918	49 22' 34"	01 03' 40"W.	M.C.B.+ (Hows.)	4	155 mm (6.1") Hows. Range 13,000x. Practical rate of fire about 5 r.p.m. Wt. of shell 95 lbs. Wide staggered trapezoid layout. Hows. mounted in open circular pits, 35' diam, 65-120x apart, probably with concrete beds. Bty faces VIRE estuary. Accommodation and storage - underground concrete shelters and magazines on gun posn. Huts in rear. O.P. - underground concrete shelter centrally situated in rear of emps. O.P. - unknown, presumably on the coast W of GRANDCAMP. Road serviced. Communications: buried cable, presumably also wireless. Sec.Armt: three 20 mm AA guns. Ident: ? Army Static Coast Troop. Dummy at 532923.
586388	49 36' 22"	00 13' 45"E.	Fd. Tp. Dummy		Unocc posn for 4-gun Fd. Tp. Centre line E. Open emps 18' diam.
586938	49 23' 47"	00 59' 22"W.	M.C.B.	6	155 mm (6.1") French guns, probably type GPF. Range 25,000x. Practical rate of fire about 2 r.p.m. Wt. of shell 95 lbs. Centre line 309°. Arc of fire ? 180°. Guns on wheeled mountings, the wheels being secured to the central pivot of a concrete emp about 40' diam; 70-90x apart. Guns 4 and 5 have been moved from emps and CASEMATES 36'x 42' u/o near the empty emps. No. 4 is under way and ground being broken for No. 5. Each gun is camouflaged with netting; there is no turret or gun shield. Bty sited to form a V with apex towards coast. Road serviced.
586938	49 23' 47"	00 59' 22"W.	M.C.B.	6	Contd. B.O.P. - reinforced concrete shelter on headland in front of gun posn. Flank O.Ps - locations unknown; presumably near PTE et RAZ DE LA PERCEE and E of GRANDCAMP. Shelters and magazines - underground; reinforced concrete 3'3" to 6'6" thick. Connected with gun emps by trenches partly covered over. Huts for off-duty personnel and administrative personnel in rear of gun posn. Sec.Armt: three?20 mm AA guns in emps on roofs of concrete shelters (still u/o). Communications - L/T (buried cable); presumably also W/T. Ident: 2 Troop, 832 Army Coast Btn. Dummy at 572935.
623934	49 23' 37"	00 56' 20"W.	Coast Watcher. Dummy		Surface range (miles) against: destroyers 11.7, coastal craft 8.8. 1 Coast Watcher, 2 Giant Wuerzburg, 1 Standard Wuerzburg, 1 Freya, 100' a.s.l. Three 1t AA guns and one S/L.

A detailed Intelligence Plan dated 14 April from within the same files covering Maisy – Les Perruques battery and it includes reference to the guns at Foucher's farm at the bottom of the picture.

MAISY I
Medium Howitzer Troop
Interservice Target
No: 9/J/7

Ref Map: GSGS 4250/6E6/533918
Geographical Coordinates: 49° 22' 34" N. 01° 03' 40" W.
Height above sea level: 20 metres.

Four ?155mm (6.1 in) Howitzers. Range 13000 yards.
Weight of Shell ?82 lbs. Rate of fire ?2 r.p.m.
Guns mounted in open circular pits, 35 ft diameter with concrete gun platforms, 65 – 120 yards apart.
Accommodation: Underground concrete shelters and magazines.
Command Post: Underground concrete shelter to rear of battery.
Secondary Armament: Three light AA guns.

MAISY II(a)   Field Troop   Interservice Target No: 9/J/39

Ref Map: GSGS 4250/6E6/531914
Geographical Coordinates: 49° 22' 13" N. 00°03' 47" w.
Height above sea level: 20 metres.

Four 775mm (2.95 in) guns. Range 10,300 yards. Weight of shell 13 lbs.
Rate of fire 8 – 10 r.p.m.
Guns in rough earthen emplacements 20 – 25 ft diameter, 27 – 35 yards apart.
This is probably a temporary position for 528916 (MAISY II, Interservice Target No: 9/J/8), a part of which is visible on this photo to the North West.

| F.1015 | 533918 | 49 22' 34" | 01 03' 40"W. | M.C.B.+ (Hows.) | 4 | 155 mm (6.1") Hows. Range 13,000x. Practical rate of fire about 5 r.p.m. Wt. of shell 95 lbs. Wide staggered trapezoid layout. Hows. mounted in open circular pits, 35' diam, 65–120x apart, probably with concrete beds. Bty faces VIRE estuary. Accommodation and storage – underground concrete shelters and magazines on gun posn. Huts in rear. C.P. – underground concrete shelter centrally situated in rear of emps. O.P. – unknown, presumably on the coast W of GRANDCAMP. Road serviced. Communications: buried cable, presumably also wireless. Sec.Armt: three 20 mm AA guns. |
| | | | | Dummy | | Ident: ? Army Static Coast Troop. Dummy at 532923. |

The Intelligence map for Maisy II – La Martinière battery, again from the same files.

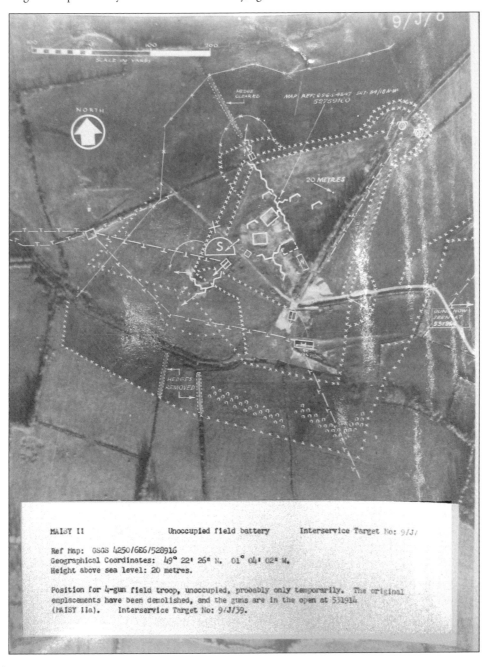

MAISY II   Unoccupied field battery   Interservice Target No: 9/J/

Ref Map: GSGS 4250/6E6/528916
Geographical Coordinates: 49° 22' 26" N. 01° 04' 02" W.
Height above sea level: 20 metres.

Position for 4-gun field troop, unoccupied, probably only temporarily. The original
emplacements have been demolished, and the guns are in the open at 531914
(MAISY IIa).   Interservice Target No: 9/J/39.

| F.1015 | 528915 | 49 22' 24" | 01 04' 06"W. | Fd.Tp. | | Unocc, possibly only a temporary posn for 4-gun Fd. Tp. Open circular pits about 25' diam; 45-55x apart. Staggered arc layout. Bty faces VIRE estuary. Accommodation and storage; underground concrete shelters and magazines still u/c. CASEMATES 35'x 40' u/c facing NNW; spaced 48x apart. O.P. – unknown. Ident: ? Div.Fd.Tp. There is some evidence that one or two additional troops have practised going into action in fields to the W. of this posn. Dummy at 527923. |
| | | | | Dummy | | |

| F.1015 | 531914 | 49 22' 14" | 01 03' 47"W. | Fd. Tp. | 4 | ? 75 mm (2.95") Fd. guns. Range 13,000x. Practical rate of fire 6-8 r.p.m Wt. of shell 13 lbs. Centre line NW. Staggered layout. Rough open earthen emps 20-25' diam; 32-35x apart, sited in an open field. Probably only a temporary posn. |

Dated 14 April again there is confirmation of operational orders for the Navy which state the Rangers are to attack the 'Coastal Batteries at Grandcamp and protect flank.'

TOP SECRET   OPERATION NEPTUNE—NAVAL ORDERS
(Short Title : ON)

ON 1.—General Outline of the Operation—*continued*

The Assaults

32. The following simultaneous main assaults will be made at H hour :—

Approximate Location.	Division.	Naval Force.	No. of Brigades or R.C.T. Assaulting.
OUISTREHAM ..	.. 3 Div.	S	1
COURSEULLES ..	.. 3 Canadian Div. ..	J	2
ASNELLES ..	.. 50 Div.	G	2
ST. LAURENT ..	.. 1 Div. (U.S.) .. .. 29 Div. (U.S.).	O	2
VARREVILLE ..	.. 4 Div. (U.S.)	U	1

Assaults will also be made by Commandos and Rangers as follows at or shortly after H hour.

Approximate Location.	Unit.	Associated Naval Force.	Task.
OUISTREHAM ..	One Commando ..	S	Occupation of town and capture of C.D. battery.
LANGRUNE ..	One Commando ..	S	Mopping up.
LANGRUNE ..	Three Commandos ..	S	Advance across river ORNE.
BERNIERS ..	One Commando ..	J	Mopping Up.
GRANDCAMP ..	Two Ranger Battalions	O	Capture C.D. batteries and protect flank.

TOP SECRET   5

OPERATION NEPTUNE—NAVAL ORDERS
(Short Title : ON)

ON 8.—Instructions for Bombarding Forces—*continued*

Table B.—Battery Targets for Night, Heavy and Medium Bombers prior to H Hour

Night Heavy Bombers (up till Civil Twilight)

Target	Map Reference
POINTE DU HOE	586937
LA PERNELLE	365200
FONTENAY SUR MER	368044
MORSALINES	354139
ST. MARTIN DE VARREVILLE	405980
SALLENELLES	155776
HOULGATE	256809
BENERVILLE	422107
BARFLEUR	394228
RIVA BELLA	117797

2. Timing will be arranged so that those batteries which are the greatest menace to the Assault Forces are bombed during the period when Assault Forces reach the lowering position, subject to the necessity for bombing certain batteries early in the night in order to avoid endangering airborne troops.

Medium Bombers (between Civil Twilight + ten minutes and H hour)

Target	Map Reference
3. LA PERNELLE	365200
POINTE DU HOE	586937
MAISY	533918
RIVA BELLA	117797
OUISTREHAM	103779
MONT FLEURY	918861

TOP SECRET

OPERATION NEPTUNE—NAVAL ORDERS

(Short Title : ON)

ON 8.—Instructions for Bombarding Forces—*continued*

Table C.—Battery Targets for Naval Bombardment

Instructions regarding the timing of naval bombardment are laid down in ON 8, paragraph 32.

2. The detailing of ships to the targets listed below is the responsibility of Task and Assault Force Commanders.

3. Task and Assault Force Commanders are at liberty to propose amendments or to make last minute adjustments to the list in the light of latest intelligence, but Allied Naval Commander-in-Chief must be kept informed, in order that the re-briefing of spotting aircraft (Table E) can be arranged.

4.

Target Name	Map Reference
BARFLEUR	394228
LA PERNELLE	365200
MORSALINES	354139
OZEVILLE	343057
CHATEAU DE COURCY	362054
FONTENAY SUR MER	368044
EMONDVILLE	359023
MAISY II	531914
MAISY I	533918
POINTE DU HOE	586937
VILLERVILLE	486156
BENERVILLE	422107
HOULGATE	256809
RIVA BELLA	117797
OUISTREHAM	103779
COLLEVILLE SUR ORNE	076782
MOULINEAUX	972808
MONT FLEURY	918861
VER SUR MER	917844
ARROMANCHES I	848853
ARROMANCHES II	846848
LONGUES	797871
VAUX-SUR-AURE	792831

The US Army Intelligence produced a highly detailed map section of the Vierville beach defences and inland obstacles showing minefields, trenches, barbed wire and emplacements. Maps such as this were being updated regularly with any changes to beach obstacles and defences.

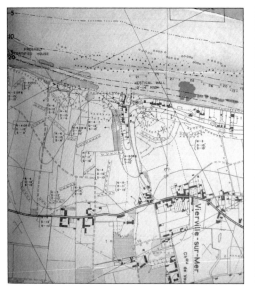

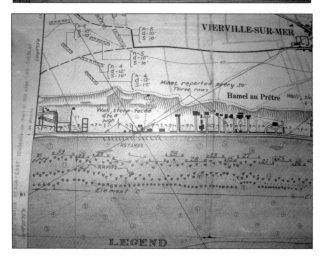

Shown here is the 15 April 'Alert Order' which provides detailed orders relating to the completion of paperwork. It was accompanied with a distribution list and the comment: *The Commanding Officers of the 2nd and 5th Ranger Battalions are furnished the necessary information directly, for their residues in the build-up.* One copy was sent to the Commanding Officer of both the 2nd and 5th Battalions.

HEADQUARTERS V CORPS
APO 305, U. S. ARMY

:AUTH: CG, V CORPS
:DATE: 15 April 44:
:INIT:

381 (C)

15 April 1944

Issue No. 2: Copy No. 50 of 60 Copies.

SUBJECT: Alert Order.

TO   : See Distribution.

1. Your command is alerted effective this date. Elements of certain of the commands contained in the distribution of this letter were alerted by letter, this headquarters, subject: "Alert Order", dated 23 March 1944. The provisions of the previous Alert Order remain in force for the elements effected thereby. The following provisions pertain to your command, less the elements previously alerted.

2. Commanding Officers of V Corps Units as listed in paragraph 4a thru k, letter this headquarters, dated 8 April 1944, subject: "Troop Assignment", will alert all subordinate units attached to their respective commands in the above reference, less the elements previously alerted. The subordinate units will be alerted without delay notwithstanding the fact that attachment in the above reference is effective 20 April 1944.

3. On or after 21 April 1944, units will receive a movement warning from the Transportation Corps. This movement warning will allow five or more days before actual movement.

4. Units will comply with instructions as issued by ETO during the period of movement and processing from Concentration Areas through the Marshalling areas to the Embarkation Points.

5. Units will move in the number of groups and at the strength in personnel and vehicles to be included in extracts from First U.S. Army Consolidated Build-Up Priority Tables, extract copies of which will be forwarded to you under seperate cover at the earliest practicable date. You will complete as far as practicable all preparations for movement prior to receipt of these extracts.

6. Units will comply with the provisions of "European Theater of Operations, United States Army, Preparation for Overseas Movement, Short Sea Voyage", dated 10 January 1944 (corrected). Forms SOSTC 8, 8a, 9 and 10 will be completed only by units outside the limits of the Southern Base Section, SOS, based on the strengths listed in tables referred to in Par. 4. (Following the word "Remarks" near the bottom of Form SOSTC No. 8, the unit commander will insert the number of officers and men, respectively, that can travel in the unit vehicles reported on Form SOSTC NO. 10. Such personnel are included in those reported in the body of Form SOSTC No. 8.) Forms will be delivered, in duplicate, to Hq, SOS, ETO, Office of the Chief of Transportation, Movements Division, Operational Branch, APO 887, on or before 20 April 1944. These froms may be obtained from the local RTO who will also be available for assistance and advice in completing the forms. It is prescribed that the above forms be delivered by officer courier. Where several units are located in the same area or when battalion or larger unit is involved, Commanding Officers may assemble such reports and forward by one courier if delivery is not delayed. This headquarters will be notified at once when SOSTC froms have been delivered to TC/ETO and advised of the date of delivery.

7. ETO - POM - SSV.

a. Paragraphs 67, 70 & 72, ETO-POM-SSV are interpreted as follows: residues, including overstrength in personnel and organizational equipment not carried on vehicles, will be formed as a separate detachment and will complete all preparations prescribed for the parent unit. At an appropriate time the residual detachment will be separated from the parent unit for concentration in an area to be designated by ETO until time for its movement to the Marshalling and Embarkation areas, as prescribed by Combined Headquarters. Detachments that are not self-sustaining will be grouped so that they can be mutually sustaining. ETO will furnish necessary assistance. Forms SOSTC 8, 8a, 9 and 10 will be completed for each residual detachment as indicated in Consolidated Build-Up Priority Tables and delivered to the Transportation Corps as prescribed in Par. 6 above.

    b. Paragraph 107, ETO-PQM-SSV is amended to read 40 copies in all places at present prescribing 25 copies.

    c. Paragraph 108, ETO-PQM-SSV, is to be rescinded and the following substituted:

        Upon receipt of the Unit Sheet in the Marshalling Area, unit commanders will prepare Unit Party Embarkation Personnel Rosters for each Unit Party by merely ruling out the names of personnel on the original roster, not part of the Unit Party, and adding names not shown on the original roster. Eight (8) copies of Unit Party Embarkation Personnel Rosters will be prepared and turned over to the officer or NCO in charge of each such Unit Party. Upon formation of Craft or Ship Loads in the Marshalling Area, each Unit Party CO or NCO will deliver to the CO Craft or Ship Load the eight copies of the Unit Party Roster. The CO Craft or Ship Load will securely fasten all of the Unit Party Rosters so that he will have eight complete sets, which will then constitute complete craft or ship rosters (Passenger Lists). The distribution of the Personnel Embarkation Roster is as follows:

        Three copies will be handed to the Embarkation Staff Officer at the Embarkation Point. The ESO will insure that Embarkation Personnel Rosters are collected for all Craft or Ship Loads embarking. The ESO will indorse on these Rosters the date and place of embarkation and the name or number of the craft or ship. Two of these copies will be dispatched to the Central Machine Records Unit, Hq, SOS, ETOUSA, APO 887, and one copy to the AG at the Base Section in which the port is located.

        The fourth copy will be retained by the CO Craft or Ship Load and will be corrected to reflect casualties, etc., enroute. Upon debarkation this copy of the Embarkation Personnel Roster will be turned over to the first available personnel administration section for forwarding to the servicing MRU.

        The remaining four copies will be handed to the Commanding Officer of the ship.

        By command of Major General GEROW.

                                          R. B. PATTERSON,
                                          Colonel, A.G.D.,
                                          Adjutant General.

        DISTRIBUTION: (Issue No. 2)   Copy
            CG, 1st Inf Div   1
            CO, 2nd Ranger Bn   26
            CO, 5th Ranger Bn   27
            CO, 3892nd QM Trk Co   11

---

15 April 1944

Both Battalions undergoing ATC Training as per 'RANGERS Training Schedule'.

A Company 5th Rangers – Braunton Camp, North Devon.

5th Rangers – Companies A – F, Medical and HQ – Braunton Camp, North Devon. Alerted for departure.

A, B & C Companies 2nd Rangers – Braunton Camp, North Devon. Alerted for departure.

D, E & F Companies 2nd Rangers – Swanage, Dorset. Alerted for departure.

Medical Detachment 2nd Rangers – Braunton Camp, North Devon. No change. Alerted for departure.

Headquarters Company 2nd Rangers – Braunton Camp, North Devon. No report found.

---

16 April 1944

Sunday: Both Battalions undergoing ATC Training as per 'RANGERS Training Schedule' had no allocated schedule for today.

5th Rangers – Companies A – F, Medical and HQ – Braunton Camp, North Devon. Alerted for departure.

A, B & C Companies 2nd Rangers – Braunton Camp, North Devon. Alerted for departure.

D, E & F Companies 2nd Rangers – Swanage, Dorset. No change. Alerted for departure.

Medical Detachment 2nd Rangers – Braunton Camp, North Devon. No change. Alerted for departure.

Headquarters Company 2nd Rangers – Braunton Camp, North Devon. Alerted for departure.

The Army issued an information letter on the use of paint.

> *Requisitions for paint will be submitted by units through normal supply channels. Each such requisition will indicate in specific detail the use of which the paint is intended (including the items to be painted) and will be submitted to the supply agency charged with the procurement and issue of such property.*
> *Signed – Eisenhower. 16th April 1944.*

Issued on 16 April all units within the 1st Infantry Division received their individual orders. [Author: I have included these in full as they are a significant document in themselves and show the wider activities of the other units under the control of the 1st Infantry Division. Of note is the fact that the Rangers alone were issued the objectives of the Coastal Batteries along the Omaha Sector – West along the coastline and again we see the order to **reach the 'D-Day Phase Line' before dark on D-Day. No order exists to remain at Pointe du Hoc and block the 'highway'.** Of particular note is the order No.6 on page 6 to attack the Batteries (plural) at Maisy. (The US National Archives hold the original of this document).]

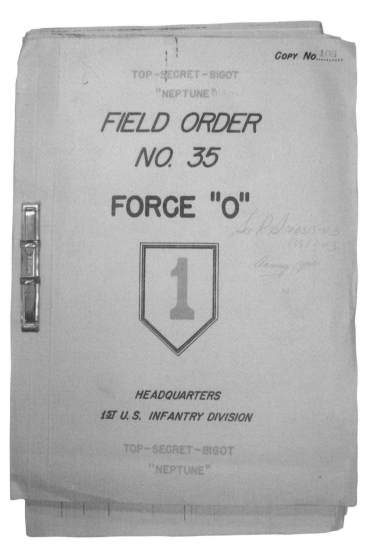

TOP-SECRET   BIGOT
                                    "NEPTUNE"

q 1st US Inf Div   : TOP-SECRET :
PO 1, US Army   :Authority: CG:
6 April 1944   :1st US Inf Div:
                                                          :16 April 1944 :
OPY NO. __108__   :Initials: /rfe:

NNEX #.......2)
          :   INTELLIGENCE ANNEX
O FO #......35)

aps: GSGS 4250, 1/50,000, FRANCE,
      Sheets 6E/6, 6F/2, 7E/5, 7F/1.

. SUMMARY OF ENEMY SITUATION.

   See current G-2 Estimate.

. MISSION.

   The 1st US Infantry Division, less Regimental Combat Team 26, with
   Regimental Combat Team 116 and other troops attached, will make
   the initial assault on Beach OMAHA at H-hour on D-day with two
   Regimental Combat Teams abreast, reduce the beach defenses in its
   zone of action, secure the Beachhead Maintenance Line, secure
   the D-day phase line by two hours before dark on D-day. It will
   cover the landing of the remainder of the V Corps and will be
   prepared to participate in the extension of the beachhead to
   the south and the southwest.

. ESSENTIAL ELEMENTS OF INFORMATION.

   a. Is there a third infantry regiment of the 716th Division; what
       is its strength and location?

   b. Have enemy rocket launching units and additional mobile artill-
       ery been brought into the beachhead, and, if so, in what
       strength and what positions?

   c. Has the enemy established a defensive position running north
       and south of LONGUEVILLE?

   d. Has the enemy established a defensive position between TRE-
       VIERES and BAYEUX, north or south of the AURE?

   e. What is the condition of the fords and bridges over the AURE
       from ISIGNY east to the DROME River?

   f. Is route LA CAMBE-DOUET, across the AURE flooded area passable
       for vehicles and/or foot troops?

   g. What is the condition of the light bridges over the VIRE at
       its mouth?

                              - 1 -
                         TOP-SECRET
                          "NEPTUNE"

TOP-SECRET NEPTUNE

BIGOT

h. Is the area where the AURE River flows underground southeast of MT. CAUVIN passable for tanks and/or motor vehicles?

i. Are there enemy reserves concealed in the CERISY or MOLAY forests?

j. Has the main road ISIGNY-BAYEUX been blocked or mined?

k. Has the main road LES MOULINS-TREVIERES been blocked or mined?

l. Is there any movement of enemy forces from BAYEUX area?

m. Are there any indications of the use of toxic chemicals by the enemy?

n. What proportion of civilian population remains in the assault area; is it cooperative?

4. RECONNAISSANCE AND OBSERVATION MISSIONS.

a. CT 16.

(1) Prior to seizure of objectives on highground north of AURE:

(a) Reconnoiter Beach 46 between 670905 and 700893 and report extent of minefields, condition of AT ditches, underwater obstacles, and other obstacle which prevent immediate exit from the beach.

(b) Reconnoiter Beach exit roads to CABOURG (697883), COLLEVILLE (688881) and along the RUQUET River to ST LAURENT (665895), and report prepared defense condition of roads, minefields and road blocks.

(c) Reconnoiter COLLEVILLE and CABOURG villages and location of enemy units encountered, prepared enemy defenses, movements along road ETREHAM-RUBBY (705863), BELLE-FONTAINE (703856)-MOSLES and SURRAIN (674858)-COLLEVILLE.

(d) Reconnoiter Le GD HAMEAU (705882) and STE HONORINE (718881) and report strength, location of enemy units encountered, prepared enemy defenses and demolitions preventing traffic circulation.

(e) Reconnoiter ground west of HUPPAIN (741873) and MT CAUVIN (735852) and report strength and location enemy units encountered, movements along BAYEUX-PORT-EN-BESSIN road, VAUCELLES-EIREHAM road and BAYEUX-MOSLES road.

- 2 -

TOP-SECRET NEPTUNE

TOP-SECRET NEPTUNE

BIGOT

(f) Reconnoiter area where the AURE flows underground southeast of MT CAUVIN and report whether it is a suitable crossing for vehicles or tanks.

(g) Reconnoiter ST LAURENT-FORMIGNY-TREVIERES road to high ground north of TREVIERES and report strength and location of enemy troops encountered, prepared enemy defenses, minefields, road blocks and other obstacles.

(2) After seizure of objectives on high ground north of AURE:

(a) Reconnoiter TREVIERES and crossings over River AURE vicinity L'ETARD (628839) and TREVIERES and roads TREVIERES-RUBERCY (658818) and TREVIERES-MICAUBEVILLE (605817). Report conditions of bridges, possible fords for vehicles, demolitions, enemy positions vicinity TREVIERES and first contact with enemy south of the AURE.

(b) Reconnoiter MOSLES-BEAUMONT (689809) road and ridge north of BEAUMONT and report strength and location of enemy units encountered, prepared enemy defenses, minefields, enemy movements south of the TORTONNE River.

(c) Reconnoiter MOSLES-TOUR-EN-BESSIN-VAUCELLES road and report strength and location enemy units encountered, prepared enemy defenses, condition of bridge over the DROME at VAUCELLES (765808) and enemy movements over the BAYEUX-VAUCELLES road.

b. CT 116.

(1) Prior to capture of ISIGNY:

(a) Reconnoiter Beach 46 between VIERVILLE and LES MOULINS. Report presence of underwater obstacles, mined areas and condition of obstacles preventing exit from beach including AT ditch at LES MOULINS and sea wall.

(b) Reconnoiter road exits from beach to VIERVILLE and ST LAURENT and report mined areas, road blocks and demolitions.

(c) Reconnoiter VIERVILLE and ST LAURENT and report strength and location of enemy units encountered, prepared enemy positions and demolitions capable of affecting traffic circulation.

- 3 -

TOP-SECRET NEPTUNE

BIGOT

(d) Reconnoiter LA MARE ANGOT (527903) and GEFOSSE-FONTENAY (512912) areas and report strength and location of enemy defenses, minefields and obstacles.

(e) Reconnoiter vicinity light bridge over the AURE, its mouth and report strength and location one encountered, condition of defenses, capacity of bridge and enemy movements on the west side of the bridge.

(f) Reconnoiter LOUVIERES (635902)-ASNIERES (623905) area and report strength and location enemy units encountered, prepared enemy defenses, minefields and enemy movements vicinity LONGUEVILLE (600877).

(g) Reconnoiter vicinity LONGUEVILLE-LA CAMBE and report strength and location enemy units, prepared enemy defenses and condition of battery position being erected 1000 yards northeast of LONGUEVILLE (600877).

(h) Reconnoiter the ridge west of LA CAMBE (5788) and LA CAMBE-ISIGNY road and report strength and location enemy encountered, minefields and prepared defenses on the outskirts of ISIGNY.

(1) Reconnoiter road LA CAMBE-DOUET (555745) over inundated area and report passability for vehicles, and enemy movements to the south of the inundated area.

(j) Reconnoiter ISIGNY and AURE crossing and report enemy resistance and condition of bridges.

(2) After the capture of ISIGNY:

(a) Reconnoiter west to establish contact with VII Corps.

(b) Subsequent missions to be assigned by 29th Division.

c. CT 18.

(1) Prior to seizure of objectives on high ground south of AURE:

(a) Reconnoiter area of objective on the ridge north of BEAUMONT and report strength and location of enemy encountered, prepared enemy defenses and movements of enemy troops on the ridges to the east and in the valley of the TORTONNE River

- 4 -

BIGOT

to the south.

(b) Reconnoiter FORMIGNY-VAUCELLES road and report strength and location enemy encountered, prepared defenses, mined areas and obstacles; report enemy movements observed east of the DROME along the BAYEUX-VAUCELLES road,

(c) If no enemy forces are observed west of the DROME, reconnoiter east along the main road until contact is established with enemy or friendly troops and report details of contact.

(2) After seizure of objectives on high ground south of AURE:

(a) Reconnoiter ridges to the east to the DROME, and report strength, type and location of enemy units encountered, prepared enemy defenses and enemy movements.

(b) Reconnoiter south on the ridge along the west bank of the DROME until contact is established and report strength, type, location and mobility of enemy units encountered.

(c) Reconnoiter roads RUBERCY -LE MOLAY-BALLEROY until contact is made and report strength, location, type and mobility of enemy forces encountered, prepared positions and artillery.

d. Rangers.

(1) Reconnoiter enemy positions at POINTE ET RAZ DE LA PERCEE and at the Radar Station, and report strength and location enemy encountered, condition of defenses and enemy movements vicinity of ST PIERRE DU MONT.

(2) Reconnoiter battery position on POINTE DU HOE. Report condition of battery, strength and location enemy encountered, and prepared enemy defenses.

(3) Reconnoiter new battery position east of POINTE DU HOE at 598934 and report type and condition of artillery, if present, and strength and location enemy encountered.

(4) Observe ST PIERRE DU MONT and road to GRANDCAMP and report strength and location enemy encountered and prepared enemy defenses.

(5) Reconnoiter ST PIERRE-GRANDCAMP road and report condi-

- 5 -

tion of road through flooded area, prepared enemy defenses covering road and prepared enemy defenses, and enemy movements in GRANDCAMP.

(6) Reconnoiter GRANDCAMP-MAISY area and report strength, location of enemy encountered, condition of defenses in GRANDCAMP and of the battery positions southwest of MAISY, and enemy movements along the road ISIGNY-MAISY.

e. Division Artillery.

Observe and report locations and movements of enemy forces and location, strength, calibre and degree of activity of enemy artillery.

f. Tank Units.

In addition to reconnaissance missions assigned by units to which attached, tank units will report by most rapid means available, type, strength and movements of enemy armor encountered, and location and nature of minefields, anti-tank obstacles and enemy anti-tank weapons.

g. Tank Destroyer Units.

In addition to reconnaissance missions assigned by units to which attached, tank destroyer units will report by most rapid means available type, strength and movements of enemy armor encountered and location and nature of enemy minefields, anti-tank obstacles and anti-tank weapons.

h. Engineer Units.

In addition to reconnaissance missions assigned by units to which they may be attached, engineer units will report by the most rapid means available location and nature of enemy minefields, road blocks, demolitions, prepared dem-

i. Antiaircraft Units.

Antiaircraft units will report by most rapid means available number, type, altitude and direction of movement of all enemy planes observed.

z. All Units.

(1) Report locations of hostile artillery with full details as to number and type of pieces.

(2) Report all identifications of enemy units.

(3) Report presence toxic chemicals in assault area.

(4) Report all points from which wide observation of assault area may be obtained.

(5) Report condition of all crossings and fords suitable for vehicles over the AURE, DROME and TORTONNE.

(6) Report presence of hostile reconnaissance parties to include size and movements.

(7) See Division SOP.

5. MEASURES FOR HANDLING PRISONERS OF WAR AND CAPTURED DOCUMENTS.

a. Prisoners of War.

(1) Division SOP except as follows:

(a) Initially Prisoners of War will be evacuated from Division Cage to returning craft by 5th Engineer Special Brigade. After establishment Army enclosure evacuation to it -- in no case to Corps enclosure.

(b) Prisoner of War personal effects will be evacuated through interrogation channels and reports sent to intelligence agencies concerned; other documents through intelligence channels without delay, except Soldbuch which remains with prisoner.

(2) All Prisoner of War interrogation teams will question prisoners on enemy plans for use of gas.

b. Captured Enemy Materiel.

Division SOP

6. MAPS.

a. All planning and briefing maps will be issued through intelligence channels.

b. Operational Maps.

(1) Maps will be distributed in the quantities and scales indicated in letter, 1st US Army, 7 March 1944, subject: "Map Supply and Distribution". A breakdown based upon this letter is given in Appendix 1 which will serve as a guide as to what units may expect to receive.

Page 1 of 4 Pages   TOP SECRET   BIGOT
                                     "NEPTUNE"

Hq 1st US Inf Div   :   TOP SECRET   :
APO #1, U.S. Army   :Authority of   :
16 April 1944   :CG,1st US Inf Div:
                                                         : 16 April 1944   :
ANNEX #6)   :Initials (illeg.) :
              : PREARRANGED AIR AND NAVAL GUNFIRE SUPPORT PLAN (TENTATIVE) Copy No. 03
TO FO #35)

1. Naval gunfire support ships and craft, tactical air force units, field
    artillery, and tank units will support the initial assault and subse-
    quent advance inland of the 1st US Infantry Division.

    a. Naval Support Ships: To protect shipping from attack by enemy air-
        craft, surface forces and submarines, and the support by bombardment
        of the initial assault and subsequent advance inland.

    b. Fire Support Craft: To furnish, during the approach to the beaches,
        area fire on and in rear of beaches; direct fire on strong points
        and beach defenses; after landing, to fire on flanks and rear areas
        or as directed by Task Headquarters Ship.

    c. Air Support: By bombing, to neutralize batteries, cut lanes in wire
        and minefields, and to neutralize strong points.

2. INITIAL ORGANIZATION FOR COMBAT (TENTATIVE)

    a. Naval Support Ships

        (1) 1 Battleship:

             RAMILIES   4 x 15 inch guns @ 106 rounds per gun
                                6 x 6 inch guns @ 180 rounds per gun

        (2) 3 Cruisers:

             BELLONA   8 x 5.25 inch guns @ 200 rounds per gun
             BLACK PRINCE   8 x 5.25 inch guns @ 200 rounds per gun
             GLASGOW   12 x 6 inch guns @ 200 rounds per gun

        (3) 10 Destroyers:

             8 Fleet Type - 6 ships, 4 x 4.7 inch guns @ 250 rounds per gun
                           - 2 ships, 6 x 4.7 inch guns @ 250 rounds per gun

             2 Hunt Type   4 x 4 inch guns @ 250 rounds per gun

    b. Fire Support Craft

         5 LCG(L)   - 2 x 4.7 inch guns @ 240 rounds per gun
         9 LCT(R)   - 1000 x 29 pound rockets
        24 LCS(S)   - 2 x.50 caliber Machine Guns and 48 x 29 pound rockets
        16 LCT(A&HE)-32 x M-4 Tanks - 1 x 3 inch gun each @ 200 rounds per gun
         2 LCT(CB) - Demolition charge (load unknown)
         9 LCT(5)   - 36 x 105mm Self-propelled, M-7, @ 100 rounds per gun.

                              - 1 -
                           TOP SECRET
                           "NEPTUNE"

c. Air Support Controlled by First United States Army, Targets Allotted in V Corps Area

(1) Night heavy bomber force - 1 mission of 250 tons.
(2) Night medium bomber force - 2 missions, amount to be announced.

d. Air Support Controlled by V Corps

(1) Day heavy bomber force - 4 missions, 180 tons per mission.
(2) Day medium bomber force - 5 missions, 36 tons per mission.
(3) Day fighter-bomber force - 4 missions, 12 planes each, 6x60 pound rockets per plane.

3. FIRE SUPPORT

a. Heavy Gunfire Ships

(1) H-40 minutes until mission accomplished:
(a) Counterbattery on Battery No. 1, POINTE DU HOE (586938)
(b) Battery No. 5, MAISY (533918).
(c) Battery No. 10, BEAUVAIS (792631).
(d) Battery No. 16, MAISY (525915).
(e) Ships that complete counterbattery tasks prior to H-hour will fire on beach defense targets.

(2) After H-hour they will be prepared to answer calls for fire from Naval Shore Fire Control Party.

(3) From H-hour to H / 1 hour, when not engaged otherwise, they will keep harrassing fire on TREVIERES (643839) and ISIGNY (50263N)

b. Destroyers

H-20 minutes to H-hour will deliver close-support fire from position on flank. One ship will be prepared to keep neutralizing fire on PORT EN BESSIN from H-40 minutes to H / 3 hours.

c. Support Craft

(1) LCG(L) accompany leading wave on flanks and in boat lanes. Mission to take under direct fire targets of opportunity as soon as visible and within range. Fire is transferred to flank targets when forced to lift for safety of troops. No indirect fire will be used.

(2) LCT(R) take position in boat lanes and deliver fire at approximately H-3 minutes on assigned targets when leading wave is approximately 500 yards from shore. As soon as rockets have been fired, craft will clear boat lanes. Six will roll and stand by on call from headquarters ship. Assignments and targets are:
(a) 3 craft on COLLEVILLE on line between 702891 and 685895.
(b) 1 craft on area at 676896.
(c) 2 craft on LES MOULINS on line between 672901 and 662907.
(d) 2 craft on VIERVILLE SUR MER on line between 657910 and 649918.
(e) 1 craft on area at 637928.

(3) LCG(8) accompany assault wave and fire on targets of opportunity distributed along entire beach.

(4) LCT(AVRE) following leading wave will take under fire targets of opportunity on their respective beaches. Primary targets - concrete emplacements; secondary targets - houses and beach installations.

(5) LCT(5) with 105-mm "Priest" Self-propelled take position in boat lanes about 3000 yards in rear of leading wave. Commence fire at about H-30 at which time they should be approximately 9000 yards from beach. Lift fire at H-5 to targets on high ground. At H-hour clear boat lanes. Targets: Neutralizing and fire beyond beach line in line with movement of craft on respective beaches. 58th Field Artillery Battalion on area 684912; 62d Field Artillery Battalion on area 694691.

d. Air Support (Tentative)

(1) Night heavy bomber force: Between H-5 hours and H-110 minutes on Battery No. 1, POINTE DU HOE (586938).

(2) Night medium bomber force: Between H-80 and H-40 on Battery No. 1, POINTE DU HOE (586938) and No. 5, MAISY (533918).

(3) Day heavy bomber force: H-25 to H-hour on strong points commanding beach. Tentative targets (637926), (649916), (666903), and (668895).

(4) Day medium bomber force: H-25 to H-hour breach lanes in-fire and minefields. Tentative location (649916), (677901), (688895), and (681896), (665907).

(5) Day fighter-bomber force: H-25 to H-hour on strong points commanding beaches. Tentative targets (653912), (684908), (667906). and (678897).

e. Target Designation

(1) General:
(a) The Lambert Grid will be used for naval target designation, using 1/50,000 maps and charts and 1/25,000 vertical mosaics.
(b) Gridded obliques will be furnished naval gunfire spotters to facilitate target identification, but Norton coordinates will not be used for target designation.
(c) Obliques marked to show location of known targets will be furnished to all craft firing on point targets in order to facilitate target identification.

4. NAVAL SHORE FIRE PARTIES

a. Attached to 1st United States Infantry Division - Nine parties, 294th Joint Assault Signal Company.

BIGOT

TOP SECRET "NEPTUNE"

Copy No. _____

Page 1 of 5 Pages

FIELD ARTILLERY

Hq 1st US Inf Div
APO #1, U.S. Army
16 April 1944

ANNEX #7)
TO FO #35)

Maps: GSGS 4347, Scale 1/25,000, FRANCE

1. a. See Intelligence Annex 2 to Field Order 35, 1st US Infantry Division.

   b. (1) See operations overlay, Annex 1 to Field Order 35, 1st US Infantry Division.

      (2) D/1 190th Field Artillery Group Headquarters and Headquarters Battery, 190th Field Artillery Battalion and 186th Field Artillery Battalion lend and are attached to 1st US Infantry Division Artillery upon arrival.

      (3) D and D/1 635th Tank Destroyer Battalion lends, and D/3 (approximately) 103rd Antiaircraft Artillery (Automatic Weapons) lands, and both are attached to 1st US Infantry Division Artillery upon arrival.

   (4) Naval Shore Fire Control Parties:

      (a) Nine parties are attached and will land with the 1st US Infantry Division on basis of one per Infantry Battalion.

      (b) Nine parties are attached to 29th Infantry Division, two of which will land with Ranger units, remainder with infantry battalions of 29th Division.

      (c) In addition to Naval Shore Fire Control Parties, Naval liaison officers will be attached and landed as follows:

         1. One with 7th Field Artillery Battalion.
         2. One with 62d Field Artillery Battalion.
         3. One with 32d Field Artillery Battalion.
         4. One with 111th Field Artillery Battalion.
         5. One with 58th Field Artillery Battalion.
         6. One with 110th Field Artillery Battalion.
         7. One with 1st US Infantry Division Artillery.
         8. One with 29th US Infantry Division Artillery.

2. The 1st US Infantry Division Artillery and attached units will land on schedule D-day and support the attack of the 1st US Infantry Division.

   It will have the following attachments:

-1-

TOP SECRET "NEPTUNE"

Page 4 of 4 Pages

TOP SECRET "NEPTUNE"

BIGOT

   b. Attached to 29th United States Infantry Division - Nine parties, 29th Joint Assault Signal Company, two of which will be allotted to Ranger units.

   c. Artillery Air Observation Posts used to adjust naval gun fire will operate through Battalion Fire Direction Center and attached naval liaison officers.

5. AMMUNITION

   Commanding Officers, 58th and 62d Field Artillery Battalion (Armored) and 745th Tank Battalion (medium) will requisition and load on craft following ammunition in addition to basic load for support firing afloat:

      Self-Propelled Battalion - 100 rounds per Howitzer
      Tank M-4 - 160 rounds high explosive shell per tank firing.

6. SIGNAL COMMUNICATIONS

   a. Radio and frequencies as prescribed by current Signal Operating Instructions.

   b. Smoke signals of colors to be designated later will be used to lift naval gun fire in case of radio failure. Its meaning "Cease firing". gunfire falling too close to friendly troops".

HUEBNER
Maj Gen

OFFICIAL: [signature]
GIBB
G-3

-4-

TOP SECRET "NEPTUNE"

Also issued on the 16 April is Field Order No 35 – it orders the Rangers to reach the Phase Line two hours before dark on D-Day.

UNCLASSIFIED

"NEPTUNE"

Page 1 of 10 Pages

Ref No.
ZA-104

Hq 1st US Inf Div
APO #1, U.S. Army
16 April 1944

:   :
:By authority of — :
:CG, 1st US Inf Div:
:16 April 1944   :
:Initials: Full.   :

Field Order Number 35

Maps: GSGS 4250, 1/50,000, FRANCE,
       Sheets 6E/6, 6F/2, 7E/5, 7F/1.

Copy No. _____ 155

1. a. For information of the enemy see current intelligence plan and G-2
        Annex, Annex 2.

    b. (1) The First US Army, associated US and Allied naval and air forces,
             and the British Second Army, will conduct a simultaneous assault
             on the continent of Europe with the mission of establishing a -
             beachhead from which further offensive operations can be develop-
             ed.

        (2) The 11th Amphibious Force will provide escort and support the
             landing of 1st US Infantry Division (reinforced), clear under-
             water mine fields and obstacles off-shore, protect the transport
             area and assist the landing with gunfire, both prearranged and
             on call. Annex 6.

        (3) The 9th US Air Force will support the attack of the 1st US Infantry
             Division, reinforced, by prearranged bombing missions prior to
             H-hour and by missions on call after H-hour. Annexes 6 and 11.

        (4) The 50th British Division will assault the beaches on the left of
             the 1st US Infantry Division and will capture BAYEUX on D-day.

        (5) The US VII Corps on the right of the 1st US Infantry Division will
             assault Beach UTAH on D-day at H-hour. The 4th US Infantry Divi-
             sion will make the assault landing. The 101st Airborne Division
             will drop on the area behind VIERVILLE (4299) – CARENTAN (3894)
             during the night of D-1, D-day, with the main objective of assist-
             ing the seaborne landing of the VII Corps.

        (6) The Provisional Engineer Special Brigade Group, consisting of the
             5th and 6th Engineer Special Brigades (reinforced), will support
             the landings of the 1st US Infantry Division. It will operate
             all shore installations necessary for debarkation, supply, eva-
             cuation, and local beach security in order to insure the con-
             tinuous movement of personnel, vehicles, and supplies across the
             beach.

        (7) The 29th US Infantry Division, less Regimental Combat Team 116,
             with Regimental Combat Team 26 and other troops attached, will
             land on Beach OMAHA behind the initial assault.

- 1 -

UNCLASSIFIED

"NEPTUNE"

2.   a.   The 1st US Infantry Division, less Regimental Combat Team 26, with Regimental Combat Team 116 and other troops attached, will make the initial assault on Beach OMAHA at H-hour on D-day with two Regimental Combat Teams abreast, reduce the beach defenses in its zone of action secure the Beachhead Maintenance Line, secure the D-day phase line by two hours before dark on D-day. It will cover the landing of the remainder of the V Corps and will be prepared to participate in the extension of the beachhead to the south and the southwest. Operations Overlay, Annex 1.

3.   a.   <u>COMBAT TEAM 116 REINFORCED</u> (See Troop List)

     (1)   Land two Battalion Landing Teams, 116th Combat Team, and one company, 2d Ranger Battalion, simultaneously at H-hour, D-day, on Beaches OMAHA, Easy Green, Dog Red, Dog White, and Dog Green, and three companies of the 2d Ranger Battalion on Beaches Baker and Charlie. Reserve Battalion, 116th Combat Team, and balance of Ranger Force to follow as directed by Combat Team Commander. Reduce beach defenses in its zone of action, seize and secure that portion of the Beachhead Maintenance Line in its zone of action, capture POINTE DU HOE, seize and secure that portion of D-day phase line in its zone of action by two hours before dark on D-day.

     (2)   Gain and maintain contact with 16th Combat Team on the left.

     (3)   Gain and maintain contact with US VII Corps on the right at the earliest possible time.

     (4)   Capture ISIGNY; organize it for all-around defense.

     (5)   Protect bridges in the vicinity of ISIGNY.

     (6)   Patrol to D / 1 phase line within its zone of action.

     (7)   See Operations Overlay, Annex 1.

"NEPTUNE"

UNCLASSIFIED

BIGOT

"NEPTUNE"

(8) Ranger Force

(a) Land three companies at H-hour, D-day at POINTE DU HOE and
destroy enemy installations in that vicinity. Be prepared
to repel hostile counter-attack and assist the advance of
the remainder of the Ranger Force and 116th Infantry.

(b) Land one company on right of Beach OMAHA, Dog Green, at H-hour,
D-day, advance rapidly to POINTE EL RAZ DE LA PERCEE.
Destroy enemy installations at that point and continue the
advance to the west, covering the right flank of the remainder of the Ranger Force.

(c) Ranger Force, less four companies above, land on Beach OMAHA,
Dog Green, as directed by Combat Team Commander, pass
through elements of 116th Combat Team; under cover of
coastal ridges, proceed rapidly via CHATEAU D'ENGLESQUEVILLE
to POINTE DU HOE where, upon arrival, in conjunction with
the three Ranger Companies landed at H-hour, capture POINTE
DU HOE, destroy enemy installations and guns at that point
(if this mission has not been previously accomplished),
assist the right Battalion Landing Team, 116th Infantry, in
the reduction of the hostile fortifications along the coast
between POINTE DU HOE and ISIGNY, and the capture of ISIGNY.

(9) The right Battalion Landing Team, 116th Combat Team, will:

(a) Land at H-hour on Beach OMAHA, Dog Green, reduce the beach
defenses in its zone of action, capture VIERVILLE SUR MER,
assist the Ranger Force in the capture of the fortifications
along the coast from the western limits of Beach OMAHA, Dog
Green to POINTE DU HOE inclusive.

(b) After the capture of POINTE DU HOE, assisted by the Ranger
Force, reduce the hostile fortifications along the coast
between POINTE DU HOE and ISIGNY; and be prepared to seize
and secure ISIGNY.

(c) Furnish necessary heavy weapons and artillery fire support
for the Ranger Force.

(10) The left Battalion Landing Team, 116th Combat Team, will:

(a) Land at H-hour on Beach OMAHA, Easy Green, Dog Red, and Dog
White, reduce beach defenses in its zone of action, capture
ST LAURENT SUR MER and the high ground (Beachhead Maintenance Line) 2,500 yards southwest of ST LAURENT SUR MER
and establish company strongpoints, prepared for all-around
defense and be prepared to augment the defense by use of
DD tanks and elements of the Engineer Special Brigade moving
into semi-prepared positions between company strongpoints.

- 3 -

"NEPTUNE"   UNCLASSIFIED

Also issued was a visual interpretation of these orders. Shown is a map overlay indicating the Rangers in the top left area at Pointe du Hoc then arrows directing them to the left to Maisy. Note the D-Day Objective Line is **again** marked on this map and again NO order exists in any of these orders to *'block the highway'*. The Rangers' missions went well beyond Pointe du Hoc as is shown.

Below is a statement of how many copies of the above orders were sent to Lt. Col. Rudder, Commanding Officer (CO) of the Ranger Force. Thus we can confirm on 16 April that he was fully aware of his unit's orders and objectives.

	No. Copies	Copy Nos.
Hq 1st US Inf Div:		
CO Ranger Force	5	226 – 230

The demand for aerial photographs for planning purposes was highly restricted to those units involved in the early operations. Requests were to be made to 'higher headquarters' and it is confirmed by this memo, that both the 2nd and 5th Battalions had their photographs at this time. The quantities of maps given to the Rangers are also shown.

AERIAL PHOTOGRAPHS.

a. All requests for planning photographs will be made to the AC of S, G-2, this headquarters.

b. Initial issue of photographs for operations will be made when available from higher headquarters. Distribution will be as follows:

```
            Div Hq.......................1
            16th Inf Regt...............4
            18th Inf Regt...............2
            116th Inf Regt..............4
            2d Ranger Bn................1
            5th Ranger Bn...............1
            Div Arty Hq.................2
            7th FA Bn...................2
            32d FA Bn...................2
            111th FA Bn.................2
            58th Armd FA Bn.............2
            62d Armd FA Bn.............2
                        TOTAL  25
```

- 8 -

"NEPTUNE"

Requests for operational photos of a specific area will be submitted as required to this Hq. Bn level can expect an approved request five hours after the request has been flown. All requests for Aerial Photos will be forwarded to the Regt S-2.

"NEPTUNE"   BIGOT

UNIT	1/4,000,000	1/1,000,000	1/500,000	1/250,000	1/200,000 Road Map	1/100,000	1/50,000	1/25,000	1/25,000 Photo Maps	1/10,000 Town Plans	1/50,000 Defense Overprint	1/25,000 Defense Overprint	1/12,500 Defense Overprint	1/5,000 Assault Maps
2d Ranger Bn		1	10	35	10	50	50			5		50	50	50
5th Ranger Bn		1	10	35	10	50	50			5		50	50	50

Authority: CG 1st US Inf Div 16 April 1944 Initials: JHL

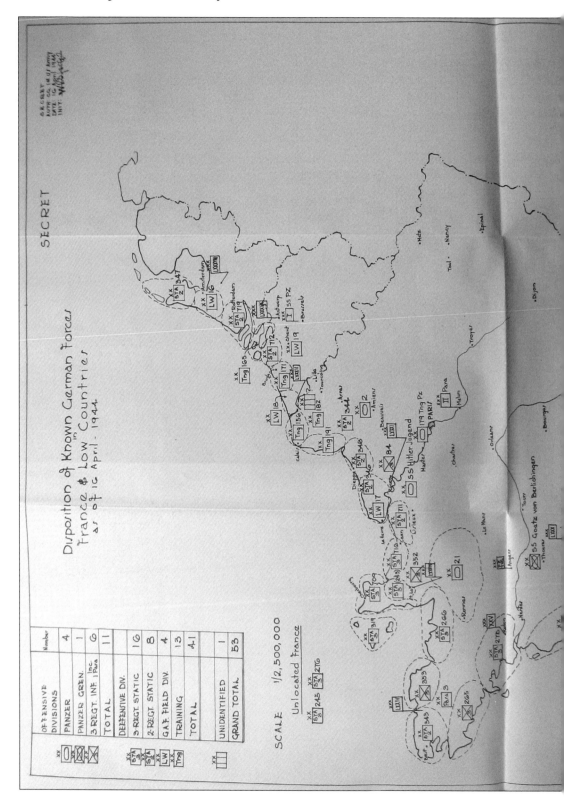

17 April 1944

Both Battalions undergoing ATC Training as per 'RANGERS Training Schedule'.

5th Rangers – Companies A – F, Medical and HQ – Braunton Camp, North Devon.

A, B & C Companies 2nd Rangers – Braunton Camp, North Devon. No change. Alerted for departure.

D, E & F Companies 2nd Rangers – Swanage, Dorset. Alerted for departure.

Medical Detachment 2nd Rangers – Braunton Camp, North Devon. No change. Alerted for departure.

Headquarters Company 2nd Rangers – Braunton Camp, North Devon.

Below: An April dated British intelligence map covering the sluice gates to the west of Pointe du Hoc, Grandcamp-les-Bains harbour and west to the Maisy Batteries.

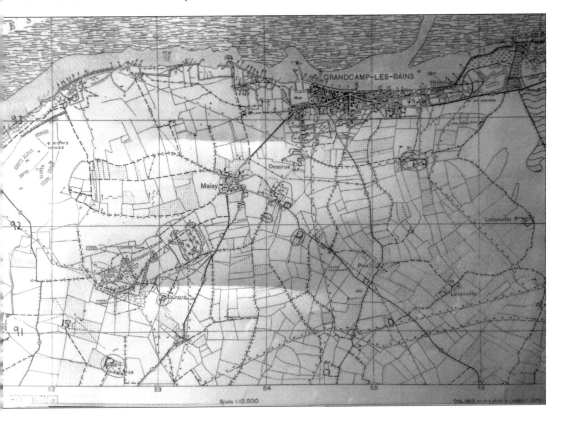

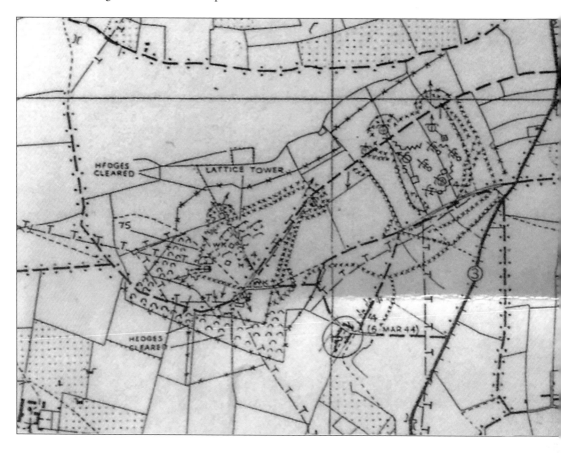

18 April 1944

Both Battalions undergoing ATC Training as per 'RANGERS Training Schedule'.

5th Rangers – Companies A – F, Medical and HQ – Braunton Camp, North Devon.

A, B & C Companies 2nd Rangers – Braunton Camp, North Devon. Alerted for departure.

D, E & F Companies 2nd Rangers – Swanage, Dorset. No change. Alerted for departure.

Medical Detachment 2nd Rangers – Braunton Camp, North Devon. No change. Alerted for departure.

Headquarters Company 2nd Rangers – Braunton Camp, North Devon. No change. Alerted for departure.

US Army issued orders related to 'Captured Materiel'

> *In the heat of combat, enemy materiel may be placed to immediate use by combat units to the extent required by the situation. Due to the difficulty of supply and maintenance, however, it is not the policy of First Army that such materiel should be retained in use – except for the immediate emergency.*

19 April 1944

Both Battalions undergoing ATC Training as per 'RANGERS Training Schedule'.

5th Rangers – Companies A – F, Medical and HQ – Braunton Camp, North Devon. No change. Alerted for departure.

A Company 2nd Rangers – Braunton Camp, North Devon. Alerted for departure.

B Company 2nd Rangers – Braunton Camp, North Devon.

1st Lt. Hanley was relieved from assignment and transferred to 1st Infantry Division, APO 1. US Army as of 18 April 1944. Alerted for departure.

C Company 2nd Rangers – Braunton Camp, North Devon. Alerted for departure.

D, E & F Companies 2nd Rangers – Swanage, Dorset. No change. Alerted for departure.
Medical Detachment 2nd Rangers – Braunton Camp, North Devon. No change. Alerted for departure.
Headquarters Company 2nd Rangers – Braunton Camp, North Devon. Alerted for departure.

Below is the regular update on the Rangers' vehicle allocation and personnel allocated to man them. These were always kept up-to-date in case there was a necessity for immediate embarkation.

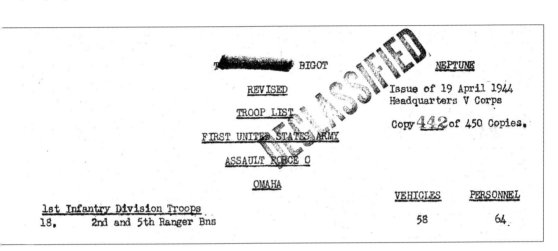

BIGOT		NEPTUNE
REVISED		Issue of 19 April 1944
		Headquarters V Corps
TROOP LIST		
		Copy 442 of 450 Copies.
FIRST UNITED STATES ARMY		
ASSAULT FORCE O		
OMAHA		
	VEHICLES	PERSONNEL
1st Infantry Division Troops		
18. 2nd and 5th Ranger Bns	58	64

20 April 1944

Both Battalions undergoing ATC Training.
5th Rangers – Companies A – F, Medical and HQ – Braunton Camp, North Devon.
A, B & C Companies 2nd Rangers – Braunton Camp, North Devon. No change. Alerted for departure.
D, E & F Companies 2nd Rangers – Swanage, Dorset. No change. Alerted for departure.
Medical Detachment 2nd Rangers – Braunton Camp, North Devon. No change. Alerted for departure.
Headquarters Company 2nd Rangers – Braunton Camp, North Devon.

The documents opposite are dated 20 April and they show the Operations Plan for the Rangers.

████████ BIGOT

Auth: CG, V Corps
Date: 20 April 1944
Initials: ████ I.J.D.

Annex 19
in 3 pages
Page No. 1

Number of Copies 125

Copy Number 92.

ANNEX 19

TO

V CORPS

OPERATIONS PLAN

NEPTUNE

RANGER PLAN

20 April 1944.

████████ BIGOT

- 1 -

 BIGOT

RANGER PLAN

1. Ranger Group, consisting of 2nd and 5th Ranger Bns, two (2) NSFCPs and one (1) Air Support Party, will operate as part of 116th CT, reinforced. (For objectives and scheme of maneuver of 116th CT, see Annex No. 21A).

2. Ranger Force A consisting of:

      Hq Det, 2nd Ranger Bn
      Co. D, 2nd Ranger Bn
      Co. E, 2nd Ranger Bn
      Co. F, 2nd Ranger Bn
      One (1) NSFCP (attached)

will land at H-hour, D-day, on Beach Charlie, companies abreast. One company will land on West portion of POINTE DU HOE. Two companies and the NSFCP will land on the East portion of POINTE DU HOE. The force will assault POINTE DU HOE directly, destroy shore batteries, assist advance of remainder of Ranger Forces.

3. Force X (Co. "C", 2nd Ranger Bn) will land on right of beach Omaha Dog Green at H-hour, D-day, advance rapidly to POINTE ET RAZ LA PERCEE, destroy installations at the pointe and continue to advance to the west covering the right flank of the remainder of the Ranger Group.

4. Ranger Force Y, commanded by CO, 5th Ranger Bn, consisting of

      Hq Det, 2nd Ranger Bn
      NFSCP
      Air Support Party
      Co. A, 2nd Ranger Bn
      Co. B, 2nd Ranger Bn
      5th Ranger Bn

will land in 2 waves. First wave consisting of:

      Hq Det, 2nd Ranger Bn
      Co. A, 2nd Ranger Bn
      Co. B, 2nd Ranger Bn
      NFSCP
      Air Support Party
      Hq Det, 5th Ranger Bn
      Co A, 5th Ranger Bn
      Co B, 5th Ranger Bn
      Co C, 5th Ranger Bn

will land on Beach Dog Green at H/28 minutes, D-day.

2nd wave consisting of remainder of Force Y will land on Beach Dog Green at H/30 minutes, proceed rapidly, in column of companies, along route paralleling the shore line, avoiding all unnecessary action, to seize POINTE DU HOE from the rear and and destroy battery installations. Two companies, 2nd Ranger Bn, will provide advance guard and flank protection for Force Y from beach to objective.

5. The Cannon platoon will land at H/120 minutes, D-day, on Beach Dog Green and will proceed along the Road VIERVILLE SUR MER - GRANDE CAMP LES BAINS to vicinity of POINTE DU HOE and be prepared to support the assault of Force Y in the capture of POINTE DU HOE.

6. Upon accomplishment of primary mission, the group will reorganize in preparation for future missions on the right flank.

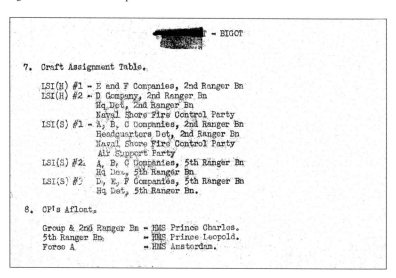

```
                            ──────── T - BIGOT

    7.  Craft Assignment Table.

        LSI(H) #1 - E and F Companies, 2nd Ranger Bn
        LSI(H) #2 - D Company, 2nd Ranger Bn
                    Hq Det, 2nd Ranger Bn
                    Naval Shore Fire Control Party
        LSI(S) #1 - A, B, C Companies, 2nd Ranger Bn
                    Headquarters Det, 2nd Ranger Bn
                    Naval Shore Fire Control Party
                    Air Support Party
        LSI(S) #2  A, B, C Companies, 5th Ranger Bn
                    Hq Det, 5th Ranger Bn
        LSI(S) #3  D, E, F Companies, 5th Ranger Bn
                    Hq Det, 5th Ranger Bn.

    8.  CP's Afloat.

        Group & 2nd Ranger Bn - HMS Prince Charles.
        5th Ranger Bn,        - HMS Prince Leopold.
        Force A               - HMS Amsterdam.
```

21 April 1944

A Company 5th Rangers – Braunton Camp, North Devon. Pvt. McGuire went from confinement in the battalion guard house and returned to Duty. Alerted for departure.

5th Rangers – Companies B – F, Medical and HQ – Braunton Camp, North Devon.

A, B & C Companies 2nd Rangers – Braunton Camp, North Devon. Alerted for departure.

D, E & F Companies 2nd Rangers – Swanage, Dorset. No change. Alerted for departure.

Medical Detachment 2nd Rangers – Braunton Camp, North Devon. No change. Alerted for departure.

Headquarters Company 2nd Rangers – Braunton Camp, North Devon.

Headquarters issued orders on the 21 April relating to the use of rations in combat.

NUTRITION

1. *Tactical situations and difficulties of supply may necessitate the issue of the emergency rations, types 'C', 'K', 'D' or '10 in-1' to combat troops for extended periods. Physical well-being and fighting efficiency will be seriously impaired under such circumstances, if troops consistently fail to eat their rations, particularly the meat, biscuit and lemon crystal components. Experience has shown that the monotony of emergency rations, especially if eaten cold, is the primary cause of loss of appetite.*

2. *All officers responsible for the feeding of troops subsisting on type 'C', 'K', 'D' or '10-in-1' rations will inform the troops of the necessity of eating the prescribed ration and will ensure that authorised heating units are available for the preparation of hot food and beverage in the event hot meals cannot be otherwise provided. Insofar as the military situation permits, troops will be allowed ample time for the cooking and eating of emergency rations and will be encouraged in their efforts to add to the palatability of their rations by variations in preparation methods.*

3. *It is imperative that troops consume an adequate diet prior to the period of use of emergency rations. All officers responsible for the feeding to troops subsisting on type 'A' or 'B' rations will give particular attention to preparation and service in unit messes so as to insure that the troops receive clean, tasty food and are not deprived of essential nutrients – because of over-cooking or failure to utilise all components of the ration. Troops will be informed of the importance of eating certain nutritionally critical items such as evaporated and dried milk, dried eggs, lemon crystals and carrots. In this respect, the responsibility of the individual soldier for his physical fitness will be stressed.*

4. *Officers of the Medical Department are specifically charged with the duty of assisting officers of the line in all measures designed to improve the nutrition of troops. The sanitary report submitted in accordance with instructions issued by the Chief Surgeon, ETOUSA, 31st January 1944 will include comments on the health of troops required to subsist on emergency rations for prolonged periods and will make recommendations concerning their subsequent nutritional rehabilitation.*

Beach recognition drawings were created indicating what the Rangers should expect to see from the sea during their landing. These were produced to help orientate the Rangers on where they had landed and the direction of their advance thereafter.

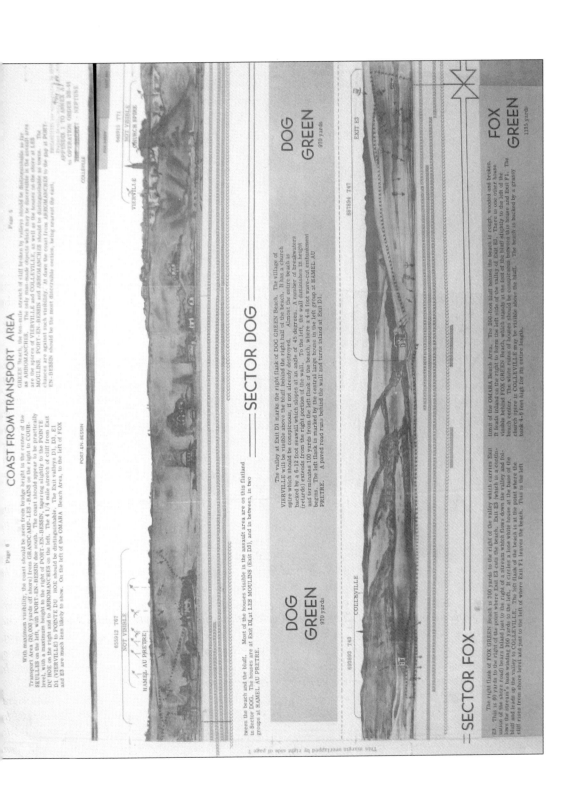

COAST FROM TRANSPORT AREA

Page 6

With maximum visibility, the coast should be seen from bridge height in the center of the Transport Area (20,000 yards off shore) from GRANDCAMP-LES-BAINS on the right to COUR-SEULLES on the left, with PORT-EN-BESSIN due south. The coast should appear to be practically level, with a maximum height to the right of PORT-EN-BESSIN, tapering slightly to the POINTE DU HOE on the right and to ARROMANCHES on the left. The 4 1/4 mile stretch of cliff from Exit D1 (VIERVILLE) to POINTE DU HOE should be distinguishable. The Exit valleys D1, D3, E1 and E3 are much less likely to show. On the left of the OMAHA Beach Area, to the left of FOX

Page 5

GREEN Beach, the ten-mile stretch of cliff broken by valleys should be distinguishable as far as ARROMANCHES. The only man-made objects which may be discernible in the assault area are the spires of VIERVILLE and COLLEVILLE, as well as the houses on the shore at LES MOULINS. PORT-EN-BESSIN and ARROMANCHES should be distinguishable as towns. The chances are against such visibility. At dawn the coast from ARROMANCHES to the top at PORT-EN-BESSIN should be the most discernible section, being nearest the east.

APPENDIX 1 TO
to OPERATION ORDER NB-44
NEPTUNE

tween the beach and the bluff. Most of the houses visible in the assault area are on this flatland in Sector DOG. The houses are at Exit D1, at LES MOULINS (Exit D3), and in between, in two groups at HAMEL AU PRETRE.

═══ SECTOR DOG ═══

The valley at Exit D1 marks the right flank of DOG GREEN Beach. The village of VIERVILLE will be visible above the bluff behind the right half of the beach. It has a church spire which should be conspicuous, if not already destroyed. Almost the entire beach is backed by a 6-12 foot seawall which slopes at an angle of 45 degrees. A number of breakwaters (retards) extends from the right portion of the wall. To the left, the wall diminishes in height and terminates 100 yards from the left flank of the beach, where the 4-8 foot wave-cut embankment begins. The left flank is marked by the central large house in the left group at HAMEL AU PRETRE. A paved road runs behind the wall and turns inland at Exit D1.

═══ SECTOR FOX ═══

23. The right flank of FOX GREEN Beach is 300 yards to the right of the point where Exit E3 cuts the beach. This is 60 yards to the right of the point where Exit E3 cuts the beach. Exit E3 which is a continuation of the shore road) bears inland just to the right of a stream which flows down the valley and follows the stream's bank winding 300 yards to the left. It circles a lone white house at the base of the bluff and leads up the valley to COLLEVILLE. The left flank of the beach is at the point where Exit F1 leaves the beach. This is the left

limit of the OMAHA Beach Area. The 200-foot bluff behind the beach is rough, wooded and broken. It leads inland on the right to form the left side of the valley of Exit E3. There is one other house visible behind FOX GREEN Beach, which stands at the foot of the bluff slightly to the left of the beach center. The white ruins of houses should be conspicuous between this house and Exit F1. The church spire in COLLEVILLE may be visible above the bluff. The beach is backed by a grassy bank 4-9 feet high for its entire length.

DOG GREEN 970 yards

DOG GREEN 970 yards

FOX GREEN 1135 yards

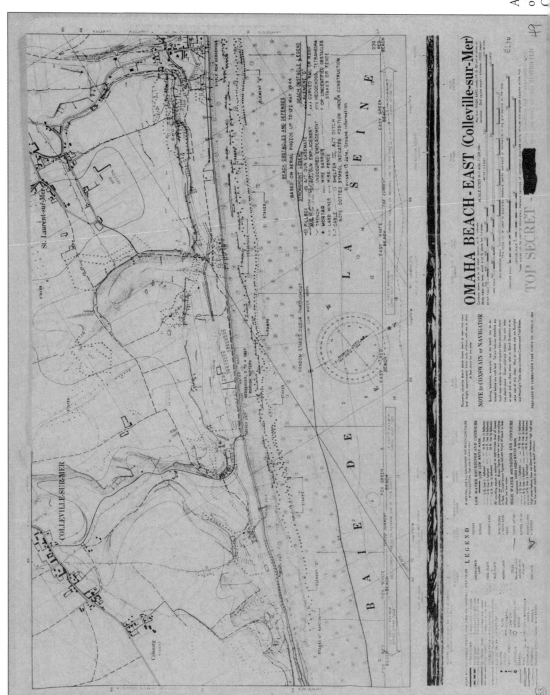

A detailed beach obstacle plan for Omaha Beach

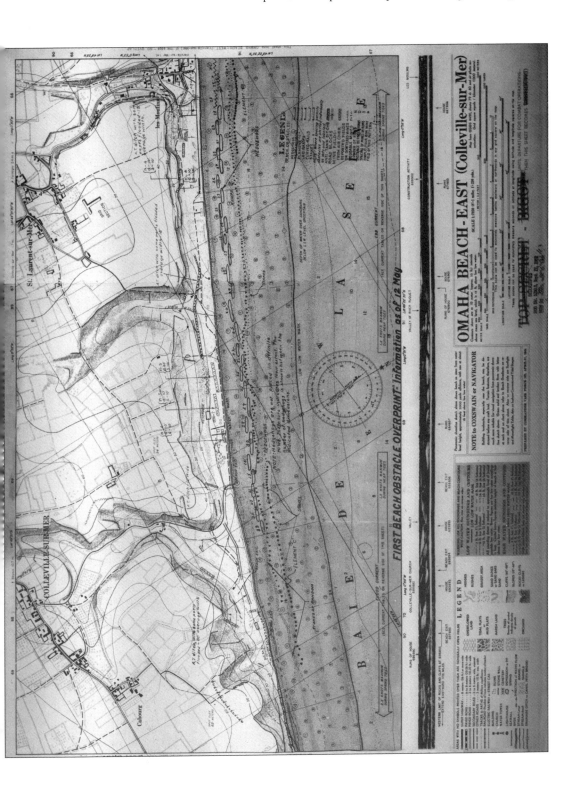

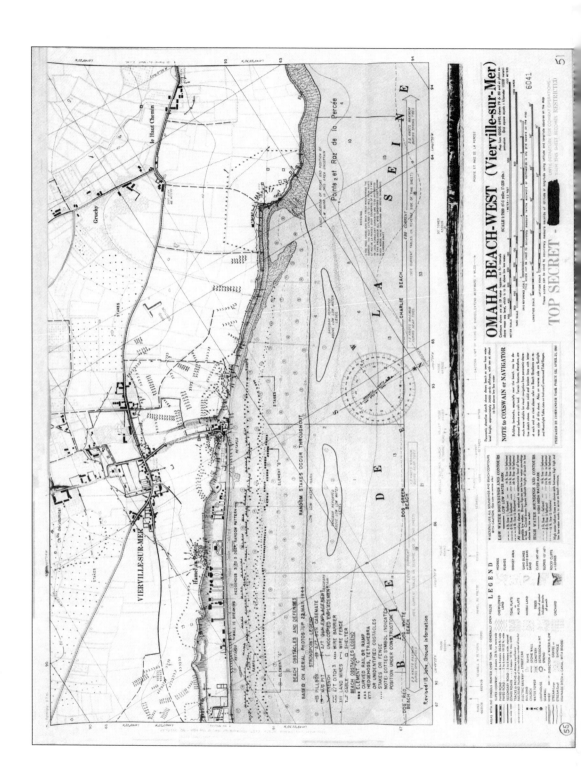

On 21 April the Top Secret Neptune Monograph was issued – it contained a comprehensive briefing of the Omaha Sector and it provided the Rangers with details for each of the emplacements they were to attack. It is shown here in full, and the areas relevant to the Rangers are highlighted in grey.

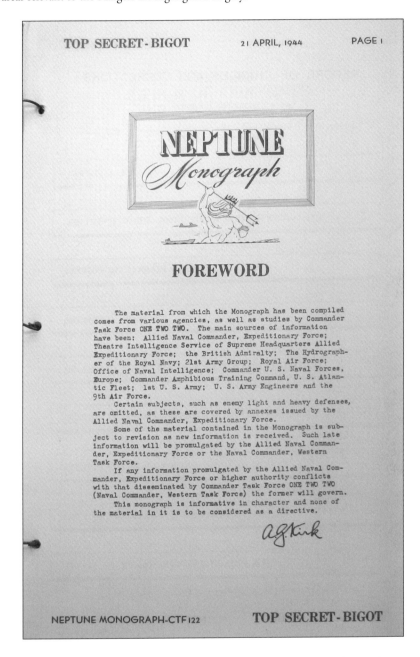

Overleaf: Pages entitled TYPICAL GUN EMPLACEMENTS reference the Pointe du Hoc battery, its observation post and gun pit type. The note at the top of the left-hand page states: *'Information for these sketches was obtained from aerial photographs taken between 18 Feb and 8 March 44 and from technical publications. Details have been approximated and should be accepted with caution.'*

The right-hand page contains information about the Longues-sur-Mer Battery (not a Rangers objective) and at the bottom of the page there is the layout for the Maisy – Les Perruques battery. The text reads: *'All of the above positions have attendant shelters and are protected by wire, trenches and minor defences. See typical layout Pointe du Hoe.'*

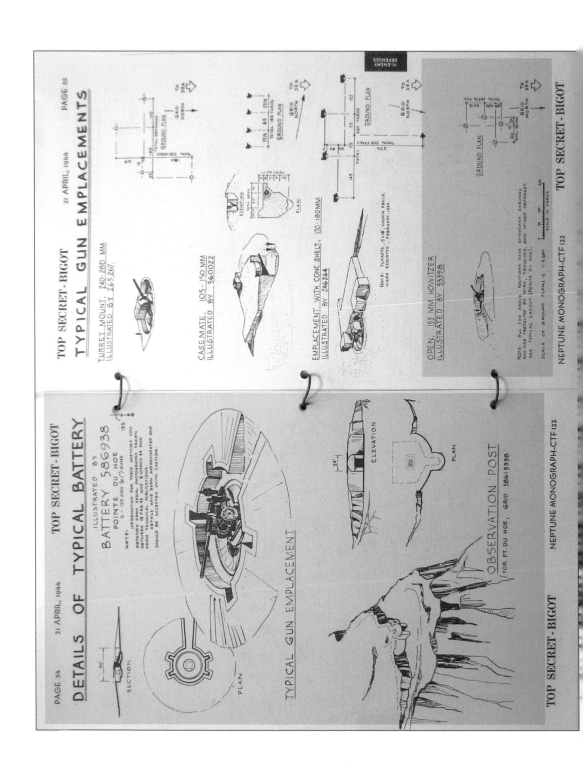

A more detailed layout for the Pointe du Hoc battery. Of particular note is the area in the centre where two of the gun positions are marked as 'GUN POSITIONS DISMANTLED' – clarifying that these were no longer positions with guns on them.

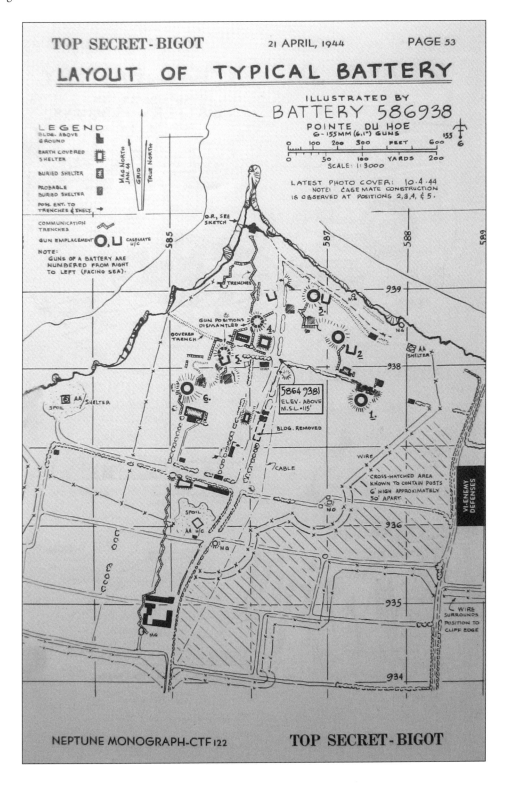

In the case of the position on the left of the two, the plan indicates that a casement is being constructed on the top of the old gun pit; a fact which concurs with the other intelligence available at the time. The elements shown as incomplete squares on the main map are in the process of being built.

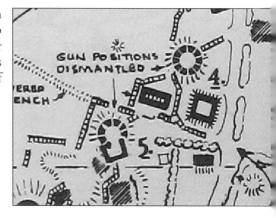

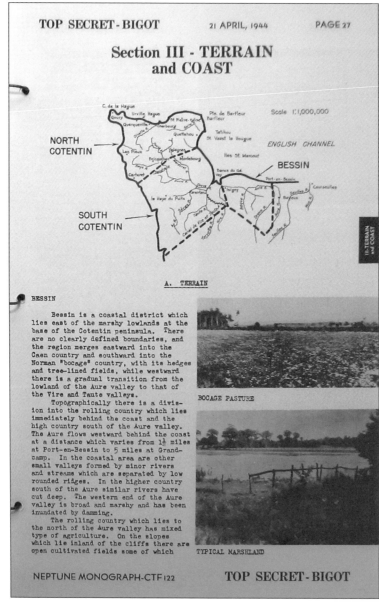

TOP SECRET - BIGOT

are bordered by low hedges or earth banks. Behind this narrow coastal belt the plateau is occupied mainly by square or rectangular pasture fields bordered by hedges, earth banks, and lines of trees.

Along the Aure valley there is a gradual transition from pasture in the east to a cultivated plain on the west, beyond which lie the alluvial pasture lowlands of South Cotentin.

The central and southern part of Bessin is more hilly and broken country which merges into true "bocage" in the south-west. There are two principal hilly regions which lie on either side of the Drome valley. On the western side the summit of the hills is crowned by the extensive Foret de Cerisy. On the flanks of this ridge and at the north-east end there are many orchards with pasture fields between; the latter are bordered by elms or ash trees for the most part, though there are occasional hedges and earthbanks.

The valleys in this hilly country are steep-sided with wooded sides and often with rich tree-lined pastures where valley bottoms widen.

Settlement in Bessin varies considerably according to situation and the underlying soils. On the hilly plateau north of the Aure there is a band of small coastal villages which are either small fishing-ports like Port-en-Bessin or Grandcamp-les-Bains or seaside resorts like Vierville-sur-Mer or St Laurent-sur-Mer; the plateau itself is occupied by scattered settlements of small farm groups which again are collected into small villages on the northern slopes of the Aure valley. The bottom of the Aure valley is unsuitable for settlement, as the ground is often soft and liable to be marshy. Bayeux is the main town of the region and is well connected by roads; it is a market centre and has only local industries connected with agriculture.

SOUTH COTENTIN

This region lies south of the hilly North Cotentin and North of the high country of the western "bocage". To the southeast lies the Bessin country.

Along the eastern coast is a belt of low-lying meadow land several miles wide, bordered on the west by a rising ridge of firmer ground. The ridge is covered with pasture land bordered with stone walls and hedges. Settlement is in scattered buildings along the coastal road and in some villages

ROLLING COUNTRY WITH TREE-LINED FIELDS, BESSIN

TYPICAL COUNTRY LANE WITH HEDGE ON EMBANKMENT

FLAT RIVER PLAIN

NEPTUNE MONOGRAPH-CTF122

TOP SECRET - BIGOT

TOP SECRET - BIGOT

with orchards on the landward side of the low land. This coastal meadow land has been inundated by artificial damming of drainage ditches to form a barrier of soft wet ground against invading troops. Most of the roads are under water.

To the southeast, around the Baie de Grand Vey, is again low lying land broken by dikes of earth construction. The estuaries of Carentan and Isigny flow through this area.

In the central part of the south Cotentin there are low rolling hills 100 ft. high or less divided by small broad stream valleys. In the north the hills are predominately pasture. The usual hedgerow borders occur between fields. The flat river valleys are a conspicuous feature and at several places broaden to form wide expanses of pasture land, sometimes quite marshy in character.

The western part of this region is composed of hard resistant rocks which give rise to a fairly thin soil of vary-ing fertility, the valleys and "pockets" being more suitable for agriculture.

Along the western coast is a belt of low sand dunes with rough pasture or heath behind. Drainage is sluggish into the numerous estuaries. The villages of the district lie on the inland side of the low sand dunes and at the foot of the pasture slopes behind.

In the south west the pasture land gives place to steep hill country east of Carteret and around La-Haye-du-Puits, these hills rise steeply from the plains. The higher ground and more infertile soils are usually occupied by heathland, though some small areas are wooded. The largest wooded areas are those of Foret de Monte Castre and Bois de Limors, the latter on low hills to the south of the pastureland. Both are woods in which dominant tree types are oak, beech and hornbeam. The market town of La Haye-du-Puits lies in a deep valley with high hills on both sides.

NORTH COTENTIN

Settlement throughout Cotentin avoids the low-lying ground of the river valleys or the infertile regions of sand dunes or coarse soils. Scattered farms are more common than nucleated villages. The larger settlements are regional market towns.

The boundary between low-lying south Cotentin and the more hilly area in the north runs roughly from Carteret on the west coast east-north-east to

LOWLAND PASTURE

HEDGED PASTURES NEAR CAP DE LA HAGUE

WALLED PASTURES NEAR GOURY

NEPTUNE MONOGRAPH-CTF122

TOP SECRET - BIGOT

TOP SECRET - BIGOT 21 APRIL, 1944 PAGE 31

dikes and drainage ditches would be additional obstacles to cross country travel.

The meadow land behind the inundated area has a relatively firm, well drained surface. During dry weather it should support vehicles over most of its area, though it may be come soft during rains. The grass covering will help support travel. Obstacles to cross country vehicle movement will be hedges, trees and walls bordering fields, which will also provide some measure of cover and concealment. There are relatively fewer orchards and woodland areas than are evident behind OMAHA.

Behind beach OMAHA is a sandy shelf which extends back to the line of bluffs behind the beach. Topping the bluffs is a rolling plateau of pastureland extending back to the AURE valley several miles inland.

The shelf back of the beach is sandy and covered with a short turf-like grass. There is an area of low dunes near the center of the beach, and one or two small marshy areas. Vehicle tracking occurs freely over this shelf except for dune and marshy areas. The grass covering would help support movement without impeding vehicle progress.

The westernmost 1500 yards of the beach is backed by a shale and shingle shelf, at the foot of the cliffs. This could be bulldozed into a passable roadway, though open to damage by waves at high tide.

The soil on the bluffs is very thin, though probably quite firm and covered with grass or turf, with scattered bushes in spots. The limey shale behind is exposed in numerous places. Vehicles would be restricted in movement by the angle of the slope, by patches of brush, and in wet weather by the slippery turf. The soil should, however support most types of vehicles.

The plateau is fairly flat and covered with a thin soil which supports cultivation and pasture land. The area is well drained and should support vehicles in cross country movement. Movement and observation will be restricted principally by field boundaries, which are composed of bushes, tree rows, earth banks or stone walls. Orchards and small patches of woodland are also obstacles to vehicle travel. Cover and concealment will be provided from air and ground view by trees and higher bushes.

III-TERRAIN and COAST

ARABLE LAND SOUTH OF CAEN

BEACH AND COAST AT VIERVILLE-SUR-MER

IV. BEACHES

c. COASTAL SECTOR DESIGNATIONS

Sector Letter	Brief description	Co-ords	Length (yards)
UTAH AREA (U)			
PETER	Village to Church	377081 – 391058	3200
QUEEN	P to Village	391058 – 407034	3300
ROGER	Q to Chalut	407034 – 415022	1900
SUGAR	R to rd.	415022 – 430000	2800
TARE	S to rd.	430000 – 445382	2800
UNCLE	T to CARENTAN Estuary	445382 – 455966	2500
VICTOR	U to CARENTAN Estuary	455966 – 455906	7400
WILLIAM	V to mouth of River VIRE	455906 – 491878	7500
OMAHA AREA (O)			
ABLE	Mouth of River VIRE to PTE DU MAIST	491878 – 527915	7600
BAKER	A to PTE DU HOE (PTE ST. PIERRE)	527915 – 587940	6900
CHARLIE	B to mouth of stream	587940 – 648917	8000
DOG	C to rd.	648917 – 667907	2400
EASY	D to rd.	667907 – 688897	2900
FOX	E to rd.	688897 – 723886	3900
GEORGE	F to PORT EN BESSIN (West break-water)	723886 – 751882	3200
GOLD AREA (G)			
HOW	G to rd (CAP MANVIEUX)	751882 – 636873	9300
ITEM	H to ASNELLES	636873 – 678868	4800
JIG	I to rd.	678868 – 907871	3200
KING	J to mouth of stream	907871 – 929868	2500
JUNO AREA (J)			
LOVE	K to rd.	929868 – 949862	2100
MIKE	L to COURSEULLES (WEST breakwater)	949862 – 968858	2200
NAN	M to ST. AUBIN	968858 – 016851	5500
SWORD AREA (S)			
OBOE	N to 105	016851 – 046835	3900
PETER	O to LION (WEST outskirts)	046835 – 068818	3000
QUEEN	P to settlement	068818 – 093805	3000
ROGER	Q to OUISTREHAM (WEST breakwater)	093805 – 119798	2900
BAND AREA (B)			
ABLE	OUISTREHAM (WEST breakwater to rd.)	119798 – 154794	4000
BAKER	A to rd.	154794 – 189797	3100
CHARLIE	B to BOULGATE (Mouth of River)	189797 – 237805	5400
DOG	C to VILLERS SUR MER (West outskirts)	237805 – 293831	7100

NOTE: When it is necessary to differentiate between sectors in different areas with the same letter, the prefix UTAH, OMAHA, GEN or BAND will be inserted, e.g., OMAHA ABLE.

(For maps showing extent of each coastal sector see Folio M at end of Monograph).

Section IV - BEACHES

GENERAL

1. Information on soundings, low water limits, gradients, sand bars, inshore currents etc., affecting the NEPTUNE AREA is regrettably scanty.

2. Tidal data is believed fairly, but not wholly, accurate.

3. The hydrographic data used in this monograph is based mainly on contour photographs taken at estimated tide levels and by photographic interpretation. Neither of these methods is absolutely accurate. Hence caution is essential in making use of the information derived from them.

4. Another factor that will affect the depth of water, as well as the width of the beaches at any stage of the tide, is prolonged onshore winds. Storms may change the height and location of sand bars.

5. The need for thorough hydrographic surveys and marking of bars as soon as possible after the assault waves have landed is imperative. Examples are the sand bars off "OMAHA" BEACH, which will not be a hazard to navigation of small craft when the water level is such that they will be visible, but would cause grounding when the tide covered them by only a few feet.

Additional Information on "OMAHA BEACH"

The rock patches at 655914, 662910, and 674903 on beach OMAHA, mentioned in "x CONSISTENCY" page 37, are low exposed areas of under-lying limey shale or shingle which are occasionally covered with sand. Shingle occurs behind the entire beach and has been reported to extend out under the sand in places. These patches should not be more than a maximum of about 8 inches above the surface of the sand.

Recent photographs show that definite sand bars occur just to seaward of the low water line on OMAHA. These are shown on Folios A and 3. The elevations of these bars are not known except that they are at or below LLW level and their horizontal position is defined only by breaking waves. This modifies paragraphs v, vii and xi. "OMAHA BEACH"

(A) BEACHES

"O M A H A" B E A C H

(COLLEVILLE - ST LAURENT - VIERVILLE)

L I M I T S

	WEST	TO	EAST
Coordinates:	"x" 637927		"m" 696893
Latitude:	49° 23' 17" N.		49° 21' 36" N.
Longitude:	0° 55' 08" W.		0° 50' 10" W.

1.   GENERAL DESCRIPTION:

"OMAHA" BEACH, 7,500 yards long, is composed of firm sand with shingle occuring from the back of the beach for a distance of about 25 yards. Several sand bars exist inside the tidal area. The beach is flanked by hard shale. At the western end, this rock formation extends 1,300 yards along the beach, and at a point 500 yards from the western end, the rocks extend 120 to 150 yards to seaward.

Except for its western end, the beach is backed by a low wavecut embankment, faced for part of its length by a masonry wall, behind which is a level, sandy grass covered shelf averaging 100 yards in width. Back of the shelf is 80-foot grass covered bluff broken by four natural valley exits, through which run roads. The western quarter of this beach is backed by a steep 80-foot cliff. A level cultivated plateau lies inland of this entire section of the coast.

The valleys are blocked by anti-tank obstacles, mines and wire, and the entire beach is defended by strong points and batteries. A line of obstacles exists along the beach at a distance of 50 to 130 yards to seaward from the back of the beach.

A detailed description follows: Refer to Folios A and B.

ii.   LENGTH: 7,500 Yds. (Coastline).
7,146 Yds. (Between coordinates).

iii.   WIDTH: Varies with the height of the tide. See SHORELINE SKETCH (Folios A and B) including TIDAL DATA and GRADIENTS on back thereof.

iv.   LANDMARKS:

(a) 647910 - VIERVILLE Steeple (100 feet high).
(b) 638926 - Tower (30 ft. high).
(c) 660595 - Valley.
(d) 678690 - Valley.
(e) 665907 - Valley.
(f) 648918 - Valley.

v.   APPROACH: Clear to seaward from low water mark. (See MAP CHART F-1015 for best data available on soundings.)

WARNINGS:

(a) POINTE DE LA PERCHE is border-

ed by a bank which, with depths of less than 5-fathoms, extends about 3/4 of a mile NE and about one mile ENE of the point. When the wind is against the tidal stream, a tide race, known as RAZ DE LA PERCHE, is formed over this bank. Under all wind conditions, turbulent currents are to be expected in this area, except during slack water.

(b) On both flanks of the beach there are underwater rocks composed of hard shale. At the western end, a strip of shale and shingle runs for 1,300 yards along the beach near the high tide mark. At a point 500 yards from the western end, a spur from this shale extends seaward 120 to 150 yards from the back of the beach.

(c) A rocky outcrop near the high water mark will be found in the vicinity of 651917.

vi. GRADIENTS: In general flat up to Mean Level (13 ft.), then increasingly steep. (See GRADIENT DATA on back of Folios A and B.)

vii. SAND BARS: A series of low sand bars exists along the entire

length of the beach. The depressions between the bars drain off as the tide recedes. The sand bars are subject to slight shifting due to storms. Most indication on bars is shown on SHORELINE SKETCH (Folios A and B).

viii. CURRENTS: See SHORELINE SKETCH (Folios A and B) (front and back.)

ix. TIDAL RANGE:

Springs: 23 feet.
Neaps :   19 feet.
Mean Level : 13 feet, above Datum, which is approximate level of low low water.

x. CONSISTENCY: Hard, well compacted sand from low water line to within 25 yards from back of beach. Beyond the sand to the back of the beach, there is shingle, averaging 6 inches in diameter. This area has an average slope of 1 in 8. In front of LES MOULINS, the shingle forms a bank 5 feet high average. The seawall west of LES MOULINS has sand and shingle piled up to a height of 2 to 3 feet. The eastern end of VIERVILLE seawall has a shingle and rock bank 4.5 feet high average. Rocks and debris occur in the western 1100 yards at the foot of the cliff. There is an outcrop at 651917 and small rock patches at 655914, 662910, and 674903.

xi. OBSTACLES:

(a) OFFSHORE -
(1) NATURAL: See par. v, APPROACH and SHORELINE SKETCH (Folios A and B).
(2) ARTIFICIAL: None.

(b) WITHIN NORMAL TIDAL AREA:
(1) NATURAL: See Par. x. CONSISTENCY.
(2) ARTIFICIAL: As of 4-9-44 1000 obstacles have been laid on the beach, forming a continuous single-row barrier 648918 to 688697, the line varying from the 11' to the 18' contour above LLW. Obstacles are of the steel hedgehog type. Further installation is anticipated. For mines, wire etc.. see ANNEX "A" - ASSAULT BEACH DEFENSE MAPS SCALE 1/12,500.

(c) BACK OF NORMAL TIDAL AREA:
(1) NATURAL:
4-6 ft. high, sloping approx. 1 in 4.
(a) 696894 to 673902: Grassy bank.
(b) 673902 to 662909: Wave-cut embankment, 4 to 8 ft. high.

(c) 662909 to 655913: Wave-cut embankment, 4 to 8 feet high.
(d) 649917 to 647919: Six-foot bank.

(e) 647919 to 637927: Vertical cliffs up to 100 feet high with debris slope and shingle at base.

(2) ARTIFICIAL:
(a) 673902 to 662909: Beach is backed by a wave-cut embankment 4 to 8 feet high with intermittent rough stone wall.

(b) 662909 to 655913: Masonry wall, 4 to 8 feet high, with 15 jetties 55 ft. long and spaced 55 ft. apart, projecting seaward at 60° angle. The surf has broken a part of the wall for a distance of 150 ft. from 65959106 to 65929109.

(c) 655913 to 655913: Wave-cut embankment, 4 to 8 ft. high, with intermittent rough stone wall.

(d) 655913 to 649917: Masonry and stone seawall, 8 to 12 ft. high, sloping approximately 45°. Nine jetties project seaward at western end of wall. These jetties are old and weathered and only pilings and a few connecting pieces remain.

(e) 649917 to 647919: A 6-foot embankment from which 6 jetties project seaward and on top of which are houses and stone fences.

(f) For obstacles of a defensive nature, see ANNEX, ANNEX "A" - ASSAULT BEACH DEFENSE MAPS, SCALE 1/12,500.

xii. EXITS:

(a) COASTAL - (On shelf between bluff and beach).
(1) 696894 to 691895: Four-foot sandy trail along coast, turning inland at 691895.
(2) 687896: Road off beach branching immediately. One fork leads inland to COLLEVILLE, the other proceeds westward as an 8-foot sandy road turning inland at 679900, continuing in this direction to 677900.
(3) 677900 to 671904: 8-foot sandy road mentioned above parallels beach 75 yards inland.
(4) 679900 to 678900: 4-foot trail continues along coast where shale road mentioned in (2) above turns inland.
(5) 671904 to 665907: 10-foot tarmac road parallels the beach.
(6) 665907 to 648917: Road mentioned in (5) above broadens into a 12-foot tarmac road paralleling the coast.

<u>WARNING</u>

This road is being washed out at 659911 by action of the sea.

(b) <u>INLAND</u>:

(1) 696893: 10-foot unsurfaced road leads up slope to strong point atop bluff and inland to village of CABOURG. At the back of the beach, this road forks to the west, and an 8-foot trail leads inland into CABOURG and COLLEVILLE.

(2) 687896: 10-foot tarmac road to COLLEVILLE.

(3) 676900: 10-foot unsurfaced road leading to ST. LAURENT.

(4) 665907: 10-foot tarmac road leaves coast at LES MOULINS inland for ST. LAURENT.

(5) 648917: 15-foot tarmac road leaves VIERVILLE inland.

xiii.   OBSTACLES TO MOVEMENT INLAND:

(a) NATURAL –

(1) BLUFF: A bluff backs the entire beach area with the exception of the easternmost end. The bluff area thus presents a continuous obstacle to tracked and wheeled vehicles, restricting their movements inland to the four exits mentioned in par. xii (b) (2), (3), (4) and (5). At the eastern end of the beach area, the slopes are believed negotiable by all

tracked vehicles and possibly lighter wheeled vehicles.

(2) FIELD BOUNDARIES: Fields on the plateau behind the bluff are bounded by hedges, rows of bushes, trees and occasionally by stone walls. Most of the fields themselves are clear of trees, but there are a few orchards and small groves.

(b) ARTIFICIAL: For road blocks, anti-tank ditches, minefields, obstacles, demolitions, etc., see ANCXF, ANNEX "A" – ASSAULT BEACH DEFENSE MAPS, SCALE 1/12,500.

xiv.   <u>DEFENSES</u>:

(a) LIGHT DEFENSES: Beach is heavily defended by light artillery units, heavy and light machine guns, mines, wire, pillboxes, demolitions etc.. Almost continuous construction activity has been noted since October 1943. For details, see ANCXF, ANNEX "A" – ASSAULT BEACH DEFENSE MAPS, SCALE 1/12,500.

(b) HEAVY DEFENSES: The beach is defended by heavy coastal batteries, located to the east and west of the beach area. For details, see:

(1) ANCXF, ANNEX "C" – TEXT AND DIAGRAM OF NEPTUNE BATTERIES.

(2) ANCXF, ANNEX "D" – TEXT AND TRACES OF COAST DEFENSES.

BEACH NEAR VIERVILLE-SUR-MER LOOKING EAST SHOWING RETARDS IN FOREGROUND (Small buildings on beach have been removed)

BEACH NEAR ST. LAURENT-SUR-MER LOOKING WEST SHOWING SHINGLE AT BACK OF BEACH (Buildings in background have been removed)

Blister gas agents are the type of chemical most likely to be encountered, although surprise attacks with tear, choking and lethal gases must be considered as a possibility.

b. ATTACKS AGAINST PERSONNEL ON OFF SHORE SHIPS. Personnel on ships which are not close in shore are less vulnerable to attacks from chemicals, but the following types must be considered possible:

(1) Armor-piercing shells from shore batteries may carry a proportion of irritant agents mixed with HE.

(2) Aircraft bombs charged with blister gas;

(3) If there is a moderate off shore wind with no fog and rain, large concentrations of choking, lethal, or nose gases released from land installations or off shore floats or submerged tanks could be in casualty producing quantities ten to fifteen miles off shore.

c. ATTACKS AGAINST PERSONNEL IN LANDING CRAFT APPROACHING THE BEACHES. If the enemy elects to employ gas, the first important chemical attack on the landing force may be directed against personnel in landing craft approaching the beaches. He may estimate that an attack at this time would cause great confusion and, in forcing the wearing of gas masks, would render the actual landing more difficult. Troops in landing craft are subject to the following types of gas attack:

(1) Blister gases from aircraft bombs with fused air-burst at 100 to 300 feet altitude;

(2) Low-level airplane spray (under 1,000 feet) with blister gas liquid, probably from intruder type planes;

(3) HE with 10% tear gas to harass personnel and force the wearing of masks;

(4) Nose gases from generators or water floats;

(5) Choking or lethal gases from rockets, particularly if there is an offshore breeze and no rain or fog.

d. ATTACKS AGAINST PERSONNEL WADING ASHORE. Personnel wading ashore must be prepared to meet all of the chemicals likely to be encountered while in landing craft approaching the beaches. In addition, the enemy may place on the surface of the water by means of floats, submerged tanks, or rockets, a mixture of 10% mustard and 90% fuel oil. Such a film on the last 50 to 100 yards to the beaches would constitute a definite chemical hazard to those having to wade ashore.

e. ATTACKS AGAINST PERSONNE ON BEACHES AND INLAND. If the enemy decides to employ chemicals against Operation OVERLORD, it is probable that he will make full use of all available chemicals and chemical weapons on the beaches and inland thus enabling him to hold ground with a small number of men until the arrival of reinforcements. Once chemical warfare has started, high HE charge in chemical shells may be used, and therefore all loud explosions upwind must be treated with suspicion. The usual smell of gas may be destroyed by HE charge or deliberately disguised or mixed with smoke. Enemy gas tactics on the beaches and inland may be summarized as follows:

(1) A fierce bombardment of gas-containing shells lasting more than two minutes, by which the enemy will attempt to attain the maximum surprise;

(2) There may be long harassing bombardments at a slow rate of fire designed to lower morale and gas discipline. But at any moment the enemy may try a surprise shoot of fierce intensity.

(3) A small number of tear gas shells over long periods, also designed to lower gas discipline; this also may be followed by a surprise shoot of great intensity when the enemy expects casualties among men who no longer trouble to adjust their masks quickly.

(4) The beaches may be contaminated. Belts of contamination are likely to be deep. Fake contamination also may be used.

(5) Chemical mines may be planted either with or separately from normal explosive mines.

(6) Gas may be mixed with smoke.

Section VI - ENEMY DEFENSES and INSTALLATIONS

A. INTRODUCTION

Coast and Beach defense along the enemy held channel coast consists of a number of well emplaced coastal and field batteries sited to cover both sea approaches and beach areas, and a line of concreted infantry strongpoints along the coast to provide interlocking fire over beaches and exits. Batteries are generally located well inland behind beach areas, and on coastal headlands. Strongpoints are spaced along the coast, thickly in areas where landing might be made, and more widely scattered along rocky or steeply sloping coastlines.

Since the beginning of the year construction activity has increased to a marked degree in the defensive belt. Batteries are being casemated with great rapidity; in some instances prefabricated concrete blocks have been laid. Existing strongpoints are being strengthened and new field defences are being built at from 1,000 to 10,000 yards inland of the coast line.

NOTE: Strongpoints are permanent positions with heavy concrete construction for defense and are usually buried for further protection. Field defences are less permanent positions comprising movable guns protected normally by wire, occasionally by mine fields, but without permanent armor. Field defenses are set up as a rule for strategic defense of highways, dumps or other military features. They are usually reserve positions.

Large quantities of steel underwater obstacles are being brought to the coast and placed in position on the beaches, and natural terrain obstacles are being supplemented by anti-tank ditches and walls to hold invading troops within the area of fire of beach strongpoints. This activity is occurring along the entire coast and is probably a result of Field Marshal Rommel's inspection of the west wall during December and January.

In the American Neptune area, this activity has resulted in the following changes: Existing batteries are being casemated, new casemated positions and new open field battery emplacements are being prepared. This activity is particularly noticeable in the North East corner of the Cotentin Peninsula. New pillboxes and shelters are being built in coastal Strongpoints; so inland Strongpoints have been begun as yet. Steel beach obstacles have been laid in parts of the area, and new anti-tank ditches and barbed wire installations are in evidence.

B. BEACH DEFENSES

STRONG POINTS, PILL BOXES, OBSTACLES, WIRE

The line of strongpoints behind the beaches provide defensive fire for the Neptune landing areas. There is no present defense in depth. Recent prepared defenses in addition to strongpoints include underwater obstacles, sea walls behind the beaches, anti-tank ditches and walls blocking valley exits (OMAHA), inundated areas blocking exits over low land (UTAH), and a liberal use of mines and wire. Most of the houses left standing on the coast have been fortified.

A typical strong point consists of a group of pillboxes, open weapon pits, and underground shelters, usually protected by wire, mines and anti-tank ditches. Flame thrower installations have been reported. On OMAHA the strong points are situated on the low land immediately behind the beach, on the beach and on the cliffs and bluffs just inland. On UTAH the strong points are located along the sea wall behind the beach. Pillboxes and shelters are usually of reinforced concrete, with a minimum thickness of 3'. Shelters are usually completely buried and pillboxes nearly so. A network of trenches connects these structures. Anti-tank emplacements or casemates and light field gun emplacements are frequently found in coastal strong points. Strong points are also found around heavy batteries and radar installations.

There are three common types of underwater obstacles (see sketch). There is a single line of "Hedgehog" obstacles on OMAHA beach between the 11' and the 18' contour above LLW, and two lines on the northern half of UTAH between the 11' and 18' contour, which extend off the beach to the north. Installation is still in progress on both beaches.

Again confirmation that there are three batteries covering both invasion beaches and all three of them are Ranger objectives – Pointe du Hoc, Maisy I and Maisy II. (Target Numbers 1, 16 and 16A).

PAGE 52   . 21 APRIL, 1944   **TOP SECRET - BIGOT**

There is a seawall immediately in back of UTAH beach which is a tank obstacle. The low wave cut embankment immediately in back of OMAHA beach is faced in part with a masonry wall. On OMAHA beach the four valley beach exits are blocked by anti-tank ditches and walls and the valley slopes are mined. On UTAH beach the exits are blocked at the sea wall by road blocks and a continuous strip of land behind the beach has been inundated blocking most of the roads inland.

Mines on OMAHA are being used in profusion to block cross country routes on the plateau above the beach as well as in the valley exits and around strongpoints; on UTAH their use has been limited principally to strongpoint borders. (Mines have been limited principally to strongpoint borders.) Mines have been observed at spacing varying from 9' to 14', generally in rows of three or more. Extensive anti-vehicle mine fields are usually protected by a bordering anti-personnel field. In some cases wire may be observed bounding the fields, but whether this is fence or barbed wire is unknown.

Wire on both beaches has been placed principally around strongpoints, where it occurs in banks of 10' to 35' in width. Narrow bands of barbed wire or fences are visible backing both beaches in spots and the tops of the UTAH seawall is strung with wire. No wire has as yet been strung between underwater obstacles, but its future use in this way is probable. Wire must be expected along tops of seawalls and across all foot and vehicle routes in either concertina rolls or barbed wire bands.

C. BATTERY STUDY
GLOSSARY OF TERMS AND ABBREVIATIONS

Gun Numbers - Guns are numbered from right to left, facing the sea.
C'SMT - Casemate - Concrete structure to house guns.

Battery Size	Coast Defense	Mobile (Troops)
Heavy	H.C.B. - 8" and over	Hy.Tp. - 8" and over
Medium	M.C.B. - 4.5" to less than 8"	Md.Tp. - 4" to less than 8"
Light	L.C.B. - Under 4.5".	Fd. Tp. - Under 4", but including 105 mm (4.14").

BTY	- Battery - over 3"	H	- HOW - Howitzer
G	- Gun	O.P. -	Observation Post
GH	- Gun Howitzer	u/c -	Under Construction
FGH	- Field Gun Howitzer	! -	Questionable or Doubtful

The order of summary information for each position is consistently adhered to, and shall not be repeated at beginning of each group list: 1st Column - Assigned Fire Priority No.; 2nd column - Grid; 3rd column - Number of Guns, Caliber (mm), Type, Range (in yds), Remarks.

GROUP I: BATTERIES WHICH COVER BOTH BEACH AREAS

16   528916   4 - ?75 Fd. Tp., 13000. Casemates u/c, facing NNW. Original position at 528915 abandoned; guns moved to temporary position at 531914; late in March 1944 2 casemates were started immediately forward of original emplacements. Range covers only westernmost sector of beach OMAHA and southern half of beach UTAH.

5   533918   4 - 155 H, 13000. Open earth revetted pits (see sketch). Covers only westernmost sector of beach OMAHA and southern half of beach UTAH.

1   586938   6 - 155-G, 25000. Open concrete pits, sunken & earth banked (see sketches). 4 C'smts u/c. 2 adj. to empls. 4 & 5 facing NNW, started in march 1944. 2 adj. to empls. 2 & 3 started in April. Range extends beyond limits of both beaches.

19   599934   4 - Gun position u/c. No guns at present. Probably a prepared position for a Fd.Tp. (105 F G H, 13000.) Assumed range will not cover beach UTAH but will reach boat lanes. (Not included in optimum lists).

Continued on Pg 58

TOP SECRET - BIGOT   NEPTUNE MONOGRAPH-CTF 122

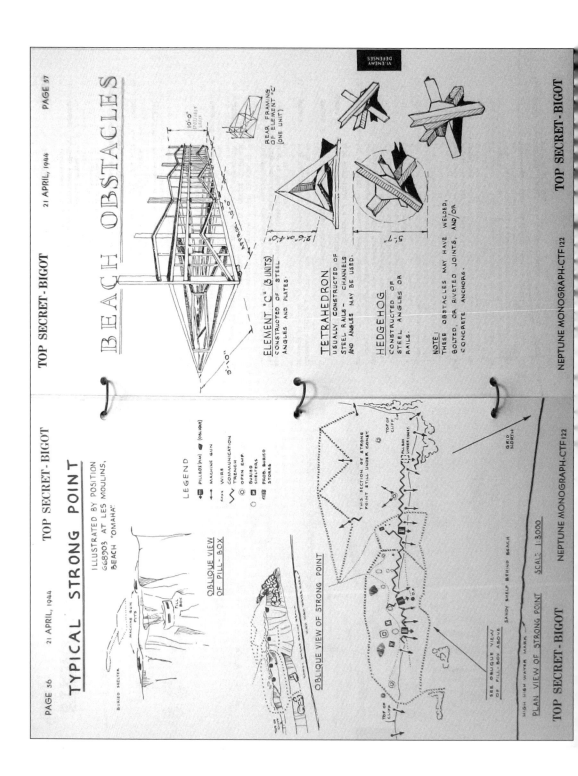

PAGE 58 — 21 APRIL, 1944 — TOP SECRET-BIGOT

(Continued from Pg 52)

Total: 18 Guns comprising 4 batteries.
2 medium batteries - Total 10 guns, including 4 casemates u/c.
1 light battery - 4 guns - 2, possibly 4, casemates u/c
1 prepared position for light battery - 4 guns.?

GROUP II - ADDITIONAL BATTERIES WHICH COVER OMAHA BEACH AND BOAT LANES
(Located in BRITISH area - omitted on optimum lists)

10 792831 4 - 1105 FGH, 13000. Open pits, possible alternative position at 791E35. Covers only easternmost sector of beach.

797871 4 - Gun casemated position u/c., probably for L.C.B.
2 Olants started early in March 1944; 3rd started late in March, and it is expected that 4th will also be constructed. 1 casemate faces 358° (grid north), and 1 faces 023° (grid north). Concrete shelters and O.P. u/c. Probable range of 13000 covers boat lanes but restricted arc of fire prohibits fire on beach.

Total 8 - guns comprising 2 light batteries; 3, possibly 4, casemates u/c.

GROUP III - ADDITIONAL BATTERIES WHICH DO NOT COVER BEACH OR BOAT LANES, BUT RANGES EXTEND INSIDE TF122 BOUNDARY
(Located in BRITISH area - omitted on optimum lists)

846849 4 - 1105 FGH, 13000. Open emplacements, sited in hedgerow. Possibly temporary position; no shelters or camouflage observed. Range is short of beach but extends approx. 2000 yds. inside T.F. 122 boundary.

848853 4 - 1105 FGH, 13000. Open earth emplacements. Range is short of beach but extends approx. 2000 yds. inside T.F. 122 boundary.

Total 8 - guns comprising 2 light batteries.

GROUP IV - ADDITIONAL BATTERIES WHICH COVER UTAH BEACH AND BOAT LANES, ALSO SWEPT AREAS FOR GUNFIRE SUPPORT SHIPS

7 246264 4 - 170 G, 3237L. Turrets in earth banked concrete 'bowls', partially surrounded by concrete shelters (see sketch). Range extends approx. 2000 yds. Inside N limit of beach. This battery has been repeatedly questioned. Radar countermeasures and disruption of communications may possibly eliminate observation for gunfire control onto T.F. 122 area. (Not included in optimum lists).

2 262267 4 - 240 or 280 G, 35000 or 40000. Turrets in open concrete emplacements (see sketch). Casemate construction. 40000 yds. (unrestricted arc of fire) covers entire area. 15000 yds. covers N half of beach. Construction on casemates was first suspected in March 1944; A rectangular excavation is being made in rear of and partly enclosing the platform of no. 3 gun. Activity at nos. 2 and 4 is concealed by elaborate camouflage. Construction for this type casemate normally requires several months, however partial construction would probably be sufficient to restrict the arc of fire from T.F. 122 area. It is not unusual for such construction work to be completed on part of a battery before starting on remaining guns. Radar countermeasures and disruption of communications may possibly eliminate observation for gunfire control onto TF122 area. (Not included in optimum lists).

15 392102 4 - 1105 FGH, 13000. Open earth revetted emplacements. Covers N 1/3 rd of beach.

TOP SECRET-BIGOT   NEPTUNE MONOGRAPH-CTF122

PAGE 59 — TOP SECRET-BIGOT — 21 APRIL, 1944

14 343057 2 - 7150 H, 14600. May possibly be only 105 FGH, 13000. Covers northern 3/4 of beach.

4 354139 6 - 155 G, 25000. Open concrete emplacements. Covers entire beach.

11 354291 3 - 150 naval const guns in turrets, 24000. (Also reported as 105 mm). Originally all 3 turrets in open emplacements but no. 1 has been casemated and arc of fire restricted from T.F. 122 area. It has been reported that nos. 2 and 3 turrets are restricted to 120° arc of fire which would prevent entire battery from firing into T.F. 122 area.; this limitation is considered questionable by several sources. Assuming unrestricted arc of fire, range falls approx. 5000 yards short of limit of beach but partially covers swept area for gunfire support ships. (Not included in optimum lists).

9 360022 4 - 105 FGH, 13000. Casemate, facing E (see sketch). Covers entire beach. Also reported as 155 mm.

361056 4 - Gun casemated battery u/c. Excavations for 4 casemates 401 x 35', facing E, were started in March. Size indicates cismte will probably house light guns, possible range 13000 which would cover practically all of beach area. (Not included in optimum list).

361080 4 - Gun casemated battery u/c. Probably for field guns. Extremely rapid progress has been made since first observed in middle of March and are already practically built. Probable range 13000 will cover N 2/3 of Beach.

1A 365200 4 - 170 G, 3237L. Open emple. 3 excavs. 74x80'. prob. for cismts facing E. Covers entire area.

3 368044 6 - 155 G, 25000. Originally open concrete emplacements: four casemates u/c., facing ENE, were started early in Feb. 44. Covers entire beach. (2 guns not included in optimum lists). 6 gun heavy A.A. battery in rough earth emplacements on S flank (3690040).

8 392277 6 - 155 G, 25000. Originally open emplacements heavily earth banked. Four casemates u/c. Range falls approx. 2000 yds. short of lles De Marcouf and N limit of beach, but covers swept area for gunfire support ships. Casemate construction started in March, laid out radially facing bearing 3470 (grid north), reported arc of fire restricted between bearing 2830 and 0590 (grid north) which prevent fire onto T.F. 122 area. Casemate construction normally requires about 4 months. It is possible that even though 4 guns may be placed in casemates before they are completely finished, the 2 remaining guns may be maintained in their original emplacements for all round fire. (Battery not included in optimum lists).

8A 394228 4 - 170 G, 3237L. New position, also considered as possibly 240 G, 35000 or 210 H, 18400. Ranges cover entire area except Howe, which falls short of beach but covers swept area for gunfire support ships.

6 405980 4 - 155 H, 13000. Originally in open emplacements begun in March 1944, facing NE. Directly behind beach and covers entire area.

18 413160 2 - ?field guns in casemates on old fort. Not considered as battery but as infantry strong point; 1 cismt. faces SSW and 1 faces NNE. Originally reported as 3-75 field guns, 13000 yds.

NEPTUNE MONOGRAPH-CTF122   TOP SECRET-BIGOT

range; and 2 unoccupied emplacements for med. guns. (Replaced by the casemates). 13000 yd. range falls just short of N limit of beach but possibly effects bont lanes, Iles De Marcouf and swept area for gunfire support ships. (Not included in optimum lists).

Total 59 - guns comprising 15 batteries.
1 Heavy battery - 4 guns in turrets, including 1, possibly 3, casemates u/c.
9 Medium batteries - 38 guns, including 6 turrets and 15 casemates u/c. 1 casemated gun at 354291 not included.
2 Light batteries - 8 guns, including 4 casemates.
3 Batteries, probably light, u/c, 9 guns, all in casemates. 1 casemate at 413160 not included.

GROUP V - ADDITIONAL BATTERIES WHICH DO NOT COVER UTAH BEACH OR BOAT LANE, BUT EFFECT INLAND MOVEMENT OF TROOPS, UTAH AREA

383174 4 - 7150 H, 14600. Open emplacements in hedgerow. Range falls approx. 2 miles short of N limit of beach.

336197 4 - 7105 FGH, 13000. Open rough emplacements. Possibly temporary position. Range falls approx. 3 3/4 miles short of N limit of beach.

339138 2 - 7105 FGH, 13000. Casemates. Facing 105° (grid north)
12 - 175 field guns, in 'miniature' casemates u/c. Position originally considered 2 med. gun bty, then enlarged to 4 temple. Two casemates were started and open emplacements altered. 1 c'mt. completed much before 2nd one, then appeared to be undergoing alteration into shelter; recent photo cover reveals that it was probably being reinforced and concrete added onto roof; 2nd casemate is now roofed over but not completely finished. The two 'miniature' casemates, approx. 25' x 30' are laid out between the two casemates. C'mts are identical with those at 360022 (see sketch). Range falls approx. 1000 yds. short of N limit of beach. Only 2 guns included in total.

344174 14 - 7150 H, 14600. Open emplacements cleverly concealed in hedgerow. Possibly temporary position. Range falls approx. 1½ miles short of N limit of beach.

343192 4 - 7150 H, 14600. Open emplacements concealed in hedgerow. Possibly temporary position. Range falls approx. 2½ miles short of N limit of beach.

358186 4 - 7150 H, 14600. Open emplacements. Possibly temporary position. Range falls approx. 2 miles short of N limit of beach.

364174 14 - 7105 FGH, 13000. Previously reported at 362174. New, possibly temporary position. Range falls approx. 2 miles short of N limit of beach.

12 - 378204 4 - 155 H, 13000. Open, earth revetted. Range falls 3½ miles short of N limit of beach.

398204 14 - Possible C.D. battery u/c. Assuming 13000, range will fall approx. 4 miles short of N limit of beach.

Total 34 - guns comprising 9 batteries, of which 3 are questionable.
5 Medium batteries (1 questionable) Total 20 guns.
3 Light batteries (1 questionable) Total 10 guns, including 2 casemates.
1 questionable battery - 4 guns.

TABULATIONS OF POSSIBLE CONDITIONS - BEACH OMAHA

Total Number of Batteries which Effect Beach and Boat Lanes
(Group I Plus Group II)

26 - Guns comprising 6 Batteries.
2 Medium Batteries - total 10 guns, including 4 casemates u/c.
2 Medium Batteries - total 12 guns, including 5, possibly 6, casemates u/c.
1 Light Batteries - total 12 guns, including 4 casemates u/c.
1 Prepared Position for Light Battery - 4 guns.

Maximum Total Number of Batteries which Effect Entire Omaha Area
(Groups I, II, and III)

34 - Guns comprising 8 batteries.
2 Medium Batteries - Total 10 guns, including 4 casemates u/c.
2 Medium Batteries - Total 20 guns, including 5, possibly 8, casemates u/c.
5 Light Batteries - Total 12 guns, including 4 casemates u/c.
1 Prepared Position for Light Battery - 4 guns.

Optimum Number of Batteries Opposed to Actual Beach and Bont Lanes
(Excluding Batteries Located in British Area, and Questionable Battery, Group 1)

14 - Guns comprising 3 batteries.
2 Medium Batteries - Total 10 guns, including 4 casemates u/c.
1 Light Battery - 4 guns, including 2, possibly 4, casemates u/c.

BEACH UTAH

Total Number of Batteries Which Effect Beach and Bont Lanes
and Swept Areas for Gunfire Support Ships
(Group I Plus Group IV)

77 - Guns comprising 19 Batteries.
1 Heavy Battery - Total 4 guns in turrets, including 1, possibly 3.
casemates u/c.
11 Medium Batteries - Total 48 guns, including 6 turrets and 19 C'mts u/c
2 Light Batteries - Total 12 guns, including 4 C'mts & 2, ? 4, c'mts u/c
4 Light Battery, probably light u/c. Total 13 guns, including 9 C'mts u/c

Maximum Total Number of Batteries which Effect Entire Utah Area
(Groups I, IV and V)

111 - Guns comprising 28 Batteries.
1 Heavy Battery - Total 4 guns in turrets, including 1, possibly 3.
casemates u/c.
16 Medium Batteries (1 questionable) - Total 68 guns, including 6 turrets.
and 19 casemates u/c.
6 Light Batteries (1 questionable) - Total 22 guns, including 6 C'mts
and 4 C'mts u/c.
4 Batteries, probably light, u/c. - Total 13 guns, including 8 C'mts u/c.
1 Questionable Battery - 4 Guns.

Optimum Number of Batteries opposed to Actual Beach and Boat Lanes
(Groups I and IV, Less Questionable Batteries)

46 - Guns comprising 11 Batteries (Partial Reduction of one).
8 Medium Batteries - Total 34 guns, including 15 casemates.
3 Light Batteries - Total 12 guns, including c'mts & 2, ? 4, c'mts u/c.

AMERICAN NEPTUNE AREA
Total Number of Batteries Which Effect Beaches Omaha and Utah and Boat Lanes
(Groups I, II and IV)

85 - Guns comprising 21 Batteries.
1 Heavy Battery - Total 4 guns in turrets, including 1. and possibly 3.
casemates u/c.
11 Medium Batteries - Total 48 guns, including 6 turrets and 19 C'mts u/c.

VI. ENEMY DEFENSES

5 Light Batteries - Total 20 guns, including 4 Cismts & 5, possibly 8, casemates u/c, probably light u/c. Total 13 guns, including 9 Cismts u/c.
4 Batteries, probably light u/c. Total 13 guns.

Maximum Total Number of Batteries which Effect Entire Area
(Groups I, II, III, IV and V)

127 Guns Comprising 32 Batteries.
 1 Heavy Battery - Total 4 guns in turrets, including 1, possibly 3, casemates u/c.
16 Medium Batteries (1 questionable) - Total 68 guns, including 6 turrets. and 19 casemates u/c.
10 Light Batteries (1 questionable) - Total 38 guns, including 6 casemates and 2, possibly 4, Cismts u/c.
 4 Batteries, possibly light, u/c. - Total 13 guns, including 9 Cismts u/c.
 1 Questionable Battery - 4 Guns.

Optimum Number of Batteries Opposed to Actual Beaches and Boat Lanes
(Groups I & IV - Less Questionable Batteries & those located in British Area)

46 Guns comprising 11 Batteries (Partial Reduction of One)
 8 Medium Batteries - Total 34 guns, including 4 casemates u/c,
 3 Light Batteries - Total 12 guns, including 4 cismts & 2, 3, 4, cismts u/c.

D. ENEMY MINES

I. MARINE MINES

The descriptions of enemy devices, mines, booby traps, etc., are of a brief informative character only and do not fully cover the subjects. They are not intended to modify any manuals or instructions, nor to be interpreted as directives as to countermeasures.

From the beginning of the war the enemy has displayed considerable energy and ingenuity in the development of new types of mines and in the adaptation of existing types of meet special conditions. There is little doubt that during operation NEPTUNE most of the familiar types - contact, acoustic, magnetic, acoustic-magnetic, and perhaps new and unknown types, will be used defensively, offensively and for sabotage purposes at ports.

It is known that many fields now exist in the NEPTUNE area, having been placed by submarines, E-boats and other craft for the defense of the enemy-held coast. In general, these comprise controlled fields at harbor entrances and at the mouths of rivers; fields of moored mines offshore in depths up to 300 fathoms, and fields of ground mines. These may be controlled, contact, acoustic, magnetic or acoustic-magnetic, and may be equipped with special devices so that they will detonate only after a given number of ships have passed over them.

Constant sweeping with all types of gear is necessary to keep channels reasonably clear of these existing fields in addition to mines dropped by aircraft or placed by submarines and surface craft during and after the assault. Even the most thorough and constant sweeping cannot guarantee a channel clear of mines.

For defense against small craft, contact mines moored on or immediately under the surface have been found as far from the enemy-held coast as the British war channel. For the same purpose the Japanese made use of a hemispherical ground mine which can be placed inexpensively and in great numbers in very shallow depths along the beaches. The Japanese frequently connected mines of this type in series by trip wires attached to sculling or other underwater obstacles for defense against landing craft and personnel.

Recent convincing evidence has been received of the existence of German 21-inch torpedo which is run to a set range and then becomes a ground mine. It can be fired either by submarines or E-boats, probably is electric, with a maximum range of three miles. It is trackless, carries about 600 pounds of explosive charge and probably is actuated magnetically. Its purpose may be to mine harbors or channels in which there has been no evidence of minelaying.

Contact mines frequently are equipped with long manilla "snag lines", which trail out from the mine and will detonate the mine on contact with a ship's hull.

Drifting mines, under the terms of the Hague Conference, are limited to one hour of life, after which they must become self-destructive. Because of the currents in the NEPTUNE area, and because they are as great a menace to friendly as to enemy craft, their use probably will be limited to harassing ships and craft in their passage across the channel. Drifting mines usually are of the contact type, and may be equipped with antennae up to 80 ft. long of copper wire, which fire the mine by sea-battery section on contact with a ship's hull.

Offensively, aircraft, surface craft and submarines probably will be used to place moored, ground and drifting mines of all types to strengthen existing mine fields, to close channels through mine fields, and to harrass ships and craft. Mines laid from aircraft may or may not require parachutes, and may have acoustic, magnetic or acoustic-magnetic units.

For sabotage purposes the enemy has made considerable use of several familiar types of mine for the destruction of port facilities. In Italy, for example, contact and other types of mines were equipped with time clocks set to detonate the mines after a certain interval, usually 80 days, and then were dropped into the water alongside docks and other port structures. Many other types of mine, including those dropped by aircraft, can be equipped with time clock devices.

The Italians made much use of special types of mines intended to be attached to the hulls of ships in port, and since it is known that the Italian experts in this field are serving with the Germans, there is a possibility that mines of this type may be encountered. These include:

Limpet Mines - The charge is carried in a metal container inside an inflated rubber ring which holds it against the ship's bottom. The charge is detonated by a time clock unless the mine aligns from its place and rises to the surface, in which case it is fired by a hydrostatic switch.

Bangalore Mines - Torpedo-shaped mine attached to the bilge keel of a ship by three C-clamps. The charge is detonated by an arming vane actuated by the forward movement of the ship and a time clock. A newer variant of this type contains the charge in an elliptical casing equipped with a guard to protect it against being swept off by a cable.

Ring Mines - These are held to a ship's bottom by suction and are said to be in two sizes, 30 and 50 cm. in diameter respectively and with charges of 11 to 13 pounds.

II. LANDMINES

These are generally either anti-tank or anti-personnel and are placed immediately below the surface of the ground to be detonated by contact. Occasionally controlled mine fields are placed, to be fired wholly or in sections as troops or vehicles pass over them. The weight of a man is insufficient to detonate an anti-tank mine.

As a rule land mines are placed in groups, with a distance of from 9 to 14 feet between mines to prevent sympathetic detonation. Mine fields are used defensively for the protection of batteries, field defenses, strong points, dumps and other military installations and are often placed on or near beaches as anti-invasion measures. Mines may be dropped from planes either with or without parachutes.

Counter measures comprise the location and removal of mines by Army Engineers or other especially trained personnel.

III. BOOBY TRAPS

In general, any enemy-held area that has not been subjected to careful search by trained personnel should be regarded as highly dangerous from the standpoint of booby traps. Booby traps may be detonated by the picking up or touching of various objects such as guns, binoculars or other equipment suitable for souvenirs, by the opening of doors or windows or shifting of objects within a house, or they may be carefully concealed and detonated by the pressure of a foot or a hand. The most efficient counter-measure against booby-traps is the training of all personnel in the grave consequence of carelessness, curiosity and souvenir-collecting in enemy territory.

Details of the Pointe et Raz de la Percée radar station which was situated on the cliffs to the west of Omaha Beach Vierville exit.

E. RADAR

Types of Enemy Radar Stations in the NEPTUNE Area which will effect the Naval Assault area are: Coastal Ship-watching Stations (C.W.) and Aircraft Reporting Stations (A.R.S.). Nightfighter Control Stations (G.C.I.) and Benito Dayfighter Control Stations (D.C.S.) are located several miles inland and are not expected to effect naval operations. Intelligence and Instructions for Radar Counter Measures are given in Annex L, Appendix 9, of Operation Plan No. 2-44.

FREYA (F). Known to operate on a frequency of 100 to 200 Mc/s, 120 to 140 Mc/s most common; pulse recurrence frequency (p.r.f.) 500/sec. or 1000/sec.; effective beam width 22º; wave length generally between 2 and 3 metres. There are a few Freya 57G apparatus on about 70 Mc/s p.r.f. 500/sec; beam width about 29º. One of these located at Cherbourg/(La Brasserie), target 46.

WUERZBURG (W). Generally 550 to 580 Mc/s; also can be 460 to 500 Mc/s; p.r.f. 3500 to 5000/sec. but normally is 3750/sec; effective beam width about 11º; wavelength 53 cm.

CYLINDER CHIMNEY (GH(C)). 120 to 140 Mc/s; p.r.f. 500/sec; effective beam width about 10º; wavelength 2.4 meters.

LARGE COASTWATCHER (L.C.W.). Probably 90 Mc/s; p.r.f. 500/sec; beam width about 20º — relatively new — radio characteristics and performance not known with certainty.

COASTWATCHER (C.W.). 365 to 390 Mc/s; p.r.f. 500/sec. (1000/sec, on old models); effective beam width about 10º; wave length about 80 cms.

GIANT WUERZBURG (G). Generally 550 to 580 Mc/s; but also can be 460 to 500 Mc/s; p.r.f. 1750 to 2000/sec. pos- sible, but normally is 1875/ sec.; effective beam width 7º; wavelength 53 cm.

Diagram labels: OCTAGONAL WOOD CABIN; POLE FREYA; LARGE COASTWATCHER; LIMBER FREYA; STEEL CABIN; 45'10'4' WIDE 10'10'TO HIGH FRAME COVERED WITH WIRE NETTING; 10'DIAM SHEET METAL PARABOLOID REFLECTOR; 24'DIAM. GIRDER WORK PARABOLOID; LARGE CABIN MOUNTED ON CONC BASE WITH TURNTABLE; 6'DIAM. 150 OR HOME MADE TUBULAR STEEL CYLINDER; COASTWATCHER

The following stations adjacent to the coastline from Cap d'Antifer to Cherbourg are the known enemy radar stations which effect the NEPTUNE Assault Area. Numbers preceeding each station name are those assigned in appendix XII to HEUBARB OPERATIONS. Ranges are based on best possible estimates against coastal craft. For destroyers add 5 miles, and for battleships add 9 miles to ranges given. Ranges are given in Nautical Miles.

BRITISH NEPTUNE AREA

31. CAP D'ANTIFER/SEMAPHORE - Top of cliffs - (C.W.) - Range: 14.5 miles.
49º 41' 10" N. 000º 09' 55" E - Grid 549481 - 330' above sea level (a.s.l.)
1 Freya Wuerzburg and 1 Coast Watcher.

32. CAP D'ANTIFER - Top of cliffs - 3 sites - (A.R.S.) - Range: 16 miles.
49º 40' 49" N. 000º 09' 46" E - Grid 547473 - 350 (a.s.l.)
1 Freya and 1 Giant Wuerzburg.

2nd site, 500 yards S.E.
1 Freya and 1 Giant Wuerzburg.

49º 40' 24" N. 000º 09' 45" E. - Grid 546467 - 350'(a.s.l.)
1 Chimney, cylinder type.

35. LE HAVRE/CAP de la HEVE - Top of cliffs - (C.W.) - Range: 15 miles.
49º 30' 42" N. 000º 04' 00" E - Grid 459296 - 340'(a.s.l.).
1 Large Coastwatcher and 1 Coastwatcher.

38. HOULGATE/SEMAPHORE - ¼ mile inland - (C.W.) - Range: 17 miles.
49º 18' 22" N. 000º 03' 45" W - Grid 255812 - 375' (a.s.l.).
1 Giant Wuerzburg.

39. CAEN DOUVRES LA DELIVRANDE - 3 miles inland - (A.R.S.) - Range: 13.5 miles.
49º 17' 13" N. 000º 24' 24" W. - Grid 004800 - 265' (a.s.l.)
2 Giant Wuerzburg and 1 Freya.

49º 17' 42" N. 000º 24' 17" W. - Grid 006808 - 200' (a.s.l.)
1 Chimney, box type.

40. ARROMANCHES - Top of cliffs - (C.W.) - Range: 12 miles.
49º 20' 25" N. 000º 36' 57" W. - Grid 854865 - 200' (a.s.l.)
1 Giant Wuerzburg and 1 Coastwatcher.

AMERICAN NEPTUNE AREA

41. POINTE et RAZ de la PERCEE - Top of cliffs - (C.W.) - Range: 8.8 miles.
49º 23' 37" N. 000º 56' 20" W. - Grid 623934 - 100' (a.s.l.).
2 Giant Wuerzburg, 1 Coastwatcher (pinpointed) and 1 Freya, pole type.

44. BARFLEUR/LE VICEL - 1½ miles inland - (C.W.) - Range: 17 miles.
49º 37' 30" N. 01 18'.15" W. - Grid 370203 - 345' (a.s.l.).
1 Large Coastwatcher and 1 Giant Wuerzburg.

45. CHERBOURG/CAP LEVY - ¼ mile inland - (C.W.) - Range: 8.25 miles.
49º 41' 44" N. 01 28' 12" W. - Grid 254287 - Approx. 50' (a.s.l.)
1 Giant Wuerzburg (reported 90' (a.s.l) and 1 Coastwatcher.

46. CHERBOURG/FERMANVILLE (LA BRASSERIE) - 1 mile inland - (A.R.S.) Range:20 Mi.
49º 40' 05" N. 01º 28' 10" W. - Grid 254257 - Approx. 450' (a.s.l.).
1 Chimney, cylinder type (pinpointed), 2 Giant Wuerzburg and 3 Freyas.

There are only 4 stations within the AMERICAN NEPTUNE Area. 1 just West of Beach OMAHA and 3 in the NE corner of the Cherbourg Peninsula. The total pieces of apparatus known to be in this area at the present time are: 1 Chimney, cylin- der type, 6 Giant Wuerzburgs, 1 Large Coastwatcher, 2 Coastwatchers, and 3 Freyas.

B. GRANDCAMP
(Admiralty Chart 2073, Folio 16)
(Map-Chart F-1015)
(Channel Pilot, Part II)

Latitude : 49° 23' 23" N.
Longitude: 1° 02' 55" W.

i.   GENERAL DESCRIPTION

GRANDCAMP, completed in 1926, is a small refuge port for fishing craft lying NE of BAIE DU GRAND VEY (or VAY) about 1 mile W. of POINTE DE MAISY. The port consists of an entrance channel protected by two diverging reinforced concrete jetties and a rectangular drying basin. Both channel and basin dry out at 8 to 10 ft. The eastern, western and southern sections of the basin are suitable for berthing.

The approach to the port is over a rock bank extending slightly west of POINTE DE MAISY and eastward beyond GRANDCAMP village. These rocks dry out at 2 feet (seaward edge) to 8 feet (inshore edge). It is doubtful whether ships drawing more than 10 feet or more than 40 feet of beam can enter the port.

For best available data on soundings, location of buoys and other navigational hazards, consult Admiralty Chart 2073, Map-Chart F-1015 and Channel Pilot, Part II. The entrance to the basin is controlled by a double boom.

ii.   APPROACH

The coast from a point about 1¼ miles SW of POINTE DE MAISY to a point 2 3/4 miles E. of POINTE DE MAISY is bordered by a rocky bank, known as ROCHES DE GRANDCAMP, which dry out at 2 feet (seaward edge) to 8 feet (inshore edge). The rocks extend in places for 2,000 yards offshore. For details, consult Admiralty Chart 2073 and Channel Pilot, Part II. Caution is suggested when referring to Map-Chart F-1015, as three breaks shown through the rock bank on the Map-Chart are not distinct enough on aerial photography to warrant the assumption that such breaks exist. Ships drawing 10 feet will be able to clear the banks at high water.

iii.   ANCHORAGE

There is no sheltered anchorage during onshore winds from W through N. to E.

TOP SECRET - BIGOT

PAGE 74   21 APRIL, 1944   TOP SECRET-BIGOT

iv. TIDES & CURRENTS:

(a) TIDES:
Springs: 22 feet.
Neaps: 18 feet.
Mean Level: 13 feet.

(b) CURRENTS:
The tidal streams at the edge of the dangers off the coast appear to be very little known.

v. WEATHER
No local peculiarities.

vi. DOCKING FACILITIES
Entrance channel, 59 feet wide, lies between two diverging reinforced concrete jetties. The channel dries out at 8 to 10 feet, and leads into the basin via a passage 49 feet wide. All quays are about 4 feet above H.W.L.

(a) EAST QUAY: Vertical face; 300 feet long. Surface is tarred. The quay is provided with bollards. A dredged channel appears to lead from the entrance to the quay.

(b) SOUTH QUAY: Reinforced concrete wharf approximately 330 feet long and 48 feet wide. The main road leading east-west runs along the rear of the quay.

(c) WEST QUAY: Stone-faced, sloping approximately 500' and about 300 feet long and 48 feet wide at top. Anchorage chains lie off this quay.

vii. DRYING-OUT
Entrance channel and basin dry out at 8 to 10 feet.

viii. SILTING
No information.

ix. ESTIMATED DAILY CAPACITY
At capture: 200 tons.
Plus 7 days: 300 tons.
Plus 90 days: 300 tons.

x. PLANT REQUIRED
At capture: 2 cranes.
Plus 7 days: No change.
Plus 90 days: No change.

xi. SHIPPING CAPACITY
At capture: 1 coaster.
Plus 7 days: 1 coaster.
Plus 90 days: Same (believed unsuitable for further development).

xii. CLEARANCE OF PORT AREA
There is no railway at the port. Nearest rail point is the narrow gauge line at ISIGNY. The main road, BAYEUX-VIERVILLE-ISIGNY-CARENTAN, passes along south side of the basin.

xiii. REPAIR FACILITIES
Careening Stage in NW angle of basin, 131 x 114 feet. There are 4 boat builders reported. "One small shipyard is reported capable of building wooden vessels up to 20 feet in length.

xiv. GOVERNMENT & MUNICIPAL BUILDINGS
TOWN HALL, on road to BAYEUX.
POST OFFICE, on coastal road near head of harbor.

THE HARBOR AT GRANDCAMP-LES-BAINS AT LOW WATER

TOP SECRET-BIGOT   NEPTUNE MONOGRAPH-CTF 122

21 APRIL, 1944   TOP SECRET-BIGOT   PAGE 75

xv. UTILITIES
(a) ELECTRICITY - 3-phase 50 cycles A.C. 115/200 volts supplied from CAEN by SECTEUR ELECTRIQUE DU BESSIN.

(b) GAS - No report.

(c) WATER - Small waterworks. Most houses use well water. position unknown.

(d) SANITATION - No report.

xvi. BILLETS
HOTEL DU GUESCLIN, Quai Crampon (26 rooms). GRAND HOTEL, Quai Crampon (34 rooms). There are two smaller hotels and 10 villas for rent.

xvii. GARAGES
GOUDOUX, Rue Ecole (40 cars).
GOUBERT, Route Maisy. GRAND HOTEL, Quai Crampon. (4 cars).

xviii. DUMPS AND PARKS
There is no suitable area in the immediate vicinity of the harbor, or among the buildings of the village. To the south, there are pasture fields and small orchards where trucks might disperse and find cover.

xix. WAREHOUSES & STACKING SPACE
No information.

xx. ENEMY OBSTRUCTION
Entrance to channel is controlled by a double boom which, in turn, is covered by a light gun at end of eastern mole.

xxi. PORT DEFENSE
(a) "T" 549933
Infantry position on coast in built-up area of town. 1 pillbox.

(b) "T" 545932
Infantry position in built-up area of town. 2 pillboxes. 1 light gun at the end of eastern mole. 1 gun probably field-type reported on coast in this area.

(c) "T" 546912 - 543932
Wall approximately 6 feet thick and 6 feet high along south side of harbor.

(d) "T" 543932 - 542932
Elements "0" continue line of wall above from west side of road. (Appears to follow outline of harbor). Possibly some hedgedope.

(e) "T" 543934
Further stretch of Elements "0" running south from west mole.

(f) "T" 543933
Road leading from quayside blocked, probably by knife-rests.

VII-SMALL PORTS

GRANDCAMP-LES-BAINS: ENTRANCE TO HARBOR AT HIGH WATER

TOP SECRET-BIGOT   NEPTUNE MONOGRAPH-CTF 122

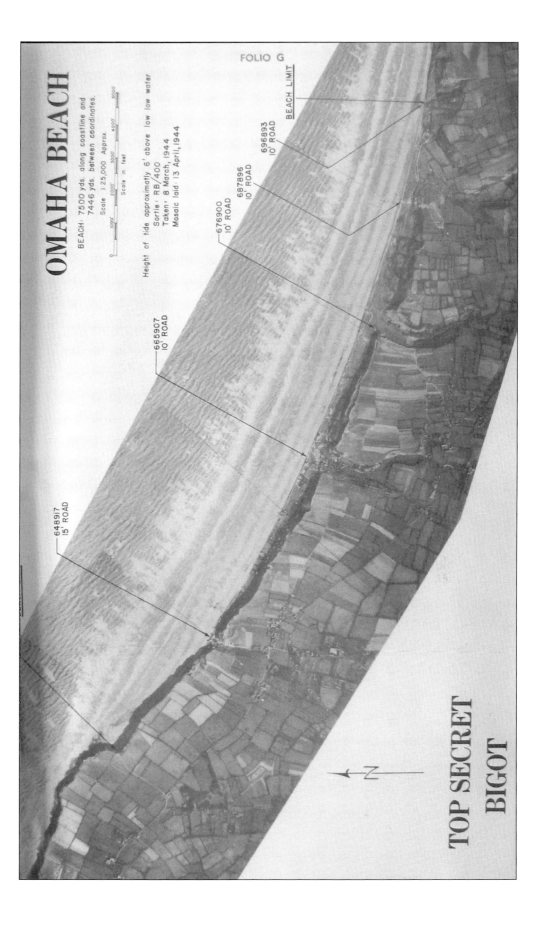

OMAHA BEACH

BEACH: 7500 yds. along coastline and
7446 yds. between coordinates.

Scale 1:25,000 Approx.

0   1000   2000   3000   4000   5000
Scale in feet

Height of tide approximately 6' above low low water
Sortie: RB/400
Taken: 8 March, 1944
Mosaic laid 13 April, 1944

FOLIO G

BEACH LIMIT

696893
10' ROAD

687896
10' ROAD

676900
10' ROAD

665907
10' ROAD

648917
15' ROAD

N

TOP SECRET
BIGOT

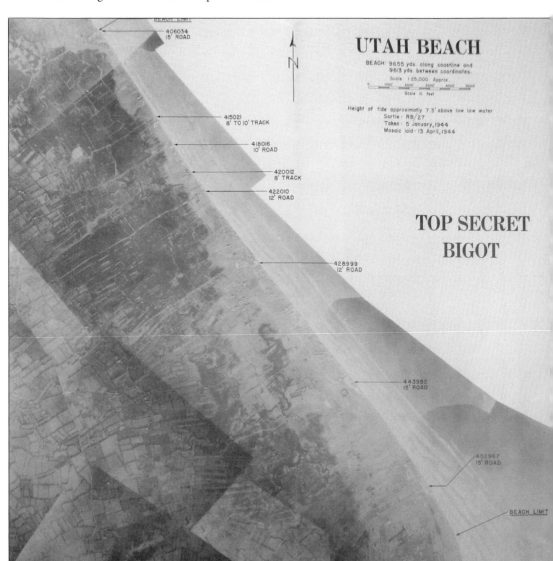

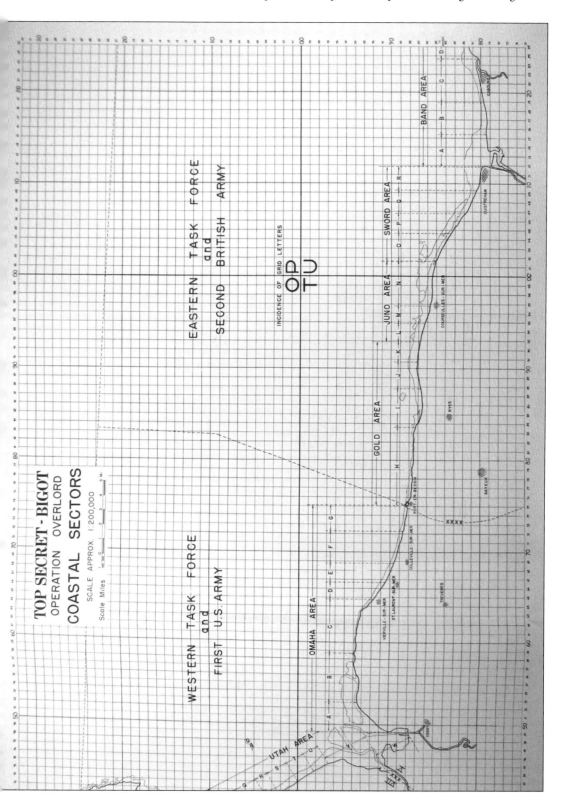

TOP SECRET - BIGOT
OPERATION OVERLORD
COASTAL SECTORS

SCALE APPROX. 1:200,000

Scale Miles

WESTERN TASK FORCE
and
FIRST U.S. ARMY

EASTERN TASK FORCE
and
SECOND BRITISH ARMY

INCIDENCE OF GRID LETTERS

OP
TU

UTAH AREA

OMAHA AREA

GOLD AREA

JUNO AREA

SWORD AREA

BAND AREA

UTILISE

VIERVILLE-SUR-MER

ST LAURENT-SUR-MER

COLLEVILLE-SUR-MER

PORT-EN-BESSIN

TREVIERES

BAYEUX

RYES

COURSEULLES-SUR-MER

OUISTREHAM

CABOURG

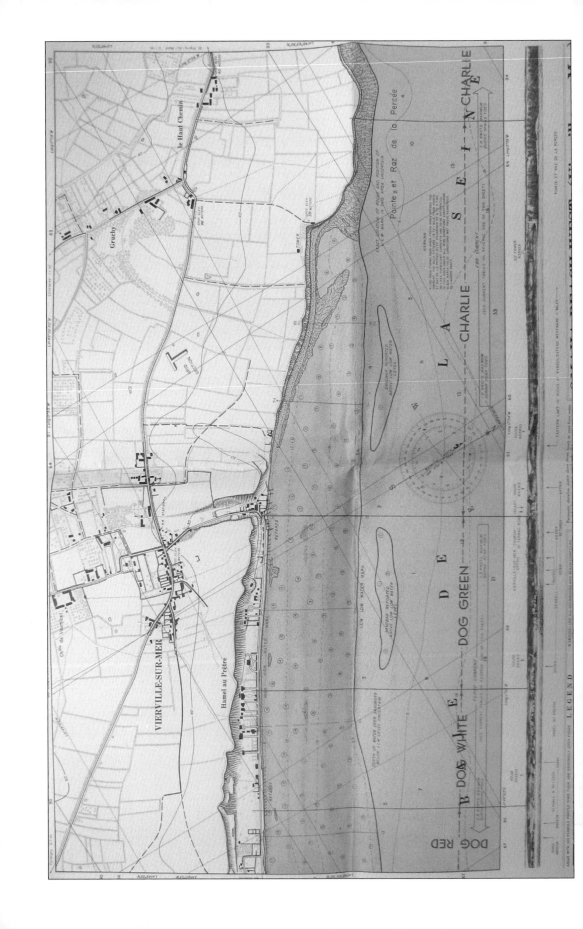

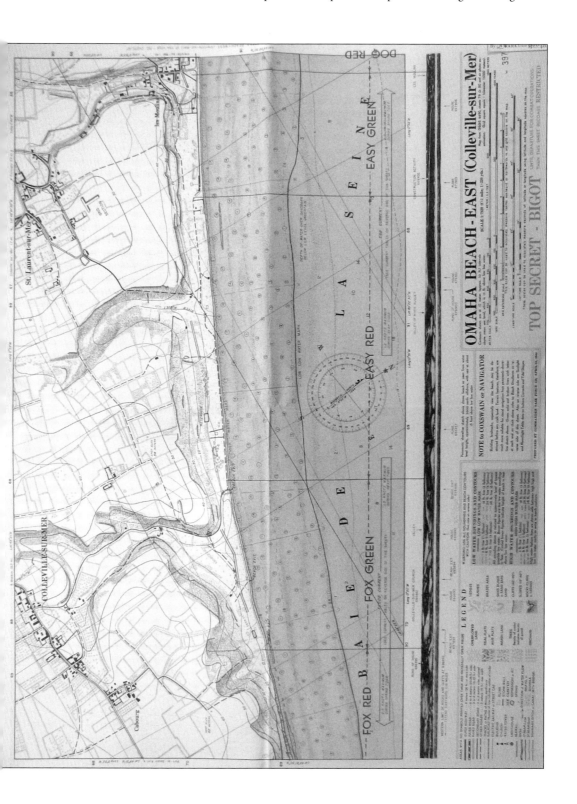

The Navy provided detailed assault 'Area Diagrams' to indicate which ships would be patrolling in which areas. Within reason the Rangers should at any given time know which ships were likely to be on station within their sector of operations – and therefore which ships could be called upon to offer fire support when necessary. The Navy vessels were to follow strict guidelines for operational areas – and only use lanes which had previously been cleared of mines by minesweepers.

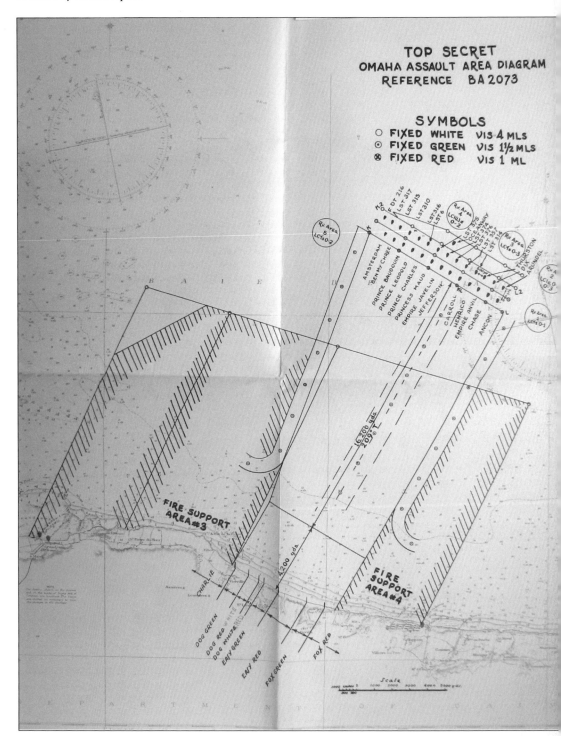

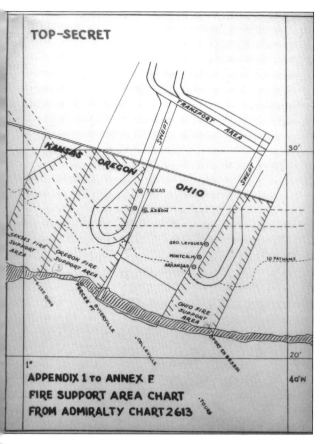

TOP-SECRET

KANSAS

OREGON

OHIO

TRANSPORT AREA

SWEPT

SWEPT

TEXAS

GLASGOW

GEO. LEYGUES

MONTCALM

ARKANSAS

KANSAS FIRE SUPPORT AREA

OREGON FIRE SUPPORT AREA

OHIO FIRE SUPPORT AREA

VIERVILLE

COLLEVILLE

30'

10 FATHOMS

20'

1°

40'W

APPENDIX 1 TO ANNEX E
FIRE SUPPORT AREA CHART
FROM ADMIRALTY CHART 2613

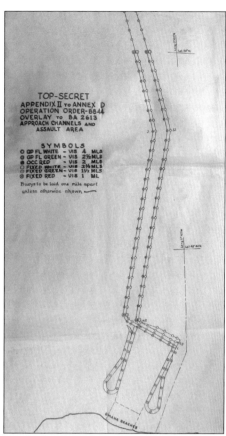

TOP-SECRET
APPENDIX II TO ANNEX D
OPERATION ORDER-BB44
OVERLAY TO BA 2613
APPROACH CHANNELS AND
ASSAULT AREA

SYMBOLS

GP FL WHITE – VIS 4 MLS
GP FL GREEN – VIS 2½ MLS
OCC RED – VIS 2 MLS
FIXED WHITE – VIS 2½ MLS
FIXED GREEN – VIS 1½ MLS
FIXED RED – VIS 1 ML

Buoys to be laid one mile apart
unless otherwise shown

OMAHA BEACHES

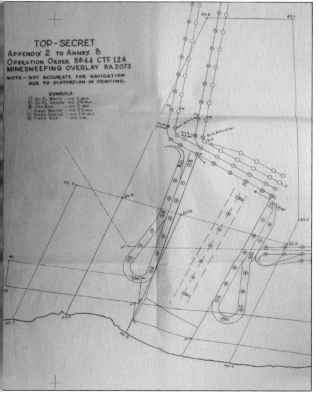

TOP-SECRET
APPENDIX 2 TO ANNEX B
OPERATION ORDER BB44 CTF 124
MINESWEEPING OVERLAY BA 2073
NOTE – NOT ACCURATE FOR NAVIGATION
DUE TO DISTORTION IN PRINTING.

SYMBOLS

GP FL WHITE – VIS 4 MLS
GP FL GREEN – VIS 2½ MLS
OCC RED – VIS 2 MLS
FIXED WHITE – VIS 2½ MLS
FIXED GREEN – VIS 1½ MLS
FIXED RED – VIS 1 ML

22 April 1944

5th Rangers – Companies A – F, Medical and HQ – Braunton Camp, North Devon.

A, B & C Companies 2nd Rangers – Braunton Camp, North Devon. Alerted for departure.

D, E & F Companies 2nd Rangers – Swanage, Dorset. No change. Alerted for departure.

Medical Detachment 2nd Rangers – Braunton Camp, North Devon. No change. Alerted for departure.

Headquarters Company 2nd Rangers – Braunton Camp, North Devon.

> *Army Orders: 22 April: 'no casualty information of any kind will be included in any correspondence written to relatives and friends by personnel in this theatre subject to Military Law.'*

A detailed map showing the predicted traffic circulation on D-Day and beyond. The '1st Objective' line for PM was emphasised as it would allow the follow-on units to land within a safe zone.

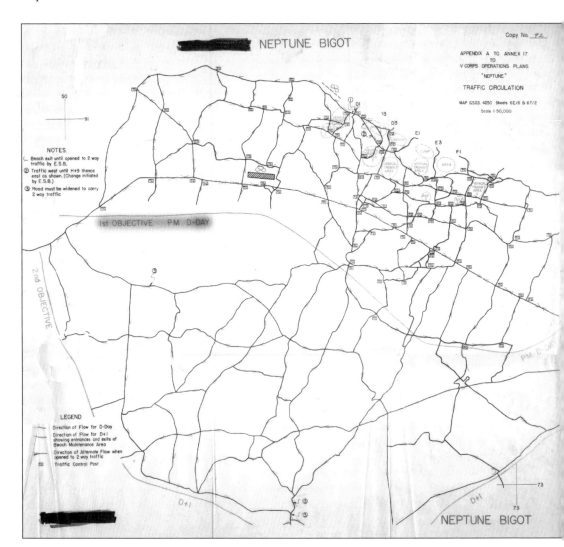

23 April 1944

5th Rangers – Companies A – F, Medical and HQ – Braunton Camp, North Devon.

A, B & C Companies 2nd Rangers – Braunton Camp, North Devon. Alerted for departure.

D, E & F Companies 2nd Rangers – Swanage, Dorset. No change. Alerted for departure.

Medical Detachment 2nd Rangers – Braunton Camp, North Devon. No change. Alerted for departure.

Headquarters Company 2nd Rangers – Braunton Camp, North Devon. No change. Alerted for departure.

US Army HQ issued various orders relating to the entitlement of certain individuals to view Top Secret documents.

7.   SAFEGUARDING TOP SECRET INFORMATION.

    a.   TOP SECRET information will not be discussed with another officer until that officer's classification with respect to the particular operation has been verified by an inspection of his classification card and WD AGO Form 65-1.

    b.   No person is entitled solely by virtue of his rank or position to have knowledge or possession of classified matter. Such matter is entrusted only to those individuals whose official duties require such knowledge or possession.

            By command of Major General GEROW:

                                    IRWIN J. BEGMAN,
                                    2nd Lt., A.G.D.,
                                    Asst. Adj. Gen.

DISTRIBUTION: Special.
                   List on file, G-2 Section.

Rangers Lt. Col. Carter, Major Max Schneider and Captain Harvey Cook were specified as BIGOT-NEPTUNE qualified officers on 23 April 1944.

Copy No. 21

                                           Auth: C.C., V Corps
             HEADQUARTERS V CORPS   Date: 23 April 1944
                                            Initials: _____

                                  23 April 1944.

                        List No. 2
            (Supersedes List No. 1, 8 Dec. 1943)   **DECLASSIFIED**

            PERSONNEL CLASSIFIED BIGOT-NEPTUNE

2nd Ranger Bn

Lt. Col. Owen H. Carter
Major Max F. Schneider
Capt. Harvey J. Cook

Separate to the activities of the US Army, each evening the British Police in each region produced a report of enemy Action within their area and delivered it to the Chief Constable. The following report relates to the bombing of Dorchester and was of special relevance to the Rangers as it came very close to the location of their camps.

```
         Incidents in the DORCHESTER DIVISION
            on the night of 23rd/24th April, 1944.
         ----------------------------------------

    Report Crashed Landing of enemy aircraft at 0230hours. 24.4.44.
at Saltern Wood, Arne - Map reference 400077 believed to be Junkers
88 - all crew killed.
    Sergt. Oliver has three Identity Discs.
    Region informed.

    Two bodies have so far been identified for the R.A.F.Officer, the
other body or bodies are a mass of pieces and the military are
  burying them on the spot.     H.Q.informed


    From P.C.Symonds, Wool & passed to H.Q.

    Exploded bomb found in open ground 200 yards east of Frampton
Arms, Moreton. Crater 3'6" deep x 14'-10" diameter. Pieces of
incendiary found. Believed to have been dropped at 0200 hours 24.4.44.
                -----------------------------
```

The US Army also recorded these same bombing incidents within their files.

S-E-C-R-E-T

A record of enemy air attack during this pre-invasion period reveals no serious damage done. Attacks were roughly a week apart, from 16 April through 28 May, with none made after that date. The record follows:

April 20th (0030) – Enemy aircraft made landfall in Portland. Scattered incidents, light damage.

April 24th (0100) – Approximately 70 enemy aircraft made landfall in Portland. Scattered incidents reported in area.

May 7th – Light air attack over Portland. No damage reported.

May 14th – Light air attack over Portland. No damage reported.

May 15th – Approximately 30 enemy aircraft came up from the south to Portland. Bombs were dropped at Fortunes Well and Chesil Beach. No damage or casualties reported.

May 28th – Approximately 30 hostile aircraft came in over Portland under cover of our returning bombers. Pathfinder flares were dropped. Approximately 15 bombs were dropped in the Portland-Weymouth area. Mines were also laid in Portland Harbor. Twenty LCT's damaged (seven considerably damaged, remainder light damage). Two LCV(P)'s sunk and various light damage was done to a number of other ships and landing craft. Damage mentioned was the result of underwater explosions, presumably mines. Portland Harbor closed for a day to all shipping until harbor was swept.

Service to the Assault Force

The mission of the Portland-Weymouth Base was set out by COMLANCRAB11TH-PHIB by letter dated 8 May and quoted in part as follows:

"1.   In the forthcoming operation the U.S. Naval Commitment will be the Western Task Force, comprised of assault Forces 'O' and 'U' and follow-up Force 'B'. These forces will be predominatly American with British units attached; ships and craft of almost all classes will be included.

"2.   It is planned that Portland will serve as the principal base for Force 'O' during the assault and follow-up and the subsequent build-up. Units of the Control Force and Force 'U' will also base there.

"3.   The mission of U.S. Naval Advanced Amphibious Base, Portland-Weymouth will be:

(a) Prepare, assemble, maintain, and provide logistic support to U.S. Naval Forces basing there.
(b) Carry out naval phase of loading of military and naval forces in accordance with operation orders.
(c) Sail ships and craft in accordance with operation orders.
(d) Receive U.S. ships and craft for unloading of survivors, casualties, prisoners, etc.
(e) Operate with FOIC Portland TURCO in the build-up."

24 April 1944

5th Rangers – Companies A – F, Medical and HQ – Braunton Camp, North Devon.

A, B & C Companies 2nd Rangers – Braunton Camp, North Devon. Alerted for departure.

D, E & F Companies 2nd Rangers – Swanage, Dorset. No change. Alerted for departure. (Bombing raid on Swanage on this day.).

Medical Detachment 2nd Rangers – Braunton Camp, North Devon. No change. Alerted for departure.

Headquarters Company 2nd Rangers – Braunton Camp, North Devon.

Pvt. Stanley J. Partyka was attached for Duty, rations and quarters from the 293rd Joint Signal Co. APO 230 US Army.

Alerted for departure.

Another set of police reports concerning bombing in the Swanage and Dorchester areas – again very close to the Rangers' camps.

At 0220 hours on 24.4.44. 2 H.E. bombs believed 1000 K.G. exploded on open ground 500 yards north-west of Glebe House, Corfe Castle. Craters 44' x 20' and 36' x 15'. No damage.

2 A.B. 1000-2 containers on Common north of Wareham I.B.S.E.N SODA EXPLOSIVE TAIL, slight damage to P.A.I.

AI 0200 hours 24. 4.44. a large container full of incendiaries fell on the Recreation Ground, Swanage, close to Shore Road, the container failed to open and was buried. Incendiaries burning in crater 15' x 6'. Slight damage to Public Conveniences.

At 0200 hours 24. 4. 44. a container marked A.B.500-1. 392. FD 1 was found at Moor Road, Swanage. Large numbers of S.D.1 bombs were found over a large area, search made in daylight, up to present 16 found unexploded and 280 exploded. Extensive damage to property. No casualties reported.

WIMBORNE POLICE DIVISION. At 0210 hours on 24-4-44 during an 'Alert' a number of S.D's were dropped at Charlbury Farm, Chalbury. 128 craters were counted. Six U.X. S.D. 1s in a field S.W. of farm. No casualties or damage. Container marked A.B. 500-1 found in field.
At the same time and date a number of S.D's and A.B.s fell fell at Hinton Martel. 125 craters found and a large number of I.B.s some of steel nose type. One person injured. Slight damage to property. Two U.X. S.D.1s container A.B. 1000-2 found. House, bungalow, garage and outbuildings damaged.

DORCHESTER POLICE DIVISION. Crashed Enemy Aircraft. At 0230 hours on 24-4-44 at Salterns Wood, Arne Map Ref.400077 – an enemy aircraft, believed Junkers 88. All crew killed. 3 identity discs found. Two identifiable bodies conveyed to Wareham mortuary. Military guard provided. R.P.S.O. Reading and R.A.F. Intelligence notified.

During an the 'Alert' period a number of believed S.D.1s wereddropped on Swanage town. All precautions were immediately taken and the organised police search is at present in progress Up to the time of the submission of this report no casualties have been reported and the matter is well in hand. A further report will follow.
I am, Sir, Your obedient Servant,

Major. Chief Constable of Dorset.

Confirmation of the Rangers' medical allocations for up to D-Day + 3.

SECTION II   -- BIGOT

SUPPLY

2. Medical Supplies.

    Basic Planning Data for Medical Components.

        (1) T/E Equipment - All units will carry ashore essential T/E Medical equipment for the assault.

        (2) Additional Equipment - The following additional equipment will be carried ashore by units indicated through D ∕ 3. These items are intended for use during the assault phase and will be carried as additional equipment on unit transportation. Items not used during the assault will be turned in to the beach medical dumps.

Litter, folding, wood, or litter, straight, steel

12 - per Inf Bn; Arty Bn; Chem Bn; Engr Bn.
24 - per Ranger Bn.
180- Per Med Bn (Inf Div); Med Bn (Engr Spec Brig).

Chest, M.D., No. 1

2 - per Coll Co.
4 - per Clr Co.
6 - per Med Bn (Engr Spec Brig).

Splint Set

1 - per Inf Bn; Arty Bn; Chem Bn; Engr Bn; Ranger Bn.
5 - per Coll Co.
10- per Med Bn (Engr Spec Brig).

Blanket Set Small

3 - per Inf Bn; Arty Bn; Chem Bn; Engr Bn; Ranger Bn.
4 - per Coll Co; Clr Co.
10- per Med Bn (Engr Spec Brig).

        (3) Special Units - Special units in waterproof containers will be carried ashore by enlisted Medical Department personnel for units indicated thro D ∕ 3, as follows:

1 - unit per Inf. Bn; Arty Bn; Chem Bn; Engr Bn; Ranger Bn.
2 - Units per Coll Co., Division.
4 - units per Clr Co., Division
6 - units per Med Bn (Engr Spec Brig).

    Units will consist of approximately eight (8) small containers, which personnel may float ashore using the containers for buoyancy where required. Each unit will provide the following:

ITEM	UNIT	AMOUNT
Dressings, first aid, large	each	50
Dressings, first aid, small	each	50
Gauze, plain, sterilized, comp.	pkg	50
Bandage, gauze, 3-inch	each	50
Sulfanilamide, crystalline	pkg	10
Morphine Tartrate, syrettes	box	25
Serum, normal human plasma, dried	pkg	7
Sulfadiazene, USP, 7.7 gr tabs	1000	1
Halazone, 1/10 gr tabs (100 in)	bottle	1
Sterile gauze packet (impregnated with boric acid or vaseline)	each	1

        (4) Blank Forms and Stationery - Units will carry a thirty (30) day supply of blank forms and stationery. Resupply will be through the Army Medical Depot.

On the 24 April Major General Huebner was issued with operational orders for the forthcoming FABIUS 1 D-Day training operation.

```
                    ELEVENTH AMPHIBIOUS FORCE            SECRET

    S-E-C-R-E-T

         ELEVENTH AMPHIBIOUS FORCE, UNITED STATES FLEET

                    WAR DIARY - APRIL 1944

    24 April 1944 -  Commander Eleventh Amphibious Force issued Operation Order
                     Z-44 for Training Exercise designated FABIUS I.

                     Task Groups were assigned as follows:

                     124.1 - Landing Force - Major General HUEBNER, U.S. Army.
                     124.2 - Shore Party - Brigadier General HOGE, U.S. Army.
                     124.3 - Assault Group O-1 - Captain FRITZSCHE, U.S. Coast Guard,
                             and Captain IMLAY, U.S. Coast Guard, (Deputy).
                     124.4 - Assault Group O-2 - Captain BAILEY, U.S. Navy, and
                             Captain WRIGHT, U.S. Navy, (Deputy).
                     124.5 - Assault Group O-3 - Captain SCHULTEN, U.S. Navy and
                             Commander UNGER, U.S. Coast Guard, (Deputy).
                     124.6 - Assault Group O-4 - Commander DENNIS, Royal Navy.
                     124.7 - Escorts - Captain SANDERS, U.S. Navy.
                     124.8 - Gunfire Support Craft - Captain SABIN, U.S. Navy.
                     124.9 - Bombardment Group - Captain JONES, U.S. Navy.
                     124.10 - Sweeper Group.
                     124.11 - Far Shore Service Group - Captain PERCIFIELD, U.S. Navy.
```

25 April 1944
5th Rangers – Companies A – F, Medical and HQ –
Braunton Camp, North Devon.
A, B & C Companies 2nd Rangers – Braunton Camp, North Devon. Alerted for departure.

Maurice Prince: *We ran several problems in conjunction with the Royal Navy and then we underwent exercises concerning a simulated flank protection of a division. To finish off this phase of training, we underwent a two day and night exercise. We combined our amphibious knowledge with our fighting skill on land. It was a tough, rough problem and very realistic. This problem gave us our first inkling of what we were to expect when the day of invasion rolled around.*

It was during this exercise that we first boarded our mother ship which was eventually to bring us across the channel. It was there we struck up our first friendship with this boat and got our first taste of being aboard a ship of this type.

D Company 2nd Rangers – Swanage, Dorset.
Alerted for departure.
Paragraphs 1a) and b) of letter, HQ V Corps, subject, 'Desertion' dated 21 April 1944, was read to the members of D Company present at a formation of the Company at 1300 hours, on 25 April 1944. Additionally the US Army issued regulations on dealing with Absent Without Leave (AWOL) personnel to unit commanders.

Status of absentees.

a)   *An absentee will be carried on the rolls as AWOL until he returns to military control or until the expiration of one year from date of absence. At the expiration of one year he will be dropped from the rolls as AWOL and his records will be completed and forwarded to The Adjutant General, Washington 25, DC.*

b)   *The rolls on which an absentee is so carried will be those of the organisation from which he absented himself, unless that organisation departs from the United Kingdom. Effective on such departure, each absentee is hereby transferred to, and will be taken up and carried on the rolls of either:*
   1)   *10th Replacement Depot, SOS, ETOUSA, if other than air force personnel, or*
   2)   *12th Replacement Control Depot, if air force personnel.*

c) *Alerted or departing unit will NOT drop an absentee as AWOL. Such unit will take necessary steps so that, in event that the absentee does not rejoin unit before his embarkation, his name will be cancelled from the passenger list.*

    1) *Extract Copy of Morning Report (WD AGO Form No 44) certified by the company commander, showing the change in status from duty to AWOL and the fact of transfer to the appropriate depot specified above.*

    2) *Service Record.*

    3) *Other pertinent records.*

    4) *Personal effects, if any.*

    5) *Letter explaining the circumstances. If any record referred to above is not immediately available, the letter will indicate clearly what officer has custody of such record and when it will be transmitted.*

When an unauthorised absentee is apprehended or surrenders, an immediate report thereof will be made by the best available means of communication to the commander of the base section within which such apprehension or surrender took place.

E & F Companies 2nd Rangers – Swanage, Dorset. No change. Alerted for departure.

Medical Detachment 2nd Rangers – Braunton Camp, North Devon. No change. Alerted for departure.

Headquarters Company 2nd Rangers – Braunton Camp, North Devon.
Paragraphs 1a) and b) of letter, HQ V Corps, subject, 'Desertion' were read to the members of HQ company present at a formation of the Company on 25 April 1944. Alerted for departure.

Dated 25 April, a very firm directive was issued by Lt. General Smith concerning the dissemination of intelligence information, in particular the paragraph highlighted in grey. On a 'once daily' basis Army Groups were to be made aware of the previous 24 hours' intelligence picture with regards to the German positions in their related areas. These had to contain the latest information available at any one time and these reports were to be delivered to Supreme Allied Headquarters (SHAEF) daily.

SUPREME HEADQUARTERS
ALLIED EXPEDITIONARY FORCE
Office of the Assistant Chief of Staff, G-2.

SHAEF/502CX/INT   25th April, 1944

INTELLIGENCE DIRECTIVE)   57
    NUMBER 1   )

INTELLIGENCE REPORTS

I. OBJECT

1.   The object of this directive is to prescribe the policy and to
establish the procedure for the submission of Intelligence Reports
to this Headquarters. As such, it supersedes all previous
instructions.

II. GENERAL

2.   Nothing contained herein will be construed as changing fundamental
Intelligence Doctrines of British or American Forces, nor as removing
the responsibility for the submission to higher authority of reports
(Combat Reports, War Diaries, etc) required by existing Regulations.

3.   Every care will be exercised, where combined or joint functions
are involved, to ensure no misunderstanding due to differences in
standard practice, common usage, or terminology.

III. REPORTS REQUIRED BY SHAEF   46

4.   COSITINTREPS. Combined Operations and Intelligence Reports,
(COSITINTREPS) will be submitted as prescribed in SHAEF OPERATION
MEMORANDUM NUMBER 25 dated 24th April, 1944. For Army Groups, it is
intended that Intelligence highlights only be included in this report,
more detailed intelligence being contained in ISUMS (see below).

5.   ISUMS. Army Groups will despatch once daily, by signal, an
ISUM (Intelligence Summary) giving the complete intelligence picture
for the previous 24 hours period. The despatch of the signal will be
so timed as to arrive at this Headquarters for decoding by 0400 hours
and should contain the latest information available.

6.   SPOT INTELLIGENCE. Intelligence of an urgent nature such as the
identification of a new division will be despatched at the earliest
opportunity by Army Groups to SHAEF for G-2.

7.   COUNTER-INTELLIGENCE REPORTS. The submission of this category
of reports will be as directed in Counter-Intelligence and Censorship
Instructions (See SHAEF Intelligence Directive No. 7, "Counter-
Intelligence").

CONFIDENTIAL

CONFIDENTIAL

CONFIDENTIAL

CONFIDENTIAL

8.   OTHER INTELLIGENCE. Unless specifically covered in appropriate directives (as, for example, "Technical Intelligence") the preparation and publication of all other Intelligence Reports will be as directed by Commanders concerned.   Copies of all such daily, weekly, or special reports, specifically including Summaries, Reviews, Bulletins, Notes, Periodic Reports, Interrogation Reports, etc. produced by Army Groups and Armies, but NOT by lower formations, will be forwarded to this Headquarters through normal channels. Two copies are required.

9.   DISTRIBUTION OF REPORTS. All Headquarters will ensure that copies of pertinent Intelligence reports are received by adjacent formations.

By Command of General EISENHOWER:

W.B. SMITH
Lieutenant General, US Army,
Chief of Staff.

OFFICIAL:

J.F.M. WHITELEY,
Major-General, GS,
A C of S, G-2.

DISTRIBUTION:

As for Intelligence Directive No. 11.

Less: A C of S, G-6
       DDMI(PW), The War Office.
       IS9(WEA), The War Office.

Plus: DDMI(O), The War Office.
       MIRS, The War Office.
       Psychological Warfare Division.

This 25 April dated aerial photograph shows the west of Grandcamp-les-Bains coastline and the Maisy Batteries.

The following over flight and intelligence aerial photographs have various dates. Often the base photograph was re-used and further information was added onto them. It is easier to include them all in one place here rather than try to split them up into various dates.

AREA : 4902N (CHERBOURG)   CATEGORY : J   COASTAL DEFENCES

OBJECTIVE NO.	NAME OF PLACE	DESCRIPTION	ILLUS. NO.	MAP REFERENCE		TARGET OP. NO.	REMARKS
				GSGS SERIES & SHEET NO.	GRID REFERENCE		
COASTAL DEFENCES LOCATED ON SHEET 6R/6 (ISIGNY), G.S.G.S. SERIES 4250 (Numbers allotted: 1 - 100)							
4902N/J/1	GRANDCAMP-LES-BAINS	Defended locality	4902N/13/1	4250 6R/6	576938		
4902N/J/2	GRANDCAMP-LES-BAINS	Defended locality	4902N/13/k	4250 6R/6	565936		
4902N/J/3	GRANDCAMP-LES-BAINS	Defended locality	4902N/13/j	4250 6R/6	558933		
4902N/J/4	GRANDCAMP-LES-BAINS	Defended locality	4902N/13/h	4250 6R/6	552933		
4902N/J/5	GRANDCAMP-LES-BAINS	Defended locality	4902N/13/g	4250 6R/6	545933		
4902N/J/6	GRANDCAMP-LES-BAINS	Defended locality	4902N/6/e 4902N/13/b	4250 6R/6	538934		
4902N/J/7	MAISY	Medium Battery: 6R/6, 5391A	4902N/6/f 4902N/13/n	4250 6R/6	533918		Four 15.5 cm. guns. Dummy Battery at 529923.

AREA : 4902N (CHERBOURG)   CATEGORY : J (Page 2)   COASTAL DEFENCES

OBJECTIVE NO.	NAME OF PLACE	DESCRIPTION	ILLUS. NO.	MAP REFERENCE		TARGET OP. NO.	REMARKS
				GSGS SERIES & SHEET NO.	GRID REFERENCE		
4902N/J/8	MAISY	Field Battery: 6R/6, 5291A	4902N/6/g 4902N/13/m	4250 6R/6	528915		4 guns. Dummy Battery at 526922.
4902N/J/9	MAISY	Defended locality	4902N/6/d 4902N/13/a	4250 6R/6	524934		
4902N/J/10	GEFOSSE-FONTENAY	Defended locality	4902N/6/c	4250 6R/6	511922		
4902N/J/11	FONTENAY	Defended locality	4902N/6/h	4250 6R/6	507897		Company Headquarters
4902N/J/12	GEFOSSE-FONTENAY	Defended locality	4902N/6/b	4250 6R/6	505916		Two 10.5 cm. guns
4902N/J/13	ISIGNY	Defended locality	4902N/15/d	4250 6R/6	499857		Battalion Headquarters
4902N/J/14	ISIGNY	Defended locality	4902N/15/e	4250 6R/6	494850		Possible Company Headquarters
4902N/J/15	ST. CLEMENT	Defended locality	4902N/14/d	4250 6R/6	493876		

AREA : 4902W (CHERBOURG)   CATEGORY : J (Page 5)   COASTAL DEFENCES

OBJECTIVE NO.	NAME OF PLACE	DESCRIPTION	ILLUS. NO.	MAP REFERENCE		TARGET OP. NO.	REMARKS
				GSGS SERIES & SHEET NO.	GRID REFERENCE		
4902W/J/32	GEFOSSE-FONTENAY	Defended post	■ 4902W/6/k	4250 6E/6	511911		Small infantry position defending probably a company H.Q.
4902W/J/33	MAISY	Defended locality	■ 4902W/6/n ■ 4902W/13/p	4250 6E/6	526934		1 casemate. 3 pillboxes. 3 shelters. Position surrounded by wire. N.W. of Maisy.
4902W/J/34	GRANDCAMP	Defended post	■ 4902W/13/q	4250 6E/6	544928		Small infantry position south of Grandcamp
4902W/J/35	JUCOVILLE	Defended post	o 4902W/91/a	4250 6E/6	562892		Probable H.Q. in Chateau de Jucoville
4902W/J/36	MADELEINE	Defended locality	■ 4902W/84/k ■ 4902W/18/f	4250 6E/6	443982		2 pillboxes. 3 shelters. Two 150 mm. guns. Position protected by wire on landward side.
4902W/J/37	MADELEINE	Minefield	■ 4902W/84/j	4250 6E/6	446977		
4902W/J/38	GRANDE DUNE	Defended locality	■ 4902W/84/h	4250 6E/6	452960		4 pillboxes. 1 shelter. 3 anti tank guns. 1 light gun, probably 75 mm. Position protected by wire on landward side.

Amendment List No. 1 (Final) - April 1944   ■ = 1st Revision
                                                 o = Additional to illustrations contained in original dossier

A GSGS Intelligence Map covering the same area was made available. It is a very basic map with only topographical information. It contains no military information at all.

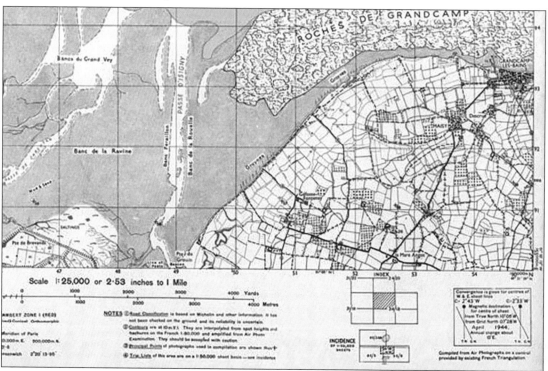

Revised Grandcamp-les-Bains intelligence photographs. They show the strongpoints in Grandcamp as well as the Maisy Batteries.

Low-level reconnaissance photograph showing the cliffs in front of the radar station at Pointe et Raz de la Percée. The radar receiver is visible on the cliff top as are two of the communication towers.

OBLIQUE FROM THE STARBOARD CAMERA, TAKEN ON SAME MISSION, SHOWS AN ENEMY WURZBURG RADAR, POLE-TYPE BEACH OBSTACLES, AND GUN POSITIONS BURROWED INTO THE CLIFFSIDE NEAR POINT DE HOE.

A 25 April dated US Army explanation of the 'TOP SECRET' control procedure. It was necessary that all officers handling Top Secret material knew what they could and could not do with it – and more appropriately – with whom they could discuss that information.

Copy No. **20**

HEADQUARTERS V CORPS

Auth: C.G., V Corps
Date: 25 April 1944
Initials: _____

25 April 1944.

SUBJECT: TOP SECRET Control Procedure.

TO   : See Distribution.

1. GENERAL.

   b. Purpose. The purpose of this letter is to present in condensed form the essential requirements of Top Secret Control Procedure.

   (2) CLASSIFICATION. a. Official matter requiring classification is graded into the following categories: (1) TOP SECRET; (2) SECRET; (3) CONFIDENTIAL and (4) RESTRICTED.

   b. In this Theatre a special system, designated TOP SECRET CONTROL PROCEDURE, has been established for the handling of TOP SECRET documents. In accordance with this procedure TOP SECRET documents pertaining to operational plans are further classified as (1) TOP SECRET plus codeword and (2) TOP SECRET BIGOT plus codeword.

   3. APPLICATION. a. The following are the general classes of documents that are graded into each of the above-named categories:
      (1) TOP SECRET.
         (a) Plans or particulars of future major or special operations. (For classification of codeword plans this Theatre, see (2) and (3) below).
         (b) Particulars of important dispositions or impending moves of our forces or convoys in connection with special operations.
         (c) Movement from a rear area in a theatre of operations to the battle or assault area.
         (d) Very important political documents.
         (e) Information of the methods used or success obtained by our intelligence and counterintelligence services.
         (f) Critical information of new and important munitions of war.
         (g) Important particulars of cryptography and cryptanalysis.
         (h) Operational code-words NEPTUNE and FORTITUDE.
         (i) Operational code-words ATLANTIS, MULBERRIES, OVERLORD, PLUTO RANKIN, CROSSBOW, if accompanied by details of their meaning or of the plans to which they pertain.
      (2) TOP SECRET plus Codeword. (e.g., TOP SECRET OVERLORD or TOP SECRET RANKIN).
         (a) The plans proper or vital parts of the plan, but not include target area or date of assault or inferences thereto.
         (b) Troop lists for an operation where sufficiently complete to indicate possible operational plans.
         (c) Detailed information concerning special equipment to be used in an operation or the technique of its employment.

-1-

(d) The plan proper or vital parts of the plan, including places and dates of Operation RANKIN "C".

(3) TOP SECRET BIGOT plus Codeword. (e.g., TOP SECRET BIGOT NEPTUNE).

(a) Operational plans which include or infer places or dates (except RANKIN "C" as indicated above).

(b) Maps covering the specific assault area infer places and must be classified TOP SECRET BIGOT NEPTUNE and safeguarded accordingly.

(c) No TOP SECRET OVERLORD document will be subject to BIGOT procedure, except those classified OVERLORD BIGOT under procedure in effect prior to 15 March 1944.

(d) TOP SECRET OVERLORD plans must be reclassified TOP SECRET BIGOT NEPTUNE when places and dates of the operation are included. Likewise, when places and dates are omitted and not inferred, TOP SECRET BIGOT NEPTUNE should be reclassified to TOP SECRET OVERLORD.

b. (1) Each document will be graded according to its own content and not necessarily according to its relationship to another document. If physically connected, the classification given to a group or file of documents will be that of the highest document therein.

(2) Administrative details growing out of TOP SECRET matter (including codeword plans) may be classified in accordance with their own contents when they do not of themselves reveal, in fact or by inference, information requiring TOP SECRET classification. When given a lower classification, such communications must not disclose the project for which the personnel, equipment or material is intended, nor contain vital parts of the plan proper, nor references to special equipment, the nature of which would divulge the plan or project.

(3) Special effort will be made by all classifying authorities to issue documents under the codeword OVERLORD rather than NEPTUNE by omitting reference to target area or date of assault or references thereto.

(4) Documents which contain an operational code-name (except NEPTUNE and FORTITUDE) and which do not disclose or infer the meaning of such operational code-name, may be classified SECRET if such classification provides adequate security.

(5) In case of new and important munitions of war, the technical service in charge of the development determines the classification.

4. CLASSIFICATION OF PERSONNEL. a. Personnel, who in the course of their duties, are required to have knowledge of operational plans will be classified in one of the following ways:

(1) TOP SECRET plus Codeword. (e.g., TOP SECRET OVERLORD; TOP SECRET RANKIN "C").

(a) Personnel required to have general knowledge of OVERLORD, exclusive of target area or date of assault.

(b) Personnel required to have full knowledge of RANKIN "C" including area and dates,

(2) BIGOT plus Codeword. (e.g., BIGOT NEPTUNE). Personnel required to have knowledge of the specific target area or date of assault of OVERLORD.

b. Personnel formerly classified as BIGOT OVERLORD will be considered as BIGOT NEPTUNE; SECRET SECURITY OVERLORD will be considered TOP SECRET OVERLORD; and BIGOT RANKIN and SECRET SECURITY RANKIN will be considered TOP SECRET RANKIN.

c. Division commanders are authorized to classify officers and enlisted men of their commands as indicated in subparagraph a. above. The respective division commanders are responsible for insuring that personnel classified by them is of unquestioned loyalty and discretion and that the number of classified persons in their commands is held to a minimum. The name, rank, serial number and assignment and type of classification will be reported to the Commanding General, V Corps, by each division commander immediately upon the classification of any officer of his command. Personnel of non-divisional units will be classified by the Commanding General, V Corps. The application for classification will include the full name, serial number, official position, and type of classification desired for each person.

26 April 1944

5th Rangers – Companies A – F, Medical –
Braunton Camp, North Devon.
Paragraphs 1a and b of letter from headquarters
V Corps. Subject: 'DESERTION' were read to the
members of A Company at a formation of the
Company at 0625 hours 26 April.

Headquarters Company 5th Rangers – Braunton
Camp, North Devon.
Pvt. Fuller and Pvt. Hall were transferred in grade to
confinement at H/L for a period of six months – at
Disciplinary Training Centre No 3, Sudbury, Derby [a military Prison].

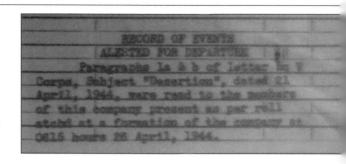

A, B & C Companies 2nd Rangers – Braunton Camp, North Devon. Alerted for departure.

D, E and F Companies 2nd Rangers – Swanage, Dorset. Alerted for departure.
Paragraphs 1a and b of letter, HQ V Corps, subject, 'Desertion' were read to the members of E Company present at a formation of the
Company at 1900 hours, on 26 April 1944.

F Company 2nd Rangers – Swanage, Dorset. Alerted for departure.
Paragraphs 1a and b of letter, HQ V Corps, subject, 'Desertion' were read to the members of F Company present at a formation of the
Company at 1900 hours on 26 April 1944.

Medical Detachment 2nd Rangers – Braunton Camp, North Devon. No change. Alerted for departure.

Headquarters Company 2nd Rangers – Braunton Camp, North Devon. Alerted for departure.

On the next page: A battery list was created for proposed air bombardment. Pointe du Hoc is listed as 6 x 155mmG
(Guns) being under construction and Maisy I is stated as having 6 x 155mm howitzers.

27 April 1944

5th Rangers – Companies A – F, Medical and HQ – Dorchester,
England. Camp D-1 APO 230 US Army.
Alerted for departure Fabius I.

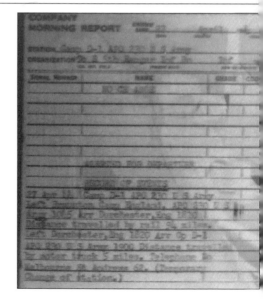

2nd Battalion Historical Narrative.

> On 27 April, Companies A/B/C moved by rail to Staging
> Area D-1 near Dorchester, Dorset, for participation in the
> Operation "Fabius I".

COAST DEFENSE BATTERIES

NO.	BATT	GRID	LOCATION	EMPLACEMENT	RANGE	AREA	PROPOSED AIR BOMBARDMENT
1	6-155G	586938	Points du Hoe	Concrete under construction	25,000	OMAHA	(a) Pre Y-day (b) Night Heavy (c) Night Medium
1A	4-170G	365201	La Pernelle	Open	30,000	UTAH	(a) Pre Y-day (b) Night Heavy (c) Night Medium (d) Fighter Bombers
2	4-240G	265267	Carneville	Turrets and casemates U/C	40,000	PENINSULA	(a) Pre Y-day
3	6-155G	368044	Fontenay	Casemates under construction. (Open)	25,000	UTAH	(a) Night Heavy (b) Fighter Bombers
4	6-155G	354139	Morsalines	Open concrete	25,000	UTAH	(a) Night Heavy (b) Fighter Bombers
5	6-155H	533918	Maisy	Open	13,000	OMAHA	(a) Night Medium (b) Fighter Bombers
6	4-155H	405980	Varreville	Casemates U/C	13,000	UTAH	Night Heavy
7	4-170G	246264	Les Movlins	Turrets	32,000	PENINSULA	(Existance doubtful)
8	6-155G	392277	Gatteville	Report Casements U/C	25,000	PENINSULA	
8A	4-170?	394228	Gatteville	Open	30,000	UTAH	
9	4-105GH	360022	Emondeville	Casemate	13,000	UTAH	
10	4-105GH	792831	Beauvis	Open	13,000	OMAHA	
11	4-150GH	354291	Pte de Neville	1 Casemate	25,000	UTAH	
12	4-150H	378204	Vicel	Open	14,600	UTAH	
13	4-105GH	848853	Ryes	Open	13,000	OMAHA	
14	4-105GH	343057	Ozeville	Open	13,000	UTAH	Day Fighter Bomber
15	4-105GH	342102	Versailles	Open	13,000	UTAH	

A Company 2nd Rangers – Braunton Camp, North Devon to Dorchester, Dorset.
A Company departed from Braunton Camp, North Devon by rail at 0900 hours and arrived at Dorchester, Dorset at 1600. Mode of travel by train. Alerted for departure – Fabius 1.

B Company 2nd Rangers – Braunton Camp, North Devon.
T/Sgt. Andrusz went from Duty to sick in Hospital.
Departed from Braunton Camp, North Devon at 0900 hours. Arrived in Dorchester, Dorset at 1600. Mode of travel by train.
Alerted for departure – Fabius 1.

C Company 2nd Rangers – Dorchester, Dorset. No change.
Departed Braunton Camp North Devon at 0900 hours. Arrived in Dorchester, Dorset by train at 1500 hours.

D, E & F Companies 2nd Rangers – Swanage, Dorset. No change. Alerted for departure.

Medical Detachment 2nd Rangers – Braunton Camp, North Devon. No change.
Alerted for departure. Departed Braunton Camp North Devon at 0900 hours. Arrived in Dorchester, Dorset by train at 1500 hours. Fabius 1.

Headquarters Company 2nd Rangers – Braunton Camp, North Devon. Record of events. Arrived at Dorchester, Dorset at 1500hrs by rail. Alerted for departure – Fabius 1.

Maurice Prince: *April 27 saw us on the move again. We were still sixty-four men and three officers strong, and strong in every sense of the word. We had trained and worked hard. We had had our fun, and now we were prepared to tackle anything the Army threw our way. Our cockiness and confidence had taken on new life.*

The following is an Army list of Embarkation camp names, numbers and grid locations. The last two columns contain the number of men allocated to each camp and then finally the number of vehicles each camp could contain. Camp D-1 Dewlish was the camp allocated to the men of the 5th Battalion and camp D-5 Broadmayne was allocated to the men of the 2nd Rangers.

AREA "D" (U.S.)					
W	D-1	DEWLISH	140/204184	1300	185
	D-3	YELLOWHAM	140/164142	1040	149
	D-6	PIDDLEHINTON "A" (c)	140/155173	1440)	
		PIDDLEHINTON "B"	140/155173	1440)	411
X	D-4	CAME HOUSE	140/143098	2170	310
	D-7	DORCHESTER (a)			
		(POUNDBURY &	140/118117	1560)	
		MARABOUT) (c)	140/120117	1500)	437
Y	D-10	KINGSTON RUSSELL	140/026107	2170	310
	D-11	WINTERBORNE ABBAS	140/043112	2170	310
	D-12	BRADFORD DOWN "A" (c)	140/078113	1750)	
		BRADFORD DOWN "B"	140/080113	870)	374
	D-13	WINTERBORNE ST MARTIN	140/081098	430	61
Z	D-2	LYCHETT MINSTER (c)	141/400139	1000	200
	D-5	BROADMAYNE "A"	140/165079	550	90
		BROADMAYNE "B"	140/166072	1620	220
	D-8	DOWN WOOD	140/124076	1300	185
	D-9	BINCOMBE (c)	140/026063	1730	247
	D-14	CHICKERELL	140/080003	1730	247
		TOTAL		25770	3736

NOTES:
(a) Area Headquarters
(b) Static Staff Only
(c) Sub-Area Headquarters
(d) May be used by RAF.

A 27 April dated reconnaissance photograph covering the Vierville exit from Omaha Beach and the Pointe et Raz de la Percée Radar Station.

27 April – European Theatre of Operations Service of Supply reports stated the following.

Camps and marshalling areas were sited and constructed near the embarkation points, so troops would be a short time and distance from their craft. The establishment of such areas would enable the tactical troops to live in reasonable comfort, under sanitary conditions, and still be ready to depart on a moment's notice. The advantage was that the tactical commander could place his plan in operation on short notice, and with a minimum of confusion and betraying of movement, as soon as weather and other variable factors became favourable.

Therefore the build up became a series of movements in phases… each step bringing the task force closer to the take-off. At the home station area the troops received basic equipment such as vehicles, clothing, weapons. This home station was called a 'BOLERO' installation, and in many cases served as a 'concentration area' as well. In the concentration area, the troops performed water-proofing of vehicles, acquisition of last minute supplies, the stripping of the administration residue personnel, and the packing and miscellany to move it to an unknown destination. Thereafter they were sent to the 'marshalling area' where issues of food, lifebelts and other operational needs were complete. Briefing, then marshalling into individual craft loads were the final stops and immediately preceded the movement to ports for loading.

Security had to be most rigid. Both British and American personnel would co-operate in preventing leaks. British police would cover towns and civilians. American soldiers would keep briefed troops inside their camps, and all unauthorised personnel outside.

This meant that Service of Supply would have to provide entertainment facilities such as movies, books, games and athletic equipment. Post Exchange supplies and mail would be uninterrupted, except that outgoing mail would be specially censored.

The camp sites were selected. This was done in such a way that every camp or group of camps was near an embarkation point. The capacity for out loading from a certain group of hards determined the size and number of camps located nearby. Each group of camps, complete with embarkation points was known as a 'marshalling area'.

Each marshalling area would have railheads for storage of all classes of supplies. Every camp would maintain a stock of food and fast moving items. Communications were planned between all camps and headquarters.

Traffic plans were established to direct and control traffic into the marshalling area, to the camps, and from the camps to the hards. Showers, laundries and bakeries completed the facilities.

Eight marshalling areas were planned, to be sprawled over Southern Base Section, from Cornwall to Hampshire, each with a letter designation. In the east, clustered around Portsmouth, Southampton, and Lymington would lay areas 'A'. 'B' and 'C'. Areas 'A' and 'B to belong to the British and area 'C' to be jointly operated by both. Area 'D' was to be an American operated area centered around Dorchester, and emptying from Portland and Weymouth.

Marshalling area construction followed two patterns. In the centre zone, areas 'A', 'B', 'C & 'D' consisted of camps ranging in capacity from 1,500 to 8,000-9,000 persons. Large mess halls, featuring mass production methods, were opened in these big camps.

Mobile bakeries produced thousands of loaves per day to assist those produced by the British. Additionally, mobile laundry units and Chemical Impregnating units were pressed into the clothes washing business as supply outstripped local supply.

American mobile shoe repair units also helped the swamped British units – as did mobile US Army shower units, which serviced the marshalling areas and outlying camps.

Roadside dumps and petrol stations were established and delivery trucks were made available in order that field force units would not have to go for petrol.

Ordnance units went to the marshalling areas to establish shops and organised roving patrols to seek out breakdowns and repair them on the spot. Spare vehicles were provided – already waterproofed – to replace any vehicle that could not be fixed within minutes. A wading pit, with water four feet high, was constructed in each marshalling area, so drivers could test the seal of their engines before departing.

Upon arrival at the designated camp, each unit was met by a representative of the camp commander. He indicated the parking areas – cleared strips beside the roadway in most cases, where hard standing had been laid by the Engineers or British personnel. The arriving troops were required to park and camouflage their vehicles. A roving camouflage patrol from a Southern Base Section Camouflage Battalion inspected completeness of the job. During this period, gasoline was supplied for filling tanks – replacing the gas used en route.

A guard was posted over the vehicles by the transient unit commander and the troops were marched to camp. The distance was generally about a half a mile to 1 mile – never over three miles.

When the unit arrived at camp, the personnel were again checked – to ensure that the number and names coincided exactly with the forecast. This was mainly information to be used in the event of casualties from enemy air-raids.

The men were then conducted to their quarters area and placed in a 'block' of tents. Cots with three blankets each were waiting for them. The Commanding Officer then received a map of the camp showing kitchens, latrines, fire points, water supply points and stating administrative procedures.

To ease the strain, the transient troops were provided every possible entertainment. Continuous movies were shown, athletic equipment distributed. Those who wished to read, easily obtained books and magazines. The 'Stars and Stripes', American news daily, was distributed to all, free of charge. Meals were excellent, featuring large quantities of beef, port, green vegetables and tasty desserts. Morale was high and the men joked about the 'last supper' and dubbed the impending operation the 'blood bath' in a good natured manner. Most of them had been waiting so, so long.

In this manner, there was assembled the entire assault and follow-up force. Task Force 'O' made up of elements of the 1st and 29th Infantry Division plus Ranger Battalions and Engineers were marshalled around Dorchester.

A period illustration of a mobile laundry covered with camouflage netting.

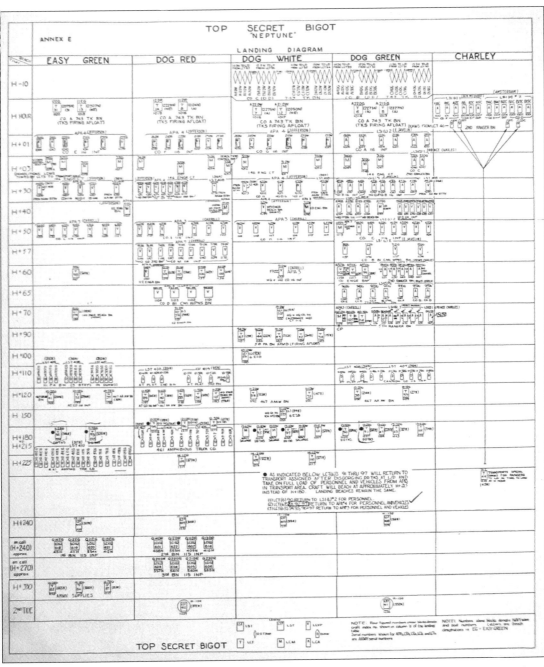

Also on 27 April a full landing plan was produced showing the Rangers' position – landing on the extreme right of Omaha Beach.

An updated illustration of expected beach obstacles – dated 27 April.

28 April 1944

5th Rangers – Companies A – F, Medical and HQ – Dorchester, England.

A, B & C Companies 2nd Rangers – Dorchester, Dorset. Alerted for departure – Fabius 1.

Maurice Prince: *Our next destination in the travels and exploits of the Rangers was to be the pleasant country side just outside the city limits of Dorchester, county of Dorset. Previously, we had always been billeted in buildings or structures, but here we were to taste the famed way of Army life, life in a tent. Since we had left the states, we had hardly seen a tent less live in one, so that now we were getting re-oriented to this old way of Army living.*

It wasn't hard to renew this style of living, as weather conditions made this outdoor life ideal. The immediate countryside with its pretty primroses, shady trees, running streams, didn't detract in the least in the joy of leading this primitive type of existence.

Our area was in an open field, which was hemmed in by tall trees, under whose cover our tents were pitched. We were fairly crowded in our homes as space was limited. The first couple of days we stayed there, we didn't have much to do. So we relaxed, refreshed and soothed our nerves by absorbing the beauty of the land.

The 29th Inf. division was also bivouacked in this vicinity. We became friendly with these men and struck up a friendly relationship. These doughs were a swell bunch of GIs. It wasn't hard to get chummy with them. It seems as though they too were here for the same reason we were. It appears that we were to pull off a gigantic amphibious exercise with both our units participating. Our outfit was to give them flank protection, which was similar to what we had trained for in the overnight problem at Braunton.

D, E & F Companies 2nd Rangers – Swanage, Dorset. Alerted for departure.

Medical Detachment 2nd Rangers – Dorchester, Dorset. Alerted for departure – Fabius 1.

Headquarters Company 2nd Rangers – Dorchester, Dorset.
The following two officers returned to Duty from Detached Service.
Captain Cleveland A. Lytle, Captain Harvey J. Cook.
The following two officers returned from Detached Service in Plymouth for Duty, rations and quarters.
1st Lt. Sylvester Vauruska, Lt. Bennie Berger (USN).
The following eleven officers returned from Detached Service in Plymouth for Duty, rations and quarters.
Sgt. Joseph J. Groth, T/4 Theodore F. Stebbins, Pfc. William J. Skelley, Pfc. Jerome O. Abare, Pvt. Francis Jakowski, Pvt. Lawrence M. McKeever, Pvt. Wallace M. Crank, Pvt. Kenneth Miller, Pvt. Henry W. Genther, T/5 Harman W. Calmes, Pvt. Irvin H. Ferriera. Alerted for departure. Fabius 1.

---

29 April 1944

5th Rangers – Companies A – F, Medical and HQ – Dorchester, England.

A, B & C Companies 2nd Rangers – Dorchester, Dorset. Alerted for departure – Fabius 1.
Fifteen enlisted men from B Company went from Duty to sick in Hospital. Alerted for departure – Fabius 1.

D, E & F Companies 2nd Rangers – Swanage, Dorset.

Medical Detachment 2nd Rangers – Dorchester, Dorset. No change – Alerted for departure – Fabius 1.

Headquarters Company 2nd Rangers – Dorchester, Dorset. Alerted for departure – Fabius 1.

---

30 April 1944

5th Rangers – Companies A – F, Medical and HQ –
Dorchester, England

A Company 2nd Rangers – Dorchester, Dorset.
No change. Alerted for departure – Fabius 1.

B Company 2nd Rangers – Dorchester, Dorset.
15 enlisted men went from Duty to sick in Hospital.
No change. Alerted for departure – Fabius 1.

C Company 2nd Rangers – Dorchester, Dorset.
No change. Alerted for departure – Fabius 1.

D Company 2nd Rangers – Swanage, Dorset.
No change. Alerted for departure – Fabius 1.

E & F Companies 2nd Rangers – Swanage, Dorset.
No change. Alerted for departure – Fabius 1.

Medical Detachment 2nd Rangers – Dorchester, Dorset.
No change. Alerted for departure – Fabius 1.

Headquarters Company 2nd Rangers – Dorchester, Dorset.
No change. Alerted for departure – Fabius 1.

Maurice Prince: *Up 'till now, our training and operations had been done by ourselves, alone. We had always simulated troops to be on our flanks, etc. Now these make-believe soldiers were to be reality and our days of simulating were to be ended. This gives one a fair idea on the workings and planning of the entire Army, as it starts progressing from the lone individual up to the division and then still farther 'till corps and armies are reached. For example, first the individual soldier is given basic training. Then he completes that, he is put into a squad, then this squad takes its place in the section, then, the section into the platoon, etc., until the end of the line is reached, where divisions become an integral part of the Corps and a complete picture of the Army is painted.*

We had a slight misfortune a day before we ran this giant amphibious problem. A few of our boys came down with stomach ailments, a slight touch of ptomaine poisoning. They had to be hospitalized. Otherwise, when time came to entruck, we were all in good shape and in the pink of condition and ready for the task at hand.

The Army issued the following instruction: *Briefing will be conducted for the build-up as prescribed for the assault – except that units will be briefed after arrival in the Marshalling Area, but before they are split into craft parties.'*

The Second Volume in this two part work continues to follow the activities of the US Army 2nd and 5th Rangers each day as they head towards D-Day. Covering the whole of May and then running into June 1944, it provides the daily Allied intelligence briefings and the evolution of Pointe du Hoc and Maisy gun batteries, as well as other Ranger D-Day targets.

Using a huge amount of period reports just as they were issued, for the first time you can assess the changes to the German coastal defence positions and monitor their threat level on a daily basis, whilst at the same time comparing them to the overall Allied invasion plans.

The closer it gets to D-Day, the more the intelligence intensifies and you see exactly what data was given to the Rangers' leadership. Preparations climax with the Slapton Sands dress rehearsal, followed by embarkation and D-Day itself – the unexpected removal of Major Lytle, the Omaha Beach landings, the Pointe du Hoc battle and three days later, the battle for Maisy.

Then the After Action Reports are all shown as they were written by everyone involved (including ALL of the Naval After Action Reports for each vessel involved). The author provides dozens of previously unseen, recently declassified Top Secret files. With documents in their original forms, there can no longer be any speculation as to the Rangers' orders and objectives. All of the Rangers' D-Day battles are laid bare.

Judge for yourself if a cover-up really did take place, and if so, by whom and for what reasons?

The groundbreaking Second Volume will challenge the way that historians look at the Pointe du Hoc battle from now on, and it sets the benchmark for any serious study of the US Rangers in Normandy.

Available now:

D-Day and the Cover-Up at Pointe du Hoc
2nd & 5th US Army Rangers
1 May-10 June 1944

Gary Sterne